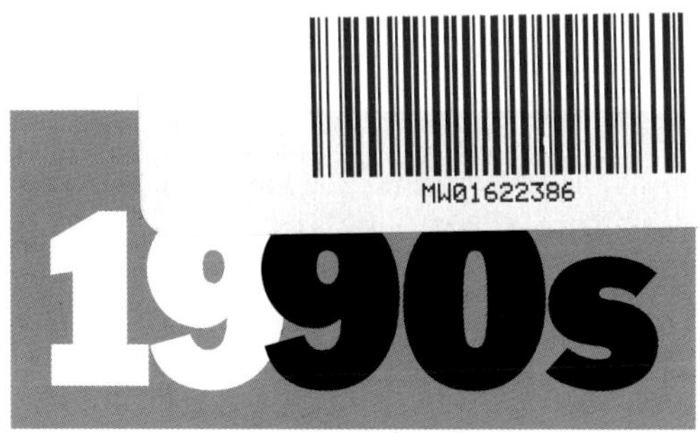

Decades of the 20th Century
Décadas del siglo XX
Decadi del XX secolo

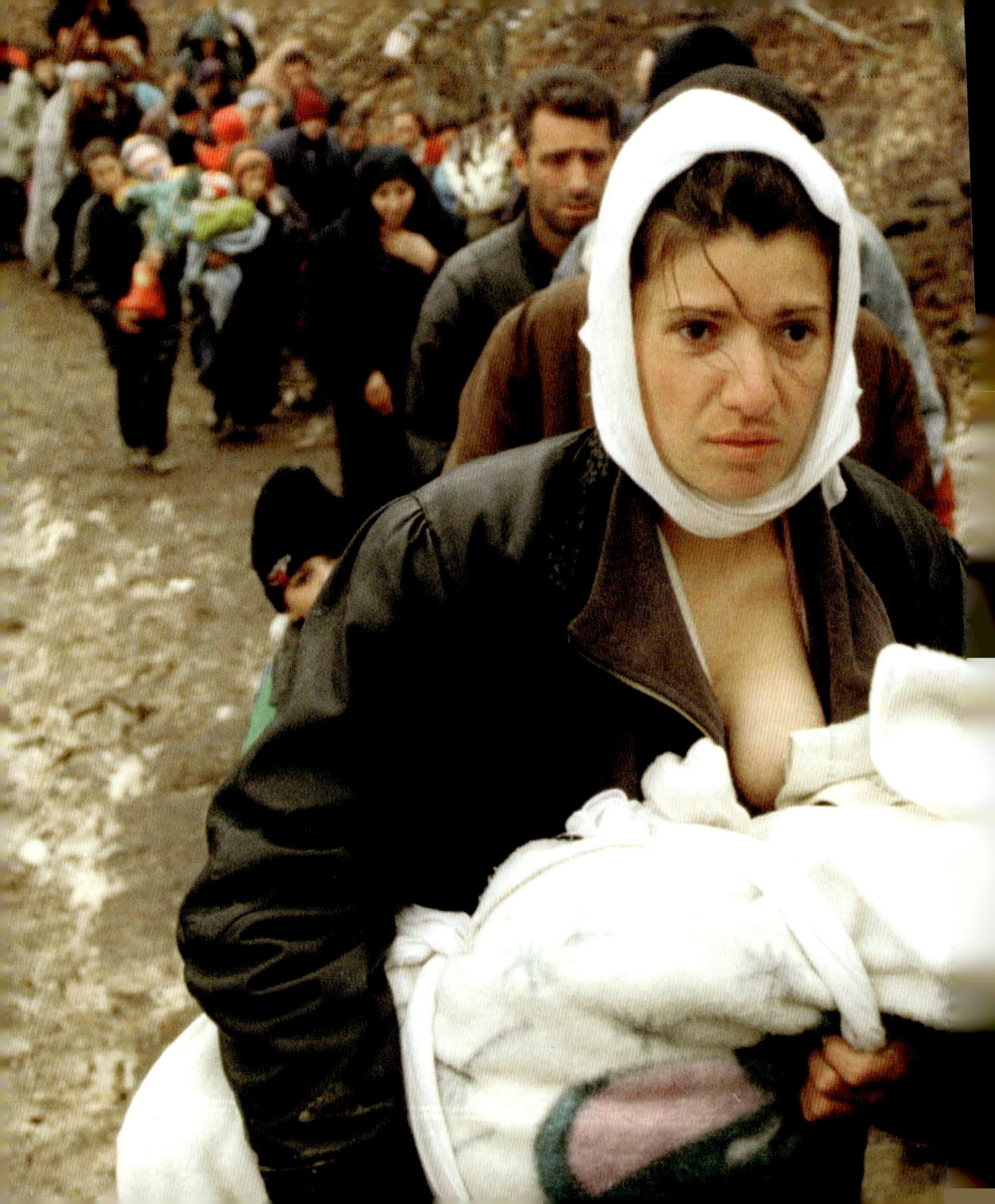

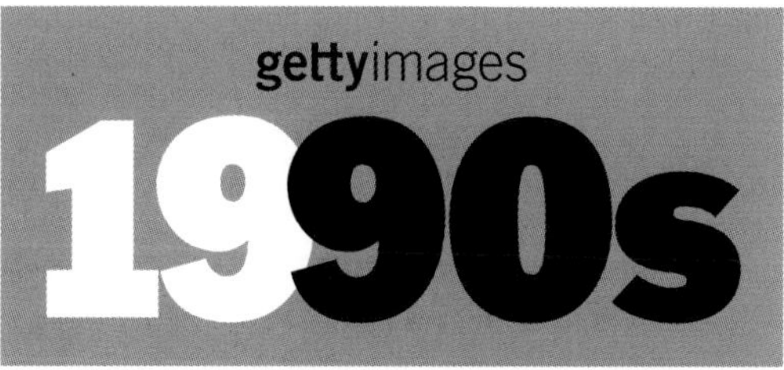

Decades of the 20th Century
Décadas del siglo XX
Decadi del XX secolo

Nick Yapp

KÖNEMANN

This book was produced by Getty Images
Unique House, 21–31 Woodfield Road, London W9 2BA

For KÖNEMANN:
Managing editor: Sally Bald
Project editors: Lucile Bas, Meike Hilbring

For Getty Images: Picture editor: Ali Khoja
Art director: Michael Rand Editor: Richard Collins
Design: Tea McAleer Proof reader: Liz Ihre

Spanish translation: Eva Vico Paredero for LocTeam, S. L., Barcelona
Italian translation: Andrea Molino for LocTeam, S. L., Barcelona
Text editing and typesetting: LocTeam, S. L., Barcelona

Printed in China

ISBN 3-8331-1153-4

10 9 8 7 6 5 4 3
X IX VIII VII VI V IV III II I

Frontispiece: A column of refugees from Kosovo trudge up Likej Mountain on their way to Macedonia, 30 March 1999. Their route was later blocked by the Macedonian army until UNHCR officials exerted pressure on the Macedonian government.

Frontispicio: Una columna de refugiados kosovares asciende penosamente por el monte Likej para dirigirse a Macedonia, 30 de marzo de 1999. Más adelante, el Ejército macedonio les bloquearía el paso, pero el ACNUR presionó al Gobierno de Macedonia para que se les permitiera la entrada al país.

Frontespizio: Profughi del Kosovo attraversano estenuati, in fila, il monte Likej per raggiungere la Macedonia, 30 marzo 1999. Più tardi vennero fermati dall'esercito macedone fino a quando alcuni funzionari dell'UNHCR fecero pressione sul governo della Macedonia.

Contents / Contenido / Sommario

Introduction

The Iron Curtain that had separated East from West for forty years was wrenched open. The Berlin Wall was smashed. Mechanical worms ground their way beneath the Channel, directly linking France and Britain for the first time in history. The Market Economy marched from strength to strength, though banks collapsed and stock exchanges hiccoughed alarmingly. In the United States, many people burnt their fingers on the latest hot properties – junk bonds. Much of Europe bound its fortunes to the new euro, while others stood by… watching, waiting and biting their nails.

Germany was reunited. In South Africa, black and white laid aside the worst of their prejudices under the wise guidance of Nelson Mandela. The old Soviet Empire fell apart. Yugoslavia tore itself to pieces. North and South Korea edged cautiously together. It was as though the tectonic plates of the earth's crust were moving uneasily as the end of the second Christian Millennium approached.

War in the Gulf brought lasting fame to 'Stormin'' Norman Schwarzkopf and Colin Powell, and momentary 'newsworthiness' to the Kurds. War in Chechnya brought misery to thousands and fame to no one. The *annus horribilis* of 1992 provoked that rare phenomenon – a royal grumble – though there were no problems in Queen Elizabeth's life that a little family therapy and a good insurance policy could not have solved. President Clinton had eight *anni mirabiles* as US President, and the smiles on his face suggested that he enjoyed every one of them.

Aung San Suu Kyi condemned the military dictatorship in Burma; in Pakistan, Benazir Bhutto was dismissed by the military. Voters in Britain supported John Major in 1992, but later rejected him in favour of New Labour's Tony Blair. Iitzhak Rabin, Prime Minister of Israel, was assassinated by a Jewish law student. Seven years after his mother's assassination, Rajiv Gandhi of India was killed by a woman who had strapped explosives to her own body.

Having announced in 1987 that he was 'bad', Michael Jackson gave people the chance to agree with him. The cult of celebrity reached new and awesome heights with the creation of 'boy' and 'girl' bands, who shot to instant fame on the basis of a single well-plugged album. Hollywood regained much of its old glamour. The number of television channels available multiplied like germs on a rotting corpse. To the masses, sport became as important as real life, as did the adventures of soap stars to millions more.

There were new inventions, new diseases, natural disasters, bombings, hijackings, deeds of high bravery and examples of crass stupidity. But the stubborn, silly, punch-drunk and wonderful human race somehow blundered on to the end of the decade, the end of the century and the end of the Millennium.

Introducción

El telón de acero que durante cuarenta años había separado los países del bloque soviético de los occidentales se eleva bruscamente y el muro de Berlín cae. A modo de lombrices mecánicas, las excavadoras se abren paso bajo el canal de la Mancha para conectar directamente Francia y Gran Bretaña por primera vez en la historia. La economía de mercado se fortalece día a día, a pesar de las quiebras bancarias y de los alarmantes sobresaltos de las bolsas. En Estados Unidos, mucha gente se pilla los dedos con los valores en boga del momento: los llamados *junk bonds*, bonos basura o sin garantía. Gran parte de Europa vincula su fortuna a la nueva moneda, el euro, mientras que el resto se mantiene a la expectativa, contempla el panorama y espera, sin dejar de morderse las uñas…

En los noventa tiene lugar la reunificación de Alemania. En Sudáfrica, blancos y negros dejan de lado sus prejuicios, guiados por la sabia figura de Nelson Mandela. El viejo imperio soviético se derrumba y Yugoslavia se desmiembra. Los Estados de Corea del Norte y Corea del Sur se aproximan cautelosamente el uno al otro. A medida que se acerca el fin del segundo milenio cristiano, parece como si las placas tectónicas de la corteza terrestre se moviesen, incómodas.

La guerra del Golfo lanza a la fama a Norman Schwarzkopf (general al mando de la operación "Tormenta del Desierto") y a Colin Powell, al tiempo que otorga un protagonismo transitorio al pueblo kurdo. La guerra de Chechenia siembra de miseria las vidas de miles de personas sin brindarle fama a nadie. Por su parte, 1992 se revela un *annus horribilis* para la familia real británica, en el ojo del huracán debido a los escándalos por los que es noticia –si bien ninguno de los quebraderos de cabeza de la reina Isabel II era en realidad un problema que unas cuantas sesiones de terapia familiar y una buena póliza de seguros no hubiesen podido solucionar–. Clinton se mantiene durante ocho *anni mirabiles* como presidente de Estados Unidos, y de su sonrisa se desprende que supo disfrutar de todos y cada uno de ellos.

La premio Nobel Aung San Suu Kyi condena la dictadura militar que impera en Birmania; en Pakistán, la primera ministra Benazir Bhutto es depuesta por las fuerzas militares. En 1992 los electores británicos respaldan a John Major, si bien más adelante le negarán su apoyo en favor de Tony Blair, militante del Nuevo Partido Laborista. El primer ministro israelí, Isaac Rabin, muere asesinado a manos de un estudiante de Derecho judío. Siete años después del asesinato de su madre, Rajiv Gandhi pierde la vida en un atentado perpetrado por una mujer que llevaba una carga explosiva ceñida a su propio cuerpo.

Tras anunciar en 1987 que era un chico *malo* ('Bad'), Michael Jackson le da al público motivos para creerlo. El culto a la fama alcanza nuevas cotas insospechadas con la creación de grupos musicales prefabricados de chicos o de chicas, que logran una ascensión meteórica gracias a un solo álbum y a una feroz campaña de *marketing*. Hollywood recupera buena parte de su *glamour* de antaño mientras las cadenas de televisión proliferan como champiñones. El deporte y las aventuras y desventuras de las estrellas de los culebrones cobran para las masas tanta o más importancia que la vida real.

Los años noventa son testigo de nuevas invenciones, de enfermedades desconocidas, de desastres naturales; presencian bombardeos, secuestros, actos de valentía suprema y ejemplos de crasa estupidez. No obstante, la terca, ridícula, maltrecha y maravillosa raza humana conseguirá avanzar a trompicones hacia el fin de la década, del siglo y del milenio.

Introduzione

Mentre il muro di Berlino andava in frantumi, l'Est e l'Ovest, che per quarant'anni avevano vissuto separati dalla cortina di ferro, assistevano alla sua disintegrazione; gli escavatori si facevano strada sotto il Canale della Manica, creando per la prima volta un collegamento diretto fra la Francia e la Gran Bretagna; l'economia di mercato diventava sempre più potente, anche se le banche crollavano e le borse barcollavano in maniera allarmante. Negli Stati Uniti molte persone pagavano lo scotto della nuova moda: le obbligazioni spazzatura, più note come junk bond. La maggior parte dell'Europa legava la propria fortuna all'Euro... E intanto c'era chi restava con le braccia incrociate... osservando, aspettando e mordendosi le unghie.

La Germania si riunificava, mentre in Sud Africa bianchi e neri si scrollavano di dosso il peggiore dei pregiudizi, sotto la saggia guida di Nelson Mandela; e se da un lato l'antico Impero Sovietico si sgretolava e la Jugoslavia si disuniva, dall'altro la Corea del Nord e quella del Sud muovevano i primi cauti passi di riconciliazione. Man mano che si avvicinava la fine del secondo Millennio cristiano il mondo era in pieno subbuglio, simile ai violenti movimenti delle placche tettoniche sulla crosta terrestre.

La guerra del Golfo servì per dare fama imperitura a *Stormin'* Norman Schwarzkopf e a Colin Powell, mentre i Curdi salivano momentaneamente alla ribalta delle cronache. La guerra in Cecenia invece portò solo miseria per migliaia di persone e non diede fama a nessuno. Con l'arrivo dell'*annus horribilis* 1992 apparve un insolito fenomeno: le rimostranze della famiglia reale, anche se, con un po' di terapia familiare e una buona assicurazione, la Regina Elisabetta non avrebbe avuto più di che lamentarsi. Invece Bill Clinton visse otto *anni mirabiles* come Presidente degli Stati Uniti, e a giudicare dall'aspetto sorridente sembra proprio che se li sia goduti al massimo.

Aung San Suu Kyi condannava la dittatura militare in Birmania, mentre in Pakistan Benazir Bhutto veniva destituita dai militari. Nel 1992 gli elettori britannici appoggiavano John Major, per preferire in seguito il New Labour di Tony Blair. Il Primo Ministro israeliano Ytzhak Rabin veniva assassinato da uno studente ebreo di giurisprudenza, mentre sette anni dopo l'omicidio di sua madre, l'indiano Rajiv Gandhi veniva assassinato per mano di una donna con il corpo ricoperto di esplosivi.

Se nel 1987, con "Bad", Michael Jackson proclamava di essere cattivo, ora il pubblico lo poteva constatare con i propri occhi. La smania di divenire celebre raggiungeva limiti impressionanti, con l'inondazione di gruppi di *boys* e *girls* che salivano alle luci della ribalta grazie a un solo album orecchiabile accompagnato da una buona operazione di marketing. Hollywood recuperava gran parte dell'antico glamour, mentre i canali televisivi spuntavano come funghi; e intanto il gran pubblico consumava sport e soap opera tanto da considerarli altrettanto importanti della propria vita.

Apparivano nuove invenzioni, nuove malattie, catastrofi naturali, bombardamenti, dirottamenti, atti di estremo coraggio ed esempi di crassa stoltezza; ma ad ogni modo la razza umana, testarda, stupida, suonata e magnifica, si apprestava a dire addio, non si sa bene come, alla fine del decennio, alla fine del secolo e alla fine del millennio.

1. Movers and shakers
Líderes y agitadores
Progressisti e agitatori

A shaky start. President Bill Clinton grimaces as his translation device fails at the beginning of his joint press conference with the Russian President Boris Yeltsin, Helsinki, 21 March 1997.

Un comienzo incierto. El presidente Bill Clinton expresa con una mueca que no funcionan sus cascos de interpretación simultánea, justo al inicio de una conferencia de prensa junto al presidente Boris Yeltsin en Helsinki, el 21 de marzo de 1997.

Un inizio incerto. Problemi con le cuffie per la traduzione provocano questa smorfia del presidente Bill Clinton in occasione della conferenza stampa tenuta con Boris Eltsin a Helsinki, 21 marzo 1997.

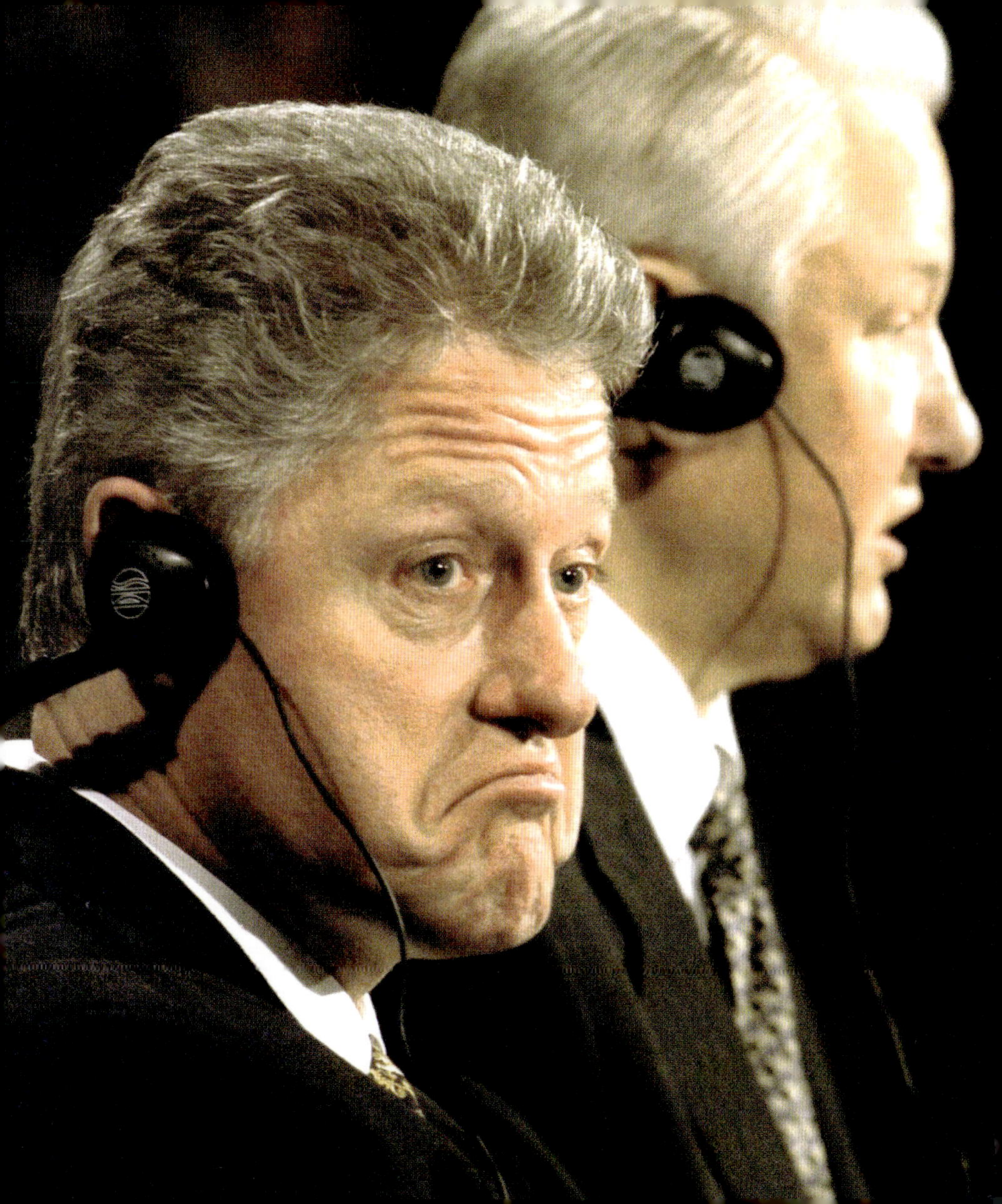

1. Movers and shakers Líderes y agitadores Progressisti e agitatori

It was a decade of change and replacement, of separation and new alliances. Nelson and Winnie Mandela, the Prince and Princess of Wales, Mikhail Gorbachev and the Russian people – all agreed to part. Mandela and Buthelezi attempted to find common ground to unite their peoples in South Africa. Iitzhak Rabin and Yasser Arafat came to an accord at Camp David. A new government in Britain brought Nationalists and Unionists to within spitting distance of each other in Northern Ireland.

Kohl and Mitterrand were replaced by Schröder and Chirac. Clinton replaced Bush. Yeltsin replaced Gorbachev. Also among the replacement heroes were the newly-elected President Walesa of Poland and President Havel of Czechoslovakia.

The Cold War came to an end, but there were plenty of new villains on the block. Saddam Hussein was considered the most scurrilous but proved elusive. General Manuel Noriega of Panama was more easily apprehended and packed off to gaol. Slobodan Milosevic of Serbia and Colonel Gaddafi of Libya proved far more intractable. The new villains rivalled their forerunners for obstinacy, as far as the West was concerned.

La década de 1990 es una época de cambios y relevos, de divisiones y nuevas alianzas. Nelson y Winnie Mandela, el príncipe Carlos de Inglaterra y la princesa Diana, Mijaíl Gorbachov y el pueblo ruso; todos deciden separarse. En Sudáfrica, Mandela y Buthelezi intentan hallar un terreno común que permita unirse a sus pueblos. Isaac Rabin y Yasir Arafat llegan a un acuerdo en Camp David, y en Irlanda del Norte un nuevo Gobierno británico logra acortar las distancias entre unionistas y nacionalistas.

Kohl y Mitterand son reemplazados por Schröder y Chirac. Clinton toma el relevo de Bush; Yeltsin sustituye a Gorbachov. Entre los nuevos dirigentes, tratados como héroes, se cuentan también los presidentes electos de Polonia y Checoslovaquia, Lech Walesa y Václav Havel.

La guerra fría toca a su fin pero aún quedan numerosos personajes malvados en escena. Sadam Husein se revela como el villano más temible, si bien destaca por ser sumamente escurridizo; en Panamá, el general Manuel Noriega resulta más fácil de atrapar y pronto acaba entre rejas. Tanto Slobodan Milosevic, en Serbia, como el coronel Gaddafi, en Libia, demuestran ser intratables. Los nuevos bellacos rivalizan con sus predecesores en obstinación, por lo que a Occidente se refiere.

Fu il decennio dei cambiamenti e delle sostituzioni, delle separazioni e delle nuove alleanze. Nelson e Winnie Mandela, il Principe e la Principessa di Galles, Mikhail Gorbaciov e il popolo russo, tutte separazioni prese di comune accordo. Mentre Mandela e Buthelezi cercavano di trovare un terreno comune per far convivere il loro popolo in Sud Africa, Yitzhak Rabin e Yasser Arafat giungevano a un accordo a Camp David. Grazie a un nuovo governo in Gran Bretagna, i Nazionalisti e gli Unionisti erano più vicini che mai nell'Irlanda del Nord.

Kohl e Mitterand venivano sostituiti da Schröder e da Chirac; Clinton subentrava a Bush, Eltsin dava il cambio a Gorbaciov. E fra i nuovi eroi si facevano spazio anche Walesa e Havel, i nuovi presidenti eletti della Polonia e della Cecoslovacchia.

Anche se la Guerra Fredda era ormai conclusa, i cattivi che restavano sulla scena erano nuovi, ma sempre numerosi. Saddam Hussein, considerato il più violento, era il più difficile da catturare. Nel caso del generale Manuel Noriega, fu più facile prenderlo e mandarlo in prigione. Slobodan Milosevic in Serbia e il colonnello Gheddafi in Libia avevano dimostrato di avere un carattere molto più scontroso. Agli occhi dell'Occidente, l'ostinazione dei nuovi cattivi rivaleggiava con quella dei loro precursori.

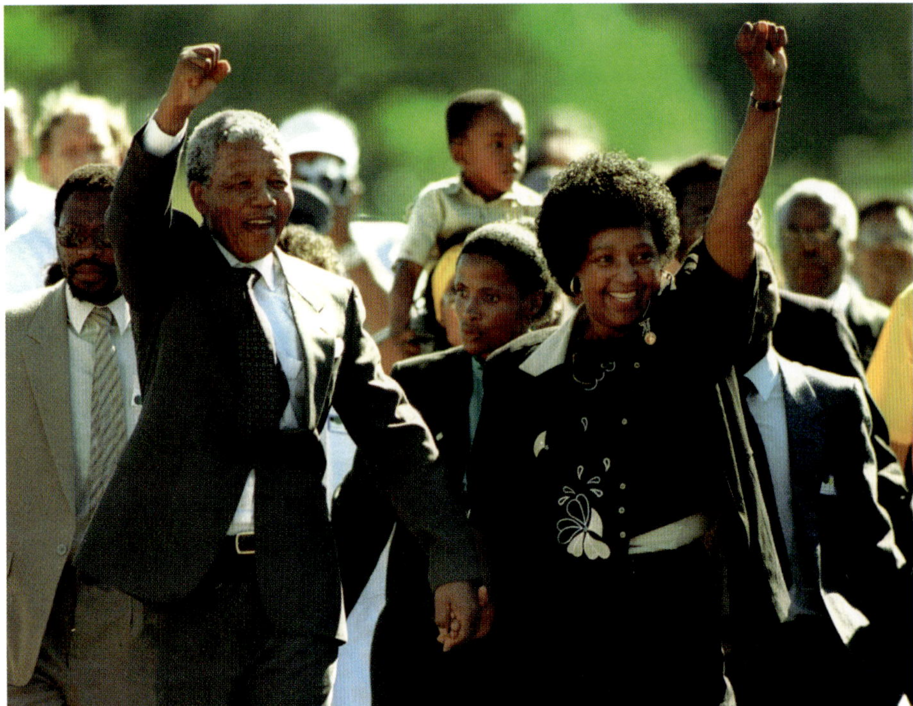

ULLI MICHEL/REUTERS/ARCHIVE PHOTOS

The end of a bitter age. Nelson and Winnie Mandela greet the crowds waiting outside Victor Verster Prison, Paarl, South Africa, 11 February 1990. It was Mandela's first day of freedom for twenty-seven years.

El final de una amarga época. El 11 de febrero de 1990 Nelson Mandela es puesto en libertad después de pasar 27 años en prisión. El futuro presidente y su mujer, Winnie Mandela, saludan a la multitud que los espera a su salida de la cárcel Victor Verster de Paarl, en Sudáfrica.

La fine di un periodo buio. Nelson e Winnie Mandela salutano la folla che li aspetta all'uscita della prigione Victor Verster di Paarl, in Sud Africa, 11 febbraio 1990. Fu il primo giorno di libertà per Mandela dopo ventisette anni.

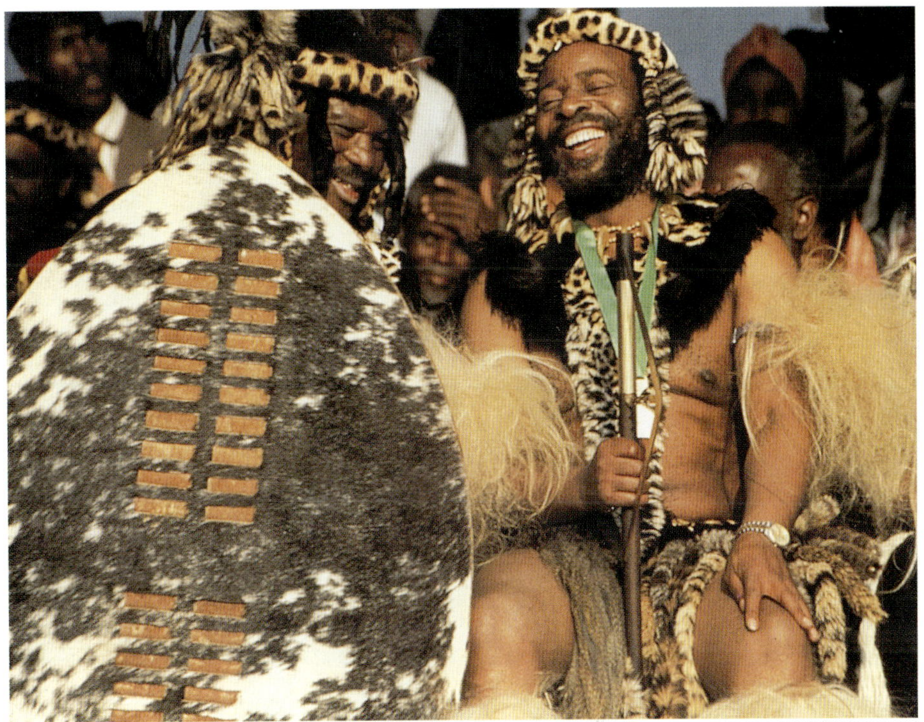

JOAO SILVA/BLACK STAR/COLORIFIC!

KwaZulu Chief Minister Buthelezi (left), with Zulu King Zwelethini, Ngoma, Africa. Buthelezi is also president and co-founder of the paramilitary Inkatha, by turn ally and opponent of Mandela.

Buthelezi (izquierda), primer ministro de la región de KwaZulu, junto al rey zulú Zwelethini en Ngoma, África. Buthelezi era también presidente y cofundador del partido paramilitar Inkatha, aliado y adversario de Mandela alternativamente.

Il Primo Ministro del KwaZulu, Buthelezi (a sinistra) e il re zulù Zwelethini a Ngoma, in Africa. Buthelezi è anche presidente e cofondatore del partito paramilitare Inkatha, a turno alleato e avversario di Mandela.

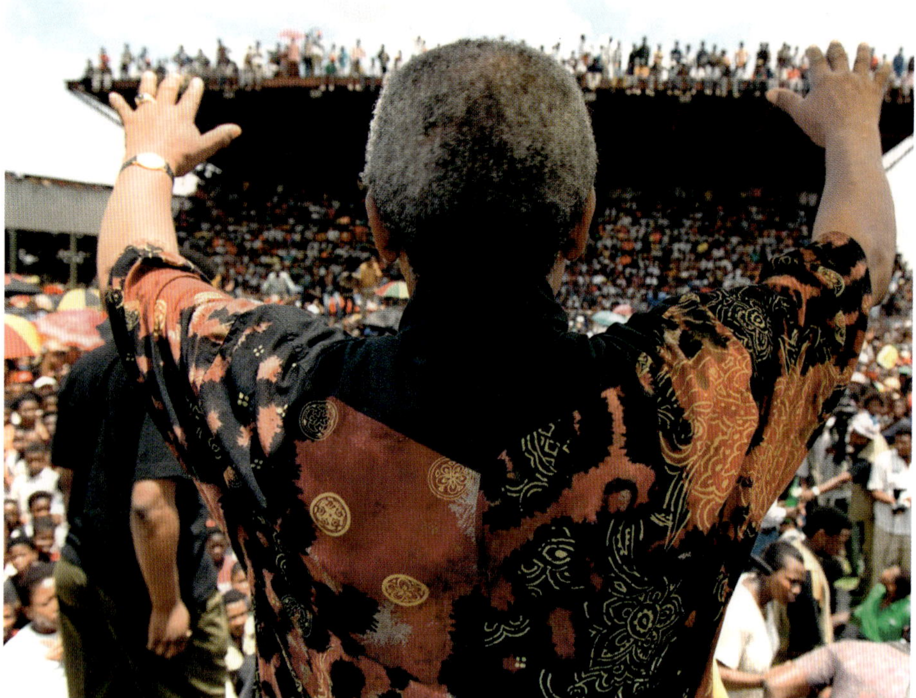

DAVID BRAUCHLI/LIAISON AGENCY

The hands of democracy. Nelson Mandela reaches out to voters at the Ikageng Stadium, Potchefstroom, Transvaal, 31 January 1994. He was campaigning in the first all-race democratic election in South Africa.

Las manos de la democracia. Nelson Mandela extiende los brazos hacia los votantes congregados en el estadio Ikageng de Potchefstroom, en el Transvaal, el 31 de enero de 1994, en plena campaña de las primeras elecciones multirraciales democráticas de la historia de Sudáfrica.

Le mani della democrazia. Durante la campagna per le prime elezioni multirazziali del Sud Africa, Nelson Mandela tende le braccia verso i propri elettori nell'Ikageng Stadium, Potchefstroom, 31 gennaio 1994.

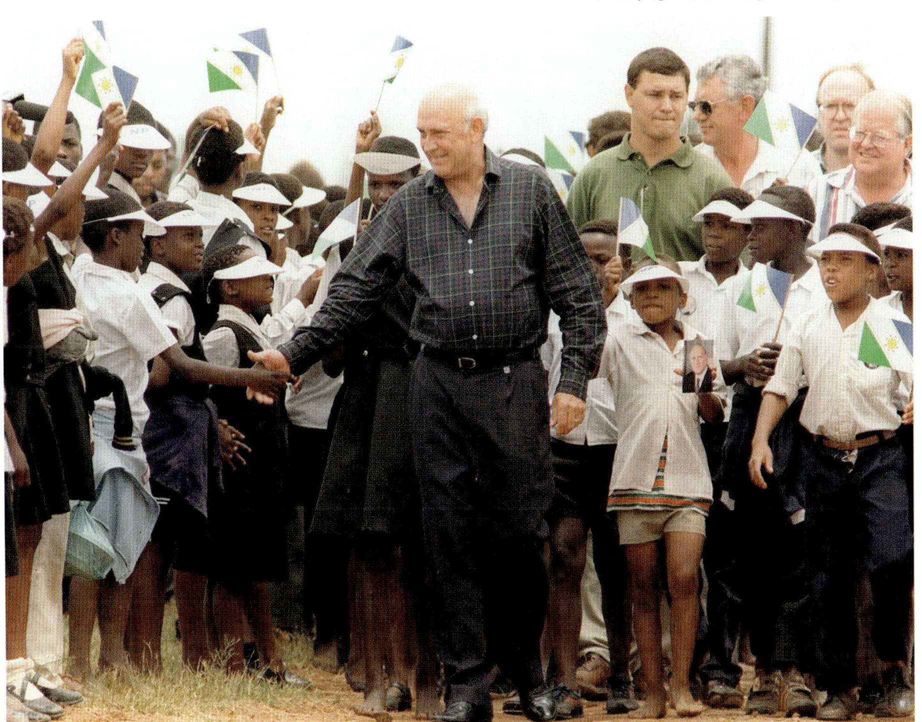

DAVID BRAUCHLI/LIAISON AGENCY

President F W de Klerk on a campaign rally at Dwarsfontein, Western Transvaal, 21 January 1994. The election was still three months away but the days of white rule were numbered.

El presidente F. W. de Klerk durante un acto de campaña en Dwarsfontein, en el Transvaal occidental, el 21 de enero de 1994. Faltaban aún tres meses para que se celebrasen los comicios pero la hegemonía blanca tenía los días contados.

Il presidente F. W. De Klerk in campagna elettorale a Dwarsfontein, nel Transvaal Occidentale, 21 gennaio 1994. Mancavano ancora tre mesi alle elezioni, ma il predominio bianco aveva i giorni contati.

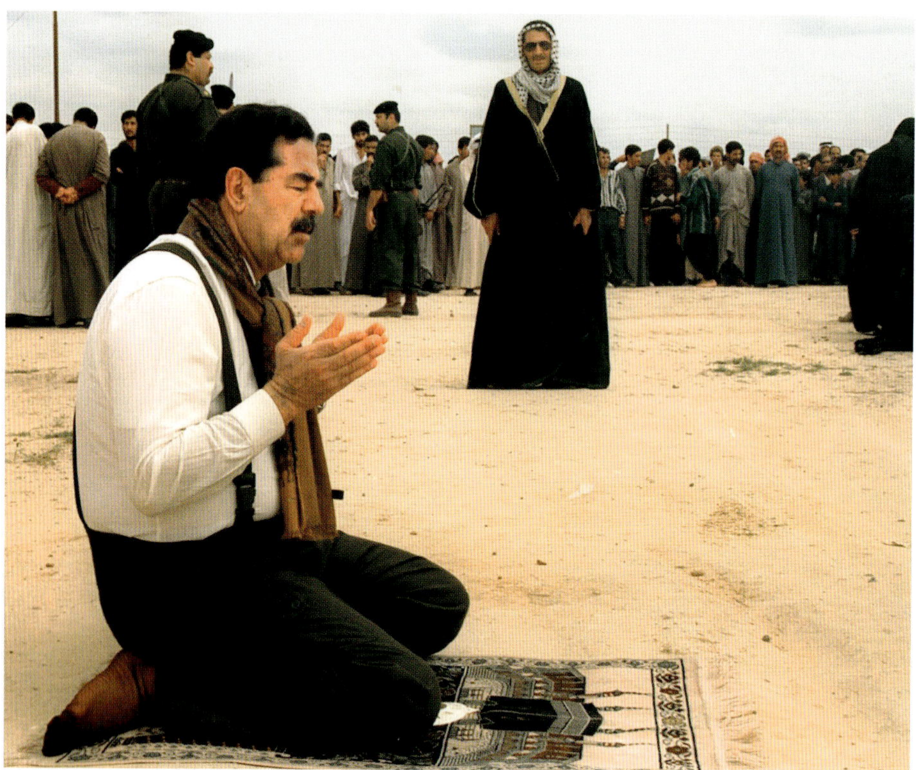

EPA/PA

Praying for Allah's help. President Saddam Hussein pauses during a tour of villages in northern Iraq, 29 March 1998. The sympathetic portrait was released by the Iraqi News Agency.

Oración para obtener la ayuda de Alá. El presidente Sadam Husein realiza un alto en su visita a diversas ciudades del norte de Irak, 29 de marzo de 1998. Esta piadosa imagen fue difundida por la agencia de noticias iraquí.

Allah aiutami tu. Il presidente Saddam Hussein durante un viaggio fra i villaggi del nord dell'Iraq, 29 marzo 1998. Questa toccante immagine è stata scattata dalla Iraqi News Agency.

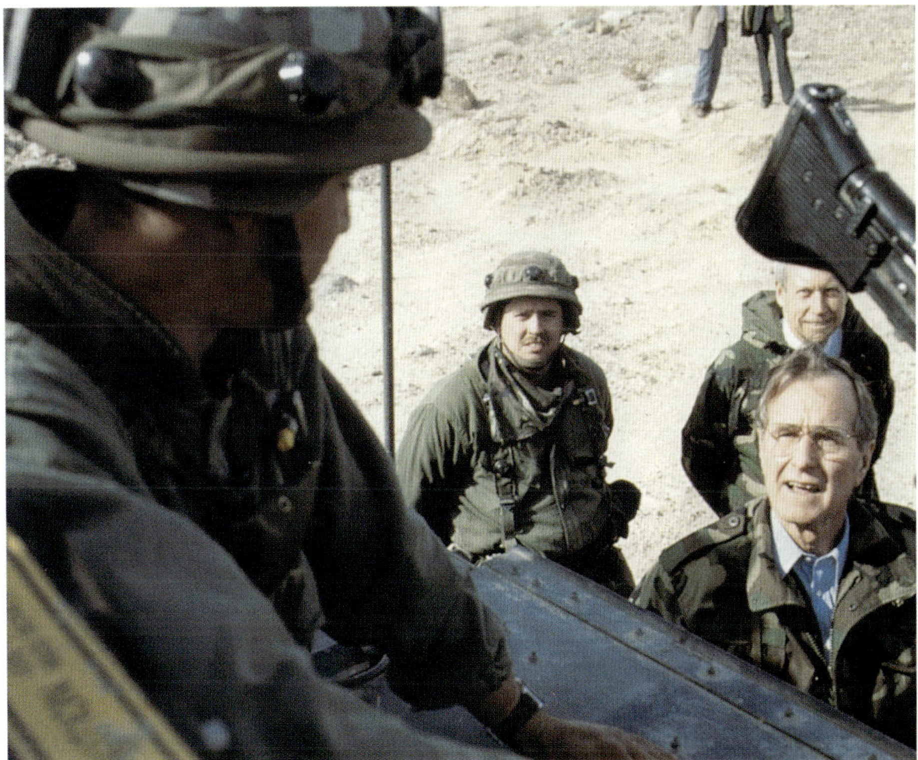

WALLY McNAMEE/WOODFIN CAMP & ASSOCIATES/COLORIFIC!

Praying for Allied help. President George Bush visits Allied troops during the Gulf War early in 1991. The fighting lasted only four days, the dying considerably longer.

Oración para obtener ayuda aliada. A principios de 1991 George Bush visita a las tropas aliadas durante la guerra del Golfo. Los combates sólo duraron cuatro días; sus funestas consecuencias, mucho más.

Alleati aiutateci voi. Il presidente George Bush fa visita alle truppe alleate durante la guerra del Golfo agli inizi del 1991. I combattimenti durarono solo quattro giorni, le perdite di vite umane molto più a lungo.

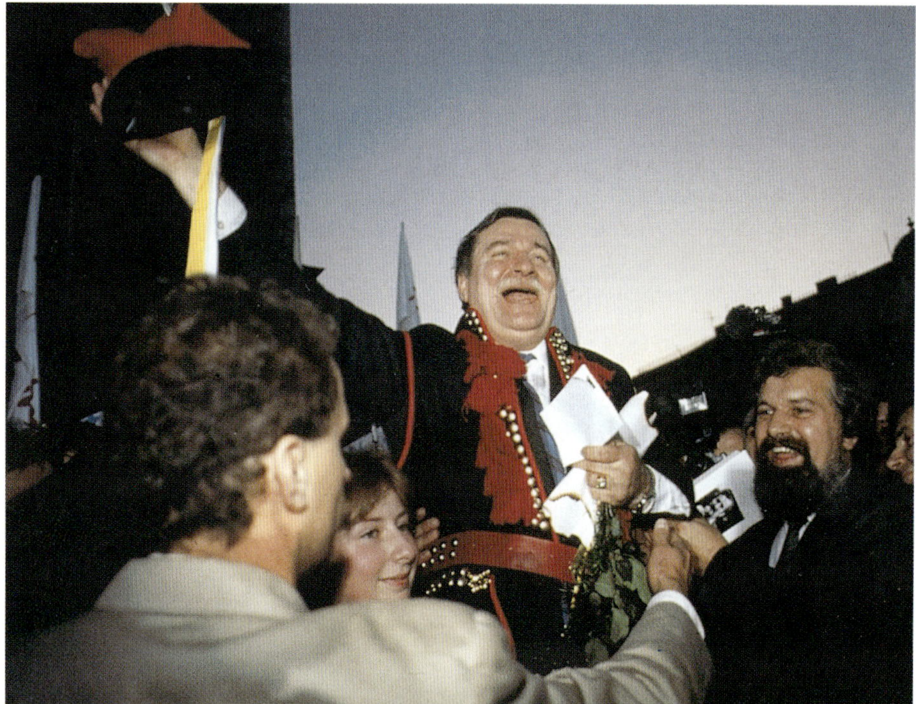

MARKUS DWORACZYK/BLACK STAR/COLORIFIC!

Careless rapture! Lech Walesa greets supporters during the Polish presidential election campaign, Cracow, 1990. His jubilation was premature but not misplaced: the former leader of Solidarity was elected.

Alegría desatada. Lech Walesa saluda a sus simpatizantes en Cracovia durante la campaña de las elecciones presidenciales polacas, en 1990. Su júbilo era prematuro pero no descaminado; el antiguo líder de Solidaridad sería elegido presidente.

Spensierata allegria! Lech Walesa saluta i propri elettori durante la campagna per le elezioni presidenziali, a Cracovia, nel 1990. Tanta esultanza era prematura ma aveva la sua ragion d'essere: l'antico leader di Solidarnosc sarebbe infatti stato eletto.

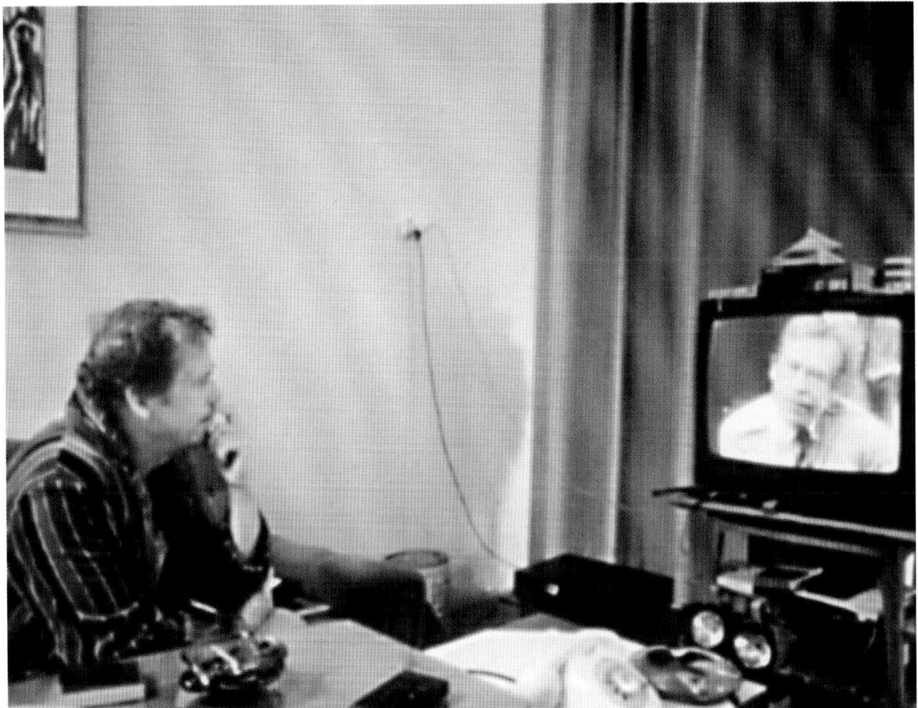

TOMKI NEMEK/ANZENBERGER/COLORIFIC!

Careful consideration. President Vaclav Havel of Czechoslovakia critically monitors his performance on a television set in Lany, 1990. He had become president the previous year, six months after being released from prison.

Un examen concienzudo. El presidente de Checoslovaquia, Václav Havel, analiza su aparición televisiva en Lany, en 1990. Havel había ocupado la presidencia el año anterior, seis meses después de ser liberado de prisión.

Pensierosa riflessione. Il presidente della Cecoslovacchia Václav Havel esamina attentamente la sua apparizione in TV a Lany, 1990. Era stato eletto presidente un anno prima, sei mesi dopo essere stato scarcerato.

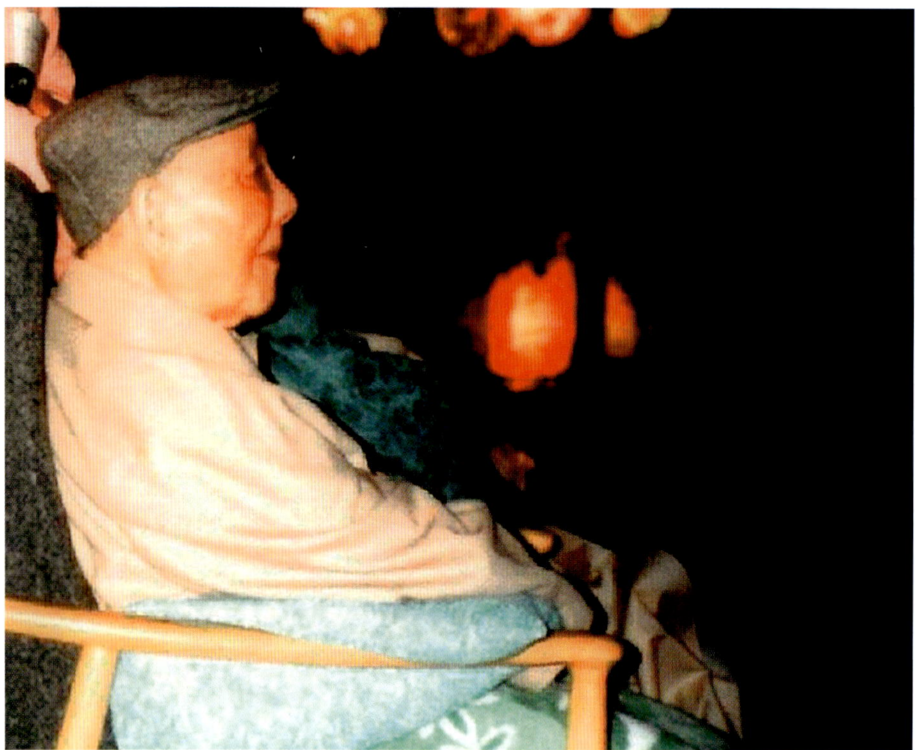

EPA/PA

Maintaining the old order. China's most powerful man, Deng Xiaoping, watches a fireworks display, 1 October 1994. He was 90 years old and head of the most populous country in the world.

Preservar el antiguo orden. El hombre más poderoso de toda China, Deng Xiaoping, contempla unos fuegos artificiales, 1 de octubre de 1994. A sus 90 años, gobernaba el país más poblado del mundo.

Mantenere l'antico ordine. L'uomo più potente della Cina, Deng Xiaoping, osserva uno spettacolo pirotecnico, 1° ottobre 1994. All'epoca aveva 90 anni ed era a capo della nazione più popolata del pianeta.

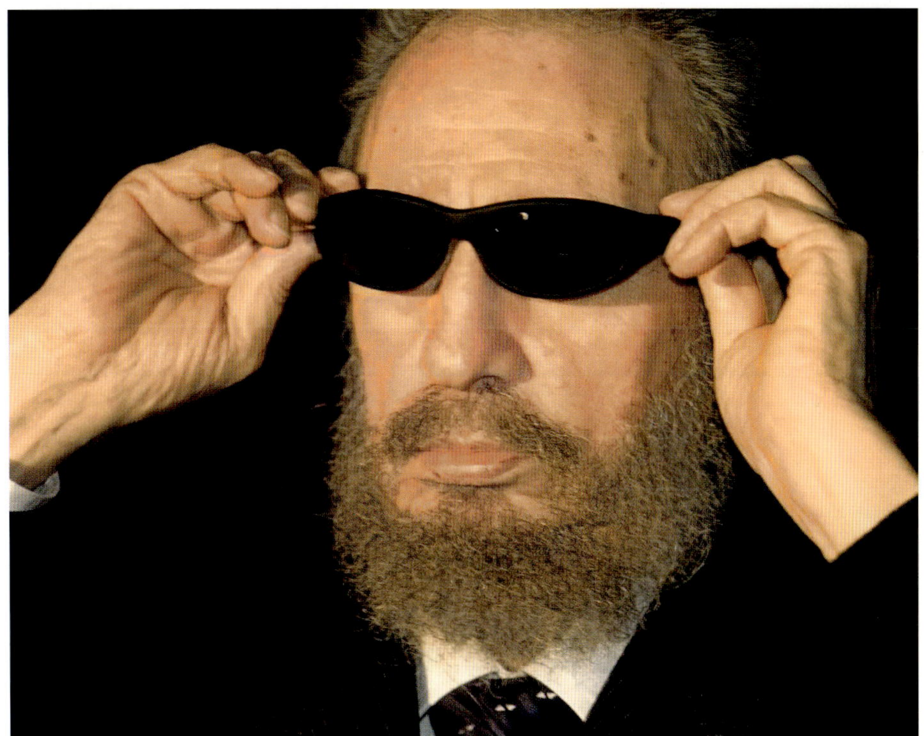

EPA/PA

Keeper of the revolution. Fidel Castro faces the media at the 9th Ibero-American Summit, Havana, Cuba, 16 November 1999. For more than forty years he has guided his country's fortunes.

El guardián de la Revolución. Fidel Castro ante los medios en la IX Cumbre Iberoamericana celebrada en La Habana, Cuba, el 16 de noviembre de 1999. Castro llevaba más de 40 años guiando el destino de su país.

Guardiano della rivoluzione. Fidel Castro, alle redini del paese per oltre quarant'anni, di fronte ai media in occasione del IX Vertice Iberoamericano a L'Avana, Cuba, 16 novembre 1999.

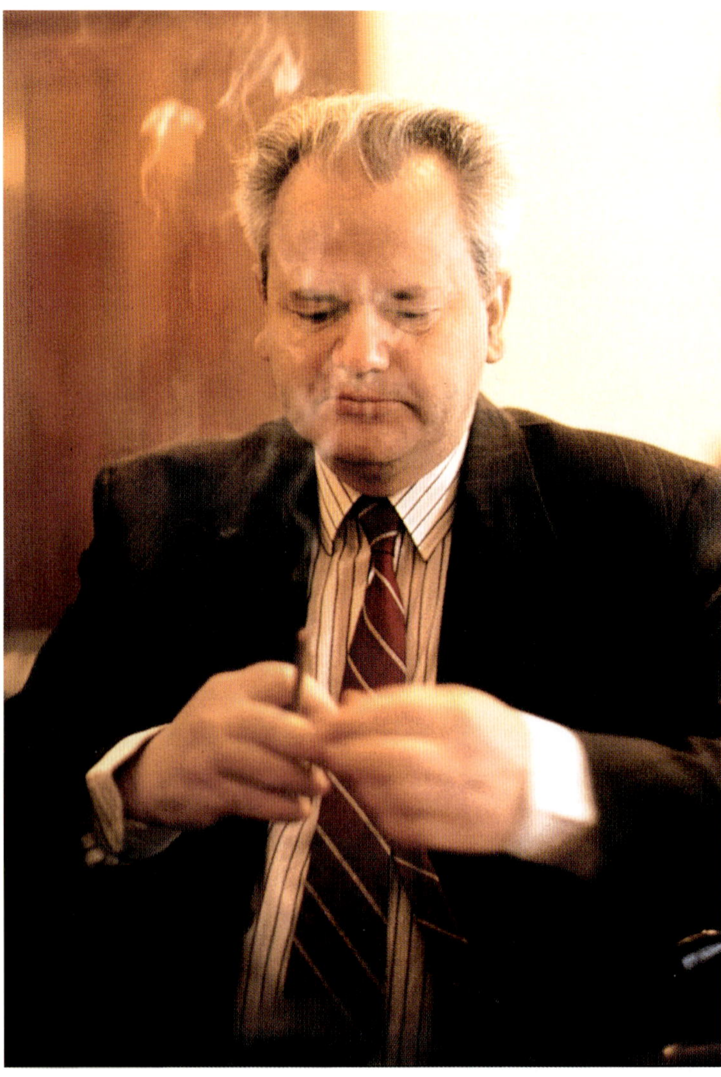

CHRISTOPHER MORRIS/BLACK STAR/COLORIFIC!

Time magazine's portrait of Slobodan Milosevic, 8 June 1992. He had just been re-elected President of Serbia, amid accusations of fraud.

Fotografía de Slobodan Milosevic aparecida en la revista *Time* el 8 de junio de 1992. Acababa de ser reelegido presidente de Serbia, a pesar de las acusaciones de fraude electoral.

L'immagine di Slobodan Milosevic mostrata dalla rivista *Time*, 8 giugno 1992. Nonostante le accuse di frode elettorale era appena stato rieletto presidente della Serbia.

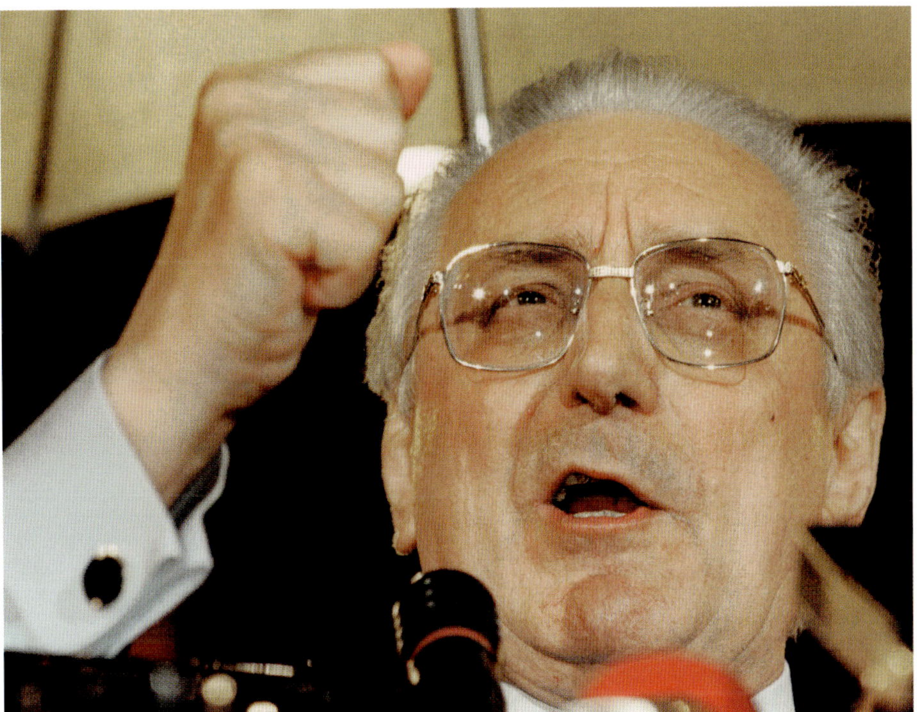

HRVOJE POLAN/LIAISON AGENCY

Franjo Tudjman, President of Croatia, on the stump during a pre-election rally of his Croatian Democratic Party (HDZ) in Zagreb's main square, 22 June 1997. The Yugoslavian Republic had irreparably broken apart.

El presidente de Croacia, Franjo Tudjman, en plena campaña electoral en la gran plaza de Zagreb, el 22 de junio de 1997, durante la gira preelectoral llevada a cabo por la Unión Democrática Croata (HDZ). La independencia de la república yugoslava era ya una realidad.

Il presidente della Croazia, Franjo Tudjman, durante un comizio tenuto sulla piazza principale di Zagabria dal proprio Partito Democratico Croata (HDZ), 22 giugno 1997. La Repubblica jugoslava era inevitabilmente destinata alla rottura.

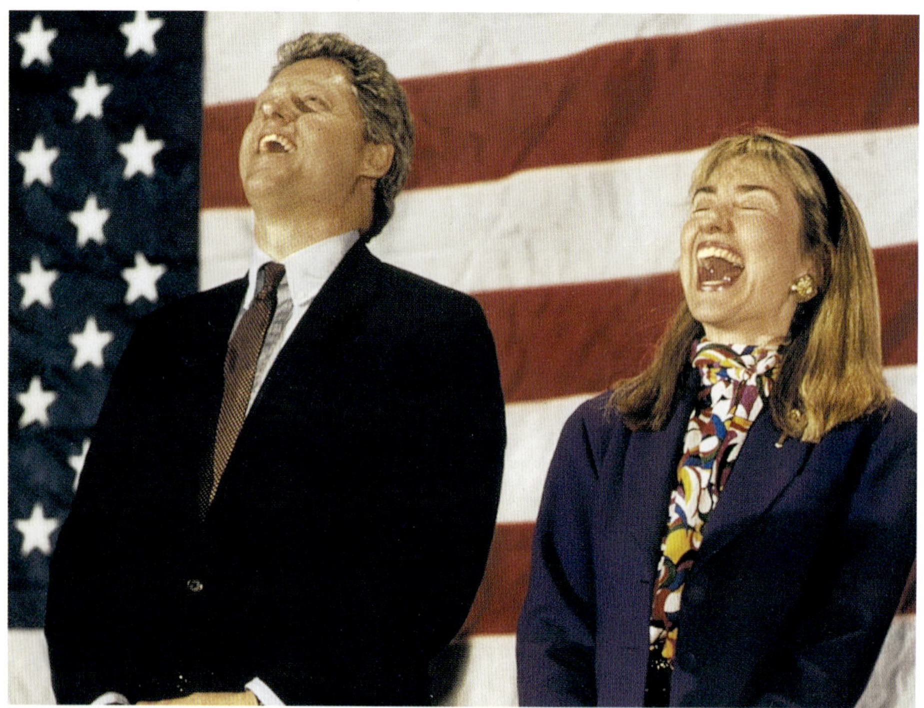

RICK FRIEDMAN/BLACK STAR/COLORIFIC!

Happy days… Bill and Hillary Clinton share a moment of joy in New Hampshire during the 1992 campaign to elect a Democratic candidate for the presidency.

Días felices… Bill y Hillary Clinton comparten momentos de gozo en New Hampshire, durante la campaña de 1992 para elegir al candidato demócrata a la presidencia de Estados Unidos.

Giorni felici… Bill e Hillary Clinton nel 1992, in un momento di allegria nel New Hampshire durante la campagna per l'elezione del candidato democratico alla presidenza.

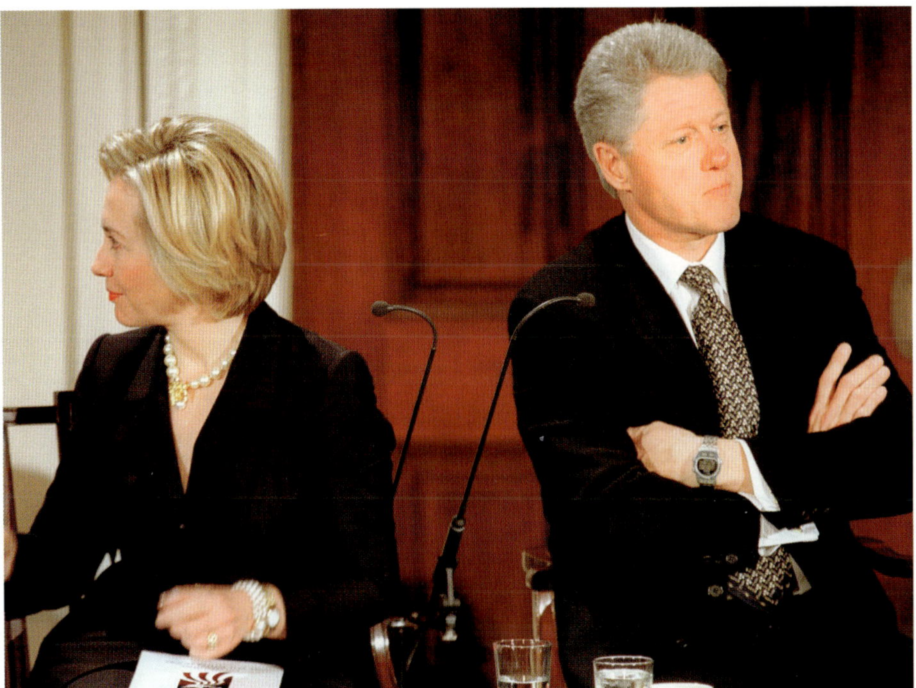

RICHARD ELLIS/LIAISON AGENCY

…but, oh, those lonely nights. Amid rumours of marital separation, the Clintons appear (back to back) at a Millennium evening lecture on 'Women as Citizens' in the East Room of the White House, 15 March 1999.

… y noches solitarias. En medio de rumores relativos a su separación, el 15 de marzo de 1999 los Clinton acuden juntos –si bien se dan la espalda– a una de las conferencias con motivo del fin de milenio sobre "Mujeres y ciudadanas", en la East Room de la Casa Blanca.

…ma quante notti solitarie. Sebbene fossero sempre più insistenti le voci che parlavano di divorzio, i Clinton appaiono assieme, ma seduti di spalle l'uno all'altro durante una conferenza delle Millennium Evenings su "Donne cittadine" nella Sala Est della Casa Bianca, 15 marzo 1999.

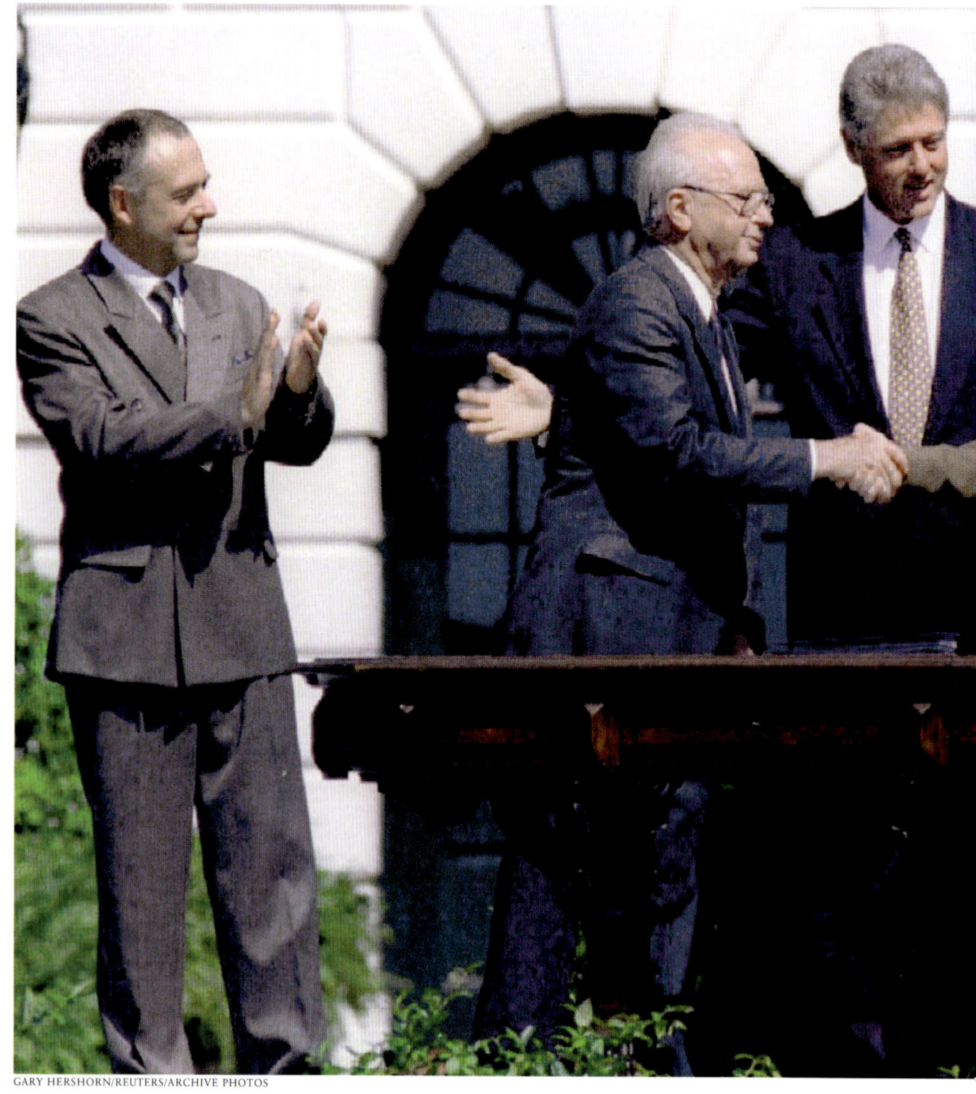

GARY HERSHORN/REUTERS/ARCHIVE PHOTOS

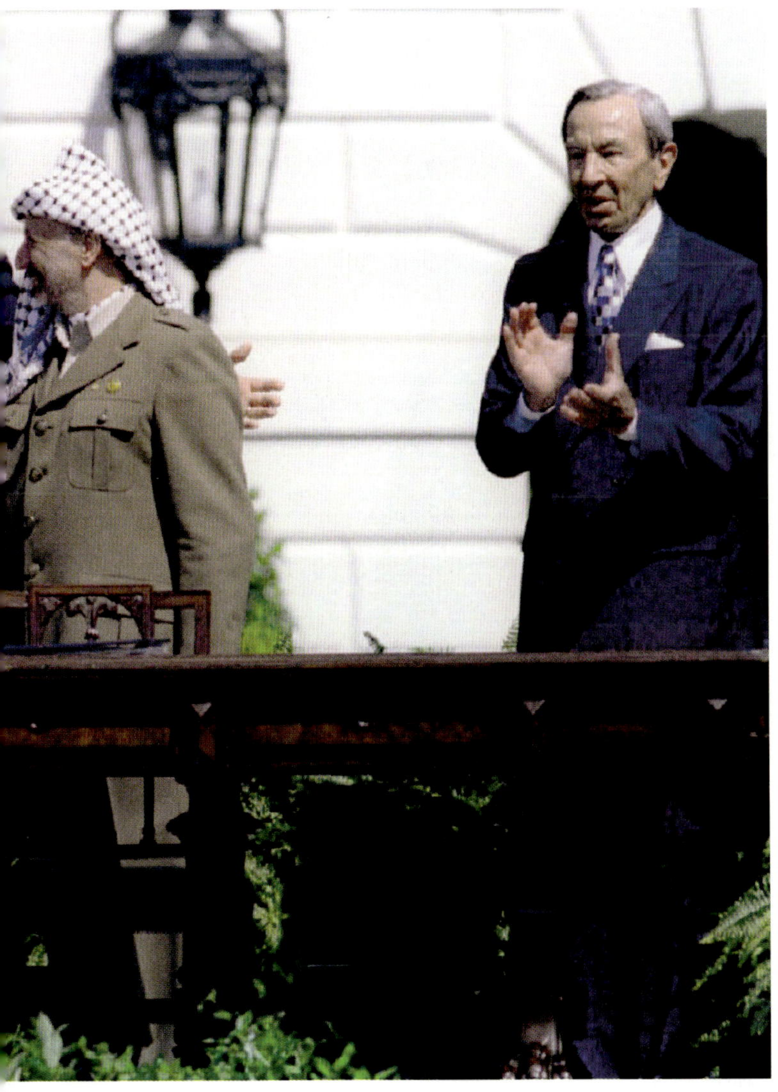

The historic handshake of Prime Minister Iitzhak Rabin of Israel (left) and the PLO chair-man Yasser Arafat at the White House, 13 September 1993.

Histórico apretón de manos entre el primer ministro israelí, Isaac Rabin, (izquierda) y el presidente de la OLP, Yasir Arafat, en la Casa Blanca, el 13 de septiembre de 1993.

La storica stretta di mano fra il Primo Ministro d'Israele Yitzhak Rabin (a sinistra) e il leader della OLP Yasser Arafat alla Casa Bianca, 13 settembre 1993.

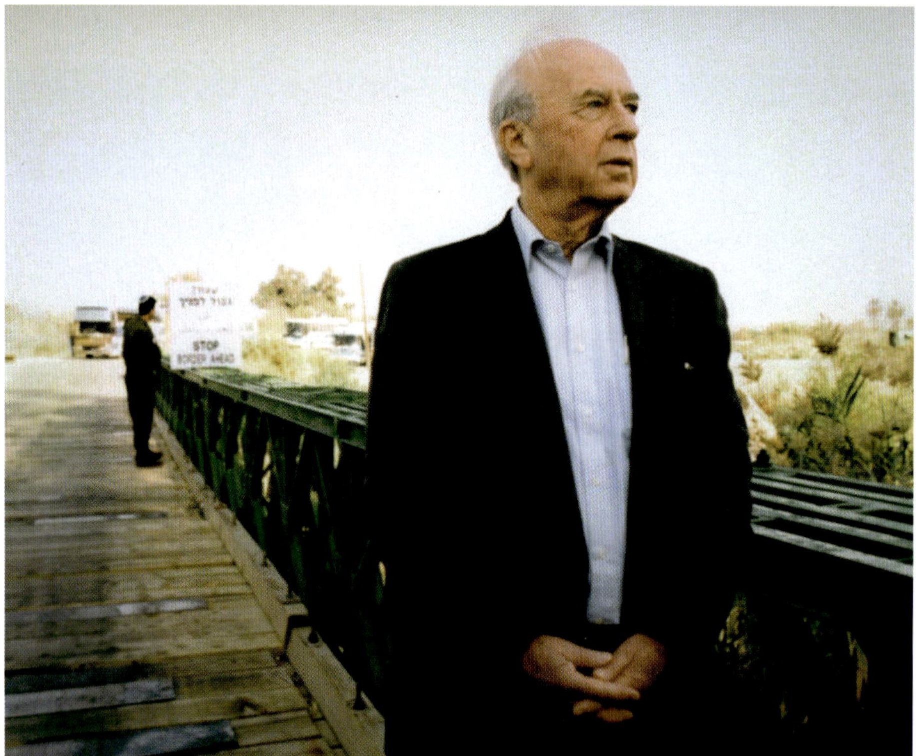

JIM HOLLANDER/REUTERS/ARCHIVE PHOTOS

Hoping for peace. Iitzhak Rabin surveys the West Bank from the Allenby Bridge on the Israel-Jordan border, 6 January 1994. Israel and the PLO had agreed to restart talks to implement the Gaza-Jericho Accord.

La esperanza de paz. Isaac Rabin observa la margen oeste del río Jordán desde el puente Allenby, en la frontera jordano-israelí, 6 de enero de 1994. Israel y la OLP habían aceptado retomar las conversaciones para llevar a la práctica el Acuerdo Gaza-Jericó.

Aria di pace. Yitzhak Rabin osserva la Cisgiordania sul ponte Allenby, alla frontiera fra Israele e Giordania, 6 gennaio 1994. L'Israele e l'OLP avevano deciso di riavviare le trattative per applicare l'accordo di Oslo su Gaza e Gerico.

Preparing for war. Benjamin Netanyahu examines a laser-sighted Tavor at the Israeli Defence Forces technology base, Tel Aviv, 2 September 1997.

Listos para la guerra. Benjamin Netanyahu examina un fusil de asalto Tavor con visor láser en la base tecnológica de las Fuerzas de Defensa israelíes en Tel Aviv, 2 de septiembre de 1997.

Aria di guerra. Benjamin Netanyahu esamina un fucile Tavor con puntatore laser durante una visita presso la base tecnologica delle Forze Armate israeliane a Tel Aviv, 2 settembre 1997.

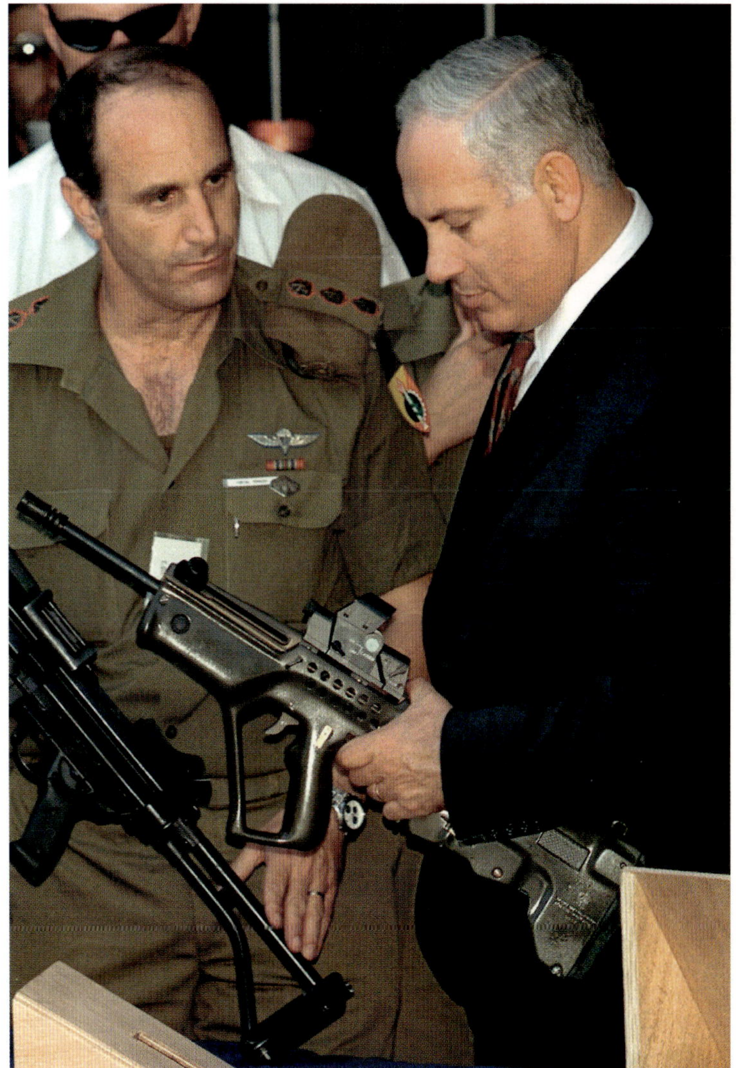

EPA/PA

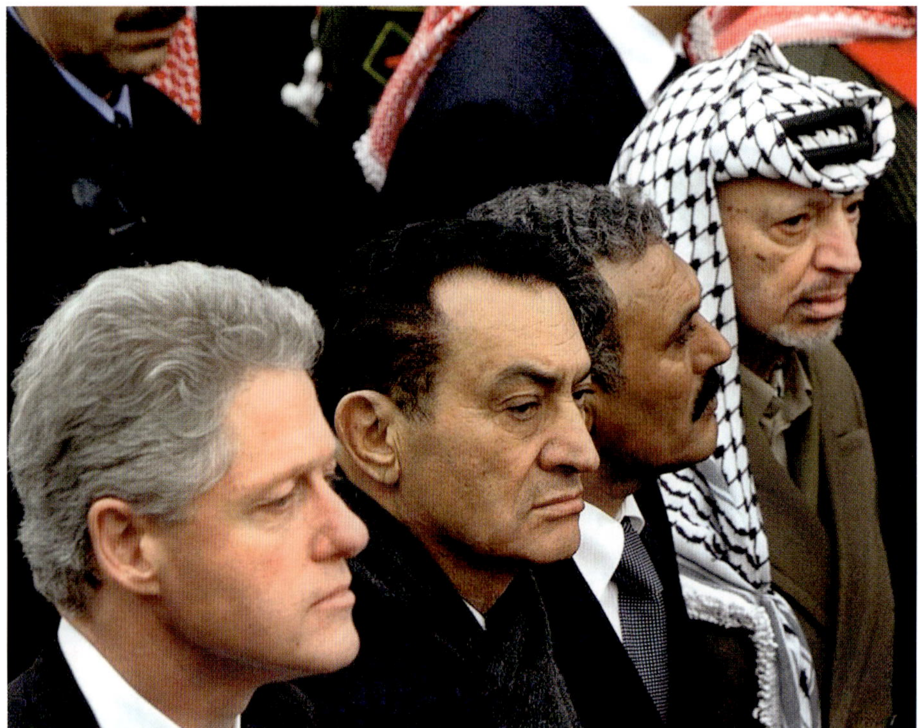

EPA/PA

Funeral of a king. (From left to right) President Clinton, Hosni Mubarak of Egypt, Ali Abdullah Saleh of the Yemen, and the PLO leader Yasser Arafat at the funeral of King Hussein of Jordan, Amman, 8 February 1999.

El funeral de un rey. (De izquierda a derecha) El presidente Clinton, el presidente egipcio Hosni Mubarak, Ali Abdullah Saleh de Yemen y el jefe de la OLP Yasir Arafat asisten al funeral del rey Husein de Jordania en Ammán, 8 de febrero de 1999.

Funerale di un re. (Da sinistra a destra) Il presidente Clinton, il presidente dell'Egitto Hosni Mubarak, il presidente dello Yemen Ali Abdullah Saleh e il leader dell'OLP Yasser Arafat durante il funerale del Re Hussein di Giordania, ad Amman, 8 febbraio 1999.

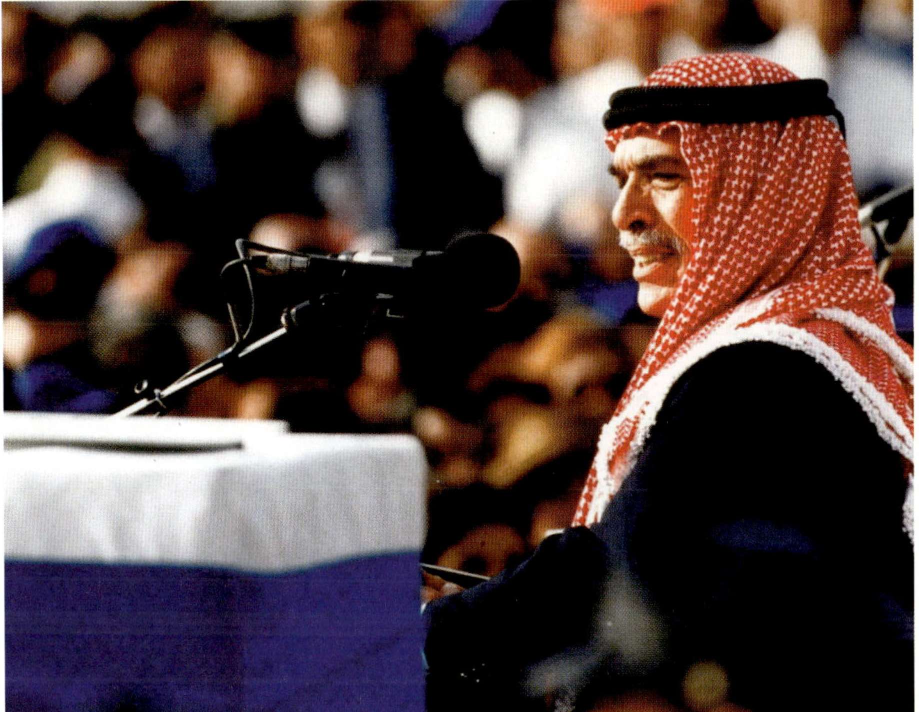

YANNIS BEHRAKIS/REUTERS/ARCHIVE PHOTOS

King at a funeral. King Hussein delivers the eulogy at the funeral of the Israeli Prime Minister Iitzhak Rabin, Jerusalem, 6 November 1995. Rabin had been assassinated – a direct result of the handshake with Arafat two years earlier.

Un rey en un funeral. El 6 de noviembre de 1995 el monarca Husein pronuncia un panegírico en el entierro del primer ministro de Israel, Isaac Rabin. Este último había sido asesinado como consecuencia directa de su apretón de manos con Arafat dos años antes.

Re a un funerale. Il Re Hussein pronuncia un elogio durante il funerale del Primo Ministro israeliano Yitzhak Rabin, a Gerusalemme, 6 novembre 1995. Rabin era stato assassinato, conseguenza diretta della stretta di mano di due anni prima con Arafat.

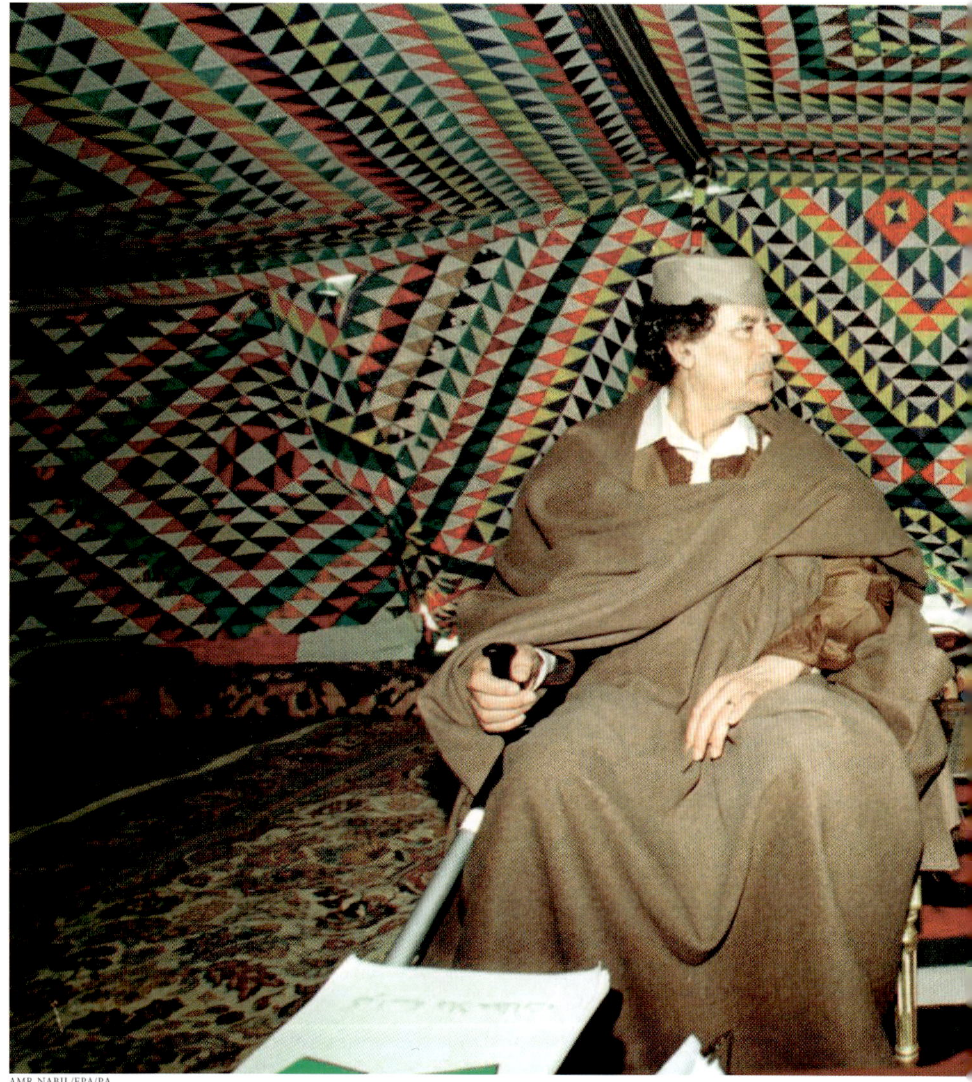

AMR NABIL/EPA/PA

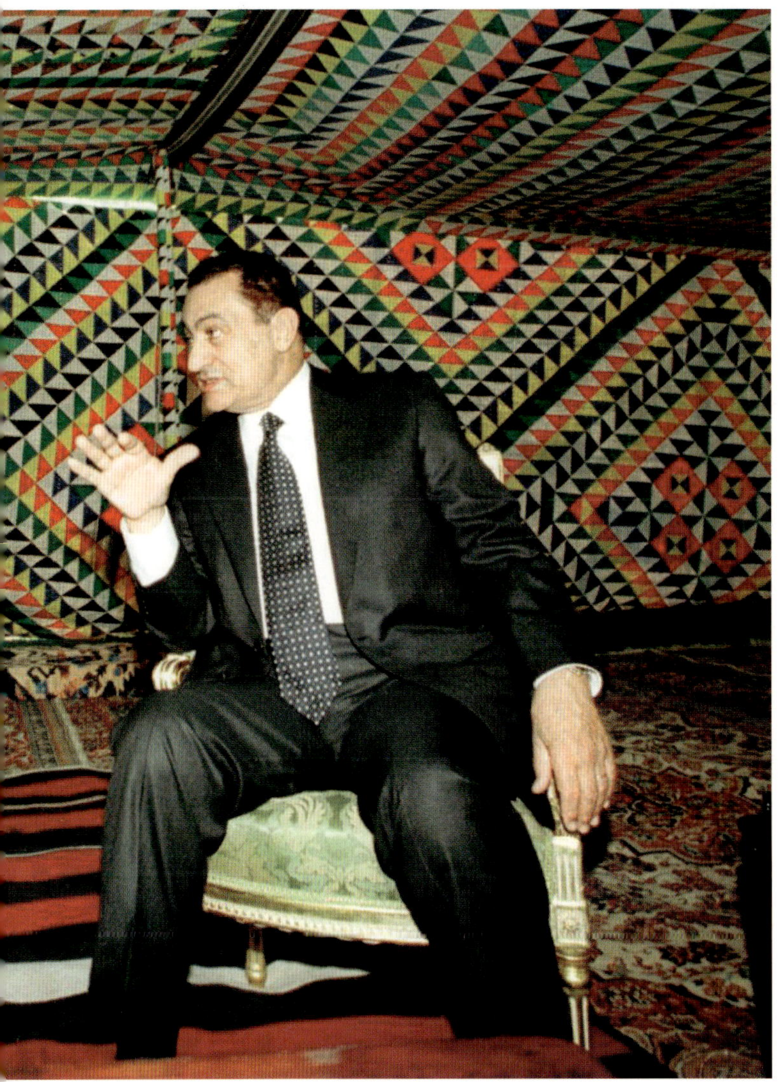

Have tent, will travel... President Hosni Mubarak of Egypt (right) meets Colonel Gaddafi of Libya in the latter's modest tent, Cairo, 6 March 1999.

Con la tienda a cuestas... El presidente egipcio Hosni Mubarak (derecha) mantiene un encuentro con el coronel Gaddafi de Libia en El Cairo el 6 de marzo de 1999. La charla tuvo lugar en la modesta tienda del mandatario libio.

Incontri sotto la tenda... Il presidente dell'Egitto Hosni Mubarak (a destra) conversa con il colonnello libico Gheddafi nella modesta tenda del secondo, a Il Cairo, 6 marzo 1999.

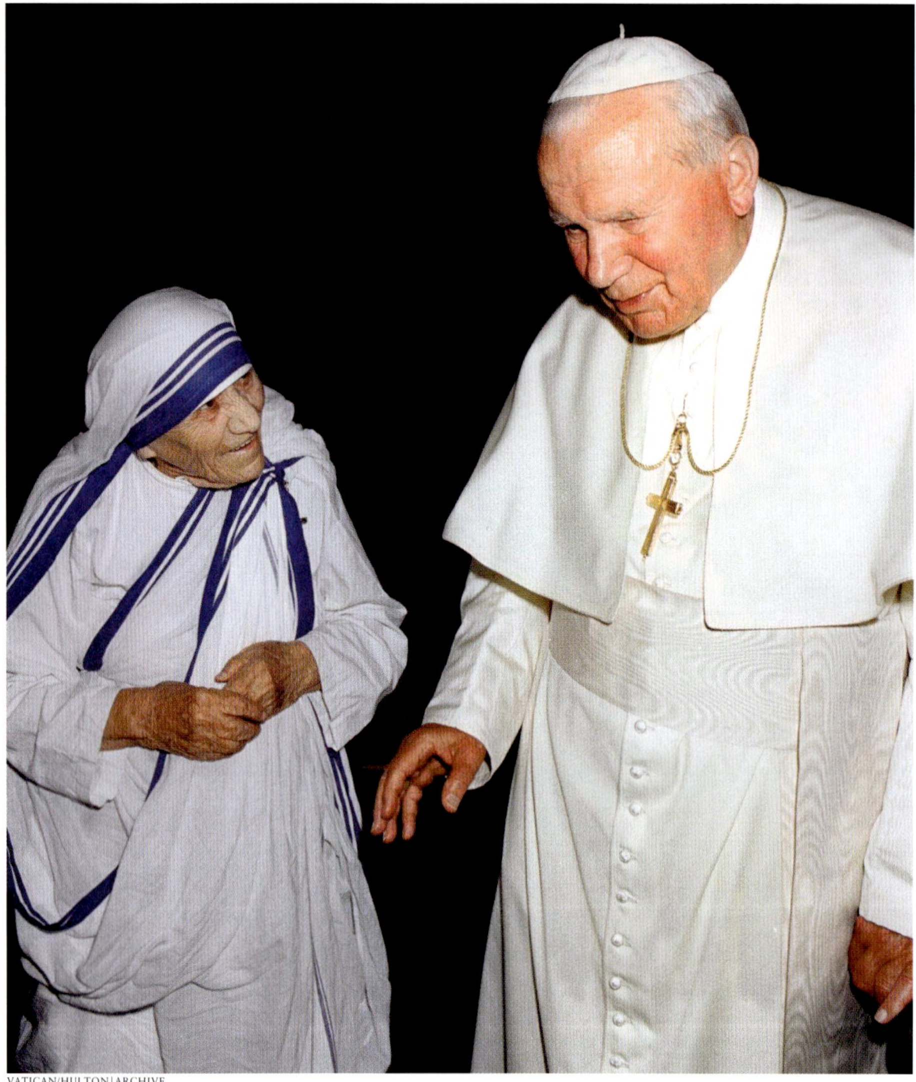

VATICAN/HULTON|ARCHIVE

(Opposite) Mother Theresa and Pope John Paul II meet at the Vatican, 20 May 1997. (Right) Sandra Tigica and Diana, Princess of Wales, Luanda, 14 January 1997.

(Página anterior) Encuentro entre la madre Teresa de Calcuta y el papa Juan Pablo II el 20 de mayo de 1997 en el Vaticano. (Derecha) Sandra Tigica y la princesa Diana de Gales en Luanda, 14 de enero de 1997.

(Pagina a fianco) Madre Teresa e Papa Giovanni Paolo II al Vaticano, 20 maggio 1997. (A destra) Sandra Tigica e Diana, la Principessa di Galles, Luanda, 14 gennaio 1997.

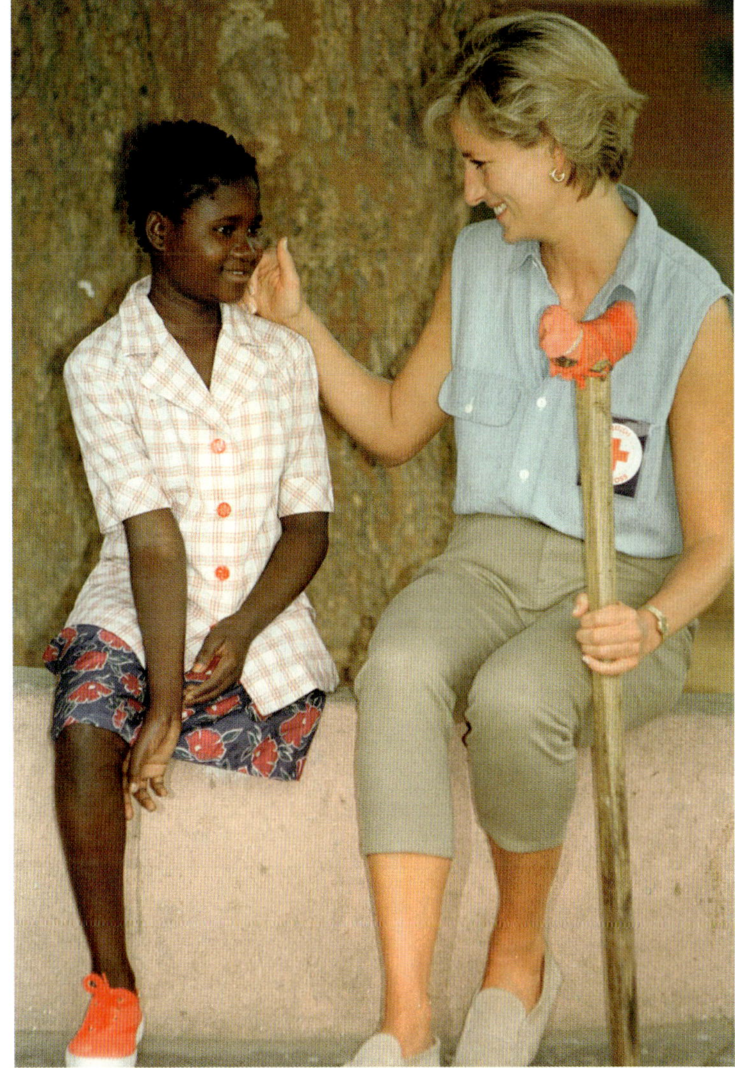

JOHN STILLWELL/PA

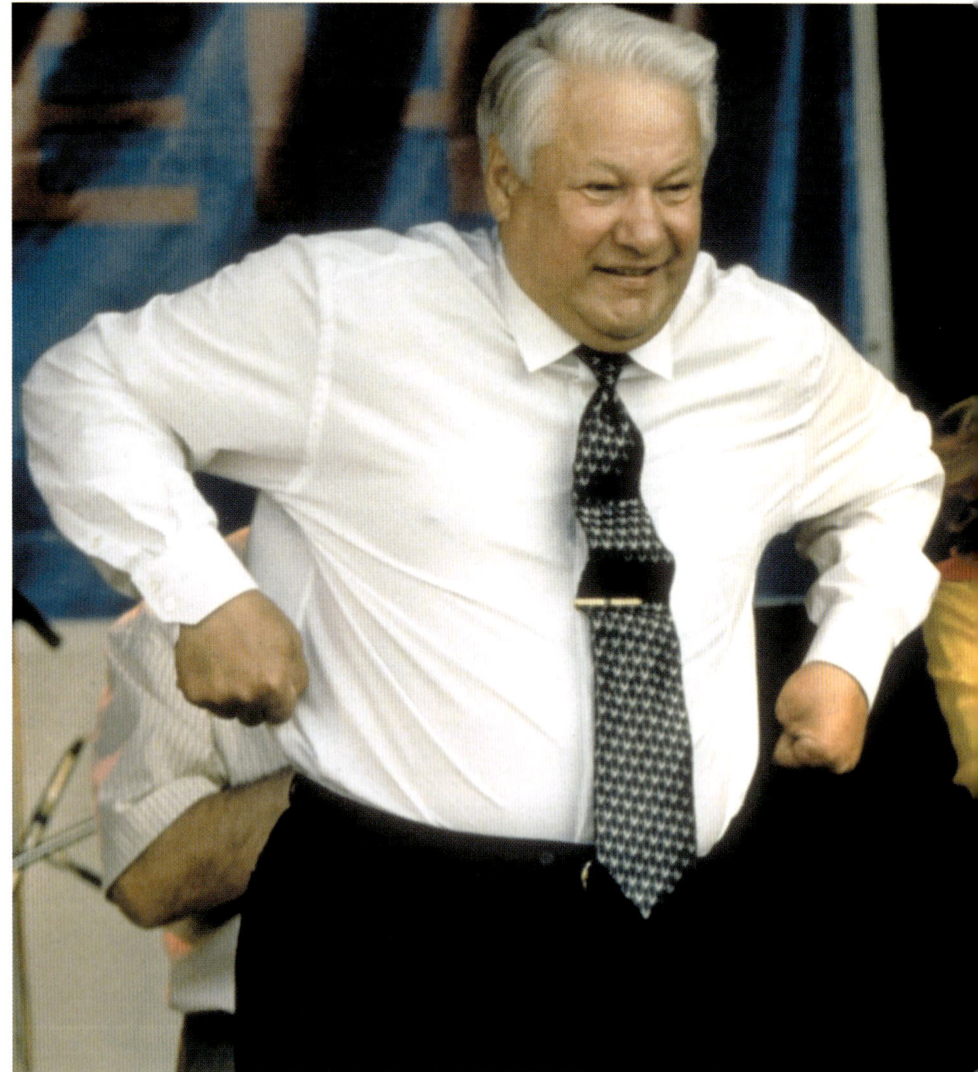

VIKTOR KOROTAYEV/REUTERS/ARCHIVE PHOTOS

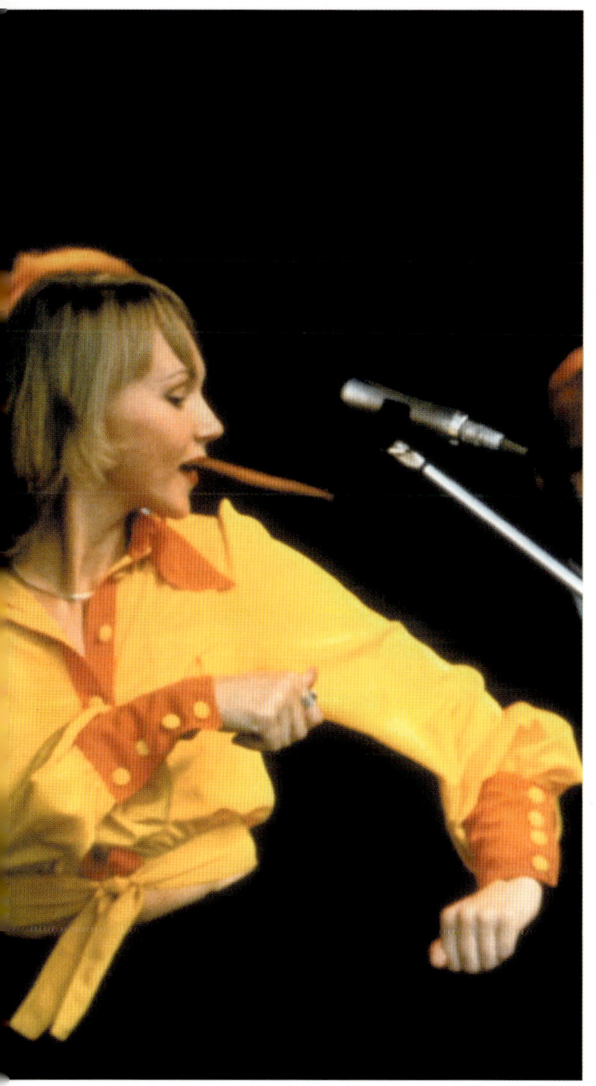

Boris steps out… President Yeltsin puts the dance floor to the test during an election rally, Rostov, Russia, 10 June 1996.

Boris se desmelena… El presidente Yeltsin se lanza a la pista de baile en Rostov, Rusia, durante una gira electoral, 10 de junio de 1996.

Boris si scatena… Il presidente Eltsin mette alla prova il palcoscenico durante una campagna elettorale a Rostov, Russia, 10 giugno 1996.

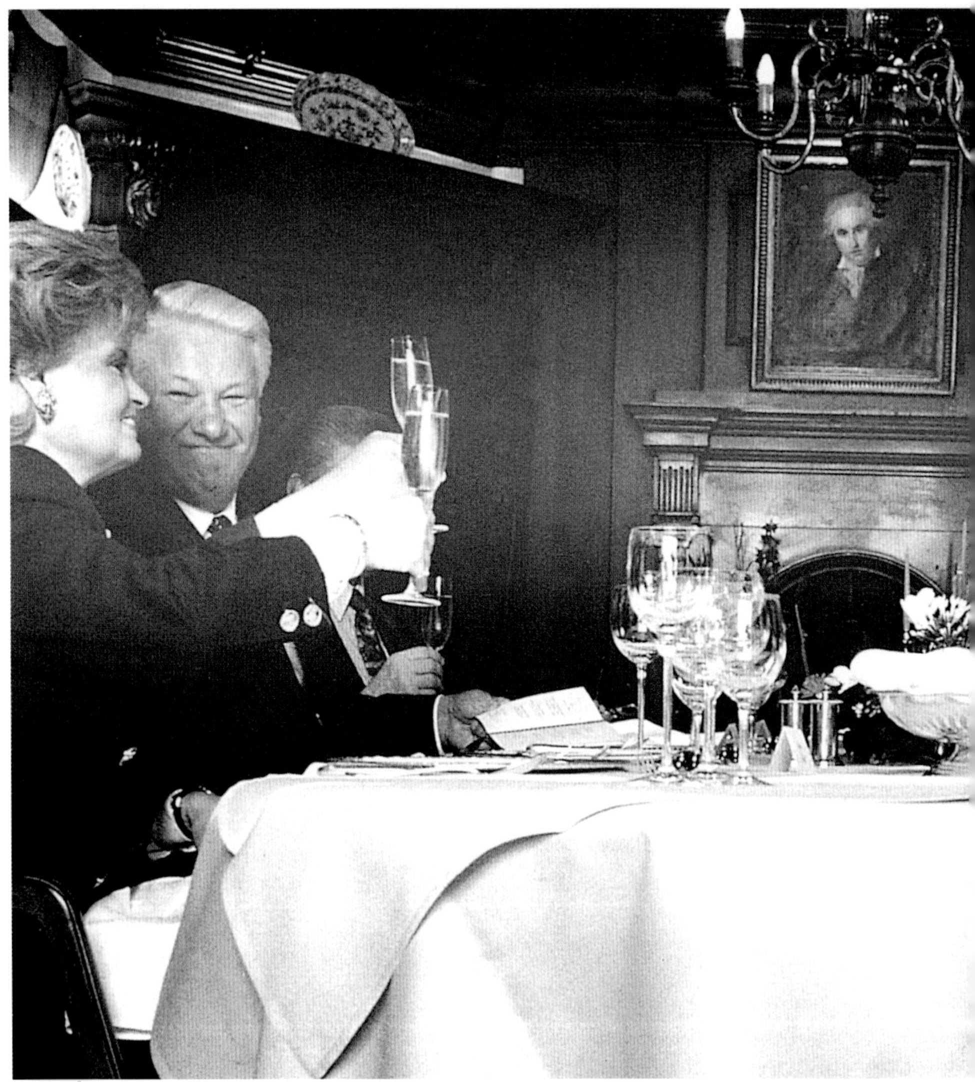

KONRAD MÜLLER/FOCUS/COLORIFIC!

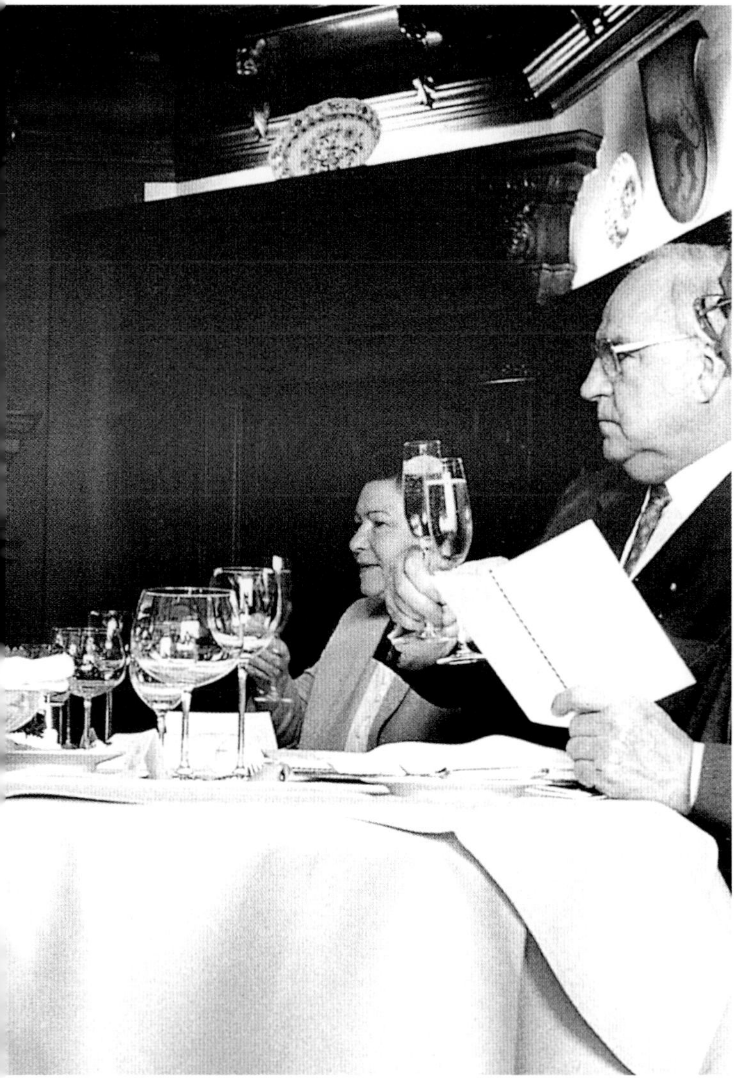

Full glasses, high hopes. The Kohls and the Yeltsins dine together in splendour at Deidesheimer Hof, 1994.

Un brindis por la esperanza. Los Kohl y los Yeltsin cenan juntos en el lujoso hotel Deidesheimer Hof, en 1994.

Bicchieri pieni di speranza. Kohl e Eltsin con le rispettive consorti, durante una sontuosa cena a Deidesheimer Hof, 1994.

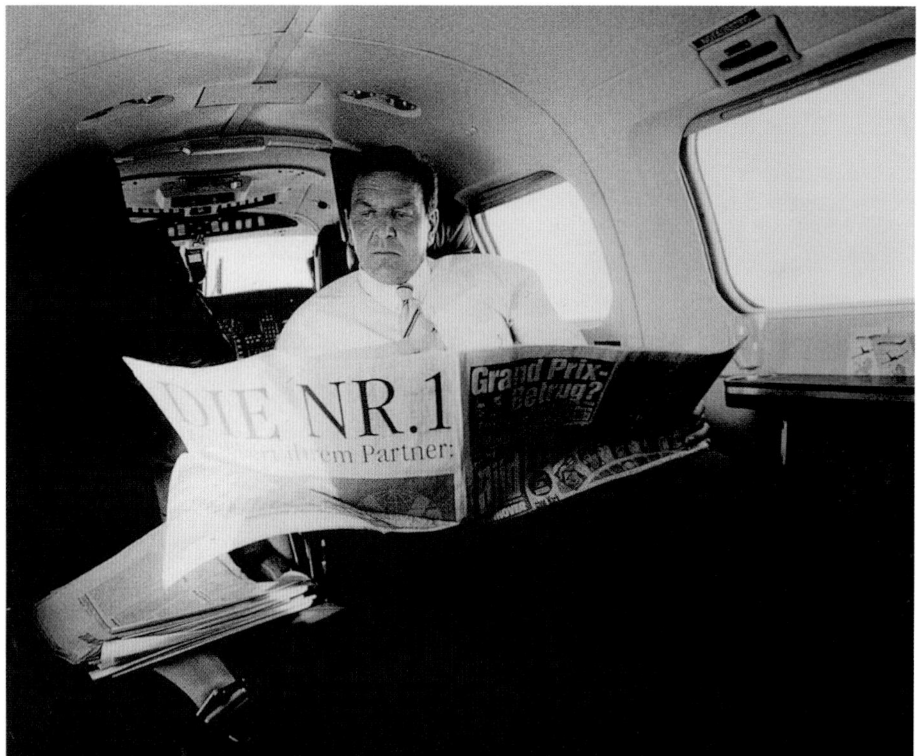

KAY DEGENHARD/FOCUS/COLORIFIC!

Off with the old… (opposite) Chancellor Helmut Kohl of Germany on holiday in Rio de Janeiro, 1991. (Above) …and on with the new. Gerhard Schröder, his successor as leader of the new united Germany, gets down to work in 1998.

Adiós al pasado… (página siguiente) El canciller alemán Helmut Kohl de vacaciones en Río de Janeiro, en 1991. (Arriba) … y bienvenido el futuro. Gerhard Schröder, su sucesor como líder de la nueva Alemania unificada, se pone manos a la obra en 1998.

Fine di un'epoca… (pagina a fianco) Il Cancelliere tedesco Helmut Kohl in vacanza a Rio de Janeiro, 1991. (In alto) …e inizio di una nuova era. Gerhard Schröder, suo successore e leader della nuova Germania riunificata, si mette al lavoro nel 1998.

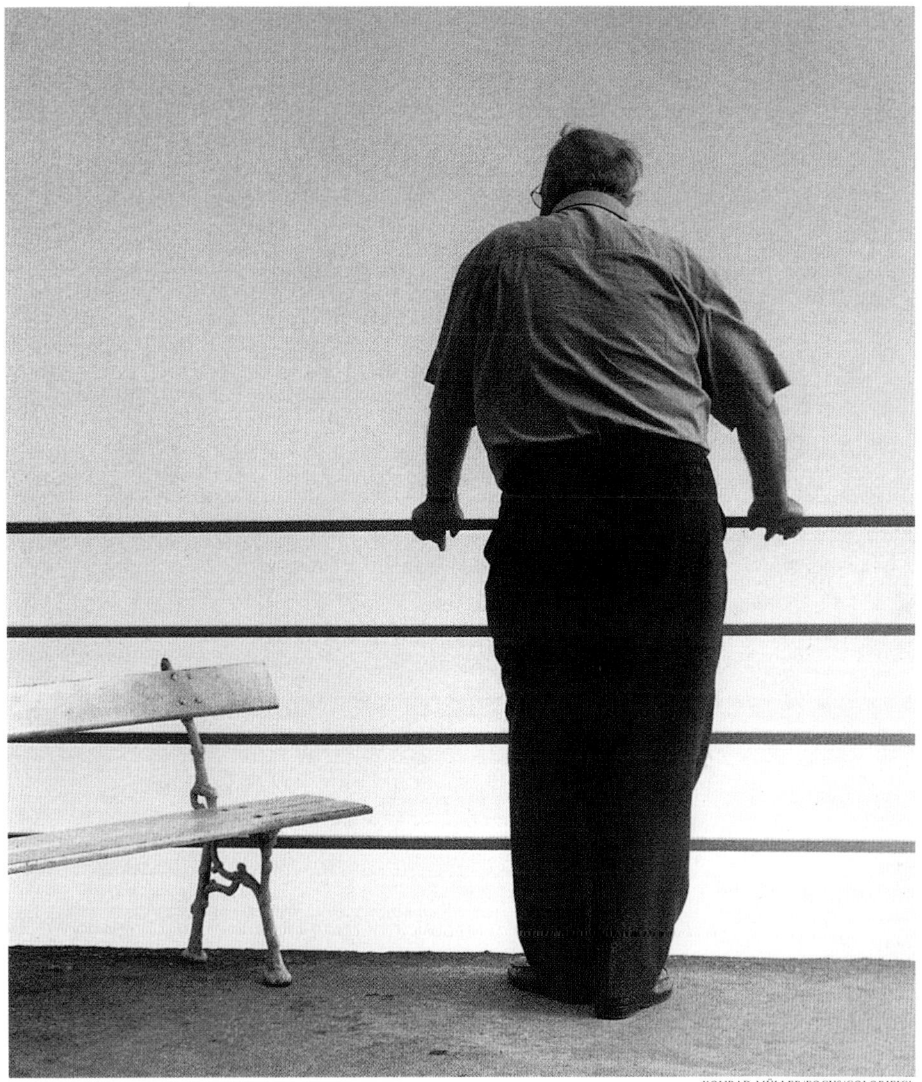

KONRAD MÜLLER/FOCUS/COLORIFIC!

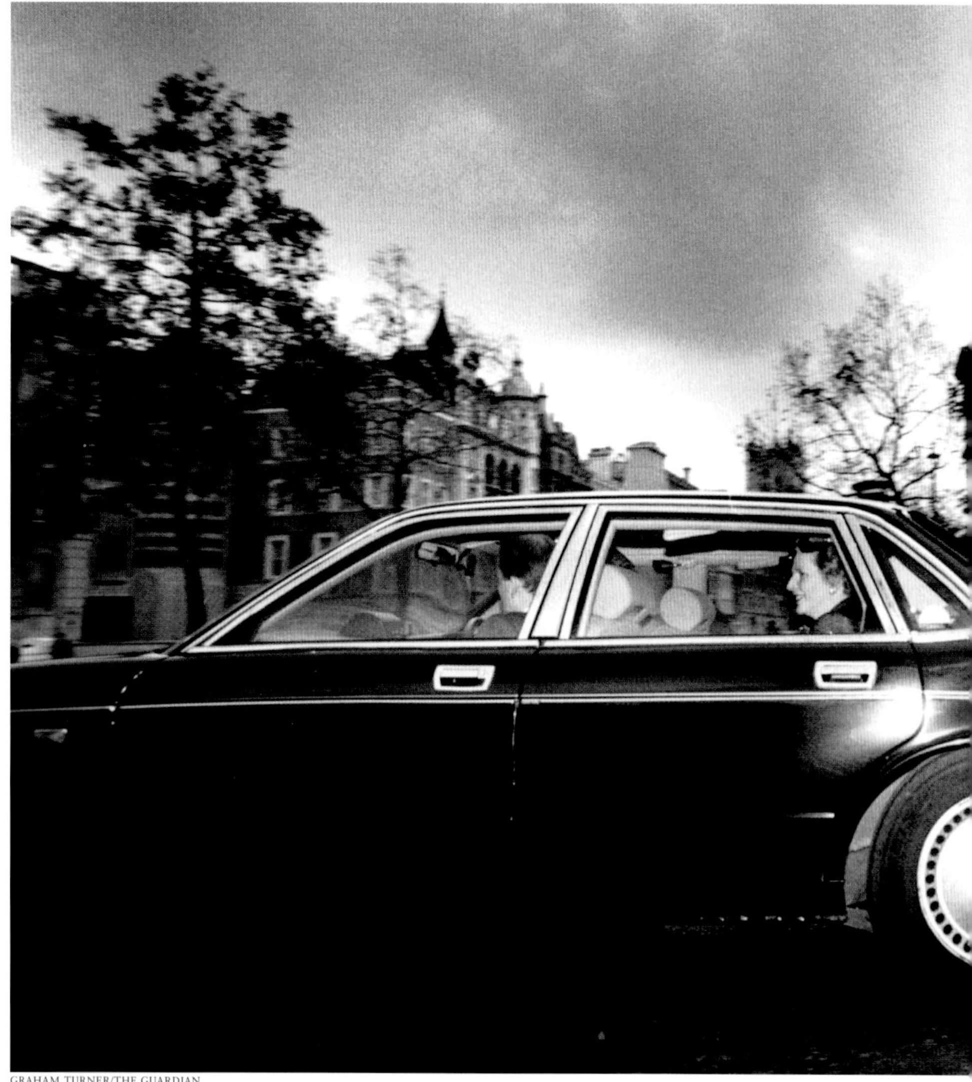

GRAHAM TURNER/THE GUARDIAN

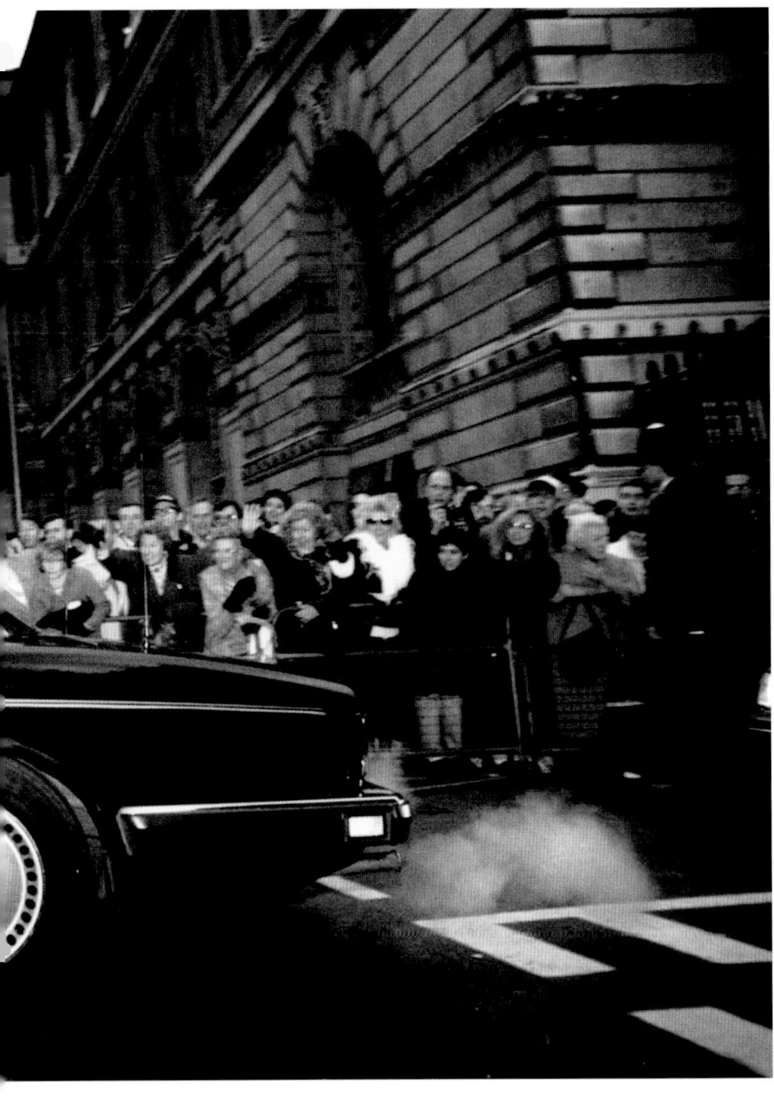

Prime Minister Margaret Thatcher leaves Downing Street for the last time, 21 November 1990. The 1980s had finally come to an end in Britain.

El 21 de noviembre de 1990, la primera ministra Margaret Thatcher sale de Downing Street por última vez. En Gran Bretaña, la década de los ochenta tocaba definitivamente a su fin.

Il Primo Ministro Margaret Thatcher abbandona definitivamente Downing Street, 21 novembre 1990. Finivano così gli anni Ottanta in Gran Bretagna.

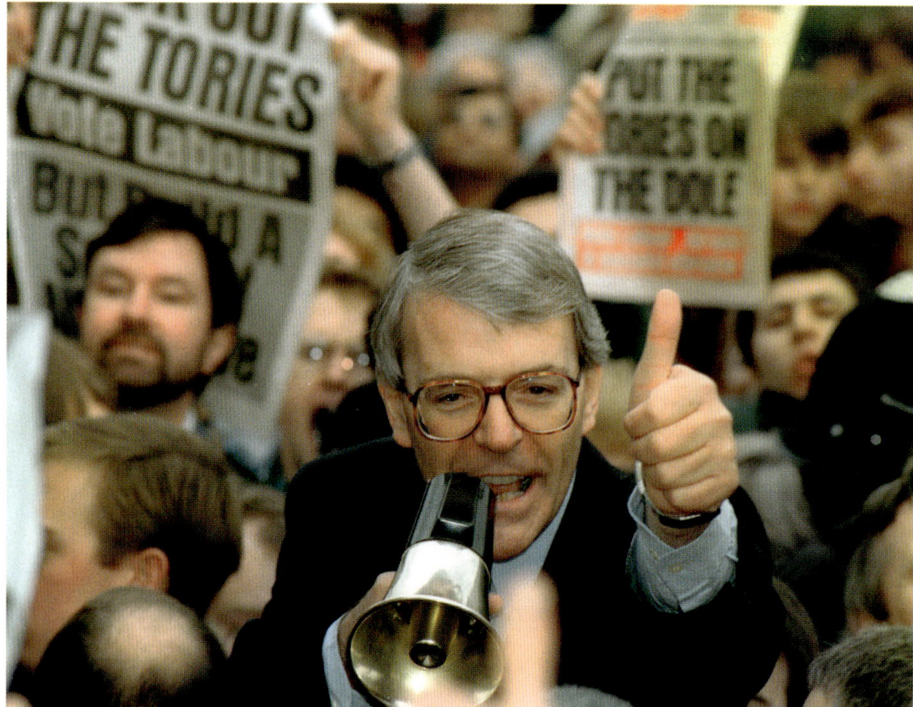

ADAM BUTLER/PA

New man, old methods. John Major takes the battle out on to the streets of Luton in the run-up to the General Election, 3 March 1992. It was a surprising, and ultimately successful, tactic.

Un nuevo hombre con viejos métodos. John Major lleva la lucha a las calles de Luton en la pugna por ganar las elecciones generales británicas, 3 de marzo de 1992. La táctica, aunque sorprendente, se revelaría eficaz.

Nuovo volto, vecchi metodi. John Major scende in campo nelle strade di Luton in occasione della campagna per le elezioni generali, 3 marzo 1992. Una tattica sorprendente ma che si rivela vincente.

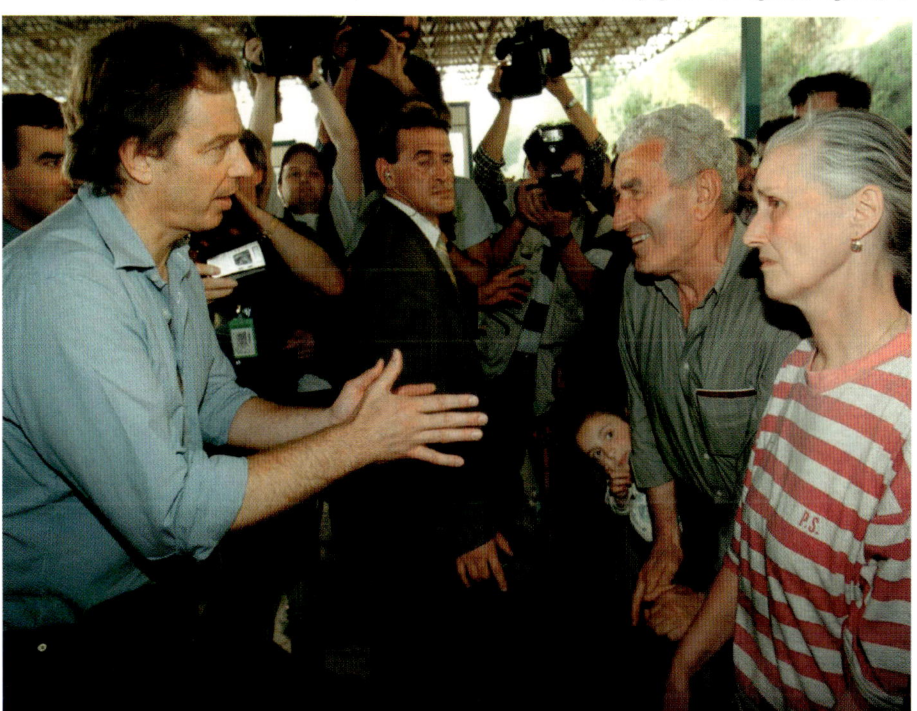

MLADEN ANTONOV/EPA/PA

New man, old problems. Tony Blair, Prime Minister of Britain, talks to Kosovar Albanian refugees, Blace, near Skopje, 3 May 1999. He was on a one-day visit to British soldiers serving with NATO forces.

Un nuevo hombre con viejos problemas. El 3 de mayo de 1999, el primer ministro británico Tony Blair habla con refugiados albano-kosovares en Blace, cerca de Skoplie durante una visita de un día a los soldados británicos al servicio de las fuerzas de la OTAN.

Nuovo volto, vecchi problemi. In occasione di una visita di un giorno ai soldati britannici dell'Esercito della NATO, il Primo Ministro della Gran Bretagna, Tony Blair, parla con i rifugiati kosovaro-albanesi a Blace, nelle vicinanze di Skopje, 3 maggio 1999.

2. Conflict
Conflictos
Conflitti

A distraught boy at the funeral of his father. A Croatian policeman, he had been killed in an ambush during the fighting that followed the Croatian declaration of independence in June 1991.

Un niño llora desconsolado en el funeral de su padre, un policía croata asesinado en una emboscada durante los enfrentamientos posteriores a la declaración de independencia de Croacia, en junio de 1991.

Un bambino disperato durante il funerale del padre, un poliziotto croato ucciso in un'imboscata durante i combattimenti che fecero seguito alla dichiarazione d'indipendenza croata nel giugno del 1991.

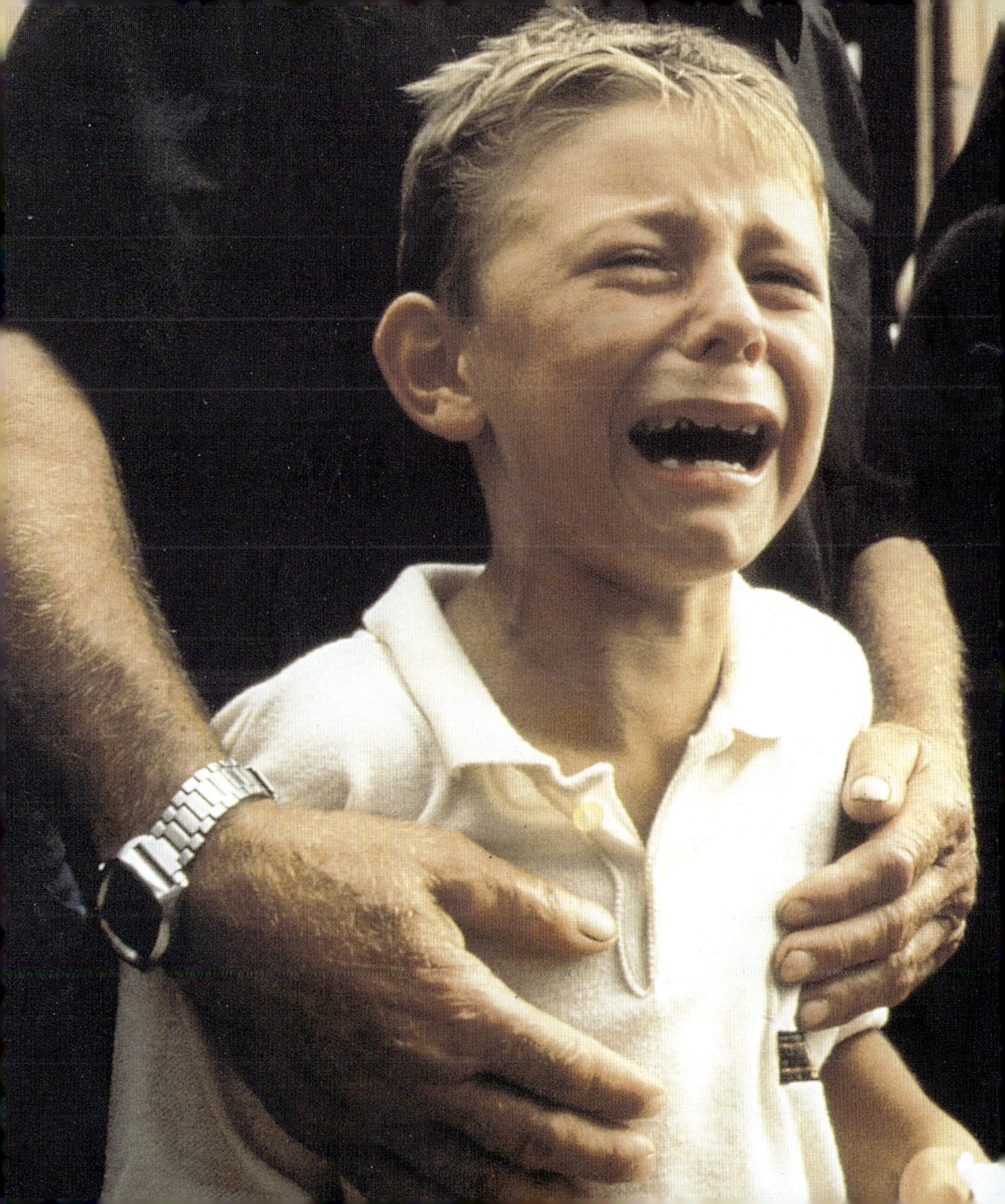

2. Conflict
Conflictos
Conflitti

There had been brave attempts to secure world peace ever since the slaughter of the First World War. Pacifists and politicians had looked to the League of Nations and the United Nations to set up an enforceable code of international law. Protesters had marched through the major cities of the world, calling for an end to nuclear weapons and for 'jaw-jaw' rather than 'war-war' as a means of settling disputes. And yet, more people died on the battlefield in the 20th century than in any other. War still dominated its last few years – in Asia, Africa, the Middle East, Central America and Europe.

Some of the conflicts were local affairs, armed struggles for the control of a country, a region, a neighbourhood. Others, like the Gulf War of 1991, featured the biggest players on the planet. War became a perverted kind of televised sport, a nightly serial for all to see in the comfort of their own homes. At whatever level they were fought, the wars seemed to prove that advances in the destructive power and sophistication of modern weaponry had not been tempered by advances in humanity or mercy. The second oldest sin in the Bible had reached potentially apocalyptic proportions.

Tras las matanzas llevadas a cabo durante la Primera Guerra Mundial, se realizan serios esfuerzos para garantizar la paz en el mundo. Los pacifistas y los políticos miran hacia la Sociedad de Naciones primero y hacia las Naciones Unidas después para establecer un código legal aplicable de ámbito internacional. Los manifestantes recorren las calles de las ciudades más importantes del mundo para pedir la desaparición de las armas nucleares y reclamar que los conflictos se resuelvan por la vía del diálogo y no por el uso de la violencia. Y aun así, en el transcurso del siglo XX más personas se dejaron la vida en el campo de batalla que durante cualquier otro siglo. En Asia, África, Oriente Medio,

América Central y Europa, los últimos años de la centuria siguen dominados por la guerra.

Algunos de los conflictos son asuntos de carácter local; pugnas armadas por el control de un país, de una región o de un territorio vecino. Otros, como la guerra del Golfo de 1991, reúnen en un mismo escenario a algunos de los hombres que mueven las fichas del planeta. La guerra se convierte en una especie de perverso deporte televisivo, un serial nocturno que los seres humanos contemplan cómodamente desde sus hogares. Las guerras, sea cual sea su magnitud, parecen demostrar que los avances del armamento moderno en lo que atañe a poder destructivo y sofisticación superan con creces los progresos del ser humano en cuanto a bondad o misericordia. El segundo pecado más antiguo según la Biblia alcanza en los noventa proporciones potencialmente apocalípticas.

Dopo il massacro provocato dalla Prima guerra mondiale, furono molteplici i coraggiosi tentativi di garantire la pace nel mondo. Gli occhi di pacifisti e di politici si concentrarono tutti sulla Lega delle Nazioni e sulle Nazioni Unite, nella speranza di creare una legislazione internazionale. Nelle principali città del pianeta, i manifestanti marciarono per esigere la scomparsa delle armi nucleari e per far sì che l'uso della parola prevalesse su quello della guerra per risolvere le controversie. Ma nonostante tutto, il XX secolo assistette a molte più morti sul campo di battaglia che nessun'altra epoca. Negli ultimi anni, la guerra continuava a predominare in Asia, in Africa, nel Medio Oriente, in America Centrale e in Europa.

Alcuni conflitti furono dovuti a problemi locali, lotte armate per il controllo di una nazione, una regione, una terra vicina; altri, come la guerra del Golfo, nel 1991, videro in azione i principali attori del pianeta. La guerra divenne così una specie di sport crudele trasmesso in TV, uno spettacolo di prima serata da guardare in poltrona. Qualunque fosse la loro importanza, le guerre sembravano dimostrare che i nuovissimi macchinari di distruzione e le sofisticate armi moderne non andavano di pari passo con una maggiore umanità e misericordia. Il secondo peccato più antico della Bibbia raggiunse così proporzioni potenzialmente apocalittiche.

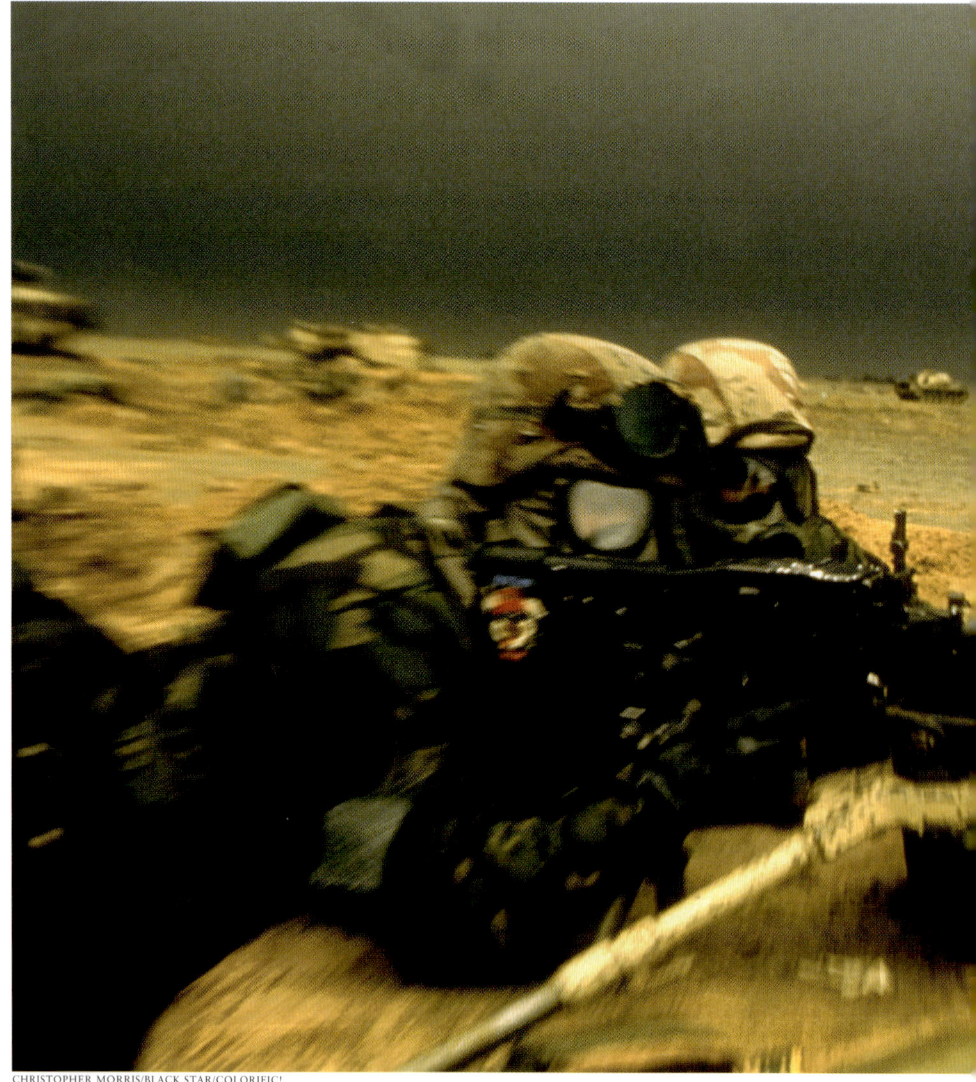

CHRISTOPHER MORRIS/BLACK STAR/COLORIFIC!

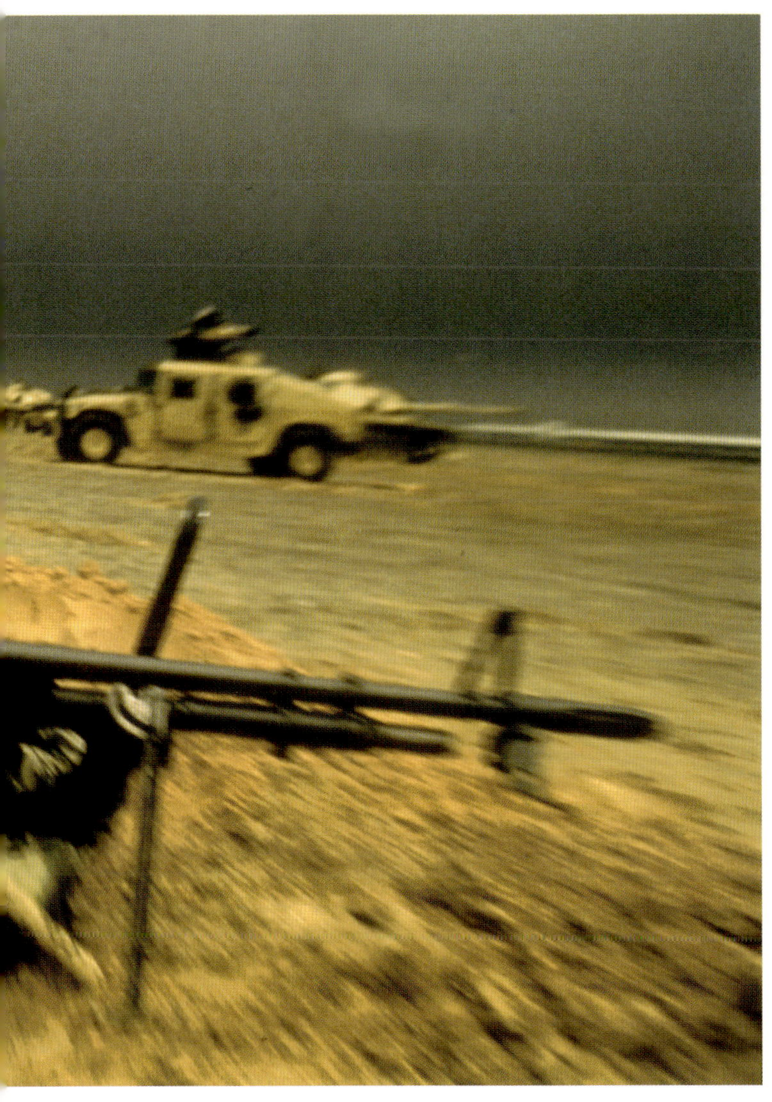

US marines in action at the height of Operation Desert Storm during the Gulf War, 26 February 1991.

Marines estadounidenses en acción en plena operación "Tormenta del Desierto", durante la guerra del Golfo, 26 de febrero de 1991.

Marines statunitensi in azione, nel momento culminante dell'operazione "Tempesta del Deserto" durante la guerra del Golfo, 26 febbraio 1991.

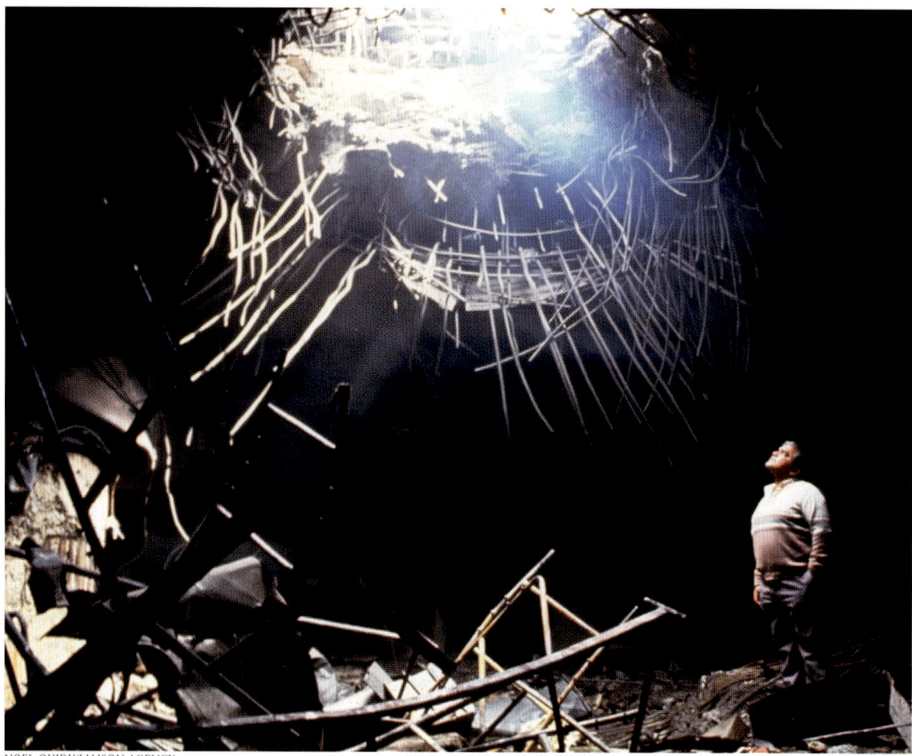

NOEL QUIDU/LIAISON AGENCY

An Iraqi civilian examines damage to a bunker inflicted by an Allied bombing raid on Baghdad, 22 February 1991. The so-called 'smart' bombs of the Allies had an embarrassing habit of hitting the wrong targets.

Un civil iraquí examina los daños causados en un búnker por el bombardeo de las tropas aliadas sobre Bagdad, 22 de febrero de 1991. Las llamadas bombas "inteligentes" tenían la fastidiosa costumbre de alcanzar objetivos equivocados.

Un civile iracheno osserva i danni provocati su un bunker, dopo un raid aereo delle truppe alleate su Baghdad, 22 febbraio 1991. Le cosiddette bombe "intelligenti" degli alleati avevano la pessima abitudine di colpire i bersagli sbagliati.

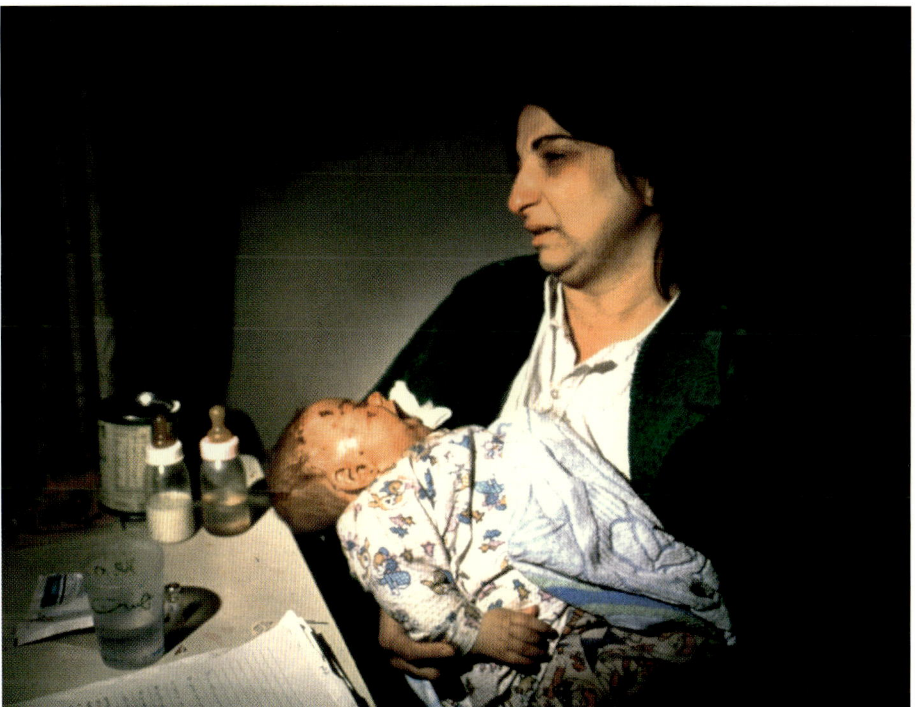

ALI YURTSEVER/LIAISON AGENCY

An Iraqi woman seeks to comfort her baby, wounded during a bomb attack on Baghdad, 7 February 1991. By the end of the war, some 250 Allied troops and more than 150,000 Iraqis had been killed.

Una mujer iraquí intenta calmar a su hijo, herido durante un bombardeo en Bagdad, 7 de febrero de 1991. Al finalizar la guerra, unos 250 soldados aliados y más de 150.000 iraquíes habían fallecido.

Una donna irachena cerca di confortare suo figlio, ferito durante un bombardamento su Baghdad, 7 febbraio 1991. Alla fine della guerra erano morti 250 soldati delle truppe alleate e più di 150.000 iracheni.

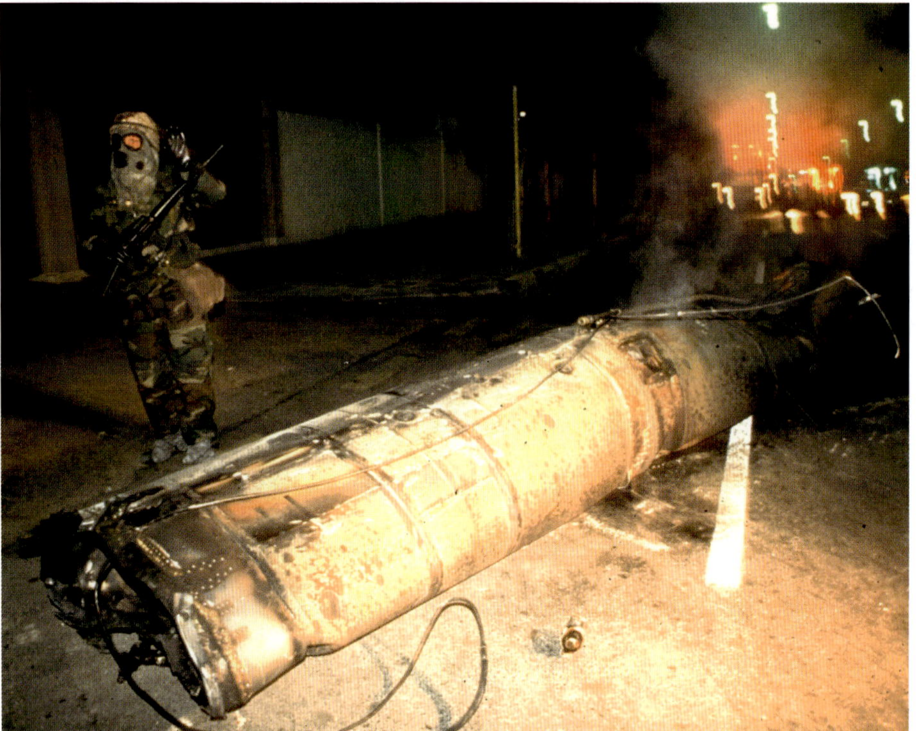

GILLES BASSIGNAC/LIAISON AGENCY

Iraq fights back. The remains of an Iraqi Scud missile intercepted by US Patriot missiles over Riyadh, Saudi Arabia, 22 January 1991. The war was just six days old and had five more weeks to run.

Irak contraataca. Restos de un misil Scud iraquí interceptado por las defensas antimisiles estadounidenses Patriot en Riad, Arabia Saudí, 22 de enero de 1991. La guerra había empezado hacía tan solo seis días y aún faltaban cinco semanas para que tocara a su fin.

L'Iraq contrattacca. I resti di uno Scud iracheno intercettato dai missili Patriot statunitensi su Riyadh, Arabia Saudita, 22 gennaio 1991. La guerra era iniziata solo sei giorni prima e doveva durare ancora cinque settimane.

ESAÏAS BAITEL/LIAISON AGENCY

An Iraqi Scud inflicts heavy damage on Tel Aviv, Israel, 22 January 1991. Such photographs helped the Allies gain the high moral ground during the propaganda struggle.

Un misil Scud iraquí causa graves daños en Tel Aviv, Israel, 22 de enero de 1991. Fotografías como esta contribuían a la victoria moral de los aliados en la lucha propagandística.

Uno Scud iracheno provoca gravi danni su Tel Aviv, Israele, 22 gennaio 1991. Foto come questa sancirono per gli alleati una vittoria morale durante la battaglia propagandistica.

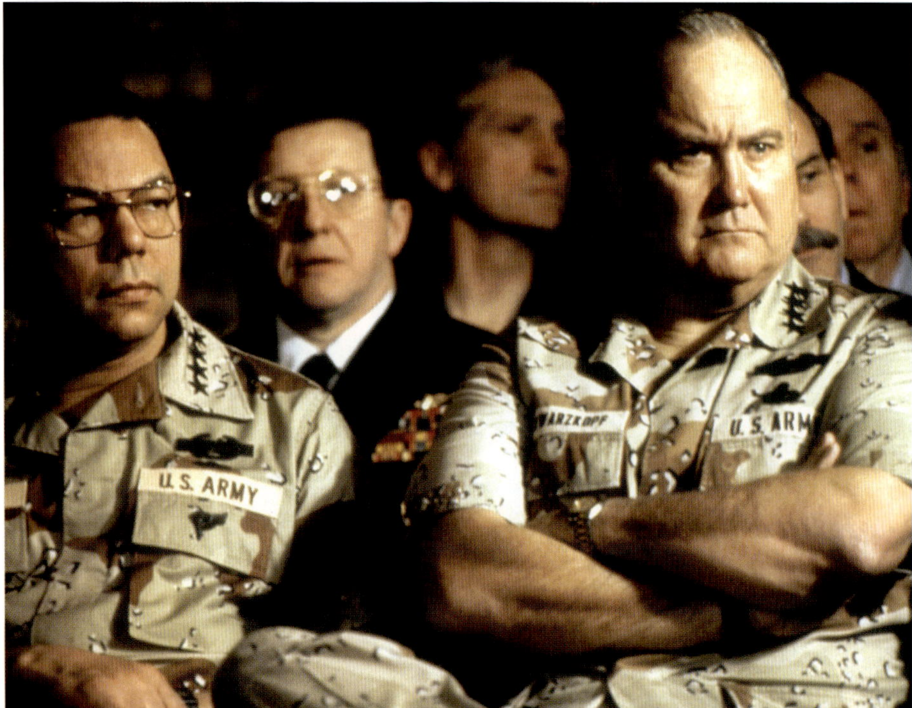

DENNIS BRACK/BLACK STAR/COLORIFIC!

(Above and opposite) Contrasting portraits of the Gulf War. (Above) American High Command: (from left to right) General Colin Powell and General 'Stormin'' Norman Schwarzkopf.

(Arriba y página siguiente) Imágenes dispares de una misma guerra. (Arriba) Altos mandos del Ejército estadounidense: a la izquierda, el general Colin Powell y a la derecha, el general Norman Schwarzkopf, conocido como "el oso del desierto".

(In alto e nella pagina a fianco) Immagini antitetiche della guerra del Golfo. (In alto) Alti comandi statunitensi: (da sinistra a destra) i generali Colin Powell e *Stormin*' Norman Schwarzkopf.

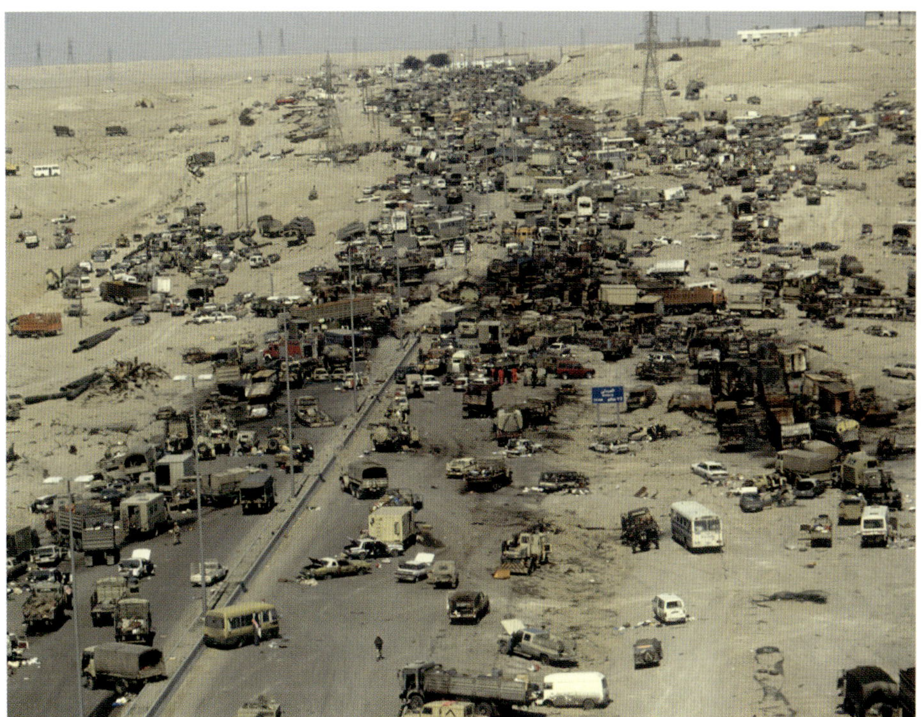

DENNIS BRACK/BLACK STAR/COLORIFIC!

The highway of death: the Baghdad–Basra road after an American bombing raid, 28 February 1991. Iraqi losses were at their heaviest in the last few days of the war, after their defence system had been all but obliterated.

La autopista de la muerte. Esta es la imagen que ofrecía la carretera que conecta Bagdad y Basora tras el bombardeo norteamericano del 28 de febrero de 1991. Las bajas entre los iraquíes fueron muy numerosas durante los últimos días del combate ya que su sistema de defensa había sido completamente aniquilado.

L'autostrada della morte: la strada che unisce Baghdad a Bassora dopo un bombardamento statunitense, 28 febbraio 1991. Le perdite più importanti per l'Iraq ebbero luogo verso la fine della guerra, quando ormai il sistema di difesa era stato completamente annientato.

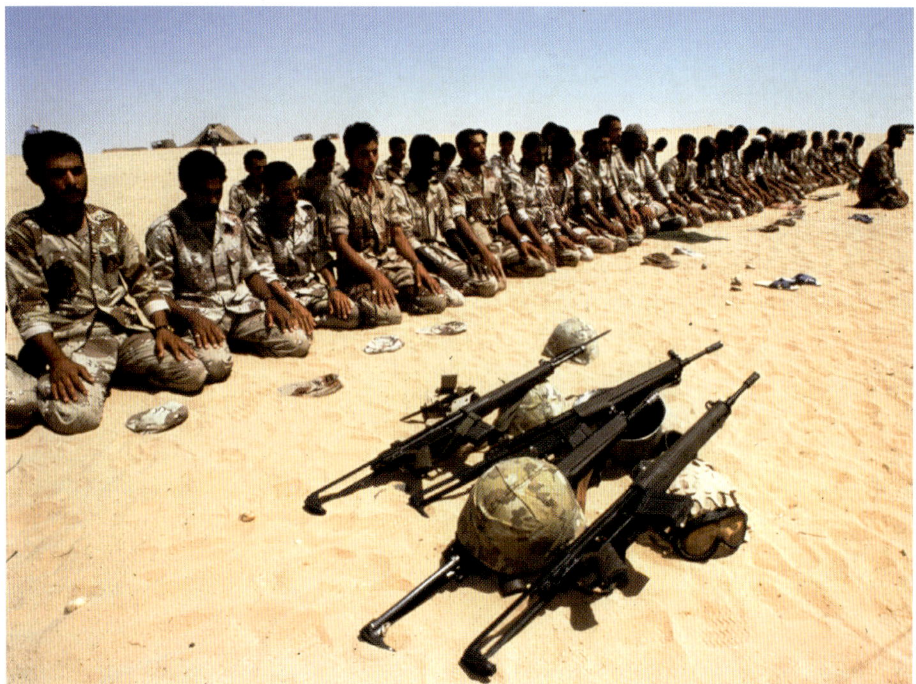

L VAN DER STOCKT/LIAISON AGENCY

Prayers of the faithful. Saudi soldiers, part of the Arab coalition forces ranged against Iraq, at prayer in the desert, 4 September 1990. The force was assembled after Saddam Hussein seized Kuwait.

La oración de los fieles. Soldados saudíes integrantes de las fuerzas de coalición árabes contra Irak rezan en el desierto, 4 de septiembre de 1990. La coalición árabe se forma tras la invasión de Kuwait por parte de Sadam Husein.

Le preghiere dei fedeli. Soldati sauditi, parte delle forze di coalizione arabe allineate contro l'Iraq, nel momento della preghiera nel deserto, 4 settembre 1990. Queste forze si radunarono dopo l'invasione del Kuwait da parte di Saddam Hussein.

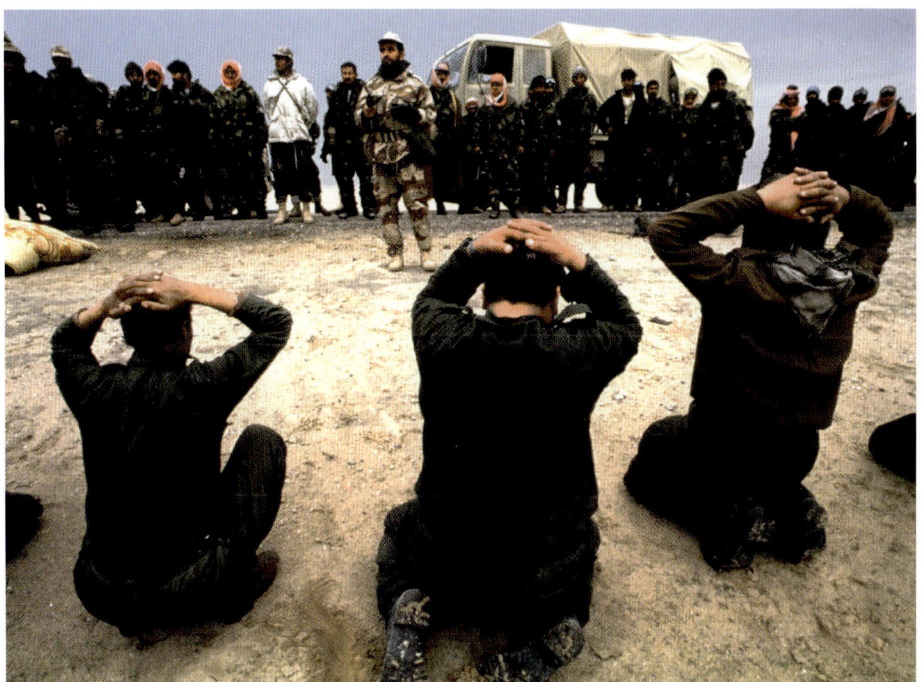

GILLES SAUSSIER/LIAISON AGENCY

Prey of the Allies. Troops of the Arab coalition confront three Iraqi soldiers taken prisoner during the liberation of Kuwait, 28 February 1991. Tens of thousands of Iraqis were captured during the operation.

Presa de los aliados. Tropas de la coalición árabe frente a tres soldados iraquíes apresados durante la liberación de Kuwait, 28 de febrero de 1991. Decenas de miles de iraquíes fueron capturados en el curso de dicha operación.

Prigionieri degli Alleati. Truppe della coalizione araba di fronte a tre soldati iracheni imprigionati durante la liberazione del Kuwait, 28 febbraio 1991. Durante tale operazione vennero catturate decine di migliaia di iracheni.

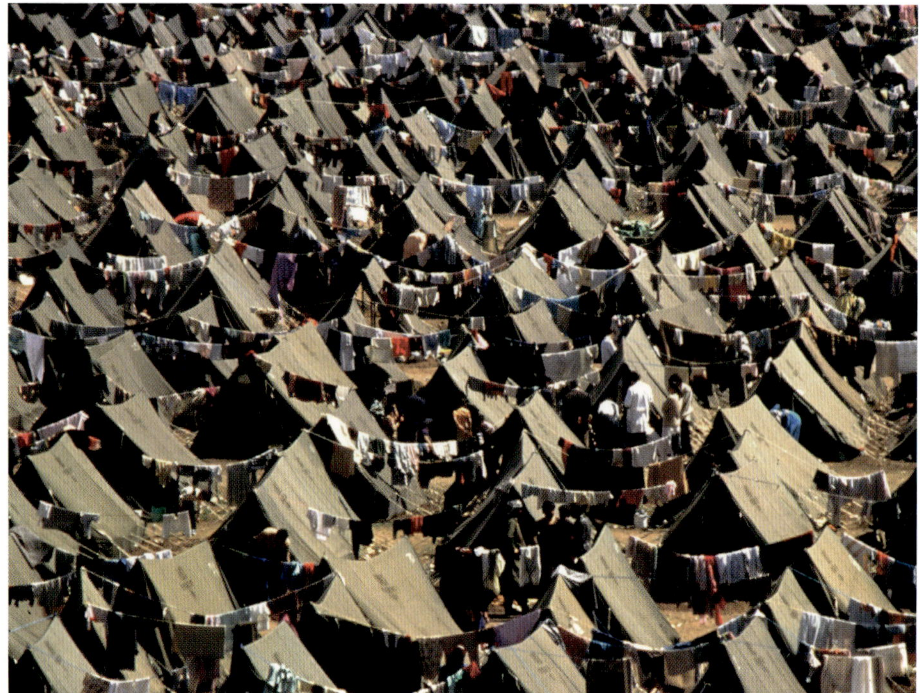

MARC DEVILLE/LIAISON AGENCY

The war against the Kurds. A section of a vast Kurdish refugee encampment at Silopi transit camp, Turkey, 17 April 1991. With the end of the Gulf War, Saddam Hussein was free to turn his wrath on opponents within Iraq's borders.

La guerra contra los kurdos. Parte de un vasto campamento de refugiados kurdos en la población fronteriza de Silopi, en Turquía, 17 de abril de 1991. Una vez acabada la guerra del Golfo, Sadam Husein era libre de dirigir su ira hacia su oponente más cercano: el pueblo kurdo de Irak.

Guerra contro i curdi. Parte di un enorme campo profughi curdo a Silopi, Turchia, 17 aprile 1991. Con la fine della guerra del Golfo, Saddam Hussein poteva tranquillamente scatenare tutta la propria ira sui suoi oppositori in territorio iracheno.

One of the hundreds of victims severely burnt during poison gas attacks by Iraqi troops in Kurdistan, 1994.

Uno de los cientos de víctimas que sufrieron graves quemaduras a causa de los ataques con gas lanzados por las tropas iraquíes sobre el Kurdistán en 1994.

Una delle centinaia di vittime con gravi ustioni provocate dagli attacchi con gas tossici perpetrati dalle truppe irachene nel Kurdistan, 1994.

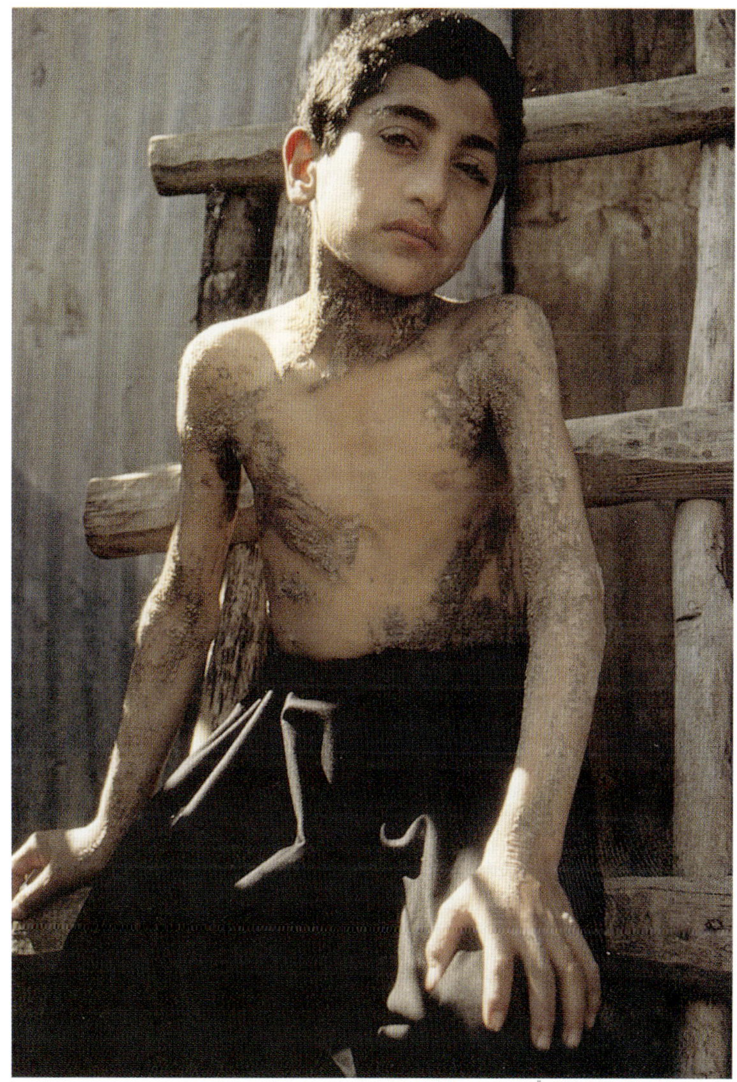

GÜNTHER MENN/FOCUS/COLORIFIC!

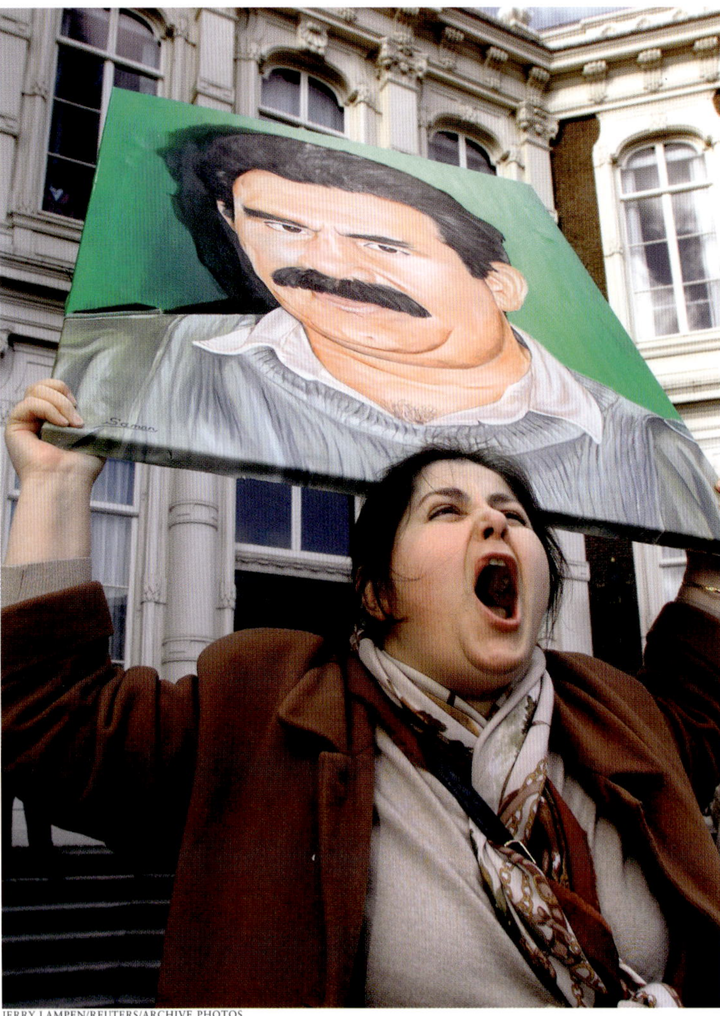

JERRY LAMPEN/REUTERS/ARCHIVE PHOTOS

A Kurdish woman holds aloft a portrait of the PKK leader Abdullah Öcalan at a protest meeting in The Hague, 16 February 1999.

Una mujer kurda sostiene un retrato del líder del PKK (Partido de los Trabajadores del Kurdistán), Abdalá Ocalan, durante un acto de protesta en La Haya, el 16 de febrero de 1999.

Una curda tiene in alto un ritratto del leader del PKK Abdullah Öcalan durante una protesta a L'Aia, 16 febbraio 1999.

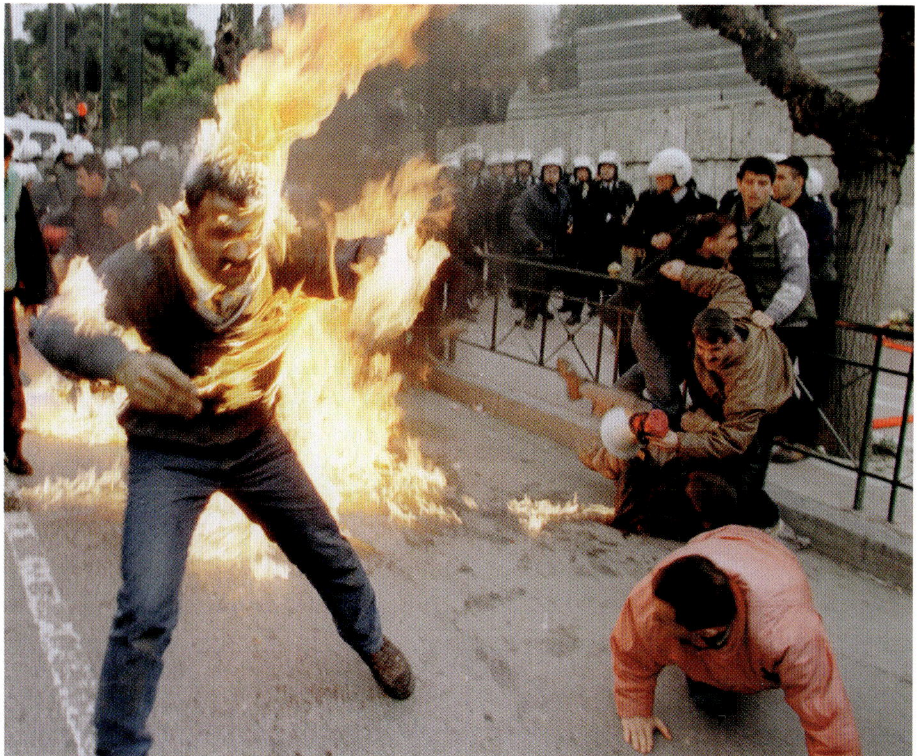

SRYROS TSAKIRIS/REUTERS/ARCHIVE PHOTOS

In an attempt to thwart attempts by Greek police to break up a Kurdish protest outside the Greek Parliament building in Athens, 15 February 1999, two of the protesters set light to themselves.

Dos manifestantes se prenden fuego frente al Parlamento de Atenas con el propósito de disuadir a la policía de intentar disolver la manifestación kurda, 15 de febrero de 1999.

Due manifestanti si danno fuoco per cercare di resistere ai tentativi della polizia greca di disperdere una protesta curda di fronte al Parlamento di Atene, 15 febbraio 1999.

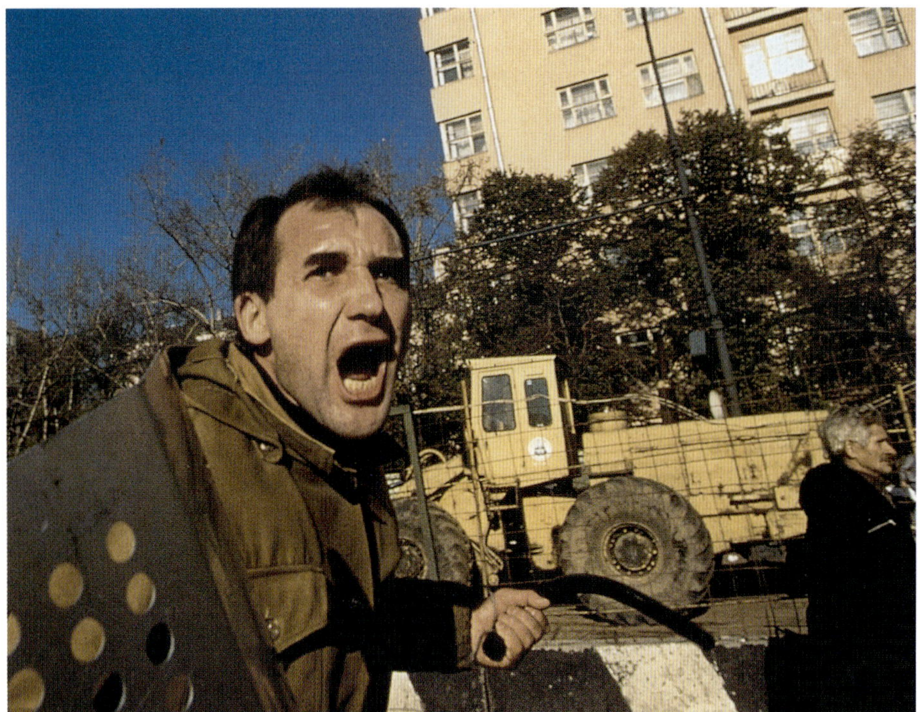

CHRISTOPHER MORRIS/BLACK STAR/COLORIFIC!

Armed with riot shield and rubber truncheon wrested from the police, a Russian protester adds passion to an anti-Yeltsin demonstration in front of the White House in Moscow, 3 October 1993.

Provisto de un escudo antidisturbios y una porra de goma arrebatados a la policía, un manifestante ruso caldea el ambiente en una manifestación antiYeltsin frente a la Casa Blanca de Moscú, el 3 de octubre de 1993.

Un manifestante russo, armato con uno scudo antisommossa e un manganello di gomma rubati alla polizia, durante una manifestazione contro Eltsin di fronte alla "Casa Bianca" di Mosca, 3 ottobre 1993.

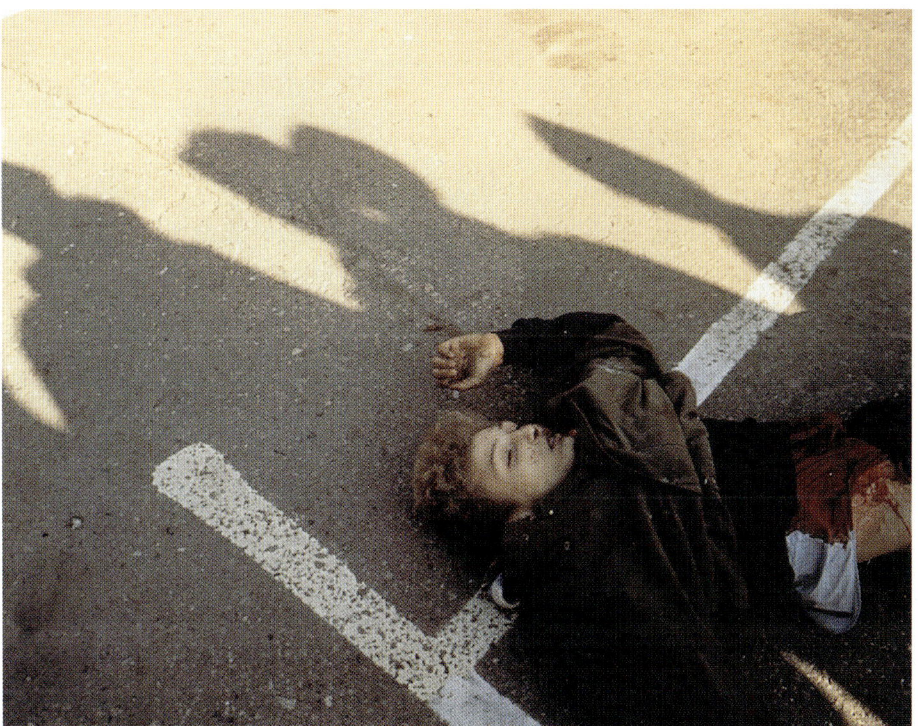

CHRISTOPHER MORRIS/BLACK STAR/COLORIFIC!

A civilian killed during the demonstration. Yeltsin's announcement that he was suspending the Russian Parliament intensified the struggle between pro- and anti-reform groups. The following morning, Yeltsin ordered tanks to fire on the rebels.

Un civil muere durante la manifestación. El anuncio de la disolución del Parlamento por parte de Yeltsin intensificó la lucha entre los reformistas y los conservadores. A la mañana siguiente, el presidente ruso ordenó que los tanques abrieran fuego contra los rebeldes.

Un civile ucciso durante la manifestazione. Non appena Eltsin proclamò la dissoluzione del Parlamento russo, si intensificarono i combattimenti fra gruppi a favore e gruppi contro la riforma. Il giorno seguente Eltsin ordinava ai carri armati di aprire il fuoco contro i ribelli.

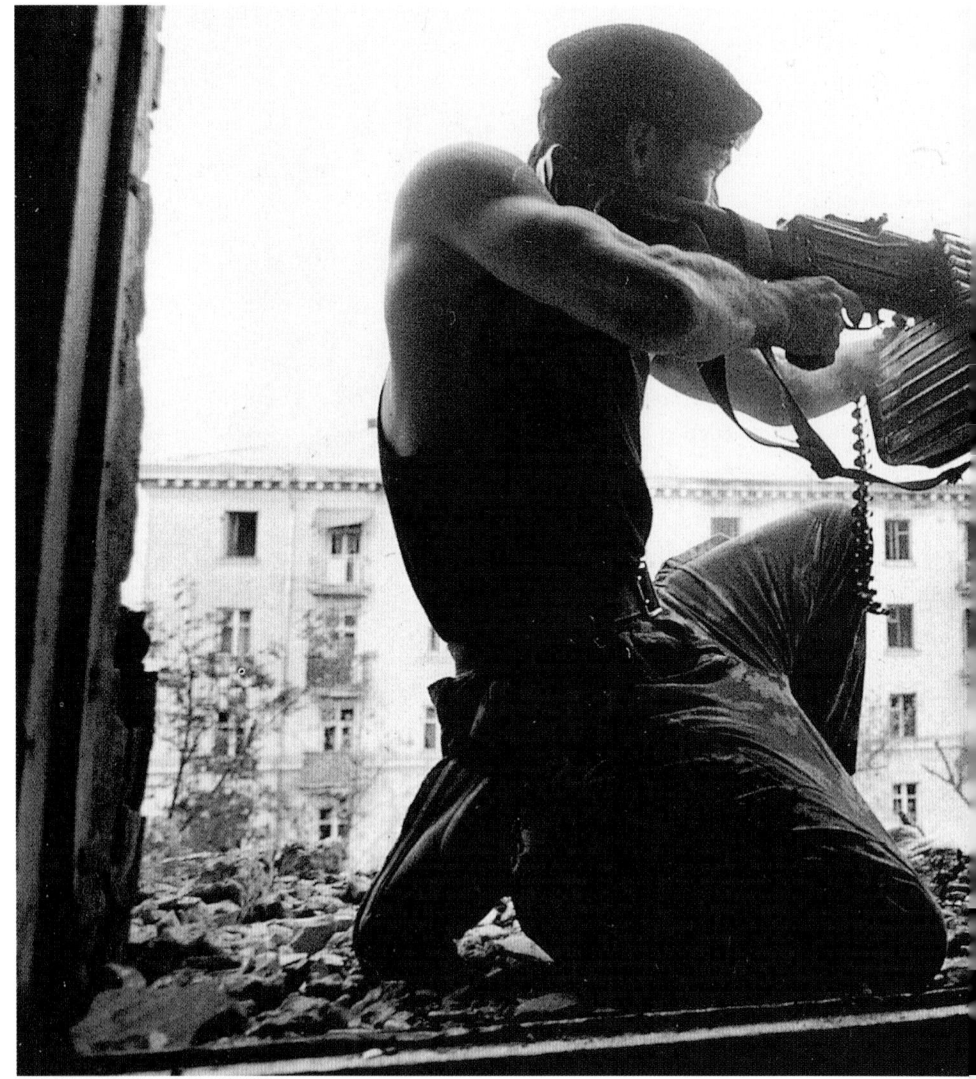

CHRISTOPHER MORRIS/BLACK STAR/COLORIFIC!

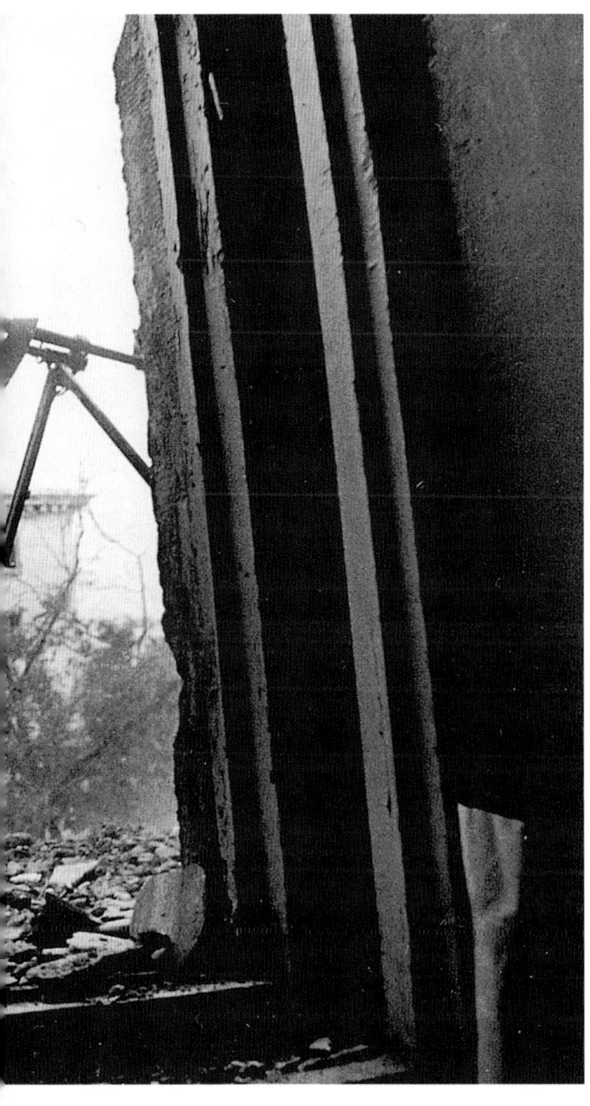

A further chapter of Russian woe. A Chechen sniper takes aim in the ruins of Grozny, 1996.

Otro capítulo en la historia de la desdicha rusa. Un tirador checheno apunta a su blanco desde las ruinas de Grozny, 1996.

Un nuovo capitolo delle disgrazie russe. Un franco tiratore ceceno prende la mira, fra le rovine di Grozny, 1996.

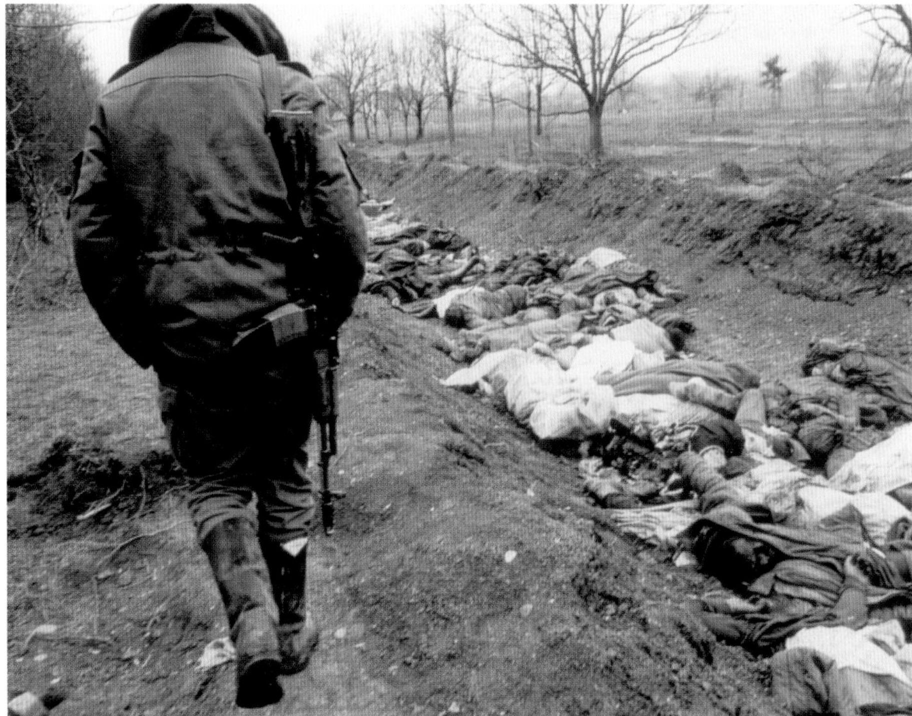

CHRISTOPHER MORRIS/BLACK STAR/COLORIFIC!

Chechen dead. A Russian soldier strides past a ditch littered with victims of the fighting in the area around Grozny, 1995. The war had begun to pick up towards the end of 1994; by February 1995, Grozny was little more than a ghost town.

Muertos chechenos. Un soldado ruso pasa junto a una fosa repleta de víctimas de los combates librados en Grozny en 1995. La guerra se había intensificado hacia finales de 1994 y, en febrero de 1995, Grozny era poco más que una ciudad fantasma.

Morti ceceni. Un soldato russo passa di fianco a una fossa piena di vittime dei combattimenti nella zona attorno a Grozny, 1995. La guerra era ricominciata verso la fine del 1994; già nel febbraio dell'anno successivo, Grozny era ridotta quasi a una città fantasma.

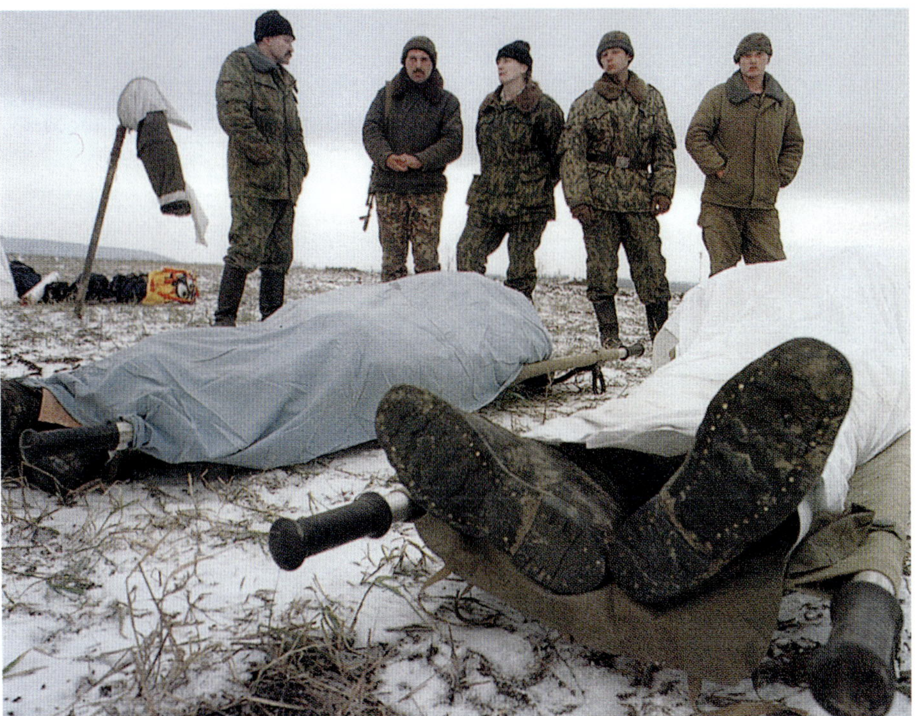

VLADAMIR VELENGURIN/REUTERS/ARCHIVE PHOTOS

Russian dead. Two days before these paratroopers were killed by grenade fire the Russian photographer Vladamir Velengurin had been chatting with them. 'A couple of minutes after I took this frame their bodies were taken away by helicopter.'

Muertos rusos. Dos días antes que estos soldados paracaidistas murieran por el impacto de una granada, el fotógrafo ruso Vladamir Velengurin había estado conversando con ellos. "Pocos minutos después de tomar esta instantánea se llevaron sus cuerpos en helicóptero."

Morti russi. Due giorni prima che questi paracadutisti venissero uccisi da una bomba, il fotografo russo Vladimir Velengurin aveva conversato con loro. "Un paio di minuti dopo aver scattato questa foto i corpi venivano portati via con un elicottero".

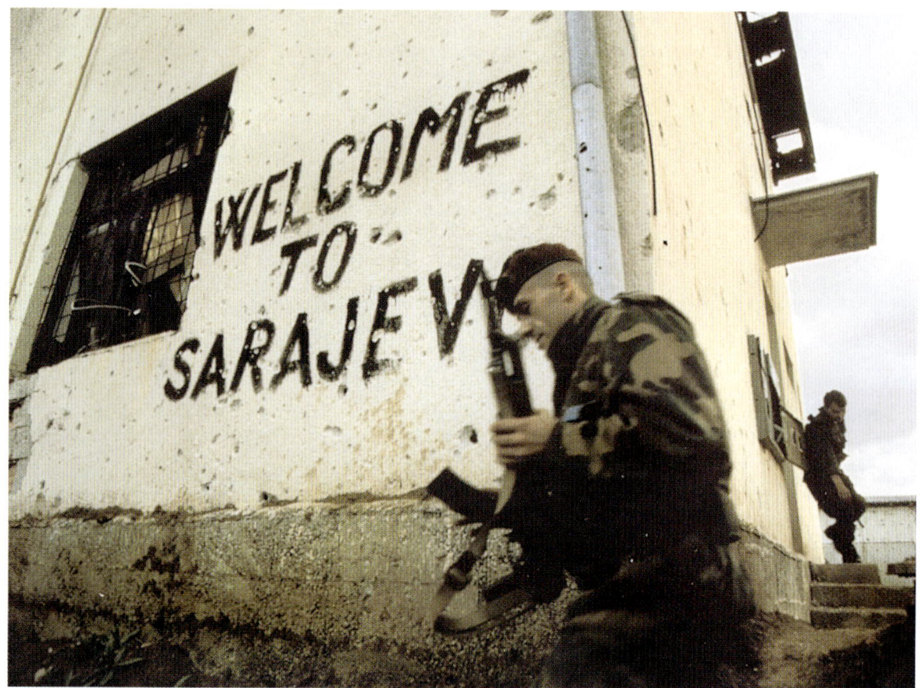

CHRISTOPHER MORRIS/BLACK STAR/COLORIFIC!

'Welcome to Sarajevo' says the slogan on the bullet-spattered wall, 19 May 1995. The dismemberment of Yugoslavia was one of the bitterest and most drawn-out events of the 1990s.

"Bienvenidos a Sarajevo" se lee en esta pared salpicada de disparos de bala, 19 de mayo de 1995. La desintegración de Yugoslavia fue uno de los conflictos más amargos y prolongados de los años noventa.

Lo slogan che appare sulla parete ricoperta di fori di pallottola dice "Benvenuti a Sarajevo", 19 maggio 1995. Lo smembramento della Jugoslavia fu uno degli avvenimenti più tristi e più lunghi degli anni Novanta.

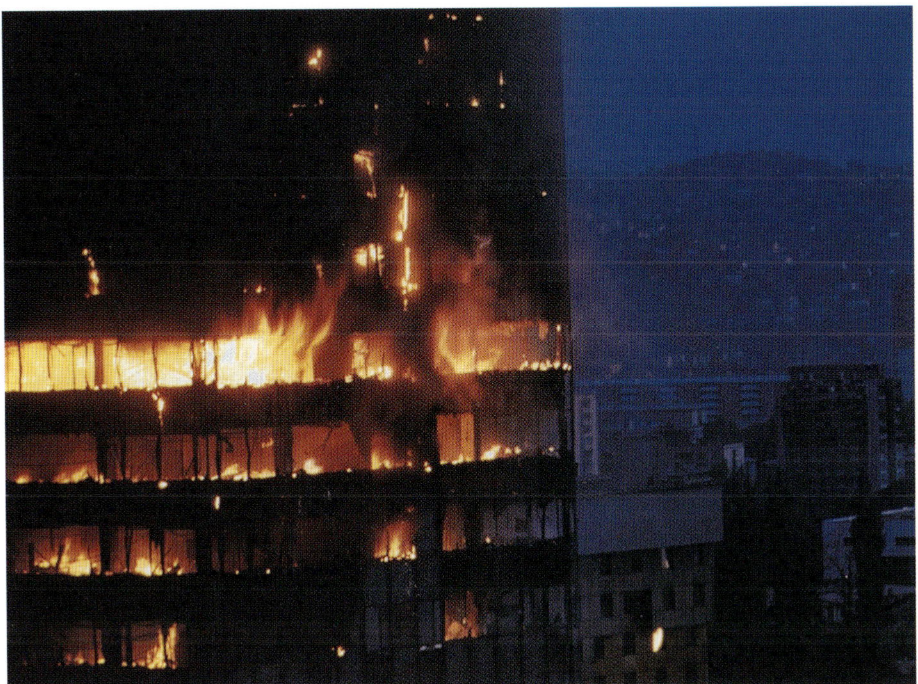

CHRISTOPHER MORRIS/BLACK STAR/COLORIFIC!

The 'spark that set the world ablaze' returns to Sarajevo, 1992. After EC recognition of Croatia and Slovenia in January 1992, Bosnia-Herzegovina declared itself independent and an ethnic powder keg exploded in the Balkans.

La chispa salta de nuevo en Sarajevo en 1992. Tras el reconocimiento de la soberanía de Croacia y Eslovenia por parte de la Comunidad Europea en enero de 1992, Bosnia-Herzegovina declaró su independencia, lo que provocó la explosión del polvorín étnico de los Balcanes.

La "scintilla che manda in fiamme il mondo" torna a Sarajevo, 1992. Dopo il riconoscimento della Croazia e della Slovenia da parte della Comunità Europea, nel gennaio del 1992, anche la Bosnia-Erzegovina si dichiara indipendente, e fa esplodere la polveriera etnica nei Balcani.

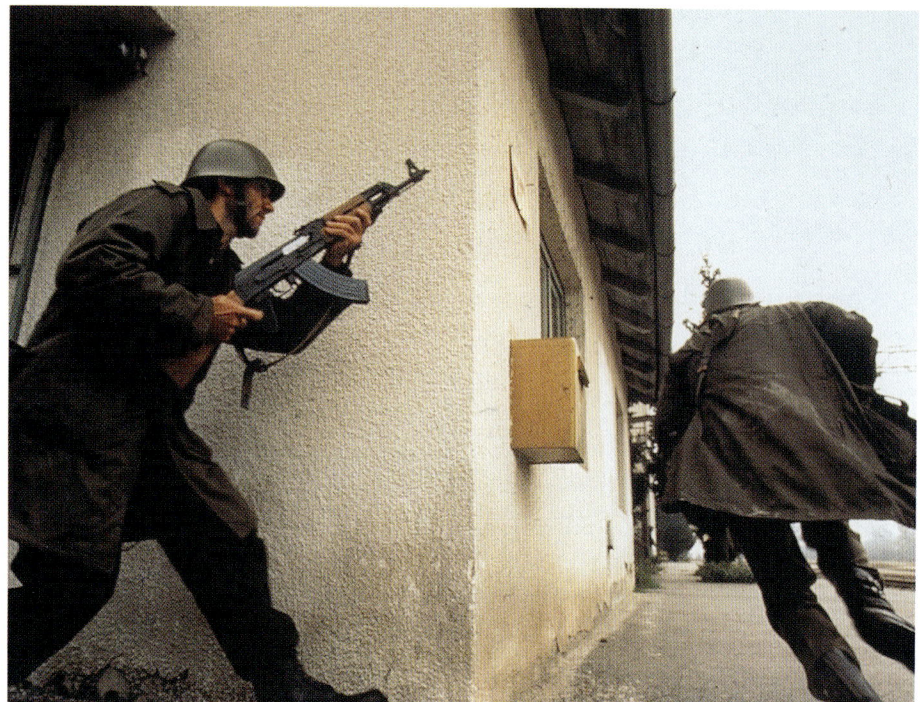

CHRISTOPHER MORRIS/BLACK STAR/COLORIFIC!

Croatian troops advance on Serb positions in Vukovar, October 1991. The photographer accompanied the soldiers until they were within close to 50 yards of the enemy.

Las tropas croatas avanzan hacia posiciones serbias en Vukovar en octubre de 1991. El fotógrafo acompañó a los soldados hasta que apenas los separaban 50 metros del enemigo.

Le truppe croate si avvicinano alle postazioni serbe a Vukovar, ottobre 1991. Il fotografo restò assieme ai soldati fino a una cinquantina di metri dalle postazioni nemiche.

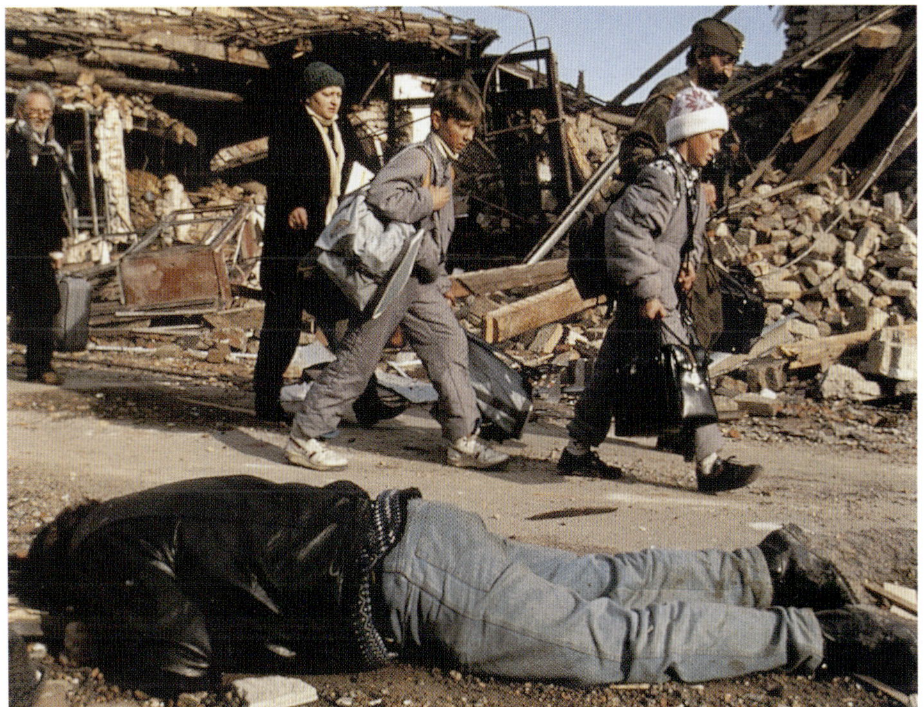

CHRISTOPHER MORRIS/BLACK STAR/COLORIFIC!

The remains of Vukovar, November 1991. Of the original 81,000 inhabitants, only 5,000 remained. Here, some of the survivors flee the city.

Las ruinas de Vukovar, noviembre de 1991. De los 81.000 habitantes que tenía la población, tan solo 5.000 lograron salvar la vida. En la imagen, algunos de los supervivientes abandonan la ciudad.

I ruderi di Vukovar, novembre 1991. Degli 81.000 abitanti che abitavano in città non ne restavano che 5.000. Nella foto, alcuni dei sopravvissuti mentre abbandonano la città.

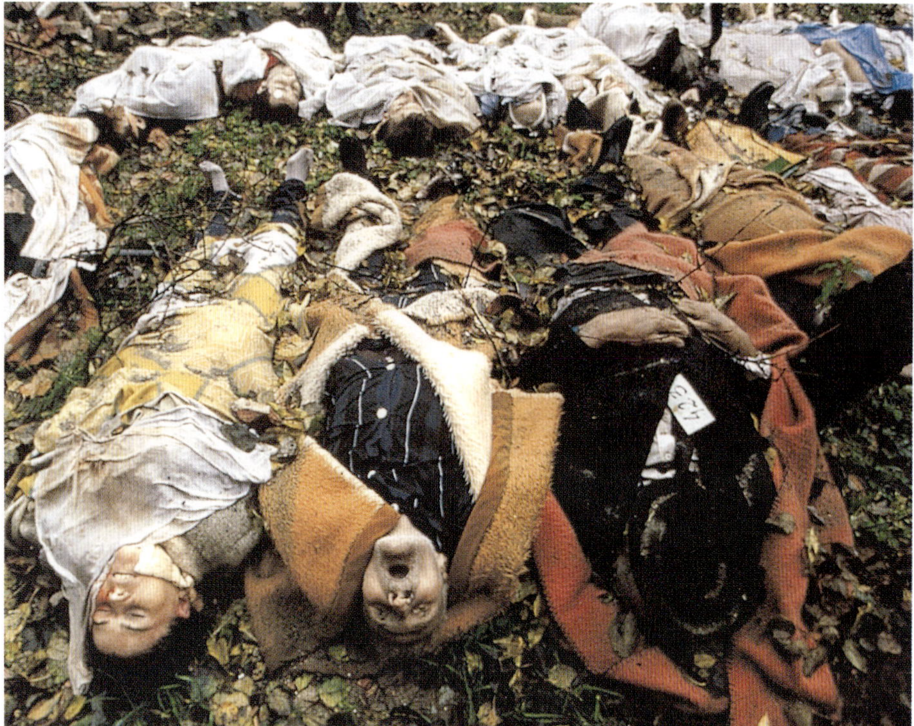

CHRISTOPHER MORRIS/BLACK STAR/COLORIFIC!

Where words fail. The bodies of slaughtered Croatian civilians – old and young – waiting to be buried, Vukovar, November 1991.

Sobran las palabras. Los cadáveres de los civiles croatas masacrados –viejos y jóvenes– esperan recibir sepultura en Vukovar, noviembre de 1991.

Senza commento. I corpi massacrati di civili croati – anziani e giovani – in attesa di sepoltura, Vukovar, novembre 1991.

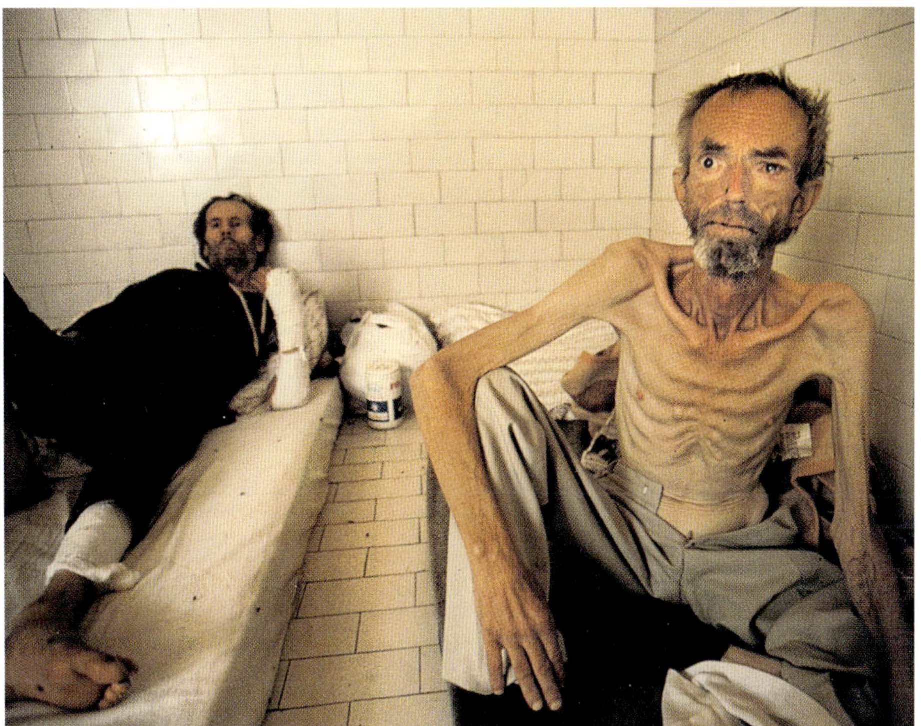

PETER NORTHALL/BLACK STAR/COLORIFIC!

The stark reality of 'ethnic cleansing' – Muslim refugees in a camp near Puropolje, Yugoslavia. Hundreds of thousands lost their homes. Tens of thousands were killed. The search to find the thousands still missing continues.

La cruda realidad de la "limpieza étnica". Refugiados musulmanes en un campamento cercano a Puropolje, en Yugoslavia. Cientos de miles perdieron sus hogares; decenas de miles perdieron la vida y aún continúa la búsqueda de los millares de desaparecidos.

La dura realtà della "pulizia etnica": profughi musulmani in un campo nelle vicinanze di Puropolje, in Jugoslavia. Centinaia di migliaia persero le loro case. Decine di migliaia furono uccisi. La ricerca delle diverse migliaia di scomparsi non è ancora terminata.

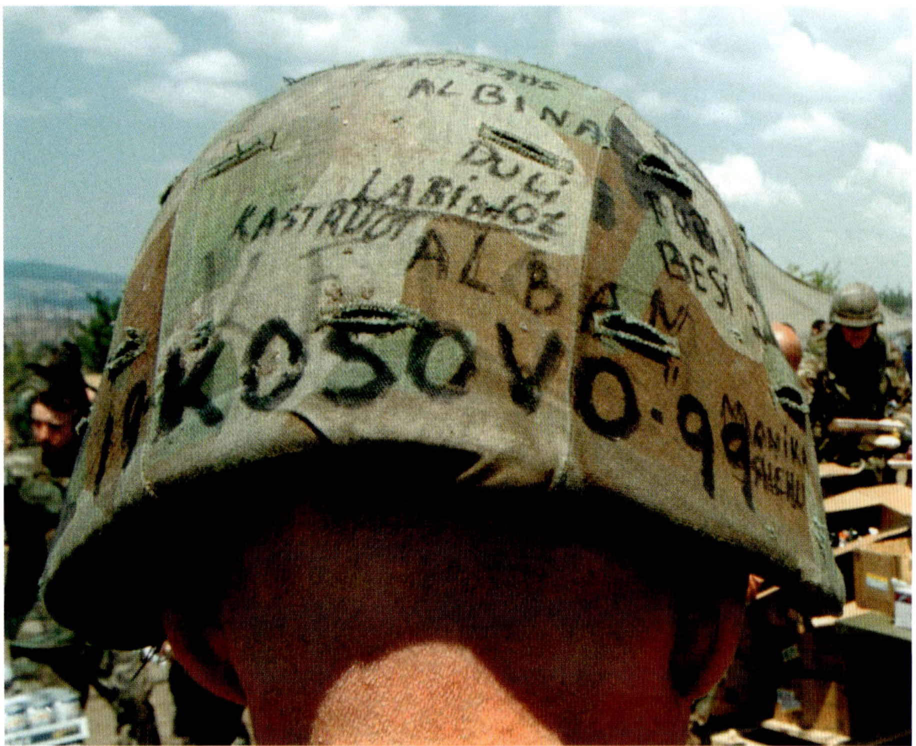

EPA/PA

The helmet belongs to an American soldier of the 26th Marine Expeditionary Unit. The names are those of Kosovan children. The picture was taken during a lunch in Gniljane (near Pristina) marking America's Independence Day, 4 July 1999.

El casco pertenece a un soldado norteamericano de la 26ª Unidad Expedicionaria de Marines y los nombres, a niños kosovares. La imagen es del 4 de julio de 1999, durante una comida en Gniljane, cerca de Pristina, para celebrar el Día de la Independencia de Estados Unidos.

L'elmetto appartiene a un soldato statunitense della 26ª Marine Expeditionary Unit. I nomi sono di bambini kosovari. La foto venne scattata a Gniljane (nelle vicinanze di Pristina) il 4 luglio del 1999 durante un pranzo in occasione della Festa dell'Indipendenza americana.

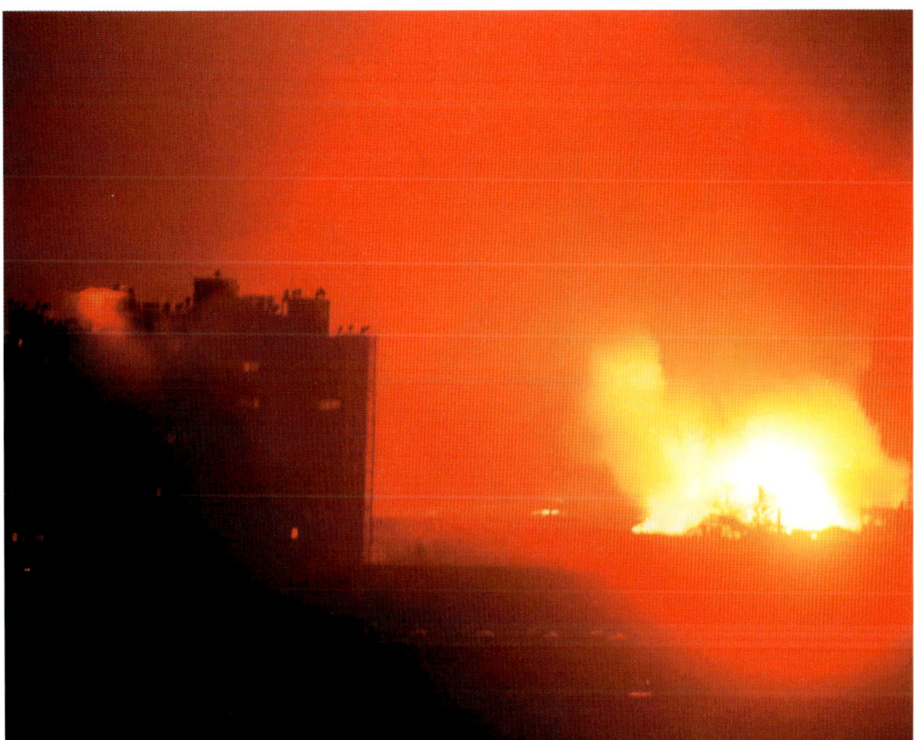

TYLER HICKS/LIAISON AGENCY

NATO air strikes set fire to the city of Pristina, Kosovo, 25 March 1999. A year later, NATO military and political leaders visited Pristina to mark the event.

El 25 de marzo de 1999, las fuerzas aéreas de la OTAN bombardean la ciudad de Pristina, en Kosovo. Un año después, líderes políticos y militares de la OTAN visitarían la ciudad para conmemorar aquellos hechos.

La città di Pristina in fiamme dopo gli attacchi aerei della NATO, 25 marzo 1999. Un anno più tardi, i leader militari e politici della NATO si recavano a Pristina per commemorare l'evento.

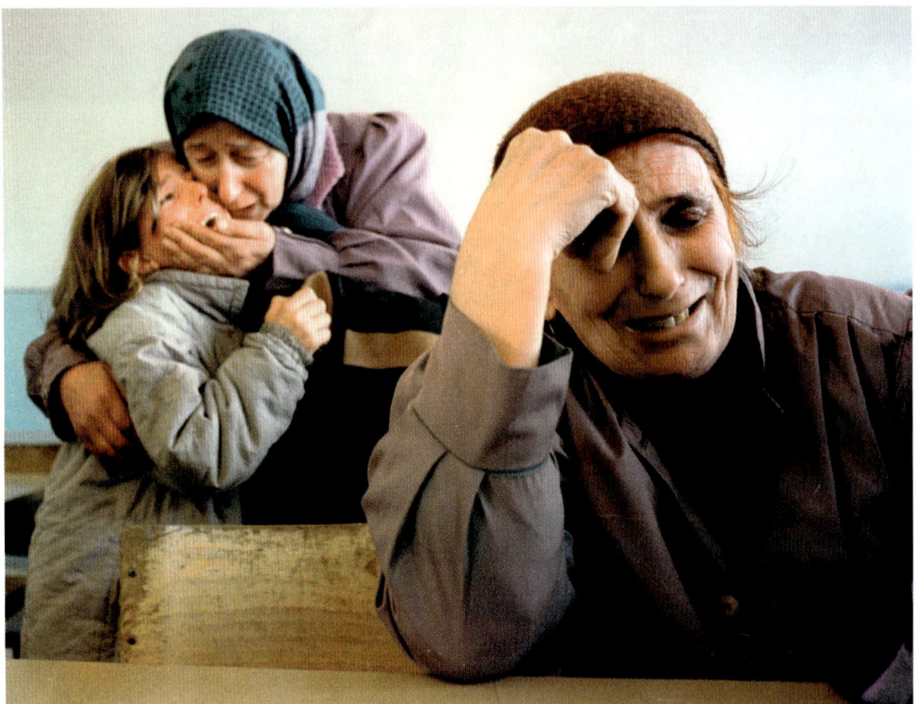

DAVID BRAUCHLI/LIAISON AGENCY

'...women must weep...' An Albanian refugee from Kosovo comforts a small girl in the village school at Bob, 30 miles south of Pristina, 2 March 1999. Fighting between Serbs and the KLA had forced them to leave their homes.

"... las mujeres deben llorar..." Una refugiada albanesa de Kosovo consuela a una niña en la escuela del pueblo de Bob, a unos 50 kilómetros al sur de Pristina, 2 de marzo de 1999. Los combates entre los serbios y el ELK (Ejército de Liberación de Kosovo) las habían obligado a abandonar sus hogares.

"...se le donne devono piangere..." Una profuga albanese del Kosovo dà conforto a una ragazza della scuola del villaggio di Bob, a 50 chilometri al sud di Pristina, 2 marzo 1999. I combattimenti fra serbi e l'ELK le costrinsero ad abbandonare le loro case.

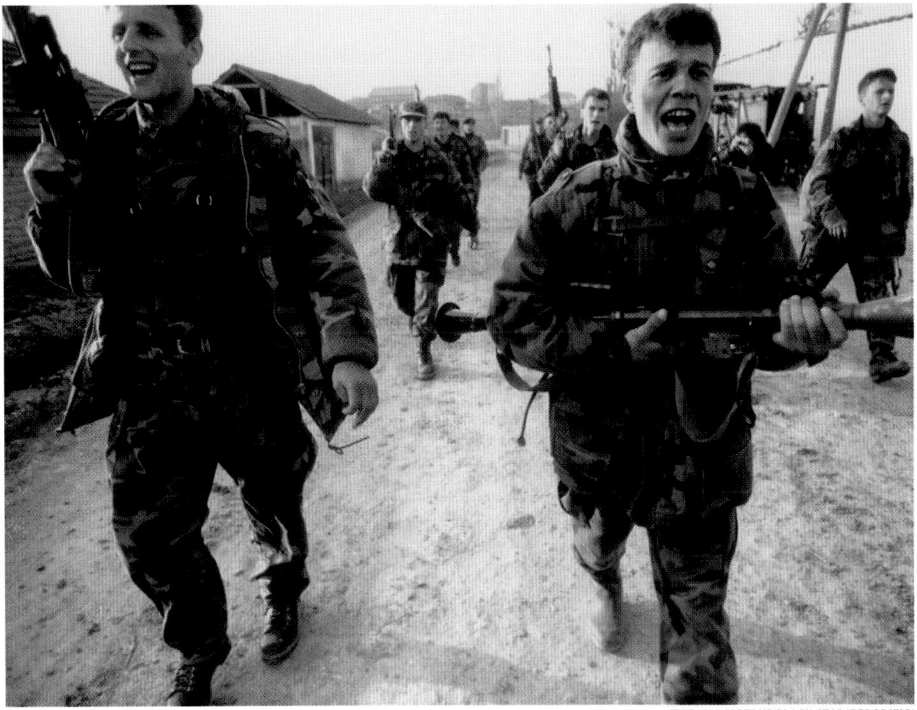

THOMAS SJOERUP/BLACK STAR/COLORIFIC!

'...must men kill and die?' Members of the Kosovo Liberation Army hurry through the streets of Svrg during a running battle with security forces, 14 March 1999.

"... ¿deben los hombres matar y morir?" Integrantes del Ejército de Liberación de Kosovo por las calles de Svrg durante los enfrentamientos contra las fuerzas de seguridad, 14 de marzo de 1999.

"...gli uomini devono uccidere e morire?" Membri dell'Esercito di Liberazione del Kosovo camminano in fretta lungo le strade di Svrg durante una battaglia contro le forze di sicurezza, 14 marzo 1999.

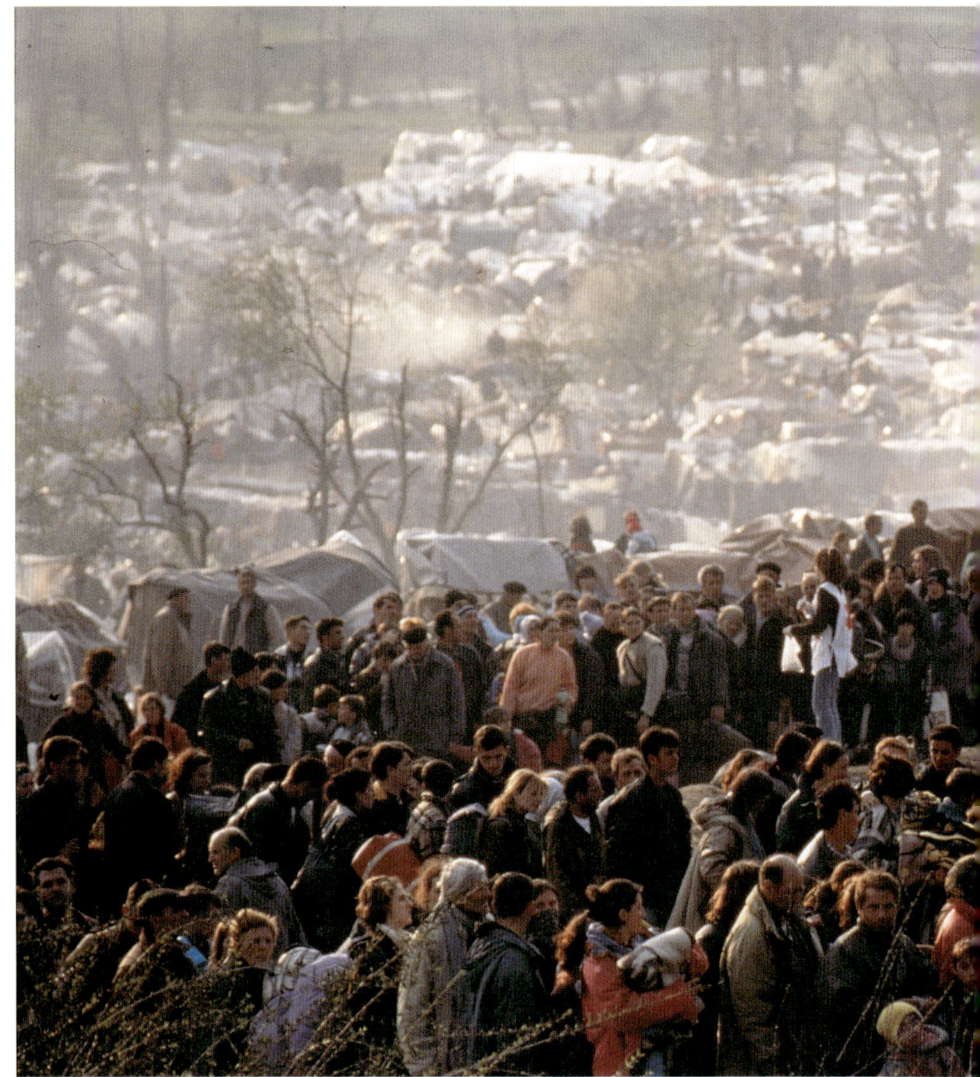

PETER TURNLEY/BLACK STAR/COLORIFIC!

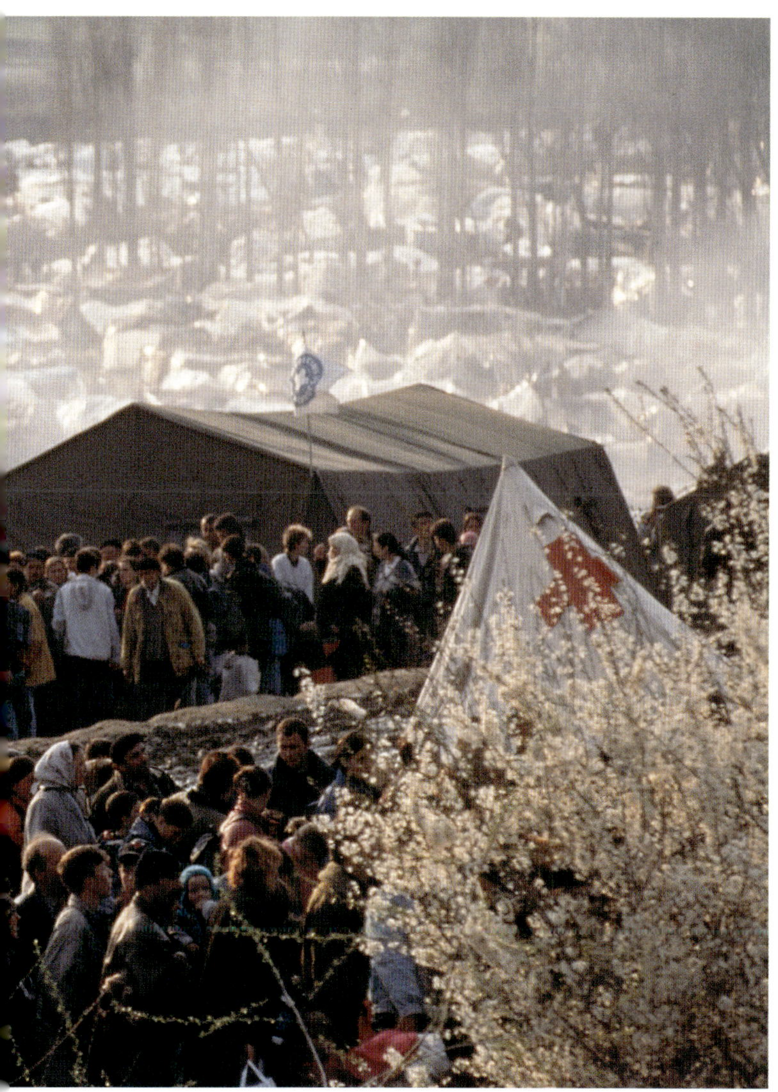

Thousands of Kosovar refugees gather in a camp near Kukes and the border with Kosovo, April 1999.

Miles de refugiados kosovares se concentran en un campamento cercano a Kukes y a la frontera de Kosovo, abril de 1999.

Migliaia di profughi kosovari si affollano in un campo nelle vicinanze di Kukes, alla frontiera con il Kosovo, aprile 1999.

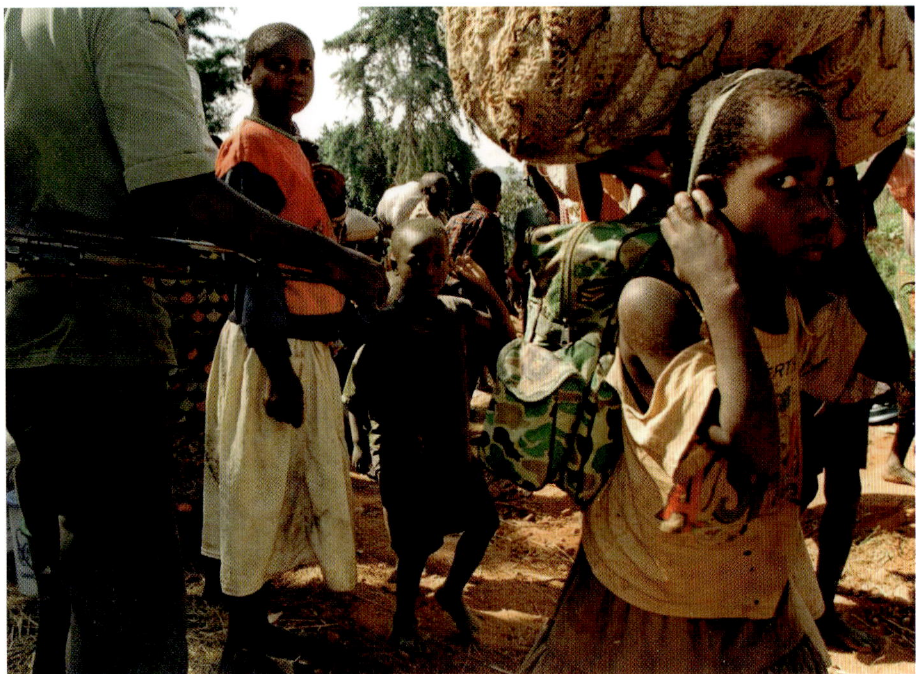

CORINNE DUFKA/REUTERS/ARCHIVE PHOTOS

Like a river in flood, refugees from the town of Uvira stream past a guard near Nyangezi, Zaire, 23 October 1996. They were fleeing from fighting between Zairean troops and Bangamulenge Tutsi rebels.

Formando una riada humana, los refugiados de la población de Uvira huyen de la lucha entre las tropas zaireñas y los rebeldes Banyamulenge de la etnia tutsi. Aquí a su paso cerca de Nyangezi, en el Zaire, el 23 de octubre de 1996.

In fuga dai combattimenti fra le truppe dello Zaire e i ribelli tutsi Bangamulenge, i profughi della città di Uvira scorrono come un fiume in piena di fronte a una guardia, nelle vicinanze di Nyangezi, Zaire, 23 ottobre 1996.

Under the protection of French soldiers, children play at the Niashishi camp, southern Rwanda, 30 June 1994.

Bajo el amparo de soldados franceses, estos niños juegan en el campamento de Niashishi, al sur de Ruanda, 30 de junio de 1994.

Protetti dai soldati francesi, alcuni bambini giocano nel campo profughi di Niashishi, al sud del Ruanda, 30 giugno 1994.

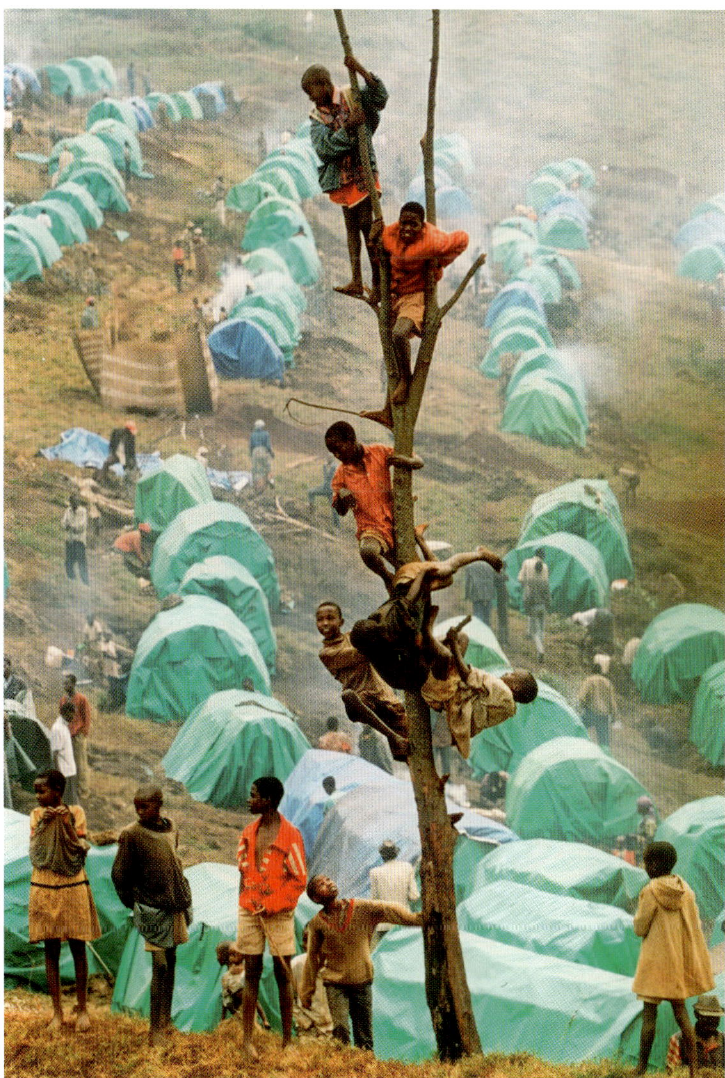

PASCAL GUYOT/EPA/PA

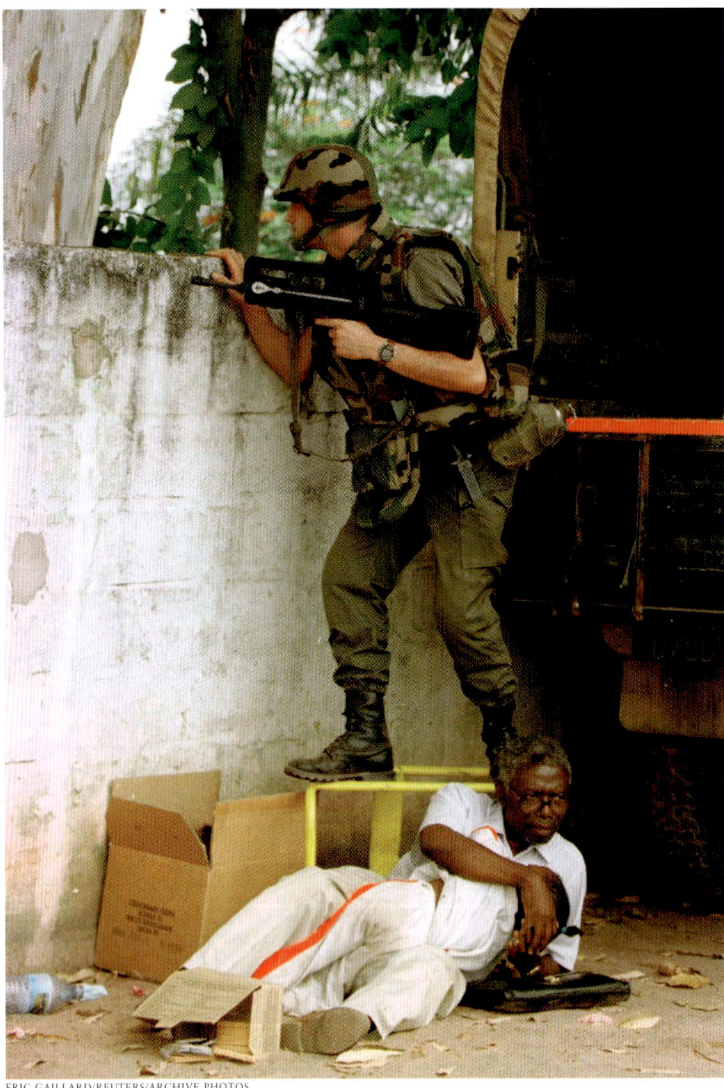

ERIC GAILLARD/REUTERS/ARCHIVE PHOTOS

Offering protection. A local man shelters a child while a French soldier mounts guard, Brazzaville, Congo, 11 June 1997.

Proteger al indefenso. Un hombre cobija a un niño mientras un soldado francés monta guardia en Brazzaville, en el Congo, 11 de junio de 1997.

Protezione. Un abitante del posto protegge un bambino mentre un soldato francese monta la guardia a Brazzaville, Congo, 11 giugno 1997.

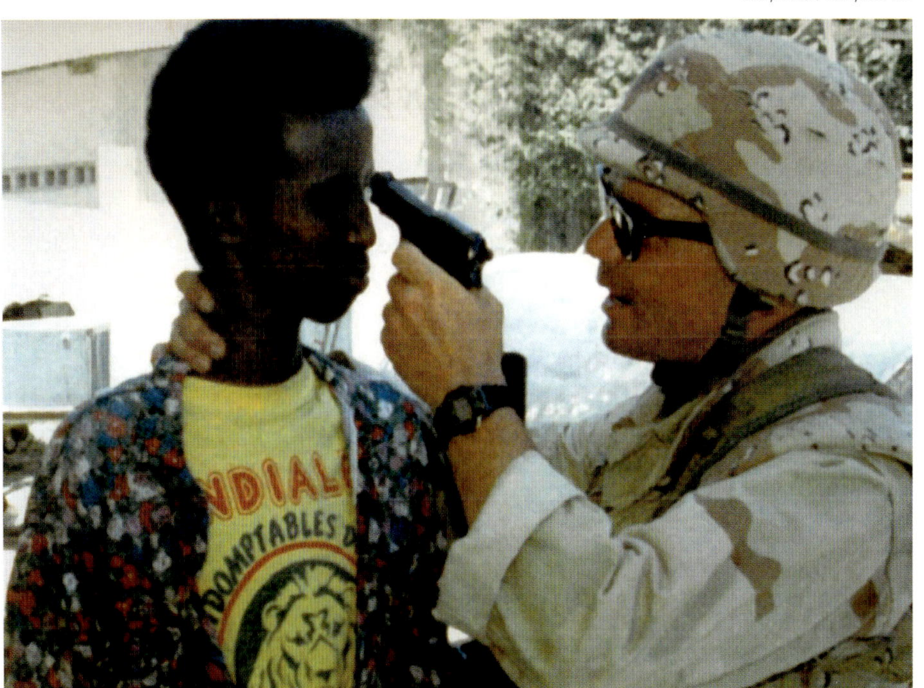

DAN ELDON/REUTERS/ARCHIVE PHOTOS

Threatening action. US marine Staff Sergeant Ken Haughen aims the pistol he has just taken from this 15-year-old Somali at the boy's head, February 1993. The incident took place on Mogadishu's 'green line'.

Amenazante. Ken Haughen, sargento de los marines estadounidenses, apunta a la cabeza de este chico somalí de quince años con la pistola que le acaba de arrebatar. El incidente tuvo lugar en la "línea verde" de Mogadiscio en febrero de 1993.

Intimidazione. Il sergente maggiore Ken Haughten, dei marine statunitensi, punta la pistola che ha appena preso a questo quindicenne somalo sulla sua testa, febbraio 1993. L'incidente avvenne lungo la "linea verde" di Mogadiscio.

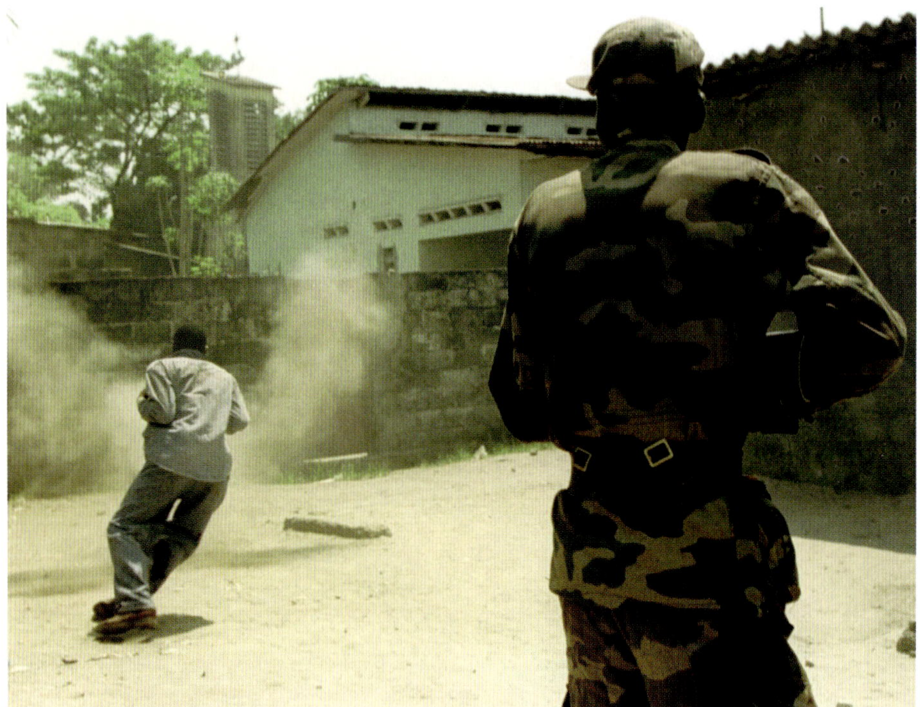

CORINNE DUFKA/REUTERS/ARCHIVE PHOTOS

Monrovia, Liberia, 8 May 1996. The story is best told in the words of the photographer, 'The nameless man had crept out of his house in search of something to eat…[he was] caught by a patrol of armed NPFL men…'

Monrovia, Liberia, 8 de mayo de 1996. Las palabras del fotógrafo relatan mejor la historia: "Este hombre desconocido había salido de su casa en busca de algo que comer … [cuando] le sorprendió una patrulla de hombres armados del NPFL (Frente Patriótico Nacional para la Liberación de Liberia)…".

Monrovia, Liberia, 8 maggio 1996. Le migliori parole per raccontare questa storia sono quelle del fotografo: "Lo sconosciuto era uscito di casa per cercare qualcosa da mangiare… [quando venne] catturato da una pattuglia del NPFL…"

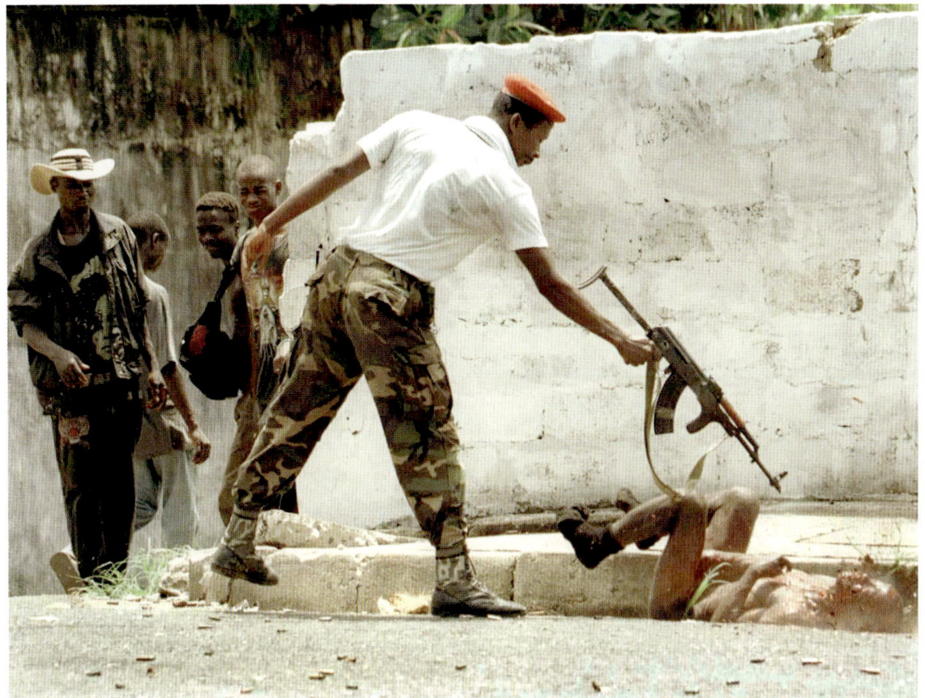

CORINNE DUFKA/REUTERS/ARCHIVE PHOTOS

'...within eight minutes he had been told to run, shot in the back, then dragged down the street and stripped down to his socks and underwear... the boss man finished him off.' At home a family waited for him to return with the food he never found.

"... en tan solo ocho minutos, lo obligan a correr, le disparan por la espalda, lo tiran al suelo y lo dejan en paños menores y calcetines... el cabecilla del grupo se encarga de acabar con él." En su casa su familia esperaba a que regresara con la comida que jamás conseguiría.

"...in soli otto minuti venne obbligato a correre, mentre i soldati gli sparavano alle spalle, poi fu trascinato lungo la strada e spogliato, lasciato in calzini e in mutande... Poi il capo gli diede il colpo di grazia". E intanto una famiglia restava in casa, in attesa del cibo che quell'uomo non riuscì a procurarsi.

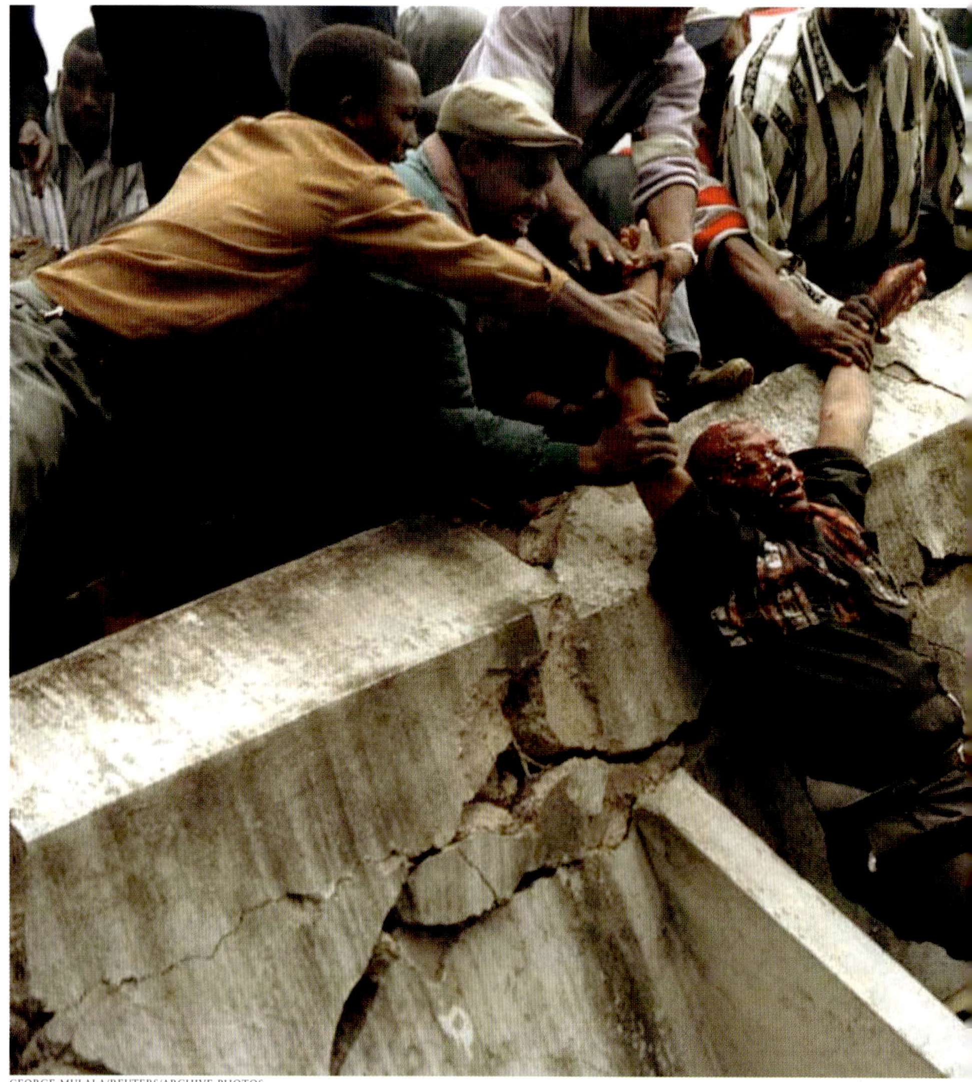

GEORGE MULALA/REUTERS/ARCHIVE PHOTOS

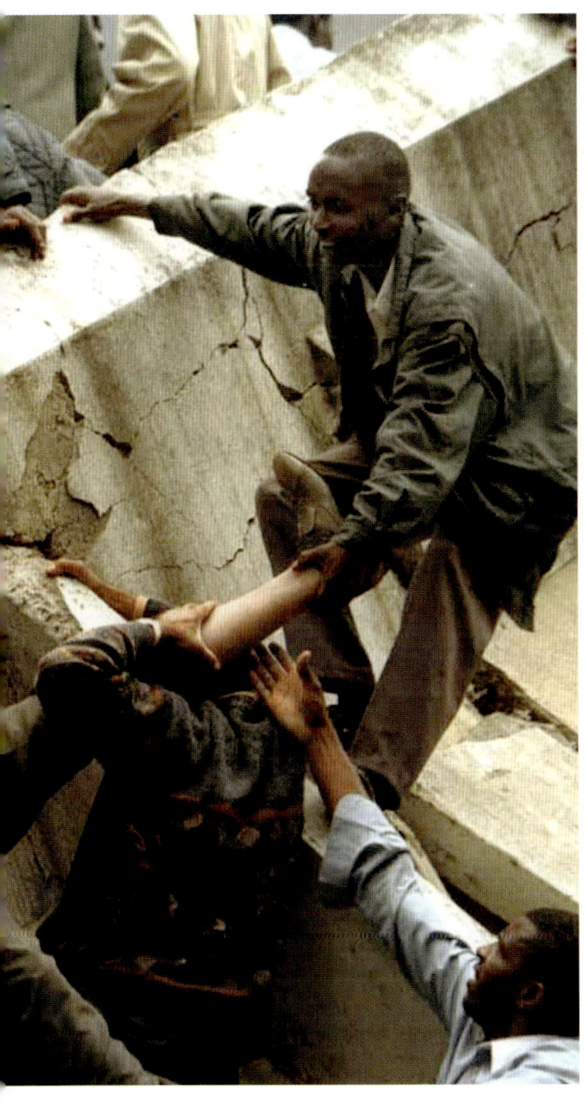

Survivors of the bombing of the US Embassy, Nairobi, Kenya, 7 August 1999. Two hundred and fifty people were killed and 5,000 injured.

Supervivientes del atentado con bomba en la embajada estadounidense de Nairobi, en Kenia. En él perdieron la vida 250 personas y 5.000 más resultaron heridas.

Sopravvissuti al bombardamento dell'Ambasciata degli Stati Uniti a Nairobi, in Kenia, 7 agosto 1999. Duecentocinquanta persone vennero uccise e 5.000 ferite.

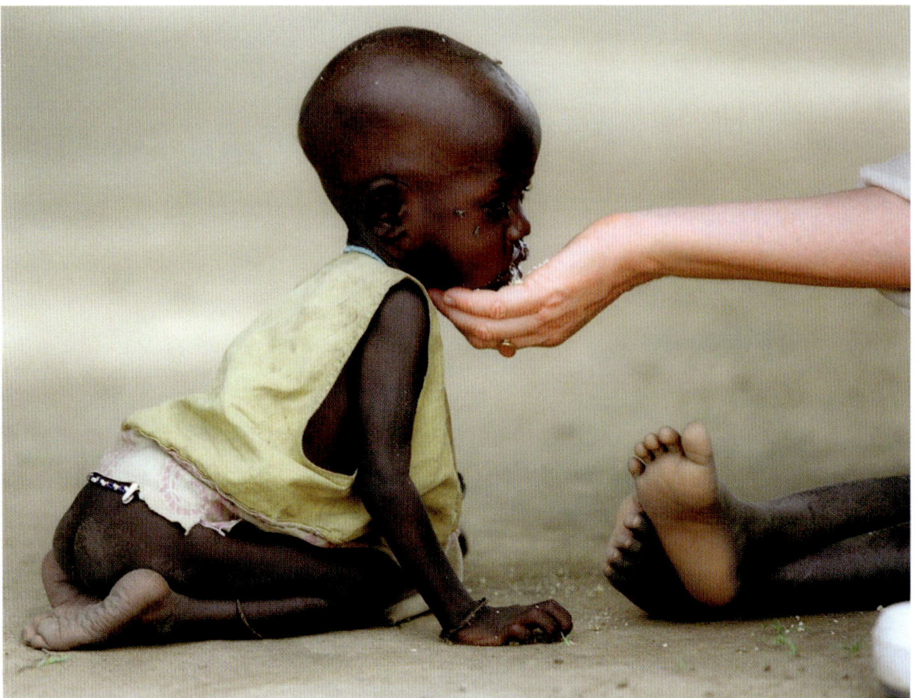

ERIC FEFERBERG/EPA/PA

A lull in the fighting. Food supplied by humanitarian aid workers is given to a baby in Akon, Bar-el-Ghazal province, Sudan, 10 October 1998. A three-month ceasefire had been negotiated in the civil war.

Una tregua en el combate. Un niño sudanés de Akon, en la provincia de Bar-el-Ghazal, recibe alimento distribuido por los equipos de ayuda humanitaria, 10 de octubre de 1998. La guerra civil se encontraba en compás de espera gracias al alto el fuego de tres meses pactado.

Una tregua nel combattimento. Un bambino mangia il cibo dato dalle organizzazioni di aiuto umanitario ad Akon, nella provincia di Bar-el-Ghazal, Sudan, 10 ottobre 1998. Era stato negoziato un cessate il fuoco di tre mesi durante la guerra civile.

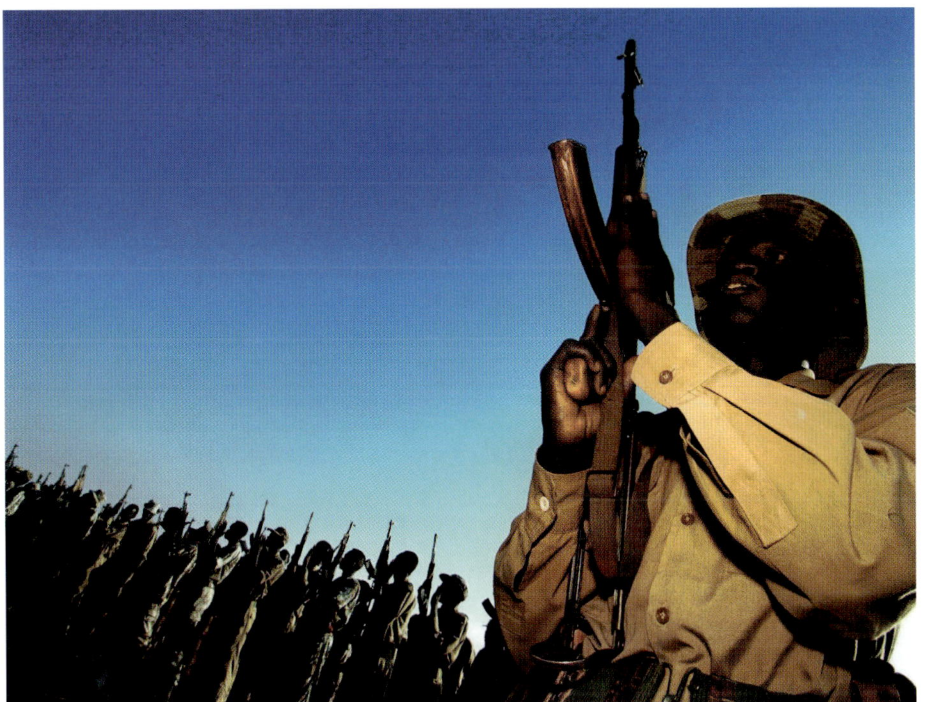

EPA/PA

Back to business. Members of the Sudanese People's Liberation Army undergo training in a 'liberated zone', eastern Sudan, 10 November 1999. The war against the Islamic Government in Khartoum had already lasted ten years.

De vuelta a las armas. Miembros del Ejército Popular de Liberación de Sudán se entrenan en una "zona liberada" al este del país, 10 de noviembre de 1999. La guerra contra el Gobierno islámico de Jartum duraba ya diez años.

Di nuovo al lavoro. Membri dell'esercito di liberazione del popolo sudanese (SPLA) si allenano in una "zona liberata", Sudan orientale, 10 novembre 1999. La guerra contro il governo islamico di Khartoum durava già da dieci anni.

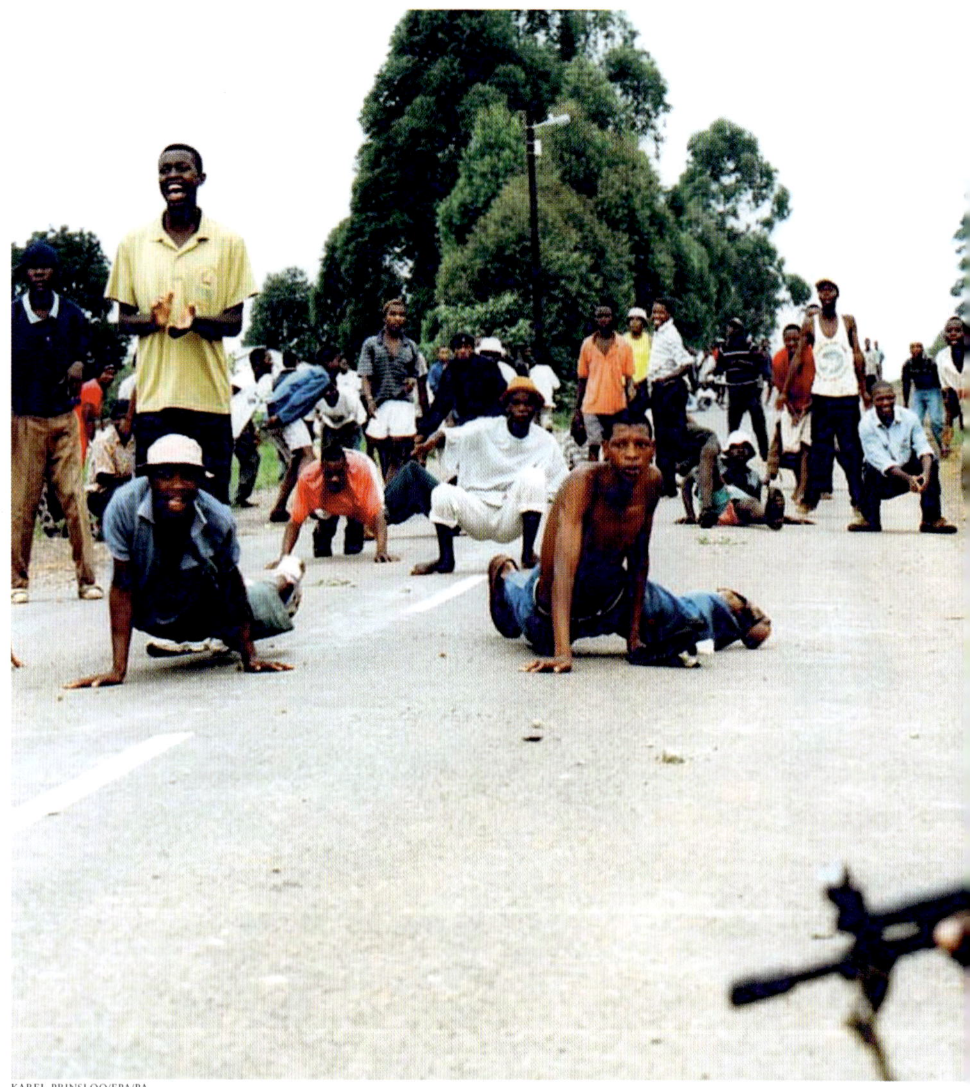

KAREL PRINSLOO/EPA/PA

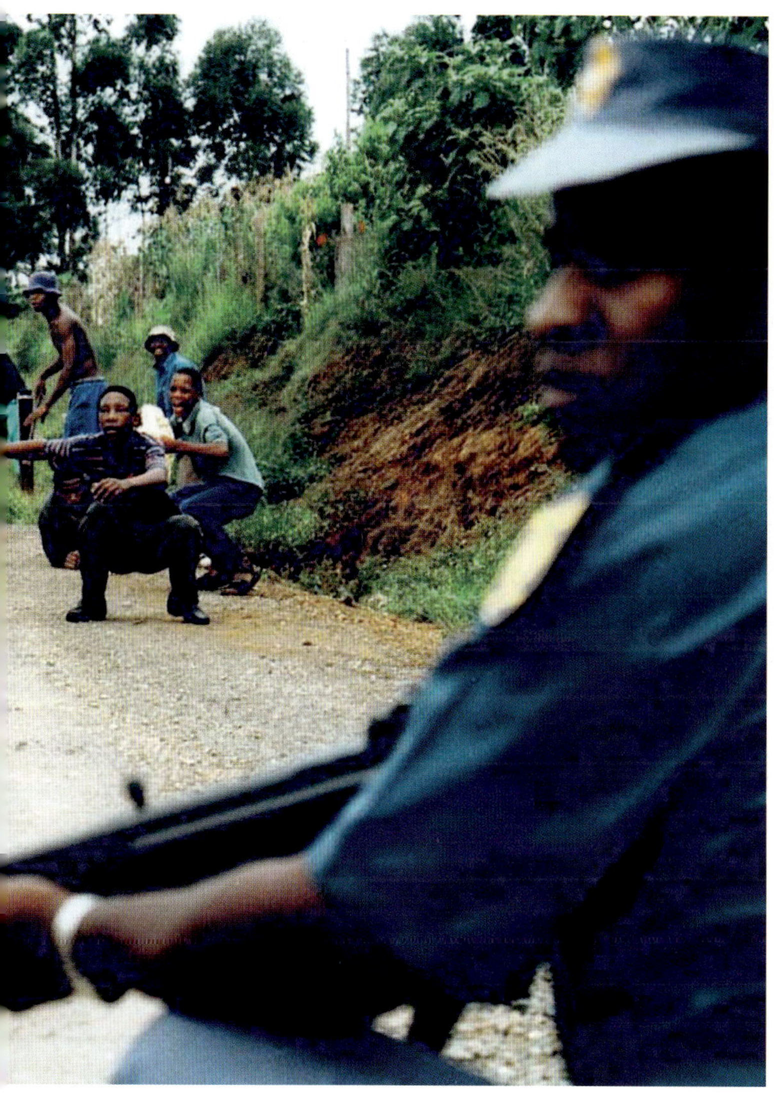

South Africans take cover during an incident between UDM and ANC supporters in the Magoda township, Richmond, 24 January 1999.

Unos sudafricanos se ponen a cubierto durante un incidente protagonizado por partidarios del UDM (Movimiento de Unión Democrática) y del ANC (Congreso Nacional Africano) en la ciudad de Magoda, en Richmond, el 24 de enero de 1999.

I sudafricani si mettono al coperto durante un incidente fra i sostenitori dell'UDM e quelli dell'ANC nella township di Magoda, Richmond, 24 gennaio 1999.

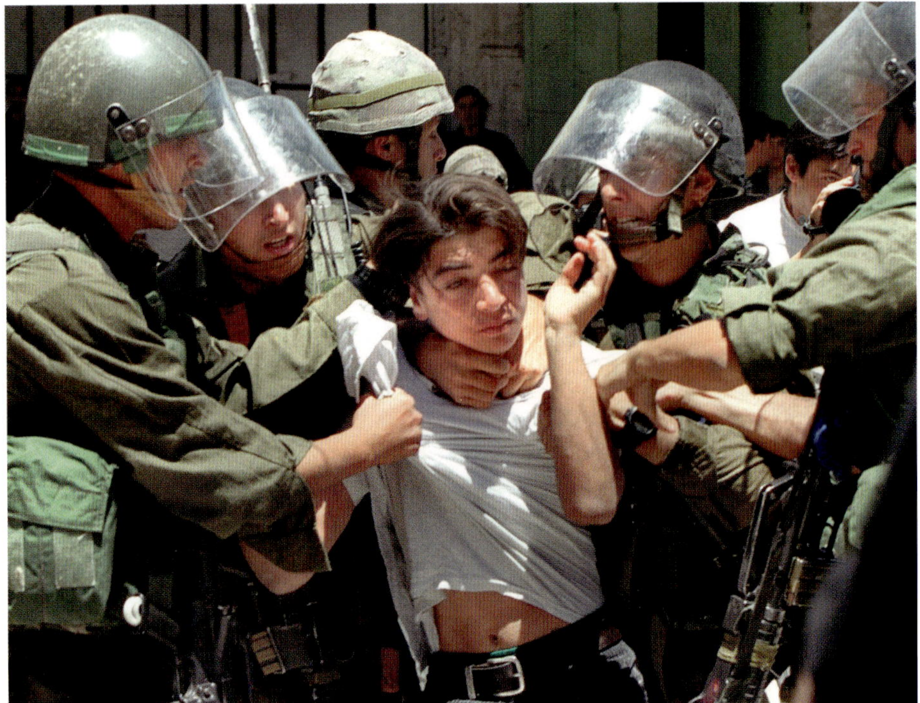

DAOUD MIZRAHI/EPA/PA

Israeli troops arrest a Palestinian in the town of Hebron, 3 June 1999. The youth had been taking part in a protest against Jewish settlement programmes in Jerusalem and the Palestinian territories.

Militares israelíes detienen a un joven palestino en la ciudad de Hebrón, 3 de junio de 1999. El chico había participado en una protesta contra los programas de asentamiento judío en Jerusalén y en los territorios palestinos.

L'esercito israeliano arresta un palestinese nella città di Hebron, 3 giugno 1999. Il giovane aveva partecipato a una protesta contro i programmi di insediamenti ebrei a Gerusalemme e nei territori palestinesi.

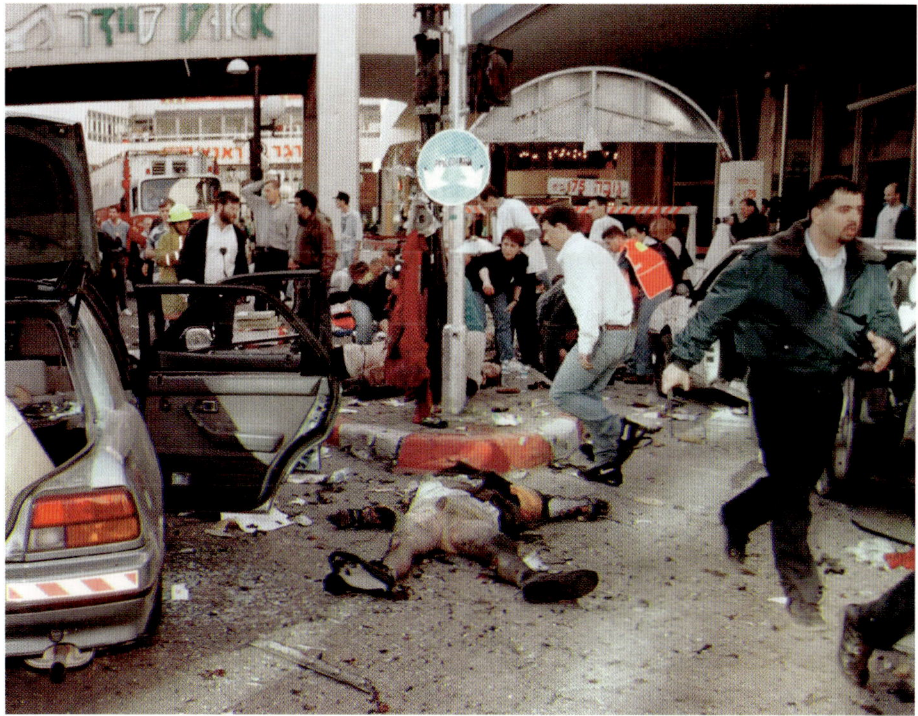

YISRAEL HADARI/REUTERS/ARCHIVE PHOTOS

An Israeli policeman (right) rushes to the aid of victims of a suicide bomb attack, Tel Aviv, 4 March 1996. Eleven people were killed and more than 100 injured. It was the fourth blast in nine days.

Un policía israelí (derecha) corre en ayuda de las víctimas de un ataque terrorista suicida en Tel Aviv, 4 de marzo de 1996. Once personas fallecieron y más de un centenar resultaron heridas. Se trataba del cuarto atentado con bomba en nueve días.

Un poliziotto israeliano (a destra) si affretta a soccorrere le vittime di un attentato suicida, Tel Aviv, 4 marzo 1996. Vennero uccise undici persone e i feriti furono più di cento. Era il quarto attentato in nove giorni.

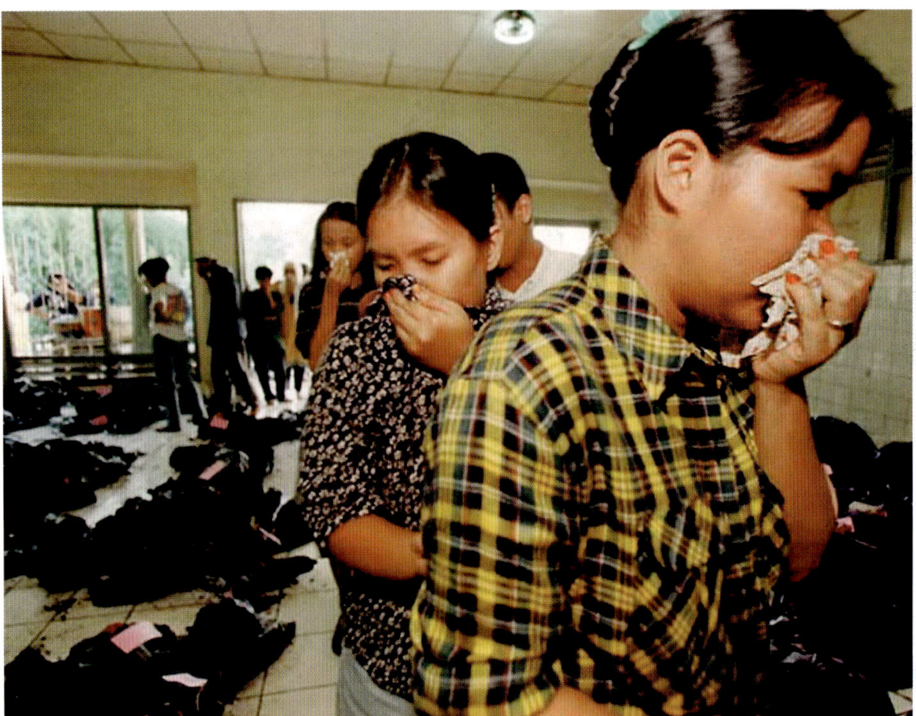

BETH SHAMITZ/LIAISON AGENCY

Students file through the city morgue, Jakarta, November 1998. The bodies they sought to identify were those killed in anti-Government riots during the last months of President Suharto's authoritarian rule.

En noviembre de 1998, unos estudiantes recorren la morgue de la ciudad de Yakarta para identificar los cuerpos de quienes habían muerto durante los disturbios antigubernamentales de los últimos meses de dictadura del presidente Suharto.

Alcuni studenti in fila nell'obitorio municipale, Giacarta, novembre 1988. Le persone che cercavano di identificare erano state uccise in sommosse antigovernative durante gli ultimi mesi del regime autoritario del presidente Suharto.

East Timorese freedom fighters stone an Indonesian armed patrol, Dili, 12 October 1999.

Los combatientes de la libertad de Timor Oriental lanzan piedras contra una patrulla militar indonesia en Dili, 12 de octubre de 1999.

I combattenti per la libertà del Timor Orientale scagliano pietre contro una pattuglia armata indonesiana, Dili, 12 ottobre 1999.

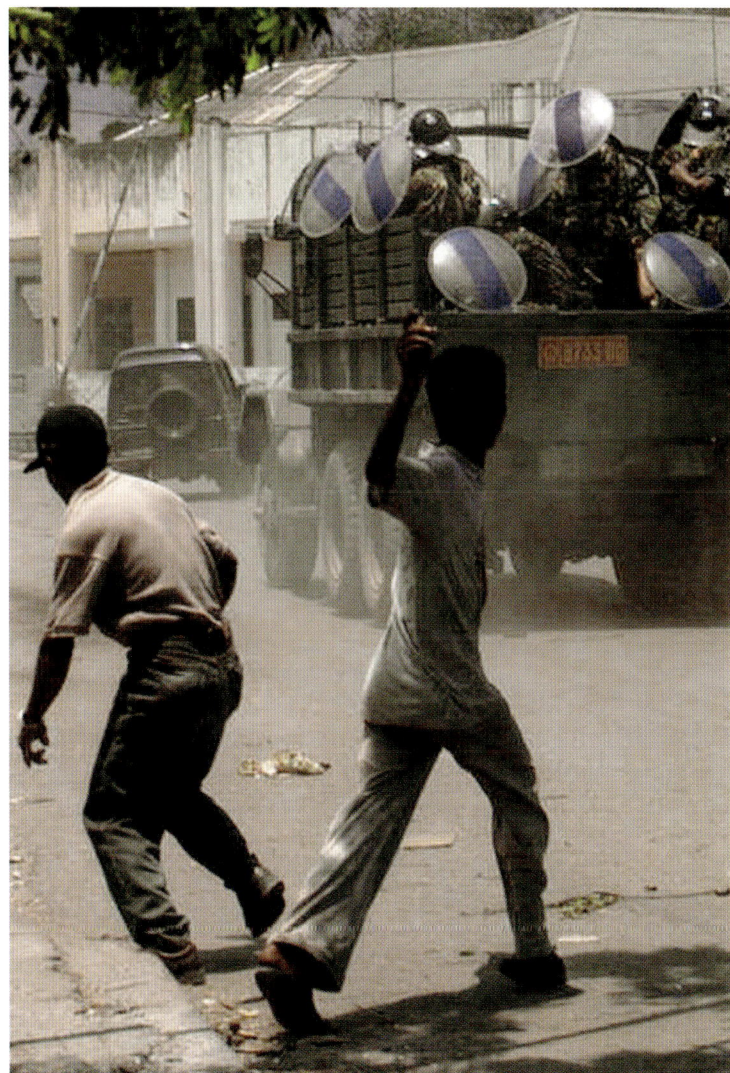

EPA/PA

3. New world order
Un nuevo orden mundial
Nuovo ordine mondiale

With a fetching touch of irony, a male visitor to the Latvian Nudist Colony in Saule seeks modesty behind the hammer and sickle, 10 June 1992. The Baltic republics had only recently achieved independence.

Con un sugerente toque irónico, este visitante de la colonia nudista letona de Saule esconde sus vergüenzas bajo la hoz y el martillo comunistas, 10 de junio de 1992. Las repúblicas bálticas acababan de lograr su independencia.

Con un simpatico tocco d'ironia, un membro della colonia nudista di Saule, in Lettonia, nasconde i propri attributi dietro la falce e il martello, 10 giugno 1992. Le repubbliche baltiche avevano da poco ottenuto l'indipendenza.

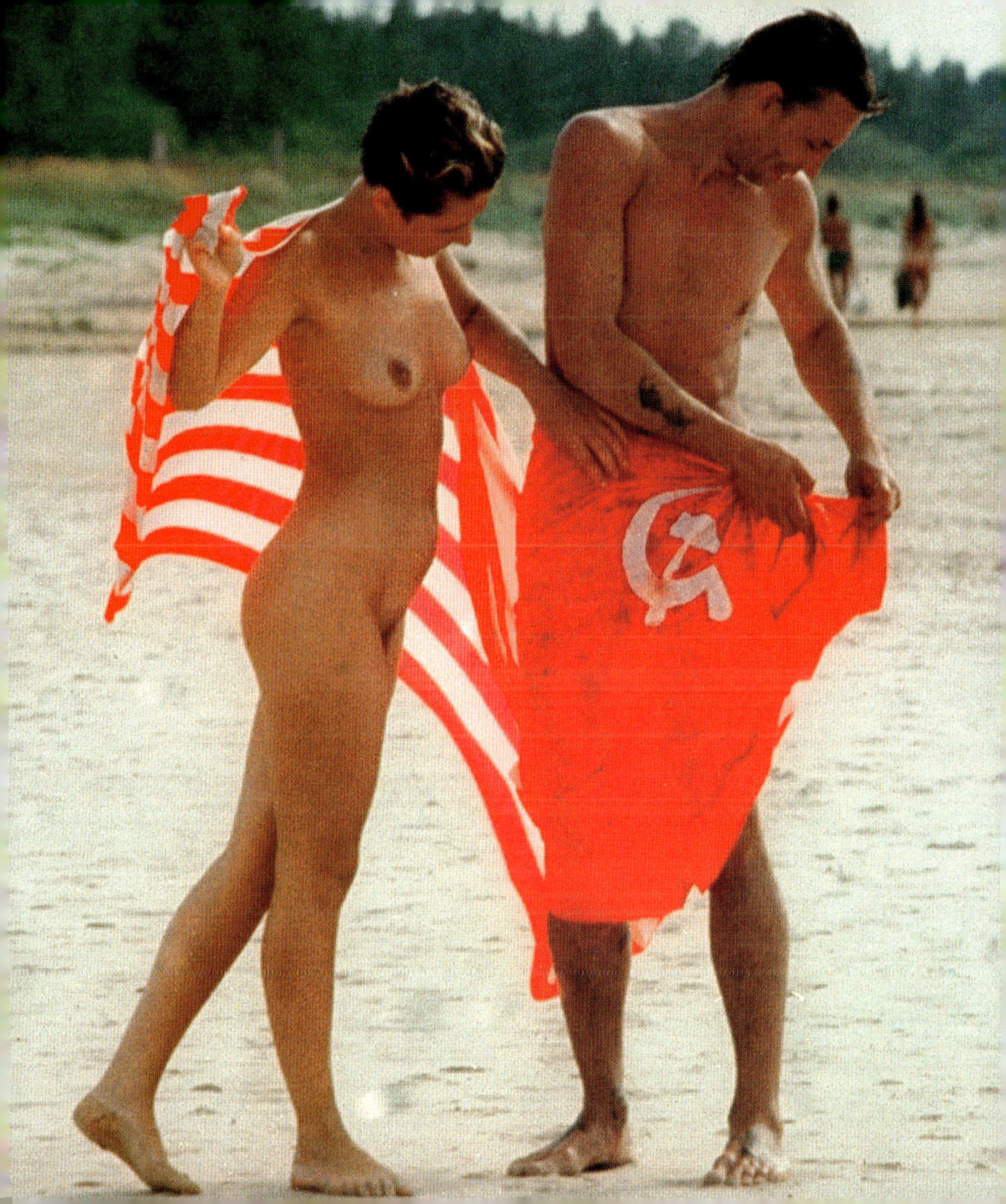

3. New world order
Un nuevo orden mundial
Nuovo ordine mondiale

For more than seventy years the Communist east and the capitalist west had built their relationship on a basis of mutual loathing and mistrust. They stockpiled weapons against each other, launched networks of spies, frightened their respective populations into submission with tales of what the other side might do if it gained the upper hand. In so doing, they maintained a world order that was tightly, if fearfully, cohesive.

All this changed with the collapse of the Communist bloc in the early 1990s. The 'evil empire' that had so excited Ronald Reagan no longer existed. In its place was a vast land of opportunity whose economic potential excited Ronald McDonald. Consumerism replaced Communism. Coke added fizz to Muscovites' vodka. Sony invaded China. Shell invaded Poland. The accountant replaced the commissar. But, while east and west merged together, old federations fragmented. Ancient nations reappeared – Latvia, Estonia, Croatia and a dozen more. To its opponents, it was as though an antibiotic had at last been found to protect the world from socialism. The free market triumphed everywhere. No more five-year plans, no more state control, no more planned economies. After a century of struggle, capitalism had emerged triumphant, and the spirit of competition reigned supreme.

Durante más de setenta años, el bloque comunista del Este y los países occidentales capitalistas construyeron su relación sobre los pilares de la desconfianza y la aversión mutuas. Acumularon armamento para ser utilizado contra el otro, fomentaron las redes de espionaje y sometieron a sus respectivos pueblos atemorizándolos con historias sobre lo que haría el otro bando si lograba la hegemonía. De este modo, se sostuvo un orden mundial fuertemente –si no alarmantemente– cohesivo. Pero todo esto cambia con la caída del bloque comunista a principios de los noventa.

El "imperio del mal" que tanto había inquietado a Ronald Reagan deja de existir y en su lugar aparece una vasta tierra de oportunidades cuyo potencial económico hace las delicias de Ronald McDonald. El consumismo sustituye al comunismo. La Coca-Cola se mezcla con el vodka moscovita; Sony invade China; Shell conquista Polonia, y el contable toma el relevo del comisario soviético. Pero mientras Oriente y Occidente se fusionan, las antiguas federaciones se fragmentan. Reaparecen las viejas naciones: Letonia, Estonia, Croacia y una docena más de estados. Los detractores del socialismo creen que por fin se ha hallado un antibiótico para proteger el mundo de dicho sistema. El libre mercado triunfa por doquier. Se acabaron los planes quinquenales, el control estatal y las economías planificadas. Tras un siglo de lucha, el capitalismo emerge triunfal y el espíritu competitivo reina con todo su esplendor.

Per più di settant'anni l'Est comunista e l'Occidente capitalista avevano basato i loro rapporti sul disprezzo e la diffidenza reciproci. Accumulavano armi da usare gli uni contro gli altri, organizzavano reti di spionaggio, mantenevano il popolo in un perenne stato di sottomissione terrorizzandolo con quello che avrebbe potuto fare l'avversario se avesse vinto la battaglia. In questo modo, mantennero un ordine mondiale strettamente e terribilmente coesivo.

Ma questa situazione cambiò con la caduta del blocco comunista agli inizi degli anni Novanta. L'impero del male che tanto aveva appassionato Ronald Reagan non esisteva più. Al suo posto si presentava un'enorme terra di opportunità, il cui potenziale economico appassionò Ronald McDonald. Così il consumismo sostituì il comunismo, la Coca Cola diede effervescenza alla vodka, Sony invase la Cina, Shell invase la Polonia e il contabile sostituì il commissario del popolo. Ma mentre l'Est e l'Occidente si amalgamavano, le vecchie federazioni si frammentavano. Così riapparvero antiche nazioni, come nel caso della Lettonia, dell'Estonia, della Croazia e di un'altra decina di stati. Per i loro avversari era come se finalmente fosse stato scoperto un vaccino per proteggere il pianeta dal socialismo. Il mercato libero trionfava ovunque, scomparivano i piani quinquennali, non c'era più controllo statale né un'economia pianificata. Dopo un secolo di lotte, il capitalismo aveva la meglio e lo spirito di competizione regnava incontrastato.

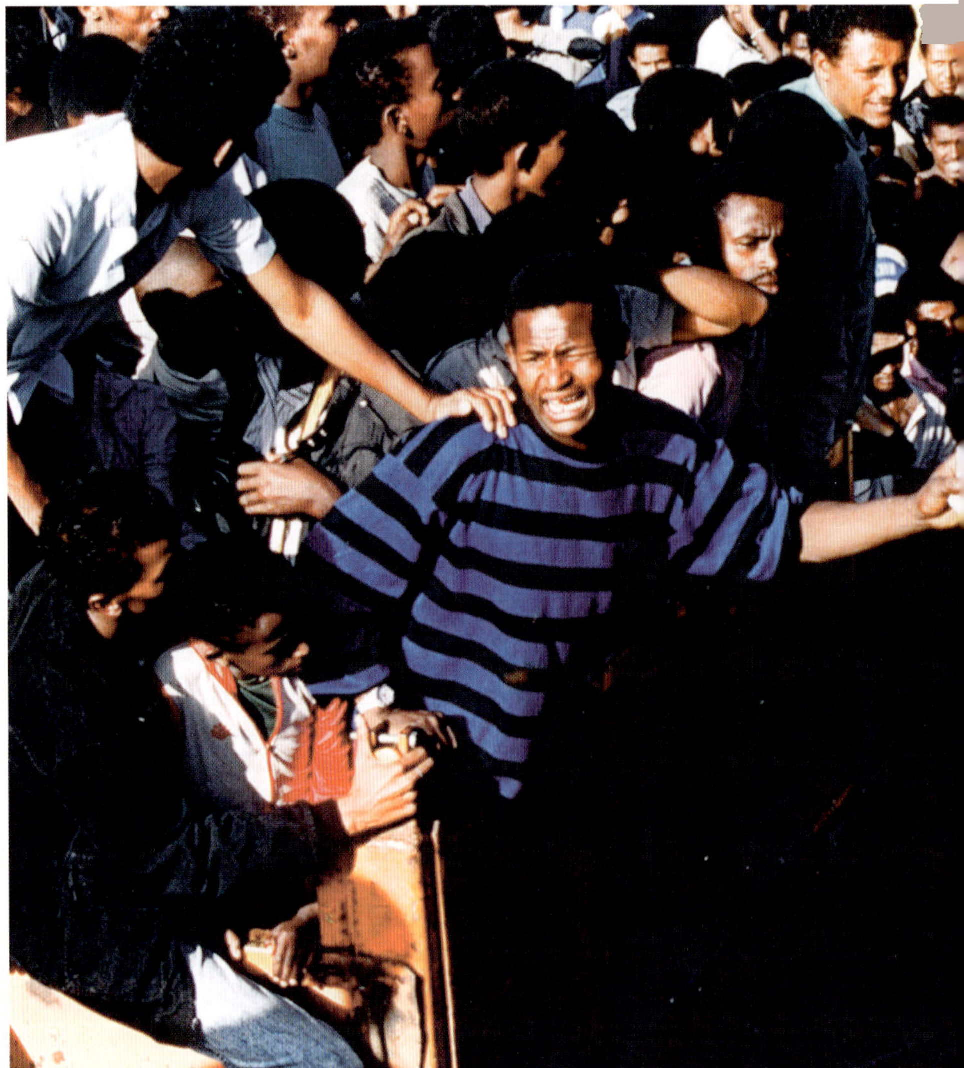

EPA/PA

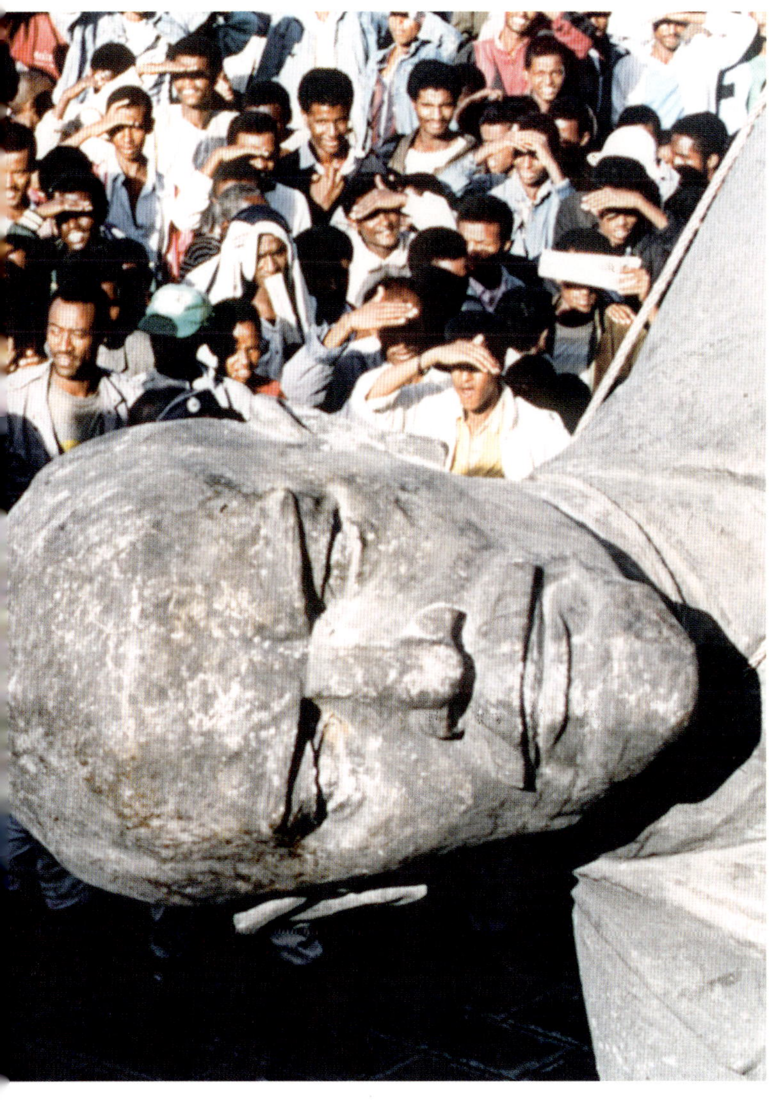

Cheering Ethiopians greet the fall of a statue of Lenin, two days after the flight of President Mengistu, 23 May 1991.

Ciudadanos etíopes celebran la caída de una estatua de Lenin el 23 de mayo de 1991, dos días después de la huida del presidente Mengistu.

Un gruppo di etiopi entusiasti applaude la caduta di una statua di Lenin, due giorni dopo la fuga del presidente Mengistu, 23 maggio 1991.

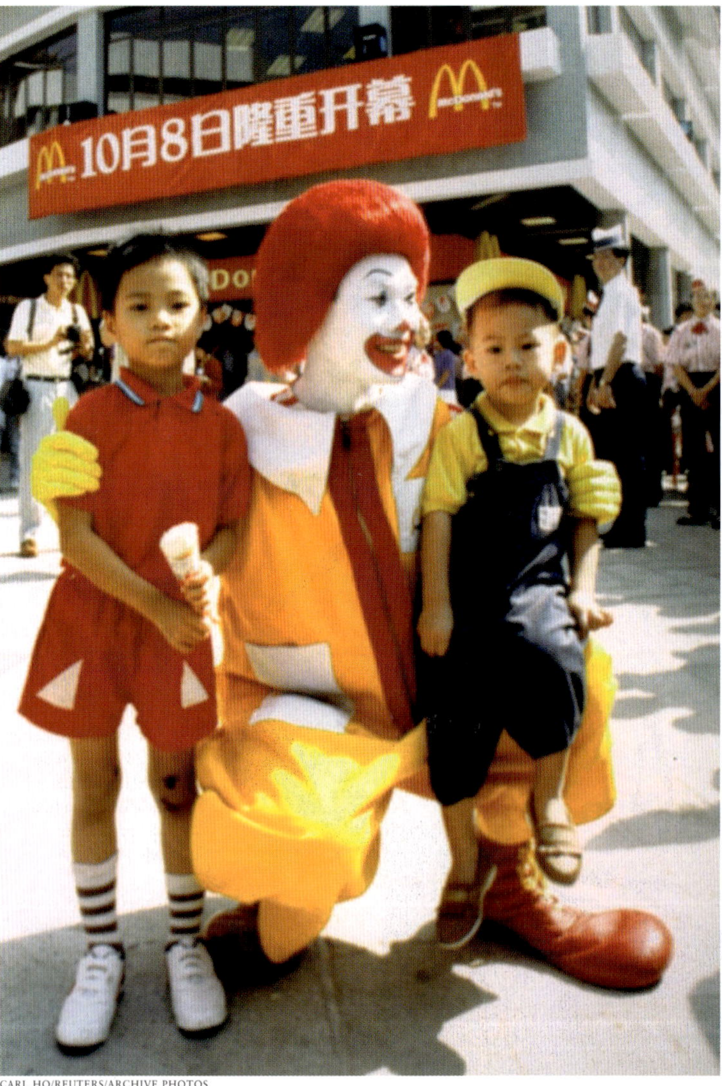

CARL HO/REUTERS/ARCHIVE PHOTOS

McFans... In the Chinese city of Shenzhen, the ubiquitous Ronald McDonald poses outside the first McDonald's restaurant in the country.

Fans de la hamburguesa... El omnipresente Ronald McDonald posa delante del primer restaurante de la cadena McDonald's abierto en China, en la ciudad de Shenzhen.

McAmici... Nella città cinese di Shenzhen, l'onnipresente Ronald McDonald posa di fronte al primo ristorante McDonald's del paese.

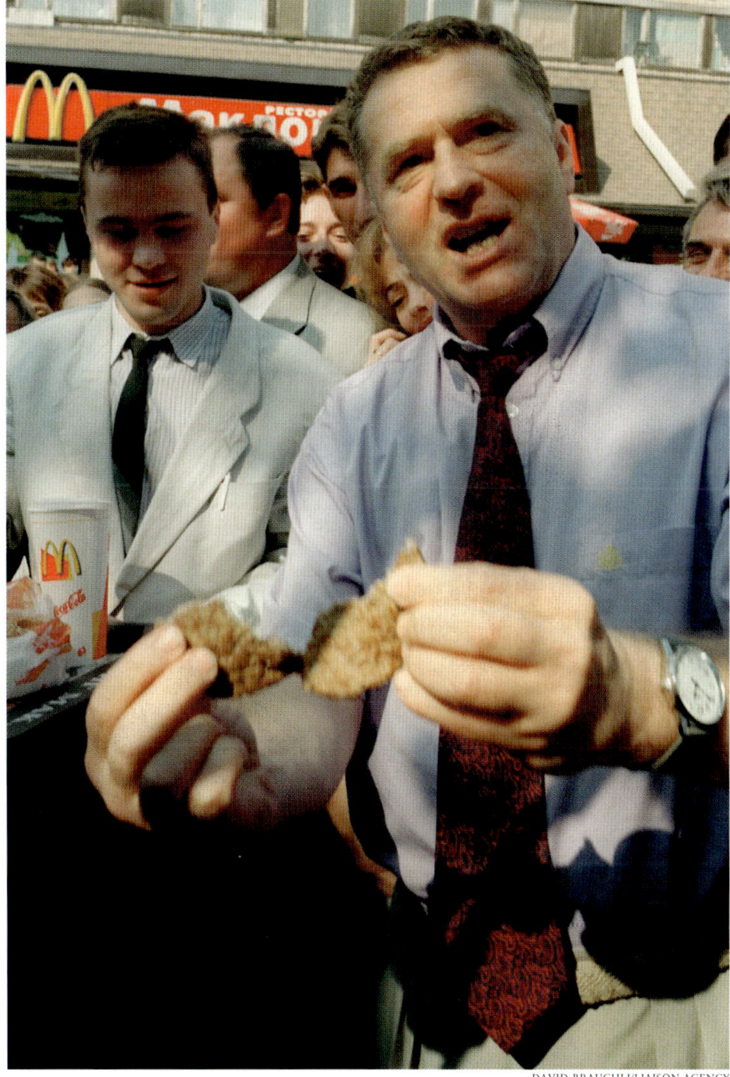

DAVID BRAUCHLI/LIAISON AGENCY

McFoes… The ultra-nationalist Duma member Vladimir Zhirinovsky enquires about the meat content of a hamburger during an anti-McDonald's protest, Moscow, 27 August 1997.

Enemigos de la hamburguesa… El diputado ultranacionalista de la Duma Vladimir Zhirinovsky protesta por la carne que contienen las hamburguesas durante una manifestación antiMcDonald's celebrada en Moscú, 27 de agosto de 1997.

McNemici… Vladimir Zhirinovsky, membro ultranazionalista della Duma, si informa sul tipo di carne contenuto in un hamburger, durante una protesta anti-McDonald's, Mosca, 27 agosto 1997.

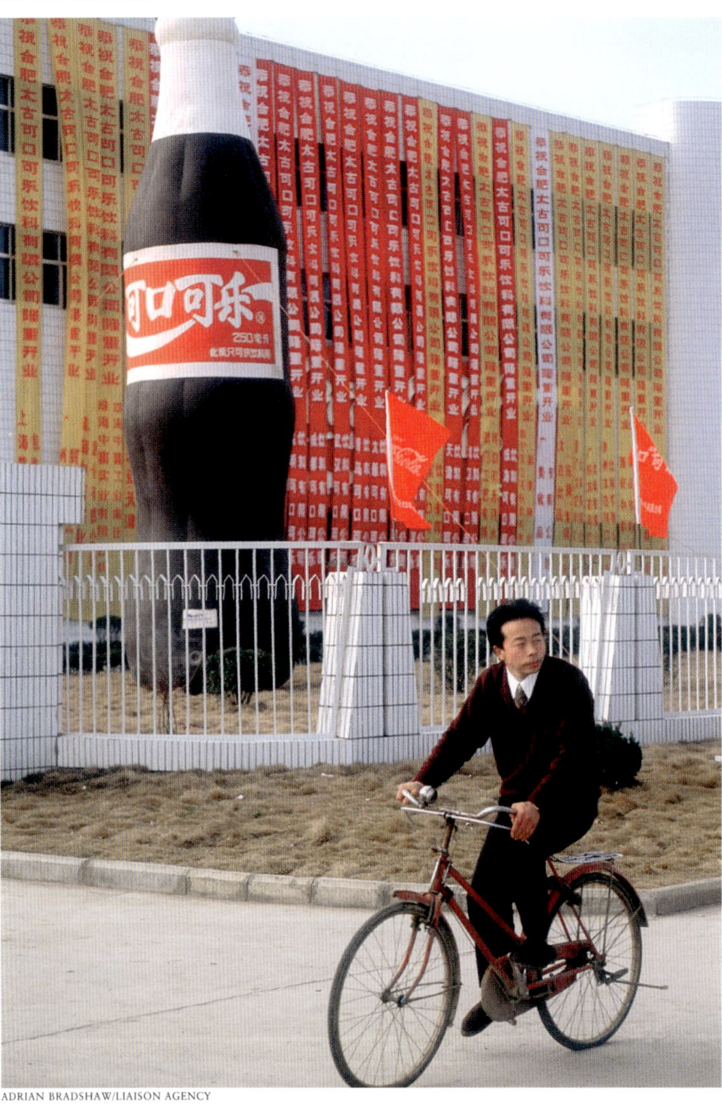

ADRIAN BRADSHAW/LIAISON AGENCY

The 'real thing'.
A cyclist passes the Coca-Cola bottling plant in Hefei, Anhui province, China, 26 February 1998.

"El gusto por lo auténtico."
Un ciclista pasa frente a la planta de embotellamiento de Coca-Cola en Hefei, en la provincia china de Anhui, 26 de febrero de 1998.

Coca-Cola di più.
Un ciclista passa accanto all'impianto d'imbottigliamento di Coca-Cola a Hefei, nella provincia cinese di Anhui, 26 febbraio 1998.

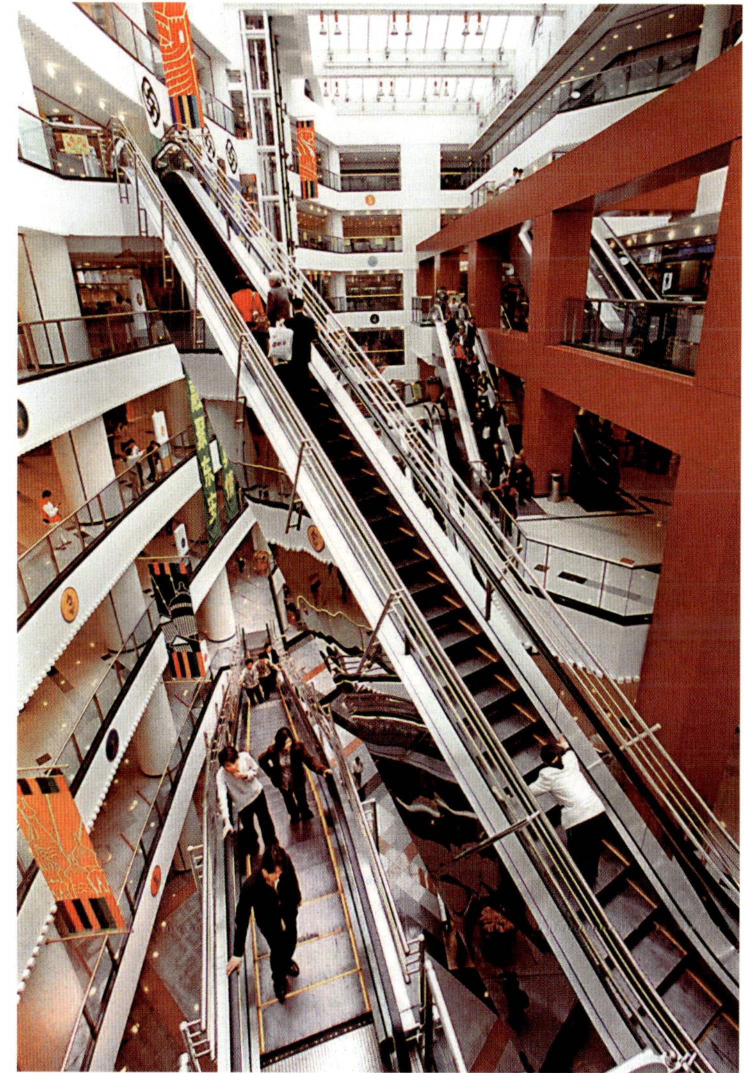

Never in the 'Thoughts of Chairman Mao' – a modern shopping complex in Beijing, China, 9 April 1998.

A buen seguro este moderno centro comercial de Pekín, en China, no figuraba entre *Los pensamientos del presidente Mao*, 9 de abril de 1998.

Cose che Mao non avrebbe mai immaginato – un moderno centro commerciale a Pechino, Cina, 9 aprile 1998.

STEPHEN SHAVER/EPA/PA

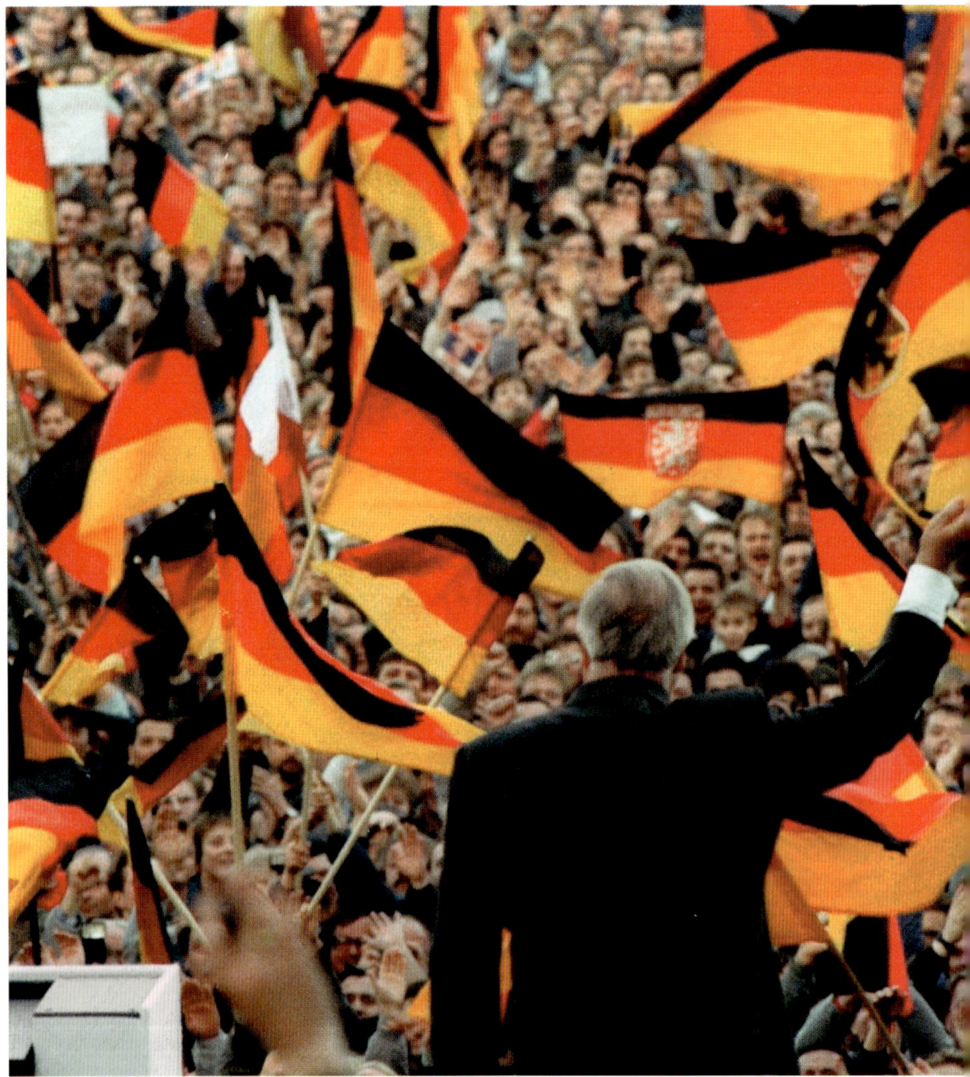

EPA/PA

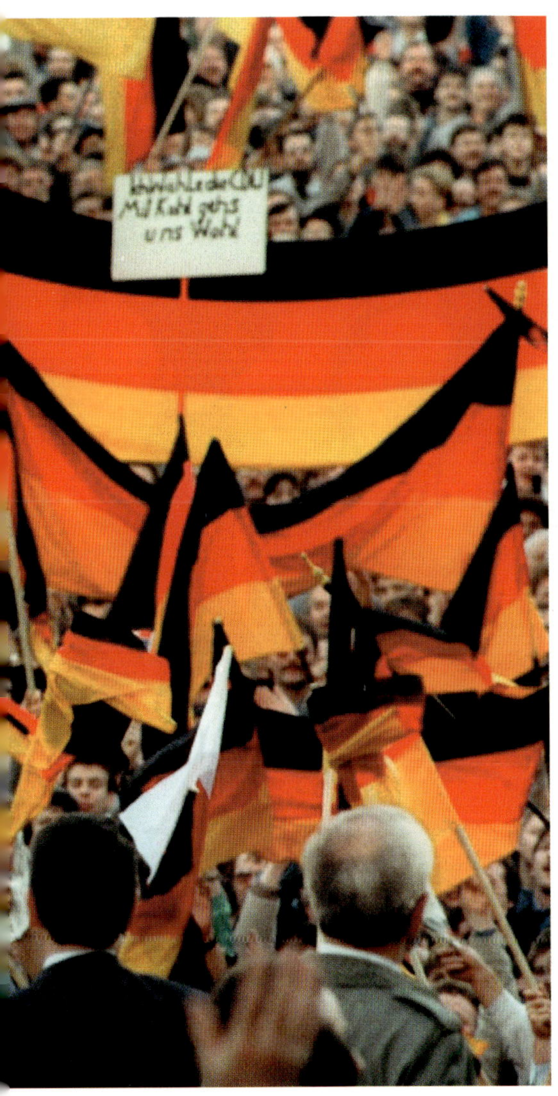

A democratic future. East Germans get their first taste of an election rally in Erfurt, East Germany, 20 February 1990. Helmut Kohl is the central figure.

Un futuro democrático. El 20 de febrero de 1990, los alemanes del Este asisten por primera vez a un acto de campaña electoral en Erfurt (Alemania del Este), cuya figura central es Helmut Kohl.

Un futuro democratico. Tedeschi della Germania Est assaporano per la prima volta una campagna elettorale a Erfurt, Repubblica Democratica Tedesca, 20 febbraio 1990. Helmut Kohl è al centro della foto.

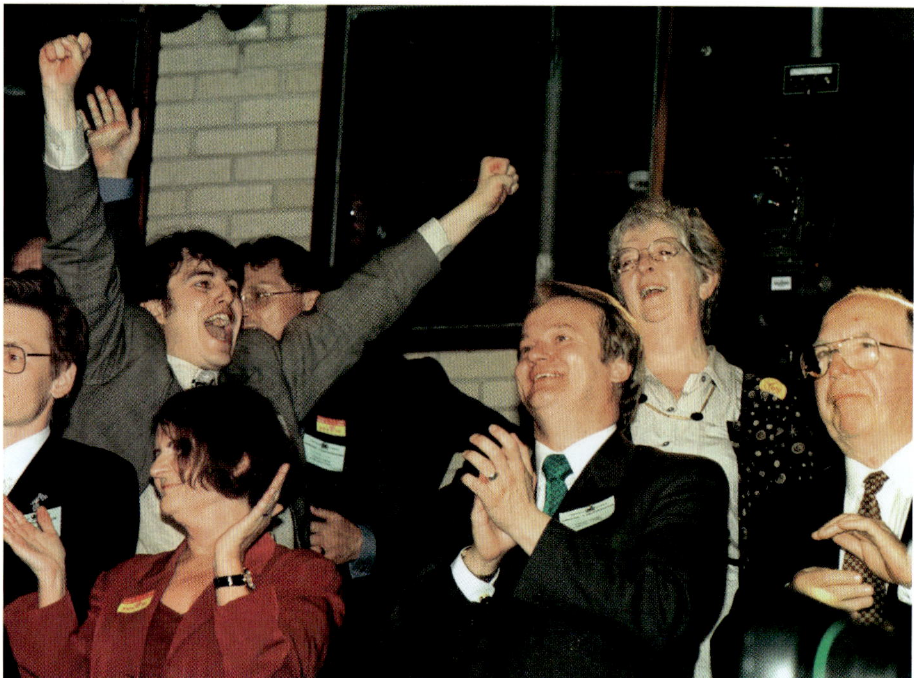

BARRY BATCHELOR/PA

The joys of devolution. Welsh supporters of devolution celebrate their victory in the referendum, 19 September 1997. The 'yes' vote ensured that a measure of self-government would return to Wales.

La dicha de la devolución. El 19 de septiembre de 1997 los partidarios galeses de la devolución celebran su victoria en el referéndum. El "sí" mayoritario garantizaba la devolución del autogobierno al País de Gales.

Le gioie della devolution. I difensori gallesi della devolution festeggiano la vittoria nel referendum, 19 settembre 1997. Grazie ai "sì", il Galles ebbe di nuovo diritto all'autogoverno.

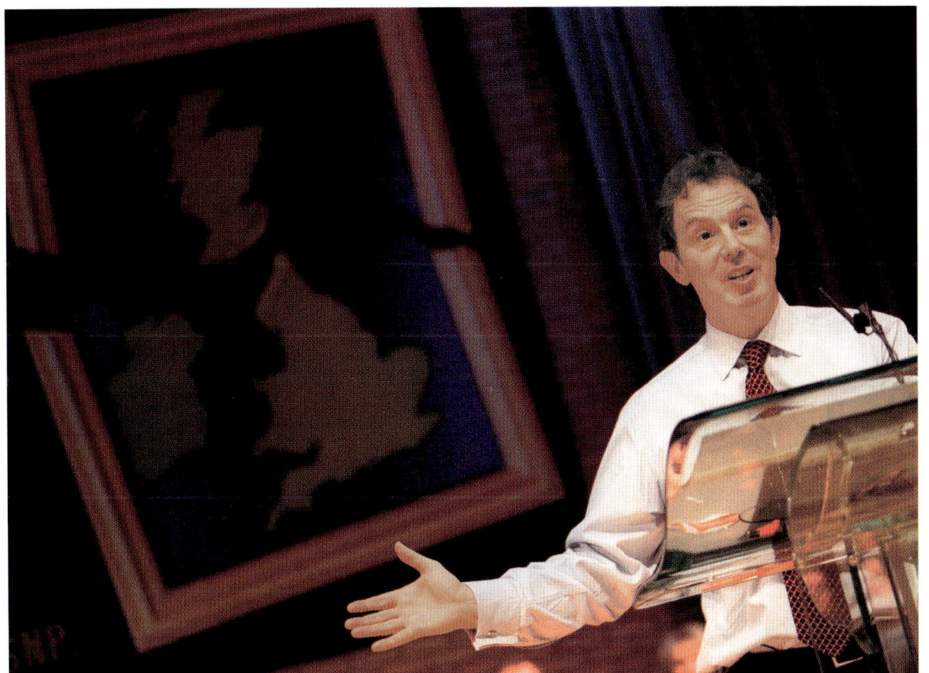

DAVID CHESKIN/PA

The perils of independence. British Prime Minister Tony Blair gives of his dramatic best at the Royal Scottish Academy of Music and Drama, Glasgow, as he counsels against Scottish independence, 5 February 1999.

Los peligros de la independencia. El 5 de febrero de 1999, en la Royal Scottish Academy of Music and Drama de Glasgow, el primer ministro británico Tony Blair condena la independencia escocesa en un acto marcadamente teatral.

I pericoli dell'indipendenza. Il primo ministro britannico Tony Blair, durante una teatrale conferenza presso la Royal Scottish Academy of Music and Drama di Glasgow, mentre parla degli svantaggi dell'indipendenza per la Scozia, 5 febbraio 1999.

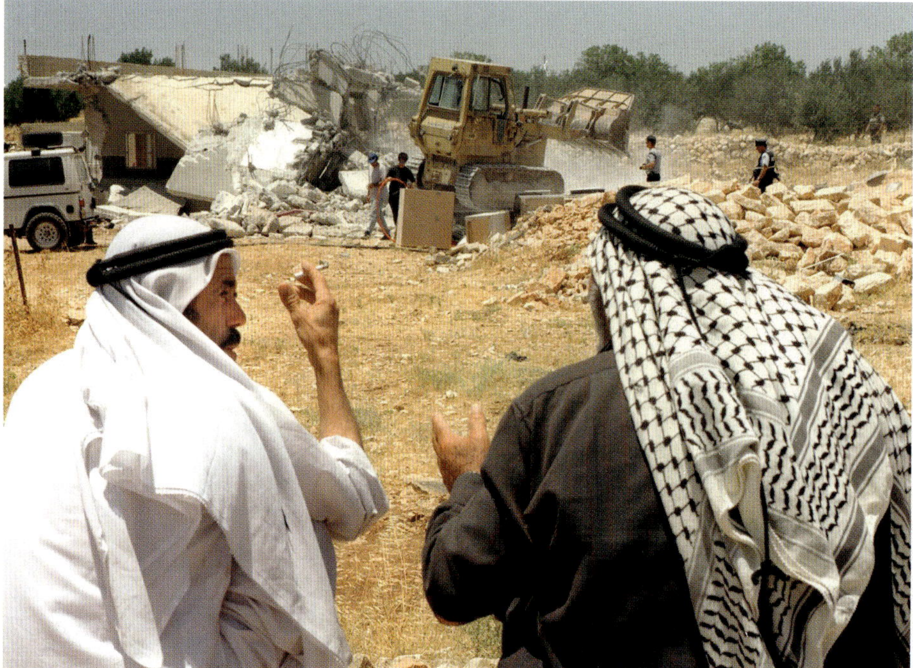

ALAN ABU HOSSAM/EPA/PA

Old homes, new ways… Palestinian members of the Isa Jibril family watch in dismay as Israeli bulldozers flatten their home in the Tekoa area of Bethlehem, 18 June 1998. In all, six houses were demolished.

Viejos hogares, nuevas formas… Miembros palestinos de la familia de Isa Jibril contemplan consternados cómo *bulldozers* israelíes derriban su casa en el barrio de Tekoa, en Belén, 18 de junio de 1998. En total seis casas fueron demolidas.

Vecchie case, nuovi percorsi… Membri della famiglia palestinese di Isa Jibril osservano avviliti i bulldozer israeliani mentre radono al suolo la loro casa, nel quartiere di Tekoa, Betlemme, 18 giugno 1998. In tutto furono demolite sei case.

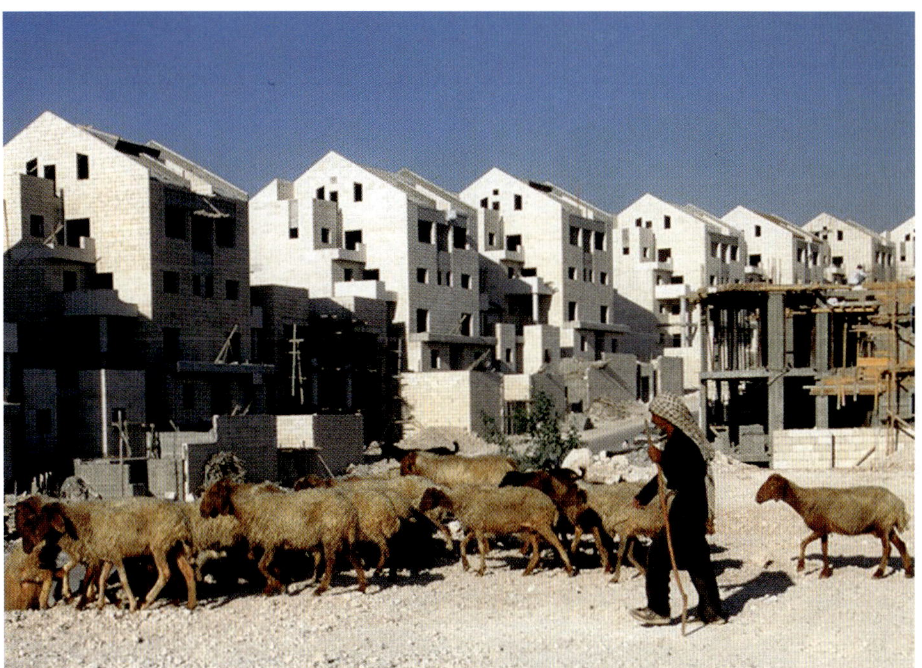

MANOOCHER DEGHATI/EPA/PA

Old ways, new homes... A Bedouin shepherd guides his flock past a new housing complex for Jewish settlers at Maale Adummim on the outskirts of Jerusalem, 12 August 1996.

Viejas formas, nuevos hogares... Un pastor beduino guía a su rebaño frente a un nuevo asentamiento de colonos judíos en Maale Adummim, en las afueras de Jerusalén, 12 de agosto de 1996.

Vecchi percorsi, nuove case... Un pastore beduino passa con il gregge accanto a un nuovo complesso residenziale per coloni israeliani presso Maale Adummium, alla periferia di Gerusalemme, 12 agosto 1996.

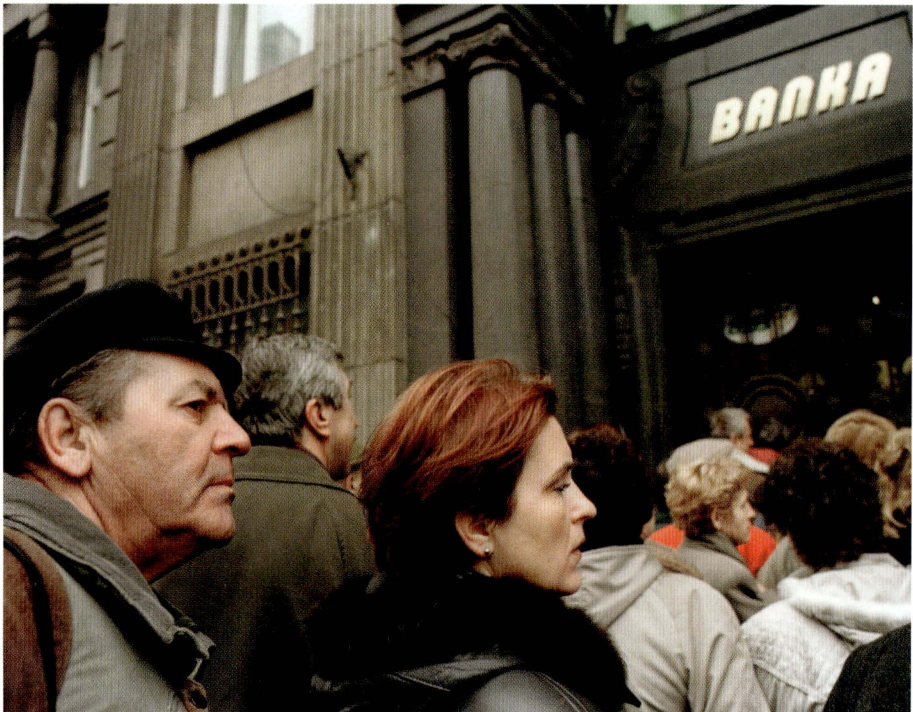

SEAN GALLUP/LIAISON AGENCY

A period of adjustment. Depositors and customers of the Czech bank Ekoagrobanka gather in front of the Prague branch after predictions that the bank was about to collapse, 11 January 1996.

Un período de ajustes. El 11 de enero de 1996, clientes del banco checo Ekoagrobanka se congregan frente a la sucursal de Praga tras propagarse el rumor de que la entidad se halla al borde de la quiebra.

Un periodo di adattamento. Depositanti e clienti della banca ceca Ekoagrobanka di fronte alla filiale di Praga dopo aver saputo che la banca stava per fallire, 11 gennaio 1996.

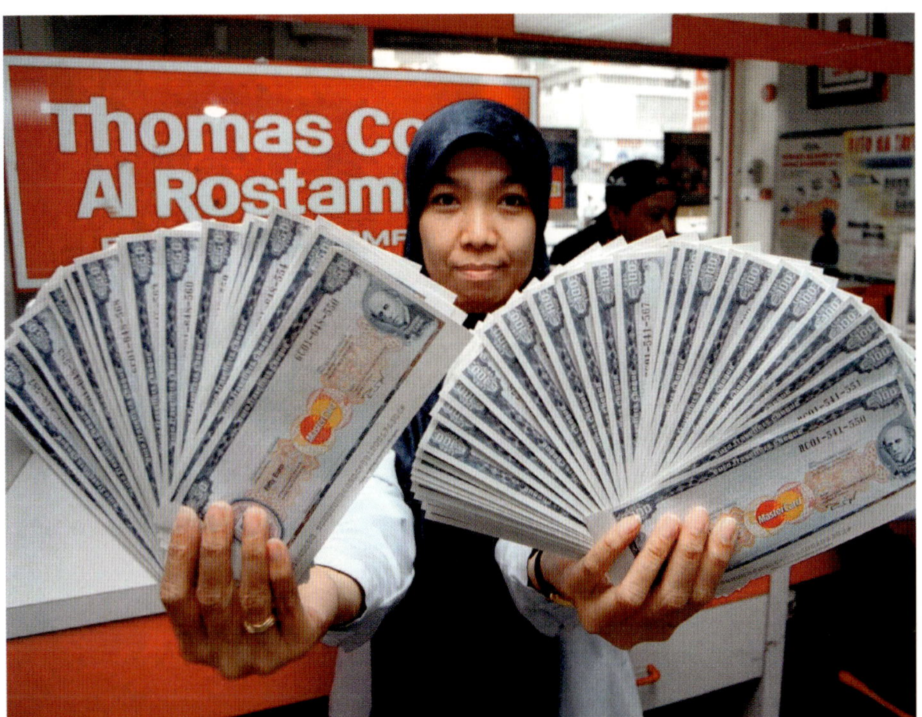

ANWAR MIRZA/REUTERS/ARCHIVE PHOTOS

A fistful of euros. Peroza Ahmad of Thomas Cook displays travellers' cheques in the new euro currency, Dubai, United Arab Emirates, 10 January 1999. The launch of the euro was greeted with rather less enthusiasm in Europe.

Un buen puñado de euros. Peroza Ahmad, de la agencia Thomas Cook de Dubai (Emiratos Árabes Unidos) muestra cheques de viaje emitidos en la nueva divisa europea, 10 de enero de 1999. En Europa el lanzamiento del euro fue acogido con algo menos de entusiasmo.

Per un pugno di euro. Peroza Ahmad dell'agenzia Thomas Cook di Dubai mostra alcuni travellers' cheque nella nuova moneta europea, 10 gennaio 1999. In Europa, il lancio dell'euro fu accolto con entusiasmo più contenuto.

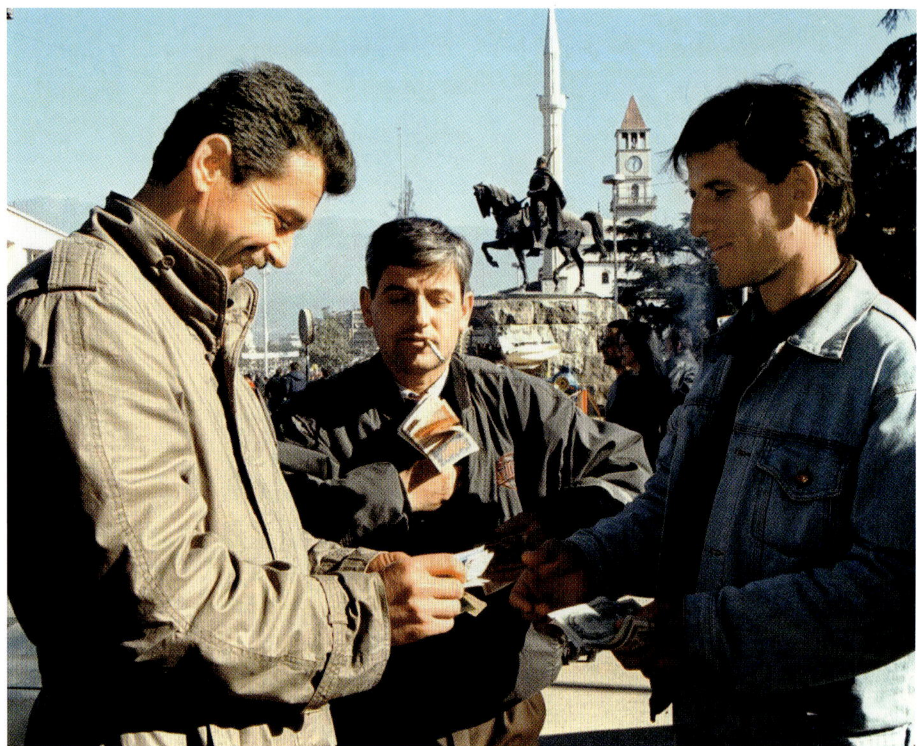

YANNIS BEHRAKIS/REUTERS/ARCHIVE PHOTOS

The curse of the pyramids. Free-market dealers trade in hard currency outside the Central Bank, Tirana, Albania, 31 January 1997. Following the collapse of pyramid investment schemes, Albanians rushed to buy 'hard' currency.

La maldición de las pirámides. Tratantes del libre mercado negocian con divisas extranjeras frente al Banco Central en Tirana, Albania, 31 de enero de 1997. Tras el hundimiento de los esquemas de inversión piramidales, los albaneses se apresuraron a adquirir divisas "fuertes".

La maledizione delle piramidi. Rivenditori sul mercato libero commerciano con valute forti di fronte alla Banca Centrale di Tirana, Albania, 31 gennaio 1997. Dopo il crollo dei piani d'investimento piramidali, gli albanesi si affrettarono a comprare valute "forti".

On the same day, Albanians sell their blood at a Tirana hospital. The exchange rate was $24 for a pint.

El mismo día otros albaneses venden su sangre en un hospital de Tirana. El medio litro se cotizaba a 24 dólares.

Lo stesso giorno, altri Albanesi vendevano il loro sangue nell'ospedale di Tirana. Il tasso di cambio era di 24 $ per ogni mezzo litro.

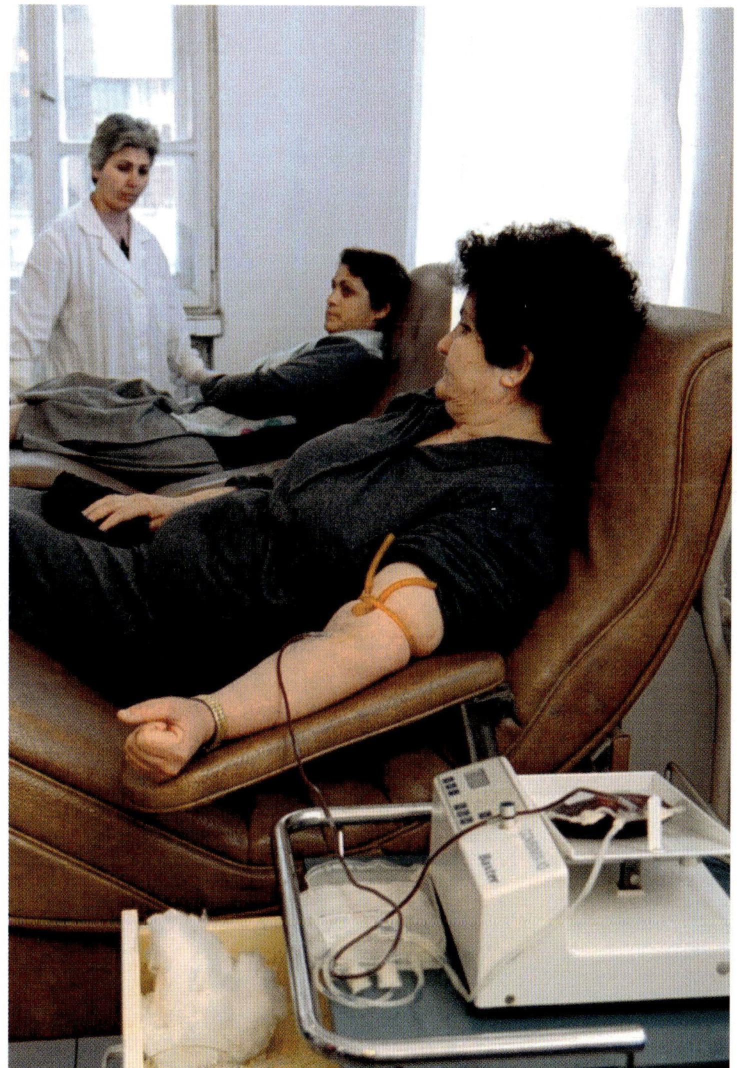

ARBEN CELI/REUTERS/ARCHIVE PHOTOS

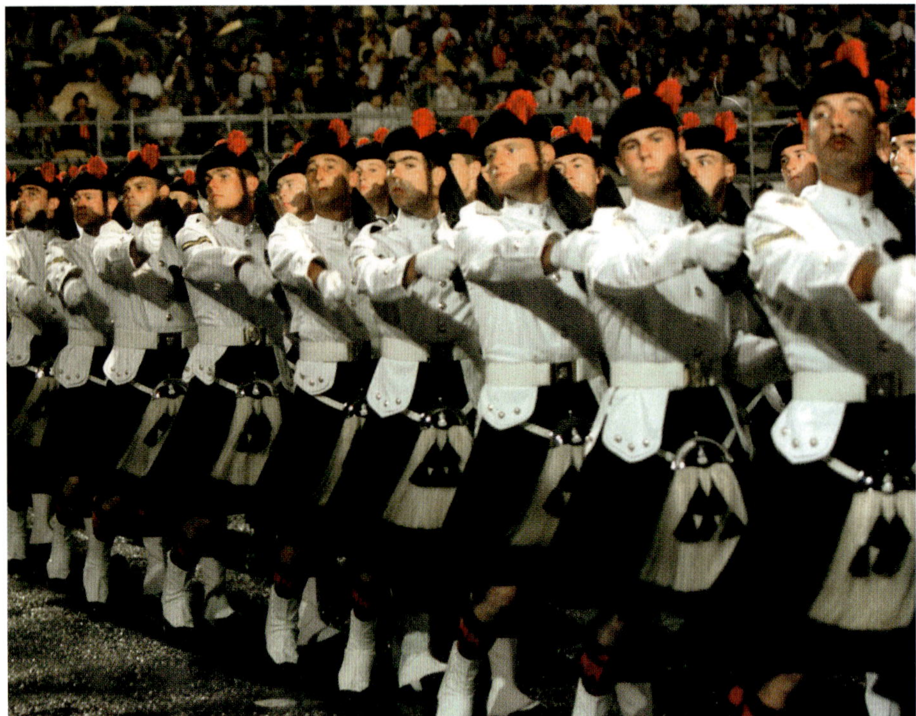

MIKE FIALA/LIAISON AGENCY

British withdrawal. Members of the Black Watch march across the parade ground at the Royal Navy headquarters in Hong Kong, 30 June 1997. It was the night when Britain relinquished control of its former colony.

Retirada británica. El 30 de junio de 1997, miembros de la Guardia Negra desfilan por la plaza de armas del cuartel general de la Royal Navy de Hong Kong. Esa noche Gran Bretaña retornaba el control de su antigua colonia a China.

Ritiro britannico. Membri del reggimento Black Watch sfilano lungo la piazza d'armi del quartier generale della Royal Navy di Hong Kong, 30 giugno 1997. Era la notte in cui la Gran Bretagna rinunciò al controllo sull'antica colonia.

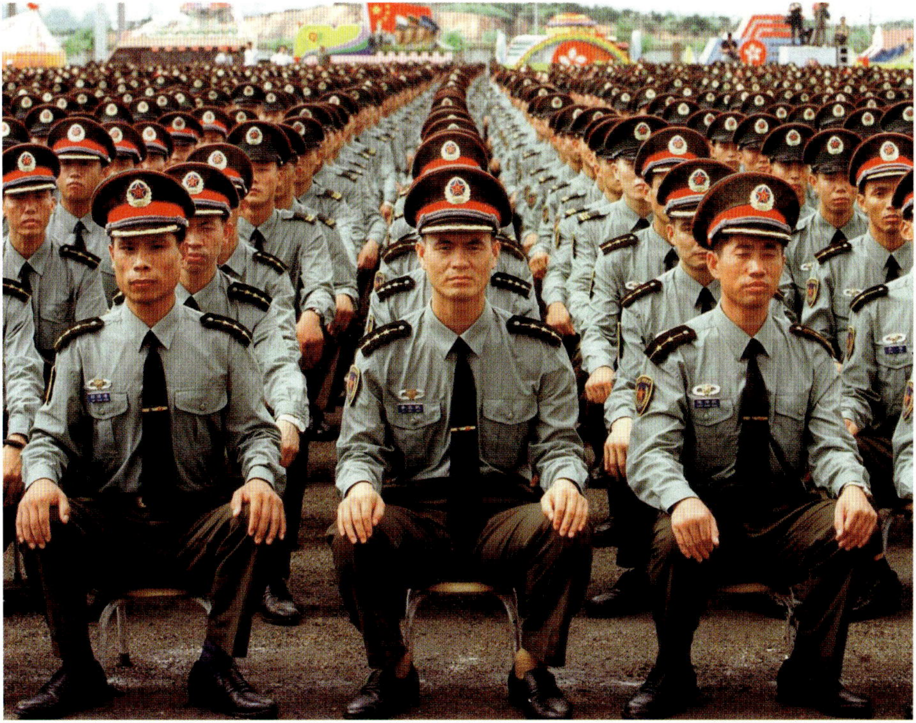

STRINGER/REUTERS/ARCHIVE PHOTOS

Chinese advance. Troops of the Chinese People's Liberation Army at a ceremony on the same day in Shenzhen, shortly before leaving for Hong Kong.

El avance chino. Tropas del Ejército Popular de Liberación de China durante una ceremonia el mismo día en Shenzhen, poco antes de partir hacia Hong Kong.

Avanzata cinese. Truppe dell'Esercito di liberazione popolare cinese durante una cerimonia tenuta lo stesso giorno a Shenzhen, poco prima di partire per Hong Kong.

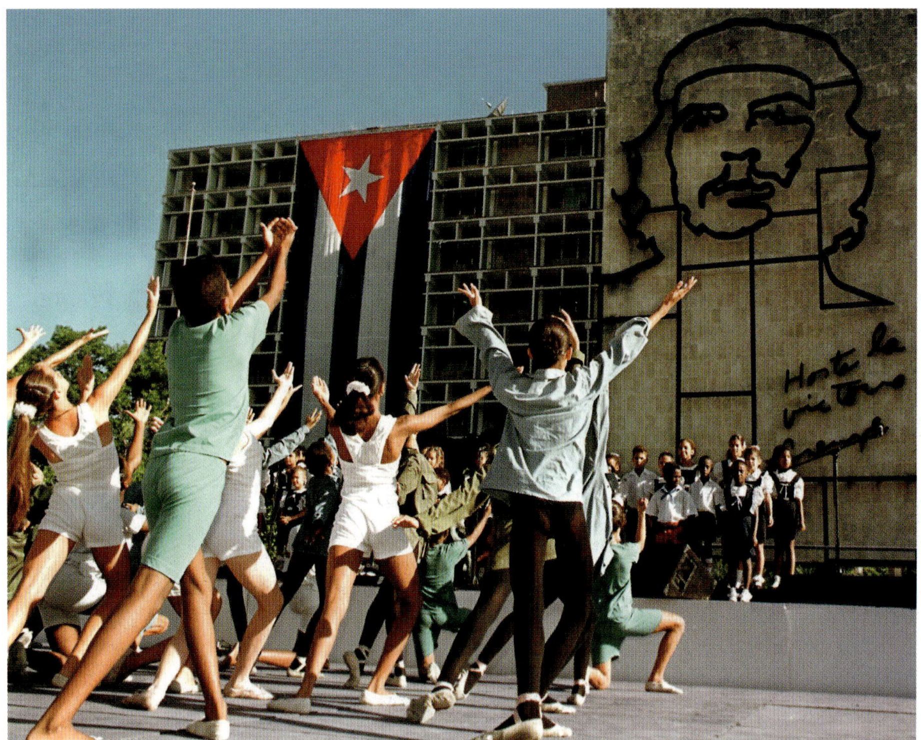

NIURKA BARROSA/EPA/PA

Happy to stay. A dance display by Cuban children to celebrate the 31st anniversary of the death of Che Guevara, Plaza de la Revolución, Havana, 8 October 1998. The image on the wall is Che's.

Felices de quedarse. Niños cubanos bailan en la Plaza de la Revolución de La Habana para celebrar el 31° aniversario de la muerte del Che Guevara, 8 de octubre de 1998. Frente a ellos, en la pared, la imagen del Che.

Felici di restare. Uno spettacolo di danza rappresentato da bambini cubani per commemorare il 31° anniversario della morte di Che Guevara, Plaza de la Revolución, L'Avana, 8 ottobre 1998. L'immagine sul muro rappresenta il Che.

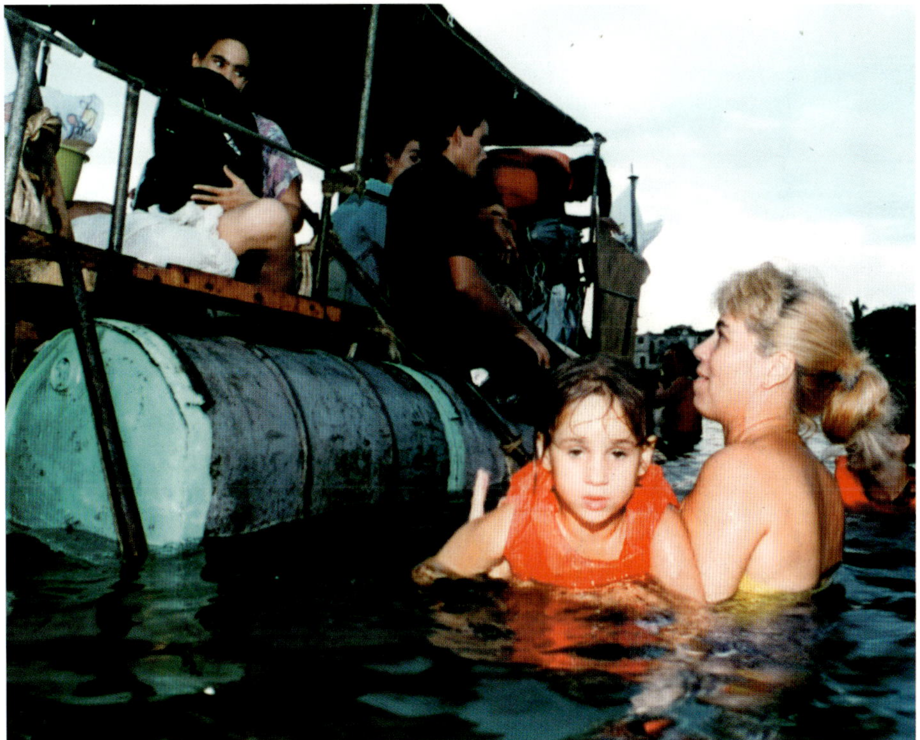

EPA/PA

Desperate to leave. A woman supports her daughter as they prepare to climb aboard an improvised raft off the coast of Cuba, 23 September 1994. They were among thousands who sought a new life in the United States.

Desesperados por marcharse. Una mujer sostiene a su hija cuando se preparan para subir a bordo de una balsa improvisada cerca de la costa cubana, 23 de septiembre de 1994. Forman parte de los miles de cubanos que partían hacia Estados Unidos en busca de una vida mejor.

Ansiosi di partire. Una donna tiene in braccio sua figlia mentre si preparano per salire a bordo di una zattera improvvisata al largo della costa cubana, 24 settembre 1994. Erano alcune delle migliaia di persone ansiose di iniziare una nuova vita negli Stati Uniti.

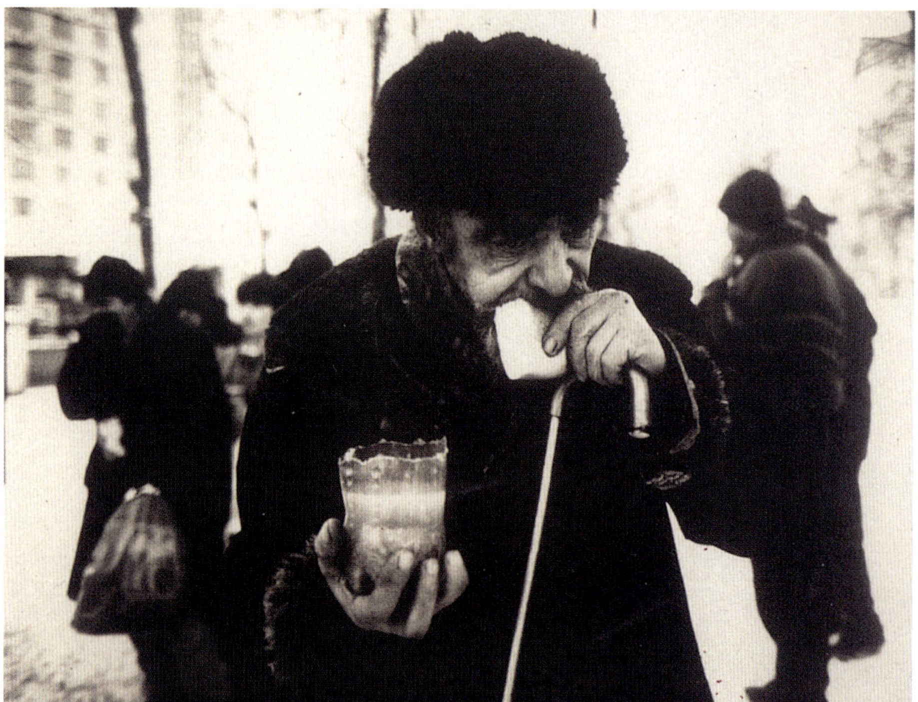

CHRISTOPHER MORRIS/BLACK STAR/COLORIFIC!

The age-old problems of cold and hunger return to the poor and elderly on Moscow's streets in the economic meltdown faced by the Russian state, 1999. Was this the best that the new order had to offer?

La crisis económica que afrontaba el Estado ruso en 1999 sembró las calles de Moscú de ancianos desfavorecidos azotados por los viejos fantasmas del frío y el hambre. ¿Era esto lo mejor que el nuevo orden podía ofrecer?

Lungo le strade di Mosca, dopo il tracollo finanziario dello Stato russo nel 1999, i poveri e gli anziani dovettero vedersela con due problemi mai risolti, il freddo e la fame. Era questo ciò che di meglio aveva da offrire il nuovo ordine?

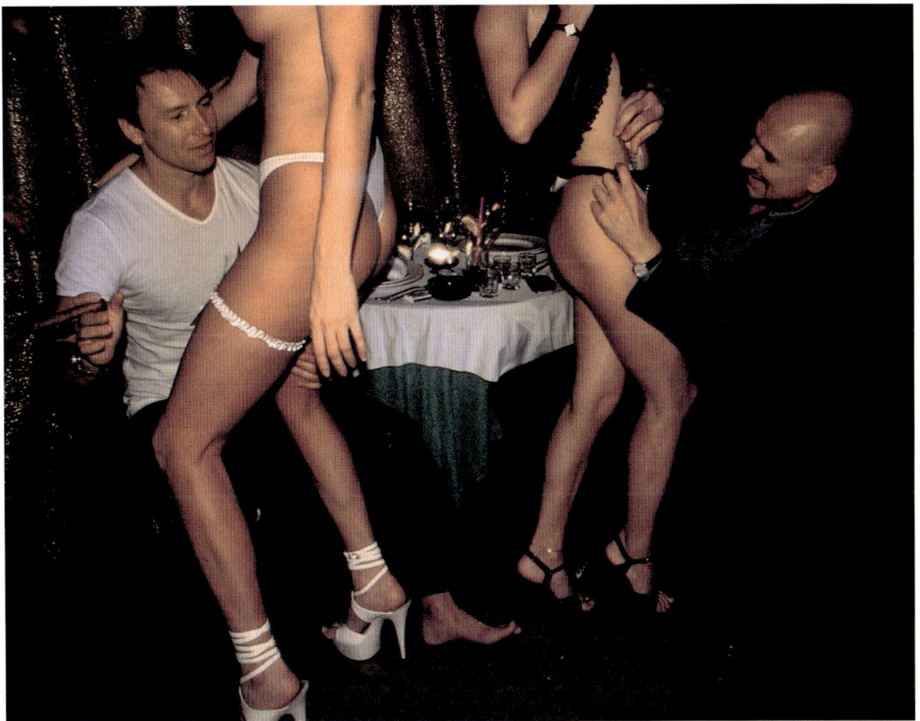

CHRISTOPHER MORRIS/BLACK STAR/COLORIFIC!

Communist hard-liners would almost certainly have labelled the protagonists in Moscow's exclusive Club Soho 'decadent hyenas'. Was lap dancing the best that the new order had to offer?

Los puristas del comunismo a buen seguro habrían calificado a estos clientes del exclusivo Club Soho de Moscú de "hienas decadentes". ¿Era este tipo de espectáculo lo mejor que el nuevo orden podía ofrecer?

Gli irriducibili del comunismo avrebbero senza dubbio definito i clienti dell'esclusivo Club Soho di Mosca come "iene decadenti". Era questo tipo di spettacoli ciò che di meglio aveva da offrire il nuovo ordine?

4. Pre-millennium tension
Tensiones de fin de milenio
Tensioni di pre-millennio

Two-month-old Namu Otani undergoes a radiation check at Tokaimura Civil Center, 8 October 1999. Two days earlier, Japan had suffered the worst nuclear accident since Chernobyl, at the JCO Nuclear Fuel Plant.

Namu Otani, un bebé de dos meses, es sometido a un control de radiación en el centro civil de Tokaimura, 8 de octubre de 1999. Dos días antes Japón había sufrido el peor accidente nuclear desde Chernobyl, en la planta de reciclaje de combustible nuclear de la empresa JCO.

Namu Otani, di due mesi di vita, viene sottoposta a un controllo delle radiazioni nel Tokaimura Civil Center, 8 ottobre 1999. Due giorni prima il Giappone aveva subito il peggior incidente nucleare dopo Chernobyl, nella JCO Nuclear Fuel Plant.

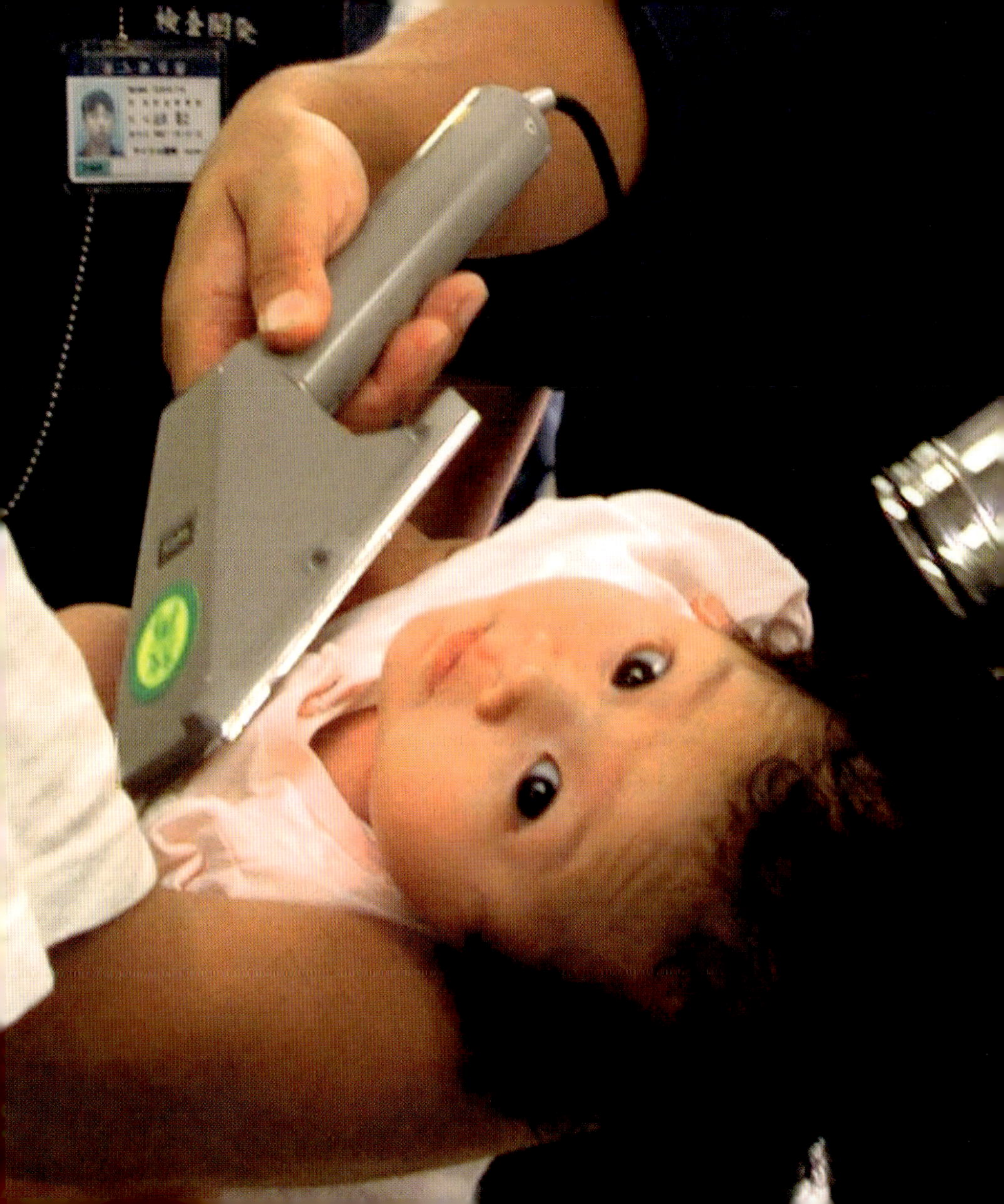

4. Pre-millennium tension
Tensiones de fin de milenio
Tensioni di pre-millennio

For much of the decade, the oncoming Millennium concentrated the minds of reformers and radicals, politicians and protesters. Every cause and every campaign seemed to be under sentence of execution – so much to be done before the year 2000, and so little time to do it. Schemers and counter-schemers locked minds over the future of the planet. There were battles over the causes and effects of pollution, over the pros and cons of genetically modified food, over the future of humanity.

Those with extreme views suggested, as the 1990s tottered towards the Millennium, that the world would soon end. There were massacres in schools at the Scottish town of Dunblane, and at Littleton, Colorado; on the subway in Tokyo; and at a tourist resort in Port Arthur. There were floods in Bangladesh and Europe, earthquakes in California and Japan. Zealots sold all they had and hurried to selected vantage points from which they could ascend en masse to heaven. In scenes reminiscent of the debauched last days of Ancient Rome, people sniffed and snorted their preferred drugs, threw caution and morality to the wild winds, ate, drank and were merry. The planet, racked by storms that could have been the result of global warming, somehow held together.

Durante buena parte de la década, el cercano nuevo milenio ocupa un lugar destacado en la mente de reformistas, radicales, políticos y manifestantes. Causas y campañas parecen estar condenadas a la ejecución inmediata; hay tanto por hacer antes del año 2000 y queda tan poco tiempo... Planificadores y antiplanificadores discuten sobre el futuro del planeta. Se genera polémica acerca de las causas y efectos de la contaminación, sobre los pros y los contras de los alimentos transgénicos y sobre el futuro de la humanidad en términos generales.

A medida que los años noventa se tambalean hacia el nuevo milenio, los más extremistas vaticinan que el fin del mundo está próximo. Se producen masacres en las escuelas de Dunblane (en Escocia) y de Littleton (en Colorado); en el metro de Tokio y en el turístico monumento de Port Arthur (Tasmania). En Bangladesh y en Europa se suceden las inundaciones, mientras que los terremotos sacuden California y Japón. Los fanáticos venden todas sus pertenencias y se apresuran a ocupar posiciones ventajosas desde las cuales poder ascender en masa a los cielos. En escenas que recuerdan a las orgías de los últimos días de la antigua Roma, muchos se olvidan de la prudencia y la moralidad, y se abandonan a la comida, la bebida, las drogas y la diversión desenfrenada. Con todo, el planeta, asolado por tormentas que bien podrían ser consecuencia del calentamiento del globo, logrará capear el temporal.

Durante la maggior parte degli anni Novanta, l'immaginario di riformatori, radicali, politici e manifestanti venne in gran parte occupato dall'imminente arrivo del nuovo millennio. Qualsiasi causa o campagna sembravano condannate a una loro immediata realizzazione – così tante cose da fare prima del 2000 e così poco tempo per farle. Previsionisti e antiprevisionisti unirono le loro menti sul futuro del pianeta. Sorsero discussioni sugli effetti dell'inquinamento, sui pro e i contro del cibo modificato geneticamente, sul futuro dell'umanità.

Per i più esagerati il mondo stava per finire, e ne era una chiara evidenza il fatto che gli anni Novanta si avvicinavano con sempre maggiore incertezza verso il nuovo millennio. Fu il momento delle stragi nella scuola della scozzese Dunblane e in quella di Littleton, in Colorado, nella metropolitana di Tokyo e in un complesso turistico a Port Arthur. Arrivò poi il turno delle alluvioni in Bangladesh e in Europa, dei terremoti in California e in Giappone. I più fanatici misero in vendita tutto ciò che possedevano, e si affrettarono ad occupare i migliori punti panoramici da dove avrebbero potuto ascendere in massa verso il paradiso. In scene di dissolutezza degne degli ultimi giorni dell'antica Roma, la gente si dava alla droga, eliminando dal proprio dizionario parole come cautela o moralità, mangiava, beveva ed era felice. E intanto il pianeta, sconvolto da tormente probabilmente provocate dal surriscaldamento globale, stava a guardare.

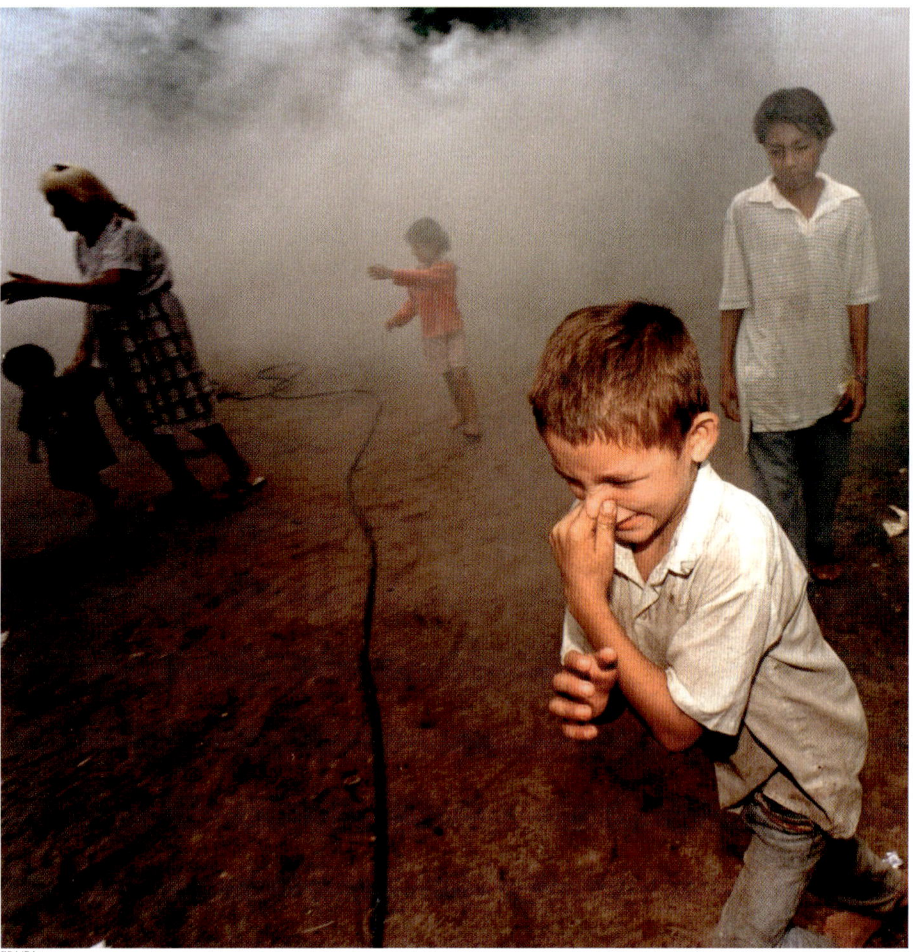

EPA/PA

(Opposite) Fumigating against malaria, El Salvador, 29 September 1999. (Right) After the deluge: a flooded cemetery in Trujillo, Peru, 12 February 1998.

(Página anterior) Fumigación contra la malaria en El Salvador, 29 de septiembre de 1999. (Derecha) Inundación en el cementerio peruano de Trujillo tras las fuertes lluvias, 12 de febrero de 1998.

(Pagina a fianco) Fumigazione contro la malaria, El Salvador, 29 settembre 1999. (A destra) Dopo il diluvio: un cimitero inondato a Trujillo, Perù, 12 febbraio 1998.

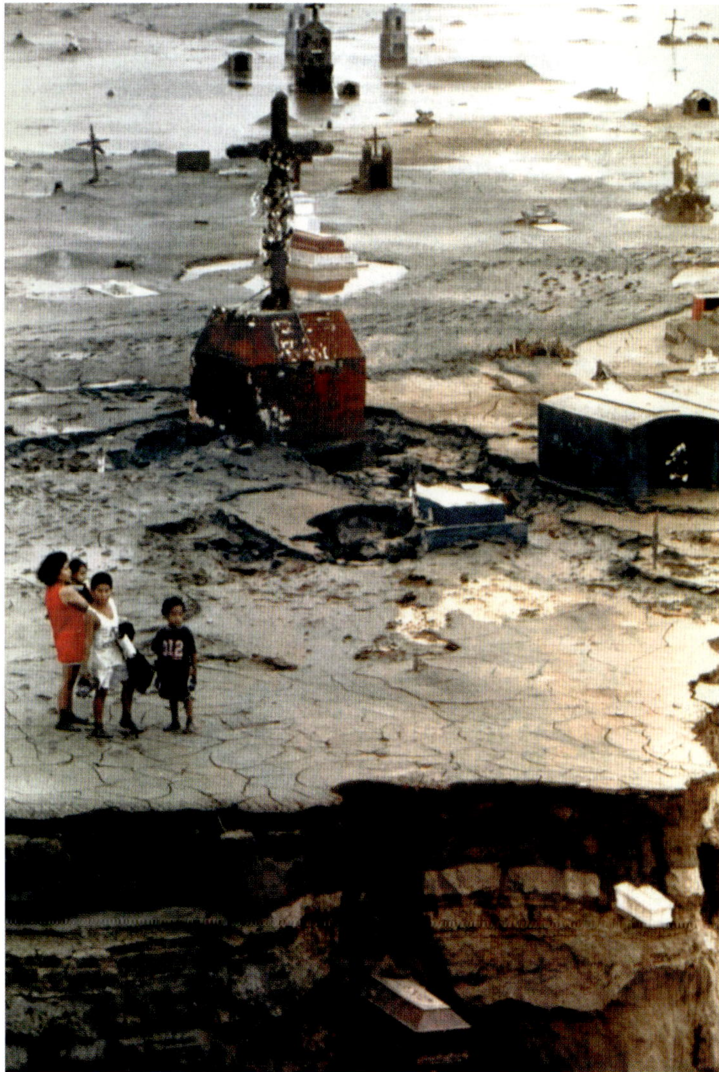

SILVIA IZQUIERDO/REUTERS/ARCHIVE PHOTOS

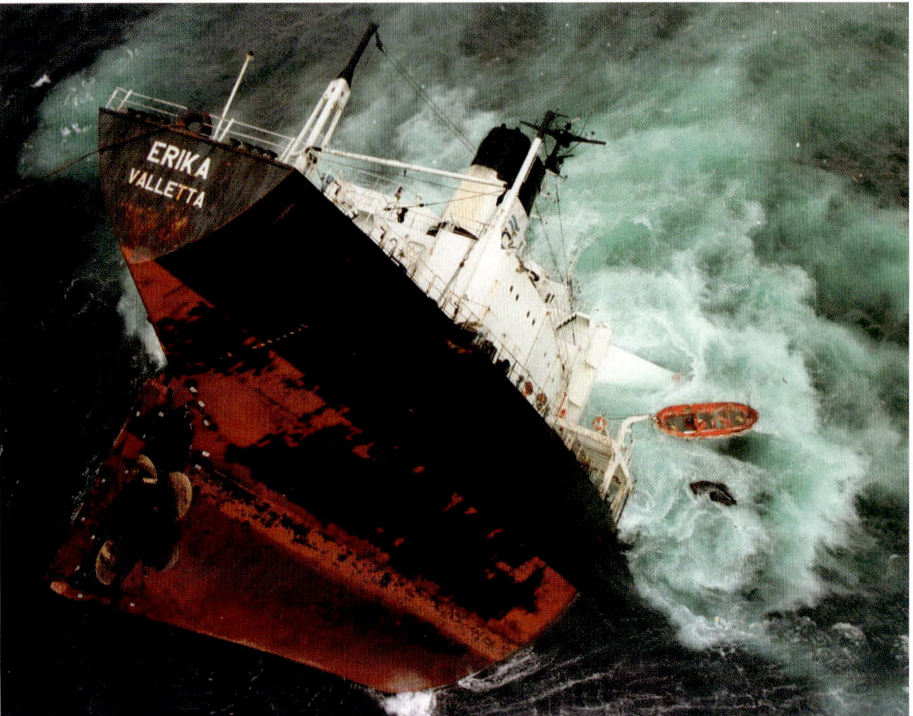

EPA/PA

(Above) The oil tanker *Erika* breaks up off the coast of Brittany, France, 12 December 1999. (Opposite) Not long after, an oil-soaked grebe is rescued from the beaches of Noirmoutier. Tens of thousands of sea-birds died.

(Arriba) El 12 de diciembre de 1999 el petrolero *Erika* se hunde frente a las costas de la Bretaña francesa. (Página siguiente) Poco después, se rescata a un somorgujo empapado de fuel en las playas de Noirmoutier. Decenas de miles de aves marinas perecieron a consecuencia de la catástrofe.

(In alto) La petroliera *Erika* affonda al largo della costa della Bretagna francese, 12 dicembre 1999. (Pagina a fianco) Poco dopo uno svasso impregnato di pretolio viene salvato sulla spiaggia di Noirmoutier. Gli uccelli morti si contarono a decine di migliaia.

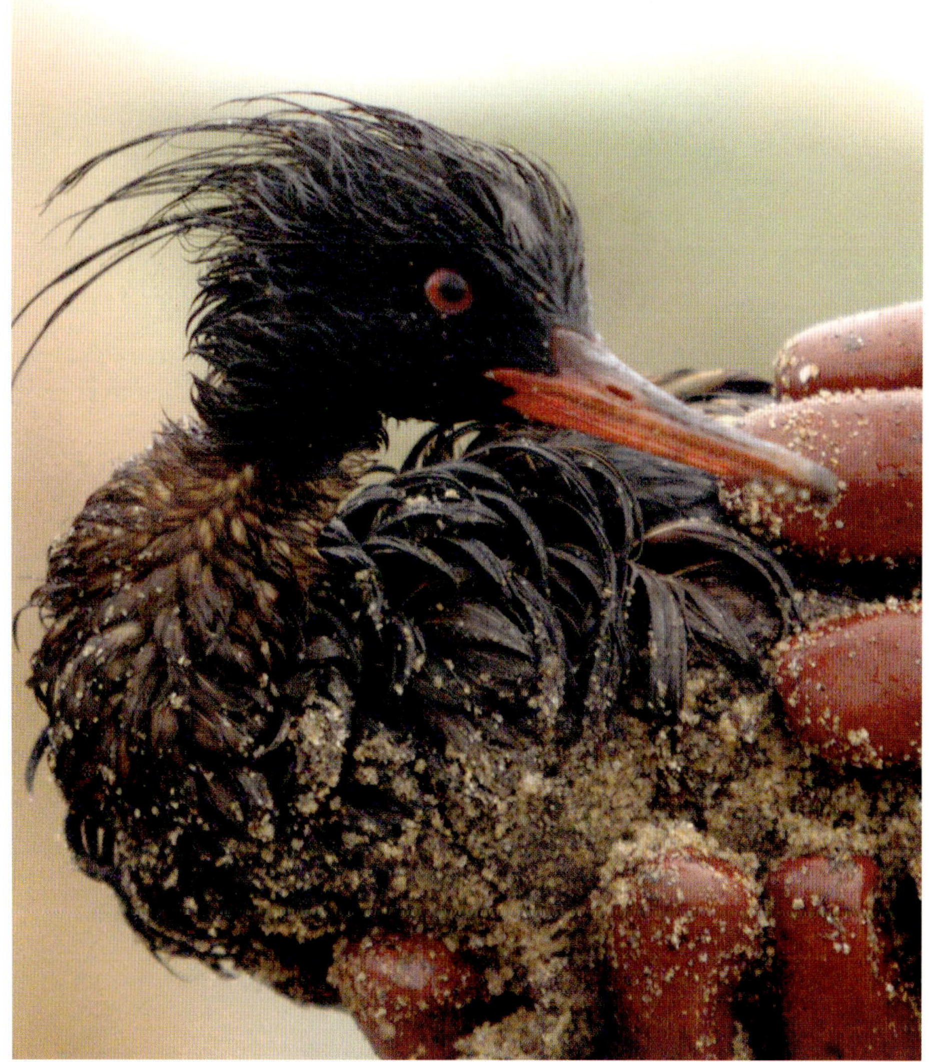

EPA/PA

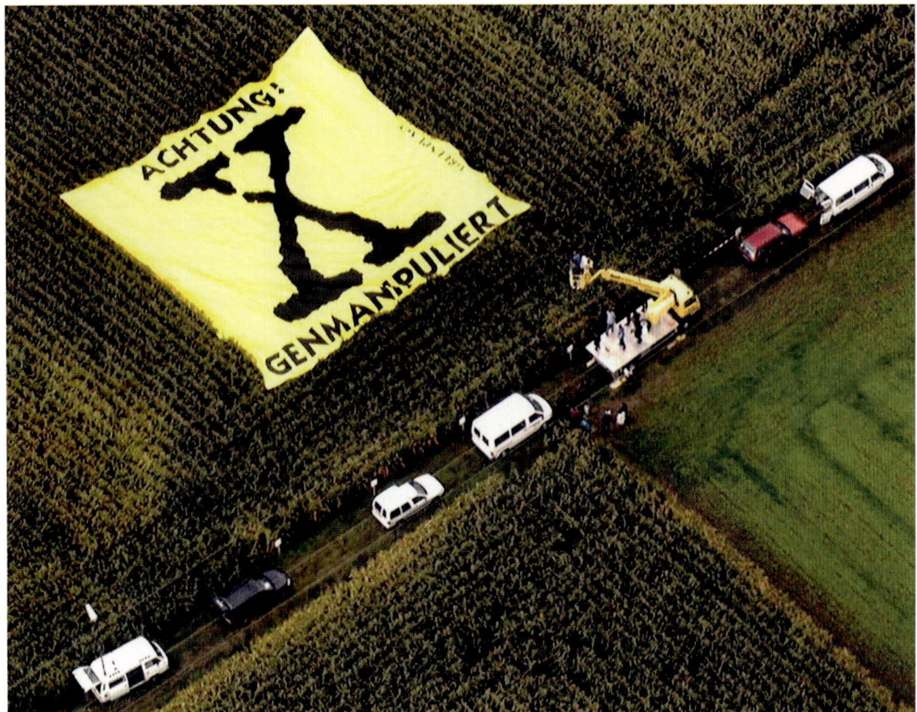

GREENPEACE/ARCHIVE PHOTOS

A new battleground. A field of corn near Freiburg, southern Germany, after Greenpeace activists had attached a warning label. The 400-metre square banner reads: 'Attention – genetically modified – X.'

Un nuevo campo de batalla. Activistas de Greenpeace colocan una pancarta de 400 metros cuadrados en una plantación de maíz cercana a Friburgo (en el sur de Alemania), la cual reza "X - Atención: Modificado genéticamente".

Un nuovo campo di battaglia. Attivisti di Greenpeace coprono un campo di mais nelle vicinanze di Friburgo, nella Germania meridionale, con un messaggio di 400 metri quadrati, su cui c'è scritto: "Attenzione! – Geneticamente modificato – X".

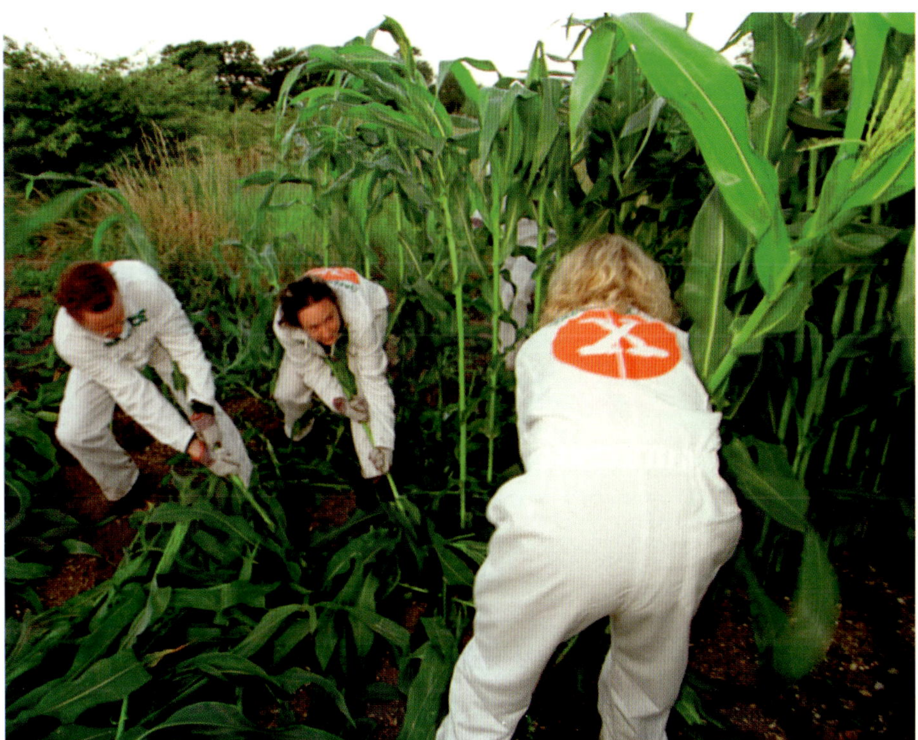

GREENPEACE/ARCHIVE PHOTOS

Greenpeace raiders destroy a GM experimental crop in Lyng, England, 26 July 1999. Thirty of them were arrested, including local farmer and Greenpeace Executive Director Peter Melchett. At their subsequent trial all were acquitted.

Miembros de Greenpeace destrozan una cosecha experimental de transgénicos en Lyng, Inglaterra, 26 de julio de 1999. Treinta de ellos fueron detenidos incluidos un agricultor de la zona y el director general de Greenpeace, Peter Melchett– pero lograron ser absueltos en el juicio celebrado posteriormente.

Attivisti di Greenpeace distruggono una coltura sperimentale geneticamente modificata a Lyng, Inghilterra, 26 luglio 1999. Furono arrestate trenta persone, fra cui un agricoltore del posto e il direttore esecutivo di Greenpeace. Durante il processo furono tutti assolti.

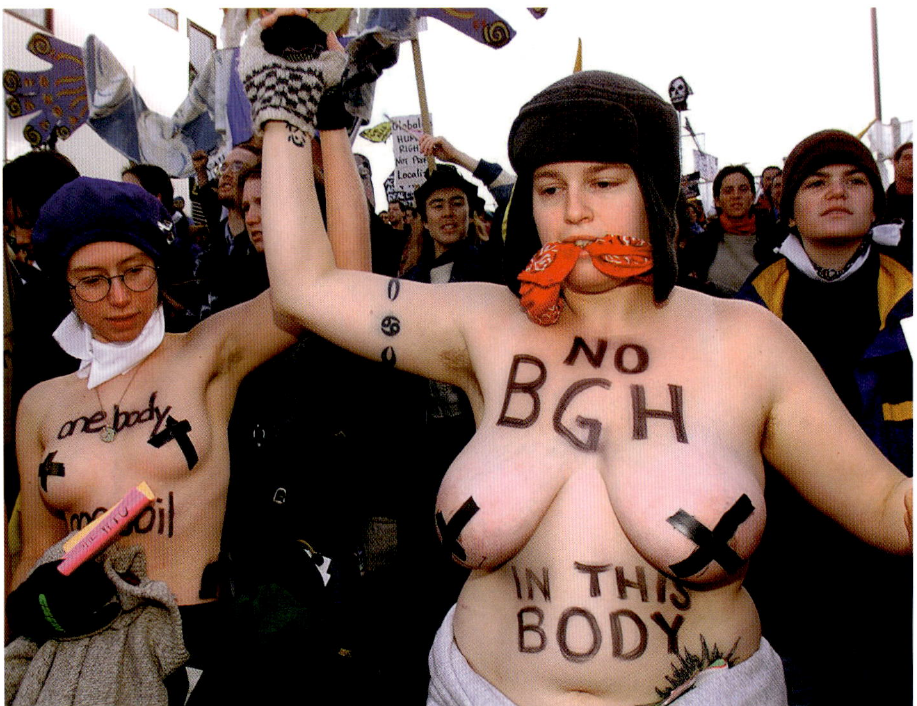

EPA/PA

Demonstrators bring the streets of Seattle to a standstill as they protest at the World Trade Organisation Summit, 2 December 1999. This section of the protest was directed against Bovine Growth Hormones (BGH).

Los manifestantes toman las calles de Seattle durante la cumbre de la Organización Mundial del Comercio, el 2 de diciembre de 1999. Estas participantes, en concreto, protestan contra las hormonas de crecimiento bovino.

Alcuni manifestanti bloccano le strade di Seattle per protestare contro il vertice dell'Organizzazione Mondiale del Commercio, 2 dicembre 1999. Questa parte della protesta si opponeva agli ormoni per la crescita dei bovini.

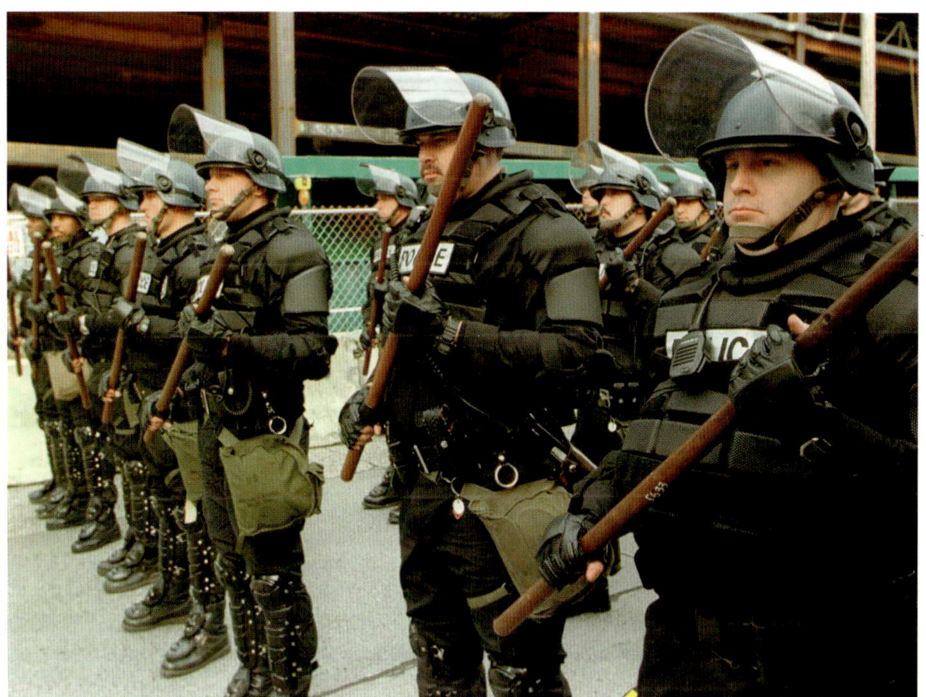

ANTHONY BOLANTE/REUTERS/ARCHIVE PHOTOS

Robocops – in reality members of the Seattle Police Department – prepare to defend the World Trade Organisation headquarters, 29 November 1999. They underestimated the number of officers needed, and the following day a curfew was imposed.

Estos “Robocops” –en verdad agentes del cuerpo de policía de Seattle– listos para defender el cuartel general de la OMC, 29 de noviembre de 1999. Los graves disturbios demostraron que se había infravalorado el número de efectivos necesarios y culminaron con la imposición de un toque de queda al día siguiente.

Robocop – in realtà membri del Dipartimento di Polizia di Seattle – si preparano per difendere il quartier generale dell’Organizzazione Mondiale del Commercio, 29 novembre 1999. Il Dipartimento di Polizia sottovalutò il numero di manifestanti, e il giorno dopo fu necessario imporre un coprifuoco.

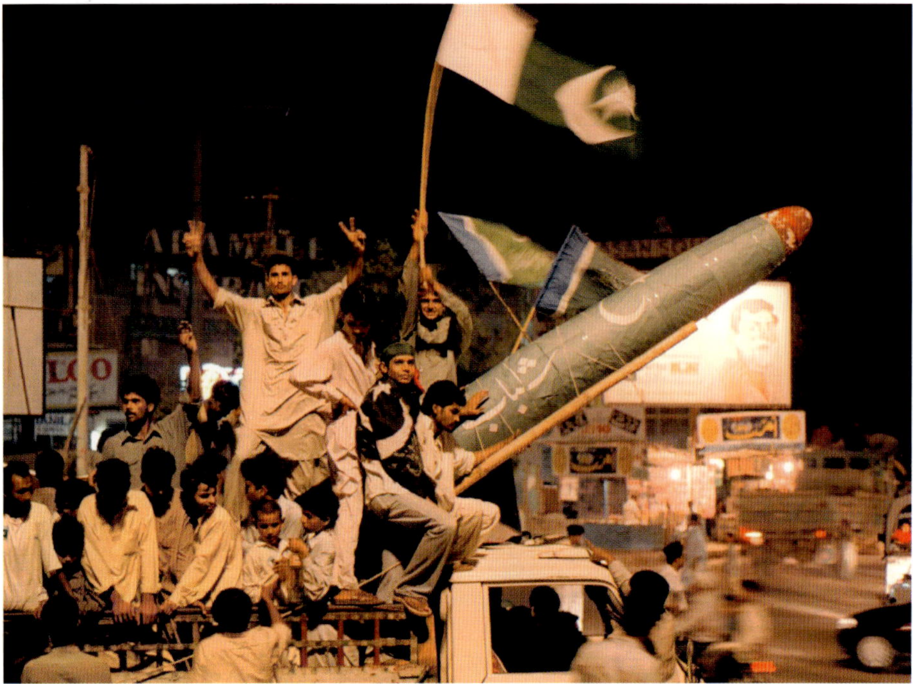

ZAHID HUSSEIN/REUTERS/ARCHIVE PHOTOS

(Opposite and above) Two perspectives on the Bomb. (Above) Pakistani youths with a model of a Ghauri missile in a night rally, Karachi, 31 May 1998. Some saw the possession of nuclear capability as a benefit to their country.

(Arriba y página siguiente) Dos puntos de vista sobre las armas nucleares. (Arriba) Jóvenes pakistaníes con la maqueta de un misil Ghauri durante una manifestación nocturna en Karachi, 31 de mayo de 1998. Algunos consideraban que poseer armamento nuclear era beneficioso para el país.

(Pagina a fianco e in alto) Due punti di vista sulle bombe. (In alto) Giovani pachistani con un modello di missile Ghauri durante una manifestazione notturna, Karachi, 31 maggio 1998. Per alcuni poter disporre di mezzi nucleari era un beneficio per il loro paese.

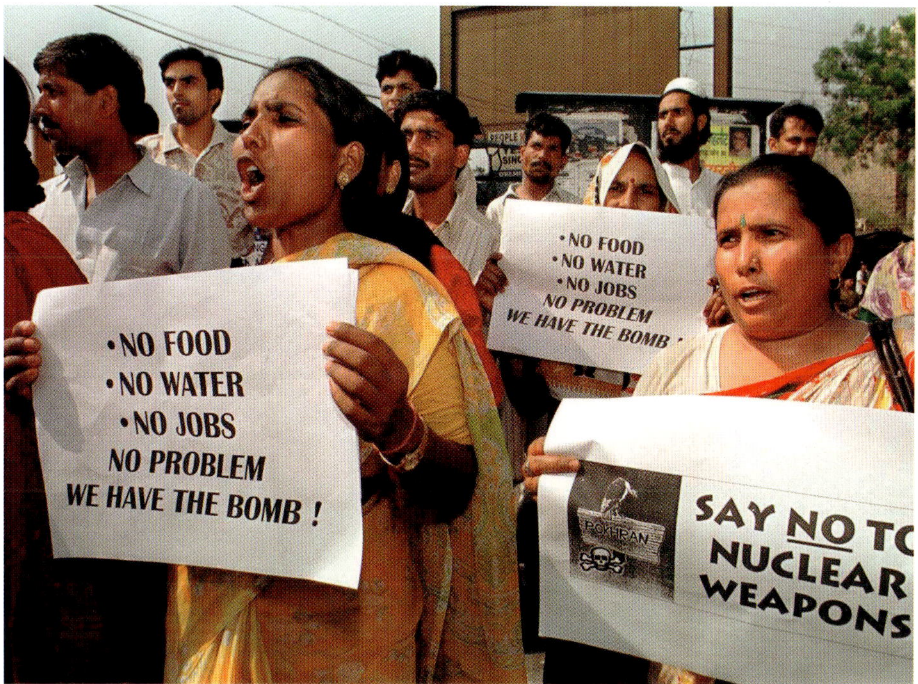

KAMAL KISHORE/REUTERS/ARCHIVE PHOTOS

Anti-bomb protesters gather in New Delhi, India, 16 May 1998 (above). The march was held following a series of underground nuclear tests by the Indian Government in the northern state of Rajasthan.

Manifestantes antinucleares se congregan en Nueva Delhi, India, 16 de mayo de 1998. La protesta tuvo lugar tras unas pruebas nucleares subterráneas llevadas a cabo por el Gobierno indio en la región del Rajastán, al norte del país.

Manifestanti antinucleari si riuniscono a Nuova Delhi, India, 16 maggio 1998 (in alto). La manifestazione fu organizzata in seguito a prove nucleari sotterranee realizzate dal governo indiano nello stato del Rajasthan, al nord del paese.

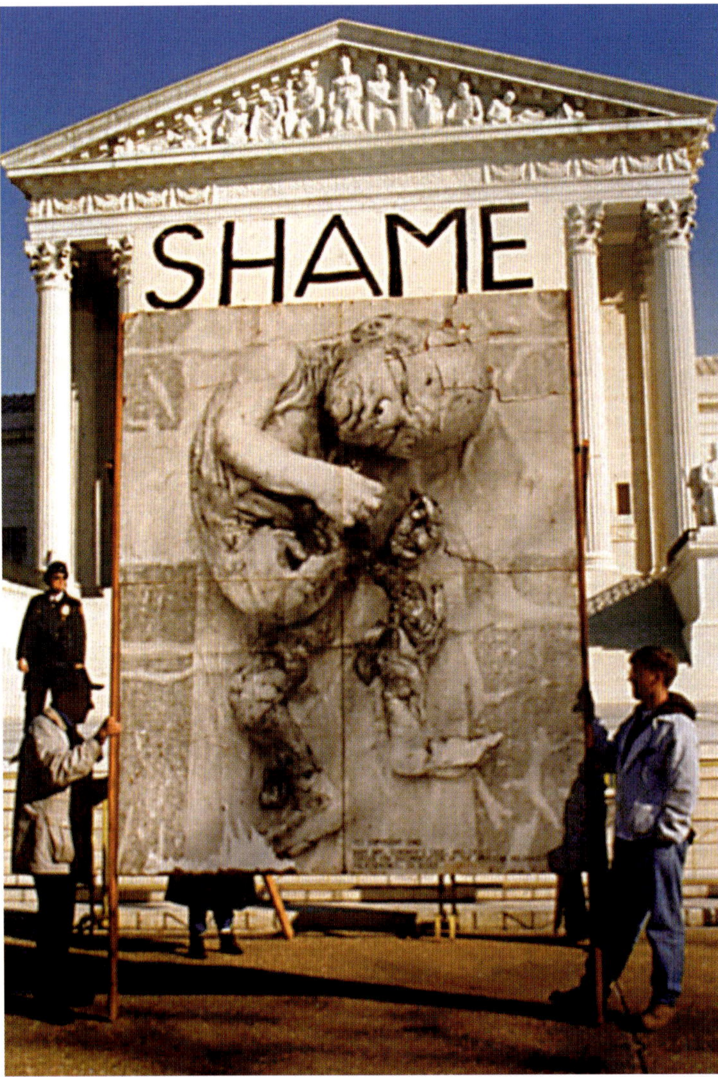

WIN McNAMEE/REUTERS/ARCHIVE PHOTOS

An anti-abortion poster is paraded outside the US Supreme Court, Washington, DC, 1996. It was the 23rd anniversary of legal abortions.

Coincidiendo con el 23º aniversario de la legalización del aborto, en 1996, sus detractores despliegan un cartel de protesta ante la Corte Suprema de Estados Unidos, en Washington DC.

Un cartello contro l'aborto, esposto di fronte alla Corte Suprema degli Stati Uniti a Washington, DC, 1996. Erano passati già 23 anni dalla legalizzazione dell'aborto.

Parodying a multinational corporation: a workman completes a giant billboard advertising the link between smoking and impotence, Hollywood, 23 April 1999.

Parodia de una multinacional. En Hollywood, un obrero trabaja en un panel publicitario gigante que advierte de la relación directa entre el tabaquismo y la impotencia, 23 de abril de 1999.

Parodia di una multinazionale: un lavoratore completa un cartellone gigante per evidenziare il legame fra il fumo e l'impotenza, Hollywood, 23 aprile 1999.

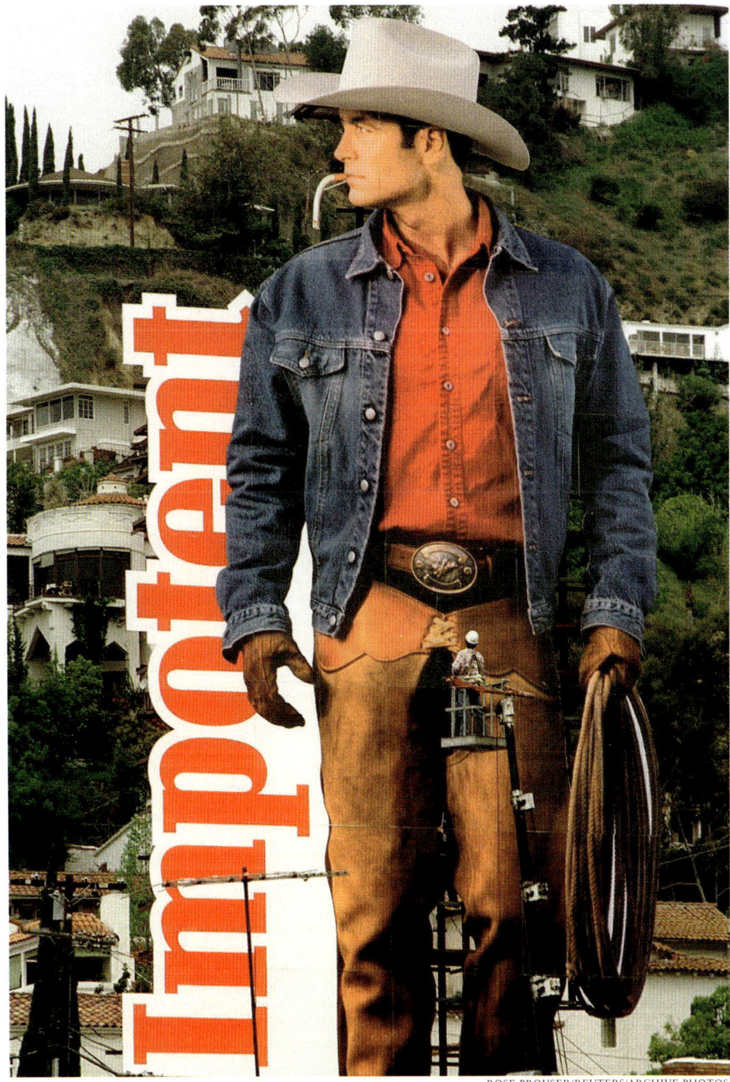

ROSE PROUSER/REUTERS/ARCHIVE PHOTOS

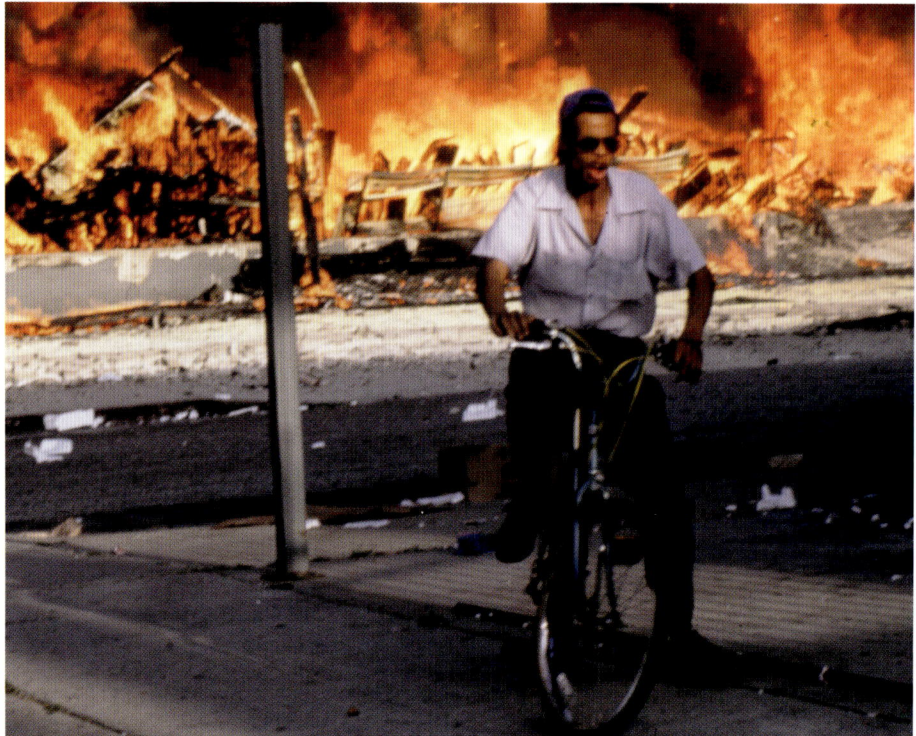

DAVID BUTOW/BLACK STAR/COLORIFIC!

Riots in Los Angeles, April/May 1992. Fifty-eight people were killed, 2,200 were injured and damage was estimated at over $1 billion. The rioting broke out soon after the acquittal of the four police officers on trial for the beating of Rodney King.

Disturbios en Los Ángeles, abril-mayo de 1992. En ellos perdieron la vida 58 personas y otras 2.200 resultaron heridas; se calcula que los daños ascendieron a más de un millón de dólares. La absolución de los cuatro agentes acusados de golpear a Rodney King desencadenó los altercados.

Sommosse a Los Angeles, aprile/maggio 1992. Furono uccise 58 persone e ne vennero ferite 2.200, mentre i danni causati ammontarono a più di un miliardo di dollari americani. La sommossa fu provocata dall'assoluzione dei quattro poliziotti accusati di aver pestato Rodney King.

Rodney King shows some of the scars that resulted from the beating of 3 March 1991. The incident was recorded by a passer-by on his video camera.

Rodney King muestra algunas de las heridas provocadas por la paliza que recibió el 3 de marzo de 1991. El incidente fue grabado por un videoaficionado que pasaba por el lugar de los hechos.

Rodney King mostra alcune delle cicatrici provocate dalle percosse ricevute il 3 maggio 1991. L'incidente venne filmato da un passante.

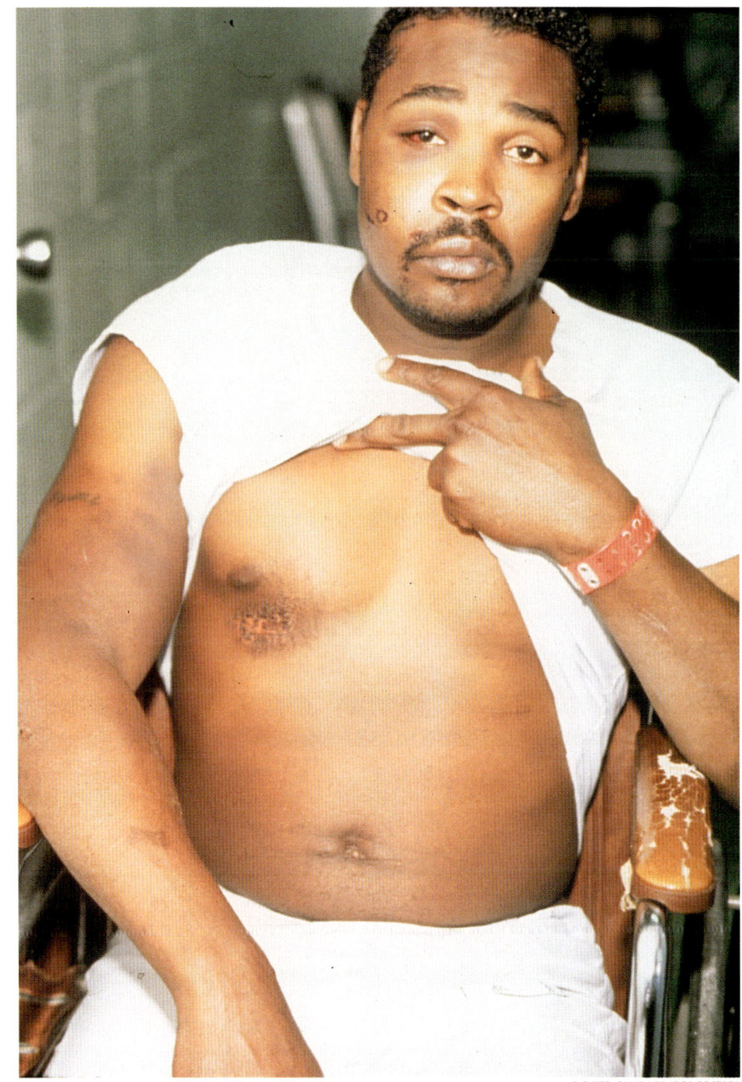

ROGER SANDLER/COLORIFIC!

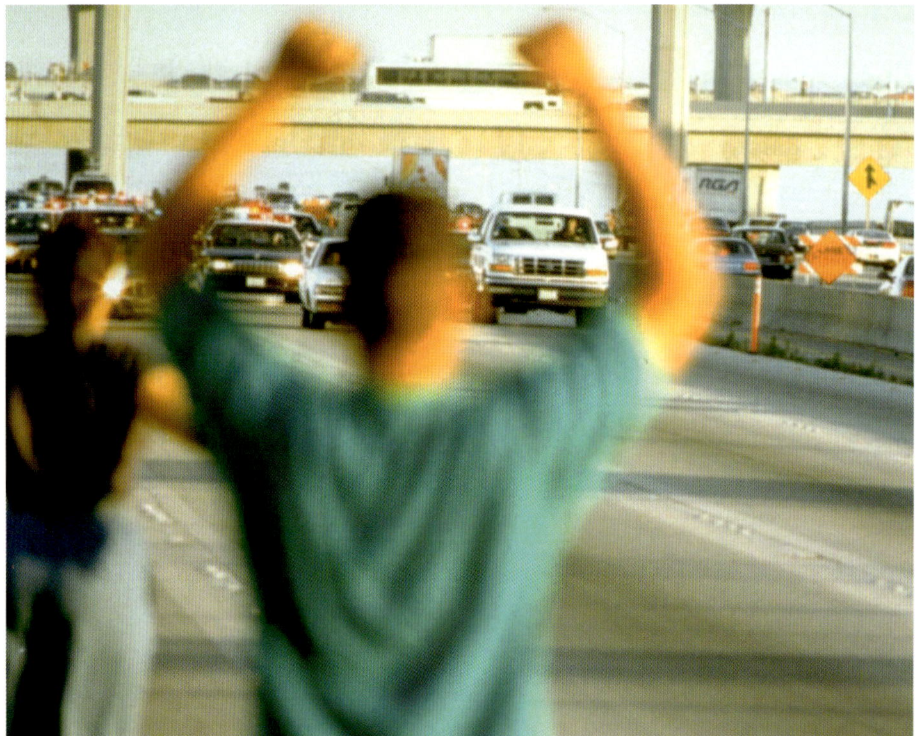

SAM MIRCOVICH/REUTERS/ARCHIVE PHOTOS

On the freeway. The jeep carrying O J Simpson is pursued by a posse of police cars along the Los Angeles Thru'way, California, 17 June 1994. The chase was just one bizarre episode in many that followed a double murder.

Por la vía rápida. El todoterreno que transporta a O. J. Simpson es perseguido por un pelotón de coches de policía a lo largo de la autopista de Los Ángeles, 17 de junio de 1994. Esta extraña persecución es solo uno de los muchos episodios acaecidos tras el doble asesinato del que era sospechoso.

Sull'autostrada. La jeep che guida O. J. Simpson viene seguita da un corteo di auto della polizia lungo la Los Angeles Thru' Way, 17 giugno 1994. L'inseguimento fu uno dei vari strani episodi che fecero seguito a un doppio assassinio.

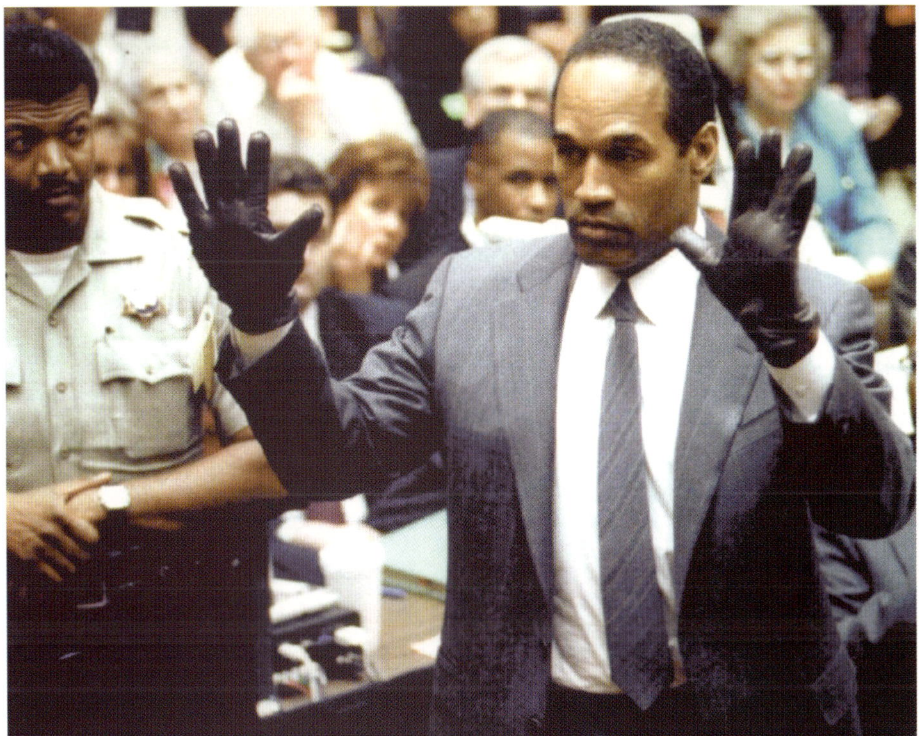

VINCE BUCCI/REUTERS/ARCHIVE PHOTOS

On the stand. O J Simpson raises his hands to the jury at his trial, 21 June 1995. The prosecution were seeking to show that Simpson's hands could fit into gloves found at the scene of the murder.

Por la vía judicial. O. J. Simpson enseña las manos al jurado durante la vista de su juicio, celebrada el 21 de junio de 1995. La acusación pretendía demostrar que los guantes hallados en la escena del crimen correspondían al tamaño de las manos de Simpson.

In tribunale. O. J. Simpson alza le mani verso la giuria durante il processo, 21 giugno 1995. L'accusa voleva dimostrare che le mani di Simpson potevano entrare nei guanti trovati sulla scena del crimine.

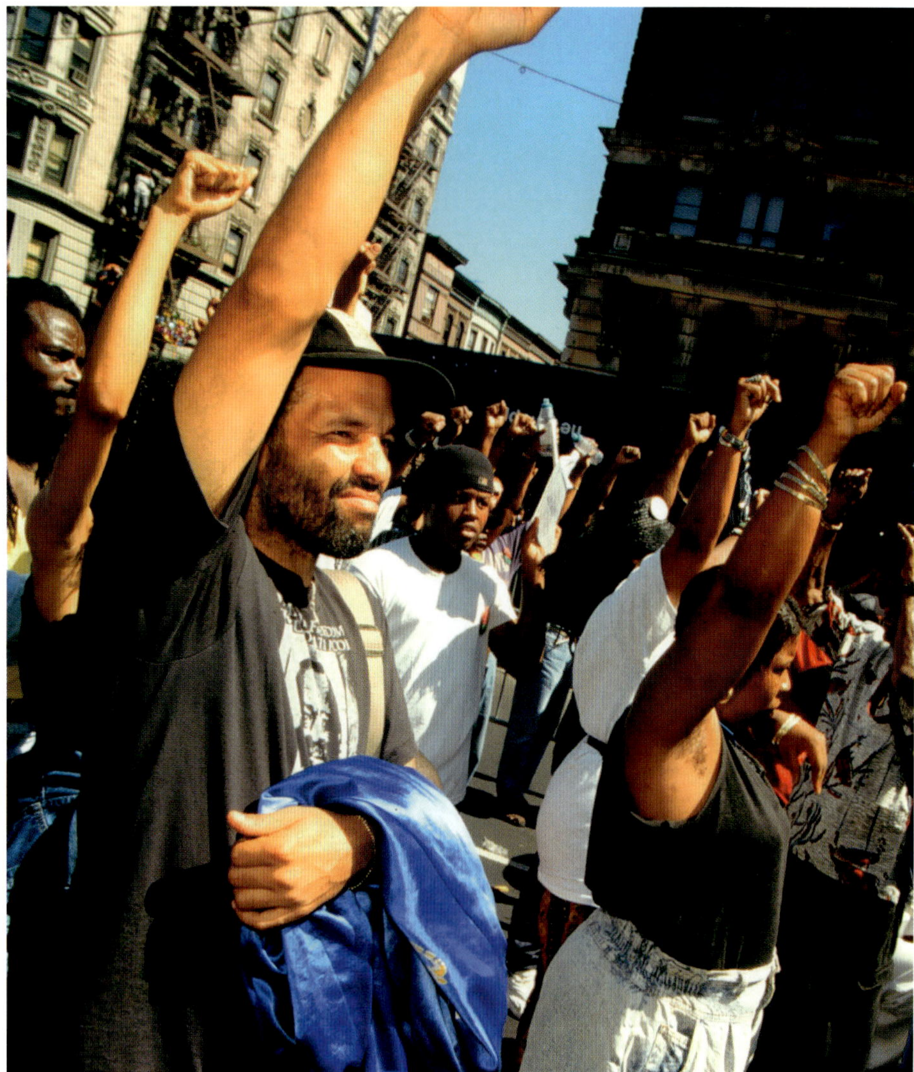

RICHARD B LEVINE/LIAISON AGENCY

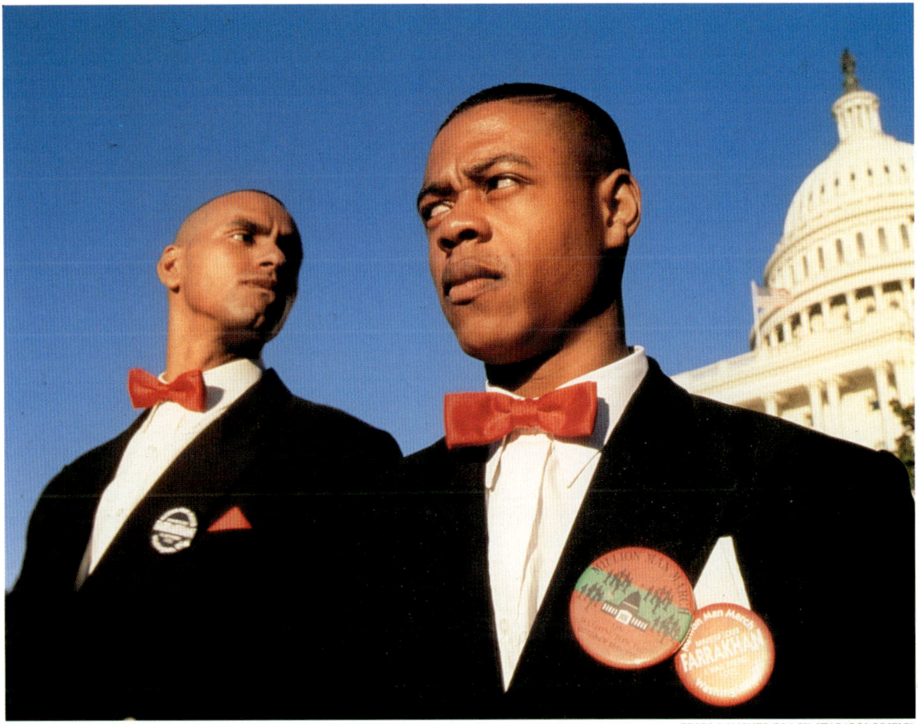

ERICA LANSNER/BLACK STAR/COLORIFIC!

Participants in the Million Youth March, Harlem, New York, 5 September 1998 (opposite), and stewards at the Million Man March in Washington, DC (above), 16 October 1995. Both marches were intended to bring attention to continued racial discrimination in the US.

(Página anterior) Participantes de la Marcha de un Millón de Jóvenes de Harlem, Nueva York, el 5 de septiembre de 1998. (Arriba) Organizadores de la Marcha de un Millón de Hombres de Washington DC, el 16 de octubre de 1995. Ambas marchas tenían como objetivo llamar la atención sobre la persistente discriminación racial en Estados Unidos.

Partecipanti alla Million Youth March, Harlem, New York, 5 settembre 1998 (pagina a fianco) e organizzatori della Million Man March a Washington, DC (in alto), 16 ottobre 1995. Tutti e due gli eventi nacquero con l'idea di far conoscere le continue discriminazioni razziali esistenti negli Stati Uniti.

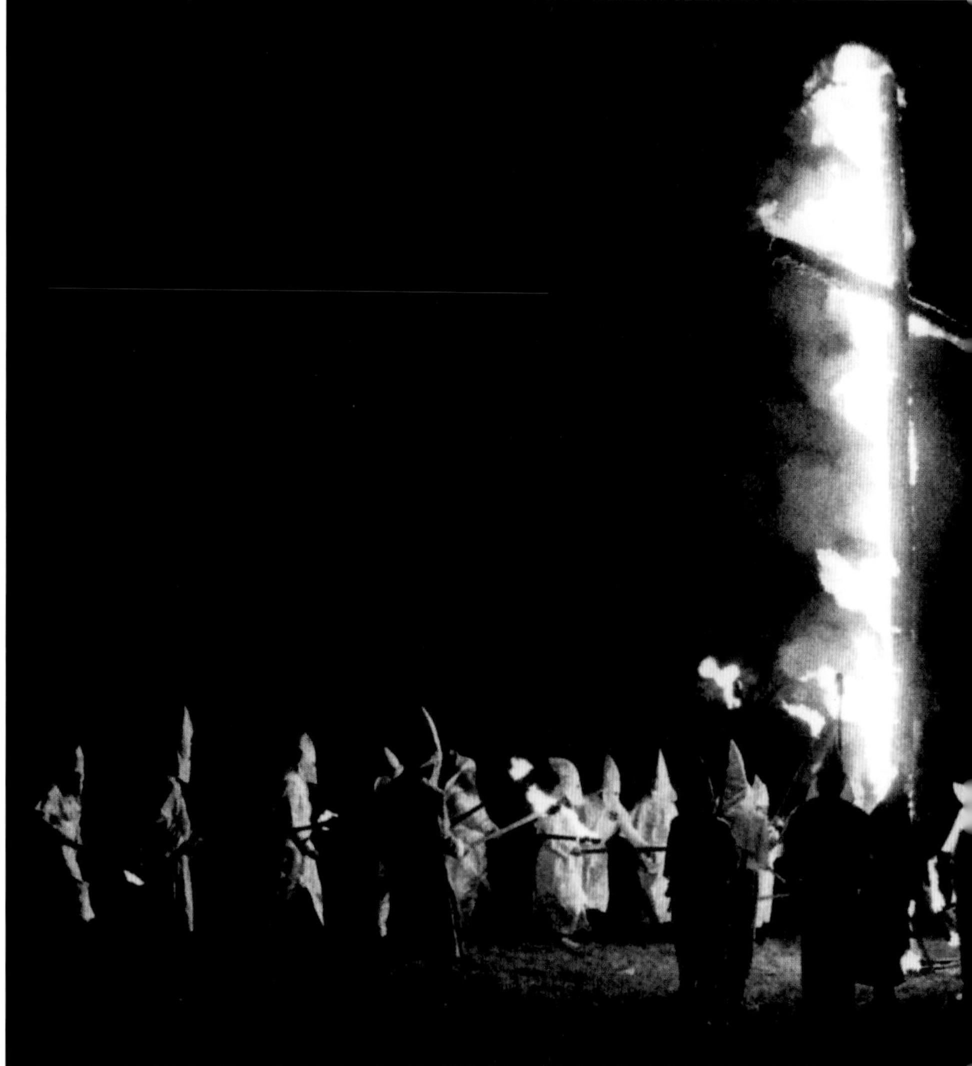

LAURA L CAMDEN/LIAISON AGENCY

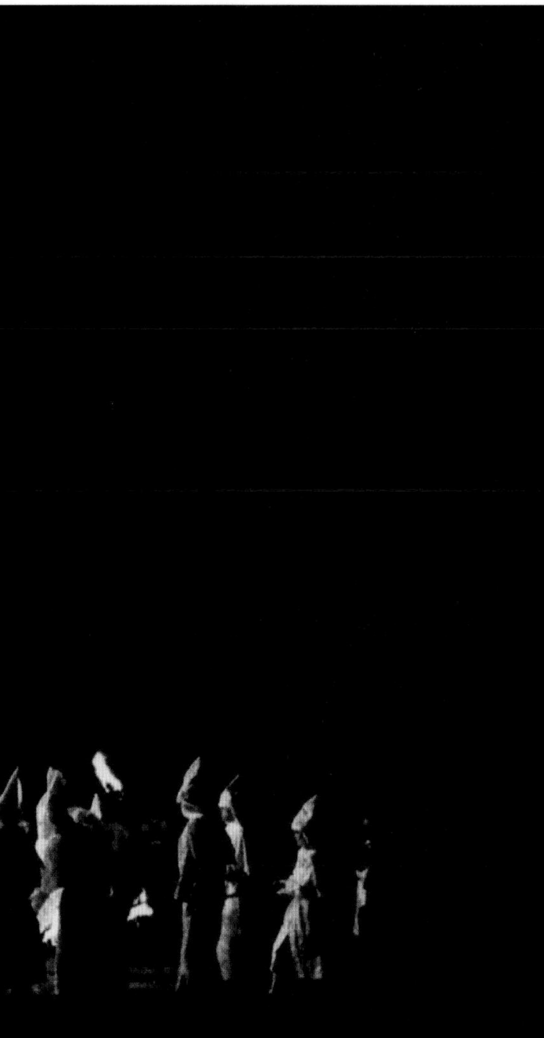

Right-wing bigots warm their memories under the Ku Klux Klan's fiery cross, Hico, near Austin, Texas, May 1994. Their numbers were dwindling.

Fanáticos de ultraderecha avivan sus recuerdos bajo la cruz de fuego del Ku Klux Klan en Hico, cerca de Austin, Texas, en mayo de 1994. No obstante, la organización contaba cada vez con menos integrantes.

Estremisti di destra ravvivano la loro memoria attorno alla croce infuocata del Ku Klux Klan a Hico, nelle vicinanze di Austin, Texas, maggio 1994. Già in quel momento il loro numero era in diminuzione.

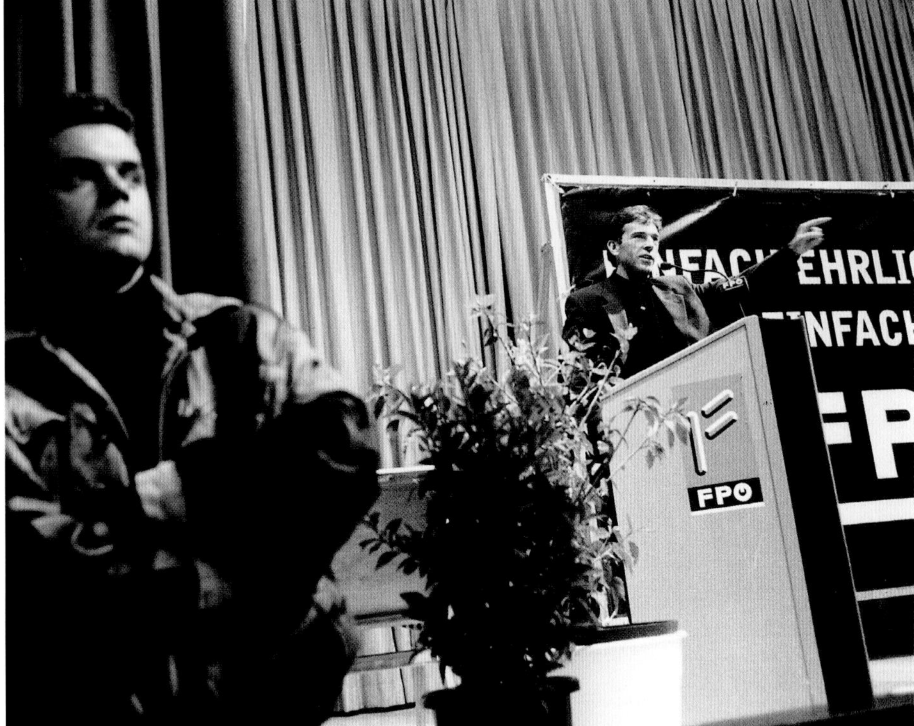

CHRISTIAN IRRGANG/FOCUS/COLORIFIC!

The right-wing politician Jörg Haider campaigns during the 1995 Austrian elections. Haider later resigned as leader of the far-right Freedom Party, but held the post of Governor of Carpinthia province in southern Austria.

El político ultraderechista Jörg Haider durante la campaña electoral austríaca de 1995. Más adelante Haider dimitiría como líder del Partido Liberal (FPÖ) –una formación de extrema derecha– pero conservaría su puesto de gobernador de la provincia de Carintia, al sur de Austria.

Il leader politico di destra Jörg Haider durante la campagna elettorale austriaca tenuta nel 1995. In seguito Haider rinunciò alla presidenza del partito di estrema destra FPO, ma mantenne il posto come governatore della Carinzia, al sud del paese.

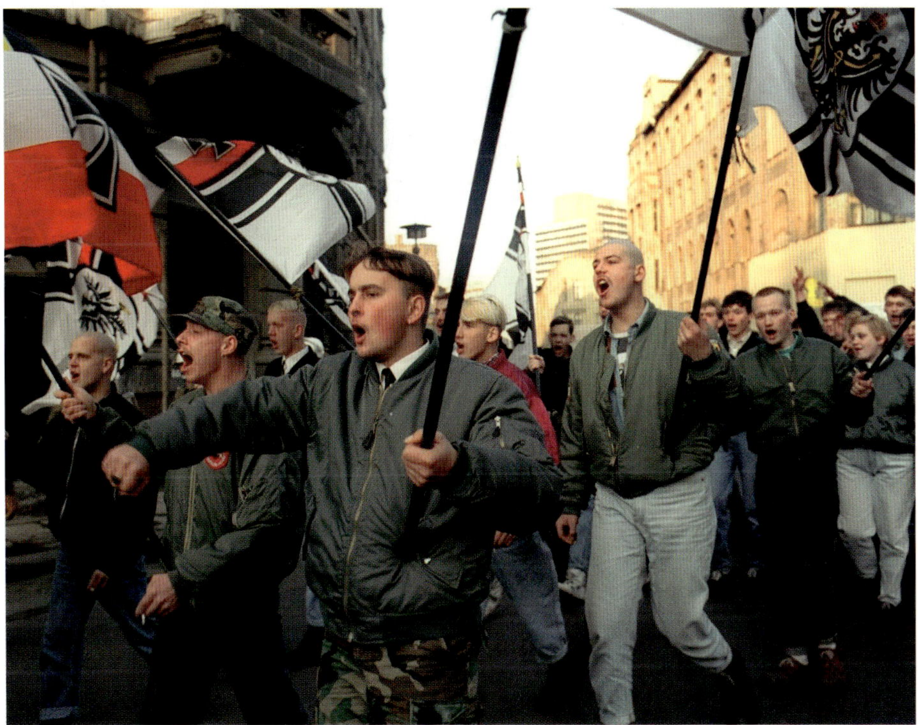

SIEGBERT HEILAND/EPA/PA

Neo-Nazis of the German People's Union parade through the streets of Halle in former East Germany, November 1995. In the Saxony-Anhalt state elections that followed they won 12.9 per cent of the vote.

En noviembre de 1995, neonazis de la Unión Popular Alemana (DVU) desfilan por las calles de Halle, en la antigua Alemania del Este. En el *land* de Sajonia-Anhalt lograron un 12,9 por ciento de los votos en las siguientes elecciones.

Neonazi appartenenti alla Deutsche Volksunion manifestano lungo le strade di Halle, nella ex Germania Est, novembre 1995. Nelle seguenti elezioni tenute nel land della Sassonia-Anhalt ottennero il 12,9% dei voti.

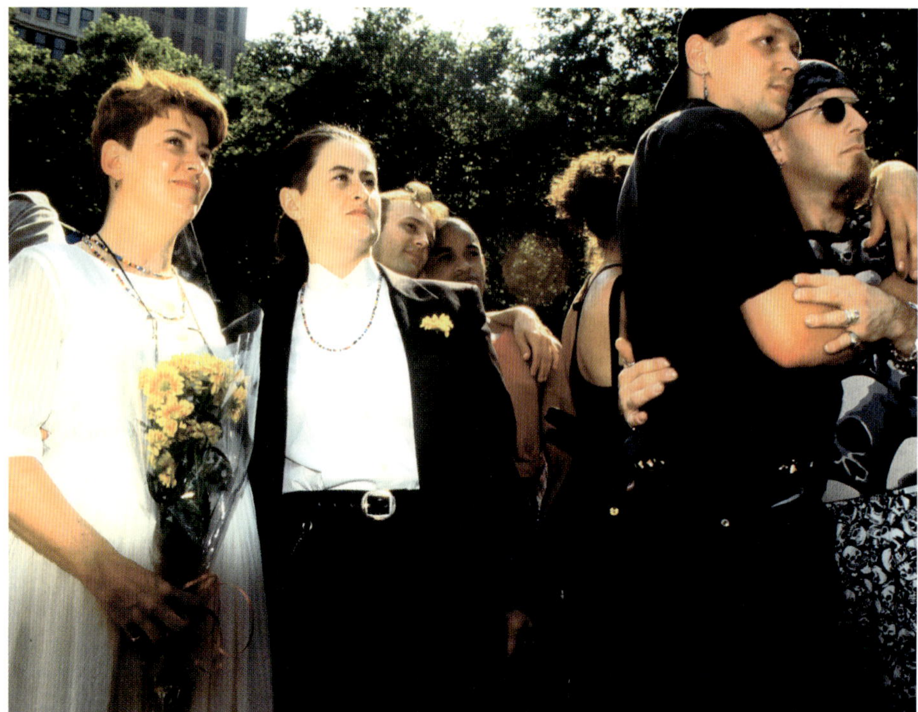

FRANCES M ROBERTS/LIAISON AGENCY

Like minds, like bodies. In the absence of legally recognised marriages, gay and lesbian couples hold 'commitment' ceremonies in Bryant Park, 16 June 1996. For an alternative American view, see opposite.

Mentes afines, cuerpos semejantes. A falta del matrimonio legalmente reconocido, parejas de gays y lesbianas celebran una ceremonia de "compromiso" en el Bryant Park, 16 de junio de 1996. Para obtener una visión norteamericana alternativa sobre el tema, véase la página siguiente.

Stesse idee, stesso sesso. In mancanza di matrimoni legalmente riconosciuti, le coppie gay e lesbiche organizzarono cerimonie di "fidanzamento" a Bryant Park, 16 agosto 1996. La pagina accanto offre un'opinione americana contrastante.

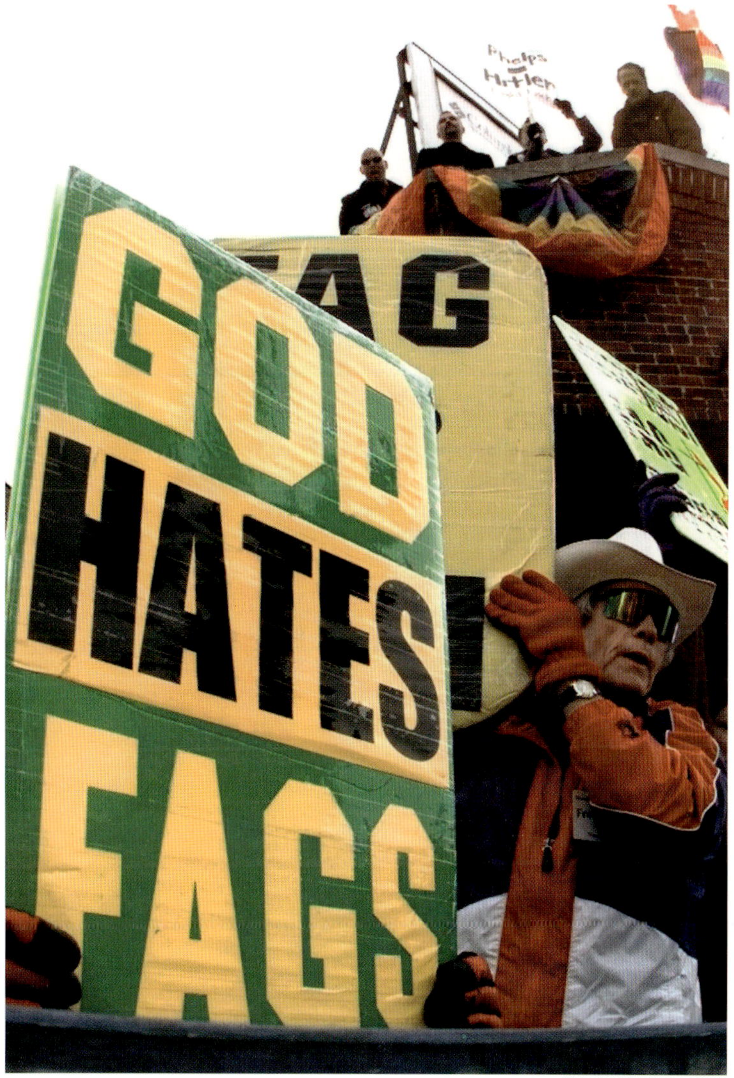

Split opinion. The Reverend Fred Phelps of the Westboro Baptist Church, Topeka, Kansas, flaunts his 'God hates fags' sign, 22 November 1998.

Opinión dividida. El reverendo Fred Phelps de la iglesia baptista de Westboro en Topeka, Kansas, enarbola una pancarta en la que se lee "Dios odia a los maricas", 22 de noviembre de 1998.

Divergenze di opinioni. Il reverendo Fred Phelps della chiesa battista di Westboro a Topeka, in Kansas, sventola lo slogan "Dio odia le checche", 22 novembre 1998.

TIM BOYLE/LIAISON AGENCY

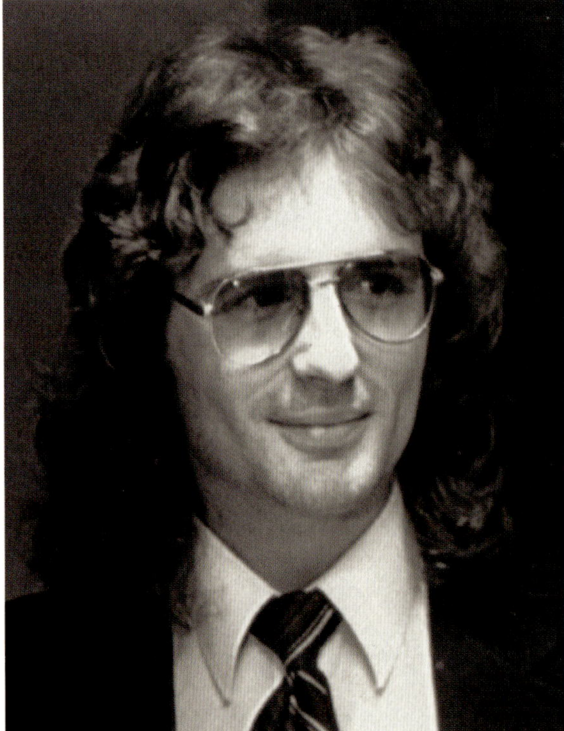

REUTERS/ARCHIVE PHOTOS

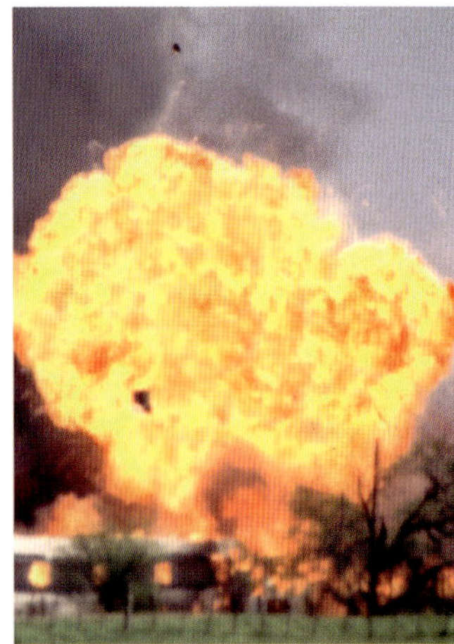

SHELLY KATZ/LIAISON AGENCY

Prophets and losses 1. (Above) David Koresh, leader of the Branch Davidian cult. In April 1993 he and his followers died during an FBI raid on the cult's headquarters at Waco, Texas (above right).

Profetas y pérdidas 1. (Arriba) David Koresh –líder del culto davidiano– y sus adeptos mueren en abril de 1993 durante un asalto de los agentes federales a la sede de la secta en Waco, Texas (arriba, derecha).

Profeti e perduti 1. (In alto) David Koresh, leader della setta dei Davidiani. Nell'aprile del 1993 morì, assieme ai suoi seguaci, durante un raid dell'FBI nel quartier generale della setta a Waco, Texas (in alto a destra).

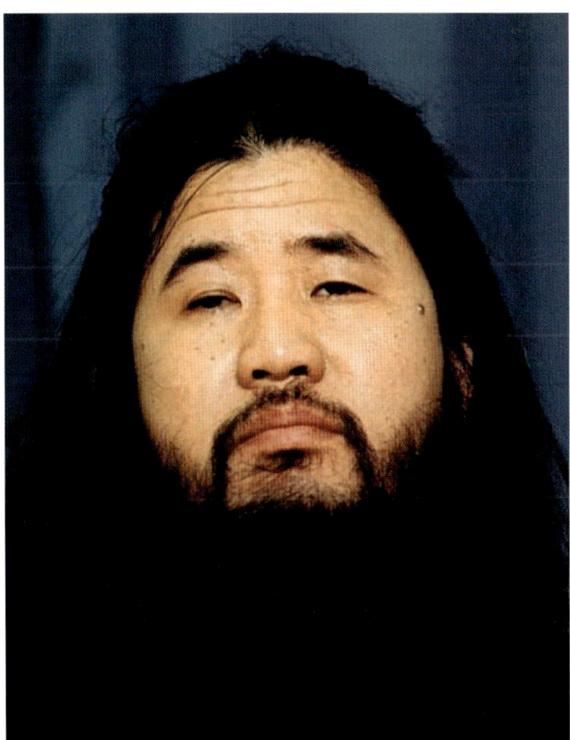

EPA/PA

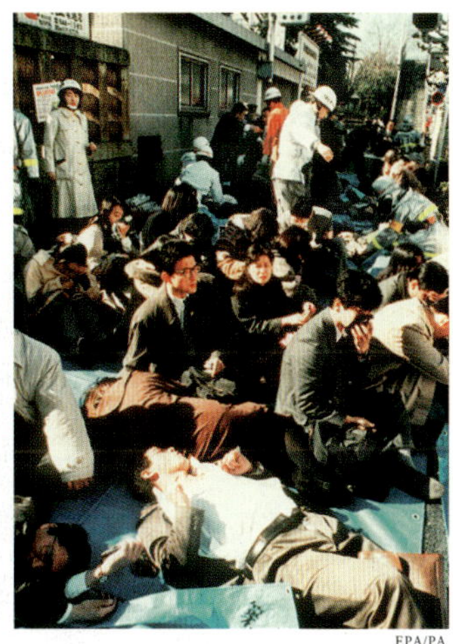

EPA/PA

Prophets and losses 2. (Above) Shoko Asahara, guru of Aum Supreme Truth, October 1990. In March 1995 Asahara released nerve gas in the Tokyo subway, asphyxiating thousands of people (above right).

Profetas y pérdidas 2. (Arriba) Shoko Asahara, gurú de la secta Verdad Suprema. En marzo de 1995 Asahara ordenó el atentado con gas sarín en el metro de Tokio, que asfixiaría a miles de personas (arriba, derecha).

Profeti e perduti 2. (In alto) Shoko Asahara, guru della setta Aum della Suprema Verità, ottobre 1990. Nel marzo del 1995 introdusse gas nervino nella metropolitana di Tokyo, asfissiando migliaia di persone (in alto a destra).

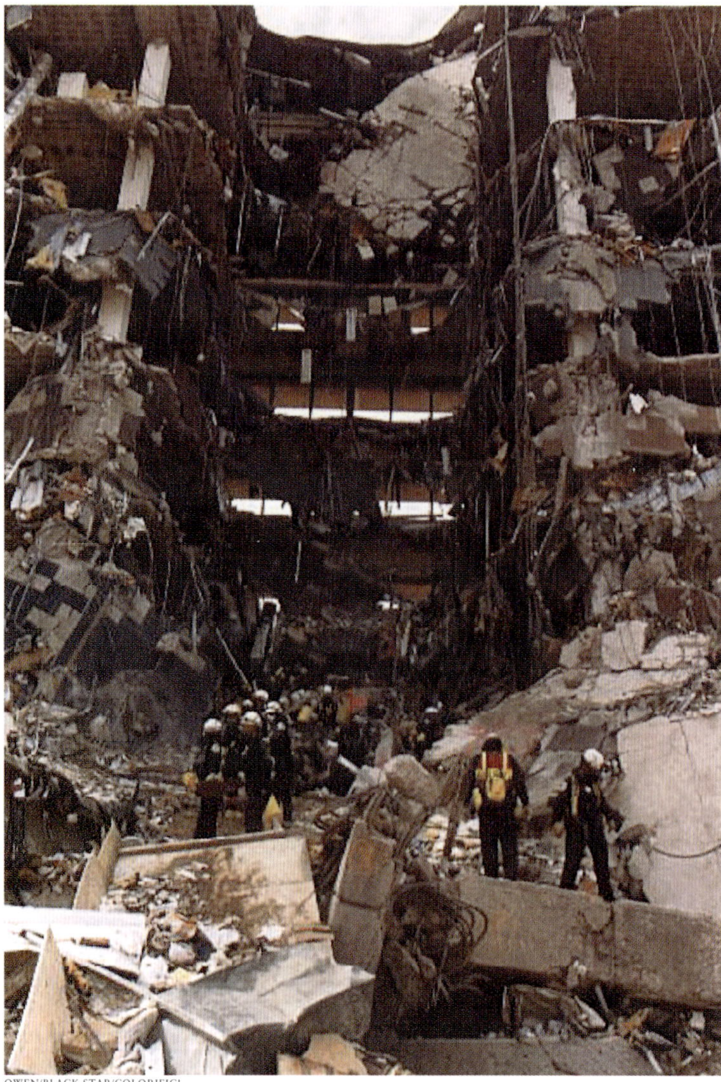

OWEN/BLACK STAR/COLORIFIC!

On 19 April 1995 a truck carrying 2,000 kilos of explosives destroyed the Federal Bureau of Alcohol, Tobacco and Firearms, Oklahoma City.

El 19 de abril de 1995, un camión que transporta 2.000 kg de explosivos destruye la Oficina Federal de Alcohol, Tabaco y Armas de Fuego, en Oklahoma City.

Il 15 aprile 1995 un camion che trasportava due tonnellate di esplosivi distrusse il Federal Bureau of Alcohol, Tobacco and Firearms di Oklahoma City.

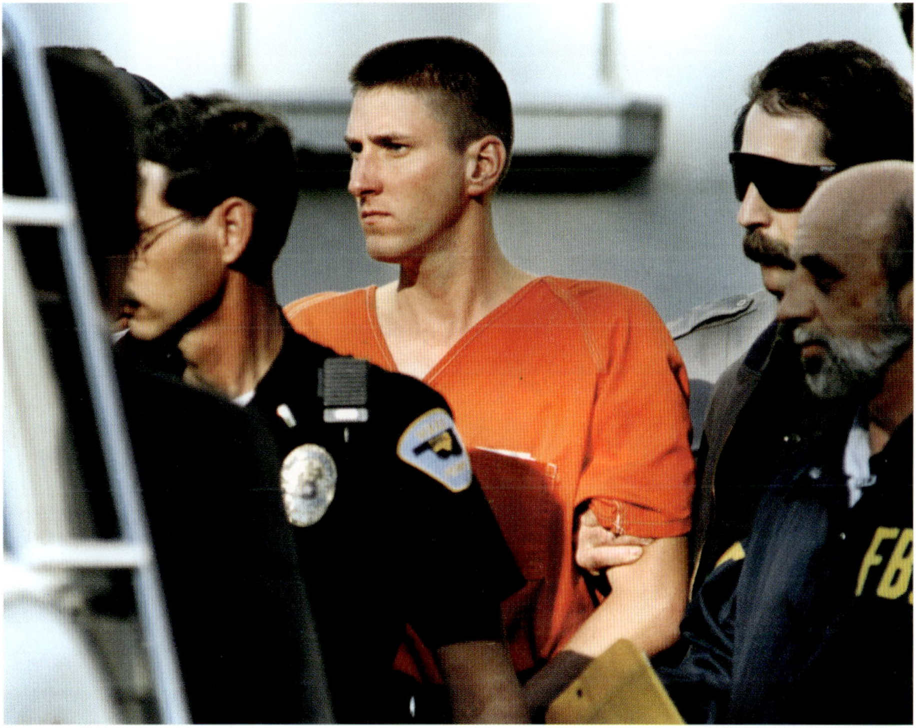

JIM BOURG/REUTERS/ARCHIVE PHOTOS

Police later arrested Timothy McVeigh for the offence. (Above) Two days after the bombing McVeigh (centre) leaves the Noble County Courthouse, accompanied by FBI agents.

La policía detiene a Timothy McVeigh por el atentado. (Arriba) Dos días después de la explosión de la bomba, McVeigh (centro) abandonaba el Palacio de Justicia de Noble County escoltado por agentes del FBI.

In seguito la polizia arrestò Timothy McVeigh per tale reato. (In alto) Due giorni dopo aver commesso l'attentato, Timothy McVeigh (al centro) abbandonava il palazzo di giustizia di Noble County, accompagnato da agenti dell'FBI.

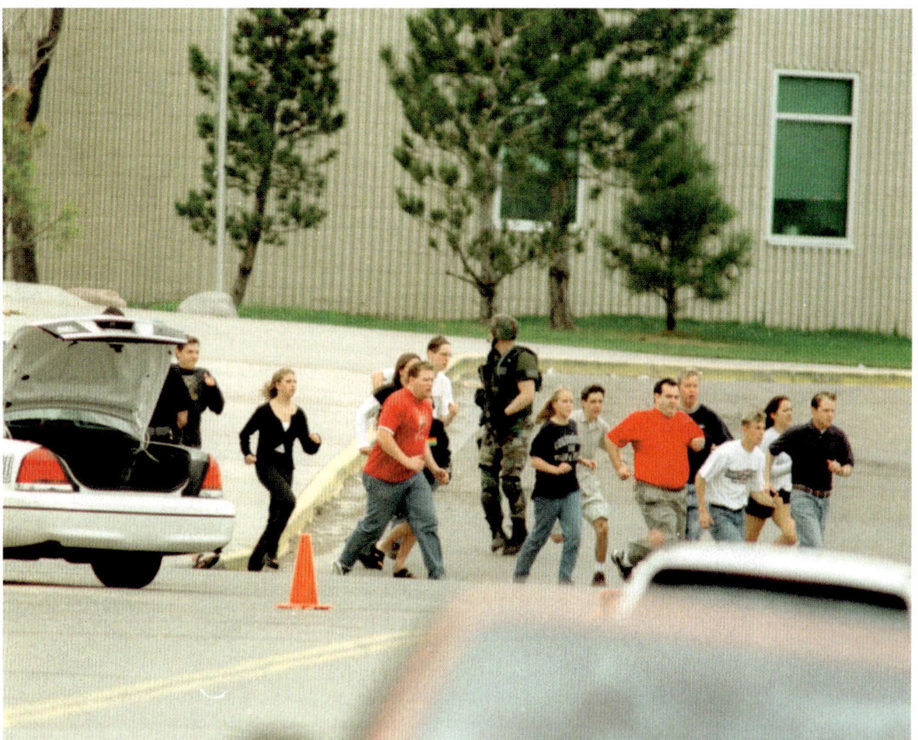

MARK LEFFINGEWELL/LIAISON AGENCY

Students at Columbine High School, Littleton, Colorado, rush for cover as shots are heard from inside their school building, 20 April 1999. Two former students, Eric Harris and Dylan Klebold, were responsible.

El 20 de abril de 1999, alumnos del instituto Columbine de Littleton, Colorado, se ponen a cubierto al oír los disparos que proceden del interior del edificio. Los autores de la matanza fueron Eric Harris y Dylan Klebold, dos ex alumnos del centro.

Studenti della Columbine High School di Littleton, in Colorado, corrono ai ripari non appena sentono gli spari provenienti dalla scuola, 20 aprile 1999. I responsabili erano due ex studenti, Eric Harris e Dylan Klebold.

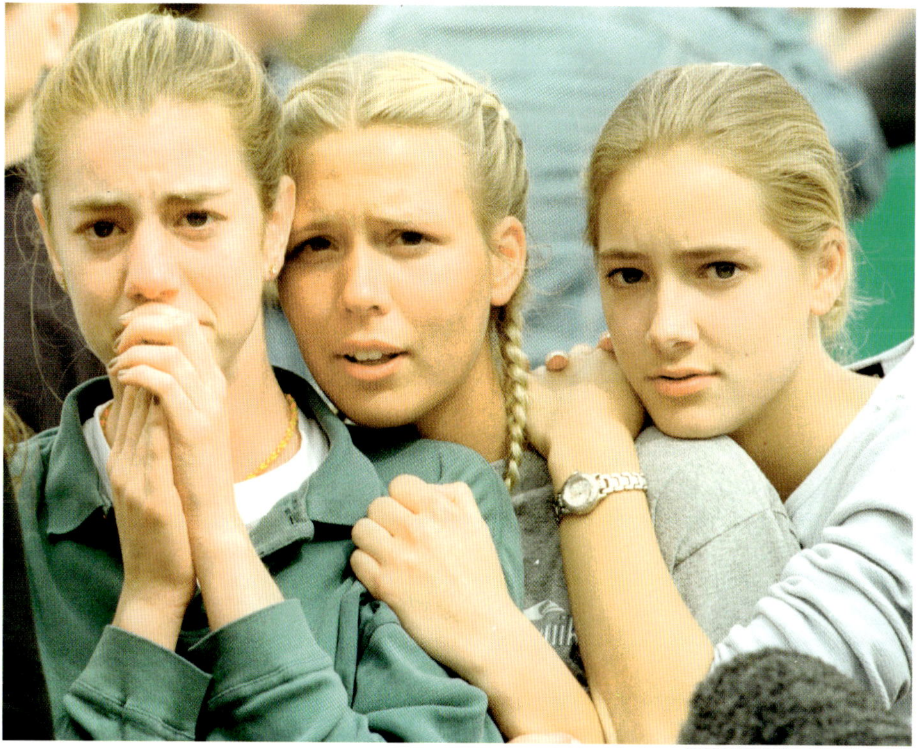

MARK LEFFINGEWELL/LIAISON AGENCY

Other students watch from safety during the evacuation of the school. If the police were baffled as to what motive the youths could have had, the world was baffled by the suggestion that other students had advance knowledge of the intended massacre.

Otras alumnas contemplan desde un lugar seguro cómo es evacuada la escuela. Mientras la policía se muestra desconcertada ante el posible móvil del crimen, el mundo se muestra consternado ante la posibilidad de que otros alumnos conociesen de antemano la intención de los jóvenes de cometer una masacre.

Altri studenti osservano, al sicuro, l'evacuazione della scuola. La polizia restava perplessa di fronte ai possibili moventi dei due giovani, mentre il mondo intero restava perplesso davanti alla notizia che i loro compagni erano già da tempo a conoscenza della strage prevista.

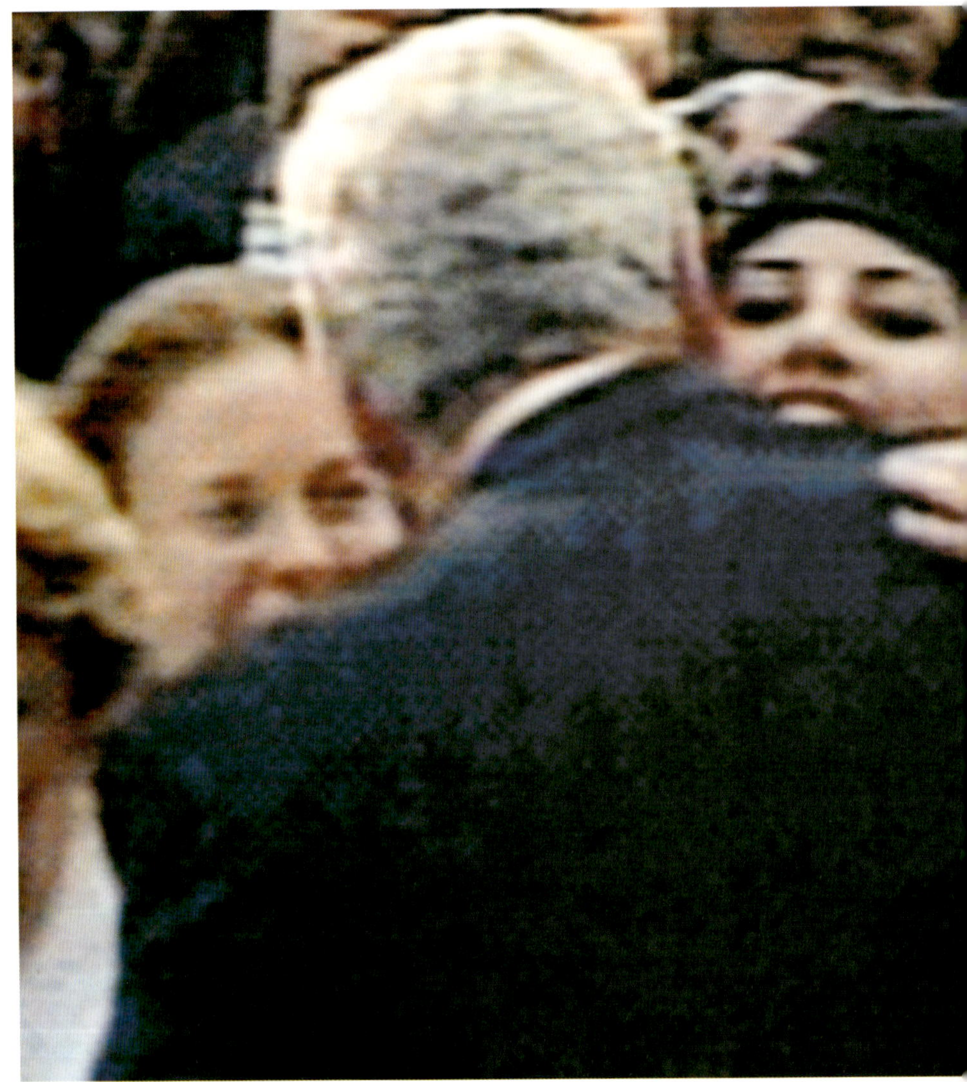

NBCTV/ARCHIVE PHOTOS

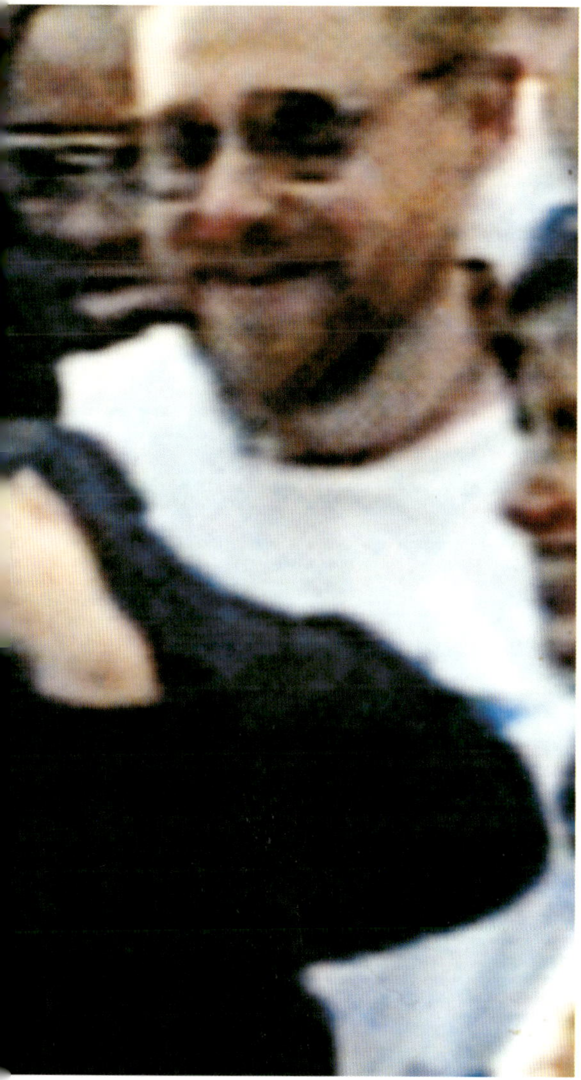

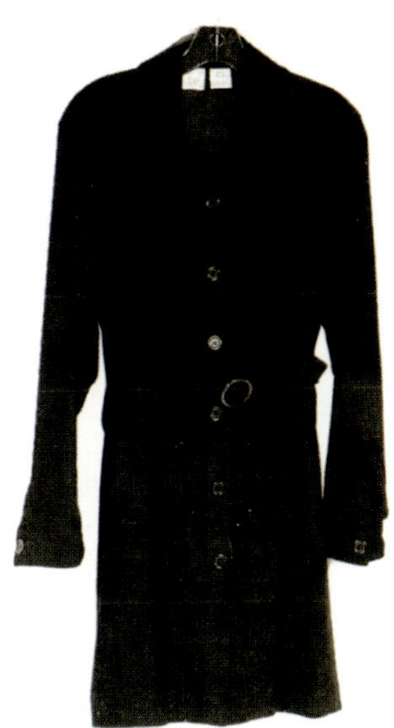

ARCHIVE PHOTOS

(Left) Lipstick on your collar… Monica Lewinsky embraces Bill Clinton outside the White House, 11 June 1996. (Above) …and stains on your dress. Lewinsky's blue dress, presented as evidence by Kenneth Starr.

(Izquierda) Carmín en el cuello… Monica Lewinsky abraza a Bill Clinton frente a la Casa Blanca, 11 de junio de 1996. (Arriba) … y manchas en el vestido. Kenneth Starr presenta como prueba el traje azul de Lewinsky.

(A sinistra) Tracce di rossetto sul tuo colletto… Monica Lewinsky abbraccia Bill Clinton davanti alla Casa Bianca, 11 giugno 1996. (In alto) …e macchie sul tuo vestito. Il vestito blu della Lewinsky, presentato come prova da Kenneth Starr.

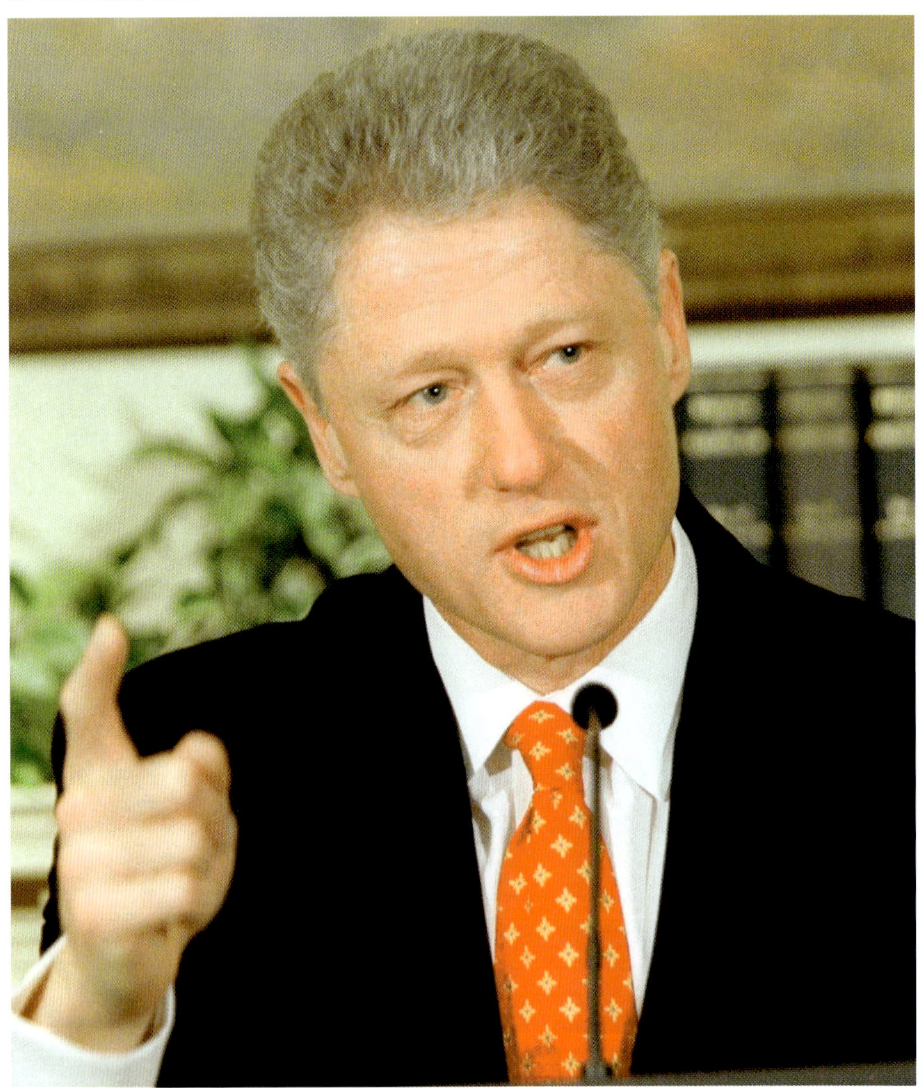

WIN McNAMEE/REUTERS/ARCHIVE PHOTOS

Stating the Presidential position… Bill Clinton (opposite) denies having sexual relationships with 'that woman', Monica Lewinsky (right).

Exponiendo la posición presidencial… Bill Clinton (página anterior) niega haber mantenido relaciones sexuales con "esa mujer" –es decir, con Monica Lewinsky– (derecha).

Chiarire la posizione del presidente… Bill Clinton (pagina a fianco) nega di aver avuto rapporti sessuali con "quella donna", Monica Lewinsky (a destra).

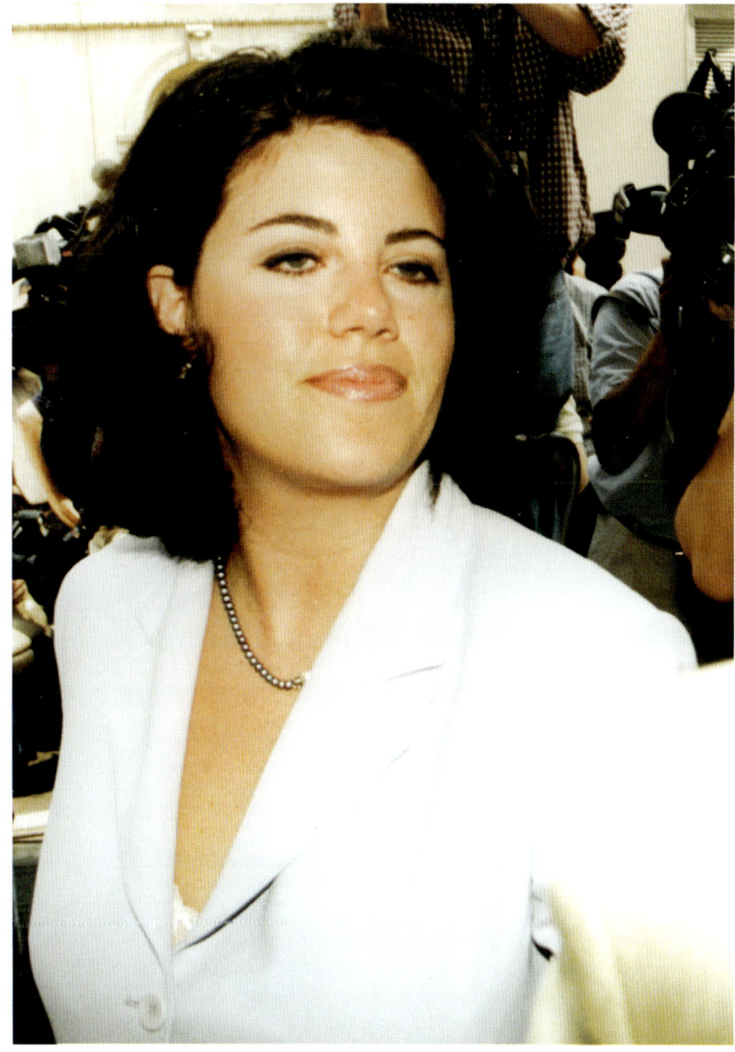

TIM AUBRY/REUTERS/ARCHIVE PHOTOS

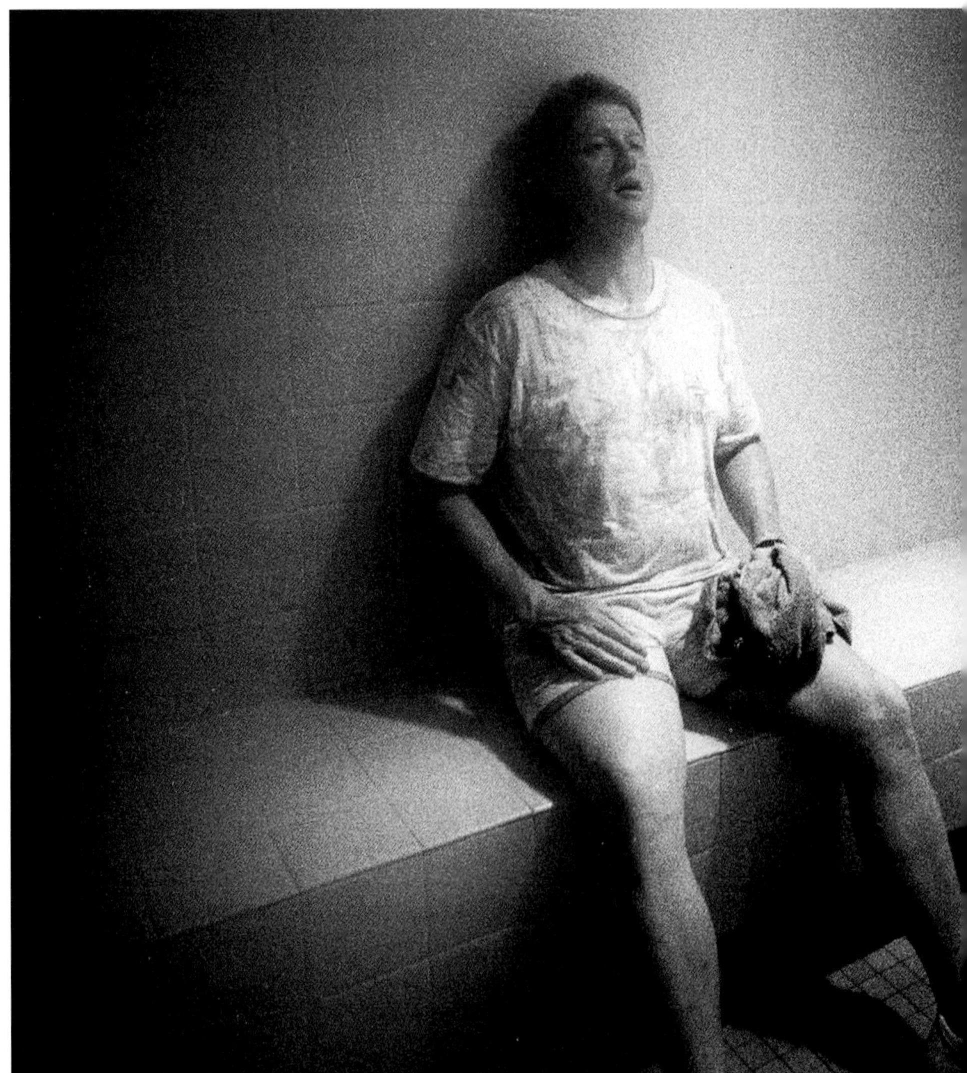

P F BENTLEY/BLACK STAR/COLORIFIC!

Bill Clinton sweats it out in the sauna of a New York City hotel during his campaign seeking nomination as the Democratic candidate, 1992.

Bill Clinton suda la camiseta en la sauna de un hotel de Nueva York durante su campaña para ser designado candidato demócrata a la presidencia en 1992.

Bill Clinton suda nella sauna di un hotel di New York durante la campagna elettorale per divenire il candidato democratico, 1992.

5. Entertainment
Espectáculos
Spettacolo

Jerry Seinfeld, stand-up comedian and star of the hugely successful TV sitcom *Seinfeld*. He claimed the show was 'about nothing', but over five series it was brilliantly crafted and superbly performed.

Jerry Seinfeld, cómico y estrella de la popular serie de televisión *Seinfeld*, emitida por la cadena estadounidense NBC. Pese a declarar que el *show* trata "sobre nada en concreto", logró mantenerse más de cinco temporadas en antena, gracias a una brillante realización y a una interpretación magnífica.

Jenny Seinfeld, attore comico e star della sitcom televisiva di grande successo *Seinfeld*. Sebbene sostenesse che "non parlava di nulla", lo show è durato per più di cinque serie brillantemente realizzate e magnificamente rappresentate.

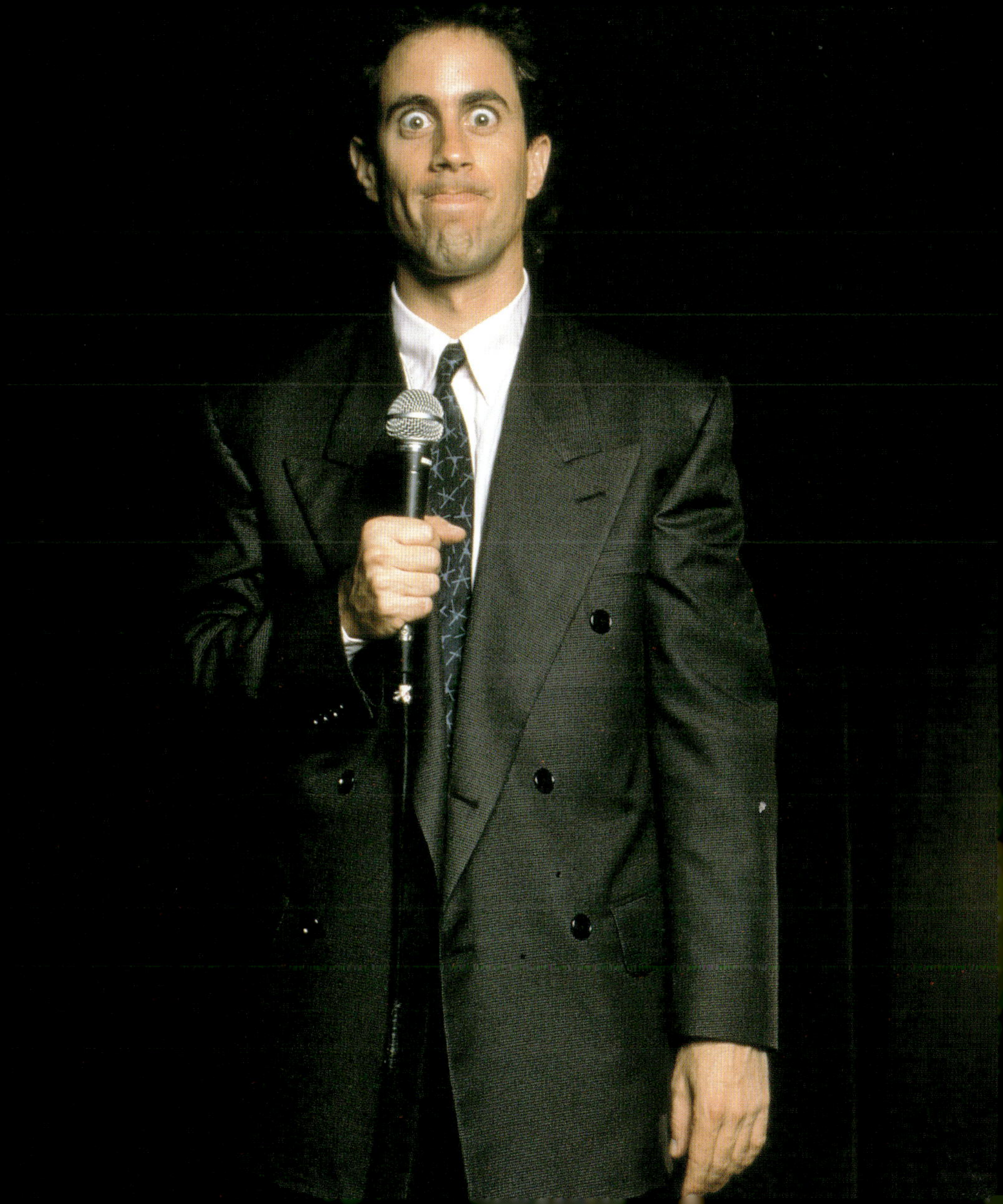

5. Entertainment Espectáculos Spettacolo

The cinema industry reached the end of the century on an upbeat note. Audiences were steadily growing, more films were being made, and Hollywood was regaining much of its glamour as well as its powers to shock. Magazines delightedly exposed the scandals that attached to the famous.

Seldom had the world-wide movie industry produced such a variety of films. Budgets soared for spectacular blockbusters, but there was a healthy market for the more modest, independently produced film. If computer animation lacked the subtlety and beauty of the best of old Walt Disney, its humour and vitality brought box office success.

At home, more people had more TVs, digital, cable or otherwise, and a plethora of channels from which to select. Such choice often meant that talent was spread a little more thinly, but every country had its popular home-grown soaps, and there were always repeats to fall back on. Now and then comedy was king, with a clutch of brilliant sitcoms from the United States, notably *Frasier*, *Seinfeld*, *Roseanne* and *The Larry Sanders Show*, and a healthy market for stand-up comedians.

There was still no business like show business.

La industria del cine alcanza el fin de siglo con motivos para el optimismo: los índices de audiencia vienen aumentando de forma constante, se realizan más películas y Hollywood recupera buena parte de su antiguo *glamour* así como su capacidad de impresionar al espectador. Por su parte, las revistas del corazón se deleitan sacando a la luz los escándalos que salpican a los personajes famosos.

Pocas veces la industria mundial del celuloide había producido tal variedad de filmes. Se destinan presupuestos desorbitados a producciones espectaculares, pero existe también un mercado saludable para las más modestas cintas independientes. La animación por ordenador, pese a carecer de la belleza y sutilidad de los viejos dibujos animados de Walt Disney, aporta a la historia un toque de humor y vitalidad que asegura su éxito de taquilla.

La gente cada vez dispone de más televisiones (digitales, por cable, etc.) que ofrecen una plétora de canales entre los que escoger, lo cual a menudo significa que el talento está más disperso que antes. No obstante, cada país cuenta con sus propias series de éxito y siempre se puede recurrir a las reposiciones. La comedia se erige en reina de la tele, con un puñado de excelentes *sitcoms* ('comedias de situación') procedentes de Estados Unidos –tales como *Frasier*, *Seinfeld*, *Roseanne* y *The Larry Sanders Show*– y buenas perspectivas para el monologuista. El negocio del espectáculo sigue siendo el mejor de los negocios.

L'industria del cinema arrivava alla fine del secolo all'insegna dell'ottimismo. Il numero di spettatori era in continuo aumento, venivano realizzati più film di prima, e Hollywood iniziava a recuperare il suo glamour e la capacità di scioccare, mentre le riviste, contentissime, si dedicavano a mettere in luce gli scandali dei personaggi famosi.

Rare volte l'industria cinematografica mondiale era riuscita a realizzare una così grande varietà di film, e intanto anche i budget dei lungometraggi di grande successo aumentavano vertiginosamente, anche se restava un mercato più sano per i film più modesti e indipendenti. Sebbene l'animazione al computer fosse priva di quella finezza e bellezza delle migliori produzioni del primo Walt Disney, il suo umorismo e la sua vitalità si rivelarono un asso vincente al botteghino.

Nelle case iniziava a dilagare la moda della TV digitale, via cavo o altro ancora, con un'infinità di canali da scegliere. Tanta varietà spesso andava a scapito del talento e della qualità, anche se poi ogni paese offriva le proprie soap opera, e di tanto in tanto poteva capitare di imbattersi in qualche replica. La commedia continuava a fare la parte del leone, con un buon pugno di brillanti sitcom provenienti dagli Stati Uniti, come ad esempio *Frasier*, *Seinfeld*, *Roseanne* e *The Larry Sanders Show*, offrendo così un buon mercato per i migliori comici.

Continuava a non esserci alcun altro business come lo show business.

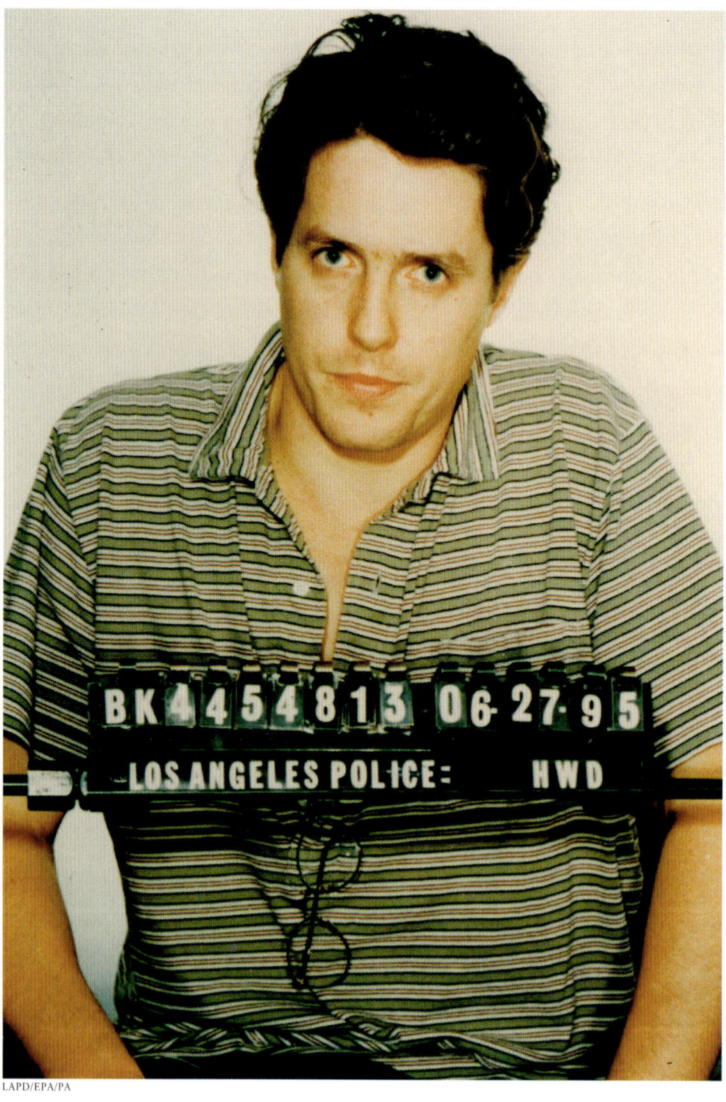

LAPD/EPA/PA

Two bookings and a scandal. Hugh Grant poses for the Los Angeles Police Department, 27 June 1995.

Dos fichas policiales y un escándalo. Hugh Grant posa para el Departamento de Policía de Los Ángeles, 27 de junio de 1995.

Due casi per la polizia e uno scandalo. Hugh Grant posa per il Dipartimento di Polizia di Los Angeles, 27 giugno 1995.

Grant and Divine Brown (right) were arrested following a *tête à groin* incident in a car on Hollywood's Sunset Boulevard.

Grant y Divine Brown (derecha) son detenidos tras ser sorprendidos en una postura comprometedora dentro de un coche en Sunset Boulevard, Hollywood.

Hugh Grant e Divine Brown (a destra) vennero arrestati dopo essere stati colti in posizioni compromettenti in un'auto, sul Sunset Boulevard di Hollywood.

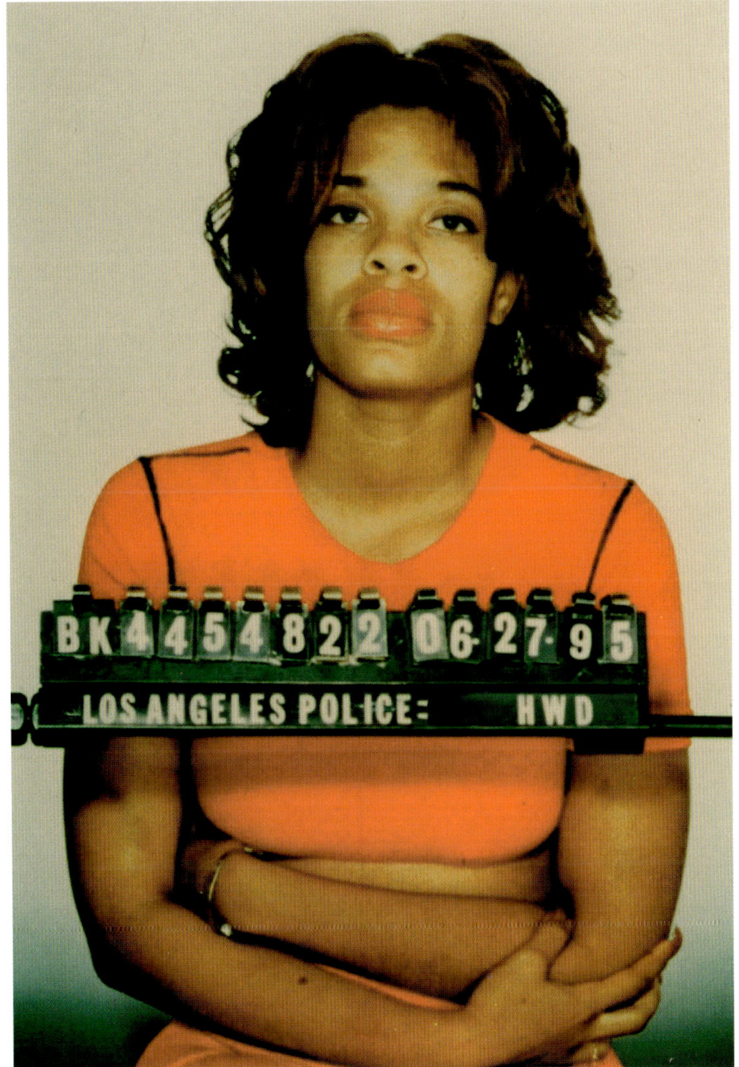

LAPD/EPA/PA

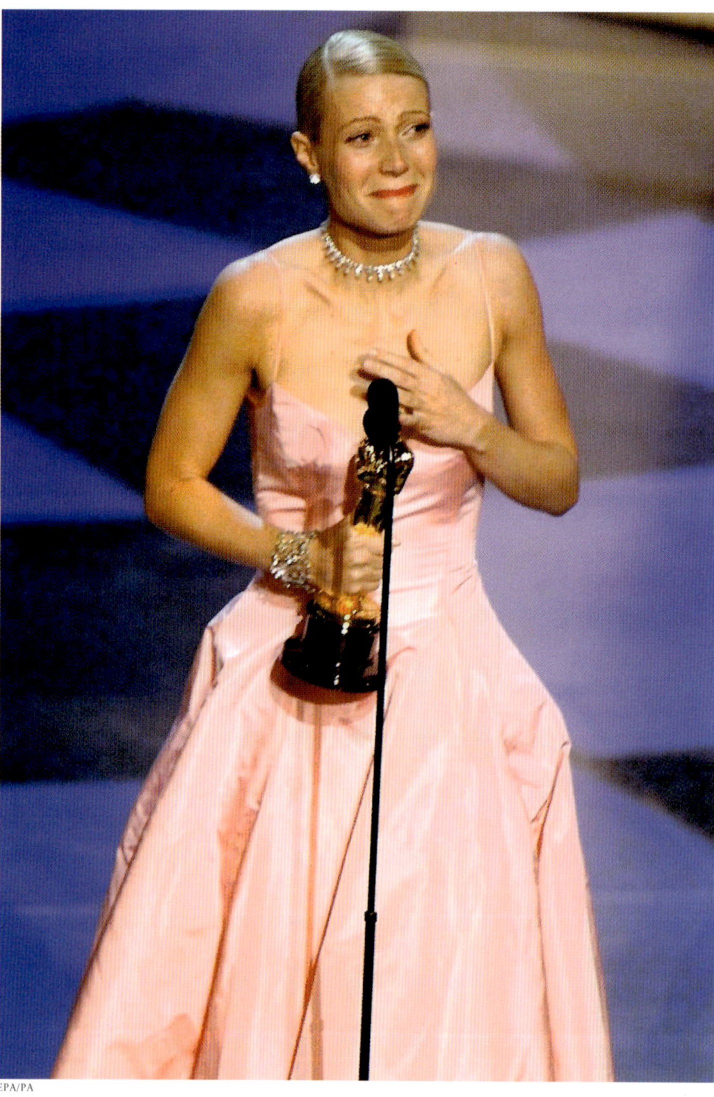

EPA/PA

Gwyneth Paltrow, in a Ralph Lauren dress, sobs as she receives the Oscar for Best Actress for her role in *Shakespeare in Love*, 22 March 1999.

Gwyneth Paltrow, vestida de Ralph Lauren, emocionada al recibir el *oscar* a la mejor actriz por su papel en la película *Shakespeare in Love*, 22 de marzo de 1999.

Gwyneth Paltrow, con un vestito di Ralph Lauren, scoppia in lacrime mentre riceve l'Oscar come migliore attrice per il suo ruolo in *Shakespeare in Love*, 22 marzo 1999.

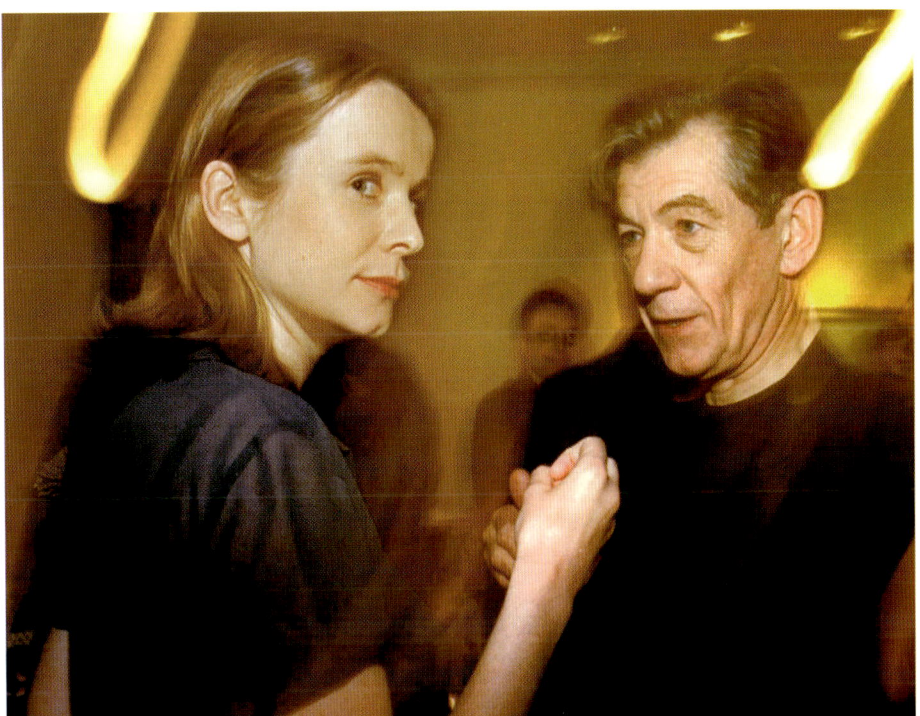

EPA/PA

Ian McKellen and Emily Watson at the BAFTA Los Angeles tea party, Santa Monica, 21 March 1999, on the eve of the Oscar ceremonies. Both had been nominated – McKellen for *Gods and Monsters*, Watson for *Hilary and Jackie*.

Ian McKellen y Emily Watson en la fiesta de la BAFTA (Academia de cine británico) en Santa Mónica, Los Ángeles, en la vigilia de la ceremonia de entrega de los Oscar, 21 de marzo de 1999. Ambos estaban nominados: McKellen por *Dioses y monstruos* y Watson por *Hilary y Jackie*.

Ian McKellen ed Emily Watson in occasione di un tea party presso il BAFTA di Los Angeles, Santa Monica, 21 marzo 1999, alla vigilia della cerimonia degli Oscar. Erano stati nominati entrambi, McKellen per *Demoni e Dei*, e la Watson per *Hilary and Jackie*.

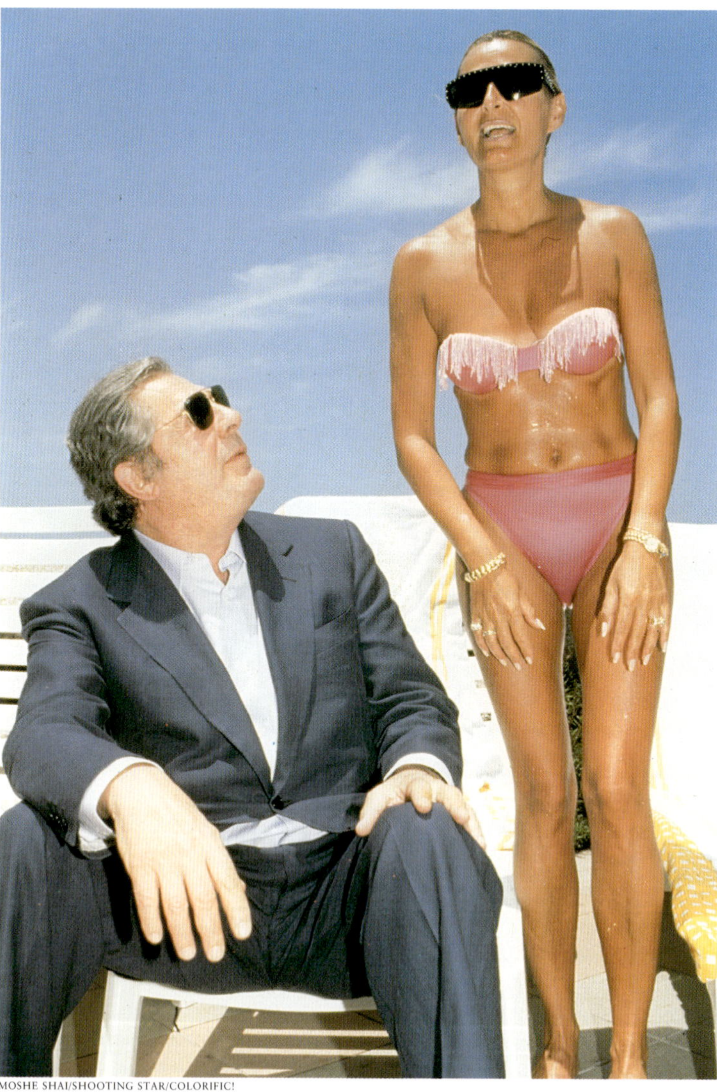

MOSHE SHAI/SHOOTING STAR/COLORIFIC!

La Dolce Vita lives again. Italian film star Marcello Mastroianni (left) admires an admirer.

Revive *La Dolce Vita*. La estrella de cine italiana Marcello Mastroianni (izquierda) admira a una admiradora.

La dolce *vita* vive di nuovo. La star cinematografica italiana Marcello Mastroianni (a sinistra) ammira un'ammiratrice.

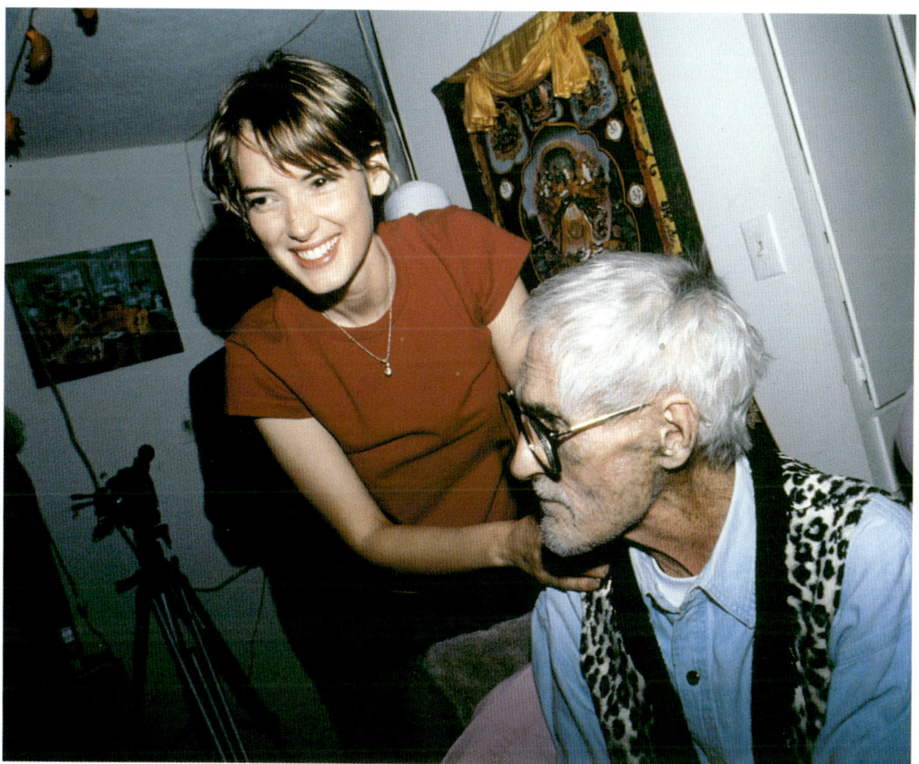

LINDSAY BRICE/VISAGES/COLORIFIC!

The Godfather LXXIV. American film star Winona Ryder with her godfather, Timothy Leary. Ryder's father, Michael Horowitz, was Leary's archivist and with him co-authored an encyclopaedia of drugs.

El Padrino LXXIV. La actriz norteamericana Winona Ryder con su padrino, Timothy Leary. El padre de Winona, Michael Horowitz, fue archivero de Leary y escribió con él una enciclopedia de drogas.

Il Padrino LXXIV. La star del cinema americano Winona Ryder, assieme al suo padrino, Timothy Leary. Il padre della Ryder, Michael Horowitz, era l'archivista di Leary e assieme avevano realizzato un'enciclopedia sulle droghe.

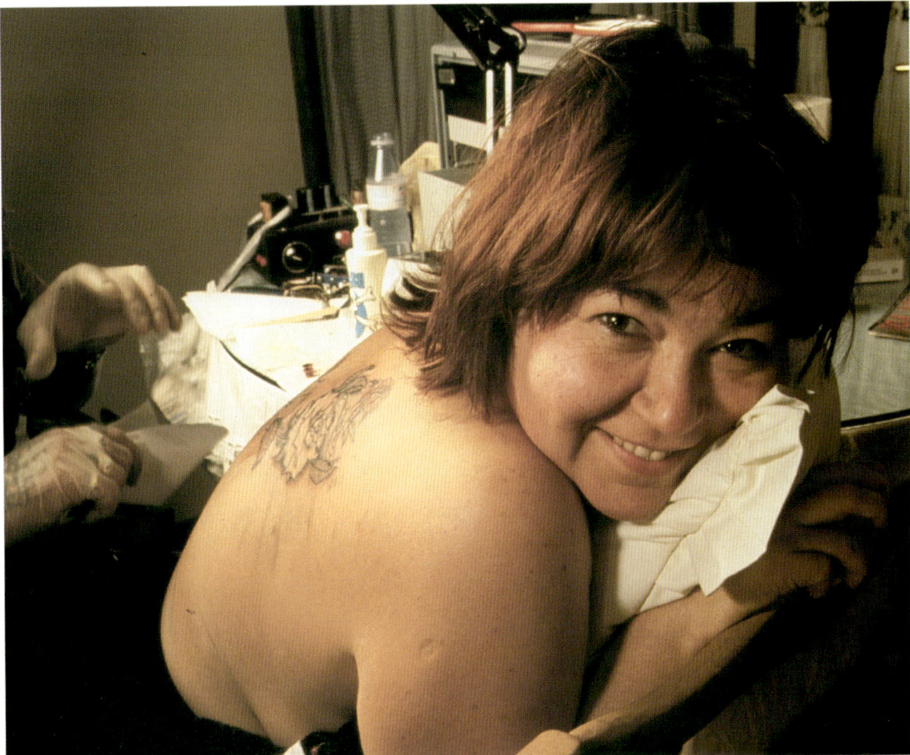

MARK RICHARDS/DOT/COLORIFIC!

In an unusually happy mood, Roseanne Barr relaxes at the tattooist's. Despite much off-screen tension and frequent rows between star and writers, the TV sitcom *Roseanne* was one of the biggest hits of the 1990s.

De un buen humor poco habitual en ella, Roseanne Barr se relaja mientras le tatúan la espalda. A pesar de la tensión sufrida fuera de cámara y de las frecuentes disputas entre estrellas y guionistas, la serie televisiva *Roseanne* fue uno de los mayores éxitos de los noventa.

Stranamente di buon umore, Roseanne Barr si rilassa dal tatuatore. Nonostante le numerose tensioni dietro le quinte e le frequenti discussioni fra l'attrice e gli sceneggiatori, la sitcom televisiva *Roseanne* fu una delle più viste durante gli anni Novanta.

The show they hate to love. Chat show host Jerry Springer (left) with two highly excitable friends.

El programa que todos odian adorar. Jerry Springer (izquierda), presentador de un popular *talk show*, junto a dos amigas fácilmente excitables.

Lo spettacolo che detestano amare. Jerry Springer (a sinistra) con due sue amiche facilmente eccitabili, ospiti di un talk show.

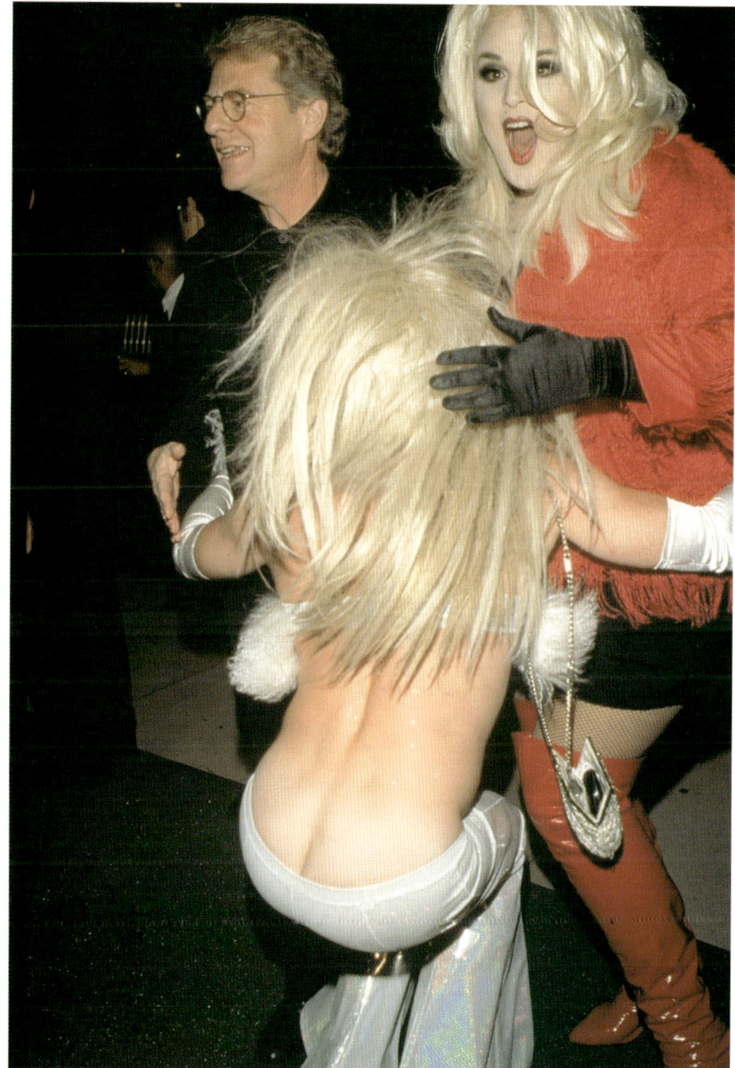

PAUL FENTON/SHOOTING STAR/COLORIFIC!

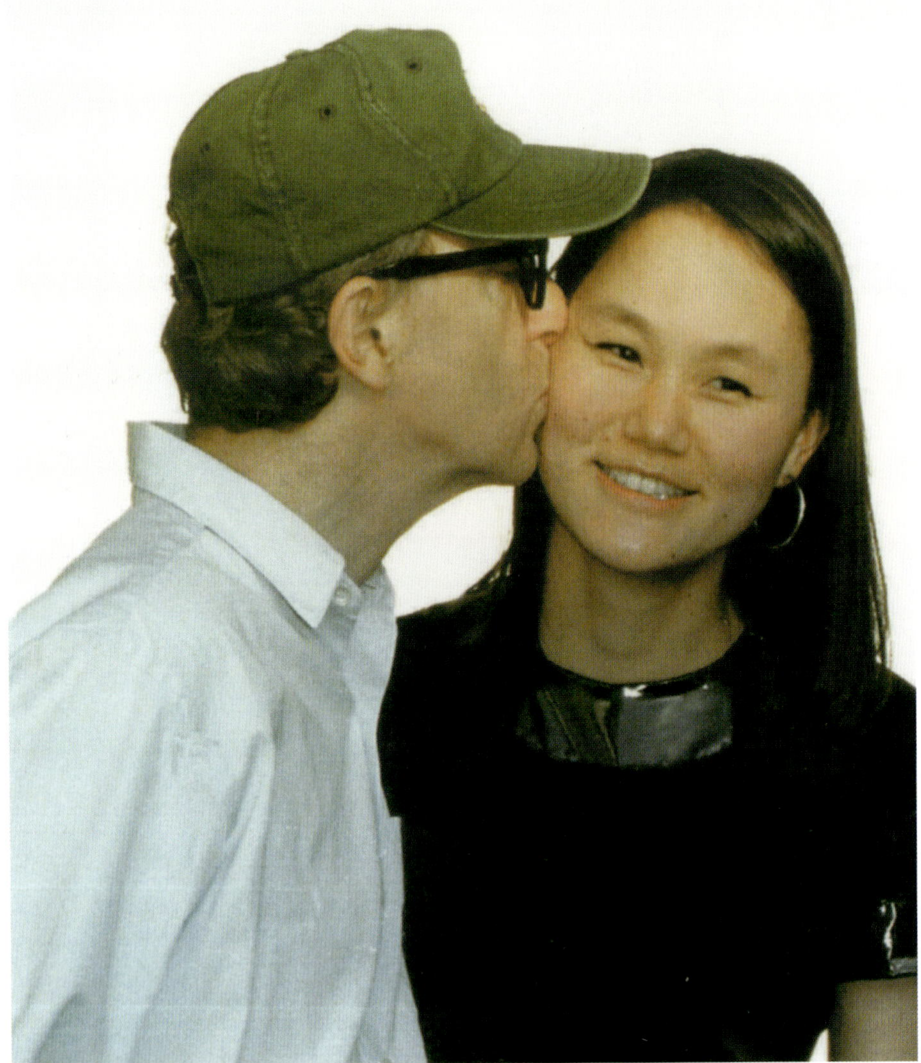

KEITH BUTLER/ONLINE USA/COLORIFIC!

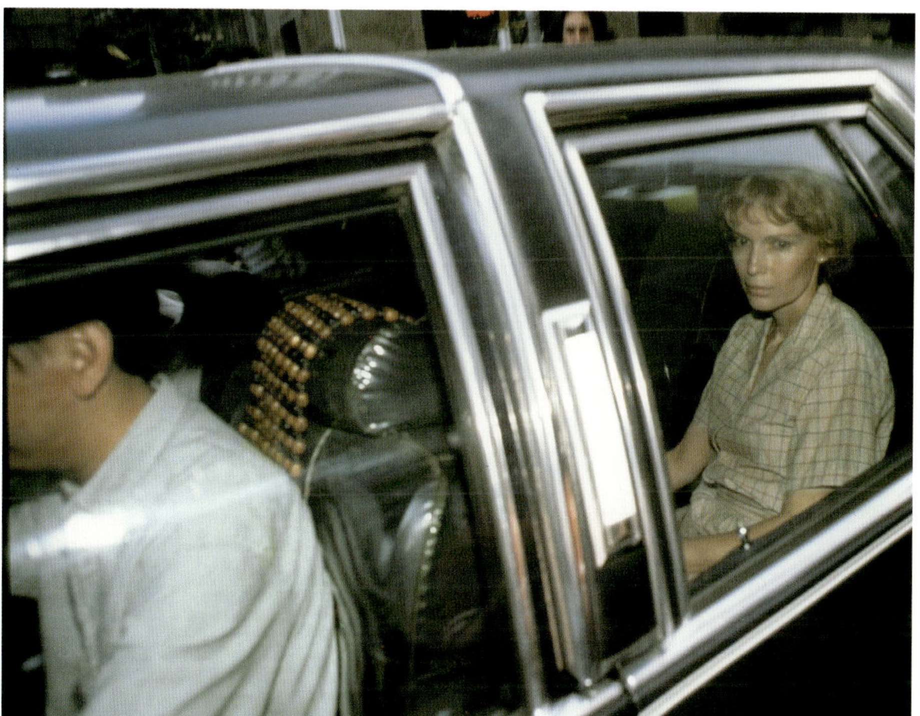

LISA QUINONES/BLACK STAR/COLORIFIC!

Husbands and wives and adopted daughters. (Above) Mia Farrow at the time of the custody hearing in which she alleged that Woody Allen (opposite, left) had sexually abused her adopted daughter Dylan, 25 August 1992. In December 1997, Allen married Soon-Yi Previn (opposite, right), another of Farrow's adopted children...

Maridos, mujeres e hijas adoptadas. (Arriba) Mia Farrow durante la batalla por la custodia de su hija adoptiva Dylan, en cuya vista judicial alegó que Woody Allen (página anterior, izquierda) había abusado sexualmente de la niña, 25 de agosto de 1992. En diciembre de 1997, Allen contrajo matrimonio con Soon-Yi Previn (página anterior, derecha), otra de las hijas adoptivas de Farrow...

Mariti e mogli con figlie adottate. (In alto) Mia Farrow all'epoca del processo per la custodia dei figli, in cui aveva sostenuto che Woody Allen (pagina a fianco, a sinistra), aveva abusato sessualmente della figlia adottiva Dylan, 25 agosto 1992. Nel dicembre del 1997 Allen sposò Soon-Yi Previn (pagina a fianco, a destra), un'altra delle figlie adottate della Farrow...

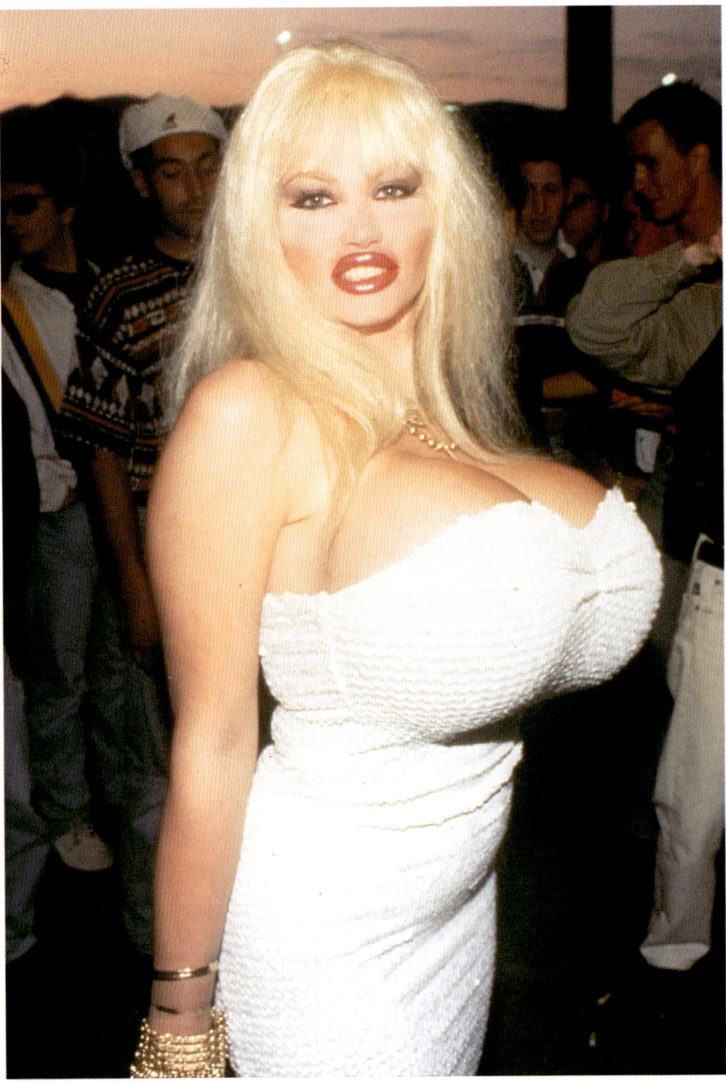

DEREK W RIDGERS/PYMCA

Lolo Ferrari, Cannes Film Festival, 1995. Reluctant porn star Lolo died of 'natural causes' five years later.

Lolo Ferrari en el festival de cine de Cannes, 1995. Empujada a convertirse en estrella del porno, Lolo fallecía por "causas naturales" cinco años después.

Lolo Ferrari, Festival di Cannes. Pornostar, suo malgrado, Lolo morì per "cause naturali" cinque anni più tardi.

Pamela Anderson, prominent star of the TV series *Baywatch*, and her husband Tommy Lee at the opening of the Hard Rock Hotel, Las Vegas. Tommy was a member of heavy metal band Mötley Crüe.

Pamela Anderson, prominente estrella de la serie televisiva *Los vigilantes de la playa*, con su marido Tommy Lee en la inauguración del Hard Rock Hotel, en Las Vegas. Tommy era componente del grupo de *heavy metal* Mötley Crüe.

Pamela Anderson, famosa star della serie televisiva *Baywatch*, assieme a suo marito Tommy Lee, alla cerimonia di apertura dell'Hard Rock Hotel, Las Vegas. Tommy era un membro del gruppo heavy metal Mötley Crue.

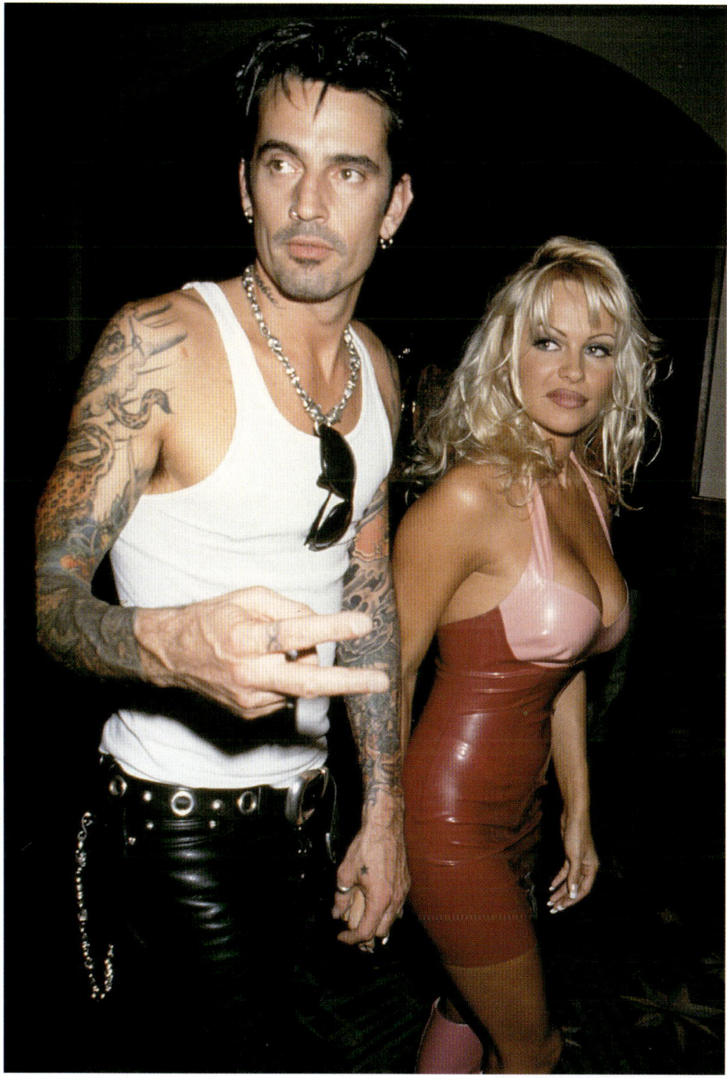

RON DAVIS/SHOOTING STAR/COLORIFIC!

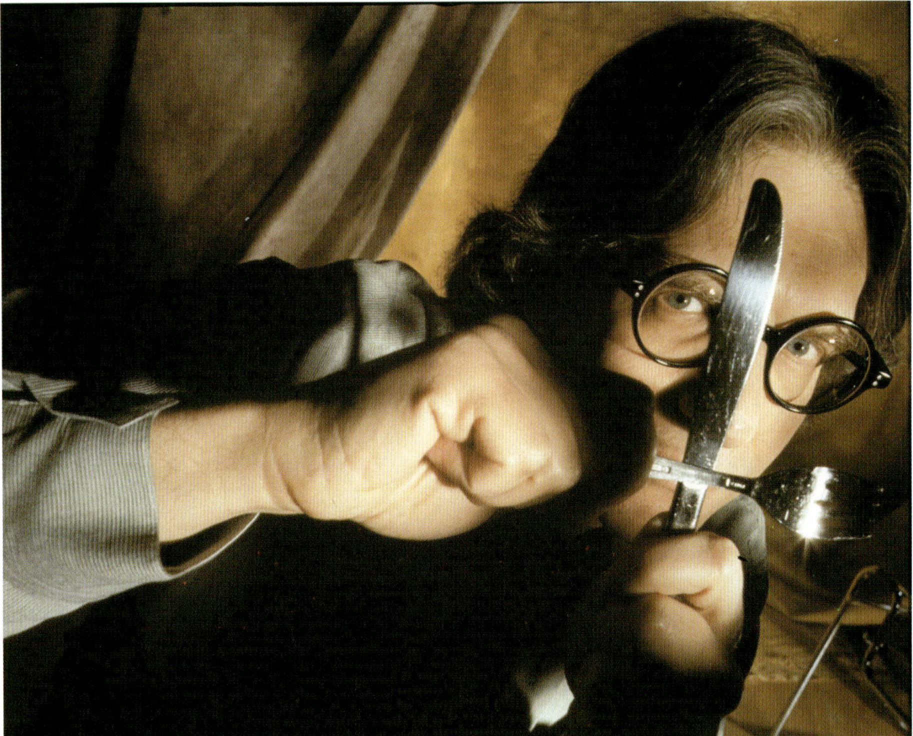

RON LEVINE/BLACK STAR/COLORIFIC!

Canadian film director David Cronenberg in defensive mode after his screen adaptation of William Burroughs' novel *The Naked Lunch* in 1992. Among Cronenberg's other films of the 1990s were *Crash* and *eXistenZ*.

El director de cine canadiense David Cronenberg con gesto defensivo tras llevar a la gran pantalla la novela de William Burroughs *El almuerzo desnudo*, en 1992. Otros trabajos cinematográficos destacados que Cronenberg realizó durante la década de 1990 son *Crash* y *eXistenZ*.

Il regista canadese David Cronenberg sulla difensiva dopo il suo adattamento per il grande schermo del romanzo di William Burroughs *Il pasto nudo*, nel 1992. Fra gli altri film di Cronenberg degli anni Novanta si possono ricordare *Crash* ed *eXistenZ*.

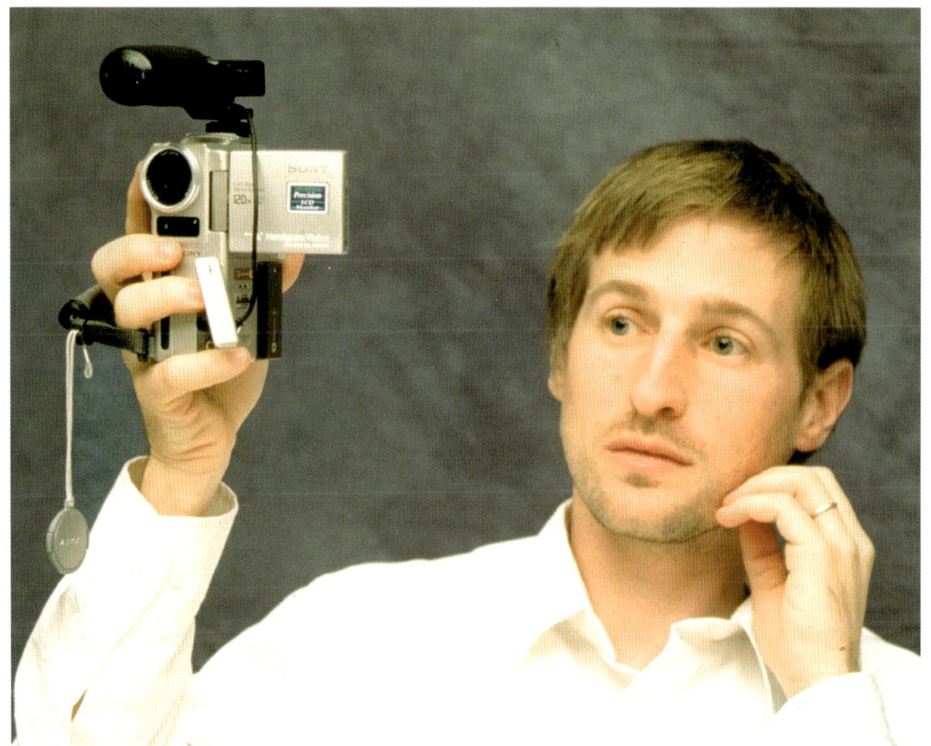

YORAM KAHANA/SHOOTING STAR/COLORIFIC!

American film director and actor Spike Jonze, December 1999. Jonze cut his film teeth on highly original pop videos, and went on the make the successful *Being John Malkovich*.

Spike Jonze, cineasta y actor norteamericano, diciembre de 1999. Jonze se estrenó grabando videoclips de música pop sumamente originales antes de rodar la célebre *Cómo ser John Malkovich*.

Il regista e attore americano Spike Jonze, dicembre 1999. Jonze iniziò ad acquisire esperienza nel mondo cinematografico con originali video pop, dopo di che continuò con la realizzazione di *Essere John Malkovich*.

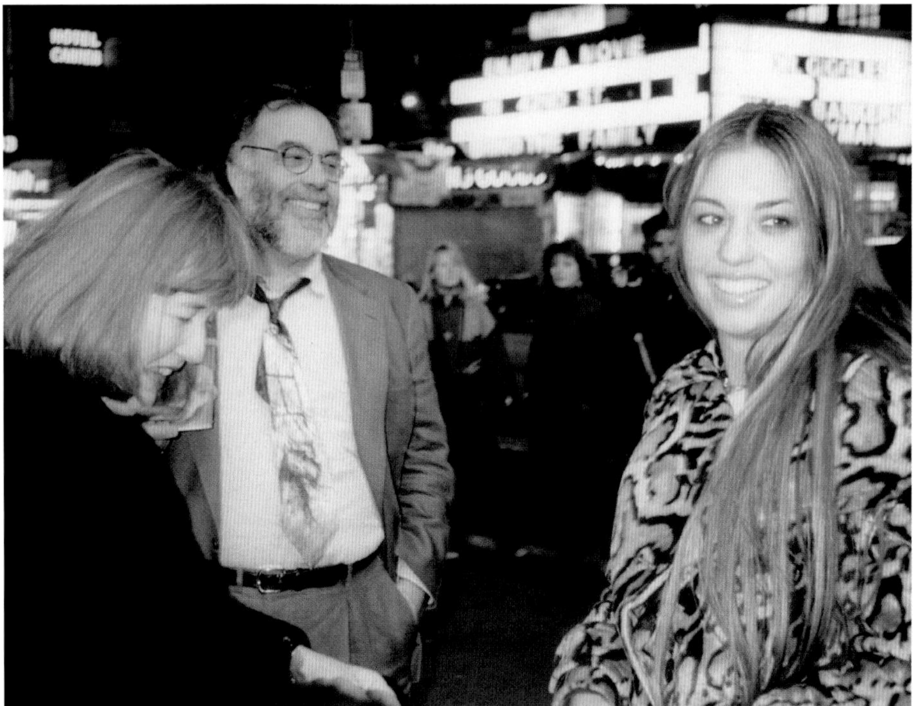

CHERYL DUNN/VISAGES/COLORIFIC!

Mr and Mrs Francis Ford Coppola (centre and left respectively) with their daughter Sofia, on a family night out in Hollywood. Sofia Coppola made her directorial debut in 1998 with *The Virgin Suicides*.

Francis Ford Coppola junto a su esposa y su hija Sofia durante una salida nocturna en familia por Hollywood. Sofia Coppola debutó como directora de cine en 1998 con el film *Las vírgenes suicidas.*

Ford Coppola assieme a sua moglie (al centro e a sinistra) e con la loro figlia Sofia, durante un'uscita in famiglia, a Hollywood. Sofia Coppola fece il suo debutto come regista nel 1998, con *Il giardino delle vergini suicide.*

John Malkovich savours success, 1997. He was the eponymous star of the 1999 movie *Being John Malkovich*.

John Malkovich saborea las mieles del éxito, 1997. Malkovich es la estrella epónima de la película de 1999 *Cómo ser John Malkovich*.

John Malkovich assapora il successo, 1997. Era la star eponima nel film del 1999 *Essere John Malkovich*.

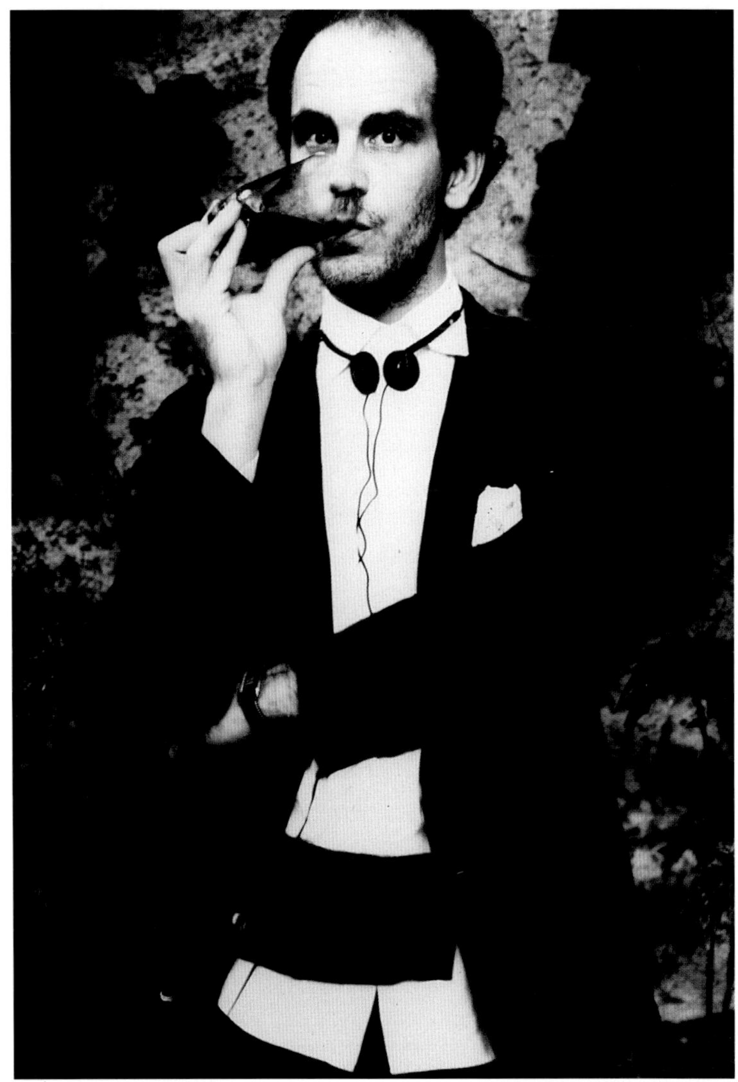

HOWARD ROSENBERG/SHOOTING STAR/COLORIFIC!

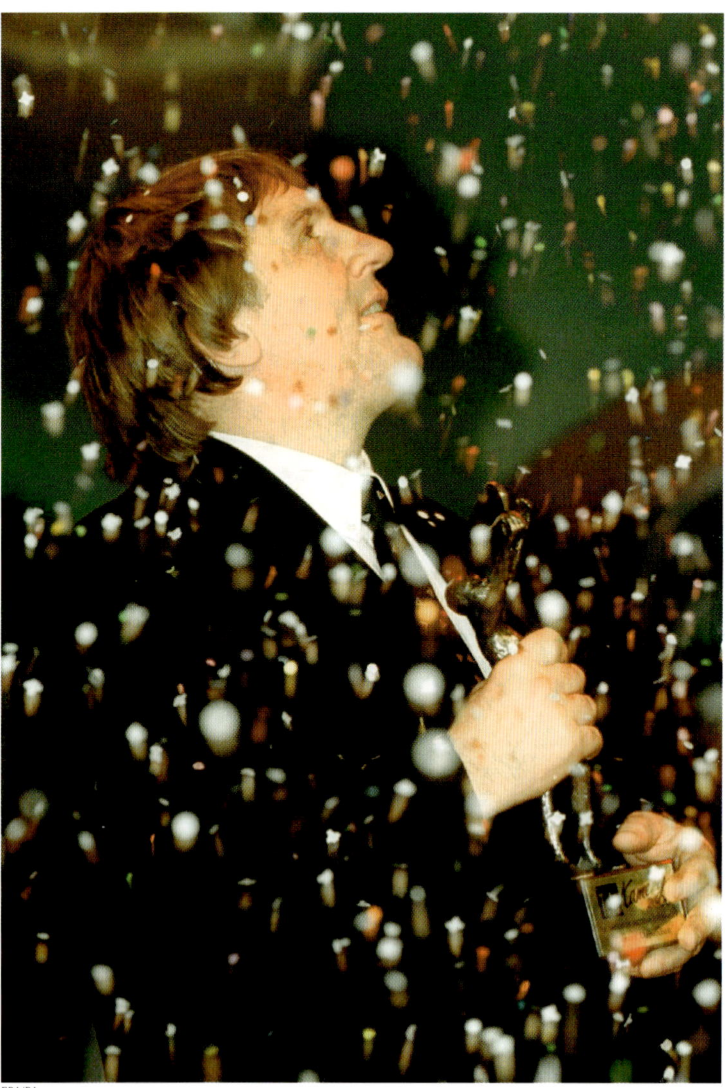

EPA/PA

Gérard Depardieu is dusted with confetti after receiving the Tele-Tydzien award in Warsaw for best foreign actor of 1999.

Gérard Depardieu bajo una lluvia de confeti tras recibir en Varsovia el premioTele-Tydzien al mejor actor extranjero de 1999.

Gérard Depardieu sotto una pioggia di coriandoli dopo aver ricevuto il premio Tele-Tydzien a Varsavia, come miglior attore straniero del 1999.

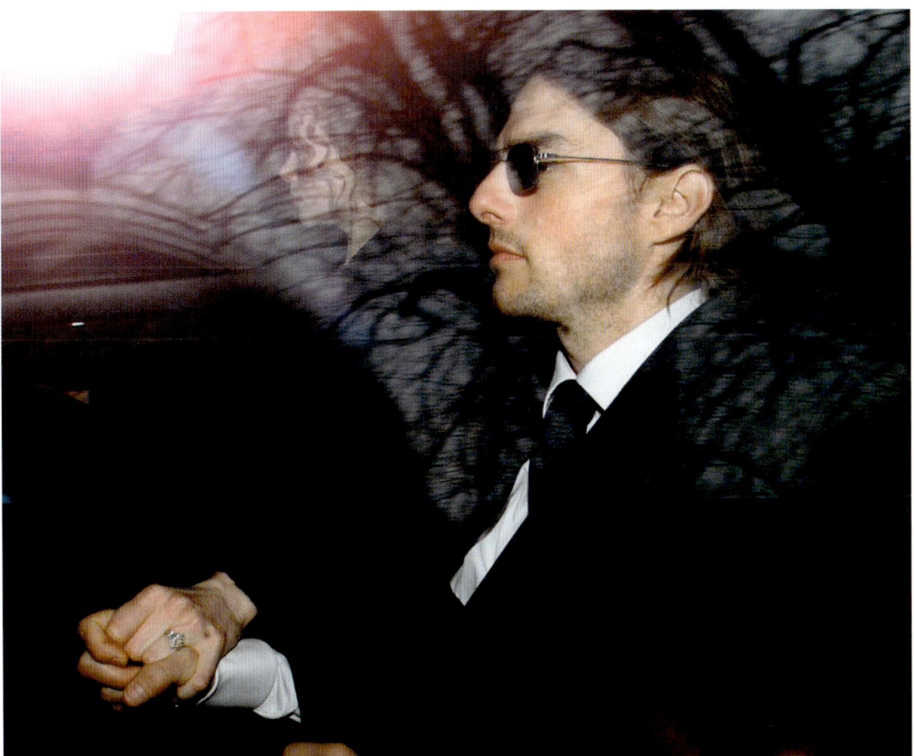

STEFAN ROUSSEAU/PA

Tom Cruise and Nicole Kidman arrive in St Albans, Hertfordshire, for the funeral of the film director Stanley Kubrick, 12 March 1999. Both had recently filmed *Eyes Wide Shut* with Kubrick.

Tom Cruise y Nicole Kidman asisten al funeral de Stanley Kubrick en St. Albans, Hertfordshire (Inglaterra), el 12 de marzo de 1999. Recientemente ambos habían trabajado bajo su dirección en *Eyes Wide Shut*.

Tom Cruise e Nicole Kidman arrivano a St Albans (Hertfordshire), per i funerali del regista Stanley Kubrick, 12 marzo 1999, con il quale avevano appena finito di girare *Eyes Wide Shut*.

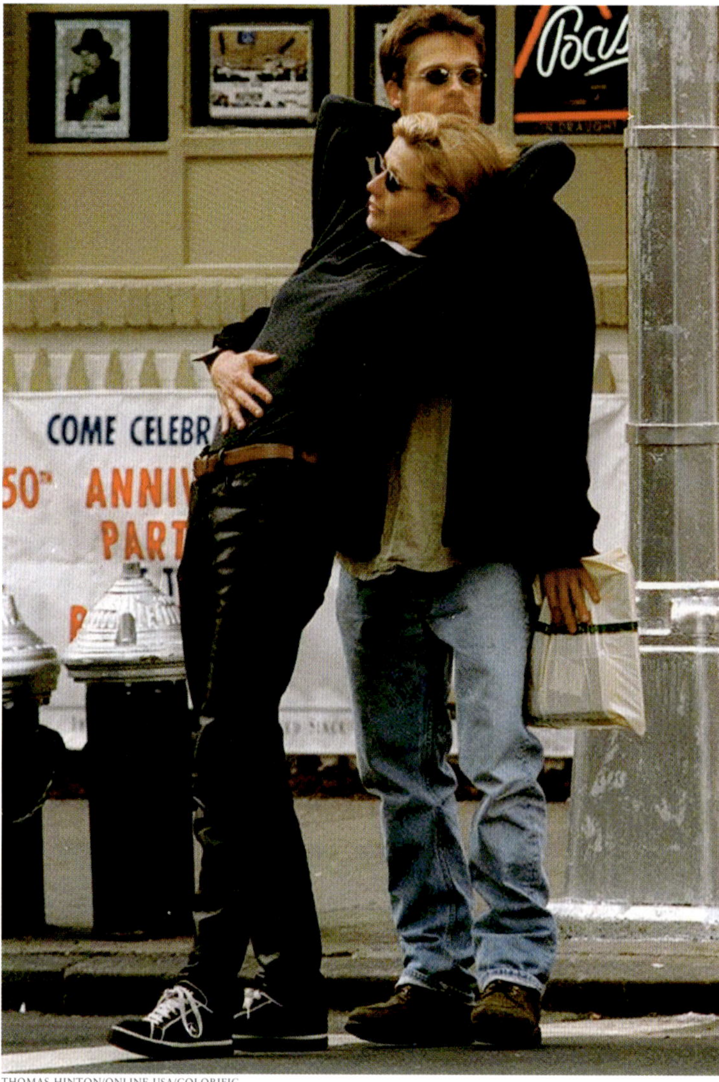

THOMAS HINTON/ONLINE USA/COLORIFIC

Brad Pitt and Gwyneth Paltrow chill out on Bleeker Street, Greenwich Village, New York, 15 June 1995.

Brad Pitt y Gwyneth Paltrow de paseo por Bleeker Street en Greenwich Village, Nueva York, 15 de junio de 1995.

Brad Pitt e Gwyneth Paltrow si rilassano a Bleeker Street, Greenwich Villane, New York, 15 giugno 1995.

Meanwhile, in another part of town… Warren Beatty on location for *Town and Country*, 15 September 1998.

Entre tanto, en otro punto de la ciudad… Warren Beatty en pleno rodaje de *Enredos de sociedad*, 15 de septiembre de 1998.

Intanto, in un'altra parte della città… Warren Beatty sul set di *Amori in città… e tradimenti in campagna*, 15 settembre 1998.

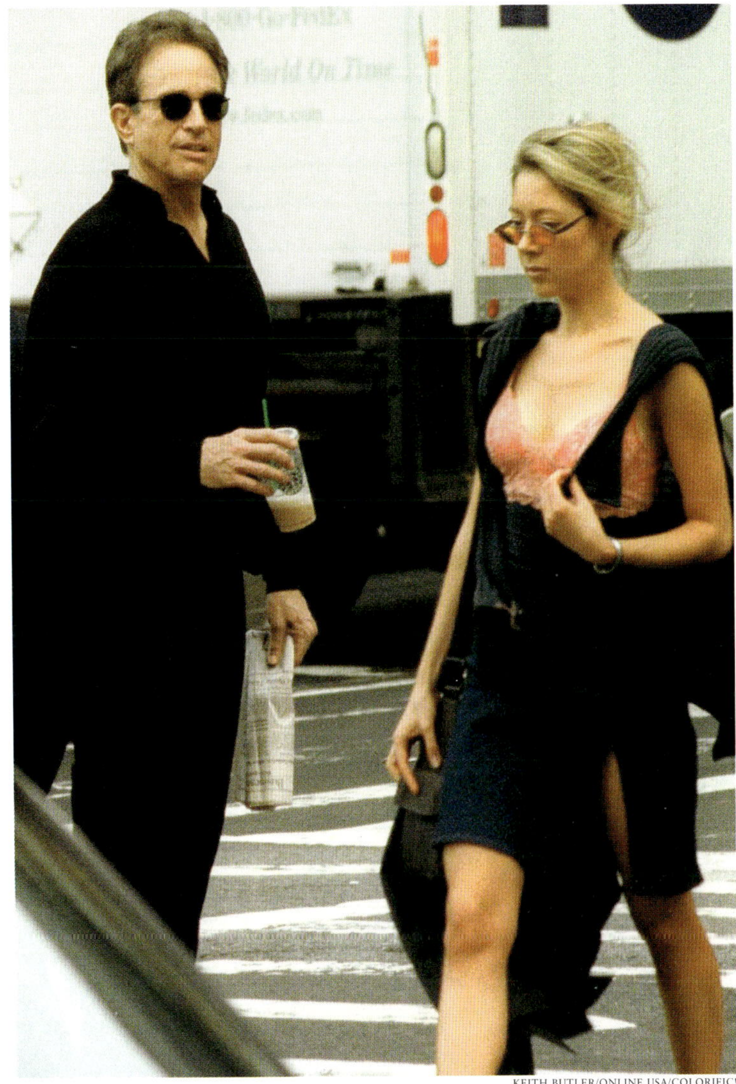

KEITH BUTLER/ONLINE USA/COLORIFIC!

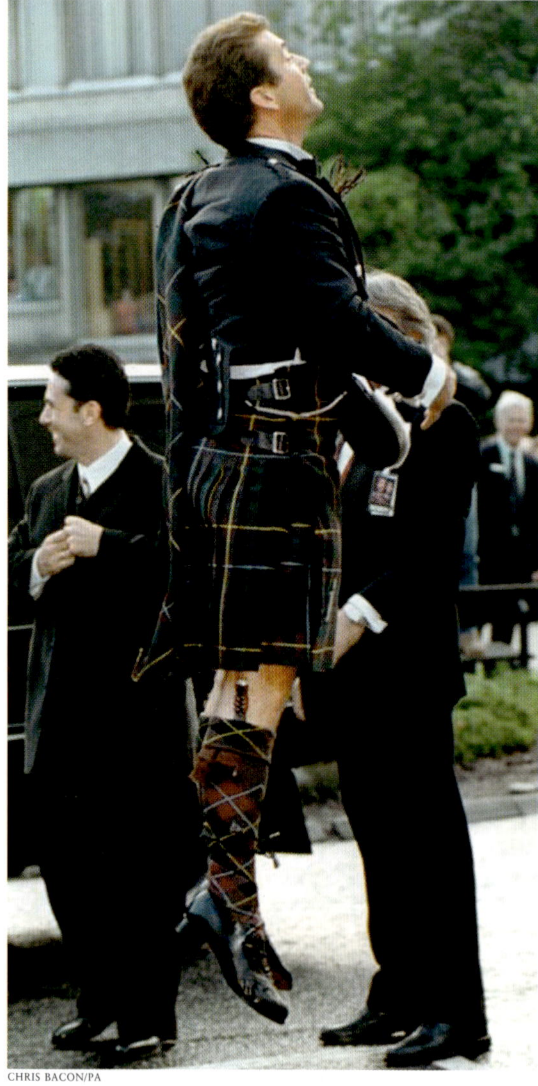

CHRIS BACON/PA

Rising stars. (Left) Mel Gibson's Highland spring at the MacRobert Arts Centre, Stirling, before the premiere of *Braveheart*, 3 September 1995. (Opposite) Roberto Benigni sweeps Helen Hunt off her feet as he celebrates his Screen Actors Guild Award, 8 March 1999.

Estrellas en alza. (Izquierda) Mel Gibson, vestido con el traje típico escocés, salta en el MacRoberts Arts Centre de Stirling, Escocia, antes del estreno de *Braveheart*, 3 de septiembre de 1995. (Página siguiente) Tras ser galardonado con el Screen Actors Guild Award, Roberto Benigni toma en volandas a Helen Hunt, 8 de marzo de 1999.

Stelle nascenti. (A sinistra) Il salto scozzese di Mel Gibson presso il MacRobert Arts Centre (Stirling), prima della première di *Braveheart*, 3 settembre 1995. (Pagina a fianco) Roberto Benigni solleva Helen Hunt dopo essere stato premiato con lo Screen Actors Guild Award, 8 marzo 1999.

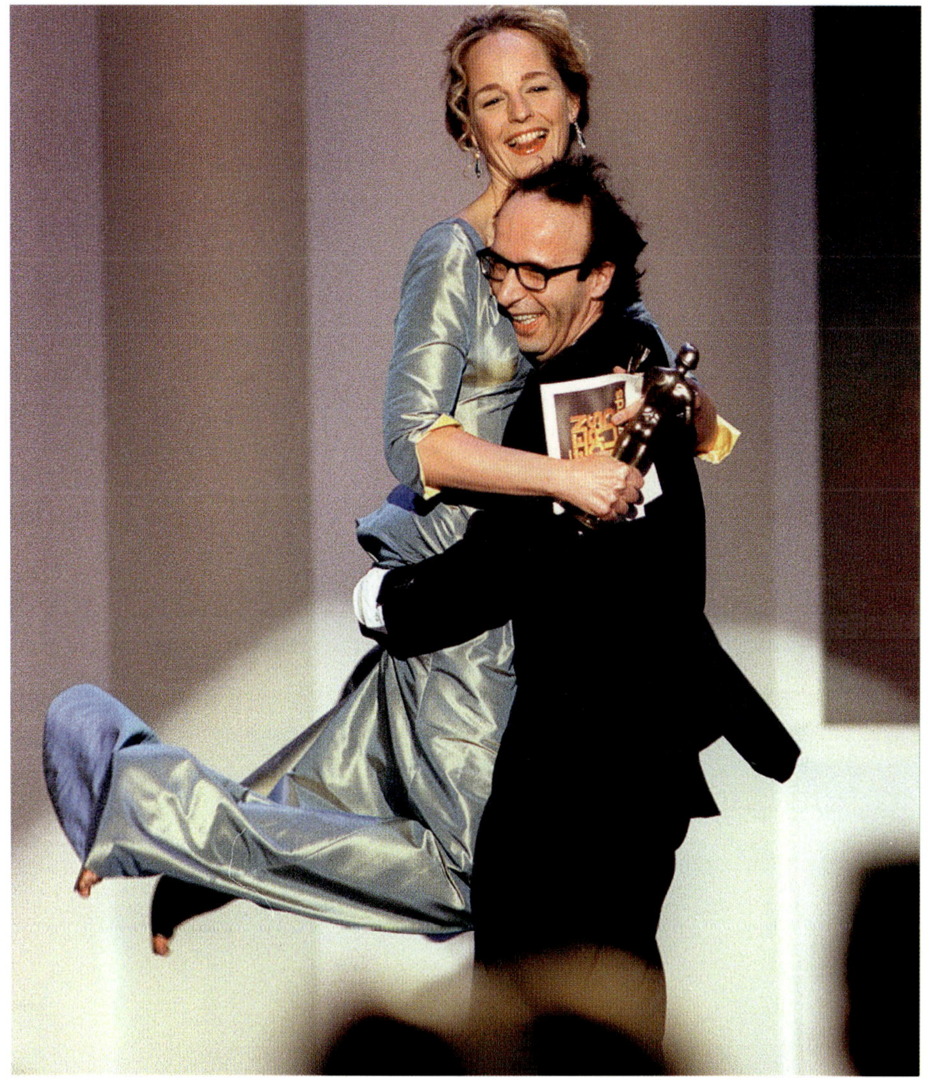

GERARD J BURKHART/EPA/PA

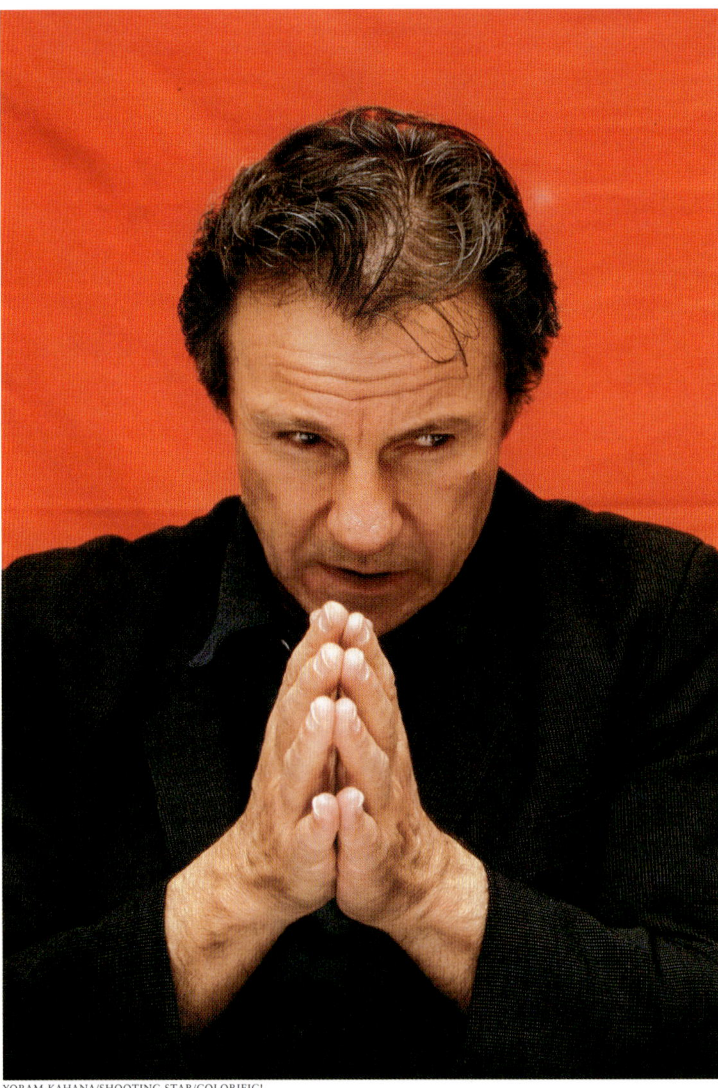

YORAM KAHANA/SHOOTING STAR/COLORIFIC!

American actor Harvey Keitel, who played the part of Mr White in Mr Tarantino's *Reservoir Dogs*.

Harvey Keitel, el actor norteamericano que da vida a Mr. White en el fim *Reservoir Dogs*, de Quentin Tarantino.

L'attore statunitense Harvey Keitel, che aveva il ruolo di Mr. White in *Le iene*, di Quentin Tarantino.

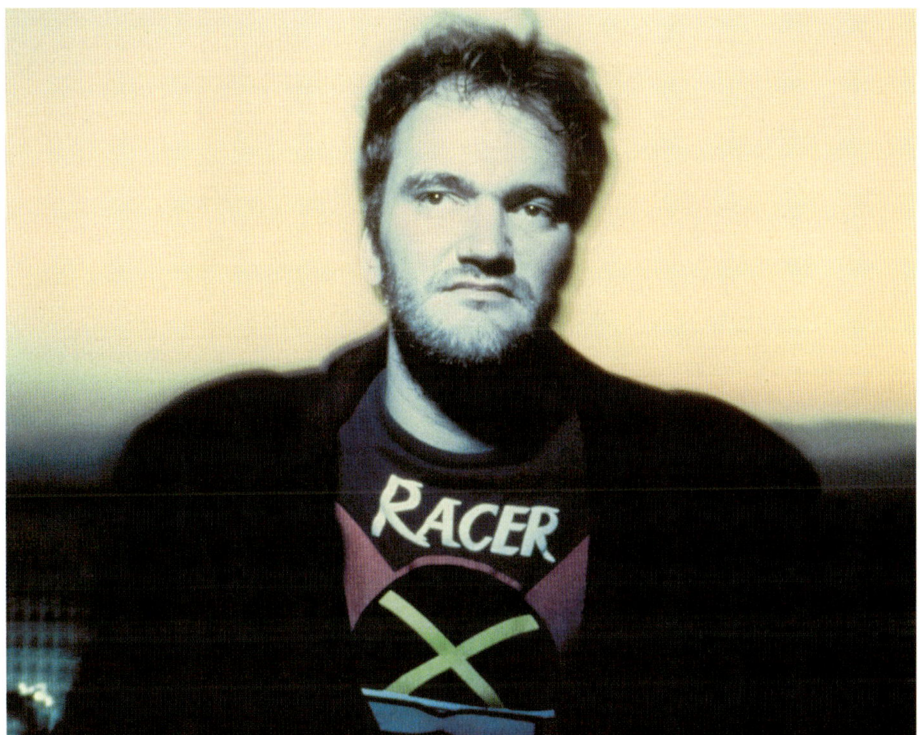

HOWARD ROSENBERG/SHOOTING STAR/COLORIFIC!

Writer, actor and director Quentin Tarantino. Critics were unsure as to whether or not the violence in films such as *Reservoir Dogs* and *Pulp Fiction* masked a lack of talent or overrode a cinematic genius.

Quentin Tarantino, guionista, actor y director de cine. La crítica no sabe si la violencia explícita de películas como *Reservoir Dogs* o *Pulp Fiction* pretende enmascarar una falta de talento o si, por el contrario, tras ella se oculta un genio del séptimo arte.

Lo sceneggiatore, attore e regista Quentin Tarantino. Le critiche non sapevano bene se dietro la maschera di violenza di film come *Le iene* e *Pulp Fiction* si nascondesse una mancanza di talento o un genio del cinema.

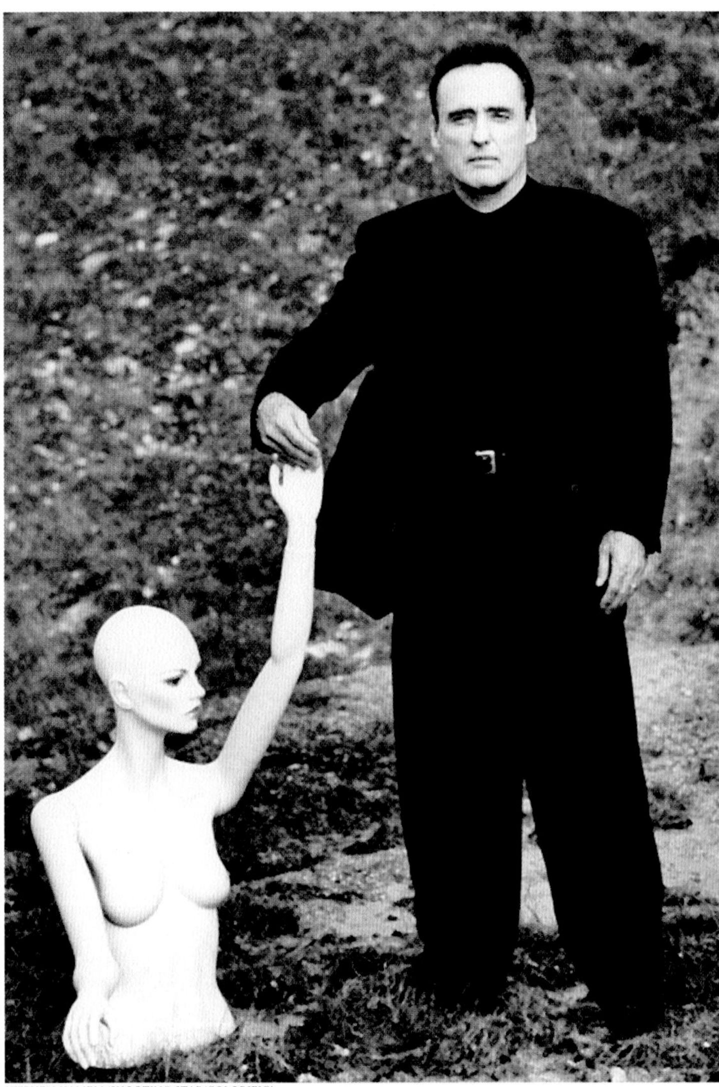

STEPHEN HAMELL/SHOOTING STAR/COLORIFIC!

Actor and director Dennis Hopper, star of many films in the 1990s including *Waterworld* and *True Romance*.

Dennis Hopper, actor y director, protagoniza numerosas películas rodadas en los años noventa, entre las que se cuentan *Waterworld* y *Amor a quemarropa*.

L'attore e regista Dennis Hopper, star di molti film degli anni Novanta, fra cui *Waterworld* e *Una vita al massimo*.

American film director David Lynch, whose 1990s credits included *Twin Peaks*, *Wild at Heart* and *The Straight Story*.

El cineasta norteamericano David Lynch rueda durante los noventa *Twin Peaks*, *Corazón salvaje* y *Una historia verdadera*, entre otros títulos.

Il regista statunitense David Lynch, autore, negli anni Novanta, di film come *Twin Peaks*, *Cuore Selvaggio* e *Una storia vera*.

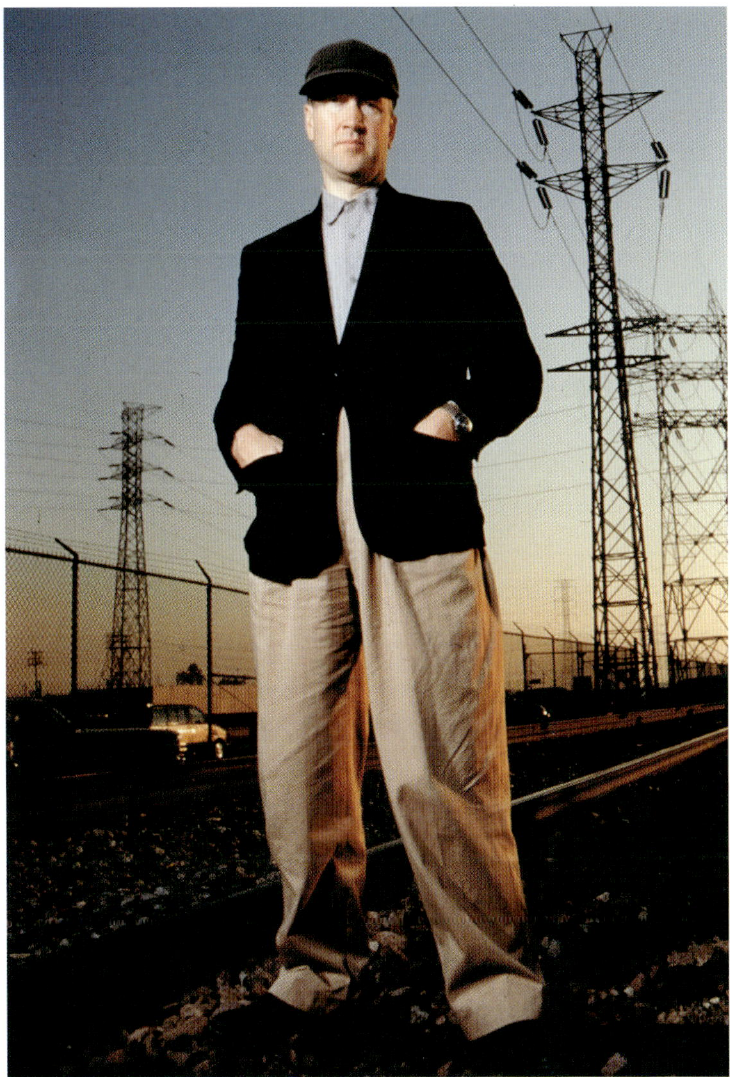

ANTHONY BARBOZA/SHOOTING STAR/COLORIFIC!

6. The Arts
Las artes
Arte

Damien Hirst and his assistants prepare some of his work for Expo 1996 at the Gogosian Gallery, New York City. Hirst was the ageing *enfant terrible* of British art during the 1990s.

Damien Hirst y sus ayudantes preparan algunas de las obras que el artista presentará en la Expo 1996 de la galería Gogosian de Nueva York. Durante la década de 1990, Hirst fue el *enfant terrible* del arte británico.

Daniel Hirst e i suoi aiutanti preparano alcune delle opere che esporrà alla Gogosian Gallery di New York per l'Expo 1996. Hirst fu il primo *enfant terribile* dell'arte britannica a maturare negli anni Novanta.

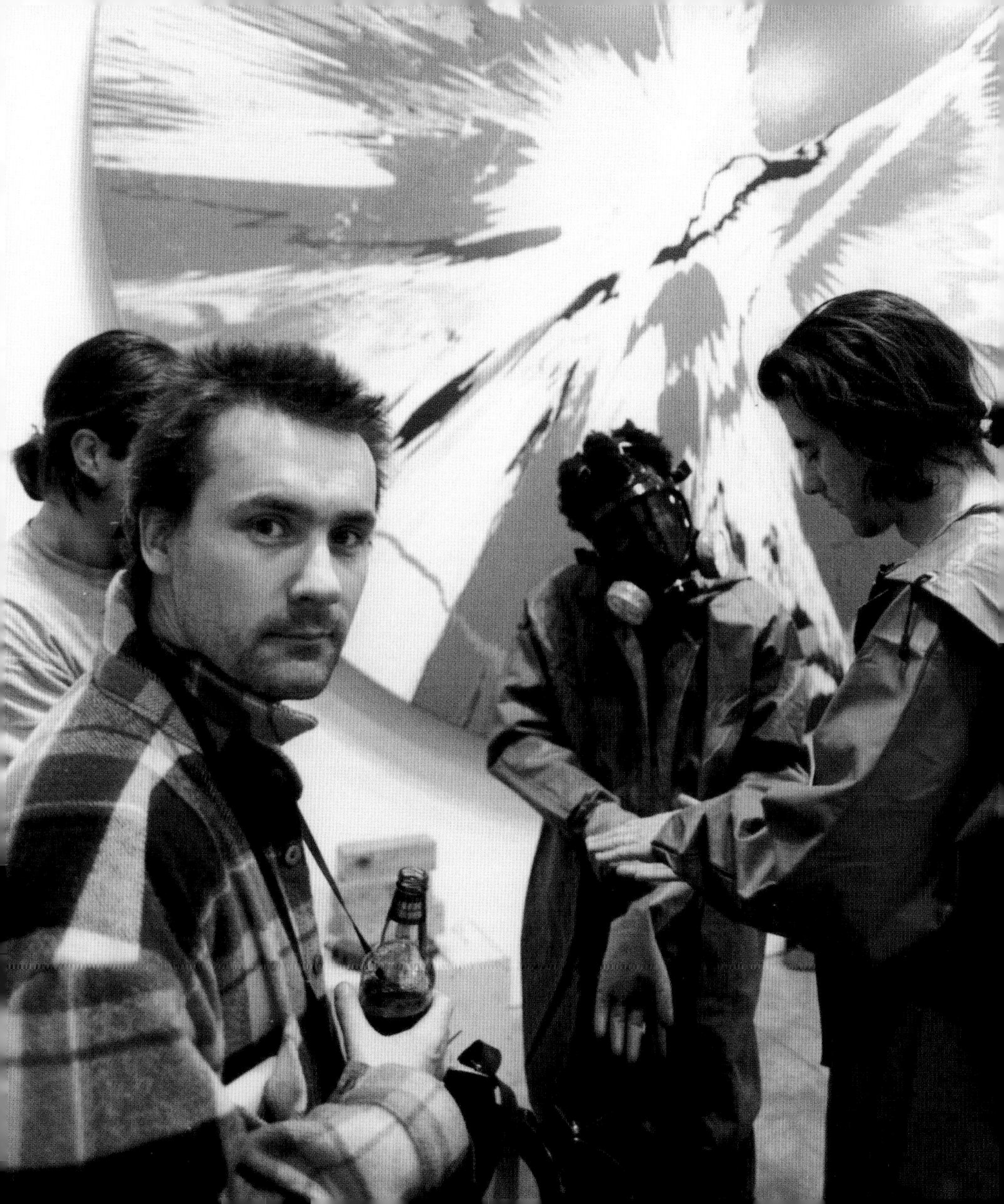

6. The Arts
Las artes
Arte

The shock tactics employed by angry young artists towards the end of the 1980s were pressed home *ad infinitum* throughout the 1990s. Paint and canvas, pencil and paper disappeared from the walls of galleries and art houses world-wide, to be replaced by structures, whole rooms and even entire houses in the guise of artistic creations. The proliferation of awards and prizes was seen by some as simply a way of indulging the glitterati, who flocked to presentation ceremonies in clothes as outlandish as the exhibits themselves.

The novel continued to die as an art form, as, it was claimed, it had been doing for well over half a century. Novelists took little notice of its alleged terminal condition. Salman Rushdie spent much of the decade in hiding from the *fatwa* imposed upon him in 1989. Martin Amis spent less time hiding from his dentist. Tom Wolfe wrote very little.

The Royal Opera House in London struggled to survive a series of financial and managerial crises, though opera and ballet had never before been so popular. A cad blew the whistle on price fixing by the leading auction houses, but all was quickly smoothed over. It was, as ever, a case of 'art for art's sake, but money, for God's sake!'

Las tácticas de choque empleadas por los artistas jóvenes y enojados de finales de los años ochenta se intensifican *ad infinitum* durante la década de 1990. De las paredes de las galerías y museos de arte de todo el mundo desaparecen pinturas, lienzos, lápiz y papel para dejar paso a estructuras, salas e incluso casas enteras a modo de creaciones artísticas. Algunos interpretan la proliferación de premios y galardones como una simple manera de complacer a los miembros de la flor y nata de la sociedad, quienes se congregan en las ceremonias de presentación de las exposiciones ataviados con prendas tan o más extravagantes que las propias piezas que en ellas se exhiben.

La novela continúa agonizando en tanto que forma de arte, si bien su enfermedad terminal ya hacía más de medio siglo que se venía anunciando –aunque los novelistas no quisieran reconocerla–. Salman Rushdie dedica buena parte de la década a esconderse de la *fatwa* proclamada contra él en 1989, mientras que Martin Amis dedica algo menos de tiempo a esconderse de su dentista. La producción literaria de Tom Wolfe es escasa.

La Royal Opera House de Londres lucha por sobrevivir a una serie de crisis financieras y de gestión en un momento en el que la ópera y el ballet gozan de una popularidad que hasta entonces jamás habían conocido. Un sinvergüenza denuncia el acuerdo de precios entre las principales casas de subastas, aunque rápidamente se echa tierra sobre el asunto. En definitiva, otro caso de "arte por amor al arte y dinero ¡por el amor de Dios!".

Le tattiche shock utilizzate da giovani e collerici artisti verso la fine degli anni Ottanta furono riproposte *ad infinitum* durante tutto il decennio successivo. Pittura e tele, matite e carta scomparvero dai muri di gallerie e case d'arte di tutto il pianeta, per lasciare spazio a strutture, stanze, e persino case intere a foggia di creazioni artistiche. La proliferazione di premi e riconoscimenti veniva vista da alcuni semplicemente come una maniera per fare contenti i rappresentanti del bel mondo che accorrevano a frotte alle cerimonie di presentazione con vestiti che avrebbero potuto fare concorrenza alle opere esposte.

Il romanzo, come forma artistica, continuava ad agonizzare dopo aver goduto di buona salute durante più di mezzo secolo, ma i romanzieri non prestarono molta attenzione alla sua presunta morte imminente. Salman Rushdie passò gran parte del decennio a nascondersi dalla fatwa emessa contro di lui nel 1989. Martin Arnis passò meno tempo a sfuggire al suo dentista. Tom Wolfe scrisse pochissimo.

La Royal Opera House di Londra cercava di mettercela tutta per sopravvivere alle varie crisi finanziarie e imprenditoriali, sebbene l'opera e il balletto non fossero mai stati così popolari. Un malintenzionato rivelò l'intesa sui prezzi con le principali case d'asta, ma il tutto venne rapidamente risolto. Era, come sempre, un caso di "arte per l'amor dell'arte, e di soldi, per l'amor di Dio!".

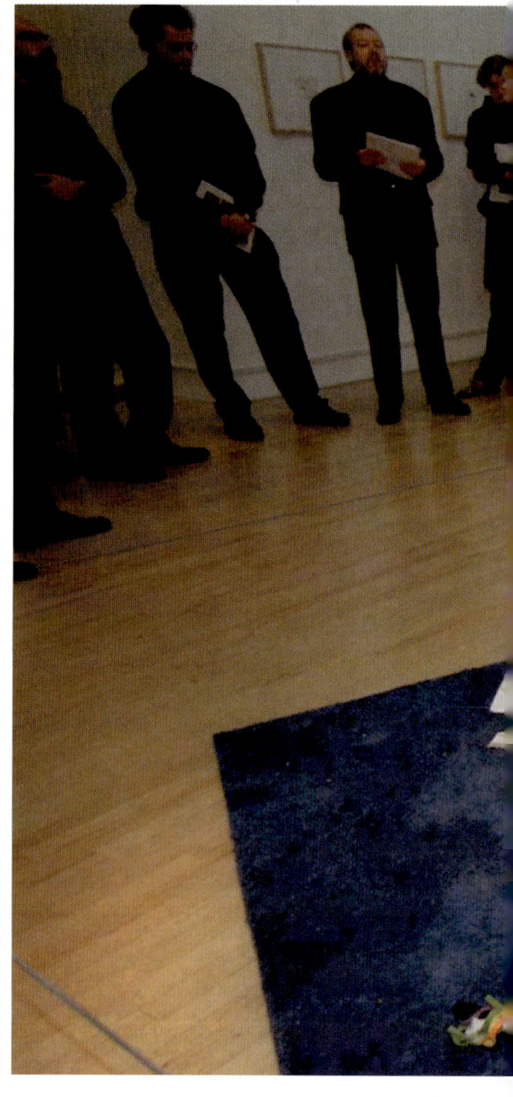

Inspired by illness, Tracey Emin's *My Bed* is shown to the press at the Turner Prize Exhibition, Tate Gallery, London, 19 October 1999.

Inspirada en la enfermedad, Tracey Emin presenta la obra *My Bed* a la prensa, con motivo de la muestra del premio Turner, en la Tate Gallery de Londres. 19 de octubre de 1999.

Prendendo come fonte d'ispirazione la malattia, *My Bed* di Tracey Emin viene mostrato alla stampa in occasione della Turner Prize Exhibition, alla Tate Gallery di Londra, 19 ottobre 1999.

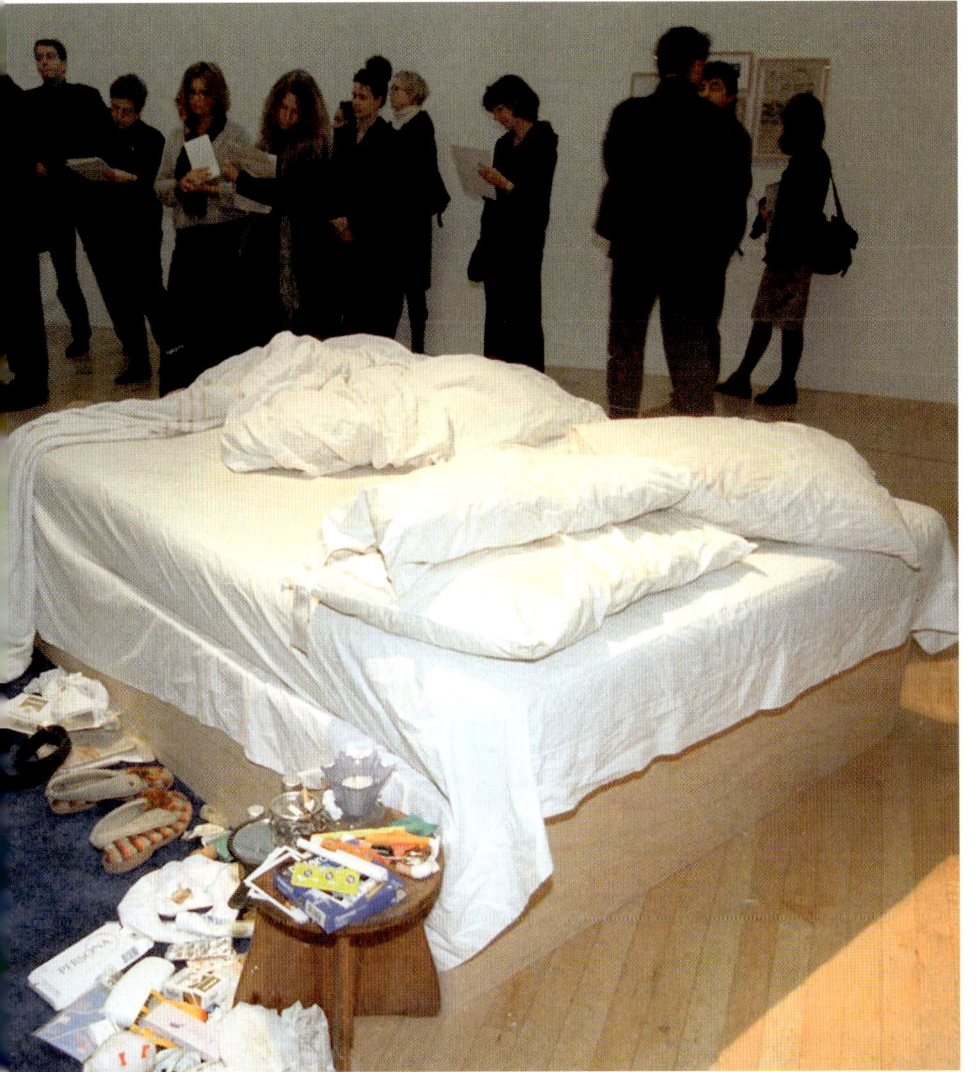

TONY HARRIS/PA

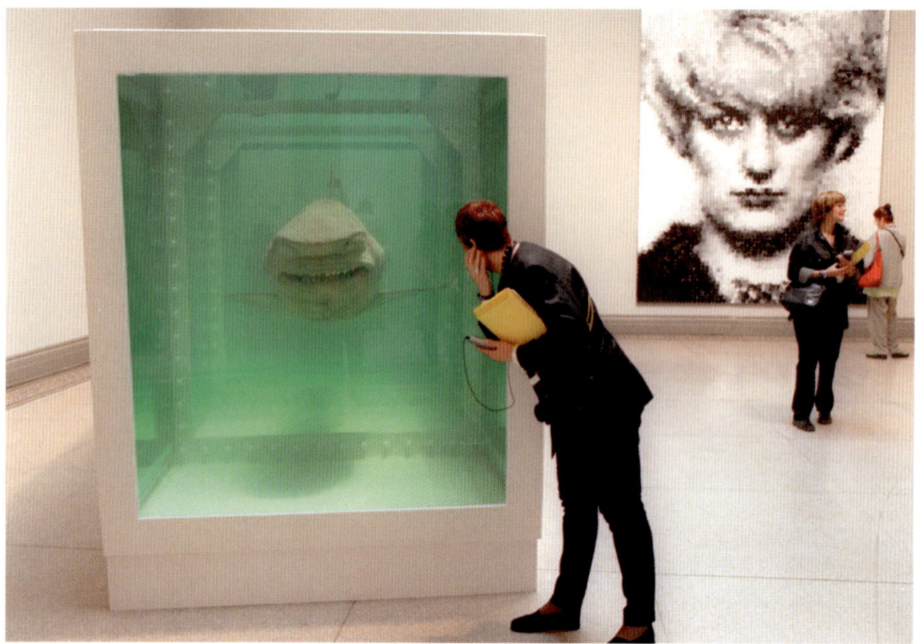

EPA/PA

The scene is the Brooklyn Museum of Art, 30 September 1999. In the foreground is Damien Hirst's *The Physical Impossibility of Death in the Mind of Someone Living*. In the background is Marcus Harvey's portrait of Myra Hindley.

Instantánea en el Brooklyn Museum of Art, 30 de septiembre de 1999. En primer término se halla la obra de Damien Hirsts *The Physical Impossibility of Death in the Mind of Someone Living* ('La imposibilidad física de la muerte en la mente de alguien vivo'), y en segundo plano, el retrato de Myra Hindley realizado por Marcus Harvey.

La scena ha luogo nel Brooklyn Museum of Art, 30 settembre 1999. In primo piano si può notare l'opera di Damien Hirst *The physical impossibility of death in the mind of someone living*. Sullo sfondo si riconosce il ritratto di Myra Hindley realizzato da Marcus Harvey.

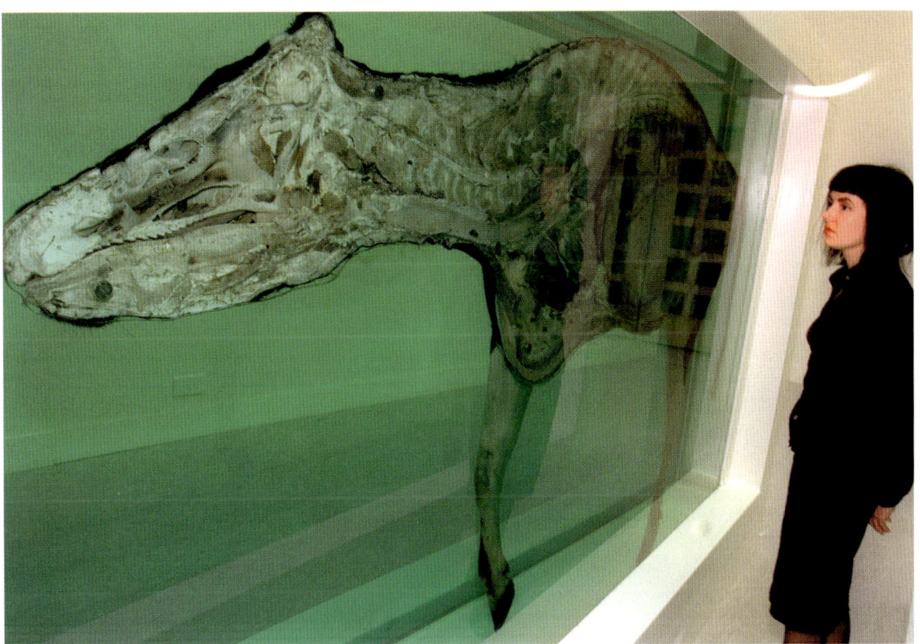

FIONA HANSON/PA

Much of Damien Hirst's work in the 1990s exhibited the versatility of formaldehyde. *Mother and Child Divided* (above), at the Tate Gallery, contained a bisected cow and calf. The Brooklyn work (opposite) contained a piece of tiger shark.

Gran parte de la obra que Damien Hirsts realizó en los años noventa muestra la versatilidad de la utilización del aldehído fórmico. *Mother and Child Divided* ('Madre e hijo divididos', arriba), obra exhibida en la Tate Gallery, muestra una vaca con un ternero en su interior partida por la mitad. La obra de Brooklyn (página anterior) contiene parte de un tiburón tigre.

La maggior parte delle opere di Damien Hirst degli anni Novanta mostravano la versatilità della formaldeide. *Mother and child divided* (in alto), nella Tate Gallery, rappresentava una mucca e il suo vitello tagliati in due. L'opera esposta a Brooklyn (pagina a fianco) raffigurava un pezzo di squalo tigre.

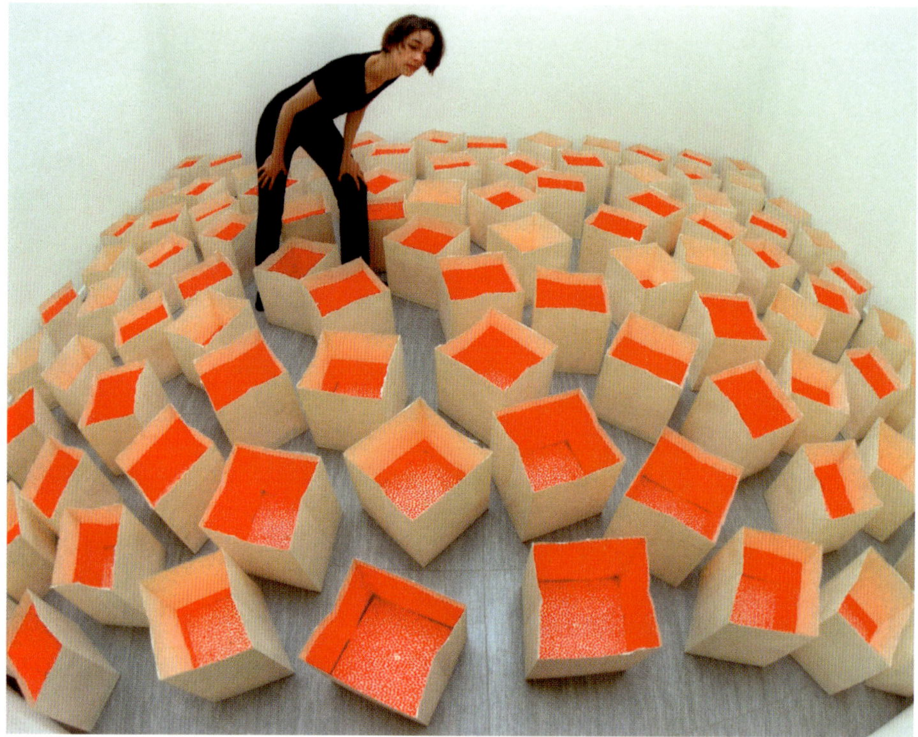

HARTMUT REEH/EPA/PA

An exhibit by the Japanese artist Fukuichi Yoshida at the Paper Art 7 show in the Leopold-Hoesch-Museum, Düren, Germany, 3 September 1998. The work covers the floor of a room with bags folded from Japanese paper.

Exposición de la artista japonesa Fukuichi Yoshida en la muestra Paper Art 7 del Leopold-Hoesch-Museum de la ciudad alemana de Düren, 3 de septiembre de 1998. La obra consiste en una serie de cajas forradas con papel japonés.

Una mostra dell'artista giapponese Fukuichi Yoshida in occasione dell'esposizione Paper Art 7 del Leopold-Hoesch Museum di Düren, Germania, 3 settembre 1998. L'opera ricopre il pavimento di una stanza con borse realizzate con carta giapponese.

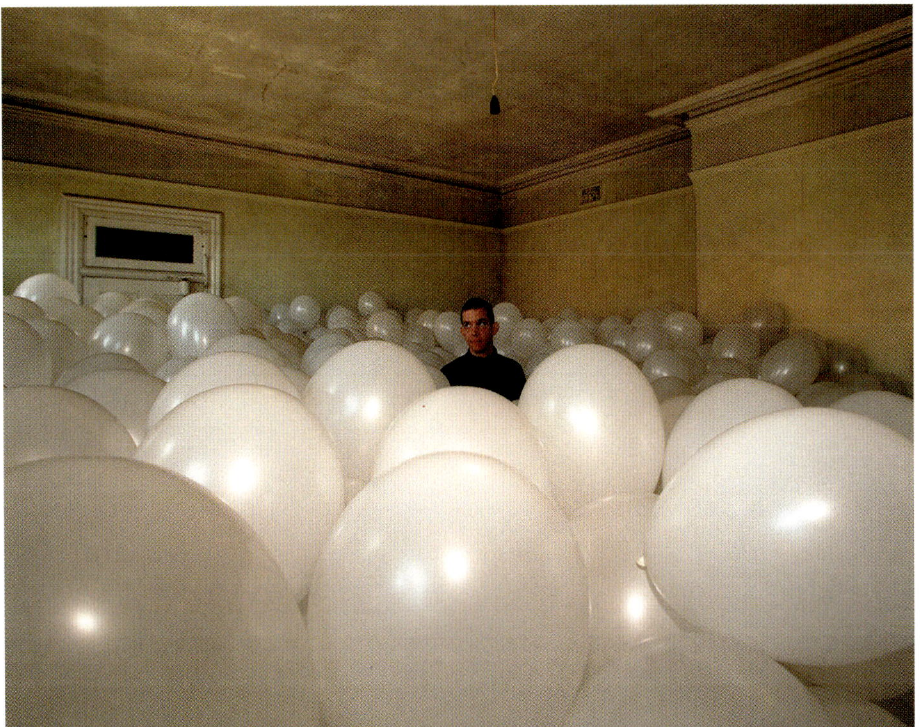

TORSTEN BLACKWOOD/PA

British artist Martin Creed peers out above the sea of 43,000 white balloons that make up his exhibit *Half the Air in a Given Space*, Goat Island, Sydney Harbour, Australia, 16 September 1998.

El artista británico Martin Creed otea por encima del mar de globos blancos (43.000) que conforma su exposición titulada "Half the Air in a Given Space" ('La mitad del aire en un espacio determinado'), la cual puede verse en Goat Island, en el puerto australiano de Sidney, 16 de septiembre de 1998.

L'artista britannico Martin Creed emerge dal mare formato dai 43.000 palloncini bianchi dell'opera *Half the air in a given space*, a Goat Island, nel porto di Sydney, Australia, 16 settembre 1998.

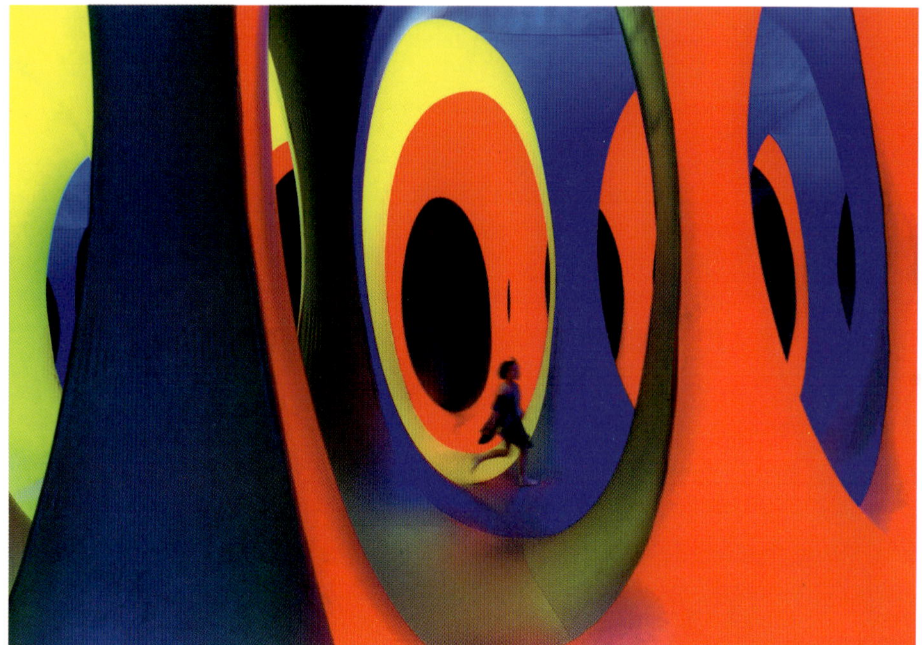

TOBY MELVILLE/PA

Confronting space. Visitors explore Maurice Agis's *Dreamspace*, a giant inflatable work of art and the largest pneumatic creation in the world, Mile End Park, east London, 15 July 1999.

Confrontación del espacio. Un visitante explora el *Dreamspace* de Maurice Agis, una obra de arte inflable y la mayor creación neumática del mundo, instalada en el Mile End Park, en el este de Londres, 15 de julio de 1999.

Affrontare lo spazio. Alcuni visitatori esplorano l'opera *Dreamspace* di Maurice Agis, un gigantesco capolavoro gonfiabile e la più grande creazione pneumatica al mondo, esposta a Mile End Park, nella zona est di Londra, 15 luglio 1999.

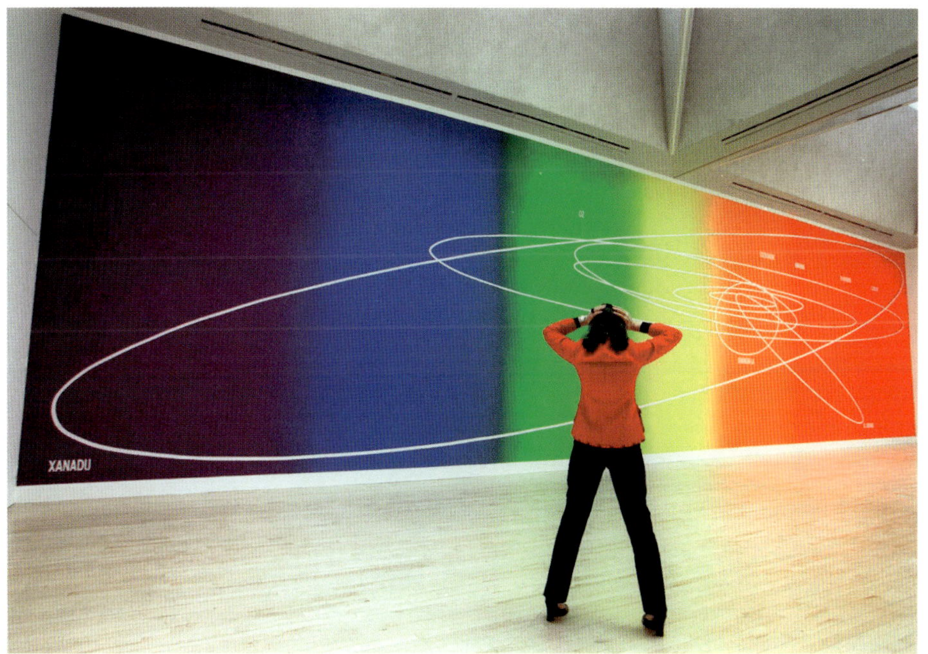

FIONA HANSON/PA

Contemplating space. Andrea Davis clasps her head in wonder at one of Simon Patterson's submissions for the Turner Prize, Tate Gallery, London, 28 October 1996.

Contemplación del espacio. Andrea Davis se lleva las manos a la cabeza en señal de admiración ante una de las obras de Simon Patterson candidata al premio Turner, en la Tate Gallery de Londres, 28 de octubre de 1996.

Contemplare lo spazio. Andrea Davis si mette le mani fra i capelli per la meraviglia, davanti a una delle proposte di Simon Patterson per il Turner Prize, alla Tate Gallery di Londra, 28 ottobre 1996.

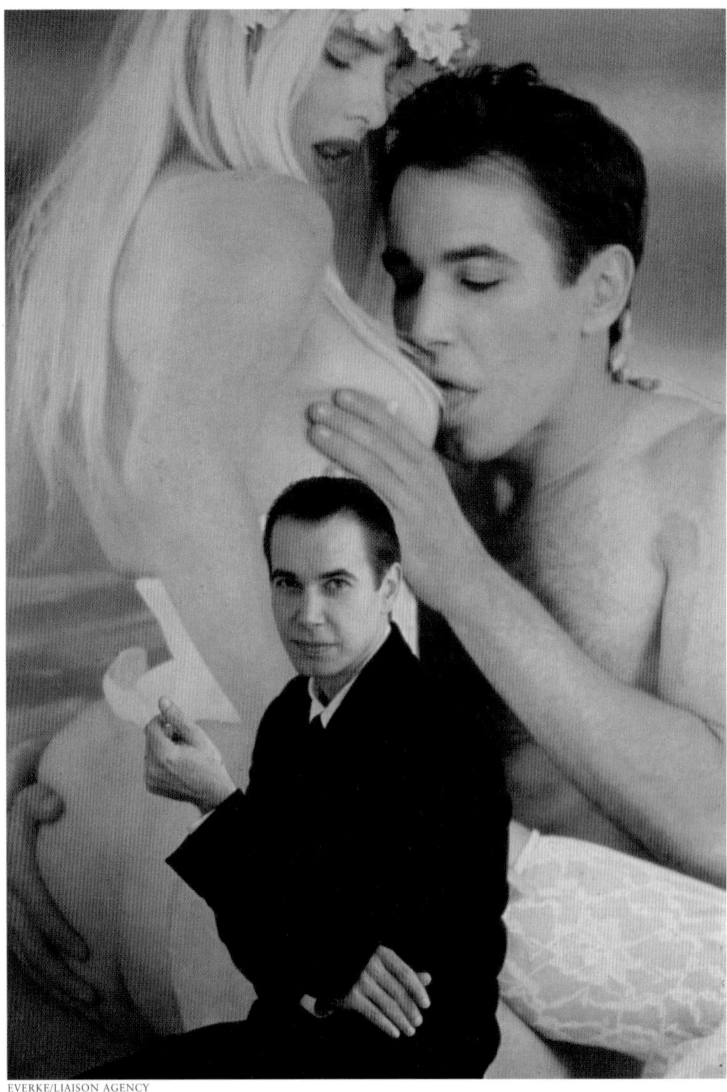

EVERKE/LIAISON AGENCY

Jeff Koons sits in front of a portrait of himself and his wife, La Cicciolina, for the X-Rated Art Show, 21 November 1991.

Jeff Koons posa frente a una fotografía de él con su mujer, La Cicciolina, para el "X-Rated Art Show", 21 de noviembre de 1991.

Jeff Koons siede di fronte a una foto che lo raffigura assieme a sua moglie, Cicciolina, in occasione dell'X-Rated Art Show, 21 novembre 1991.

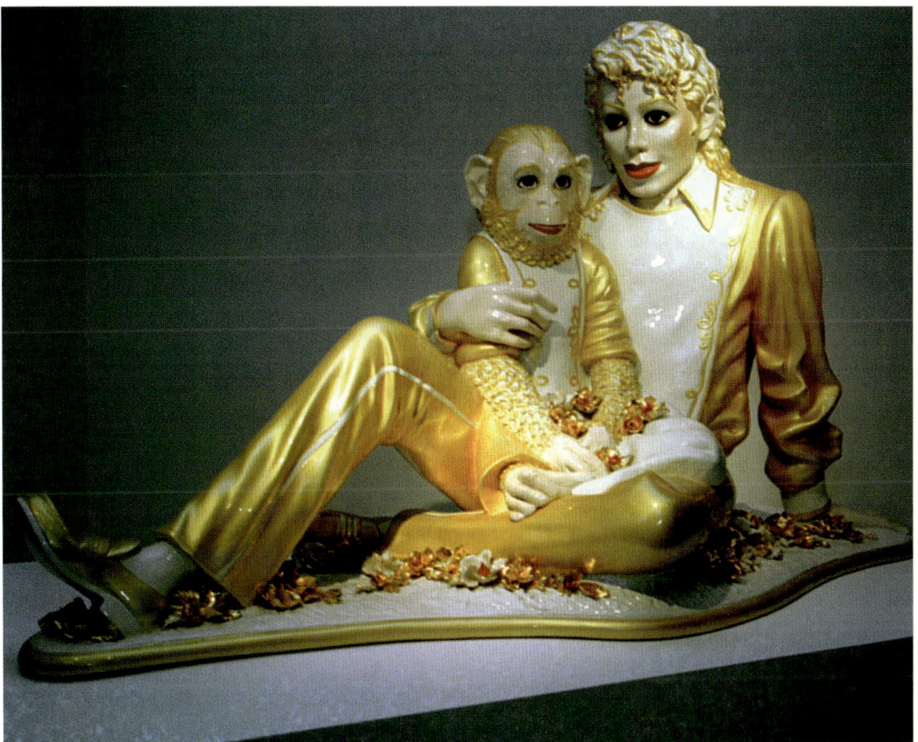

DAVID KENDALL/PA

Another medium, another icon. Jeff Koons's sculpture of Michael Jackson and his pet monkey, Bubbles, 8 December 1999. The work was part of the 'Heaven' exhibition at the Tate Gallery, Liverpool.

Otro medio para otro icono. Jeff Koons esculpe a Michael Jackson junto a su mascota, el chimpancé *Bubbles*, 8 de diciembre de 1999. La obra forma parte de la exposición "Heaven" de la Tate Gallery de Liverpool.

Un altro materiale, un'altra icona. La scultura di Michael Jackson e la sua scimmietta realizzata da Jeff Koons, esposta a Bubbles, 8 dicembre 1999. La creazione faceva parte della mostra "Heaven" della Tate Gallery di Liverpool.

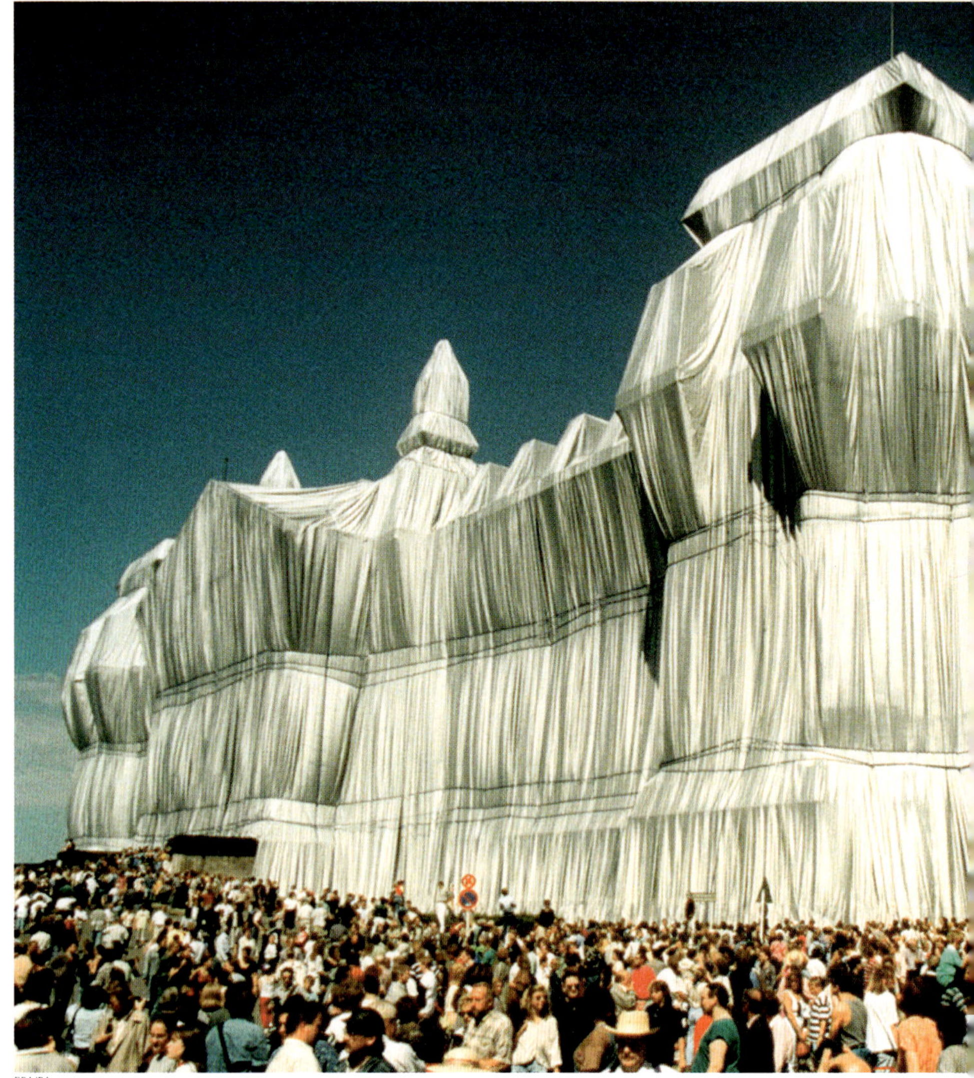

EPA/PA

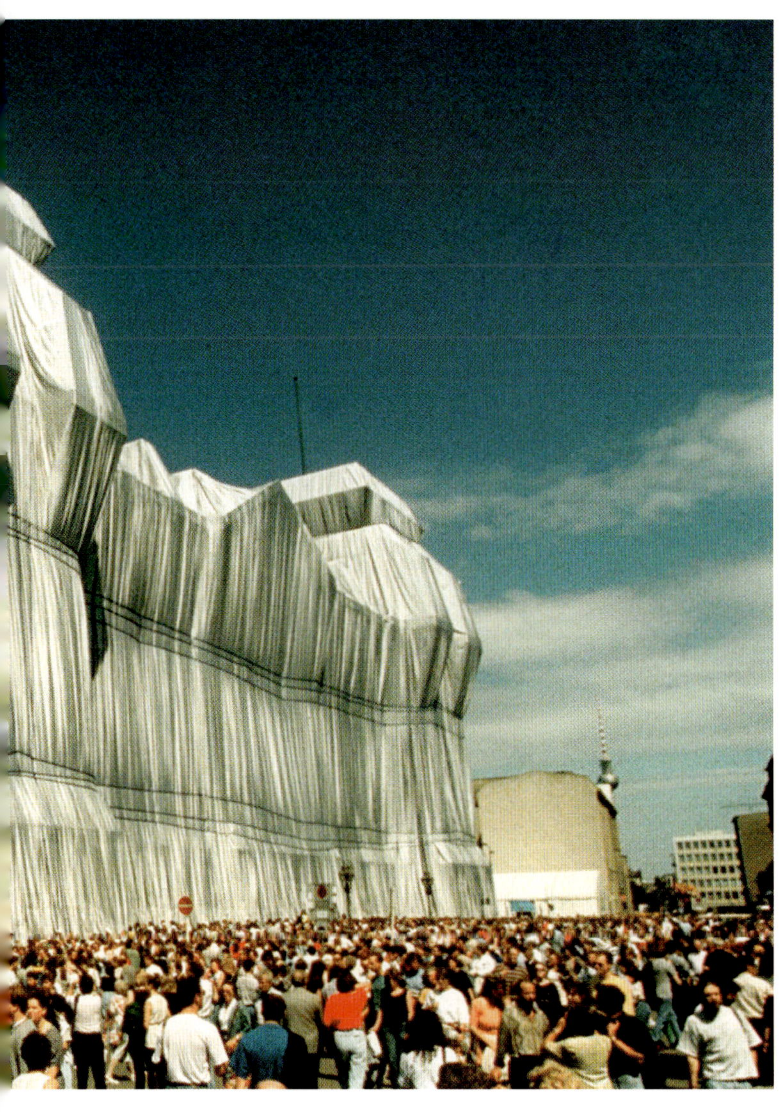

Since 1972 Christo Javacheff had been planning to wrap the Reichstag in Berlin. He finally achieved his ambition in June 1995.

Christo Javacheff venía planeando embalar el Reichstag de Berlín desde 1972. Su deseo por fin se materializó en junio de 1995.

Era dal 1972 che Christo Javacheff desiderava incartare il Reichstag di Berlino, e finalmente ci riuscì nel giugno del 1995.

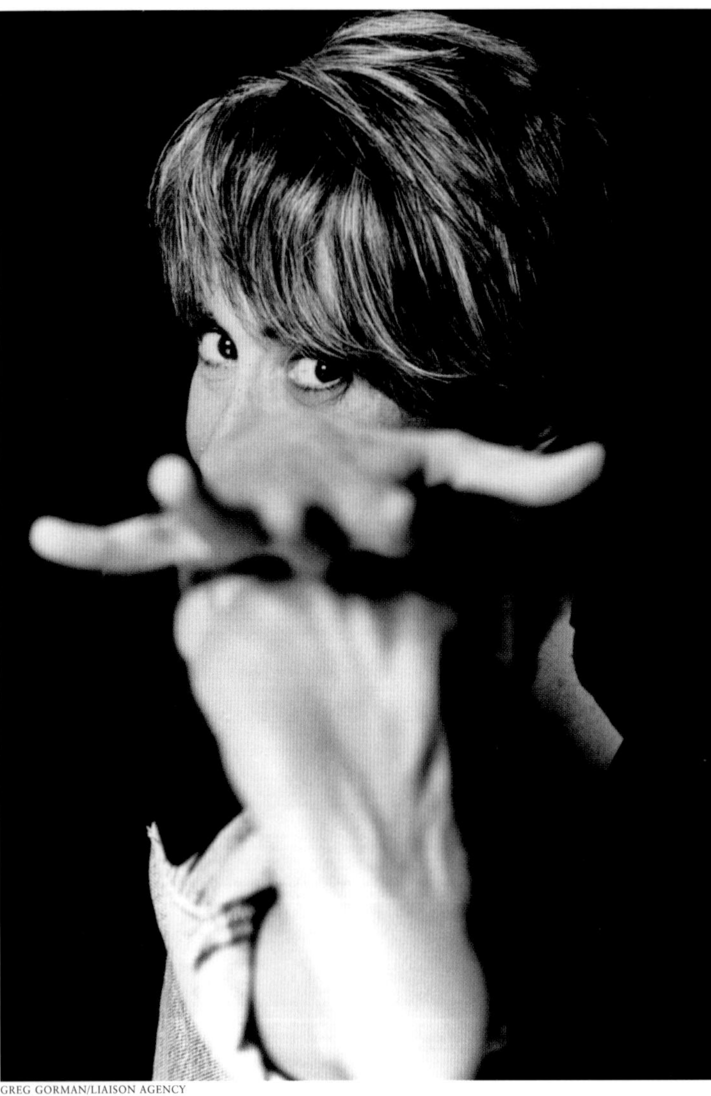

GREG GORMAN/LIAISON AGENCY

Dancing feet. American dancer, choreographer and founder of her own company, Twyla Tharp poses for the camera.

Pies para la danza. La norteamericana Twyla Tharp, bailarina, coreógrafa y fundadora de su propia compañía, posa para la cámara.

Piedi per ballare. La statunitense Twyla Tharp, ballerina, coreografa e fondatrice della propria compagnia, posa di fronte all'obiettivo.

Defending hands. US artist Julian Schnabel, painter and printmaker, best known for such works as *Portrait of José Luis Ferrer*.

Manos para defenderse. El artista estadounidense Julian Schnabel –pintor y artista gráfico– debe su fama a obras tales como *Portrait of José Luis Ferrer.*

Mani per difendersi. L'artista statunitense Julian Schnabel, pittore e incisore, più noto per opere quali *Portrait of José Luis Ferrer*.

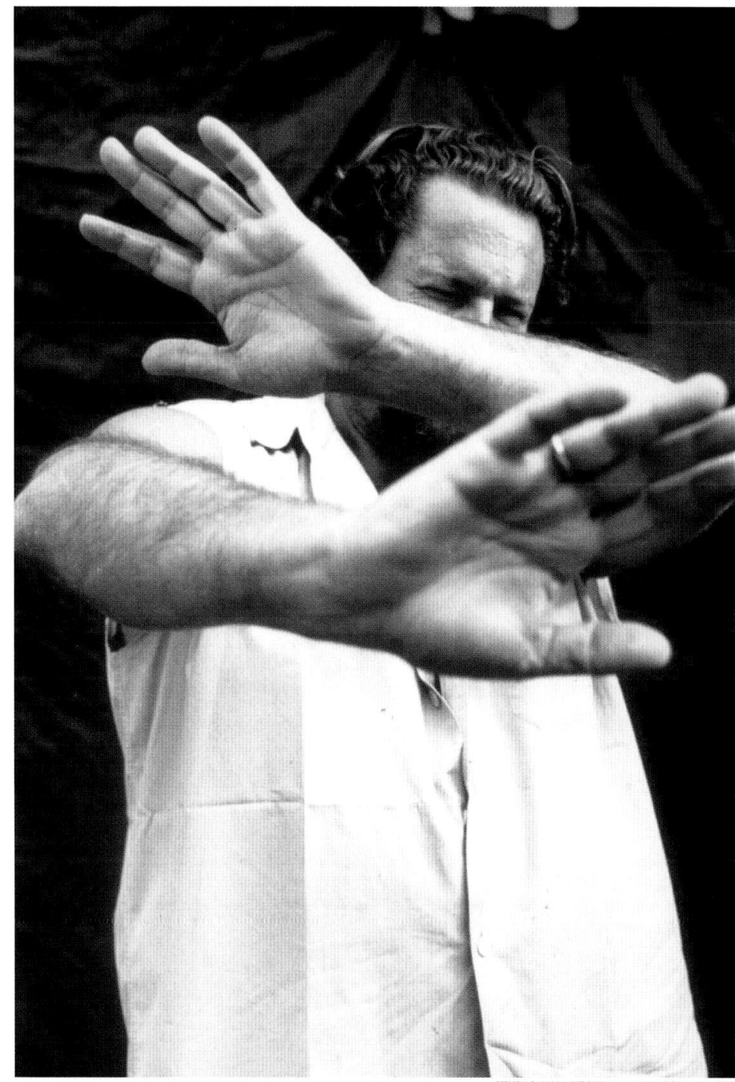

STUDIO VALLETOUX/MPA/LIAISON AGENCY

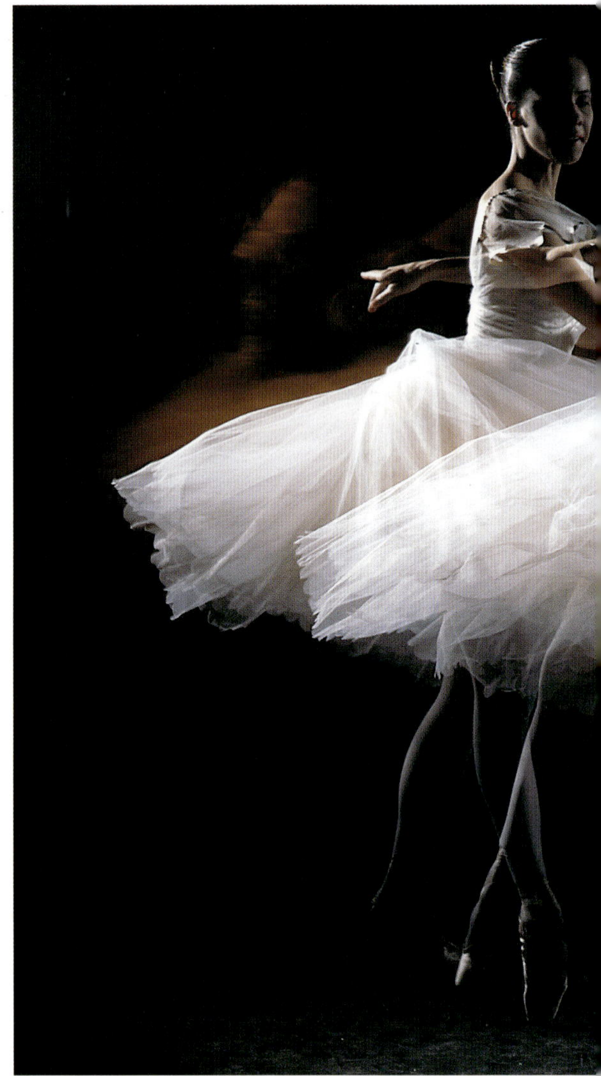

The dance goes on. A pirouetting portrait of the English ballerina Darcy Bussell.

La danza continúa. Retrato de una pirueta de la bailarina inglesa Darcy Bussell.

La danza continua. Una piroetta della ballerina inglese Darcy Bussell.

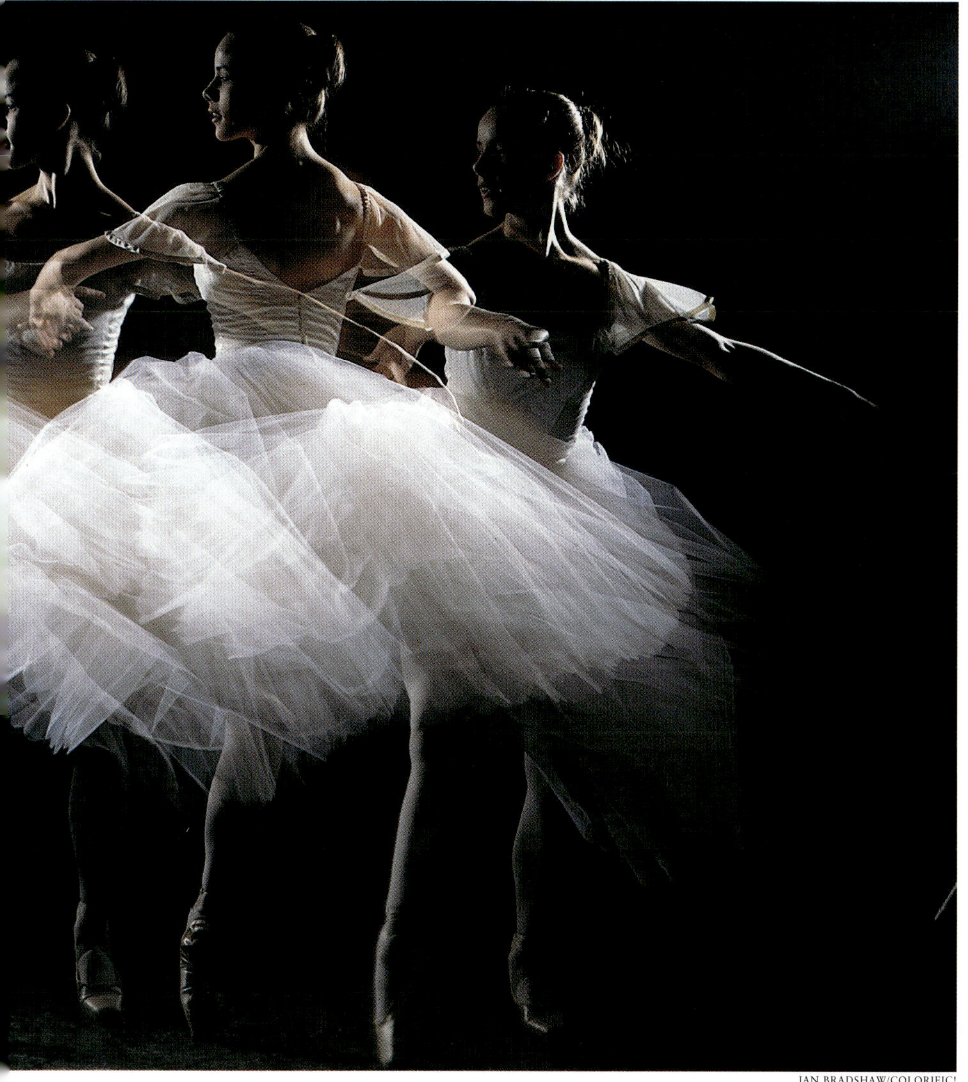

IAN BRADSHAW/COLORIFIC!

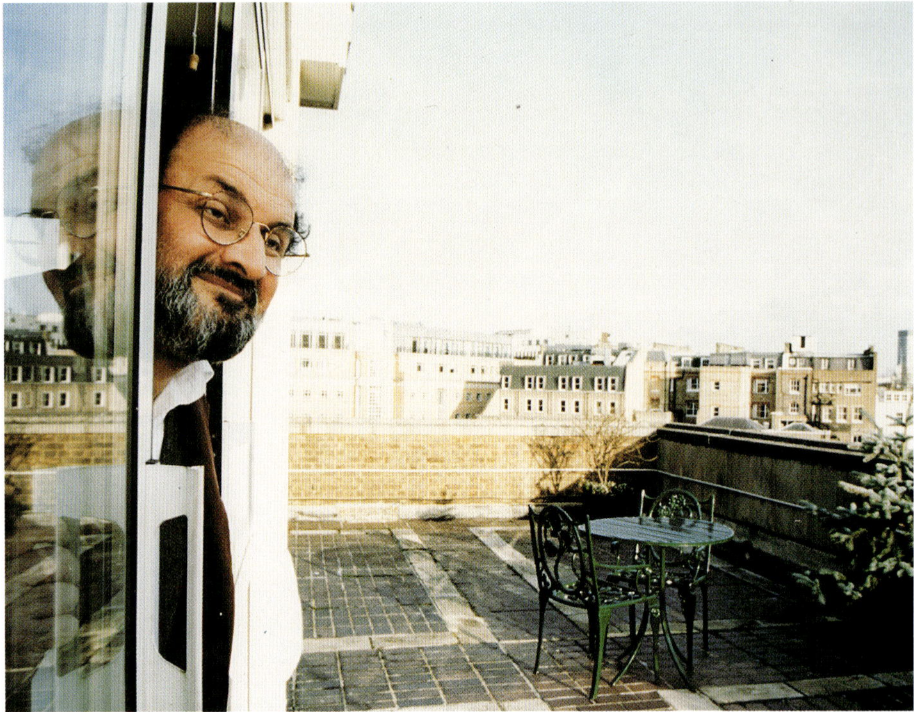

FRANCOIS DARMIGNY/SAOLA/COLORIFIC!

Emerging from his hideout, Salman Rushdie views the 1990s literary scene. His works from the decade included *Haroun and the Sea of Dreams*, *The Moor's Last Sigh*, *The Ground Beneath Her Feet* and *East, West*.

Salman Rushdie sale de su escondrijo para contemplar el panorama literario de los años noventa. Entre los libros que publica durante esta década se cuentan *Harún y el mar de las historias, El último suspiro del moro, El suelo bajo sus pies* y *Oriente, occidente*.

Salman Rushdie, mentre spunta dal suo nascondiglio, contempla la scena letteraria degli anni Novanta. Alcune delle sue opere di quel momento furono *Harun e il mar delle storie, L'ultimo sospiro del moro, La terra sotto i suoi piedi* e *Est, Ovest*.

Mouth wide shut. Martin Amis risks *Time's Arrow* on his way to (much earlier) *Success* in *London Fields*.

Como un libro abierto. Martin Amis arriesga *La flecha del tiempo* en su camino al *Éxito* (muy anterior) en los *Campos de Londres*.

Acqua in bocca. Martin Amis autore della *Freccia del tempo*, di *Success* (scritto anni prima) e di *Territori londinesi*.

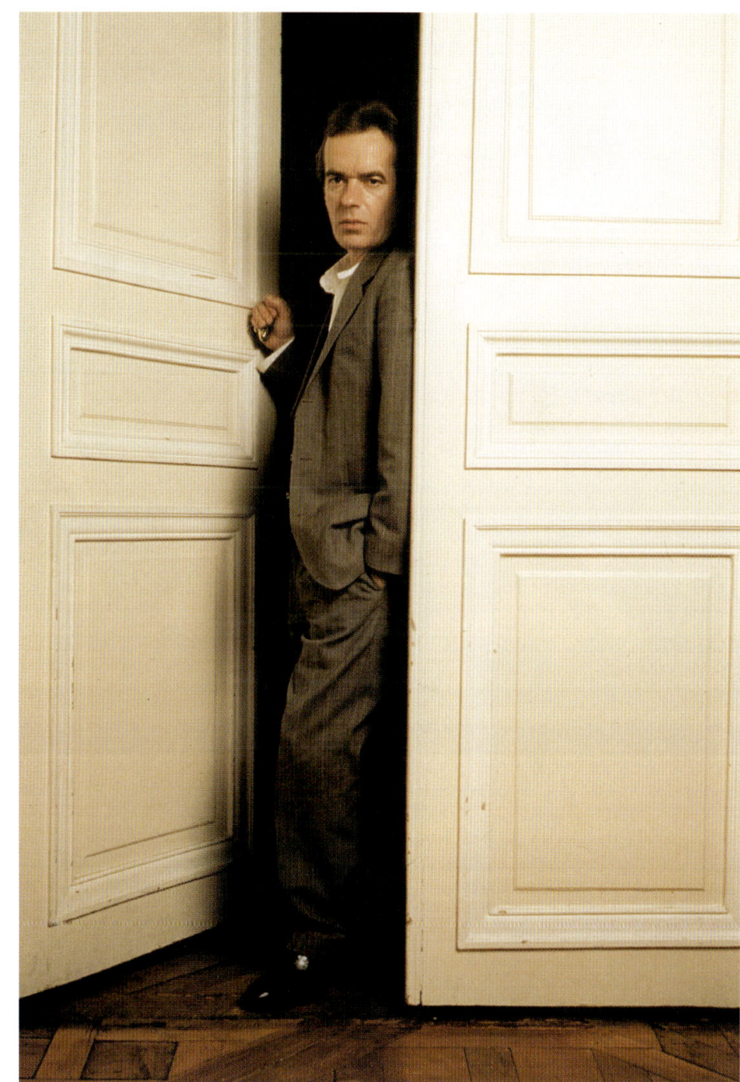

ANDERSEN/SIPA PRESS

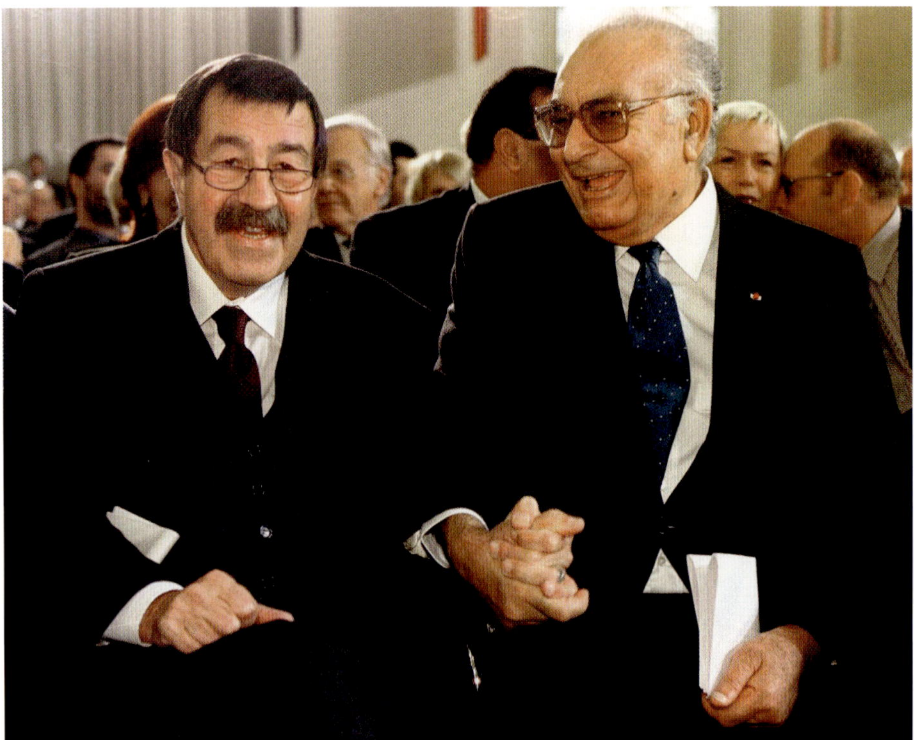

KAI PFAFFENBACH/REUTERS/ARCHIVE PHOTOS

Günter Grass (left) clasps the hand of Turkish author Yasar Kemal after the latter had been awarded the Peace Prize of the German Book Trade at the Frankfurt Book Fair, 19 October 1997.

Günter Grass (izquierda) estrecha la mano del autor turco Yasar Kemal, tras recibir este último el premio de la Paz otorgado por los libreros alemanes en la Feria del Libro de Fráncfort, 19 de octubre de 1997.

Günter Grass (a sinistra) stringe la mano dello scrittore turco Yasar Kemal quando quest'ultimo viene insignito del Premio della pace dell'Associazione dei librai tedeschi, durante la Fiera del libro di Francoforte, 19 ottobre 1997.

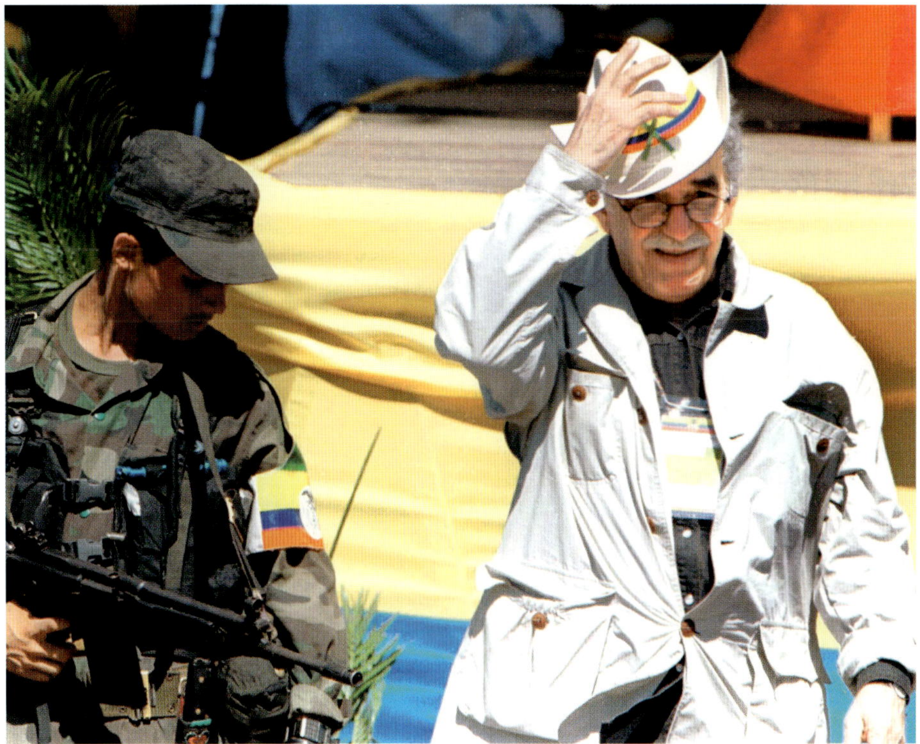

JOSE MIGUEL GOMEZ/REUTERS/ARCHIVE PHOTOS

Nobel prize-winning author Gabriel Garcia Marquez doffs his hat to a left-wing freedom fighter in San Vicente del Caguan, Colombia, 7 January 1999. The writer was on his way to take part in peace talks.

El Nobel de literatura Gabriel García Márquez sujeta su sombrero al pasar junto a un combatiente de la guerrilla en San Vicente del Caguán, Colombia, 7 de enero de 1999. Iba a tomar parte en las conversaciones de paz.

Gabriel García Márquez, vincitore di un premio Nobel, si leva il cappello davanti a un combattente per la libertà del partito di sinistra a San Vicente del Caguán, Colombia, 7 gennaio 1999. Lo scrittore si stava recando a una conferenza sulla pace, alla quale doveva prendere parte.

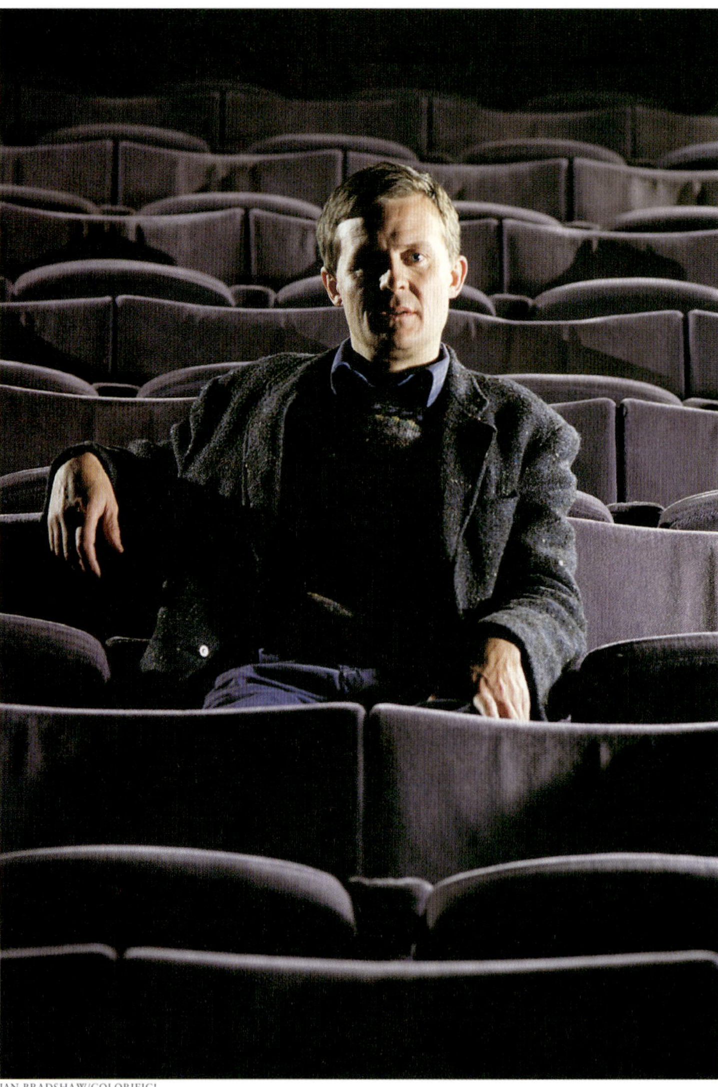

IAN BRADSHAW/COLORIFIC!

English actor, producer, playwright and film director David Hare takes a view from the stalls.

David Hare –actor, productor, dramaturgo y director de cine inglés– retratado en un patio de butacas.

L'inglese David Hare, attore, produttore, drammaturgo e regista, si accomoda in sala.

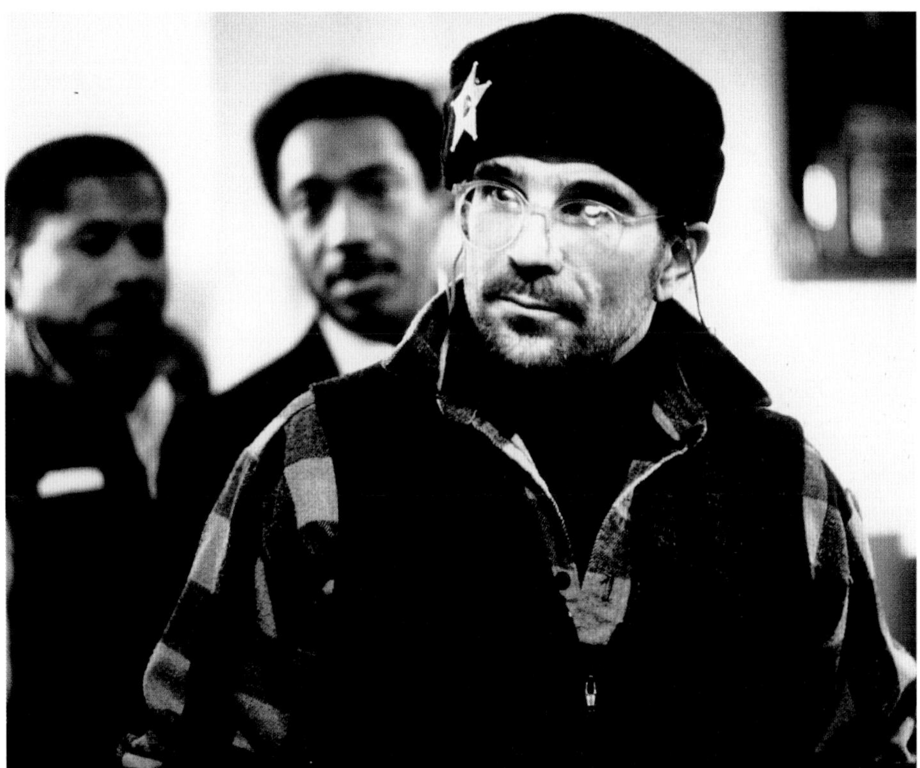

ARCHIVE PHOTOS

American playwright and film director David Mamet on the set of his film *Homicide*, 1991. Among his most successful works in the 1990s were *Glengarry Glen Ross*, *American Buffalo* and *Wag the Dog*.

El cineasta y dramaturgo estadounidense David Mamet durante el rodaje de su película *Homicidio,* en 1991. *Glengarry Glen Ross, El búfalo americano* y *La cortina de humo* son algunos de sus trabajos más aclamados durante los años noventa.

Il drammaturgo e regista statunitense, David Mamet, sul set del film *Homicide*, nel 1991. Fra i suoi più noti capolavori degli anni Novanta si ricordano *Americani, American buffalo* e *Sesso e potere*.

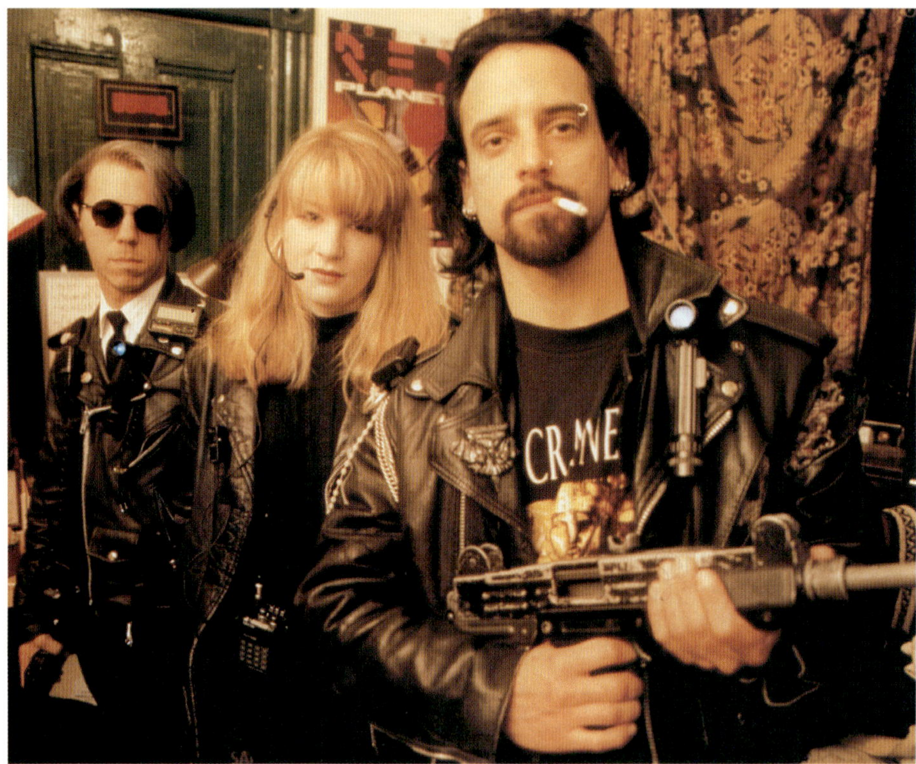

MAX RAMIREZ/BLACK STAR/COLORIFIC!

Cyberpunks, 1994. The phenomenon was created by the writer William Gibson (opposite), and the image was a weird mixture of punk, sci-fi, martial arts, soft drinks and the whole world of cyberspace.

Ciberpunks, 1994. El escritor William Gibson (página siguiente) es el creador de este curioso fenómeno: una extraña mezcla de filosofía *punk*, ciencia ficción, artes marciales y refrescos en el mundo del ciberespacio.

Cyberpunk, 1994. Il fenomeno fu creato dallo scrittore William Gibson (pagina a fianco) e il risultato fu uno strano cocktail di punk, fantascienza, arti marziali, bibite analcoliche e tutto il mondo del cyberspazio.

William Gibson, creator of the *Sprawl* series that included *Neuromancer*, *Count Zero* and *Mona Lisa Overdrive*.

William Gibson, autor de una trilogía de culto compuesta por las novelas *Neuromante, Conde Cero* y *Mona Lisa acelerada*.

William Gibson, creatore della Trilogia dello *Sprawl*, formata da *Negromante, Giù nel cyberspazio* e *Monnalisa cyberpunk*.

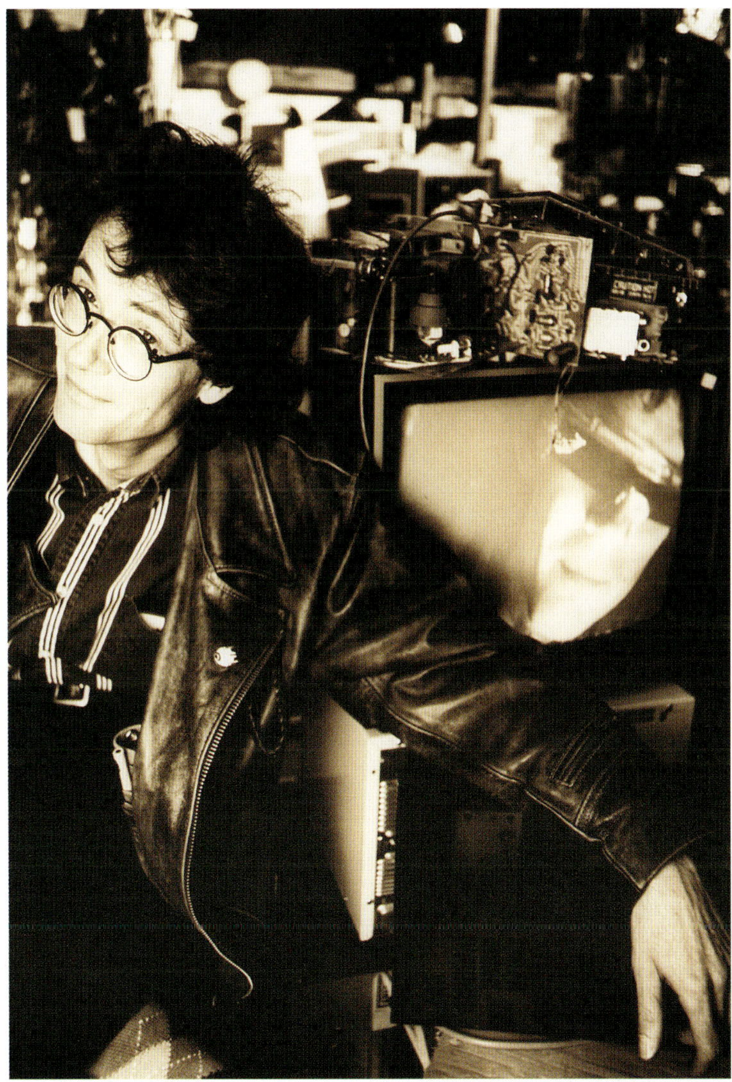

EXLEY/LIAISON AGENCY

7. Pop
La música pop
La musica pop

Keeping the flame of the 1980s alive, the American shock rocker Marilyn Manson ignites his Paris audience, 19 December 1998.

Procurando mantener viva la llama de los años ochenta, el sorprendente roquero Marilyn Manson enciende a su público parisino, 19 de diciembre de 1998.

L'impressionante cantante rock statunitense Marilyn Manson tiene viva la fiamma degli anni Ottanta infuocando i suoi fan parigini, 19 dicembre 1998.

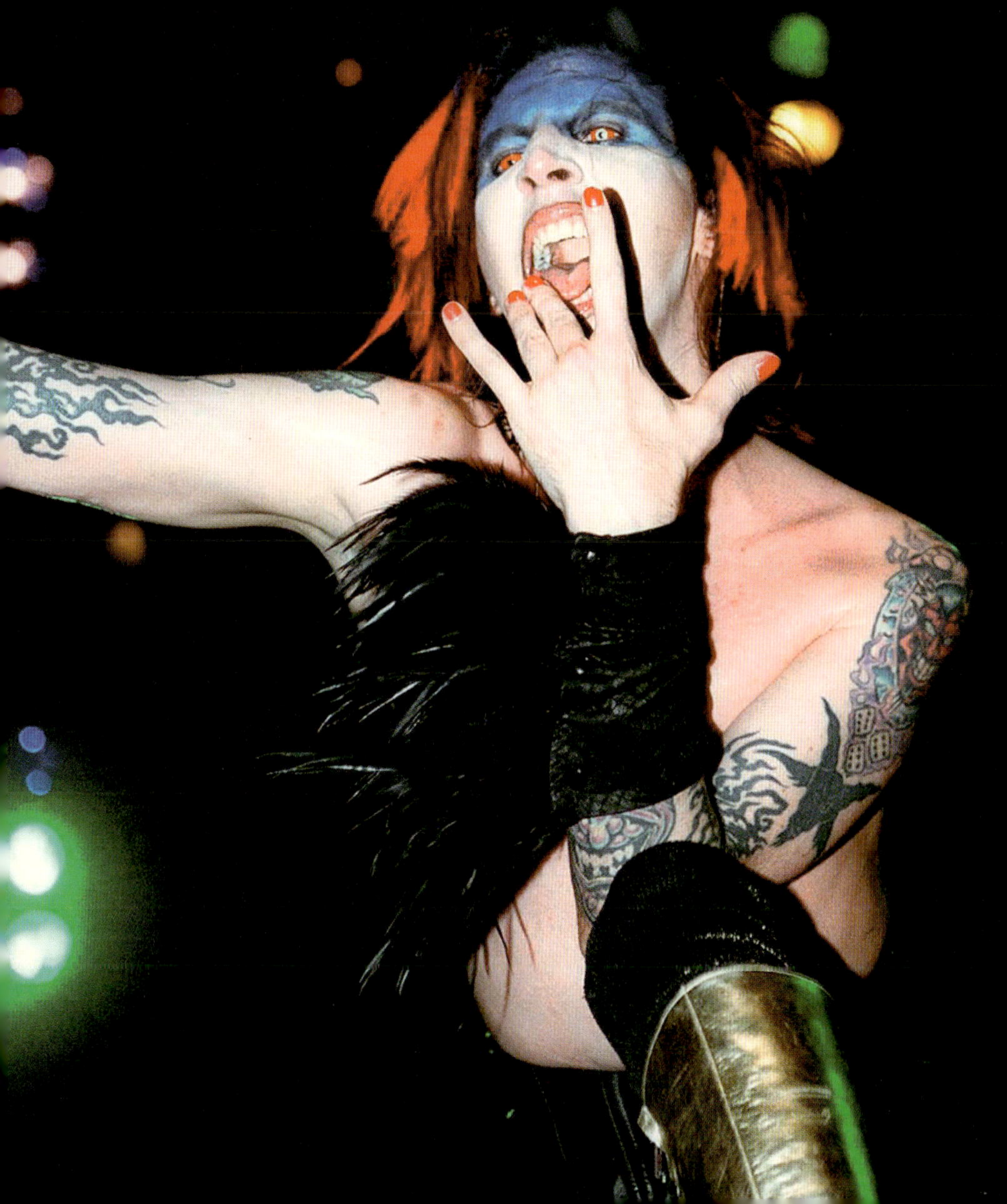

7. Pop
La música pop
La musica pop

In the ever more frantic business of pop it now took too long to discover 'talent'. Better by far for promoters and record companies to identify a niche in the market, set up a publicity machine, and then create a star band or singer from scratch. And the younger such fledgling stars could be fed into the system, the longer their careers might last. Some were all too ephemeral, but Stepz, Boyzone, Westlife and the Spice Girls were all accorded veteran status after a couple of years at the top.

There were still hard-faced, hard-line rockers on the circuit, but the new fashion was for a clean-cut image. Britney Spears tapped into the planet's thirst for morality by flaunting her virginity. The Spice Girls insisted in song that 'if you want to be my lover, you gotta get with my friends...' Michael Jackson, who reached the age of forty in 1998, was rumoured to have sinned, and his career suffered accordingly. Madonna, meanwhile, steered an erratic but successful course between propriety and impropriety.

It was okay to be gay, and Queen superstar Freddie Mercury passed into the All Time Rock 'n' Roll Hall of Fame with his death from AIDS in November 1991.

Descubrir nuevos "talentos" en la cada vez más frenética industria de la música pop es ahora más difícil que antes. Sin embargo, a las discográficas y a los promotores les resulta bastante más fácil identificar nichos de mercado, poner en marcha la maquinaria publicitaria y crear así, de la nada, un grupo o un cantante de éxito. Y cuanto más jóvenes sean estas nuevas estrellas al ser introducidas en el sistema, mayores posibilidades tendrán sus carreras de perdurar. Algunas serán verdaderamente efímeras pero Stepz, Boyzone, Westlife y las Spice Girls lograrán el estatus de veteranos tras conseguir mantenerse un par de años en los primeros puestos de las listas de éxitos.

Si bien es cierto que los auténticos roqueros de siempre continúan presentes en el panorama musical, la nueva moda que se impone es la de artistas con una imagen que roza la perfección. Britney Spears apaga la sed de moralidad del planeta haciendo alarde de su virginidad mientras que las Spice Girls reiteran en una de sus canciones que "si deseas ser mi amante, primero has de ser mi amigo...". Se rumorea que Michael Jackson –quien cumple 40 años en 1998– ha cometido ciertos pecados, lo cual perjudicará seriamente su carrera artística. Entre tanto, Madonna sigue una trayectoria errática –aunque jalonada de éxitos– que se debate entre el decoro y la obscenidad.

Ser gay está aceptado; Freddie Mercury, la superestrella del grupo Queen, pasará a los anales del *rock 'n' roll* por su prematura muerte, víctima del sida, en noviembre de 1991.

Nel sempre più frenetico mondo del pop ci voleva ormai troppo tempo per scoprire nuovi "talenti". Per i promotori e per le società discografiche era di gran lunga più interessante localizzare una nicchia nel mercato, mettere in moto la macchina pubblicitaria, e solo in un secondo momento tirare fuori dal nulla una band o un solista. E quanto più giovani erano le star da integrare nel sistema, tanto più a lungo sarebbero potute durare le loro carriere. Alcune furono troppo effimere, ma Stepz, Boyzone, Westlife e le Spice Girls divennero tutti veterani dopo solo un paio di anni in vetta alle classifiche.

Il mercato poteva offrire ancora alcuni rocker brutti, sporchi e cattivi, ma la nuova moda tendeva sempre di più verso un'immagine di bravi ragazzi con la faccia pulita. Britney Spears sfruttava la sete di moralità che aveva il pianeta, sventolando ai quattro venti la sua verginità. Le Spice Girls continuavano a dire in una delle loro canzoni che "...se vuoi essere il mio amante, devi stare con le mie amiche...". Si diceva che Michael Jackson, che nel 1998 aveva compiuto quarant'anni, avesse peccato, e la sua carriera ne pagò le conseguenze, mentre Madonna seguiva una rotta erratica, seppure piena di successi, a cavallo fra decoro e indecenza.

Essere gay non era più un problema, e la morte della superstar dei Queen, Freddie Mercury, avvenuta nel novembre del 1991, gli apriva le porte dell'Olimpo degli eterni miti del Rock 'n' Roll.

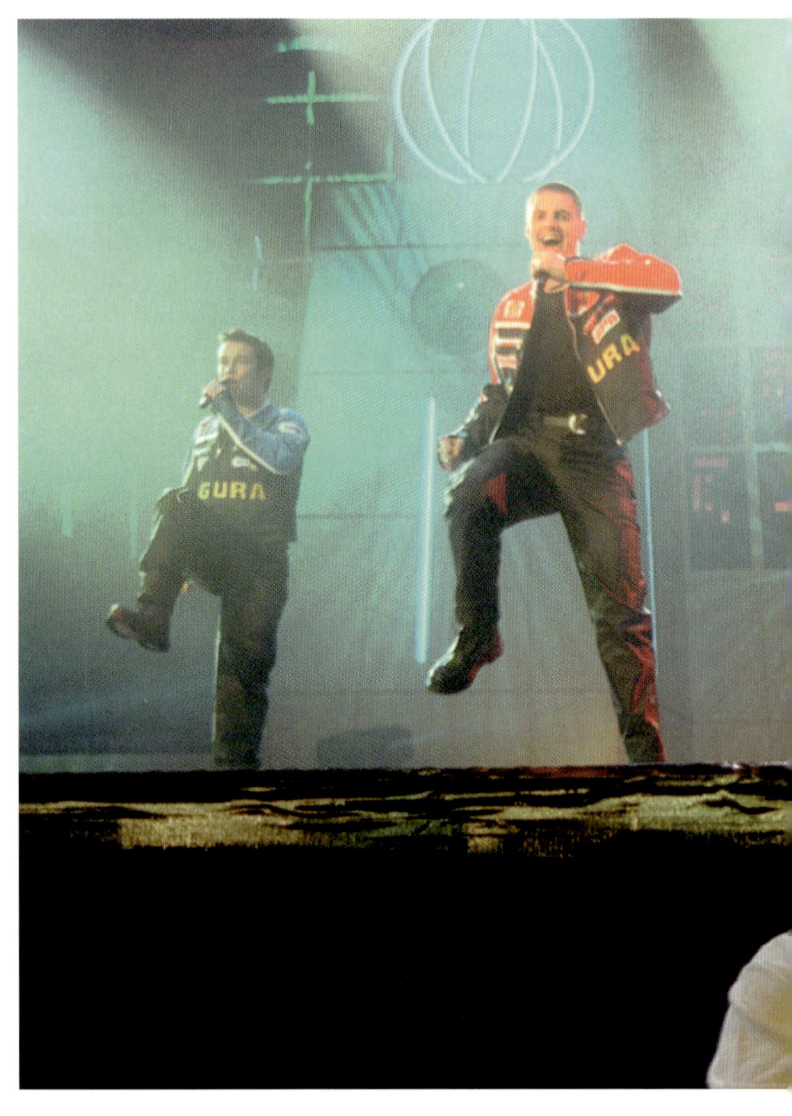

Unmoved, a security guard protects Boyzone during the *Smash Hits* 1995 Poll Winners Party, London, 3 December 1995.

Imperturbable, un guarda de seguridad se encarga de proteger a los Boyzone durante la fiesta organizada en Londres, el 3 de diciembre de 1995, por la revista *Smash Hits* para los ganadores del concurso de ese año.

Impassibile, un addetto alla sicurezza protegge i Boyzone durante lo Smash Hits Poll Winners' Party 1995, Londra, 3 dicembre 1995.

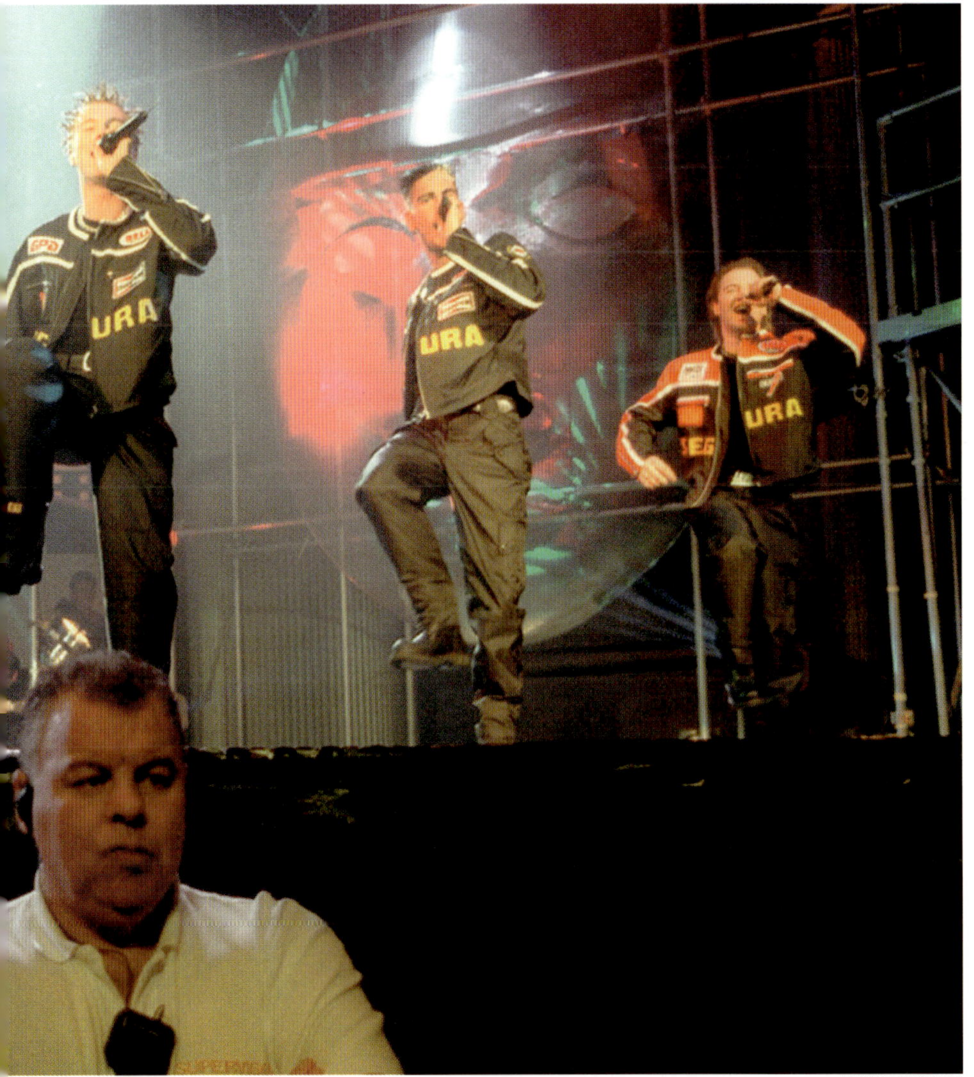

STEFAN ROUSSEAU/PA

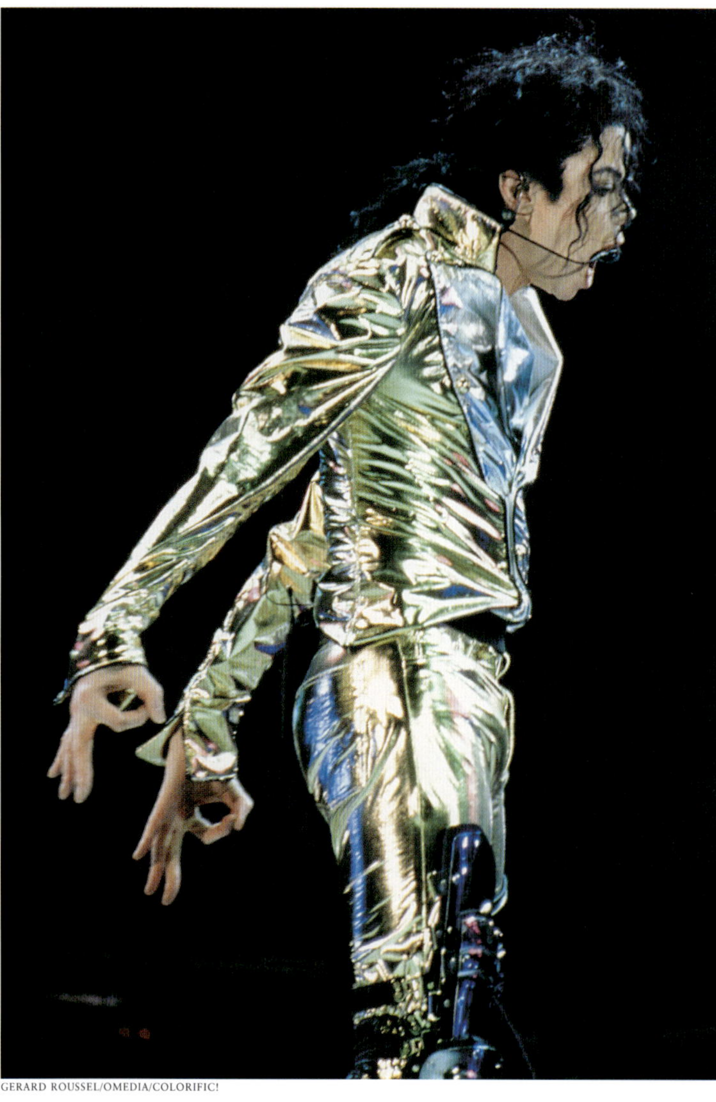

GERARD ROUSSEL/OMEDIA/COLORIFIC!

Oh, brother… Michael Jackson in full flow, HIStory World Tour, Prague, 7 September 1996.

Oh, hermano… Michael Jackson en plena actuación dentro de su gira mundial HIStory, en la ciudad de Praga, 7 de septiembre de 1996.

Oh, fratello… Michael Jackson a pieno ritmo durante il suo HIStory World Tour, Praga, 7 settembre 1996.

Oh, sister… Janet Jackson at full stretch in the Sheffield Arena, Yorkshire, April 1995.

Oh, hermana… Janet Jackson a todo gas en el Sheffield Arena de Yorkshire en abril de 1995.

Oh, sorella… Janet Jackson a tutto gas nella Sheffield Arena, Yorkshire, aprile 1995.

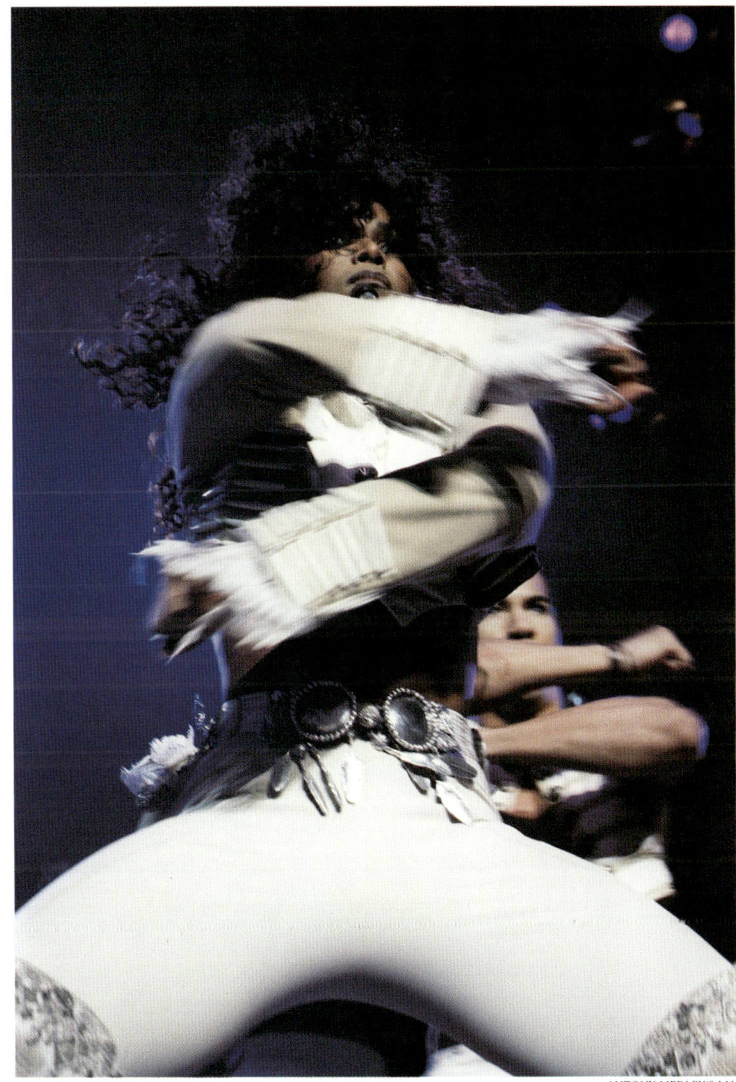

ANTONY MEDLEY/S.I.N.

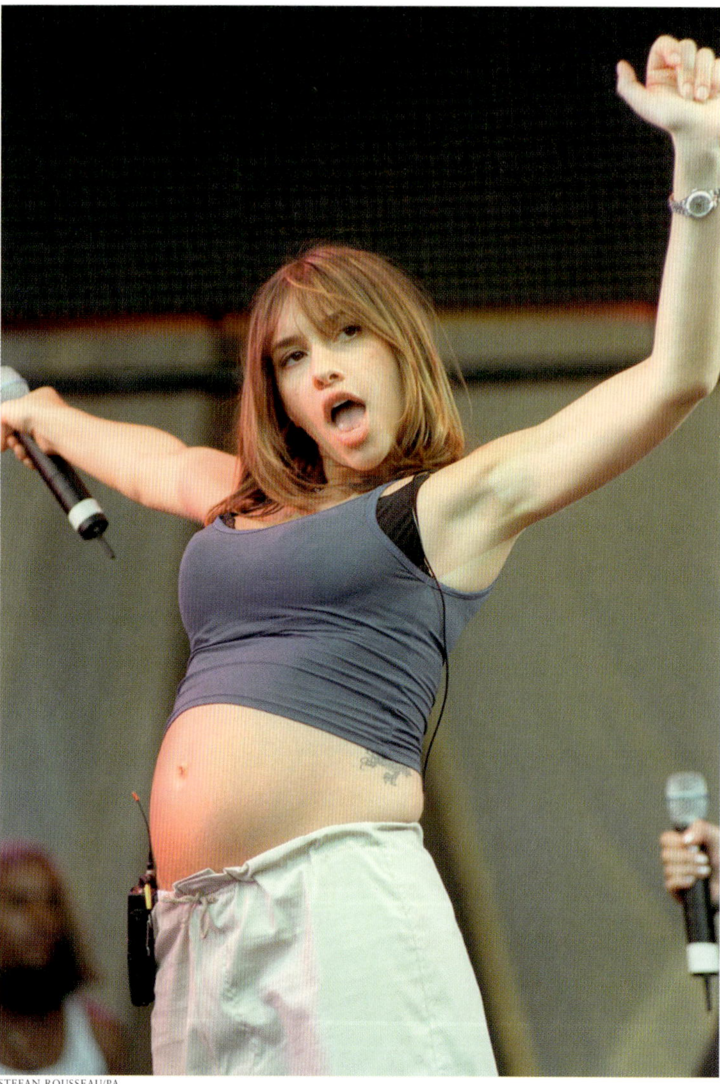

STEFAN ROUSSEAU/PA

A pregnant Melanie Blatt of All Saints on stage at the Party in the Park concert for the Prince's Trust, London, 5 July 1998.

Una embarazada Melanie Blatt del grupo All Saints en el escenario del concierto Party in the Park en Londres, 5 de julio de 1998. Los beneficios se destinaron a la organización de ayuda a la juventud del príncipe de Gales, el Prince's Trust.

Melanie Blatt delle All Saints, incinta, sul palco durante il Party in the Park in occasione del Prince's Trust, Londra, 5 luglio 1998.

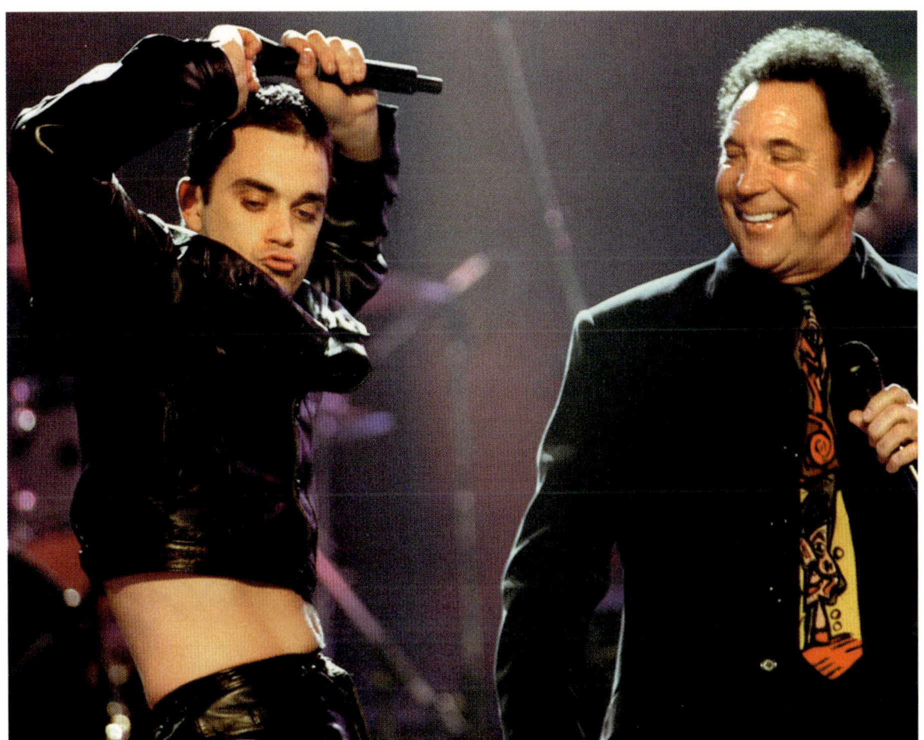

FIONA HANSON/PA

Robbie Williams (left) and Tom Jones duet at the Brit Awards, London Docklands Arena, 9 February 1998. Williams was romantically linked with another of All Saints, Natalie Appleton.

Robbie Williams (izquierda) y Tom Jones actúan a dúo en el Docklands Arena de Londres durante los Brit Awards, 9 de febrero de 1998. Williams mantenía un idilio con Natalie Appleton, otra de las componentes de All Saints.

Il duetto Robbie Williams (a sinistra) e Tom Jones durante i Brit Awards nella Docklands Arena, Londra, 9 febbraio 1998. Williams era unito sentimentalmente a un'altra componente delle All Saints, Natalie Appleton.

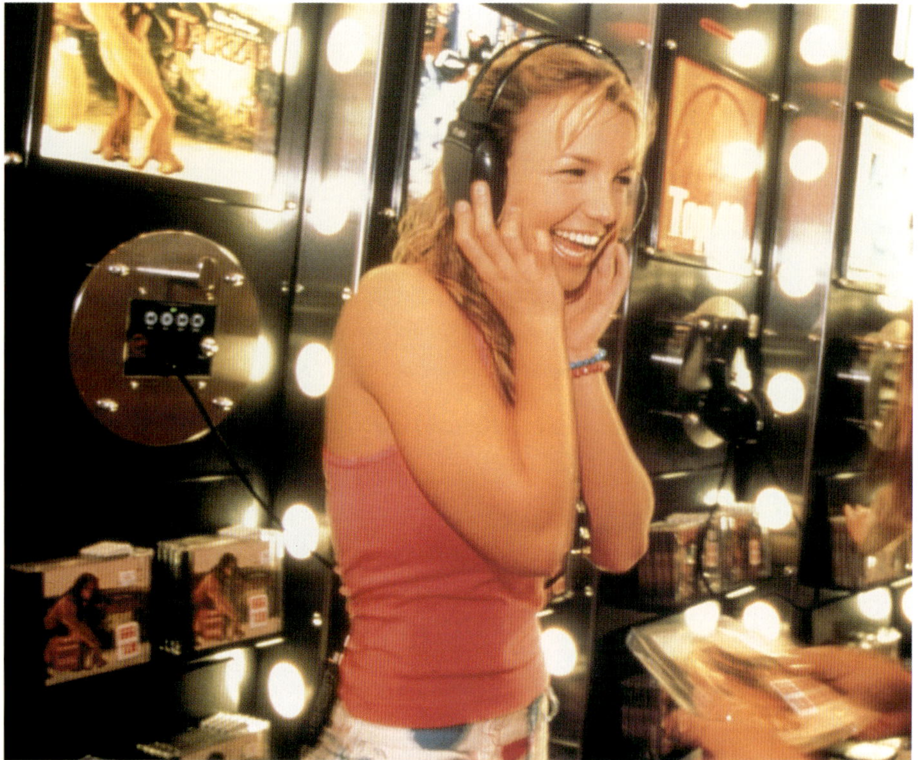

COLORIFIC!

Britney Spears enjoys a playback in 1998, the year her career took off. Following her Month in the Malls promotional tour, she released *Baby, One More Time*. The rest was instant history.

Britney Spears se divierte escuchando su disco en 1998, año en que despega su carrera musical. Tras la gira promocional Month in the Malls, lanza el sencillo *Baby, One More Time*. El resto ya es historia.

Britney Spears si diverte mentre si riascolta nel 1998, l'anno in cui la sua carriera prese il volo. Dopo il tour promozionale Month in the Malls pubblicò *Baby, one more time*. Il resto è storia dei nostri giorni.

A promotional shot of the Spice Girls for their 1997 movie *Spiceworld*. They were then at the height of their fame and success.

Instantánea de promoción de las Spice Girls con motivo de su película *Spiceworld*, de 1997. En esos momentos se hallaban en el punto culminante de su éxito y celebridad.

Una foto promozionale delle Spice Girls per il film *Spiceworld*. Erano al culmine della fama e del successo.

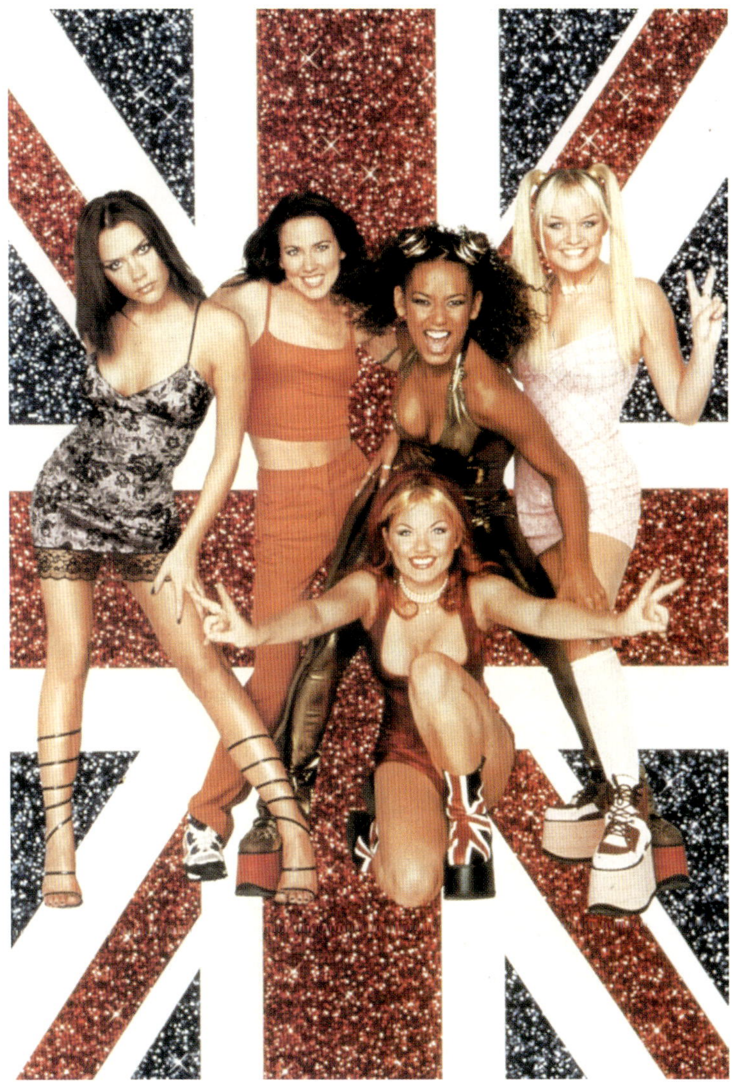

COLORIFIC!

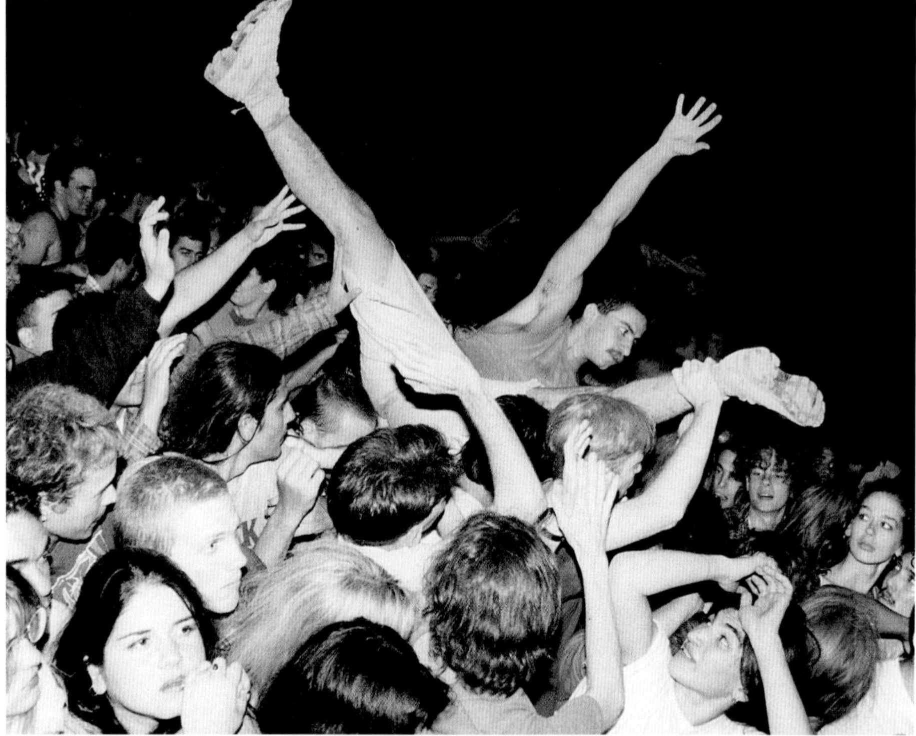

LINDSAY BRICE/VISAGES/COLORIFIC!

The fan who headed for the stars… Part of the audience at a Sonic Youth gig, 1992. They made their name with *Bad Moon Rising* in the late 1980s, and became one of the first alternative bands to hit the big time in the early 1990s.

Un fan intentando alcanzar a sus estrellas… Parte del público asistente a un concierto de Sonic Youth en 1992. La banda se dio a conocer a finales de los ochenta con su trabajo *Bad Moon Rising* y se convirtió en uno de los primeros grupos alternativos que triunfaron a principios de la década de 1990.

Fan che toccano le stelle… Una parte del pubblico durante un concerto dei Sonic Youth, 1992. Il gruppo divenne famoso grazie a *Bad moon rising*, alla fine degli anni Ottanta, e divenne una delle prime band alternative ad avere successo agli inizi del decennio successivo.

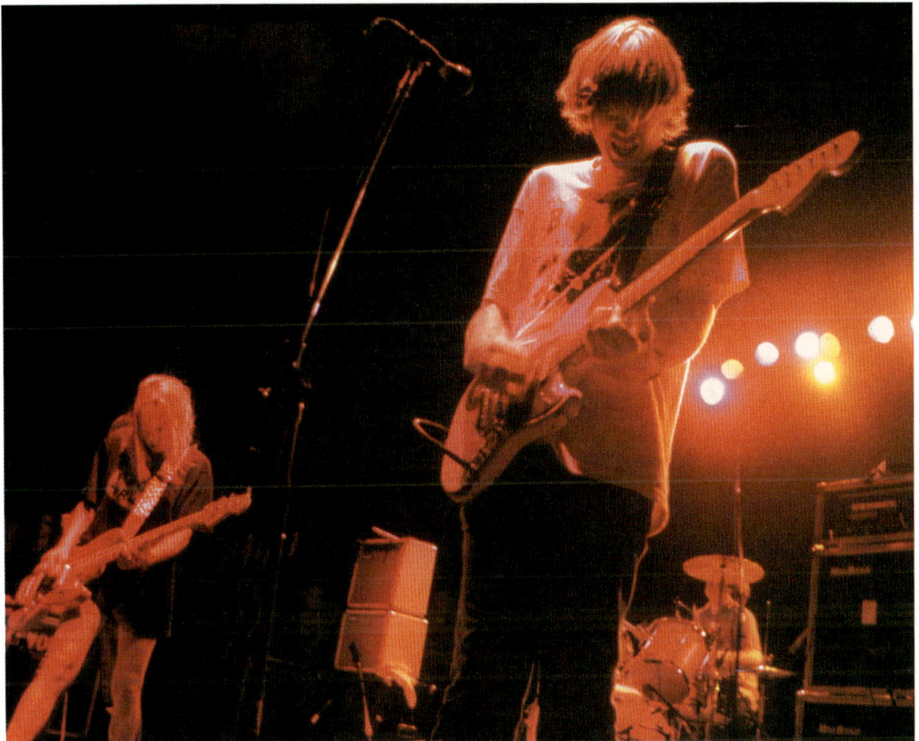

LINDSAY BRICE/VISAGES/COLORIFIC!

Sonic Youth on stage at the same concert. It was the year they released their pop-oriented hit album *Dirty*. Ahead lay *A Thousand Leaves* (1998) and *NYC Ghosts and Flowers* (2000).

Sonic Youth en el escenario durante el mismo concierto. 1992 es también el año en que lanzan su aclamado álbum *Dirty*, un disco con tintes pop, al que seguirían *A Thousand Leaves* (1998) y *NYC Ghosts and Flowers* (2000).

I Sonic Youth sul palco durante lo stesso concerto. Era l'anno in cui pubblicarono *Dirty*, album dalle melodie pop, seguito poi da *A thousand leaves* (1998) e *NYC ghosts and flowers* (2000).

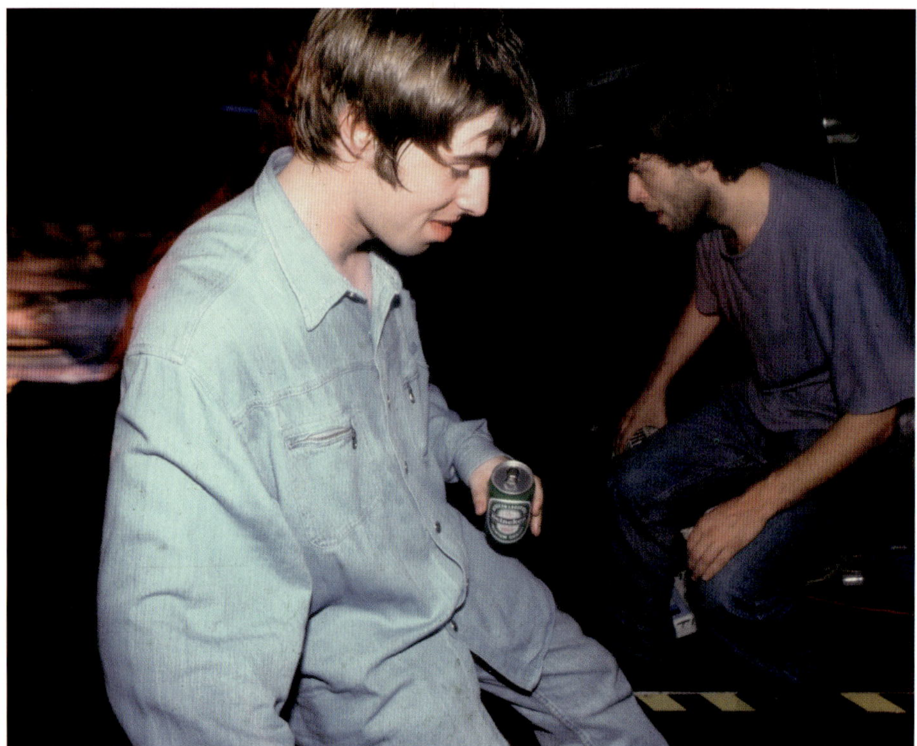

MICK HUTSON/IDOLS

The perils of pop… Noel Gallagher of Oasis left the band three times in the 1990s. He blamed his brother Liam's drinking habits for the repeated splits.

Los peligros del pop… Noel Gallagher, de Oasis, abandonó el grupo tres veces durante los noventa; lo atribuía a los excesos de su hermano Liam con la bebida.

Il rischio del pop… Noel Gallagher del gruppo Oasis abbandonò tre volte la band negli anni Novanta perché suo fratello Liam era troppo propenso a bere.

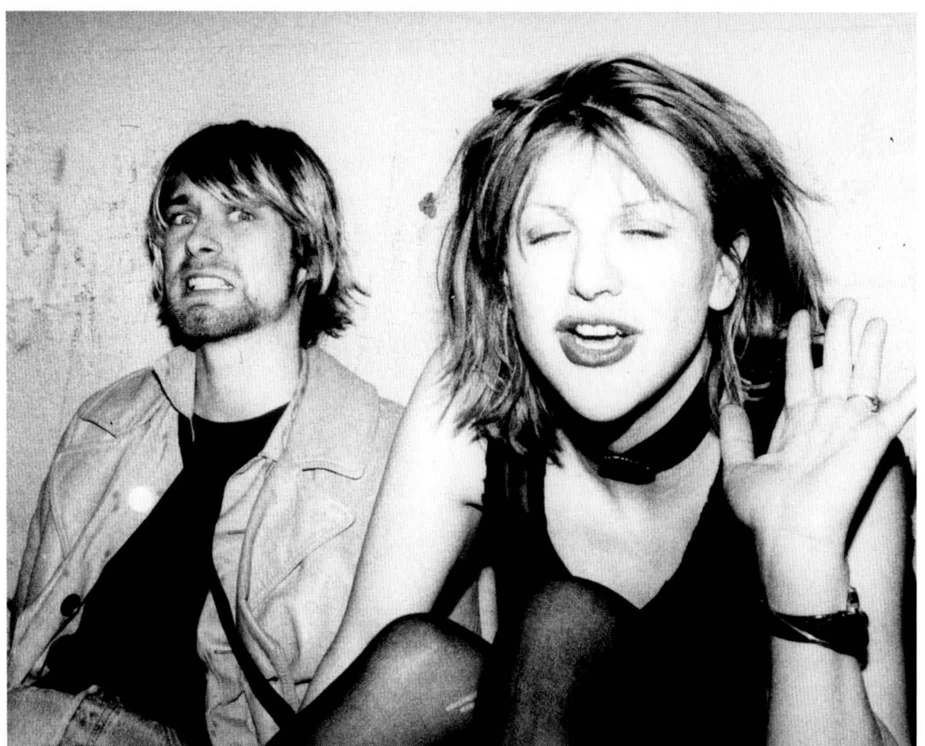

LINDSAY BRICE/VISAGES/COLORIFIC!

The tragedy of pop... Kurt Cobain of grunge band Nirvana and his wife Courtney Love of Hole. Cobain killed himself, leaving a note which ended: 'Please keep going, Courtney... I love you, I love you.'

La tragedia del pop... Kurt Cobain de la formación de música *grunge* Nirvana y su mujer Courtney Love, del grupo Hole. Cobain se suicidó y dejó una nota que acababa con las palabras: "Sigue adelante, Courtney, por favor... Te quiero, te quiero".

La tragedia del pop... Kurt Cobain della band grunge Nirvana, assieme a sua moglie Courtney Love, del gruppo Hole. Cobain si suicidò, lasciando una nota che finiva con: "Courtney non mollare... Ti amo, ti amo".

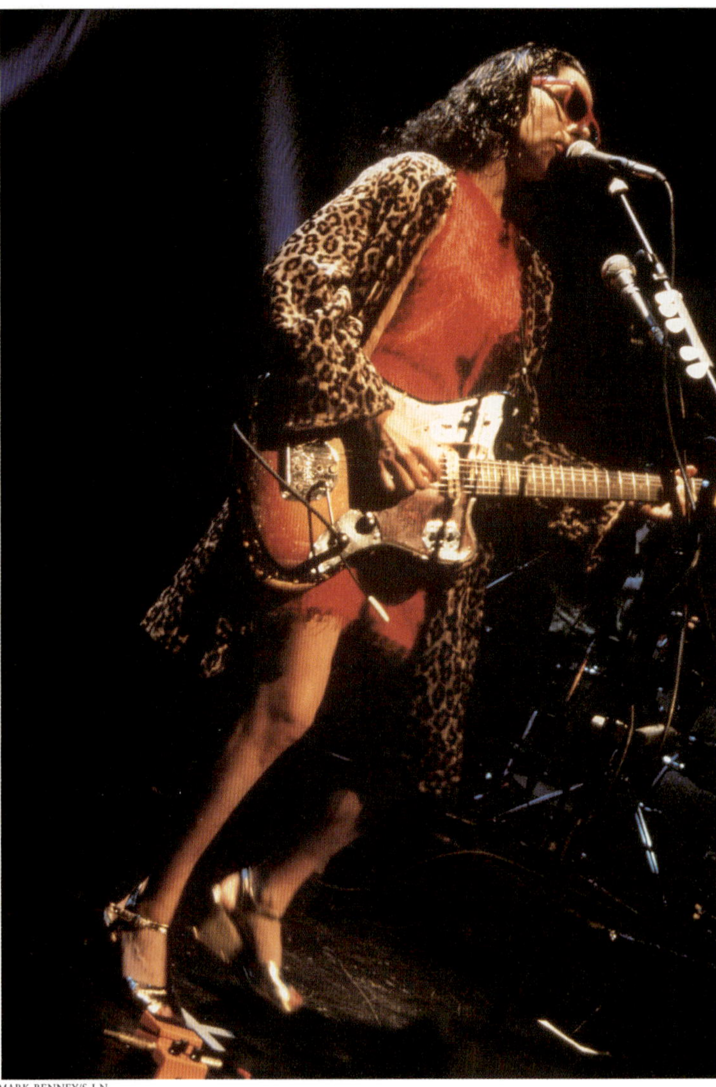

MARK BENNEY/S.I.N.

P J Harvey discovers the joys of dressing up, earning herself the label 'indie-Madonna' along the way.

P. J. Harvey descubre los placeres del disfraz y se gana el apelativo de "la Madonna *indie*".

P. J. Harvey scopre i piaceri dell'abbigliamento chic, guadagnandosi l'etichetta di "Madonna indipendente".

Prince reveals his new persona, bearing on his cheeks the self-inflicted labels 'The Artist Formerly Known As Prince' and 'Slave'.

Prince revela su nueva identidad haciéndose llamar "The Artist Formerly Known As Prince" ('El artista anteriormente conocido como Prince') y pintándose en el moflete la palabra "slave" ('esclavo').

Prince svela il suo nuovo personaggio, scrivendosi sulle guance i suoi due nuovi appellativi "The artist formerly known as Prince" e "Slave".

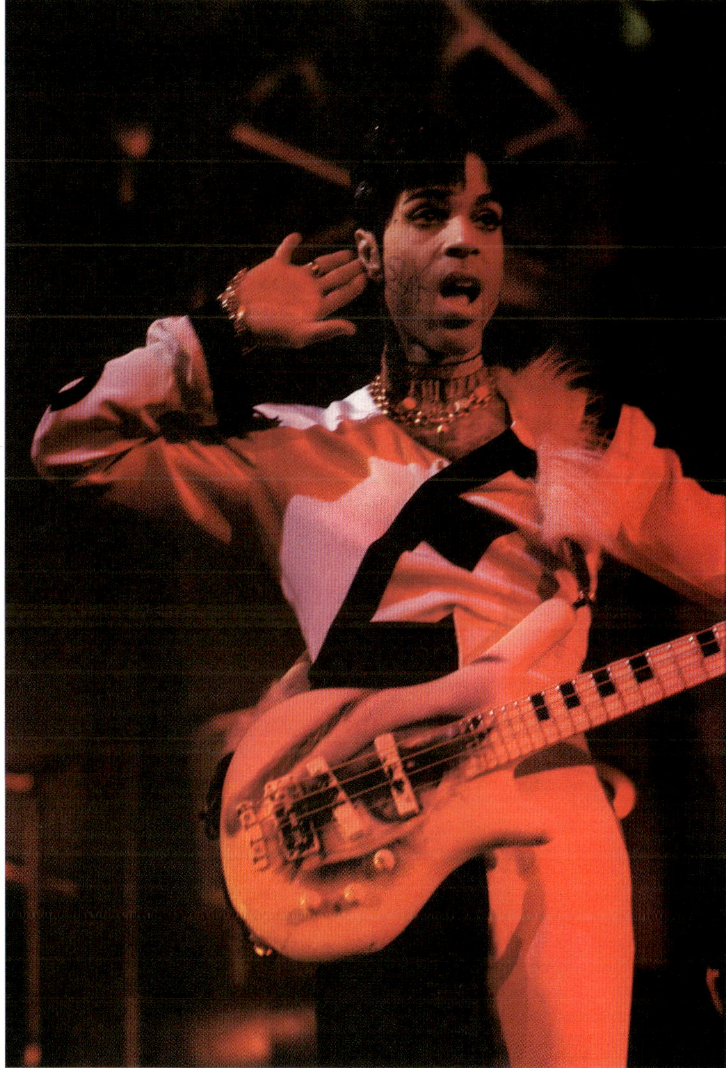

RUSSELL SACH/COLORIFIC!

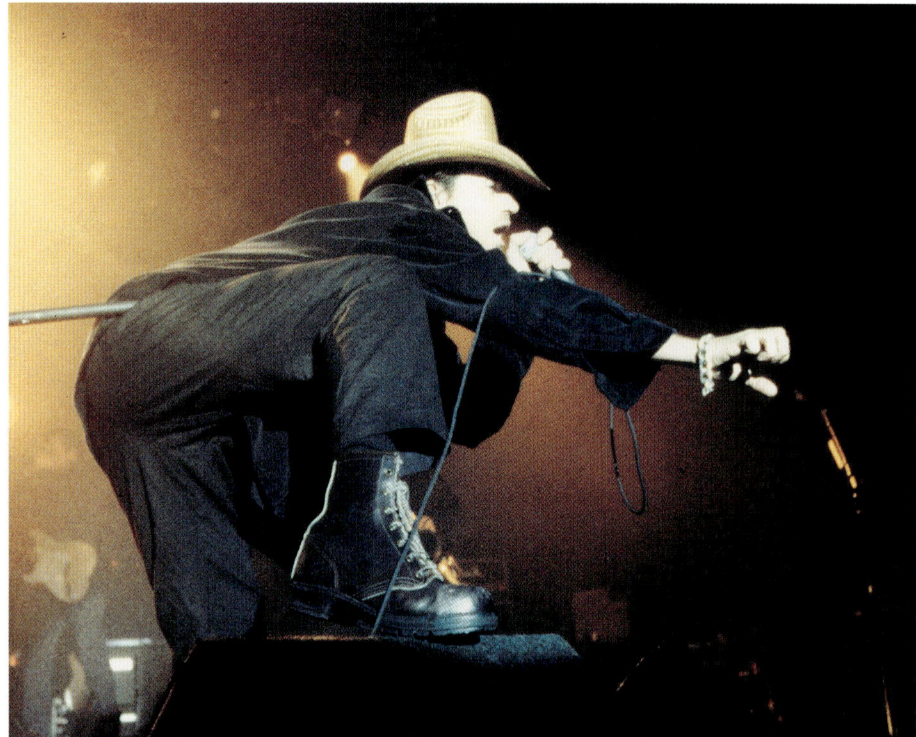

RICHARD BELAND/S.I.N.

Australian rock star Michael Hutchence of INXS at Marine Terminal 28, 19 November 1993. In an eventful but tragically short life, Hutchence partnered Helena Christensen, Kylie Minogue and Paula Yates before hanging himself in 1997.

La estrella de *rock* australiana Michael Hutchence del grupo INXS, en el Marine Terminal 28, 19 de noviembre de 1993. En el transcurso de su corta pero intensa vida, Hutchence fue pareja de Helena Christensen, Kylie Minogue y Paula Yates, antes de ahorcarse en 1997.

La rock star australiana degli INXS, Michael Hutchence, al Marine Terminal 28, 19 novembre 1993. Durante la sua movimentata, ma tragicamente breve vita, Hutchence fu il partner di Helena Christensen, Kylie Minogue e di Paula Yates, prima di impiccarsi nel 1997.

Kylie Minogue and Nick Cave. The two Australians surprised everyone by singing together on the 1996 hit single *Where the Wild Roses Grow*.

Kylie Minogue y Nick Cave. La pareja de australianos sorprendió a todo el mundo cantando a dúo el popular tema *Where the Wild Roses Grow*, en 1996.

Kylie Minogue e Nick Cave. I due australiani sorpresero tutti quanti cantando insieme, nel 1996, il single *Where the wild roses grow*.

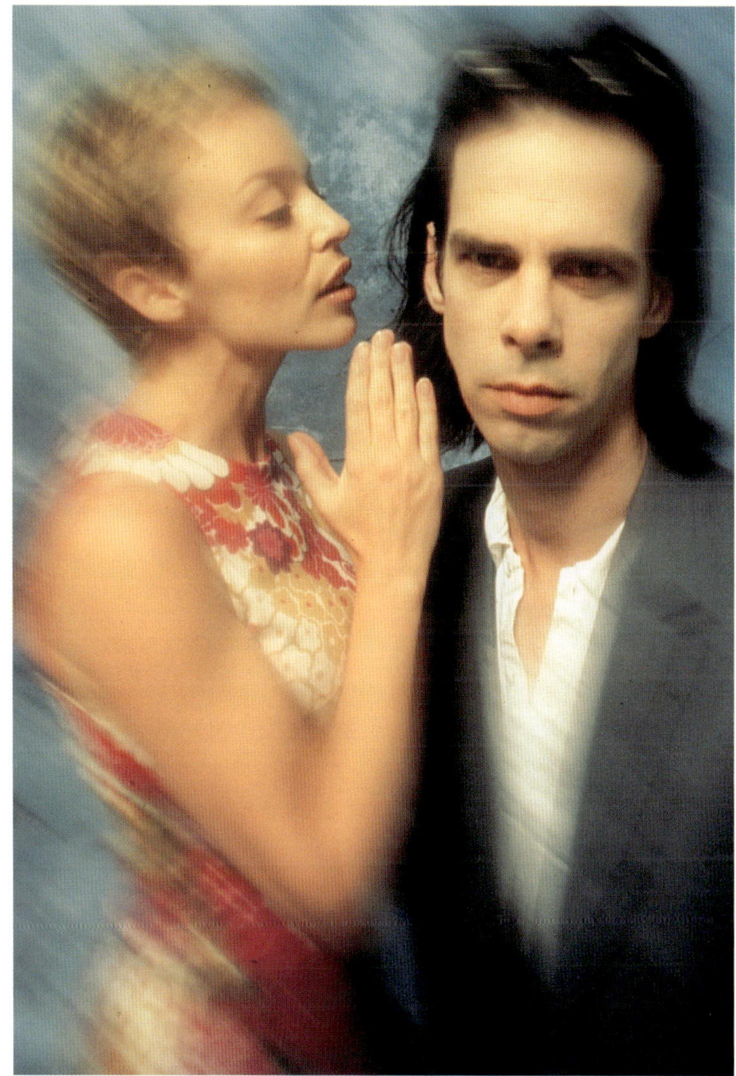

TONY MOTT/S.I.N.

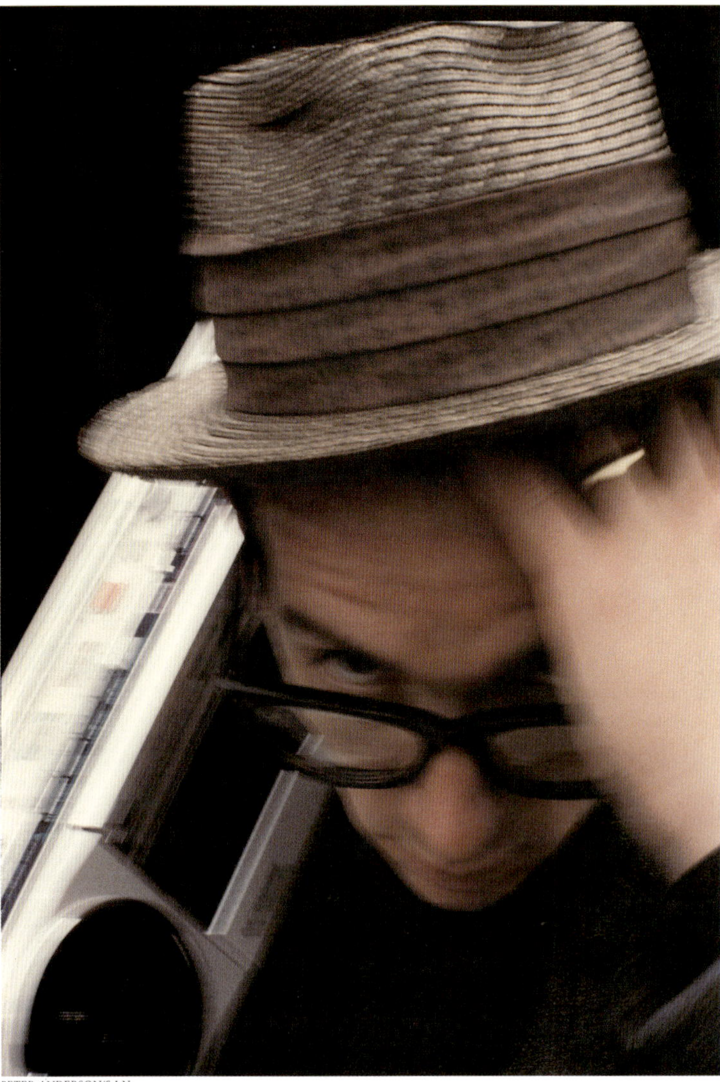

PETER ANDERSON/S.I.N.

Elvis Costello indulges his eclectic musical tastes while on the go, 1994.

Elvis Costello se entrega a sus eclécticas preferencias musicales (1994).

Elvis Costello appaga i suoi eclettici gusti musicali mentre cammina, 1994.

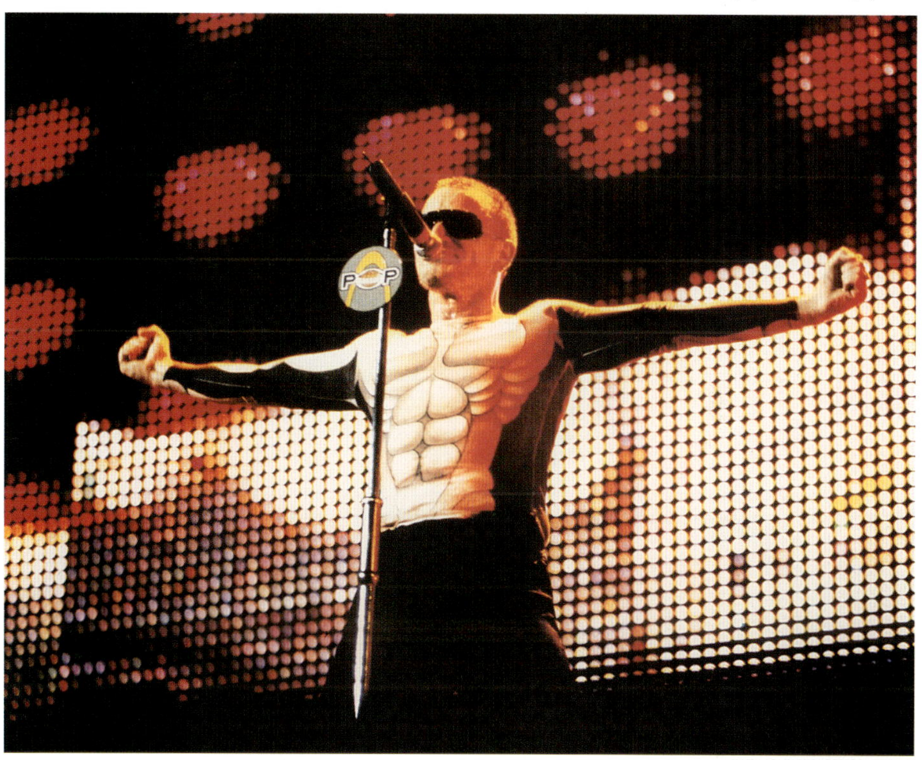

KAT MONK/VISAGES/COLORIFIC!

'It's no secret that ambition bites the nails of success.' Paul Hewson, better known as Bono of U2, here seen expounding on the meaning of 'Pop' during U2's World Tour of 1998.

"Todos saben que la ambición muerde las uñas del éxito." Paul Hewson, más conocido como Bono de U2, explica así el significado de *pop* durante la gira mundial del grupo en 1998.

"Tutti sanno che l'ambizione morde le unghie del successo". Paul Hewson, meglio noto con lo pseudonimo di Bono, degli U2, spiega al pubblico il significato della parola "Pop" durante il World Tour degli U2 nel 1998.

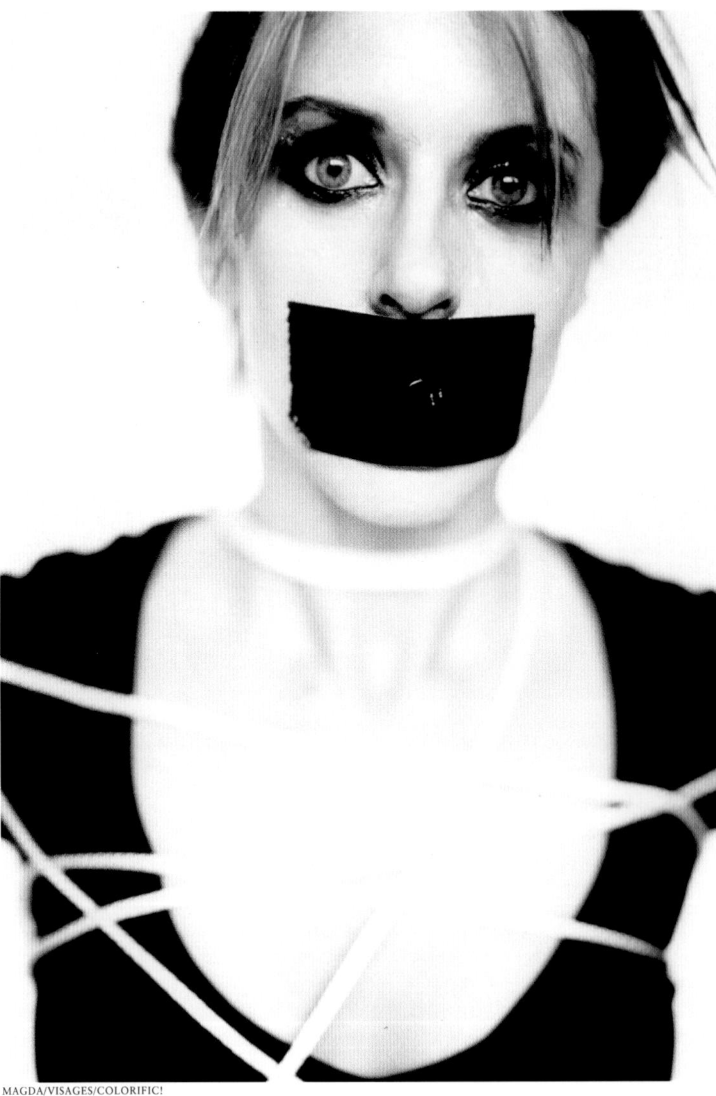

MAGDA/VISAGES/COLORIFIC!

Lo-fi indie songstress Liz Phair. Her combination of preppy looks and explicit lyrics thrilled the male music establishment.

Liz Phair, cantautora de música *indie lo-fi*. Combinando un aspecto provocativo y unas letras explícitas hacía estremecerse al *establishment* musical masculino.

La cantante indipendente lo-fi Liz Phair. La combinazione fra l'aspetto da brava ragazza e il linguaggio esplicito eccitò l'establishment musicale maschile.

Hot property from Iceland. Björk Gudmundsdottir, better known simply as Björk, who launched her solo career in 1992.

Una ardiente propuesta musical procedente de Islandia. Björk Gudmundsdottir, más conocida simplemente como Björk, inicia su andadura en solitario en 1992.

Materiale incandescente direttamente dall'Islanda. Björk Gudmundsdottir, meglio nota come Björk, iniziò la carriera solista nel 1992.

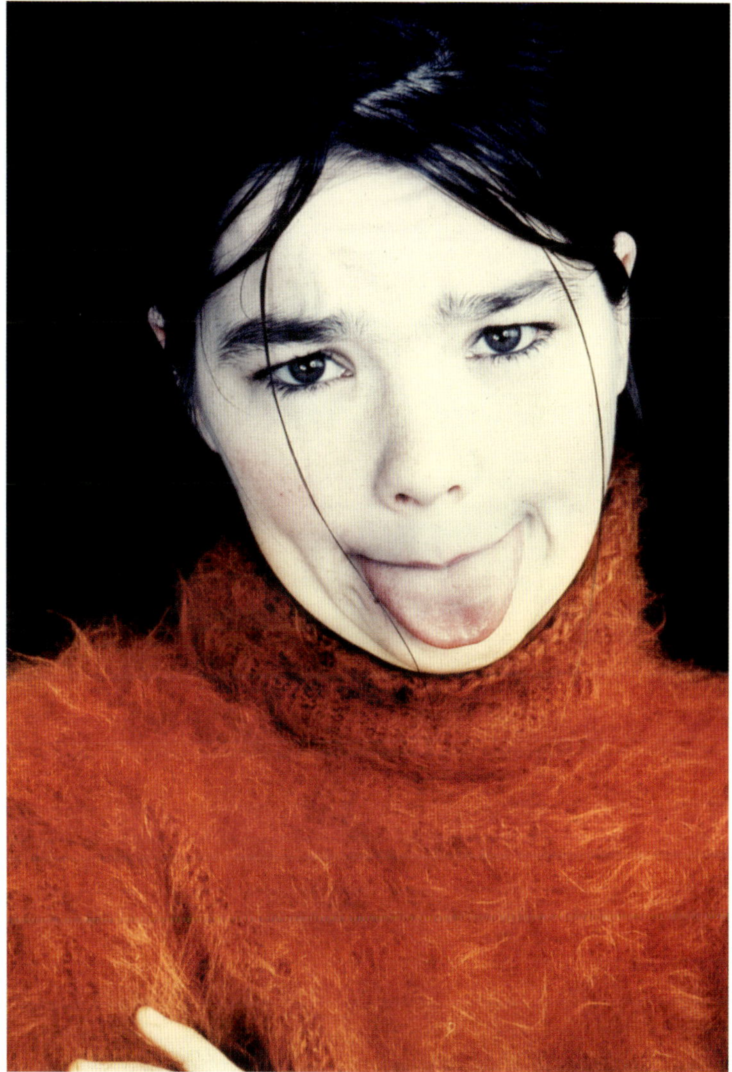

BARRY MARSDEN/IDOLS

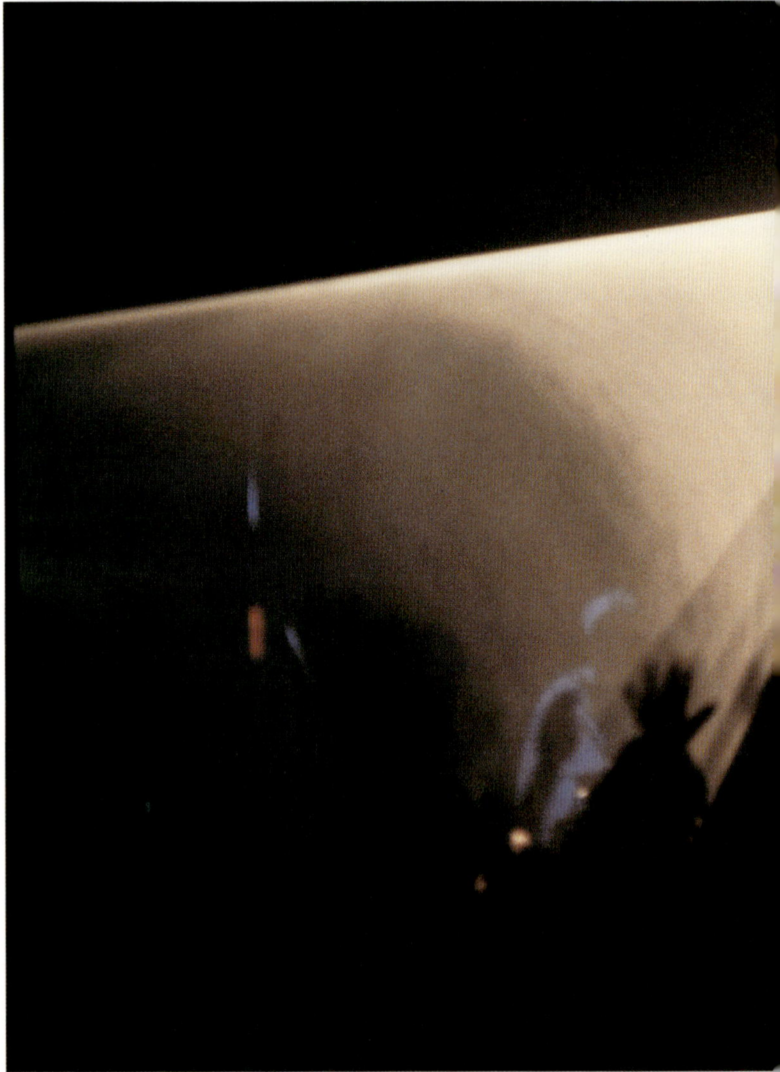

Transcendent pop. Hands emerge in silhouette from the darkness of an acid house rave.

Pop trascendente. De la oscuridad emerge la silueta de unas manos; se trata de una *rave* de *acid house*.

Pop trascendentale. Mani che si lasciano intravedere durante un rave di musica acid house.

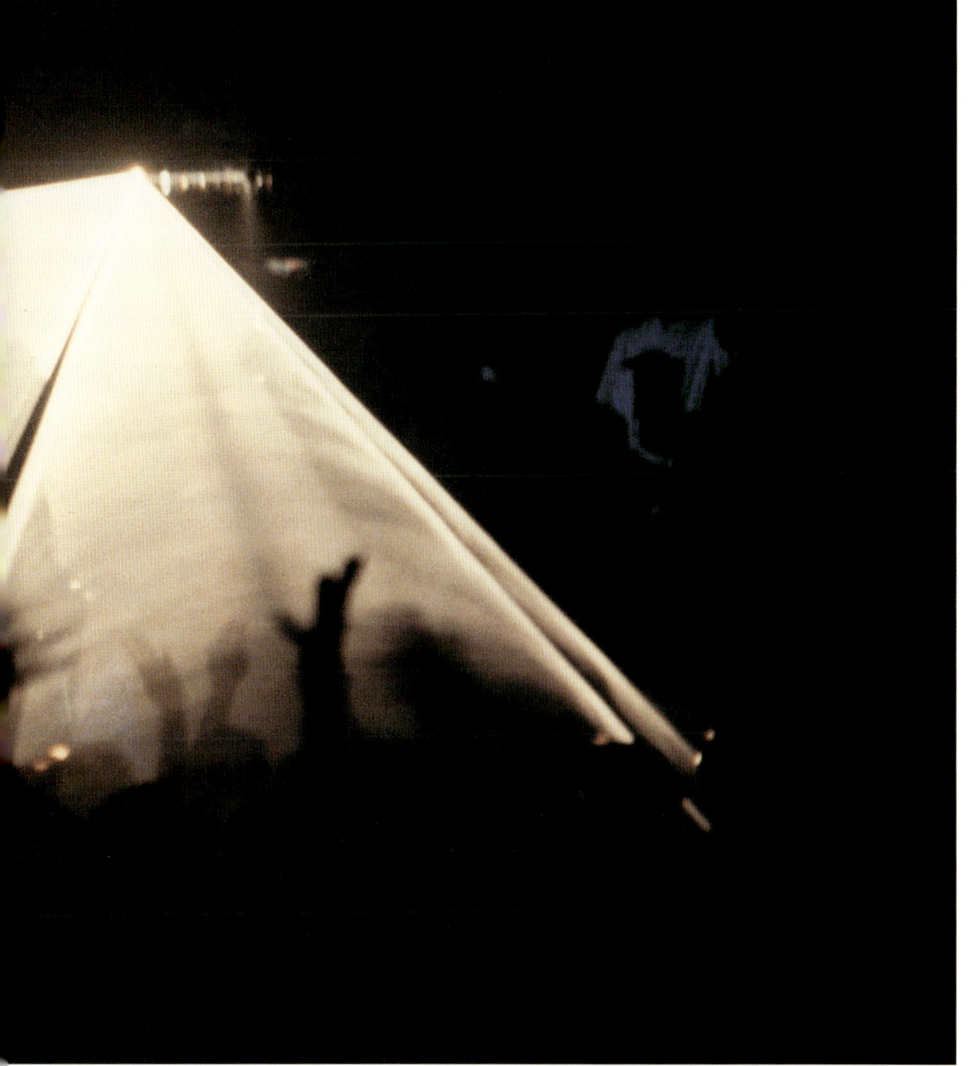

SIMON TAYLOR/S.I.N.

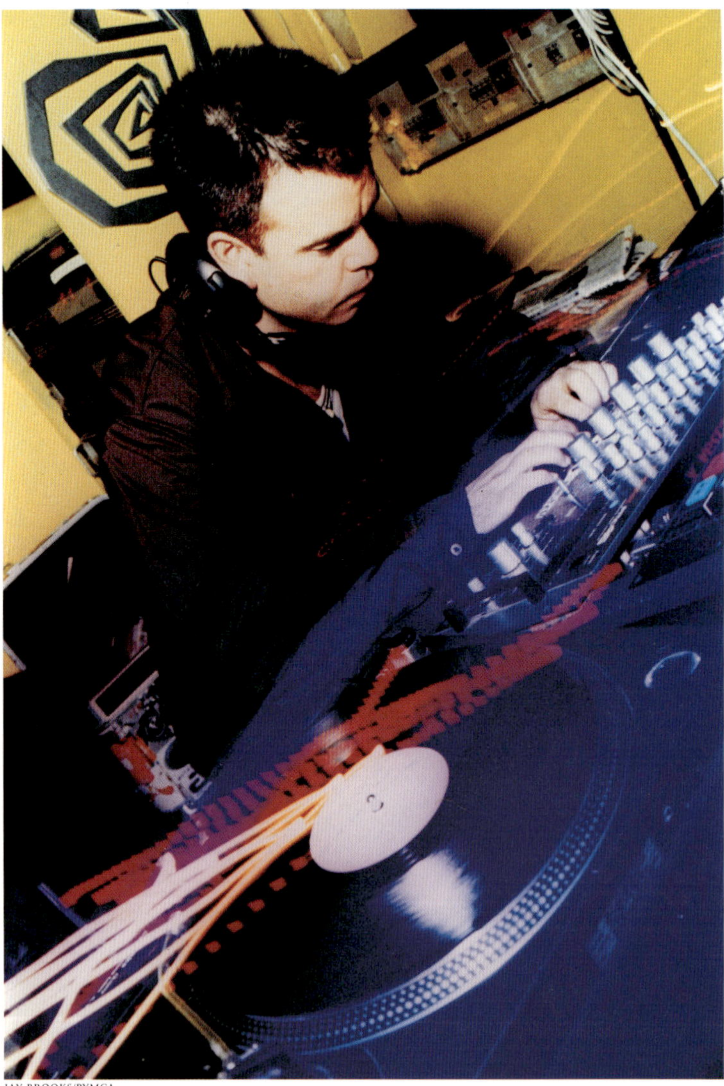

JAY BROOKS/PYMCA

House proud 1. DJ and house music producer Paul Oakenfold, who inaugurated the London super-club Ministry of Sound in the early 1990s.

El orgullo del *house* 1. Paul Oakenfold, *disc-jockey* y productor de música *house*, inaugura el archiconocido club londinense Ministry of Sound, a principios de los noventa.

Fieri dell'house 1. Il DJ e produttore di musica house Paul Oakenfold, che inaugurò il super-club londinese Ministry of Sound nei primi anni Novanta.

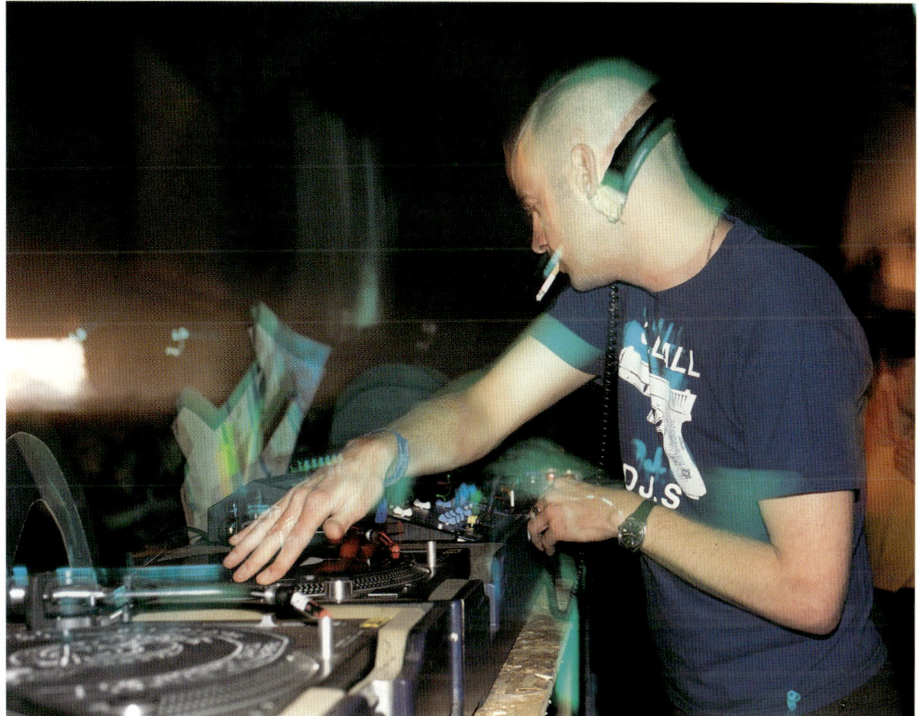

HAYLEY MADDEN/S.I.N.

House proud 2. Norman Cook, better known as Fatboy Slim, performing at the Glastonbury Festival, 1998. Cook was a proponent of the Big Beat sound. His remix of Cornershop's *Brimful of Asha* spent weeks at No. 1 in the British charts.

El orgullo del *house* 2. Norman Cook –más conocido como *Fatboy Slim* y uno de los padres del sonido *big beat*– pinchando en el festival de Glastonbury en 1998. Su remezcla del tema *Brimful of Asha* de los Cornershop permanecería durante semanas en el número 1 de las listas británicas.

Fieri dell'house 2. Norman Cook, più noto come Fatboy Slim, durante una performance al Glastonbury Festival, 1998. Cook fu uno dei creatori del sound Big Beat. Il suo remix di *Brimful of Asha*, dei Cornershop, restò diverse settimane al n. 1 delle classifiche britanniche.

8. Fashion
Moda
Moda

As a preliminary to the World Cup, ready-to-wear fashion houses organised their own football match at the Stade de France, Paris, 25 May 1998. Here the midfield is dominated by a John Galliano creation.

Como aperitivo al campeonato mundial de fútbol celebrado en París en 1998, varias firmas de moda *prêt-à-porter* organizaron su propio partido en el Stade de France, el 25 de mayo de 1998. En esta imagen una creación de John Galliano domina el medio campo.

Prima che fosse inaugurata la Coppa del mondo, le case di moda organizzarono la loro partita di calcio nello Stade de France, Parigi, 25 maggio 1998. Nella foto il centrocampo occupato da una creazione di John Galliano.

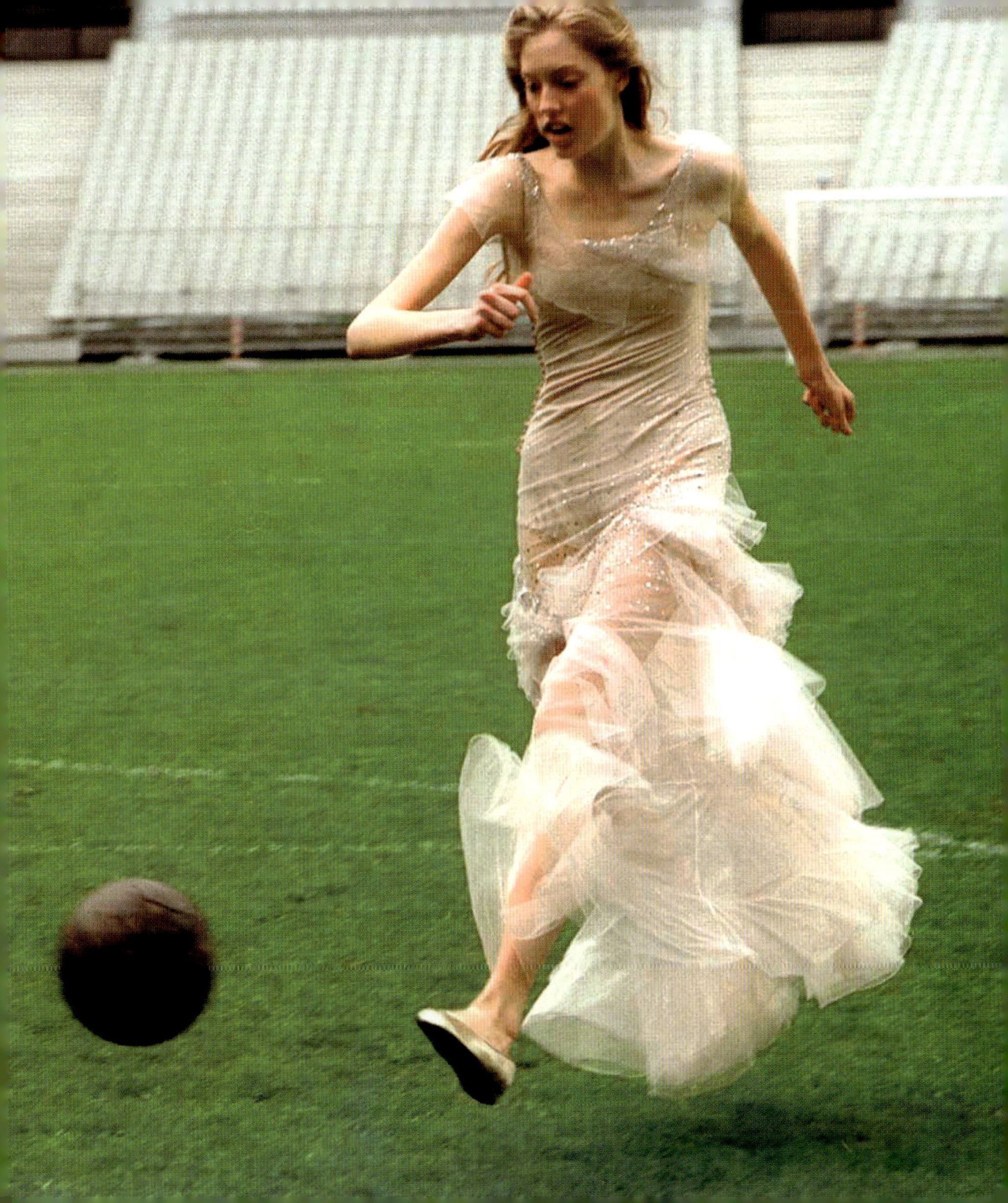

8. Fashion Moda Moda

There were beautiful clothes. There were designer clothes. And, in some cases, there were beautiful designer clothes. The Nineties were the age of the label – Armani, Gucci, Versace and dozens more. *Haute couture* came down from its lofty catwalks to reach 'off the peg' and everyday levels. Schoolchildren refused to wear school uniform unless its components came from Pierre Cardin and company. It was fashionable to be pencil slim. Supermodels such as Kate Moss and Naomi Campbell became richer and more famous than many a movie actress, but no one had more style than Diana, Princess of Wales.

Designs reflected the principles that governed the world of art. What mattered was shocking the beholder. Clothes became outrageously ugly, brilliantly bizarre, eye-catchingly eccentric in colour, material and shape. Such design, in turn, provoked a counter-fashion for a return to more folksy, homespun designs and materials.

And there were the customary revivals... of the Forties, the Fifties, the Sixties. Those in the know quietly put their Nineties clothes away, aware that the 'shock of the new' would one day become fashionably retro.

Se crea ropa espléndida. Se crea ropa de diseño. Y, en ciertas ocasiones, hasta se crea ropa de diseño espléndida. En los noventa triunfan las marcas: Armani, Gucci, Versace y otras muchas. La alta costura desciende de las elevadas pasarelas para situarse a un nivel más próximo a la confección y al *prêt-à-porter*. Los niños se niegan a vestir uniforme de colegio a menos que lo firme Pierre Cardin y compañía. La delgadez extrema está de moda. Las *top models*, como Kate Moss o Naomi Campbell, devienen más ricas y famosas que muchas estrellas de cine, si bien ninguna de ellas consigue superar en estilo a la princesa Diana de Gales.

El diseño refleja los principios que imperan en el mundo del arte: lo que realmente importa es impresionar al espectador. Las prendas se vuelven escandalosamente horribles, clamorosamente extravagantes y llamativamente excéntricas en cuanto a colores, materiales y formas. Dicha tendencia, a su vez, genera una contracorriente en el mundo de la moda que reivindica el retorno a la sencillez de los diseños y los materiales tradicionales.

También tienen lugar los inevitables *revivals*… vuelven los cuarenta, los cincuenta y los sesenta. Así, los más astutos guardan a buen recaudo su vestuario de los noventa, a sabiendas que un día esas "novedades chocantes" serán las estrellas de la moda retro.

Si indossavano bei vestiti. Si indossavano vestiti di stilisti, e, in alcuni casi, si indossavano bei vestiti di stilisti. Gli anni Novanta furono gli anni delle marche – Armani, Gucci, Versace e altri ancora. L'alta moda scese dalle eleganti passerelle per avvicinarsi al prêt-à-porter e alle marche più comuni. Gli alunni si rifiutavano di indossare uniformi a meno che fossero firmate da Pierre Cardin e compagnia. Essere magri come un chiodo faceva tendenza. Supermodelle come Kate Moss e Naomi Campbell divennero più ricche e famose di molte attrici di cinema, ma nessuna aveva più stile di Diana, la principessa del Galles.

I modelli per i capi d'abbigliamento rispecchiavano i principi del mondo dell'arte. Ciò che più contava era sconcertare lo spettatore. I vestiti divennero incredibilmente brutti, meravigliosamente eccentrici, con colori, materiali e forme appariscenti e stravaganti. E questa moda, a sua volta, provocò una controtendenza che aspirava al ritorno a modelli e materiali più semplici e senza pretese.

E apparvero i classici revival… degli anni Quaranta, Cinquanta e Sessanta. Chi se ne intendeva, zitto zitto, mise da parte anche i vestiti degli anni Novanta, sicuro che prima o poi quelle "sciocanti novità" sarebbero ritornate di moda.

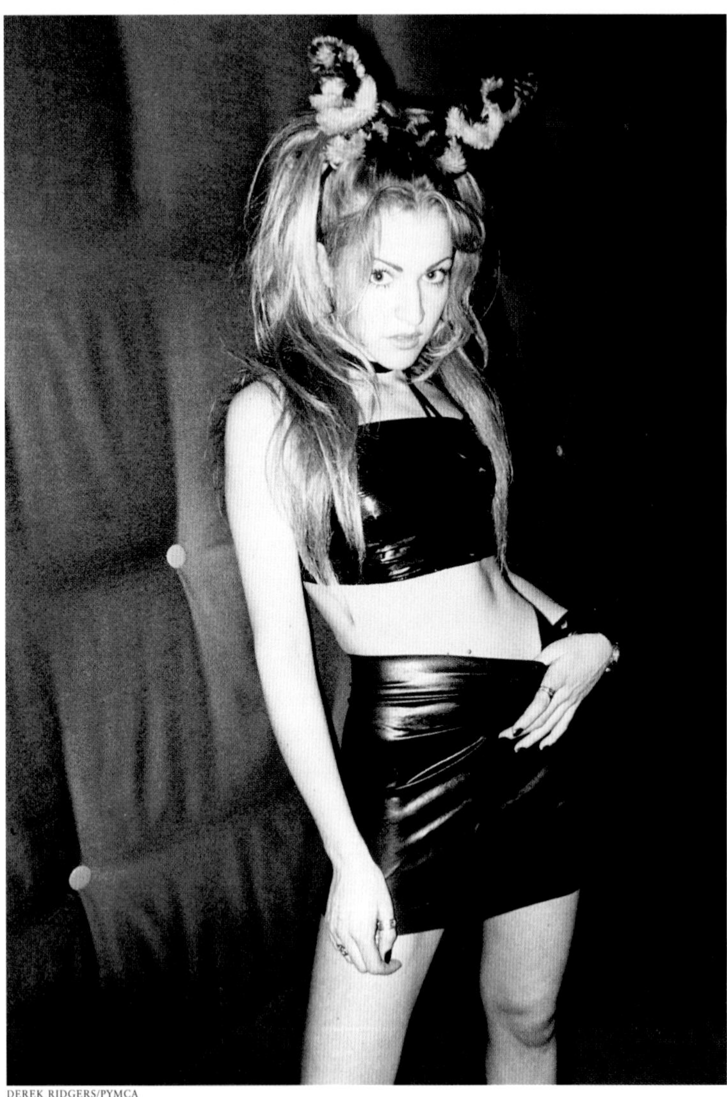

DEREK RIDGERS/PYMCA

The little girl look beloved of pop stars and 'men of a certain age'. Kerry at Submission, 1998.

La apariencia de lolita es adoptada por numerosas estrellas del pop y apreciada por "hombres de una cierta edad". Kerry en Submission, 1998.

Il look Lolita, preferito dalle pop star e dagli "uomini di una certa età". Kerry al Submission, 1998.

Hiding behind their masks, revellers dance tongue-to-tongue at the Skin 2 Ball, London, December 1995.

Ocultos tras las máscaras, asiduos del Skin 2 Ball de Londres bailan lengua contra lengua, diciembre de 1995.

Nascosti dietro le maschere, c'è chi si diverte ballando, lingua con lingua, nello Skin 2 Ball, Londra, dicembre 1995.

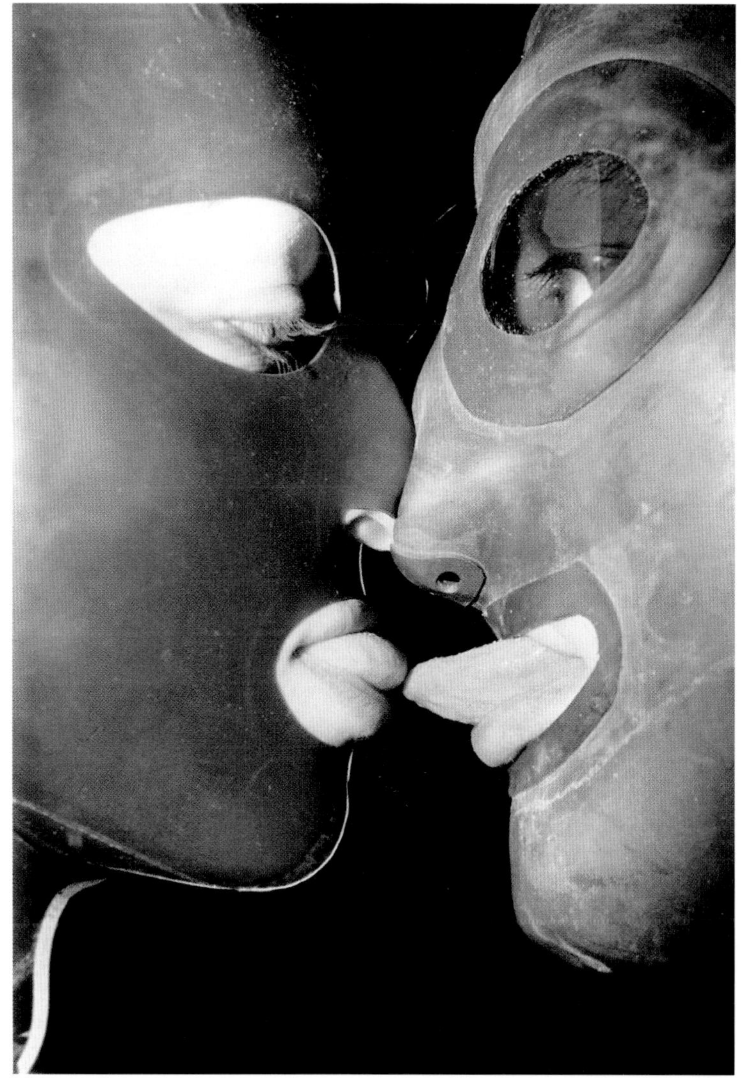

SIMON NORFOLK/PYMCA

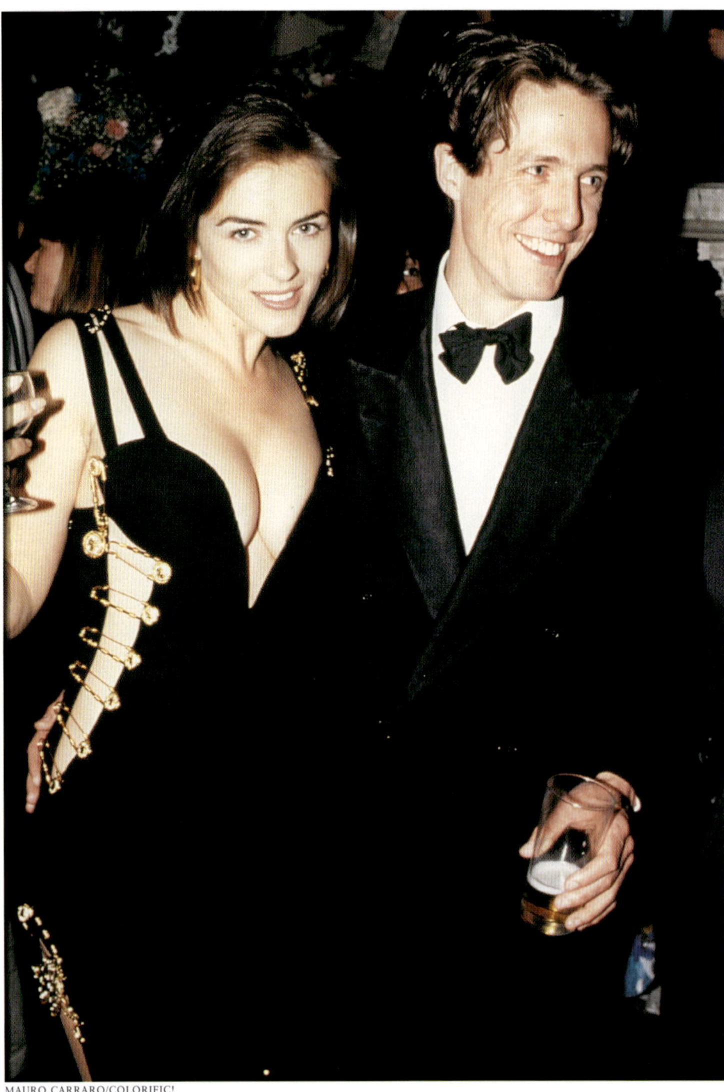

MAURO CARRARO/COLORIFIC!

In happier days, Liz Hurley and Hugh Grant arrive at the FWAF party, London, 11 May 1994. (Dress and safety pins by Versace.)

Corrían tiempos mejores para Liz Hurley y Hugh Grant cuando, el 11 de mayo de 1994, acudían juntos al estreno de *Cuatro bodas y un funeral* en Londres –tanto el vestido como los imperdibles de seguridad son de Versace–.

In un periodo più felice, Liz Hurley e Hugh Grant arrivano al party londinese per *Quattro matrimoni e un funerale*, 11 maggio 1994. (Vestito e spille da balia di Versace).

Julia Roberts arrives at the premiere of *Notting Hill*, London, 27 April 1999. Some delicate souls were upset by her armpits.

Julia Roberts asiste al estreno de la película *Notting Hill* en Londres, 27 de abril de 1999. El vello de sus axilas hirió algunas sensibilidades.

Julia Roberts arriva alla première di *Notting Hill*, Londra, 27 aprile 1999. I più sensibili restarono scandalizzati dalle sue ascelle *nature*.

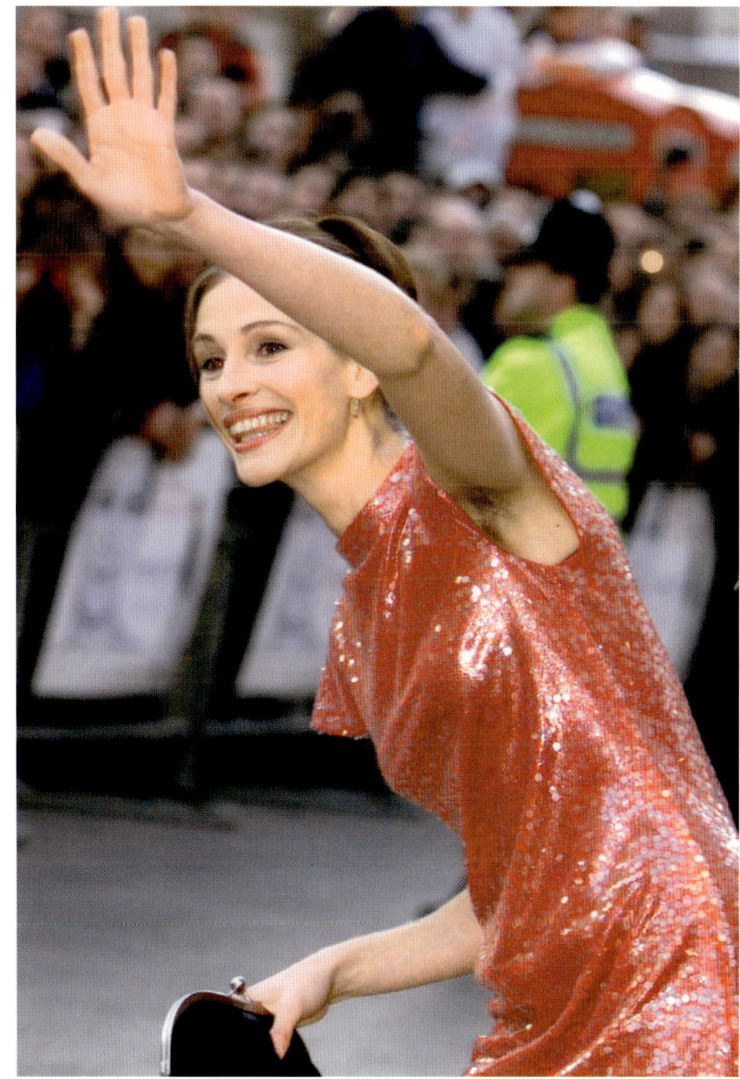

IAN WALDIE/REUTERS/ARCHIVE PHOTOS

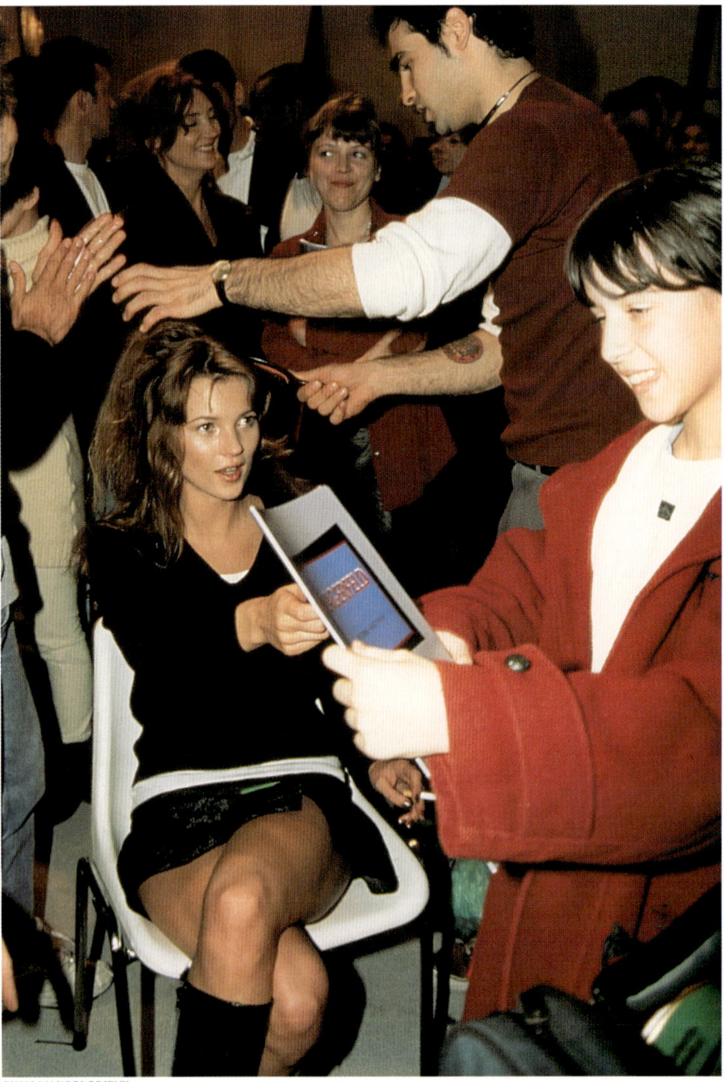

QUAN MAI/COLORIFIC!

Kate Moss relaxes in a ready-to-wear dress at the Thierry Mugler autumn/ winter show, Paris, March 1995.

Kate Moss, vestida con un modelo *prêt-à-porter,* se prepara para el desfile de la colección otoño-invierno del diseñador Thierry Mugler, en París, marzo de 1995.

Kate Moss si rilassa in un vestito prêt-à-porter durante la presentazione della collezione autunno/inverno di Thierry Mugler, Parigi, marzo 1995.

Christy Turlington (in curlers) and Naomi Campbell (reading) at the Oscar de la Renta autumn/winter show, New York City, 1993.

Christy Turlington (con rulos en la cabeza) y Naomi Campbell (leyendo) en la presentación de la colección otoño-invierno de Oscar de la Renta, Nueva York, 1993.

Christy Turlington (con i bigodini) e Naomi Campbell (mentre legge) durante la presentazione della collezione autunno/inverno di Oscar de la Renta, New York, 1993.

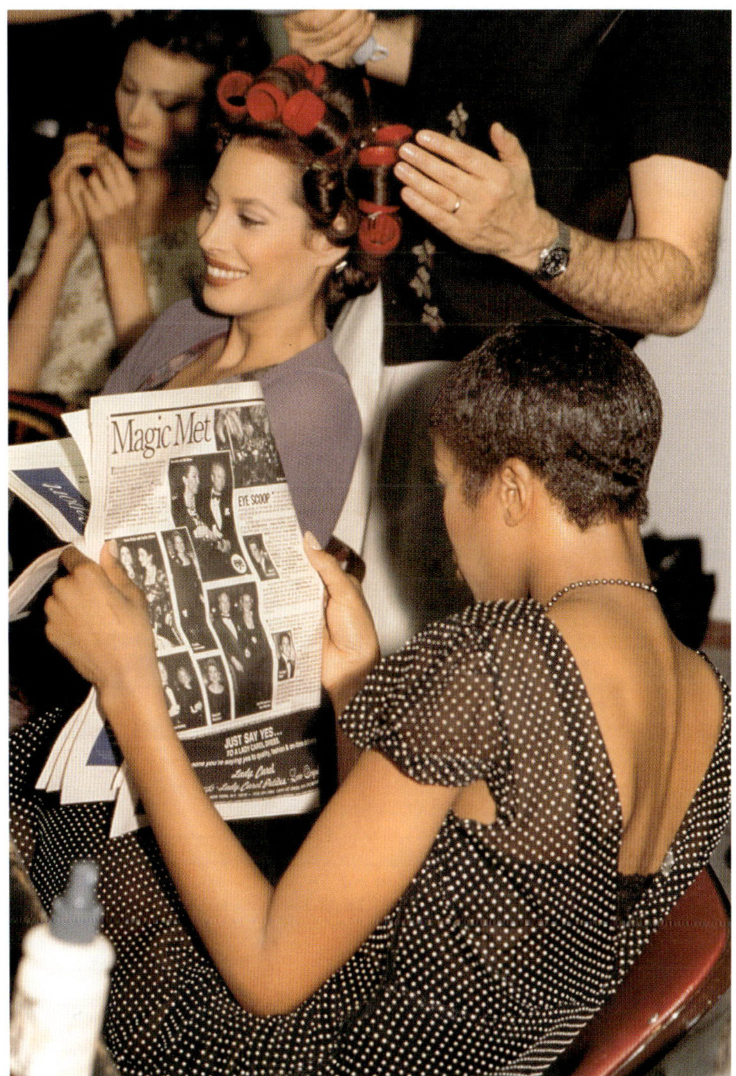

B NICE/VISAGES/COLORIFIC!

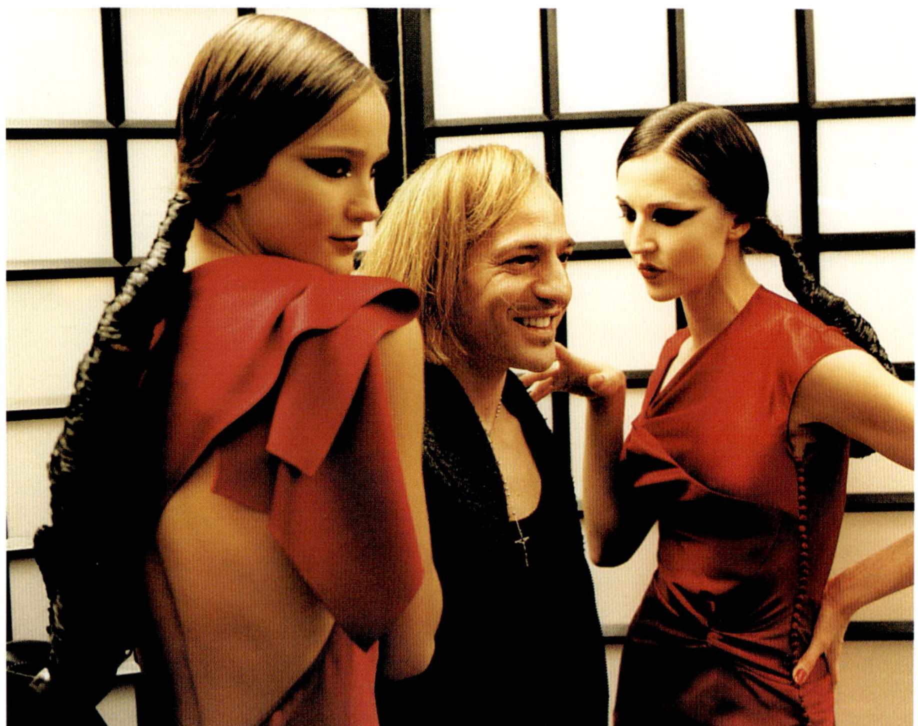

CHABASSIER/MPA/LIAISON AGENCY

The master of the bias-cut slip dress, John Galliano, with two of his models. The dresses were part of Galliano's autumn 1999 collection and exemplified his love of simplicity of design with subtle detailing.

John Galliano, maestro del corte al bies, posa con dos de sus modelos. Los trajes forman parte de su colección de otoño de 1999 y ejemplifican su gusto por la simplicidad en el diseño y los detalles sutiles.

John Galliano, maestro del taglio di sbieco, con due delle sue modelle. I vestiti facevano parte della collezione autunno dello stilista per il 1999 ed erano un esempio del suo amore per le linee semplici arricchite con eleganti dettagli.

The Stars and Stripes are put to fashionable use in another Galliano dress, from his 1993 summer collection.

Las barras y estrellas de la bandera estadounidense inspiran esta otra creación de Galliano, perteneciente a su colección de verano de 1993.

Le stelle e le strisce fanno moda su quest'altro vestito di Galliano, della collezione estate 1993.

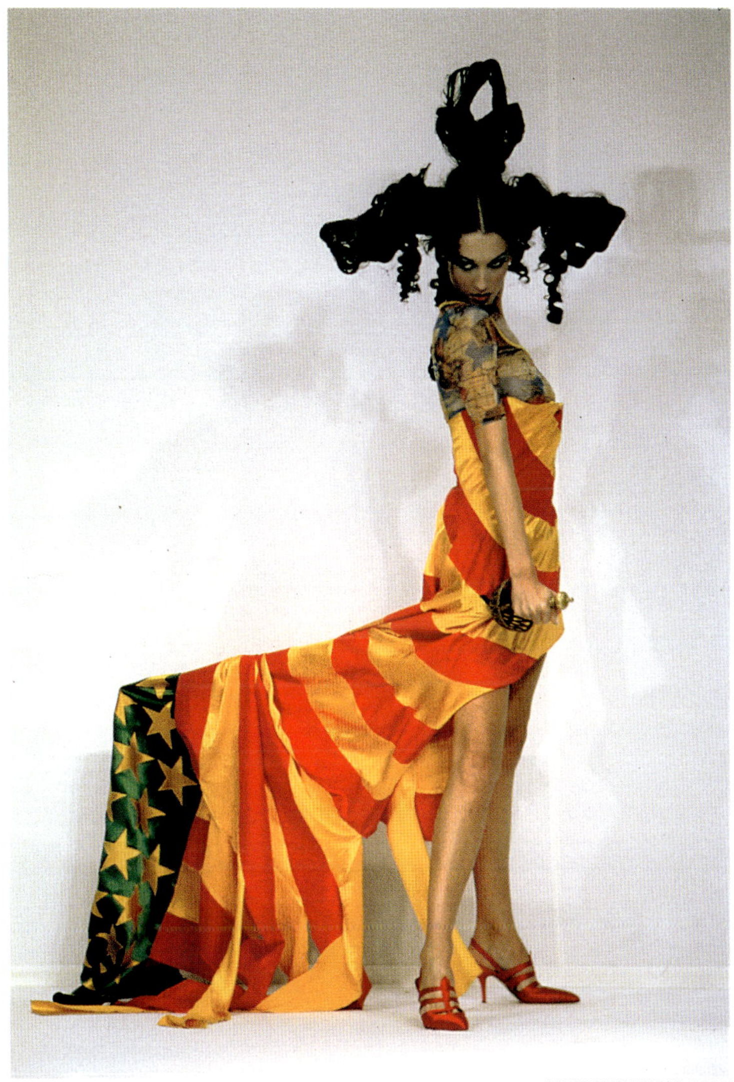

DANIEL SIMON/LIAISON AGENCY

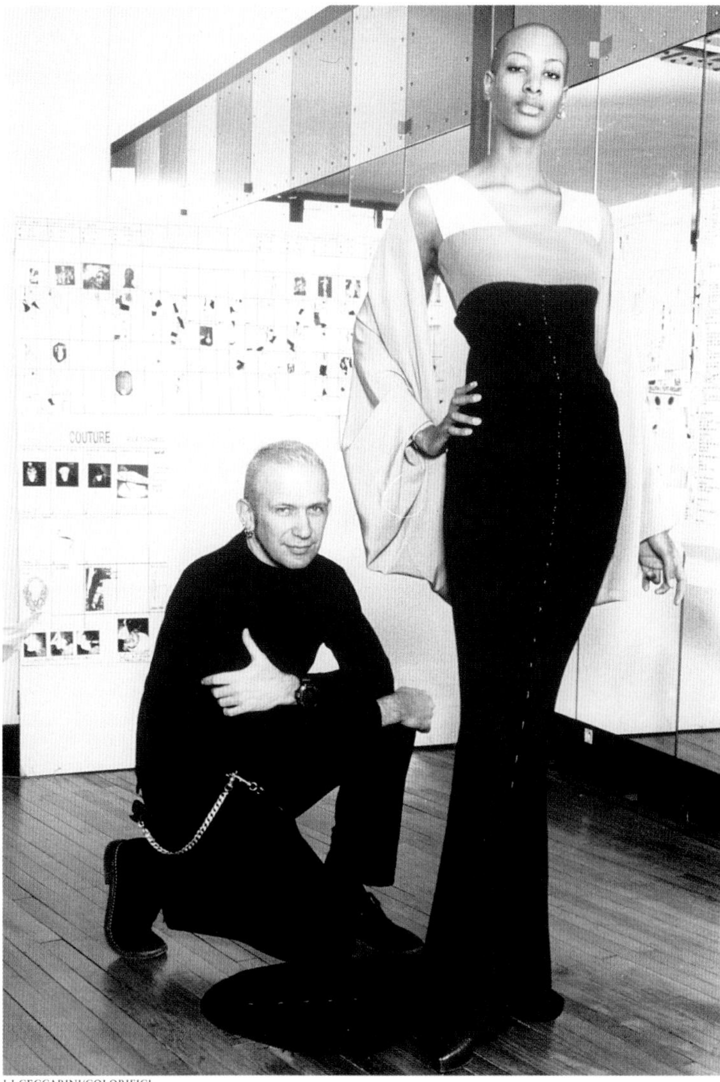

J J CECCARINI/COLORIFIC!

Jean Paul Gaultier goes down on one knee before his own creation for the spring/summer collection of 1996, Paris.

Jean Paul Gaultier arrodillado ante una de sus creaciones para su colección de primavera-verano de 1996, en París.

Jean Paul Gaultier si inginocchia di fronte alla sua creazione per la collezione primavera/estate del 1996, a Parigi.

Alexander McQueen, however, appears to have doubts about a dress he designed for the same collection.

En cambio, Alexander McQueen parece tener serias dudas sobre un traje diseñado por él para la misma colección.

Invece Alexander McQueen sembra abbia dubbi sul vestito creato per la stessa collezione.

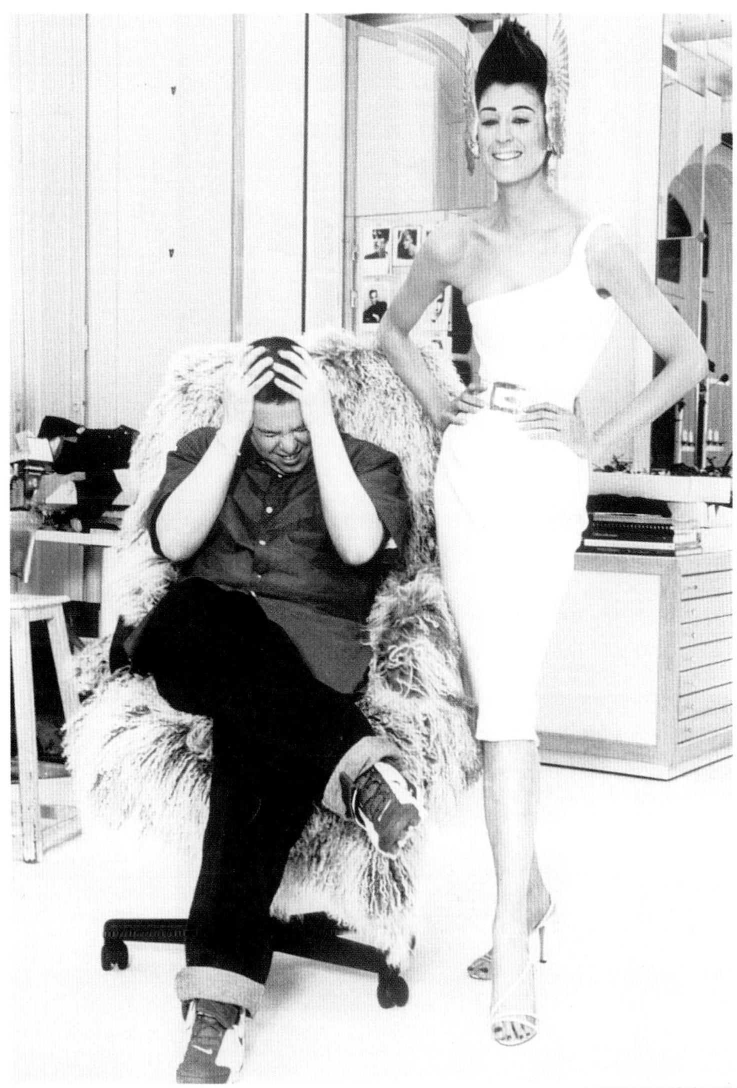

J J CECCARINI/COLORIFIC!

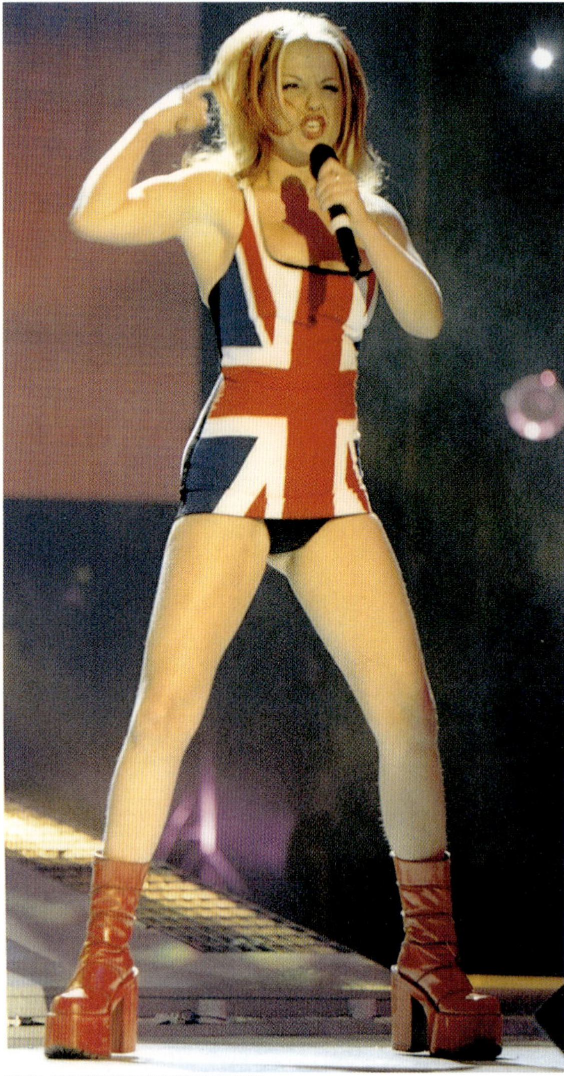

KIERAN DOHERTY/REUTERS/ARCHIVE PHOTOS

Pop goes the fashion. Ginger Spice (Geri Halliwell) sports a size 6 Union Jack at the 1997 Brit Awards.

El pop marca tendencias dentro de la moda. La Spice picante (Geri Halliwell) exhibe una camiseta de la talla 36 con los colores de la bandera británica en la entrega de los Brit Awards de 1997.

Il Pop fa tendenza. Ginger Spice (Geri Halliwell) mostra una bandiera britannica, taglia 38, durante i Brit Awards 1997.

Madonna revels in a typical Jean Paul Gaultier corset-fronted outfit on her Blonde Ambition Tour, 1990.

En su gira Blonde Ambition Tour, de 1990, Madonna luce un típico corsé de copa puntiaguda diseñado por Jean Paul Gaultier.

Madonna si diverte con il classico bustino a punte creato da Jean Paul Gaultier per il suo Blonde Ambition Tour, 1990.

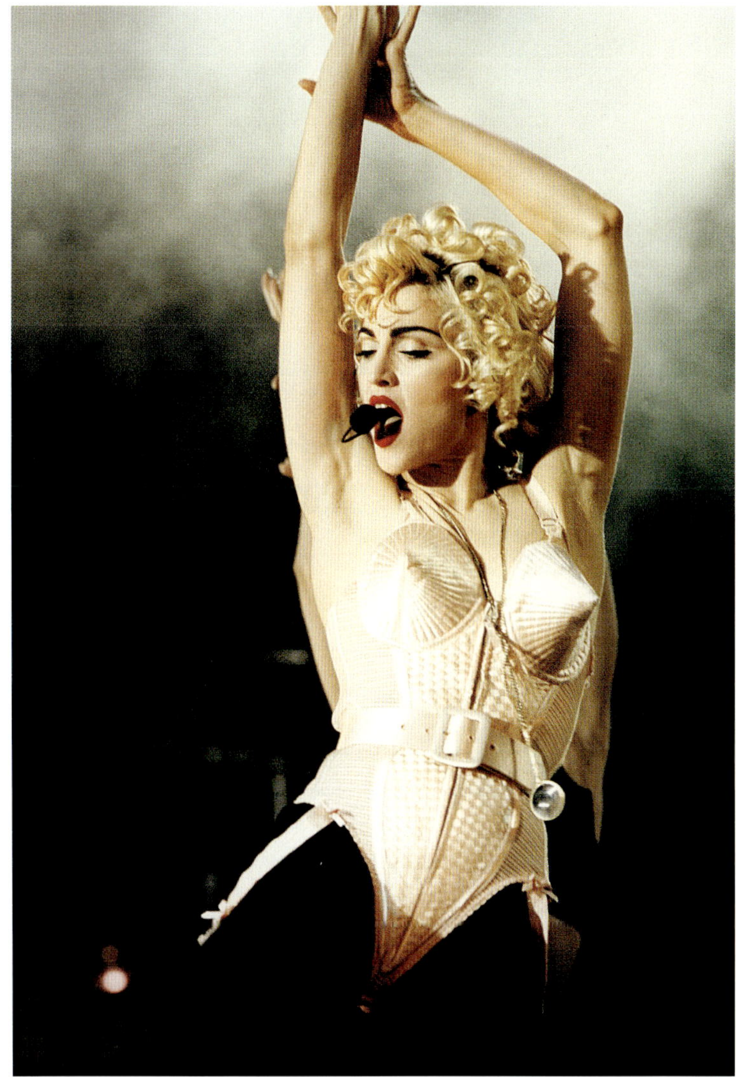

STEFANO RELLANDINI/REUTERS/ARCHIVE PHOTOS

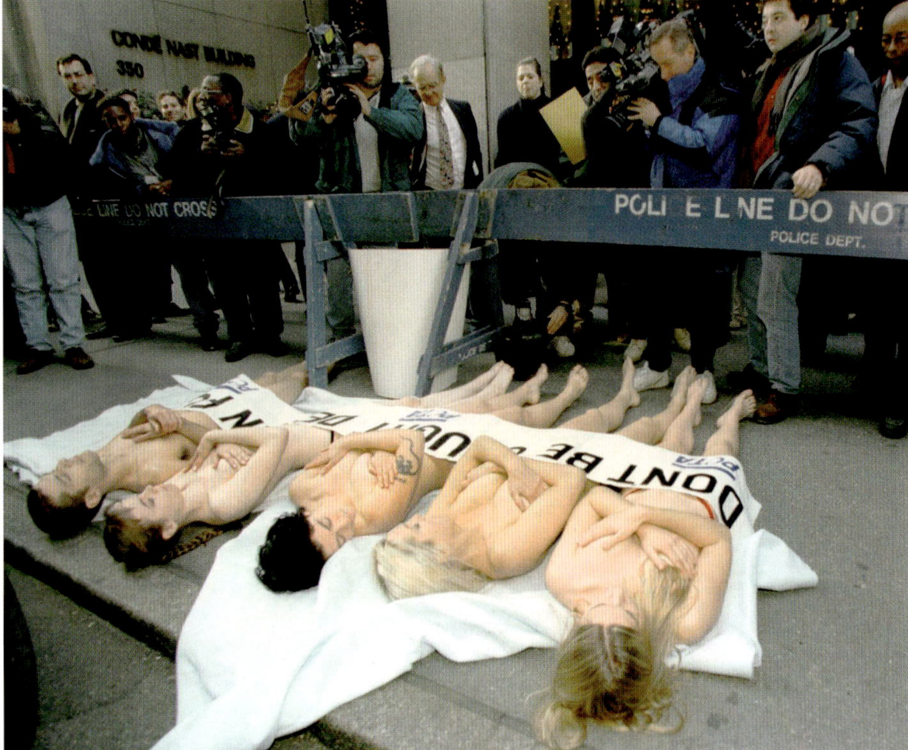

JEFF CHRISTENSEN/REUTERS/ARCHIVE PHOTOS

Members of the People for the Ethical Treatment of Animals protest group stage a naked protest outside the offices of American *Vogue*, New York City, 17 December 1997. They objected to the magazine's promotion of fur coats.

Miembros del grupo PETA (People for the Ethical Treatment of Animals) protagonizan un acto de protesta desnudándose frente a las oficinas de la revista *Vogue* en Nueva York, 17 de diciembre de 1997. Así rechazaban la publicidad que esta hacía de los abrigos de piel.

Membri del gruppo People for the Ethical Treatment of Animals protestano nudi di fronte agli uffici di Vogue America, New York, 17 dicembre 1997. Si opponevano alle pubblicità di pellicce che apparivano sulla rivista.

Modelling a protest skirt at Sonja Nuttall's show, London, 12 March 1995. The slogan reads 'Put smoking out of fashion'.

El 12 de marzo de 1995, en un desfile celebrado en Londres, Sonja Nuttall presenta una falda de protesta, cuyo eslogan reza: "Haz que el tabaco pase de moda".

Una gonna di protesta presentata durante la sfilata della collezione di Sonja Nuttall, Londra, 12 marzo 1995. Lo slogan è: "Manda il tabacco fuori moda".

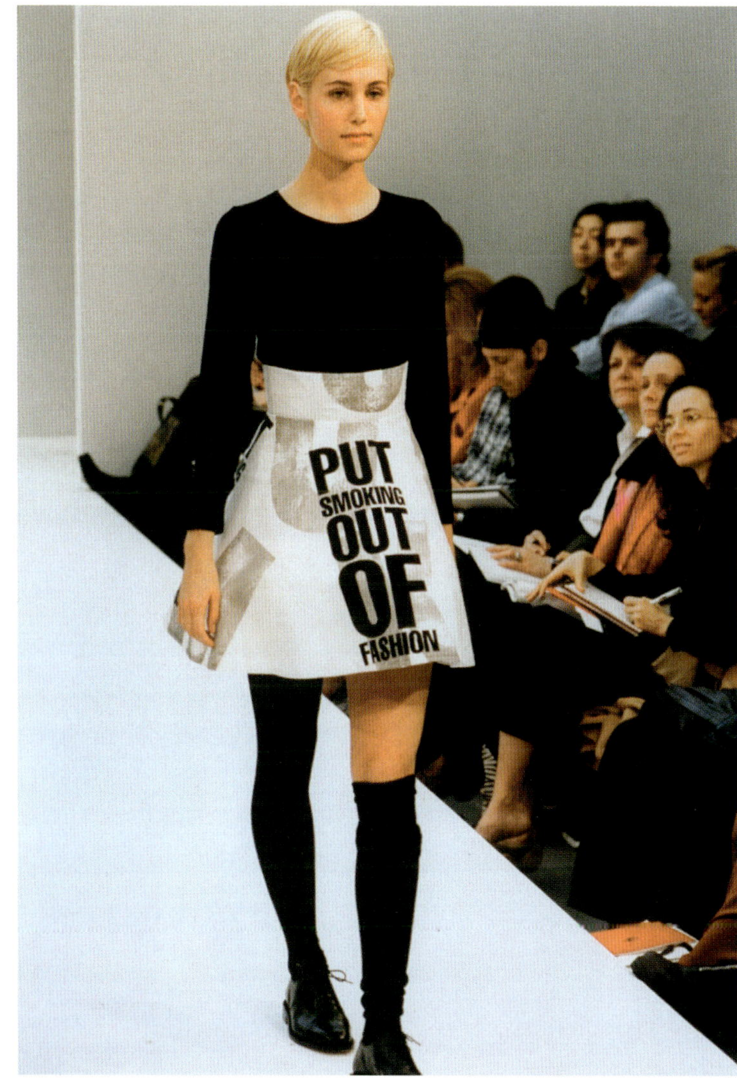

PA

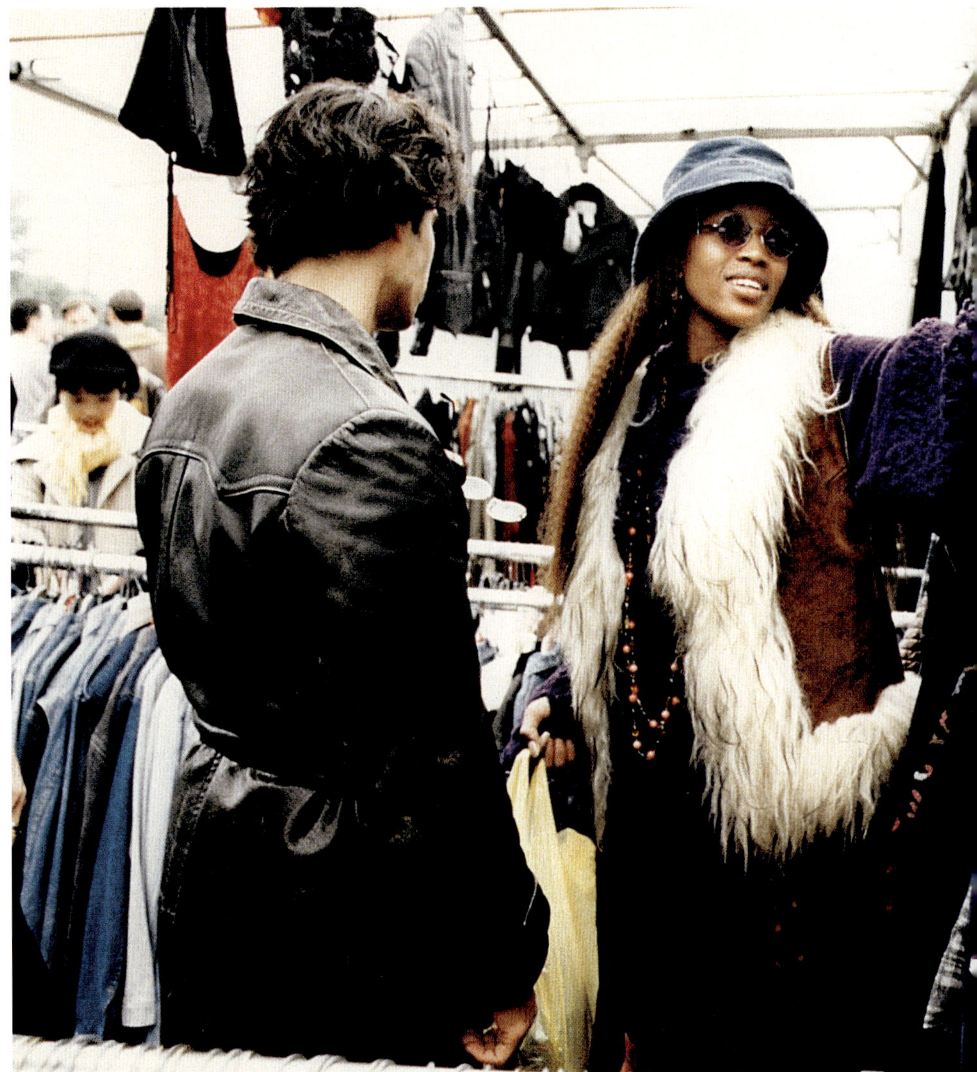

EXPRESS NEWSPAPERS/ARCHIVE PHOTOS

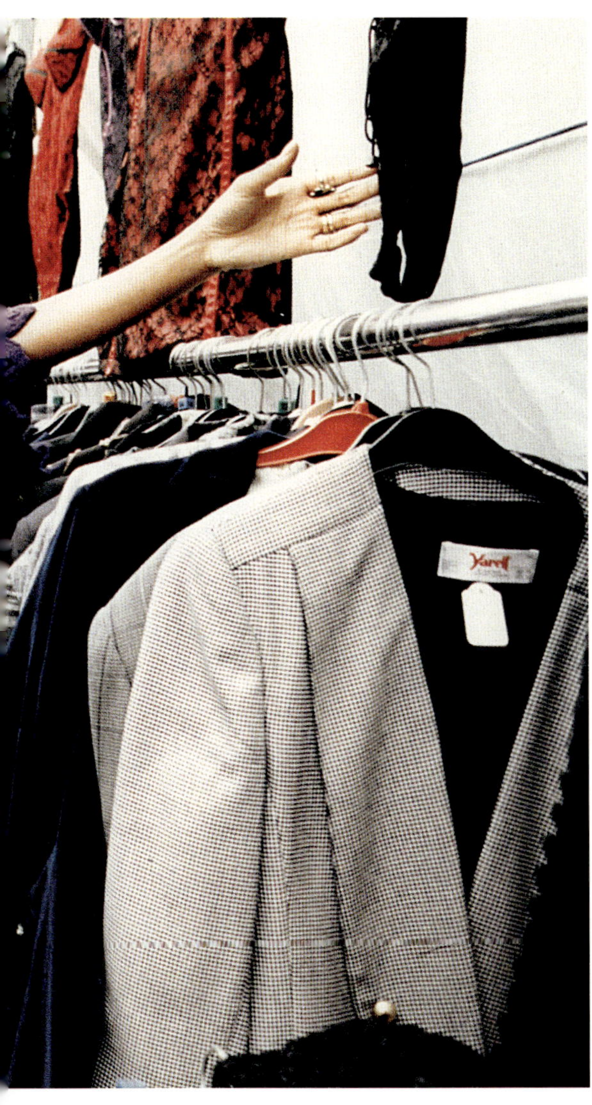

Supermodel goes second-hand. Naomi Campbell examines the delights of Portobello Market, London.

Una *top model* comprando ropa de segunda mano. Naomi Campbell se deleita con las maravillas del mercado londinense de Portobello.

La supermodella compra di seconda mano. Naomi Campbell si perde fra i piaceri del Portobello Market di Londra.

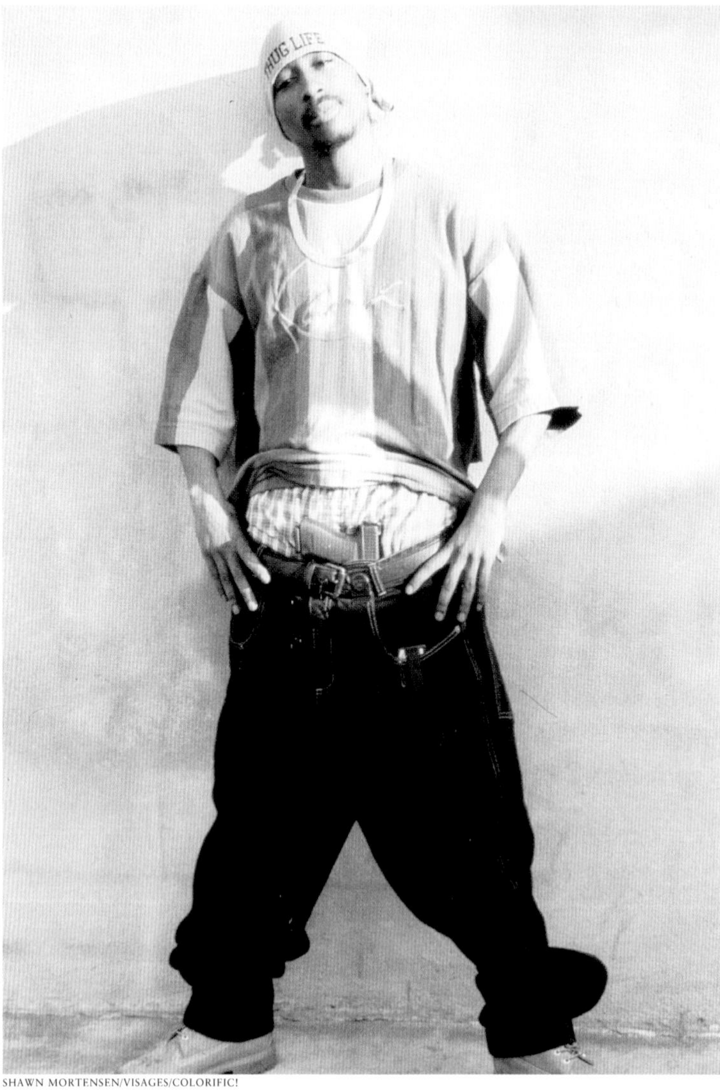

SHAWN MORTENSEN/VISAGES/COLORIFIC!

'There goes my gun.' Tupak Shakur displays the season's must-have accessory in his short-lived gangsta rap career, 1993.

"He aquí mi pistola." Tupak Shakur muestra el accesorio indispensable del rapero gángster que fue por poco tiempo, 1993.

"Attenti alla mia pistola". Tupac Shakur mostra l'accessorio essenziale nella sua breve carriera di gangster rap, 1993.

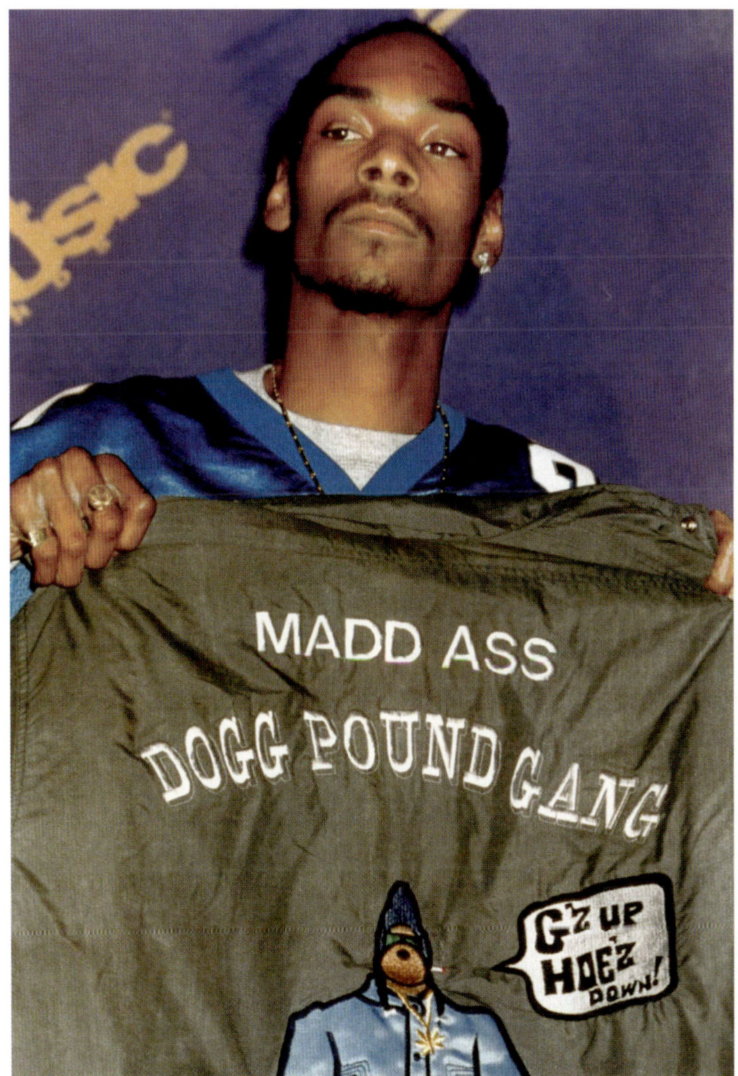

FRED PROUSER/REUTERS/ARCHIVE PHOTOS

Snoop Doggy Dogg holds up his Dogg Pound Gang jacket at the *Billboard* Music Awards, Los Angeles, 1994.

Snoop Doggy Dogg sostiene su chaqueta con el nombre de Dogg Pound Gang en los Billboard Music Awards celebrado en Los Ángeles en 1994.

Snoop Doggy Dogg tiene fra le mani la giubba della Dogg Pound Gang durante i *Billboard* Music Awards, Los Angeles, 1994.

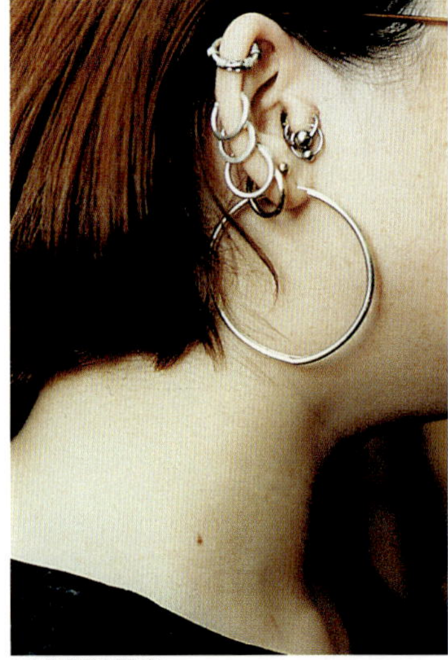

ROB WATKINS/PYMCA

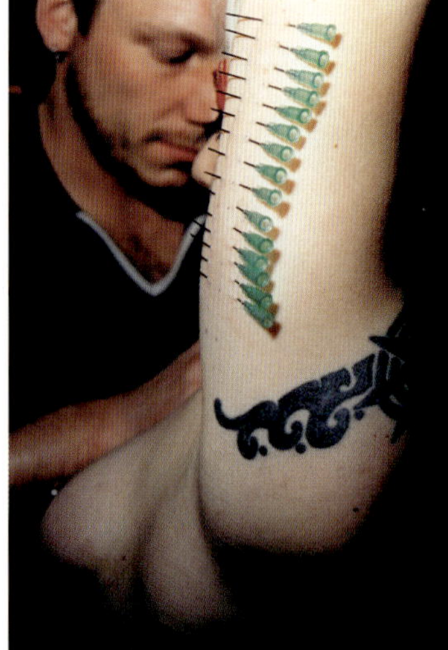

JAY BROOKS/PYMCA

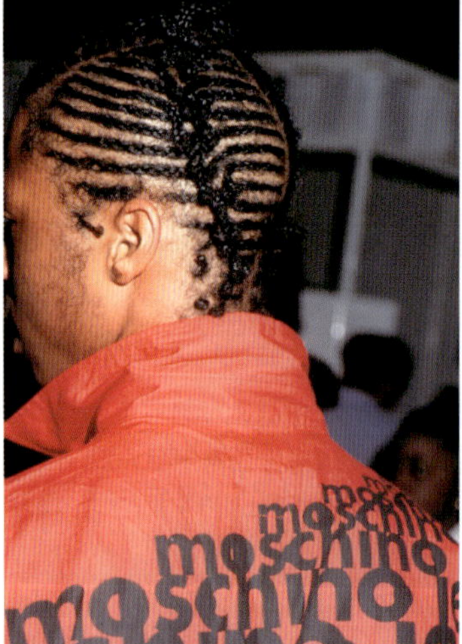

JAMES LANGE/PYMCA

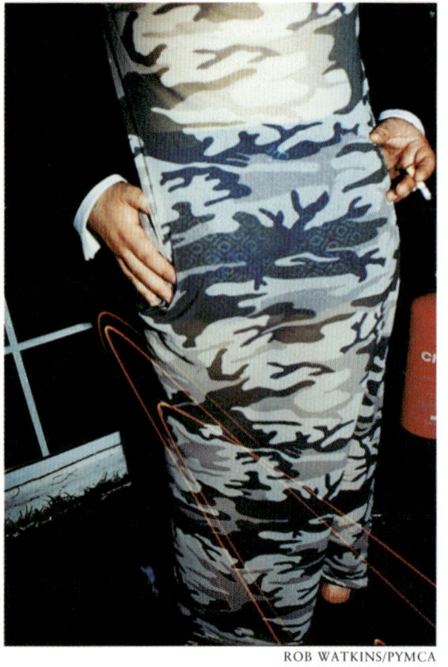

ROB WATKINS/PYMCA

(Clockwise from top left) Ear piercing; syringe piercing; a combat skirt of 1998; and Black Hair and Beauty at Alexandra Palace, London, 1999.

(En el sentido de las agujas del reloj desde arriba a la izquierda) *Piercing* en la oreja; *piercing* de agujas; falda de combate de 1998; y peluquería para personas negras en el Alexandra Palace de Londres, 1999.

(In senso orario dall'alto a sinistra) Piercing all'orecchio; piercing con siringhe; una gonna da combattimento del 1998 e Black Hair and Beauty all'Alexandra Palace, Londra, 1999.

Take a hike… Michiko Koshino models a fashionable front strap rucksack, 1999.

Para ir de excursión… La diseñadora Michiko Koshino presenta una mochila para llevar en la parte delantera del cuerpo, 1999.

In gita… Michiko Koshino sfila con uno zainetto frontale molto trendy, 1999.

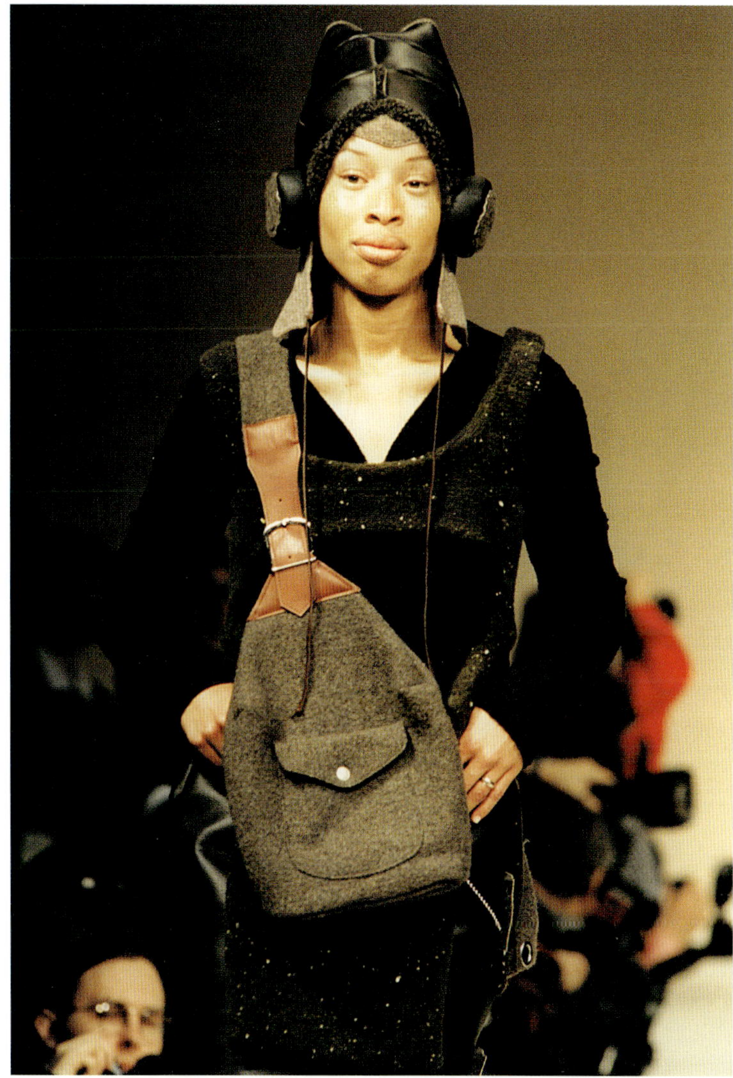

PA

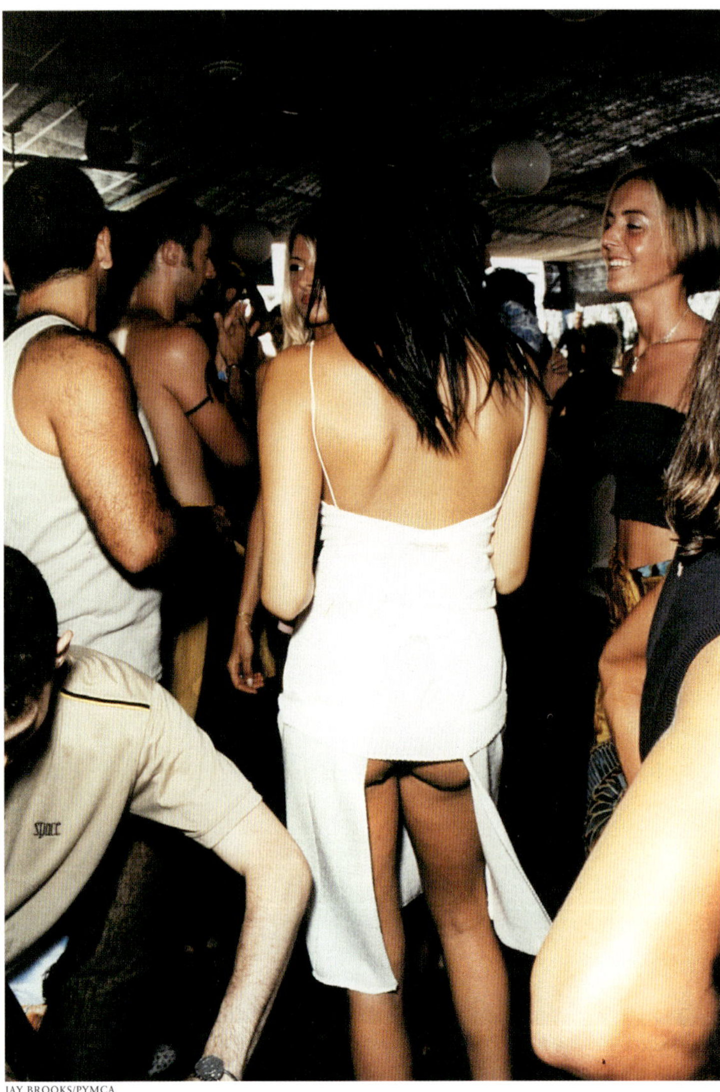

JAY BROOKS/PYMCA

Bare-cheeked face: scenes from a clubber's life. A rave, somewhere in Ibiza, 1999.

Escenas de la vida nocturna. Posaderas casi al desnudo en una *rave* en algún lugar de Ibiza, 1999.

Sedere al vento: scene di vita dei clubber, durante un rave, da qualche parte a Ibiza, 1999.

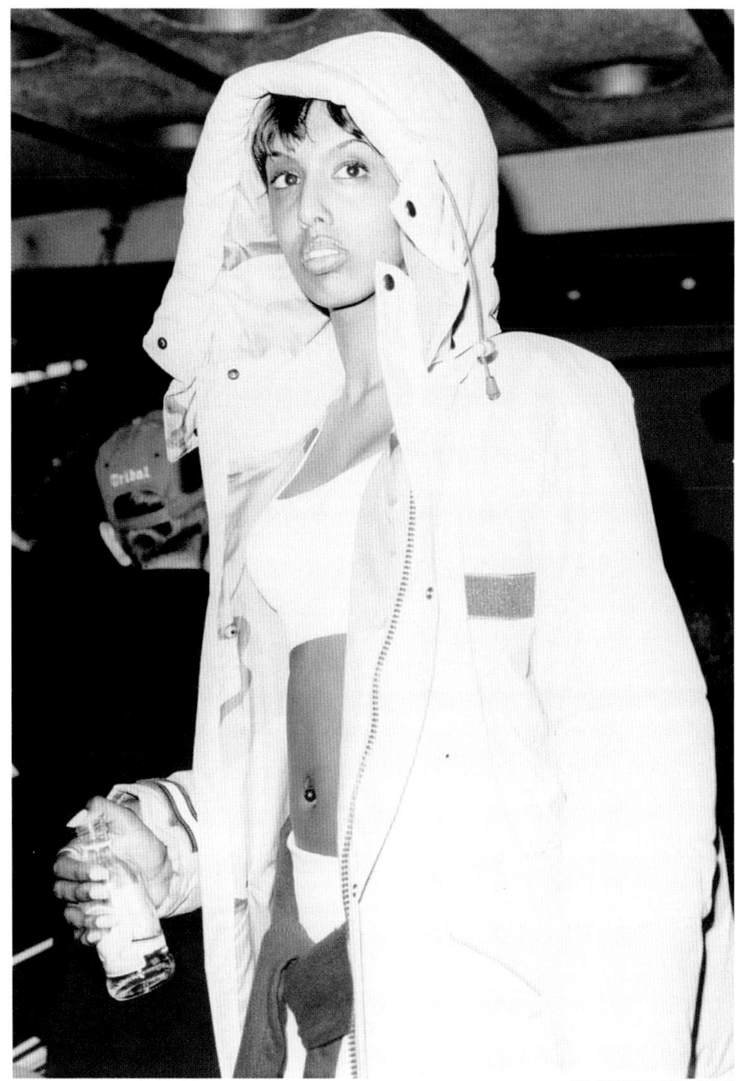

Standing up and cooling off. Designer gear, designer mineral water in Hoxton Square, London, 1994.

Algo de ejercicio y un refrigerio de marca. Ropa y agua mineral de diseño en Hoxton Square, Londres, 1994.

In piedi a rinfrescarsi. Per un abito di stilista niente di meglio che un'acqua di stilista, Hoxton Square, Londra, 1994.

LIZ JOHNSON ARTUR/PYMCA

9. Youth
La juventud
Giovani

'...and would you like that gift-wrapped?' A shop that positively bulged with something for the weekend – one of the Ann Summers sex shops, Cardiff, Wales, 1998.

"... ¿quieres que te lo envuelva para regalo?" En esta tienda se puede hallar sin duda algo para amenizar el fin de semana; se trata de uno de los *sex shops* de Ann Summers, en Cardiff, Gales, 1998.

"...vuole un pacchetto regalo?" Un negozio veramente pieno di cose per passare il week-end – uno dei sexy shop di Ann Summers, Cardiff, Galles, 1998.

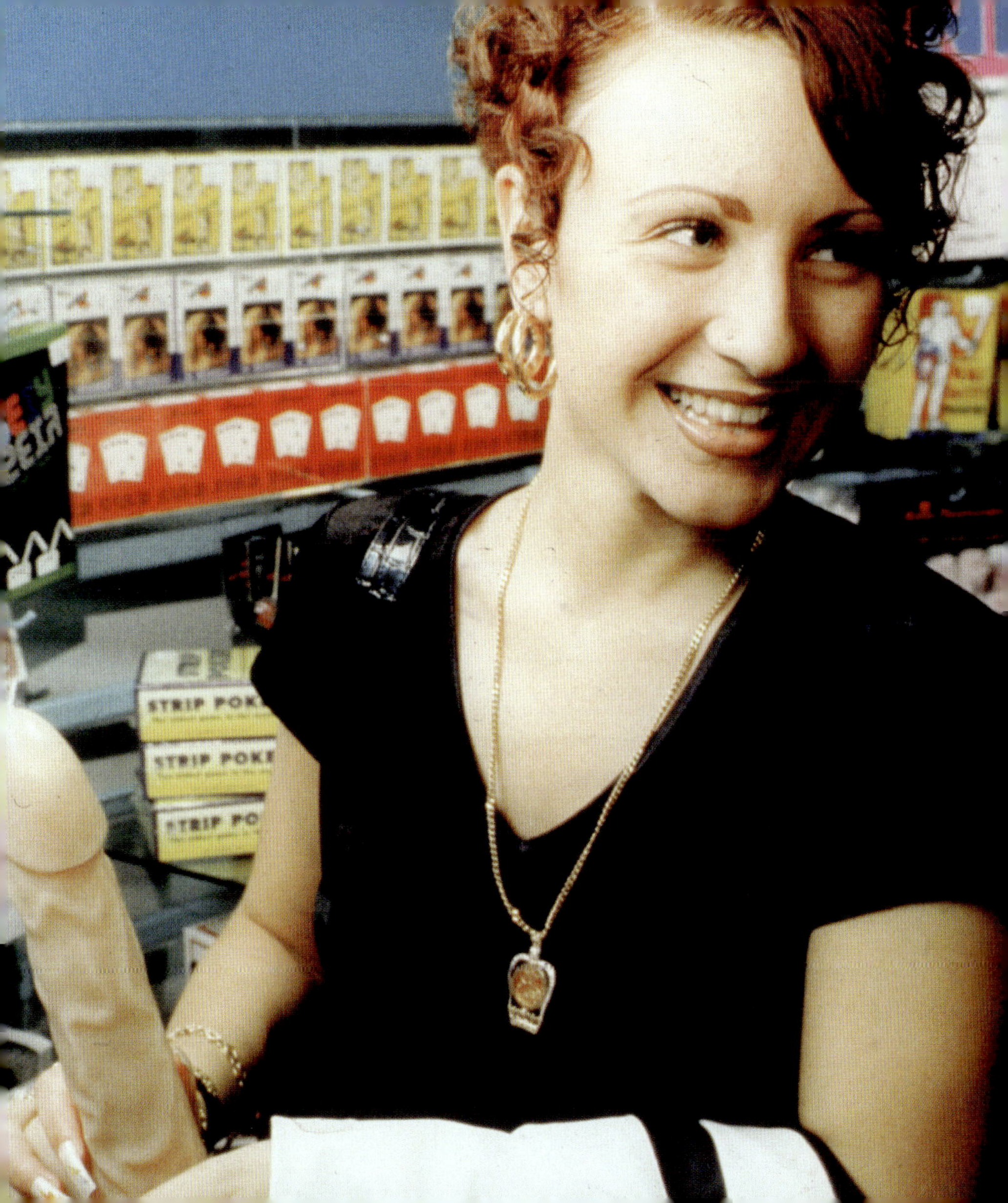
STRIP POKE
STRIP POKE
STRIP PO

9. Youth La juventud Giovani

To be young, with a job, friends, money in your pocket and a sense of purpose in life, the Nineties were a great time to be alive. Ageing populations needed youth to prime the economic pump and to inject energy and momentum into everyday living. The shops were full of the good things in life… clothes and footwear, discs, bikes, sugar-sweet alcoholic drinks, fast food, and all the trappings of that blissful entry into adult life.

To have no job meant to have no money, no power, no style, no hope. The streets of most major cities still provided a hard, cold bed for an increasing number of young people. Drugs provided desperate and momentary relief. The passing crowds provided an unceasing reminder of what could be.

But, for the lucky, life partied on. There were clubs, bars, raves, brawls, nights on the town, lads on the pull, girls on the loose. And there were plenty of role models to inspire young people with the will to succeed, to make a fortune, reach the top, snatch at fame.

Para un joven con trabajo, amigos, dinero en el bolsillo y un propósito claro en la vida, los años noventa son una época espléndida en la que vivir. La cada vez más envejecida población necesita de la juventud para impulsar la economía e inyectar ímpetu y energía a la vida cotidiana. Las tiendas rebosan de todas aquellas cosas buenas de la vida… ropa y calzado, discos, bicicletas, dulces bebidas alcohólicas, comida rápida y el resto de accesorios que adornan el feliz debut en la vida adulta.

En cambio, no tener trabajo es sinónimo de no tener dinero, ni poder, ni clase, ni esperanza. Un creciente número de jóvenes se cobija en el frío y duro lecho que ofrecen las calles de la mayoría de las grandes ciudades. Muchos buscan en las drogas un desesperado y perecedero consuelo, mientras la multitud les recuerda sin cesar lo que podrían haber sido.

Para los más afortunados, sin embargo, la vida es una fiesta continua, repleta de discotecas, bares, juerga, refriegas, salidas nocturnas, chicos predispuestos al ligue y chicas liberadas. Además, los jóvenes se inspiran en un sinfín de modelos que les infunden el deseo de triunfar, amasar fortunas, alcanzar lo más alto y saborear las mieles de la fama.

Essere giovani, con un lavoro, amici, denaro in tasca e un senso da dare alla propria vita: gli anni Novanta furono un magnifico momento da vivere. La popolazione che stava invecchiando aveva bisogno di giovani per rifocillare la macchina dell'economia e per iniettare energia e slancio alla vita quotidiana. I negozi erano pieni di cose buone della vita... vestiti e scarpe, dischi, biciclette, bibite alcoliche zuccherate, fast food, e tutto il corredo per entrare con felicità nella vita adulta.

Non avere lavoro significava non avere denaro, né potere, né stile, né speranze. Le strade delle principali città continuavano ad offrire un freddo e duro letto per un sempre maggior numero di giovani. Le droghe regalavano un disperato e momentaneo sollievo. La folla che passava dava un'idea di ciò che sarebbero potuti divenire.

Ma per i più fortunati la vita continuava ad essere una festa. Nascevano club, bar, rave, risse, serate in città, ragazzi che rimorchiavano, ragazze che si liberavano. Ed esisteva un'infinità di modelli di comportamento per ispirare giovani desiderosi di successo, di fortuna, di raggiungere il vertice e di diventare famosi.

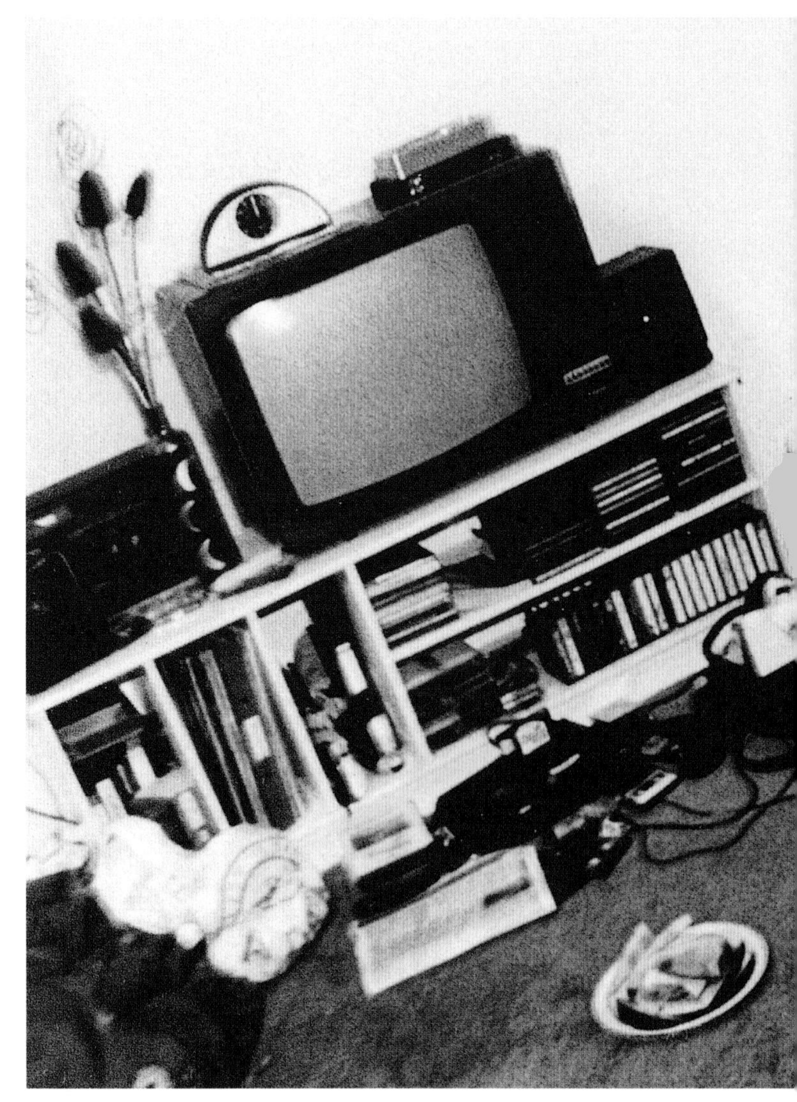

A commonplace scene: ...skinning up, London 1994. Television and drugs offered escape from the harsh realities of life for a great many young people in the 1990s.

Una escena bastante frecuente: un joven londinense liándose un porro, 1994. Para muchos chicos de la década de los noventa, la televisión y las drogas constituyen la evasión perfecta de la cruda realidad de la vida.

Una scena di vita quotidiana... Rullare una canna, Londra, 1994. Per la maggior parte dei giovani degli anni Novanta, la televisione e le droghe offrivano una maniera per sfuggire alla cruda realtà.

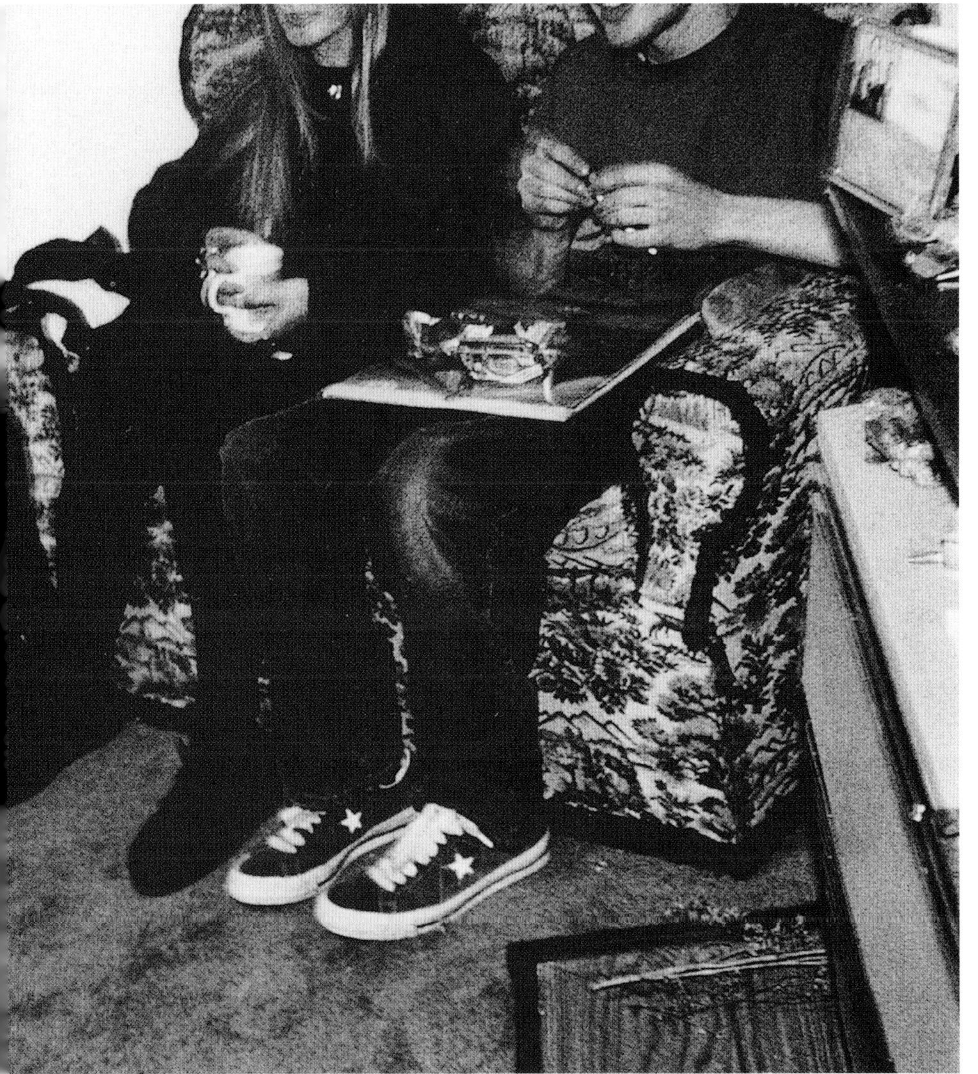

JAMES LANGE/PYMCA

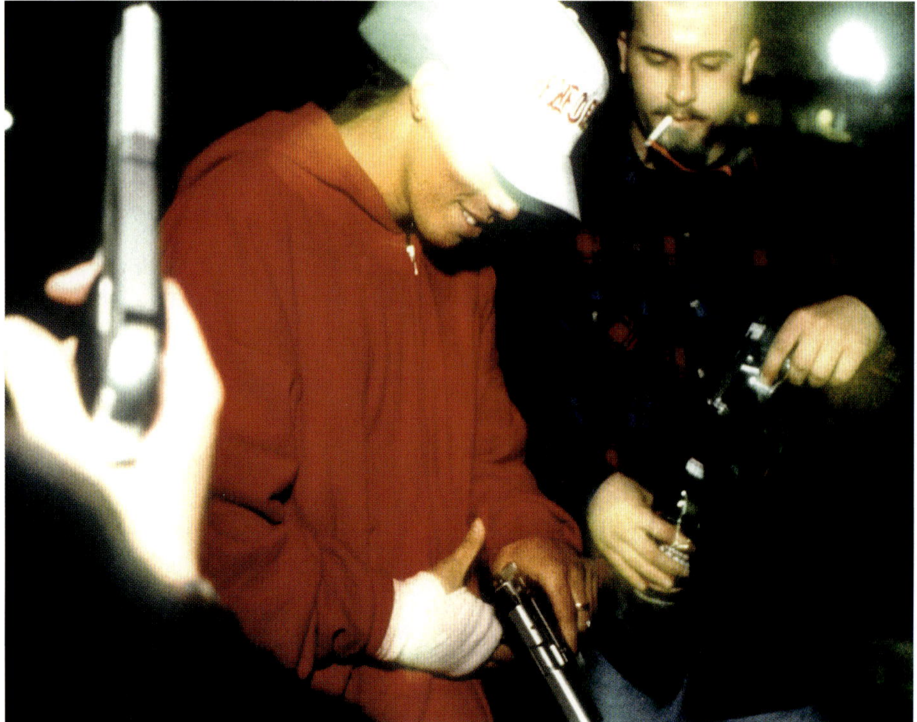

TYRONE TURNER/BLACK STAR/COLORIFIC!

Members of a teenage gang 'Dangerous Bones' check their weapons. Most such gangs were mutual protection societies against a world that young people saw as unnervingly dangerous.

Miembros de una banda de adolescentes, los Dangerous Bones, revisan sus armas. Muchas de estas pandillas nacían como grupos destinados a ofrecer protección a sus integrantes frente a un mundo que consideraban desconcertante y peligroso.

Membri di una gang di adolescenti "Dangerous Bones", mentre controllano le loro armi. La maggior parte di queste gang erano gruppi che si promettevano mutua protezione di fronte a un mondo del quale i giovani avevano una paura incredibile.

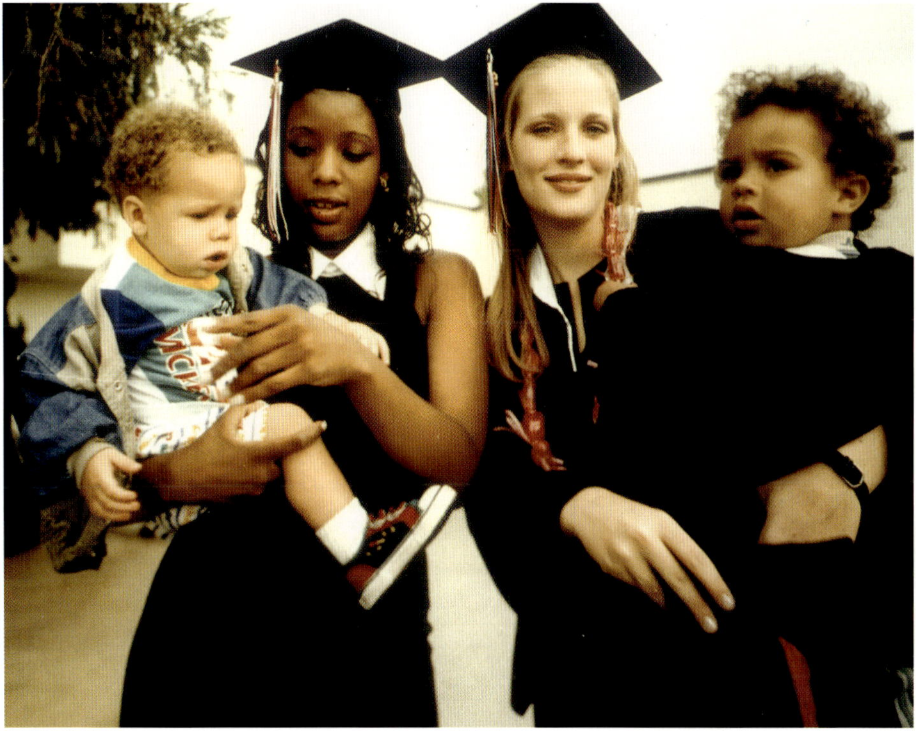

CHERYL HIMMELSTEIN/BLACK STAR/COLORIFIC!

The fruits of further education. Two teenage mothers in high school graduation day mortarboards and gowns pose with their infant children. Much of the stigma attaching to teenage pregnancy had been lifted, but the burden remained.

Los frutos de la educación. Dos madres adolescentes, ataviadas con togas y birretes, posan con sus hijos en su graduación del Instituto. Si bien los embarazos en adolescentes ya no eran un estigma, la carga para las jóvenes madres seguía siendo la misma.

I frutti di tanta educazione. Due mamme adolescenti, durante la cerimonia per la consegna dei diplomi, posano, vestite per l'occasione, con i loro figli. Sebbene non esistesse più gran parte del disonore, restava comunque il peso di essere ragazza madre.

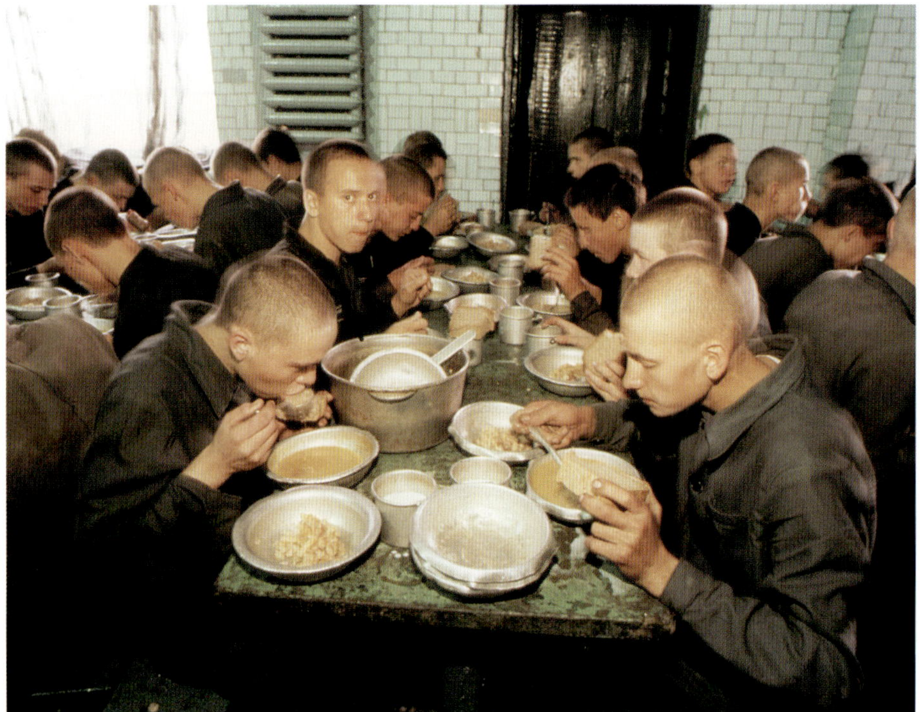

JOSEF POLLEROSS/ANZENBERGER/COLORIFIC!

(Above and opposite) Locked up on both sides of the world. (Above) Inmates at a prison colony for 16- to 18-year-olds, Mariinsk, Russia, 1992. For the most part, their crimes consisted of rape, robbery or murder.

(Arriba y página siguiente) Prisioneros en extremos opuestos del mundo. (Arriba) Internos de una colonia penitenciaria para chicos de 16 a 18 años en Mariinsk, Rusia (1992). La mayoría de estos jóvenes cumplían condena por delitos de violación, robo o asesinato.

(In alto e nella pagina a fianco) Al fresco da entrambi i lati dell'oceano. (In alto) Reclusi in una colonia penale per giovani di 16/18 anni, a Mariinsk, Russia, 1992. I reati più frequenti in cui incorrevano erano stupro, rapina e assassinio.

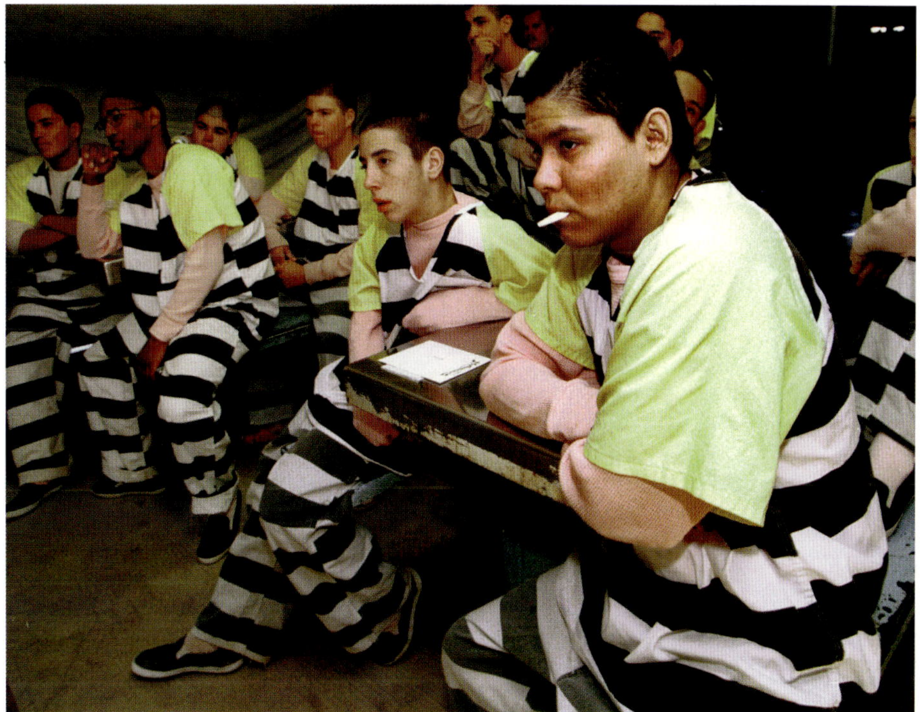

MIKE FIALA/LIAISON AGENCY

Canvas prison. (Above) Some of the 1,400 young detainees at the Maricopa County 'Pup Tent City', Phoenix, Arizona, 23 December 1998. Tent cities were set up to ease the overcrowding of conventional prisons.

Cárcel de lona. (Arriba) Varios de los 1.400 jóvenes presos de la Pup Tent City del condado de Maricopa en Phoenix, Arizona, 23 de diciembre de 1998. Estas ciudades de tiendas se creaban para descongestionar las atestadas cárceles convencionales.

Prigioni di pezza. (In alto) Alcuni dei 1.400 giovani detenuti della "Pup Tent City" di Maricopa County, Phoenix, Arizona, 23 dicembre 1998. Fu necessario creare diverse tendopoli per alleggerire la sovrappopolazione delle carceri convenzionali.

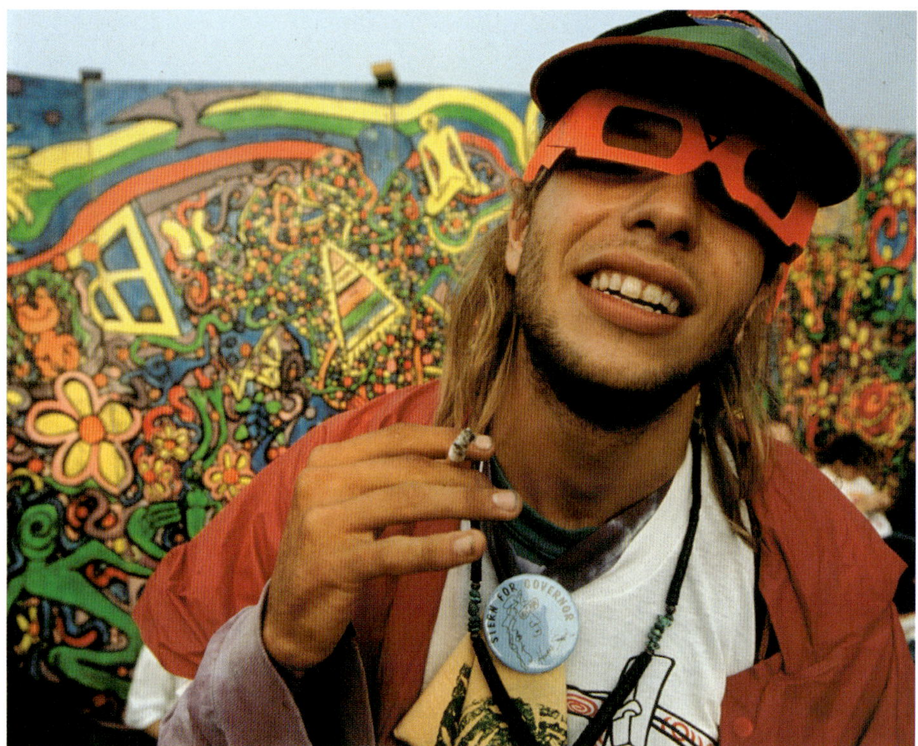

ERICA LANSNER/BLACK STAR/COLORIFIC!

Twenty-five years on from the original rock festival at Woodstock, an attempt was made to revive the spirit and freedom of those three days of peace, love and music in 1969. Even with the obligatory substances (above), the 1994 festival failed miserably.

En 1994, transcurridos 25 años desde el mítico festival de *rock* de Woodstock de 1969, tuvo lugar una tentativa de revivir el espíritu y la libertad de aquellos tres días de paz, amor y música. Ni siquiera la sustancias prohibidas de rigor (arriba) lograron evitar el estrepitoso fracaso de este acontecimiento.

Venticinque anni dopo il vero festival rock di Woodstock, si cercò di far rivivere lo spirito e la libertà di quei tre giorni del 1969 all'insegna della pace, l'amore e la musica. Il festival del 1994 fu un totale fallimento nonostante l'aiuto delle sostanze d'obbligo (qui in alto).

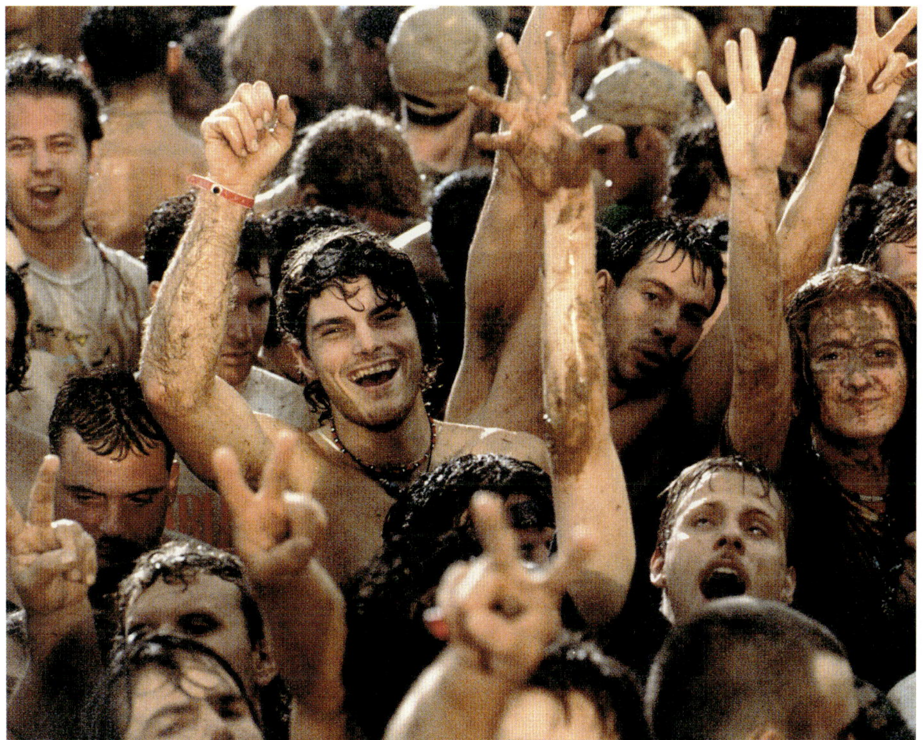

RICHARD BELAND/S.I.N.

The rain and the mud were still there, but that essential hippie culture of the late 1960s had long ago been buried under the new materialism of the late 20th century.

La lluvia y el barro también hicieron acto de presencia, pero la esencia de la cultura *hippy* de finales de los sesenta hacía ya mucho que había sido sepultada por el nuevo materialismo imperante en las postrimerías del siglo XX.

La pioggia e il fango fecero come sempre atto di presenza, ma lo spirito della cultura hippie della fine degli anni Sessanta era ormai stato sotterrato dal nuovo materialismo della fine del XX secolo.

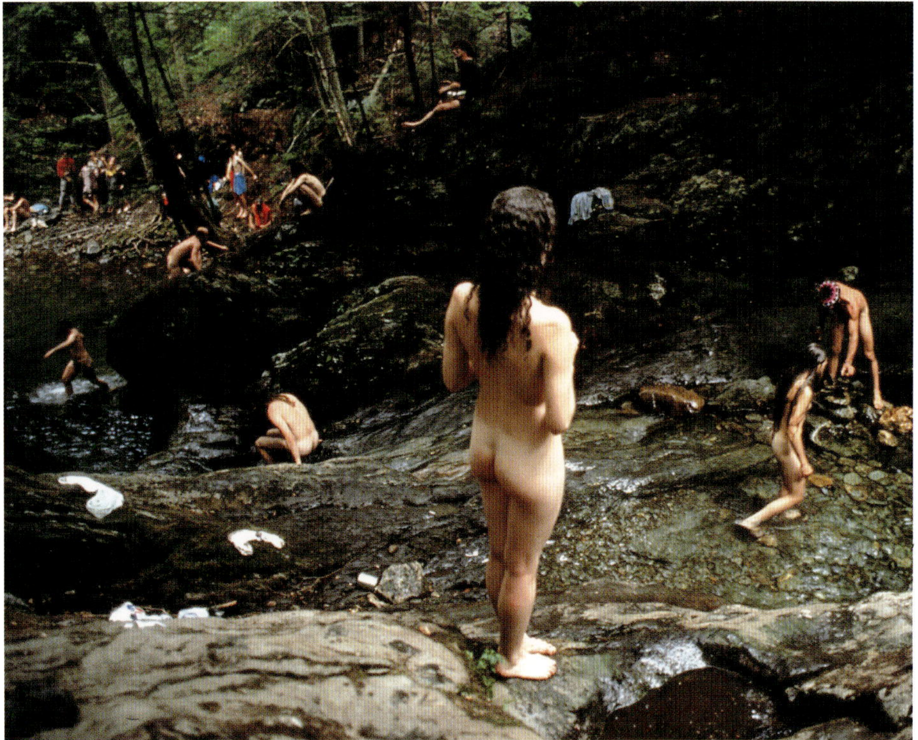

RICK FRIEDMAN/BLACK STAR/COLORIFIC!

The spirit was willing, the flesh was willing, but such events as the Rainbow Gathering at Vermont in 1991 (above) were merely brief escapes from the routine of comfortable and well-ordered life.

Tanto el cuerpo como el espíritu acogían con excelente predisposición acontecimientos como el Rainbow Gathering de Vermont en 1991 (arriba), si bien estos no significaban mucho más que una buena ocasión para escapar de la rutina de una vida cómoda y ordenada.

Sebbene l'anima e la carne lo desiderassero più che mai, eventi come il Rainbow Gathering a Vermont, nel 1991 (in alto) non erano altro che brevi fughe dalla routine di una vita comoda e perfettamente organizzata.

Nature spoils what might have been a great gig. A fan arises from the slime of the Glastonbury Festival, Somerset, 1997.

Una fan completamente embarrada en el festival de Glastonbury, en Somerset, Inglaterra, 1997. La meteorología estropeó lo que podría haber sido un fabuloso evento.

La natura rovinò quello che poteva divenire un fantastico concerto. Una spettatrice si dibatte nella melma del Glastonbury Festival, Somerset, 1997.

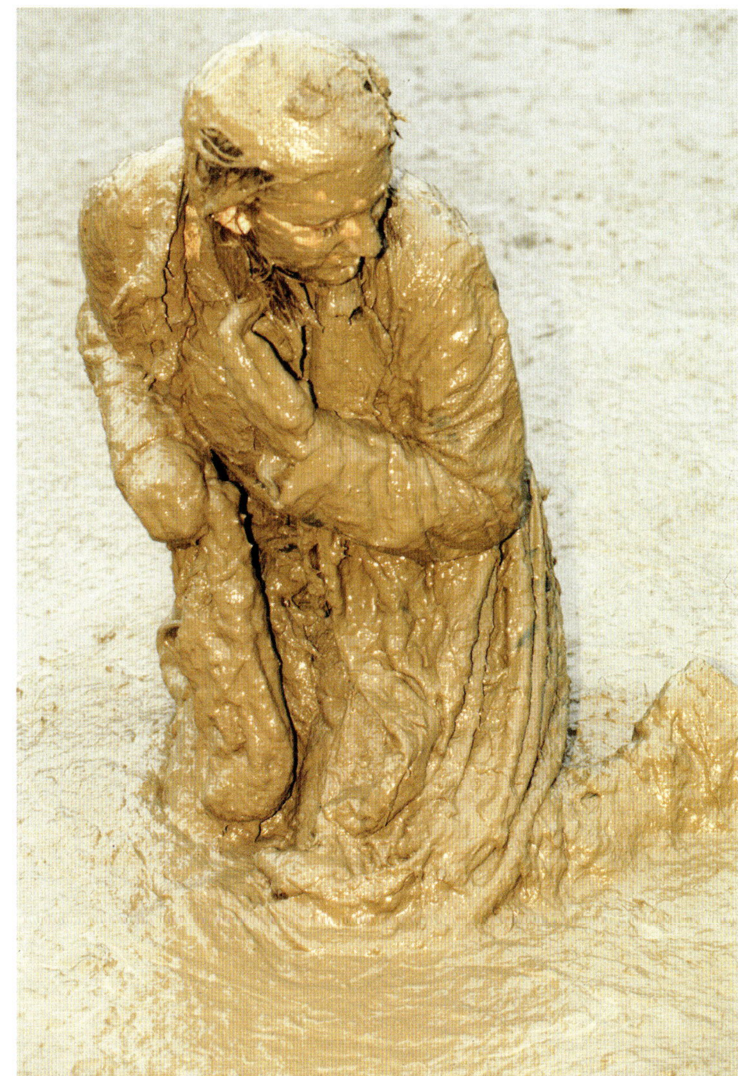

MELANIE COX/S.I.N.

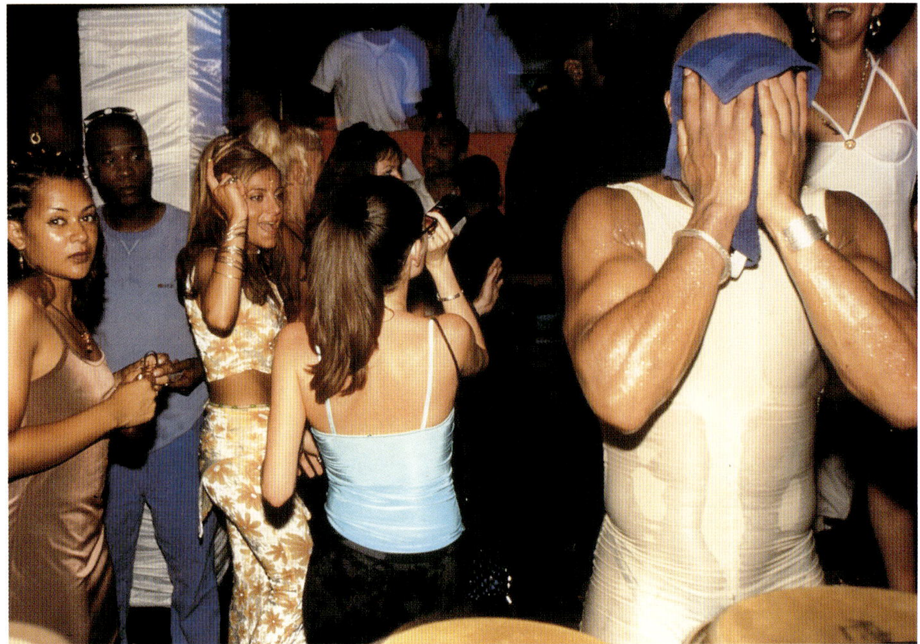

DAVID SWINDELLS/PYMCA

It's a club, an empire, and a way of life. Travis the Bongo drives regulars to steam and sweat their way through an evening at 'Twice As Nice', a British garage night started in 1996.

Un club, un imperio, un estilo de vida. En el Twice As Nice –un local nocturno británico inaugurado en 1996, en donde la música *garage* es la reina–, Travis caldea el ambiente tocando el bongó hasta que los asiduos acaban empapados en sudor.

È un club, un impero e un modo di vivere. Travis the Bongo riscalda e fa sudare gli animi durante una serata al "Twice As Nice", un club UK garage aperto nel 1996.

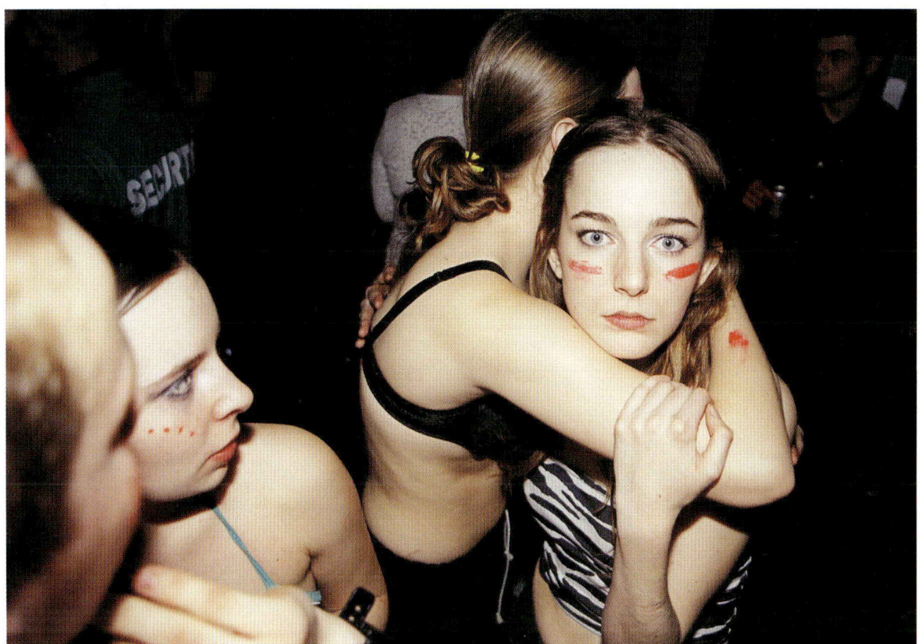

MATT SMITH/PYMCA

Out of it but still there. 'Infamous' might at Lakota, Bristol, early 1990s. Ecstacy, trip hop, Tricky and Portishead were all part of the Bristol scene at the time.

Hasta que el cuerpo aguante en el infame club Lakota de Bristol, a principios de 1990. Extásis, *trip hop*, Tricky y Portishead: todos formaban parte del panorama nocturno del Bristol de la época.

Già all'uscita, ma ancora dentro. Notte "famosa" a Lakota (Bristol), agli inizi degli anni Novanta. Ecstasy, trip hop, Tricky e Portishead facevano tutti parte della scena di Bristol del momento.

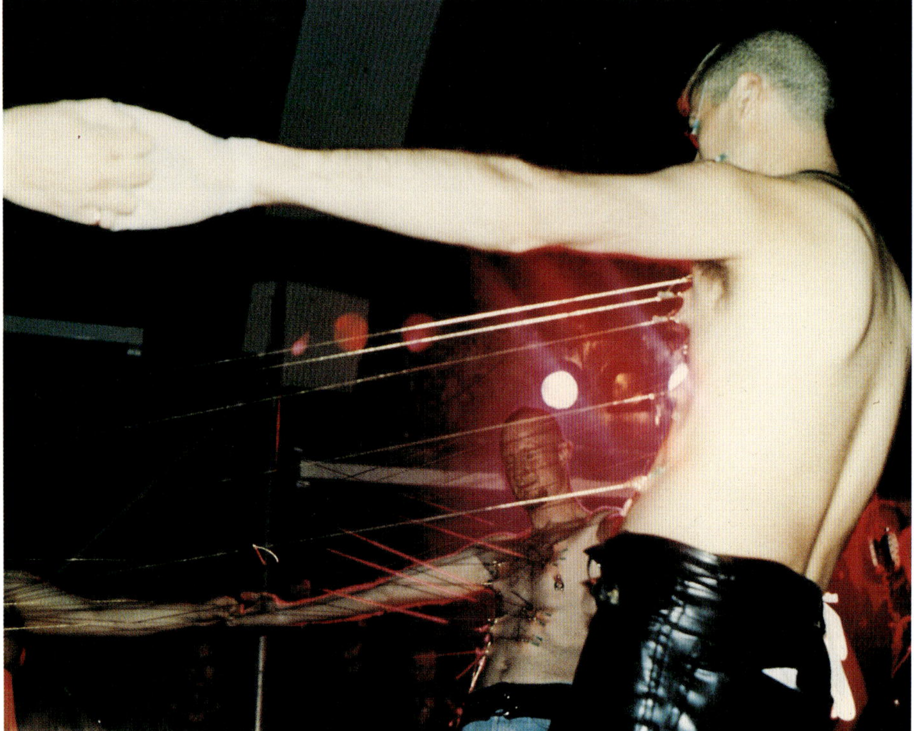

DARREN REGMER/PYMCA

Plenty of fun, but with strings attached, at the Torture Garden, London, 1998. The dividing line between pain and pleasure became hopelessly blurred for many in the 1990s.

Diversión a raudales, pero solo si hay cuerdas de por medio, en el Torture Garden de Londres, 1998. Para muchos, la línea que separa el dolor del placer quedó completamente difuminada en los años noventa.

Divertimento a più non posso, ma con le cinghie allacciate, nel Torture Garden, Londra, 1998. Per molte persone gli anni Novanta segnarono la fine del confine fra dolore e piacere.

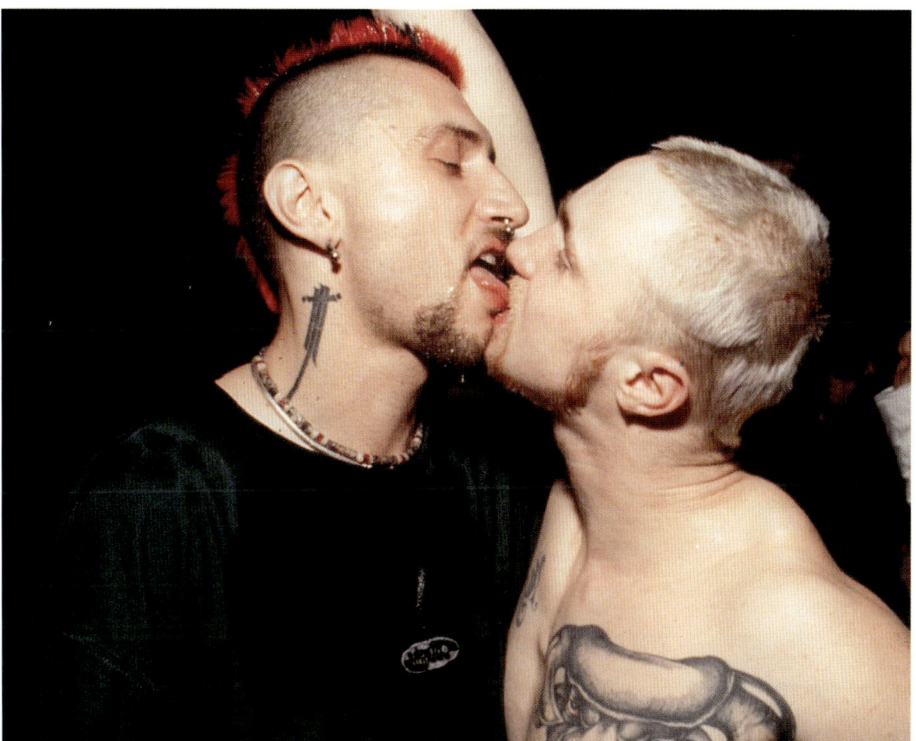

JAY BROOKS/PYMCA

The taste of true freedom in the glorious years that followed the collapse of Communism in Czechoslovakia for two revellers in a Prague club, 1998. How different from the old Party life.

Dos gays saborean el gusto de la libertad en un club de Praga en 1998, durante la época gloriosa que sucedió a la caída del comunismo en Checoslovaquia. La vida tras la desaparición del antiguo partido muestra una cara bastante diferente.

Il sapore della vera libertà, durante i magnifici giorni che seguirono il crollo del comunismo in Cecoslovacchia, per due ragazzi in un club di Praga, 1998. Che differenza con la vecchia vita del Partito.

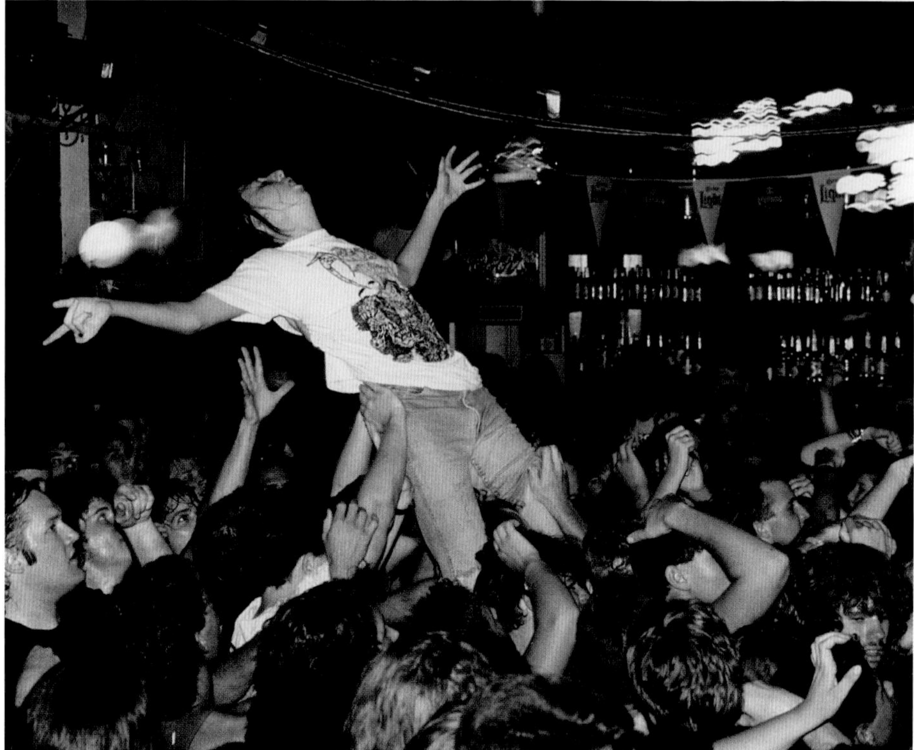

DEREK RIDGERS/PYMCA

Club or concert, it didn't matter. There was always the chance that someone would be overcome by the music, the ambience, the booze... as in this scene in Albuquerque, New Mexico, 1990.

Club o concierto; poco importa. Siempre cabe la posibilidad de que alguien se deje arrastrar por la música, el ambiente, el alcohol... como en esta escena en Albuquerque, Nuevo México, 1990.

Club o concerto, poco importava. Esisteva sempre la possibilità che qualcuno venisse esaltato dalla musica, dall'atmosfera, dall'alcol... come in questa scena di Albuquerque, Nuovo Messico, 1990.

Someone gimme a break: the Wag, one of London's top dance clubs, 1997.

Exhibición de *break dance* en The Wag, uno de los locales de este tipo de baile más en boga de Londres, 1997.

Non riesco più a fermarmi: "The Wag", uno dei migliori dance club di Londra, 1997.

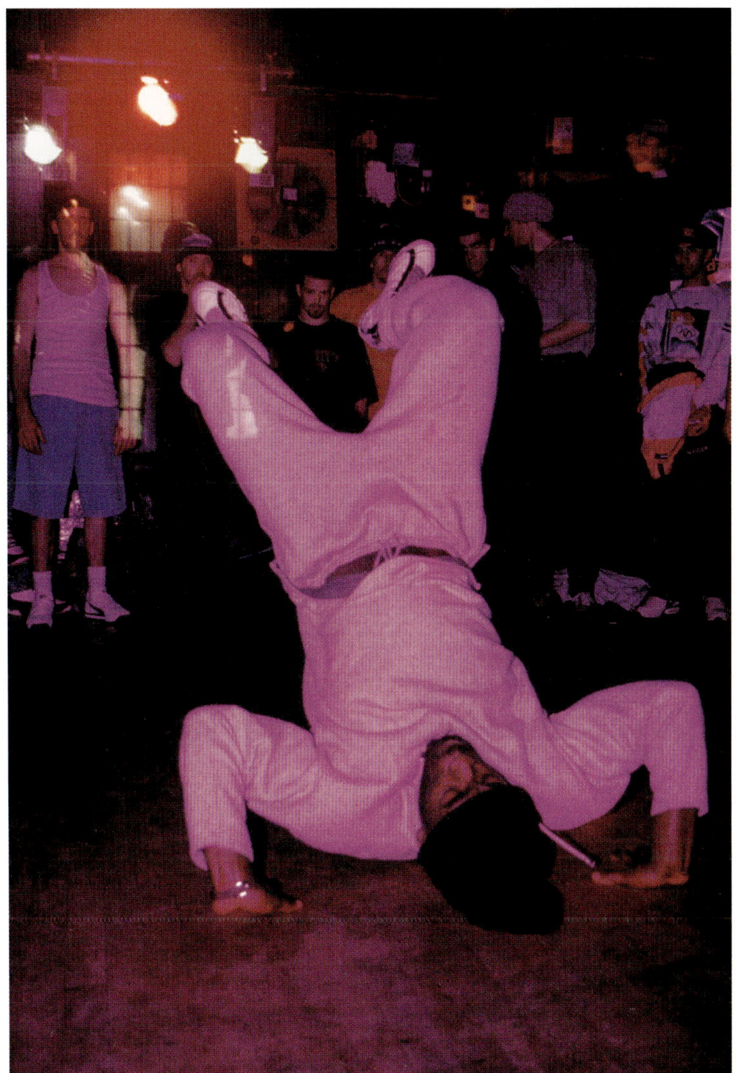

JAY BROOKS/PYMCA

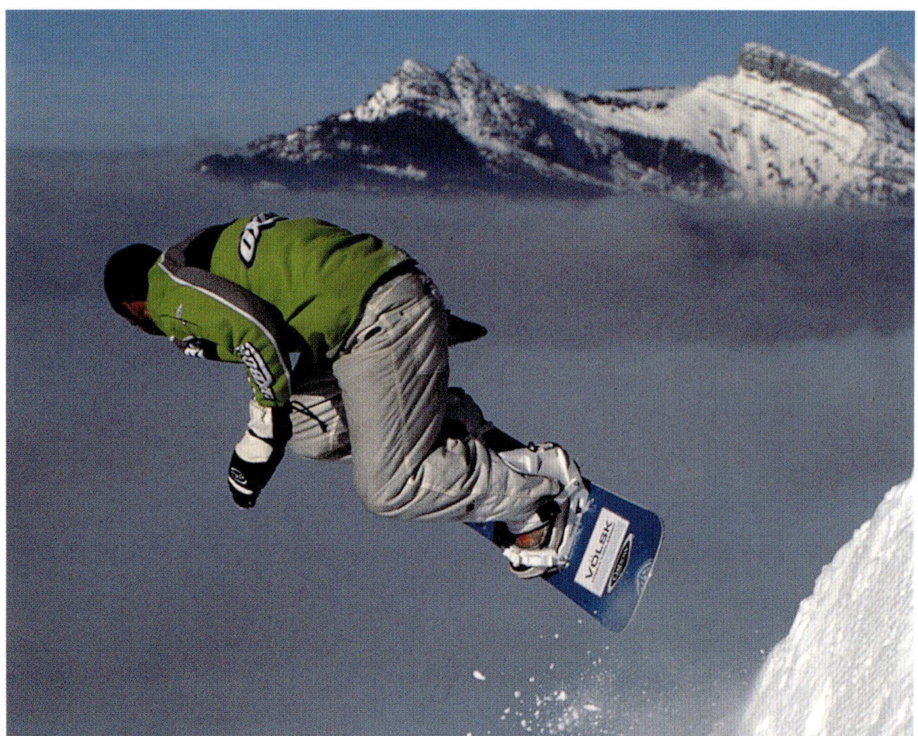

HENRY IDDON/PYMCA

Away from the club scene there was plenty of fresh air and fun for those with more bravery than sense of self-preservation. (Above) Free-riding on the snowy slopes of La Clusaz, France, 1998.

Lejos de las pistas de baile, muchos jóvenes con más arrojo que sentido del riesgo se lanzan en busca de aire puro y diversión en estado salvaje. (Arriba) Practicando el *free-ride* en las pendientes nevadas de La Clusaz, Francia, 1998.

Lontano dai club c'erano ancora aria fresca e divertimento per chi preferiva il coraggio all'istinto di autoconservazione. (In alto) Free-ride sulle cime innevate di La Clusaz, Francia, 1998.

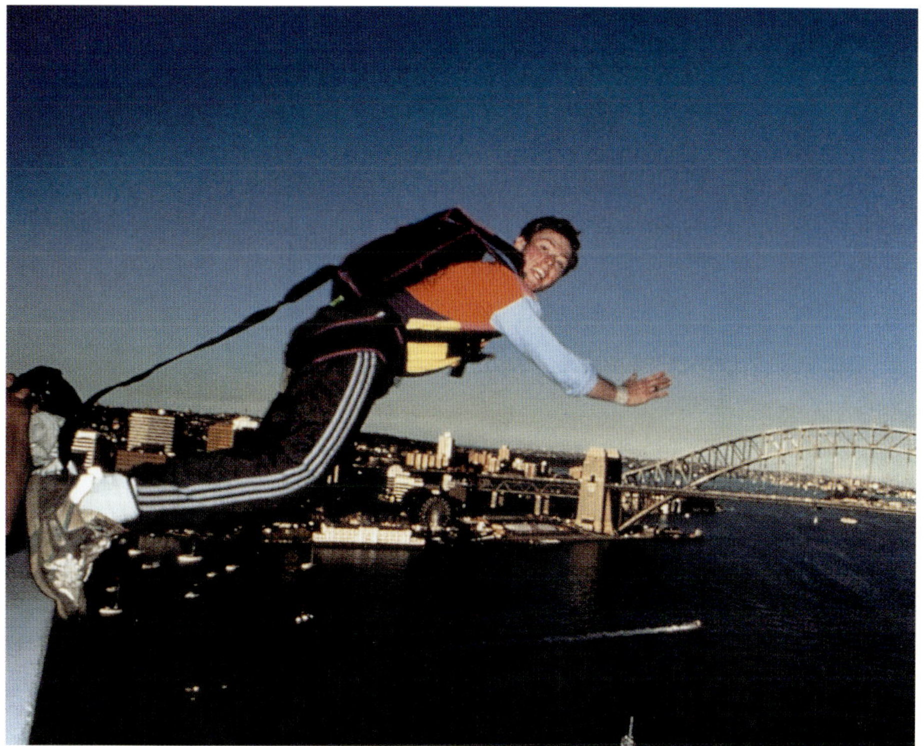

ELIO LOCCISANO/ANZENBERGER/COLORIFIC!

With not a moment's thought for the consequences of the line breaking or the strain on his spine, a base jumper takes off from the heights overlooking Sydney Harbour, Australia.

Sin pensar ni por un momento en las consecuencias de una posible ruptura de la cuerda o en lo que pueda llegar a sufrir su columna vertebral, este saltador se precipita al vacío desde las alturas que dominan el puerto de Sidney, en Australia.

Senza pensare nemmeno per un secondo alle conseguenze della rottura della corda o dello sforzo a cui viene sottoposta la spina dorsale, un base jumper prende il volo di fronte al Porto di Sydney, Australia.

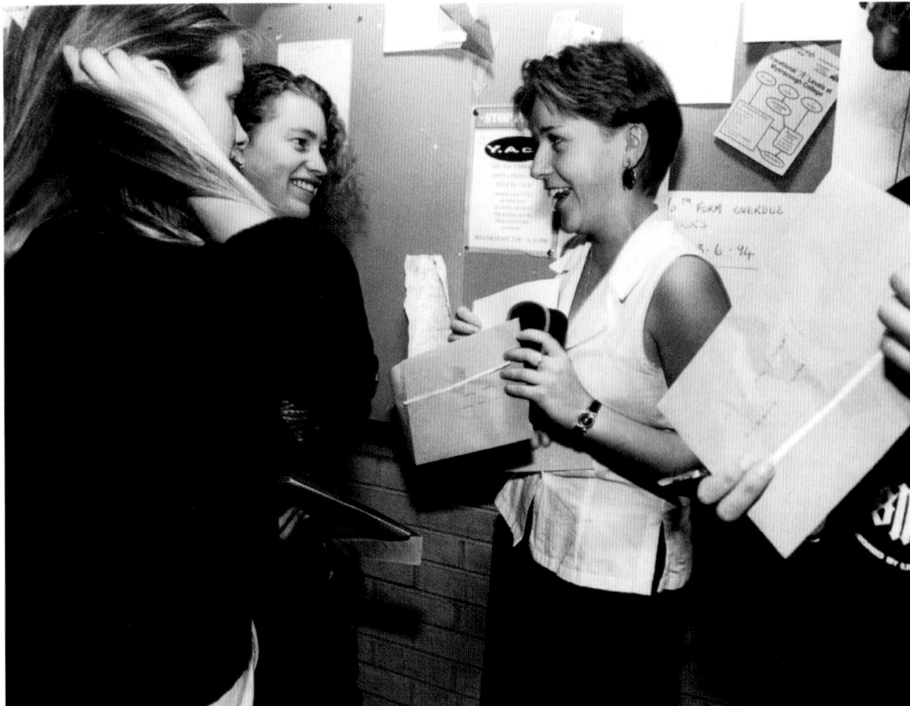

ANDY HALL

Was it all worthwhile? The day of reckoning as sixth-form students get their A-level exam results, Chenderit School, 19 August 1999.

¿Valió la pena el esfuerzo? Los alumnos de bachillerato de Chenderit School (Gran Bretaña) conocen sus notas de selectividad, 19 de agosto de 1999.

Ne valeva veramente la pena? Il giorno della verità, quando un gruppo di studenti all'ultimo anno della Chenderit School riceve i risultati dell'esame di maturità, 19 agosto 1999.

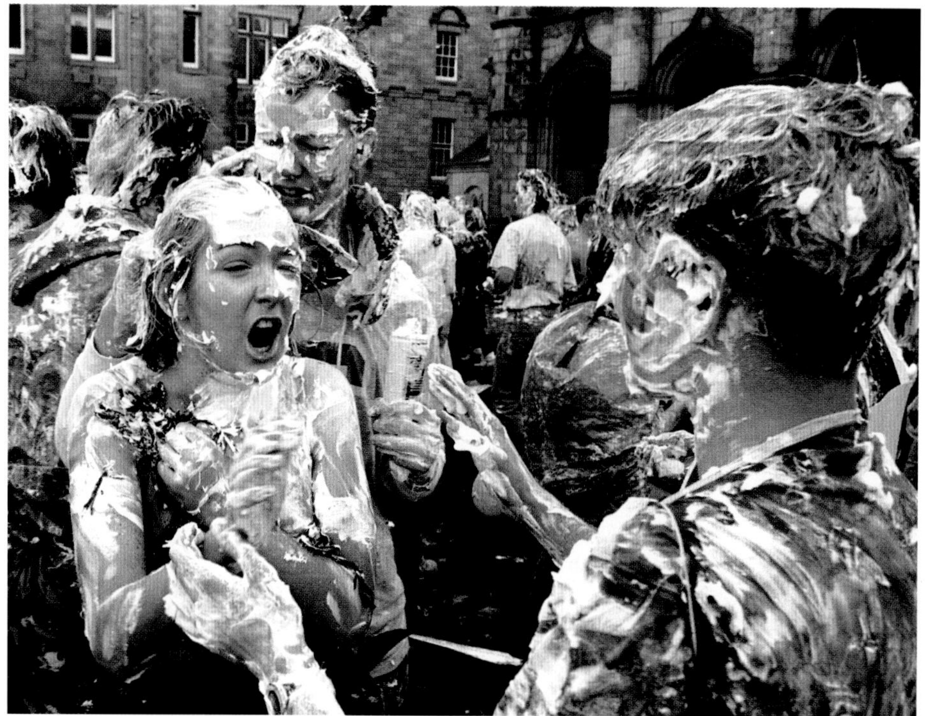

MURDO MACLEOD

And will it all be worthwhile? Freshers (first-year students) enjoy ritual humiliation in the traditionally lukewarm welcome to university by second-year students, St Andrews, Scotland.

¿Valdrá la pena *este* esfuerzo? Los estudiantes de primer año de la universidad de St Andrews (Escocia) son objeto de la típica novatada por parte de los alumnos de segundo año, que les daban la bienvenida.

E ne varrà veramente la pena? Studenti appena entrati all'università si sottopongono alla classica umiliazione del freddo benvenuto imposto dagli studenti di secondo anno a St Andrews, Scozia.

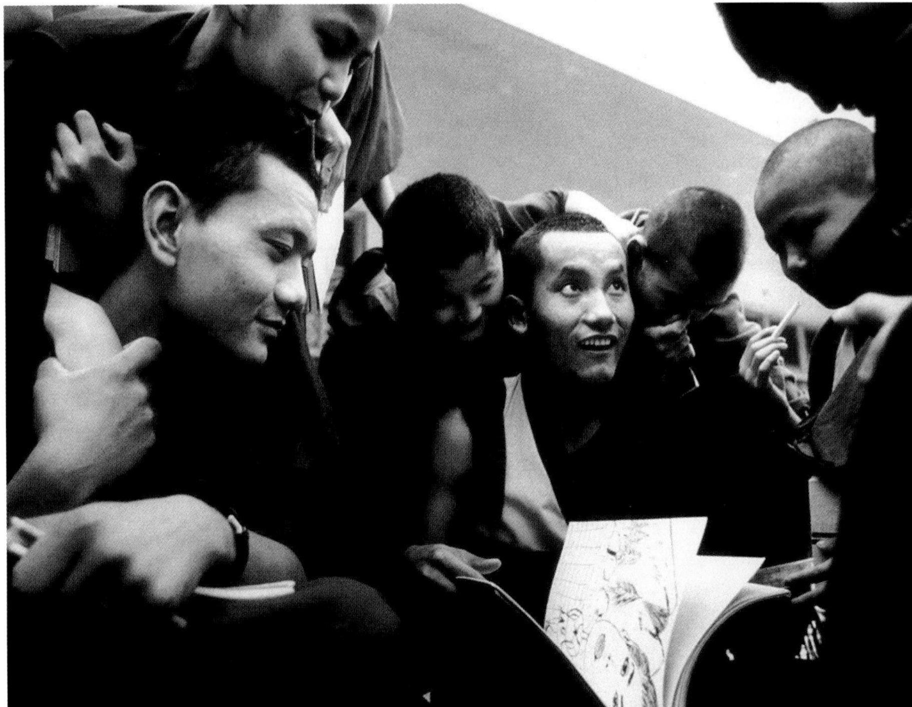

DAVID TURNLEY/BLACK STAR/COLORIFIC!

(Above and opposite) Punks and monks, a story of contrasting though related philosophies. (Above) A break in the customary meditation for Tibetan Buddhist monks at the Dharamsala Monastery, India, January 1999.

(Arriba y página siguiente) *Punks* y monjes, dos filosofías muy distintas pero con muchos puntos en común. (Arriba) Monjes budistas tibetanos del monasterio Dharamsala de la India hacen una pausa en sus sesiones de meditación habituales, enero de 1999.

(In alto e pagina a fianco) Punk e monaci, una storia di contrasti, ma con filosofie simili. (In alto) una pausa durante la consueta meditazione dei monaci buddisti tibetani nel monastero di Dharamsala, India, gennaio 1999.

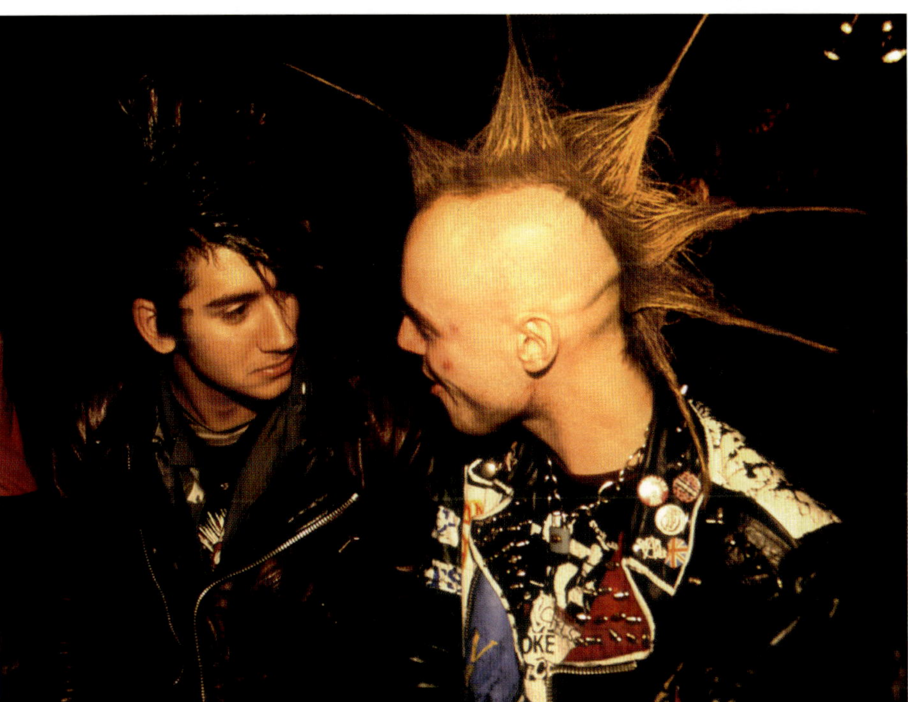

TODD YATES/BLACK STAR/COLORIFIC!

An alternative way of freeing oneself from the restrictions and routines of society. Punks on a New York City street, 1996. Though not as old as Buddhism, the Punk movement was into its third generation.

Punks en una calle de Nueva York, 1996. Si bien no tan ancestral como el budismo, el movimiento *punk* –ya en su tercera generación– constituye una manera alternativa de traspasar los límites que impone la sociedad y de protestar ante los convencionalismos sociales.

Una maniera alternativa di liberarsi dai divieti e dalla routine della società. Punk in una strada di New York, 1996. Sebbene il movimento Punk non sia così antico come il buddismo, in quel momento era già alla sua terza generazione.

10. Sport
Deporte
Sport

Ronaldo cuts a swathe through the Moroccan defence as Brazil win their Group A match 3-0 during the World Cup preliminaries in Nantes, France, 16 June 1998.

Ronaldo traspasa la defensa del equipo marroquí en un partido del grupo A, en la primera eliminatoria de la Copa del Mundo, disputado en la ciudad francesa de Nantes el 16 de junio de 1998. Brasil ganó a Marruecos por 3 a 0.

Ronaldo si apre un varco nella difesa marocchina durante i preliminari del gruppo A della Coppa del Mondo, a Nantes, in Francia, il 16 giugno 1998, quando il Brasile vinse per 3 a 0.

ROSS KINNAIRD/ALLSPORT

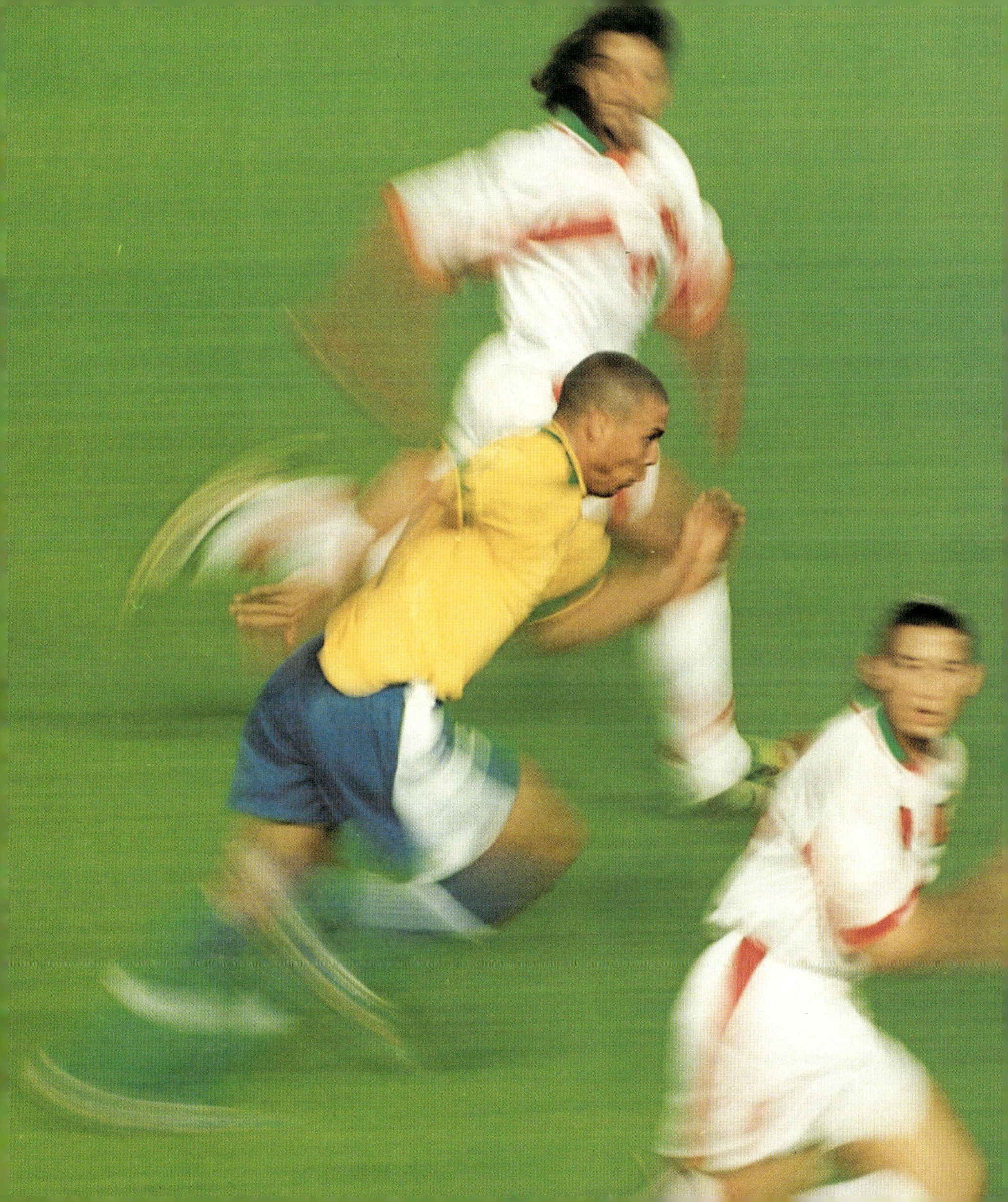

10. Sport
Deporte
Sport

Never before had so much time, money and newsprint been devoted to sport. The private lives of footballers, athletes, tennis players, boxers, Grand Prix drivers and even match-fixing cricketers were minutely examined and posted for all to see. The cult of sporting celebrity ensured that all play and no work made Jack a very rich boy.

Basketball, ice hockey, baseball and golf increased their international appeal – thanks largely to coverage by television channels which had lost out in the auctions of rights to televise the more popular sports. The Olympic Games passed by happily enough in Barcelona in 1992, but in Atlanta in 1996 they were marred by a terrorist bomb that killed two and injured well over a hundred.

Football became the greatest sporting money-spinner of all time, with a proliferation of international and continental tournaments. Players' salaries reached ludicrous levels. Managers walked a weekly tightrope, their jobs secure only while the team performed well. And it cost fans dear to watch the game they loved and to wear replica strips manufactured in the Third World.

Jamás el deporte había despertado tanto interés, movido tanto dinero ni copado tantas páginas en los periódicos como en los noventa. Las vidas privadas de futbolistas, atletas, tenistas, boxeadores, pilotos de carreras y hasta jugadores de *cricket* devienen blanco de todas las miradas y pasan a ser de dominio público. El culto a la celebridad deportiva induce a creer que cualquiera puede hacerse millonario sin trabajar si destaca en algún deporte.

Baloncesto, *hockey* sobre hielo, béisbol y golf ganan adeptos a nivel internacional, gracias sobre todo a la cobertura que ofrecen las cadenas de televisión que no consiguen los derechos para retransmitir otros encuentros deportivos más populares. Los Juegos

Olímpicos de Barcelona de 1992 son todo un éxito mientras que los de Atlanta de 1996 se ven malogrados por la explosión de una bomba terrorista que mata a dos personas y hiere a más de un centenar.

El fútbol se convierte en la mayor máquina de hacer dinero jamás inventada; proliferan los torneos internacionales y continentales, los salarios de los jugadores alcanzan cifras astronómicas y los entrenadores caminan semanalmente por la cuerda floja, pendientes del buen rendimiento de su equipo, del que depende directamente su puesto de trabajo. Por su parte, los seguidores pagan verdaderas fortunas para asistir a los partidos y para adquirir réplicas de las camisetas de sus jugadores favoritos, las cuales se fabrican a bajo coste en países del Tercer Mundo.

Mai prima di quel momento così tanto tempo, denaro e carta di giornale erano stati dedicati allo sport. Le vite private dei calciatori, degli atleti, dei giocatori di tennis, dei pugili, dei piloti di Formula 1 e persino dei giocatori di cricket venivano sottoposte a un minuzioso esame per essere poi date in pasto al pubblico. Grazie al culto per le star dello sport si dimostrò che per diventare ricchi bastava giocare e si poteva fare a meno di lavorare.

Il basket, l'hockey su ghiaccio, il baseball e il golf divennero sport di moda a livello internazionale – grazie principalmente alla diffusione che ne fecero i vari canali televisivi dopo aver perso i diritti per trasmettere sport più popolari. Le Olimpiadi di Barcellona del 1992 andarono più o meno lisce come l'olio, ma quelle del 1996 ad Atlanta vennero sconvolte da una bomba terrorista che provocò due morti e più di un centinaio di feriti.

Il calcio si trasformò nella più potente macchina per fare soldi mai esistita prima di quel momento, con la proliferazione di tornei internazionali e continentali. Gli stipendi dei calciatori raggiunsero livelli assurdi, mentre gli allenatori, che dipendevano esclusivamente dal rendimento della loro squadra, vivevano sul filo del licenziamento settimana dopo settimana. E i fan pagavano cifre astronomiche per assistere alla loro partita preferita e per indossare le magliette della loro squadra, prodotte nel Terzo Mondo.

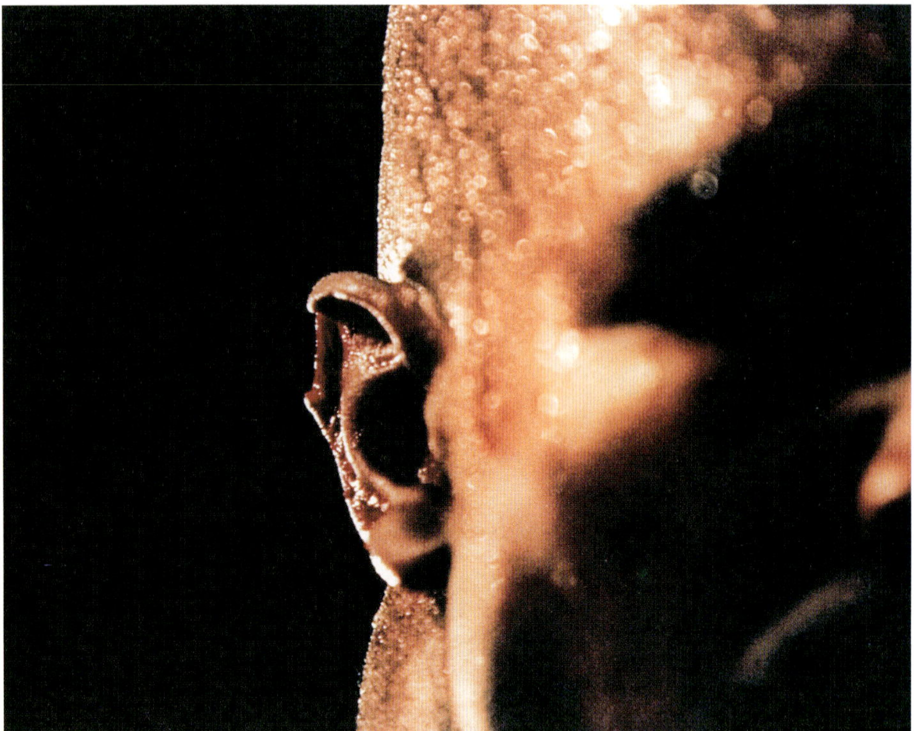

JED JACOBSOHN/ALLSPORT

The remains of Evander Holyfield's right ear after eleven rounds with Mike Tyson for the WBA Heavyweight title at the MGM Grand Garden, Las Vegas, 28 June 1997. Holyfield was not expected to win.

Así quedó la oreja derecha de Evander Holyfield tras ser mordida por Mike Tyson en el undécimo asalto del combate por el título de campeón del mundo de los pesos pesados de la WBA, disputado en el MGM Grand Garden de Las Vegas el 28 de junio de 1997. Holyfield no partía como favorito.

Ciò che resta dell'orecchio destro di Evander Holyfield dopo undici round contro Mike Tyson, che era dato per favorito per conquistare il titolo di pesi massimi della WBA al MGM Grand Garden di Las Vegas, 28 giugno 1997.

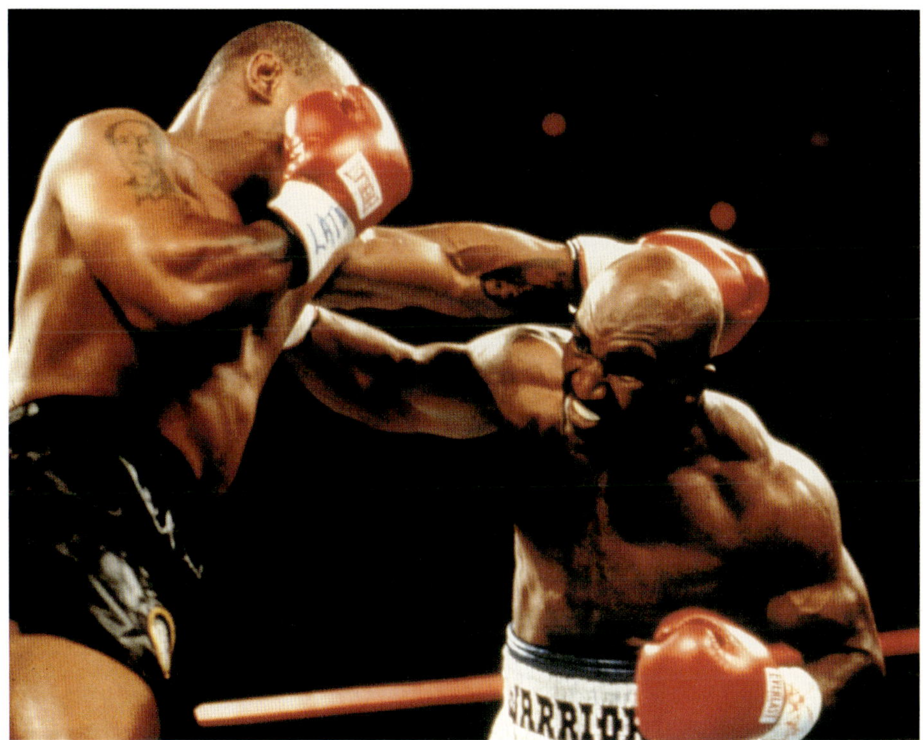

COLORIFIC!

The 1990s were not propitious for Tyson. In 1992 he was sentenced to six years in gaol for the rape of a beauty contestant in an Indianapolis hotel room. Five years later he was back in the ring, but Holyfield (right) outpunched him.

La década de 1990 no sonrió a Tyson. En 1992 fue condenado a seis años de cárcel por violar a una participante de un certamen de belleza en un hotel de Indianápolis. Cinco años más tarde volvió a los cuadriláteros pero fue derrotado por Holyfield (derecha).

Gli anni Novanta non furono favorevoli per Tyson. Nel 1992 fu condannato a sei anni di prigione per aver stuprato una partecipante a un concorso di bellezza in una camera di un hotel di Indianapolis. Cinque anni dopo tornò sul ring, ma venne vinto da Holyfield (a destra).

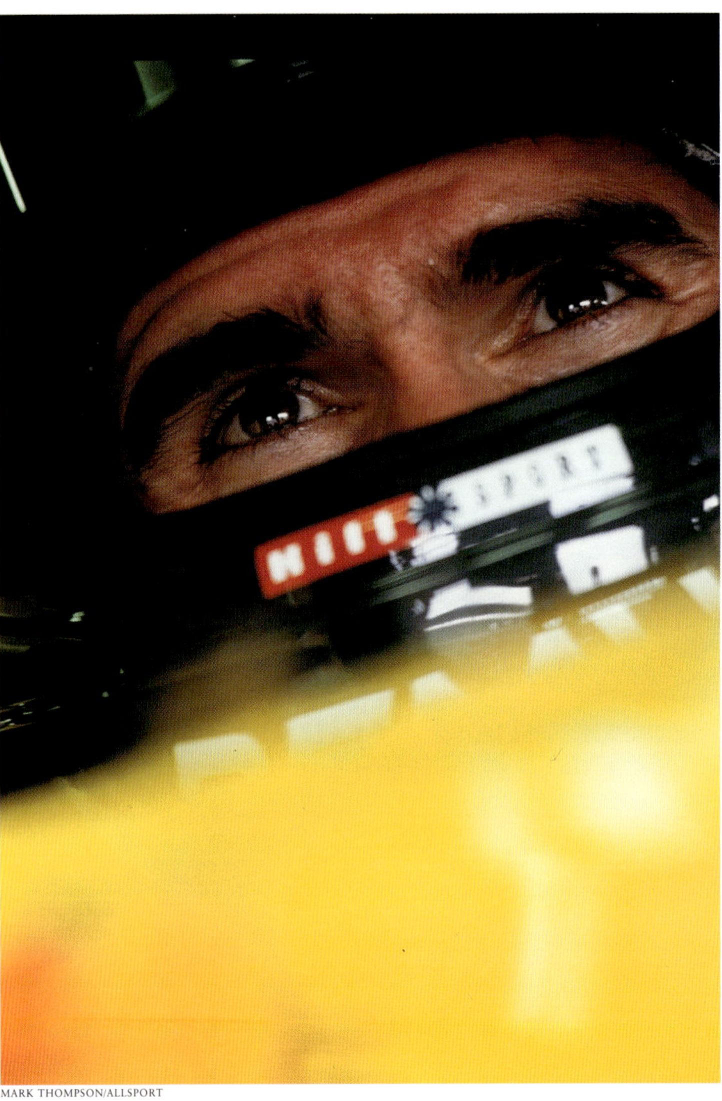

MARK THOMPSON/ALLSPORT

British Formula 1 racing driver Damon Hill at the Spanish Grand Prix, Barcelona, 30 May 1999.

Damon Hill, piloto británico de Fórmula 1, en el Gran Premio de España, disputado en Montmeló, 30 de mayo de 1999.

Il pilota britannico di Formula 1 Damon Hill durante il Gran Premio di Spagna, Barcellona, 30 maggio 1999.

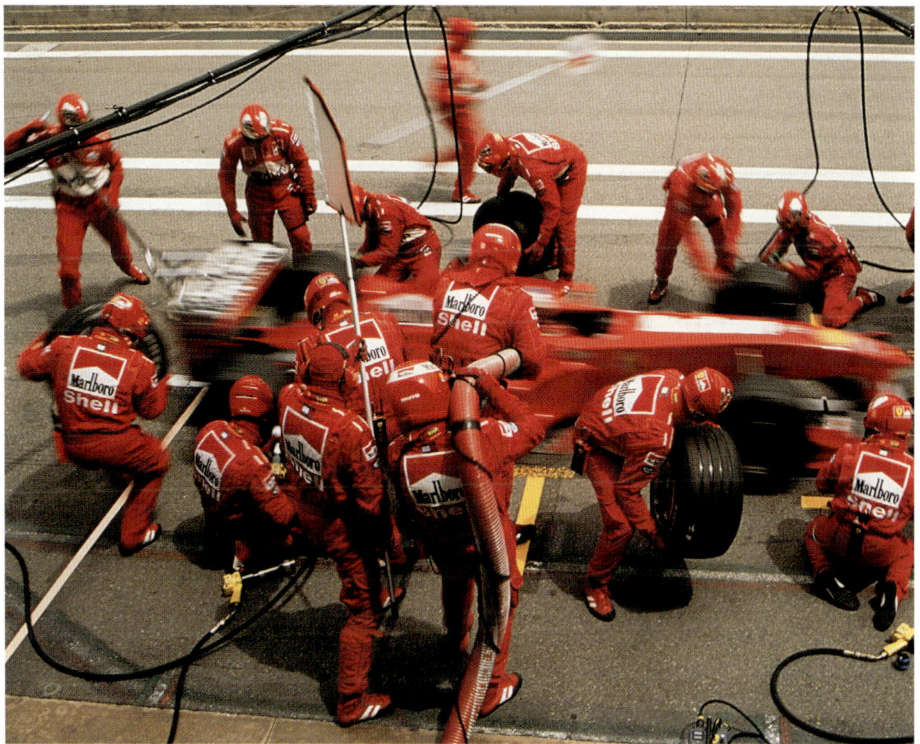

MICHAEL COOPER/ALLSPORT

Germany's Michael Schumacher takes his Ferrari into the pits during the same race. Schumacher finished third, his arch rival Hill seventh. The race was won by Mika Hakkinen in a McLaren.

El alemán Michael Schumacher realiza una parada en boxes durante la misma carrera. Schumacher acabó en tercer lugar y su gran rival, séptimo. Mika Hakkinen, de la escudería McLaren, se alzó con el primer puesto del podio.

Il tedesco Michael Schumacher entra nel box durante la stessa gara. Schumacher arrivò terzo, e il suo rivale più agguerrito, Hill, settimo. La corsa venne vinta da Mika Hakkinen su McLaren.

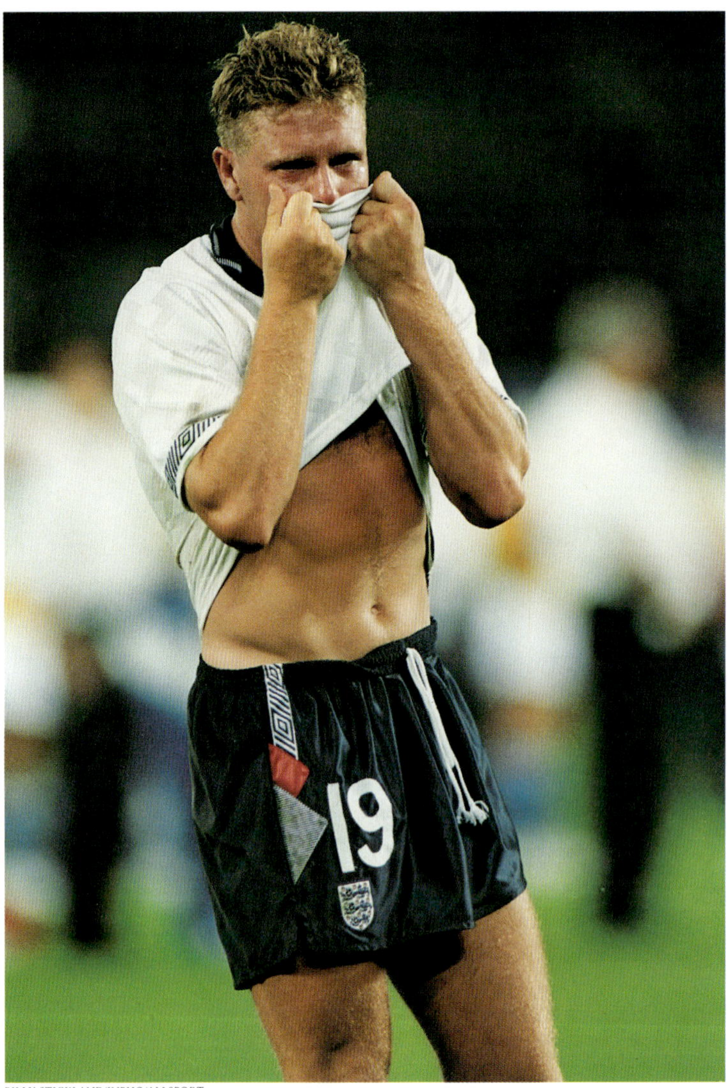

BILLY STICKLAND/INPHO/ALLSPORT

The tears of Gazza. Paul Gascoigne's heart-broken response to a yellow card during England's defeat by West Germany in the 1990 World Cup semi-final, Turin, Italy…

Las lágrimas de Gazza. La tarjeta amarilla recibida por Paul Gascoigne durante la semifinal de la Copa del Mundo de 1990 –celebrada en la ciudad italiana de Turín– desata su llanto ante la derrota inglesa frente a Alemania Occidental…

Le lacrime di Gazza. Lo sconforto di Paul Gascoigne dopo aver ricevuto un cartellino giallo, quando l'Inghilterra venne sconfitta dalla Germania Ovest durante le semifinali della Coppa del Mondo, Torino, Italia…

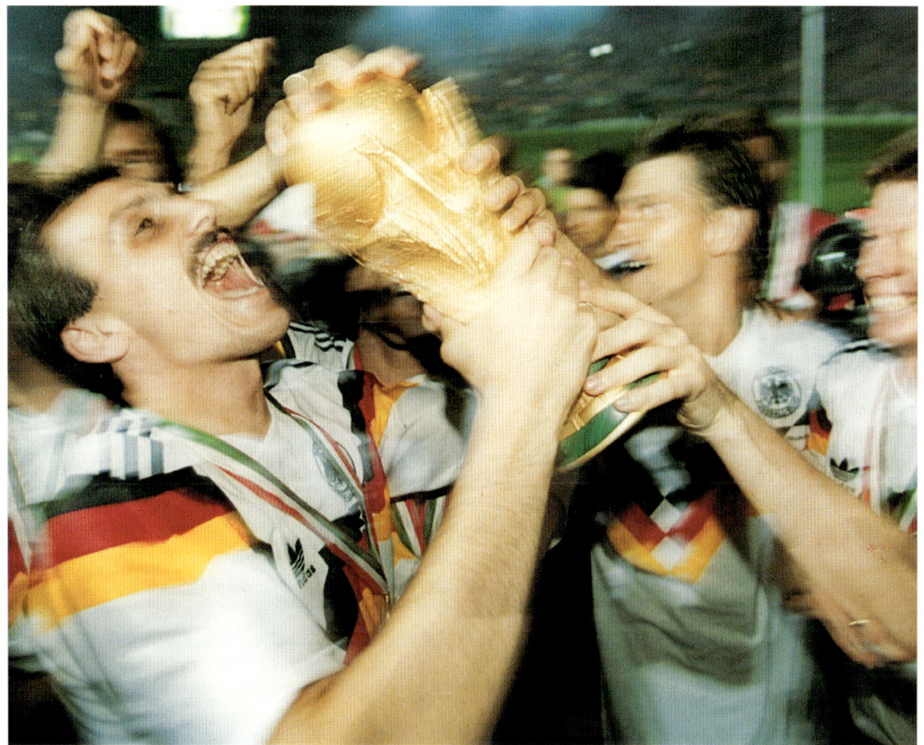

SIMON BRUTY/ALLSPORT

...and West Germany go on to win the World Cup. Jürgen Kohler lifts the FIFA World Trophy after their 1-0 victory over Argentina in the final at the Olympic Stadium, Rome, 8 July 1990.

... y Alemania Occidental se lleva la Copa a casa. Jürgen Kohler alza el trofeo de la FIFA tras vencer a Argentina por 1 a 0 en la final disputada el 8 de julio de 1990 en el estadio olímpico de Roma.

...e la Germania Ovest continua la sua corsa per vincere la Coppa del Mondo. Jürgen Kohler alza in alto la Coppa della FIFA dopo aver sconfitto per 1 a 0 l'Argentina in finale, nello Stadio Olimpico di Roma, 8 luglio 1990.

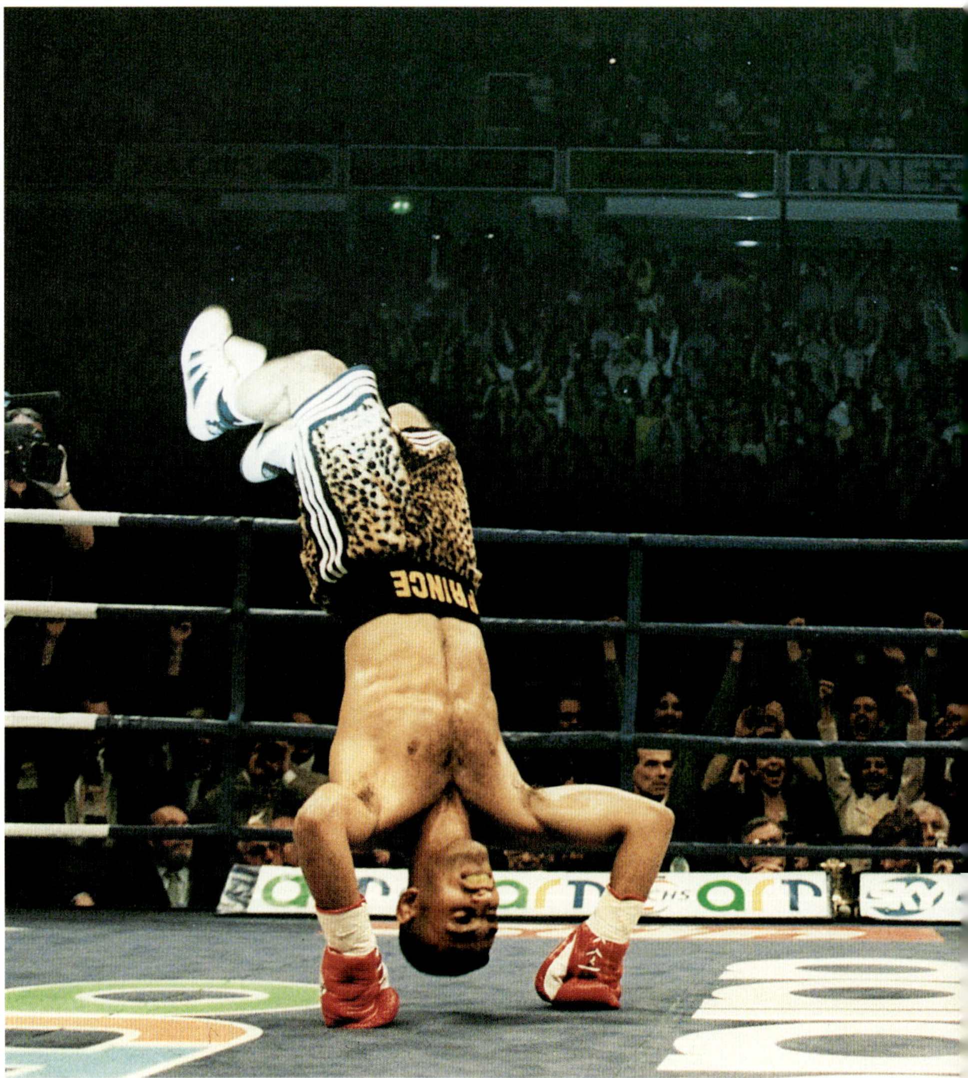

JOHN GICHIGI/ALLSPORT

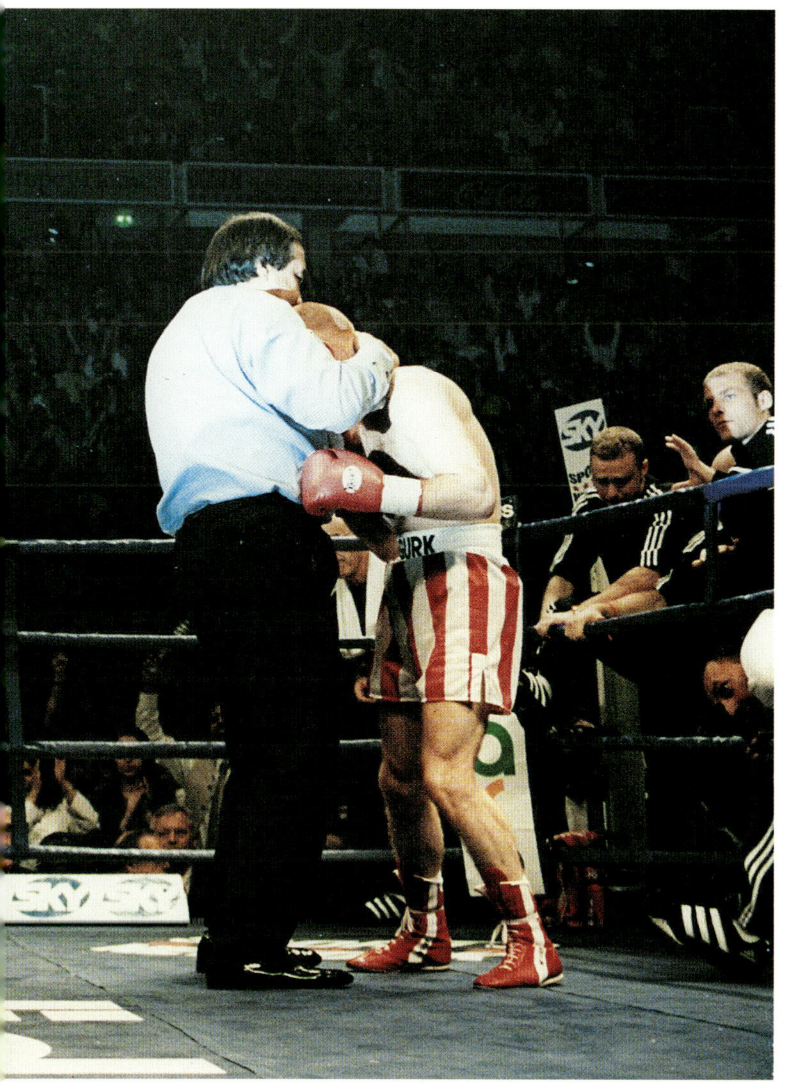

Sheffield-born Prince Naseem Hamed executes a jubilant backflip after his first round victory over Billy Hardy, Manchester, 3 May 1997.

El púgil de Sheffield (Inglaterra) Príncipe Naseem Hamed celebra con una voltereta su victoria en el primer asalto frente a Billy Hardy en Manchester, 3 de mayo de 1997.

Il principe Naseem Hamed, nato a Sheffield, fa una verticale di allegria dopo aver battuto Billy Hardy alla fine del primo round, Manchester, 3 maggio 1997.

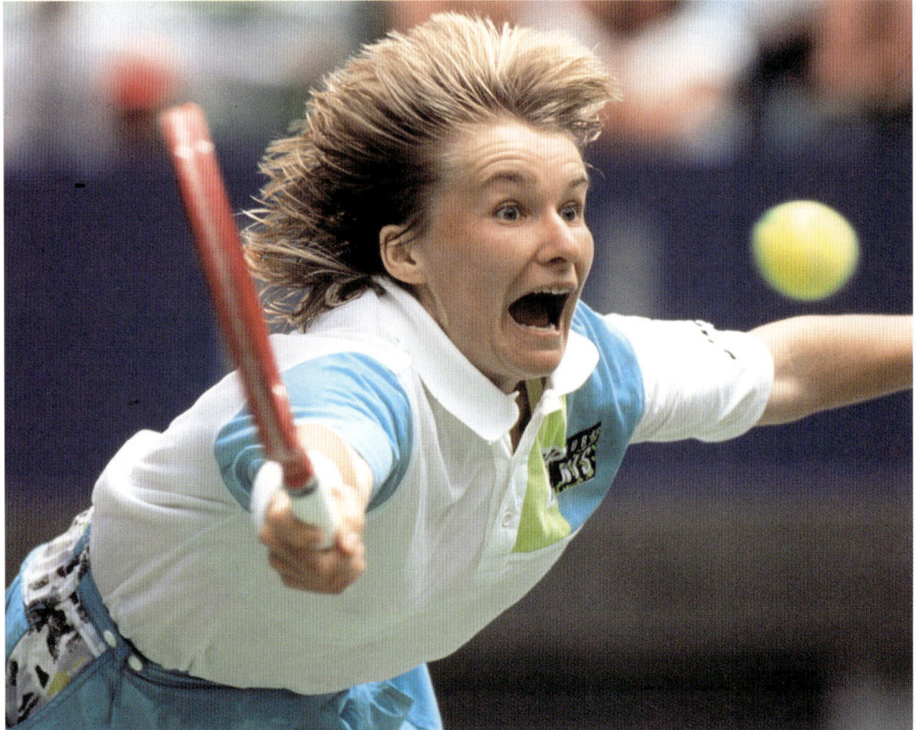

SIMON BRUTY/ALLSPORT

Eye on the ball… Jana Novotna of Czechoslovakia at full stretch during the final of the women's singles at the Grand Slam Australian Open, 1991. In 1998 she won the women's singles at Wimbledon, beating Nathalie Tauziat 6-4, 7-6.

Los ojos en la pelota… la checoslovaca Jana Novotna lucha por un punto durante la final individual femenina del Abierto de Australia en 1991. En 1998 gana en el individual femenino en Wimbledon tras vencer a Nathalie Tauziat por 6-4 y 7-6.

Occhi sulla palla… La cecoslovacca Jana Novotna si allunga al massimo durante la finale del singolare femminile degli Open di Australia, validi per il Grande Slam, nel 1991. Nel 1998 vinse la finale del singolare femminile a Wimbledon, dopo aver sconfitto Nathalie Tauziat 6-4, 7-6.

Knees on the grass… Richard Krajicek breaks the Sampras run, Wimbledon, 7 July 1996.

De rodillas sobre la hierba… Richard Krajicek rompe la buena racha de Sampras y le vence en el torneo de Wimbledon, 7 de julio de 1996.

Ginocchia sull'erba… Richard Krajicek frena le aspirazioni di vittoria di Sampras, Wimbledon, 7 luglio 1996.

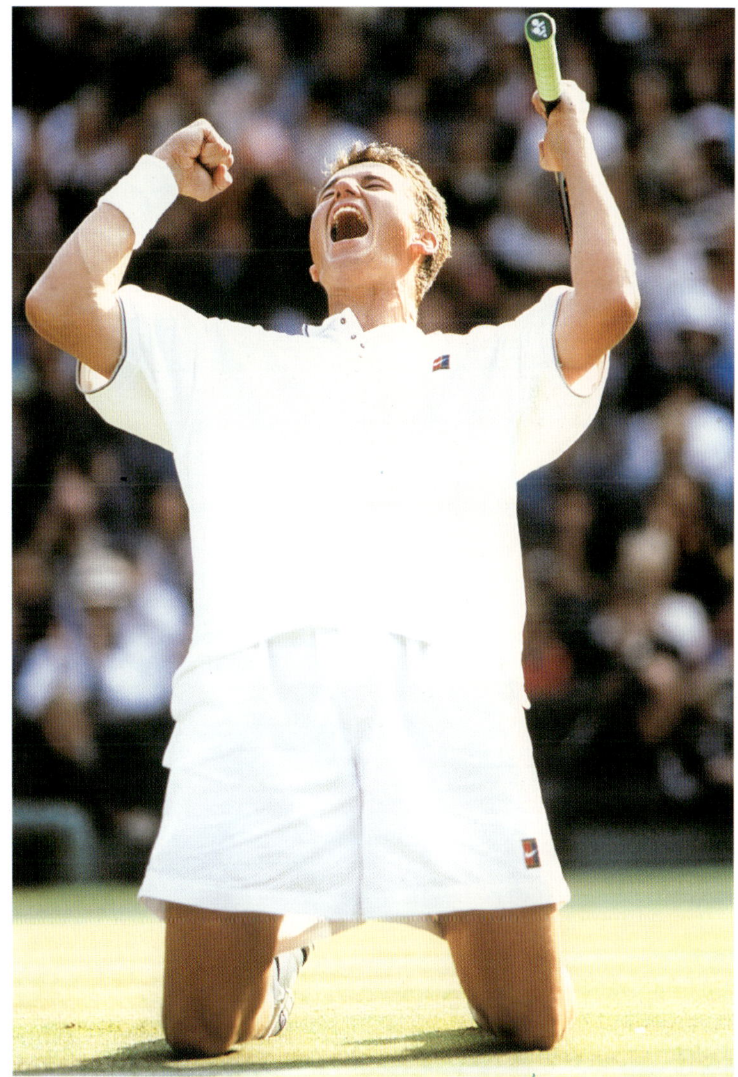

GARY M PRIOR/ALLSPORT

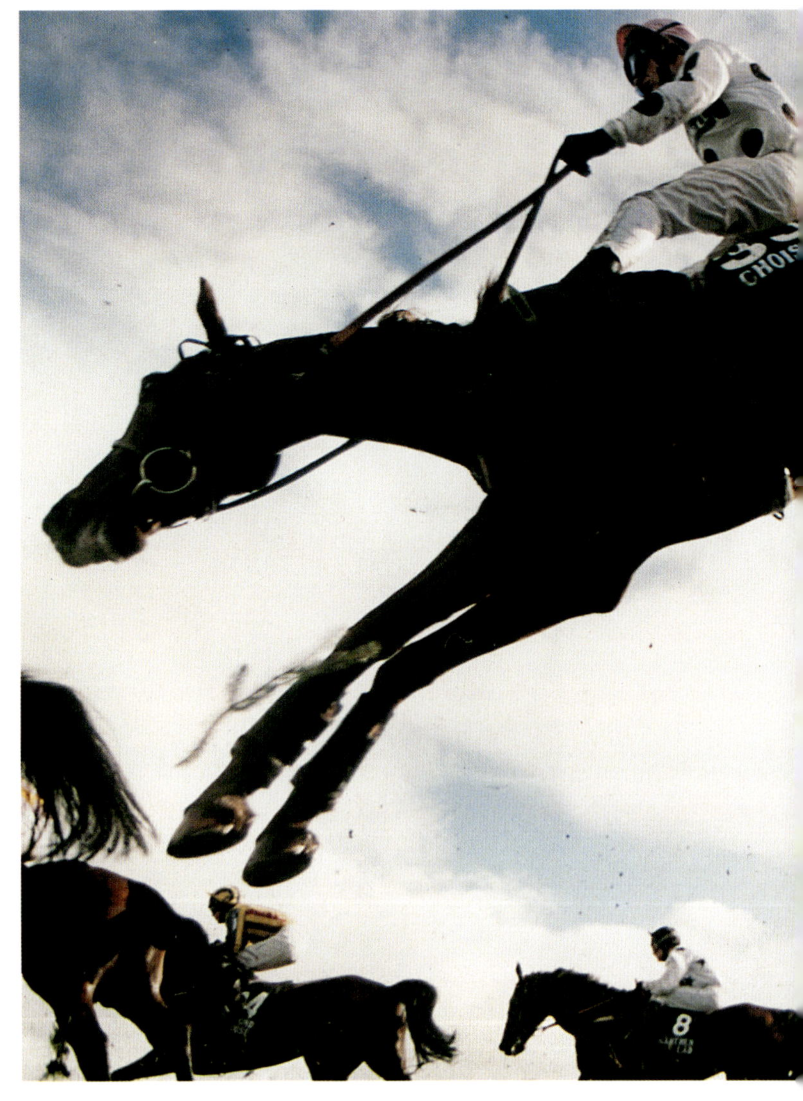

Choisty clears Becher's Brook in the 1998 Grand National, Aintree, Liverpool. Two years later Choisty won a virtual reality National on a computer.

El caballo de carreras *Choisty* salva el Becher's Brook –el temible obstáculo del Grand National– durante la carrera de Aintree (Liverpool) en 1998. Dos años después el equino se haría con un Grand National virtual, disputado por ordenador.

Choisty attraversa il Becher's Brook durante il Grand National del 1998, Aintree, Liverpool. Due anni più tardi vinse il National nella realtà virtuale di un computer.

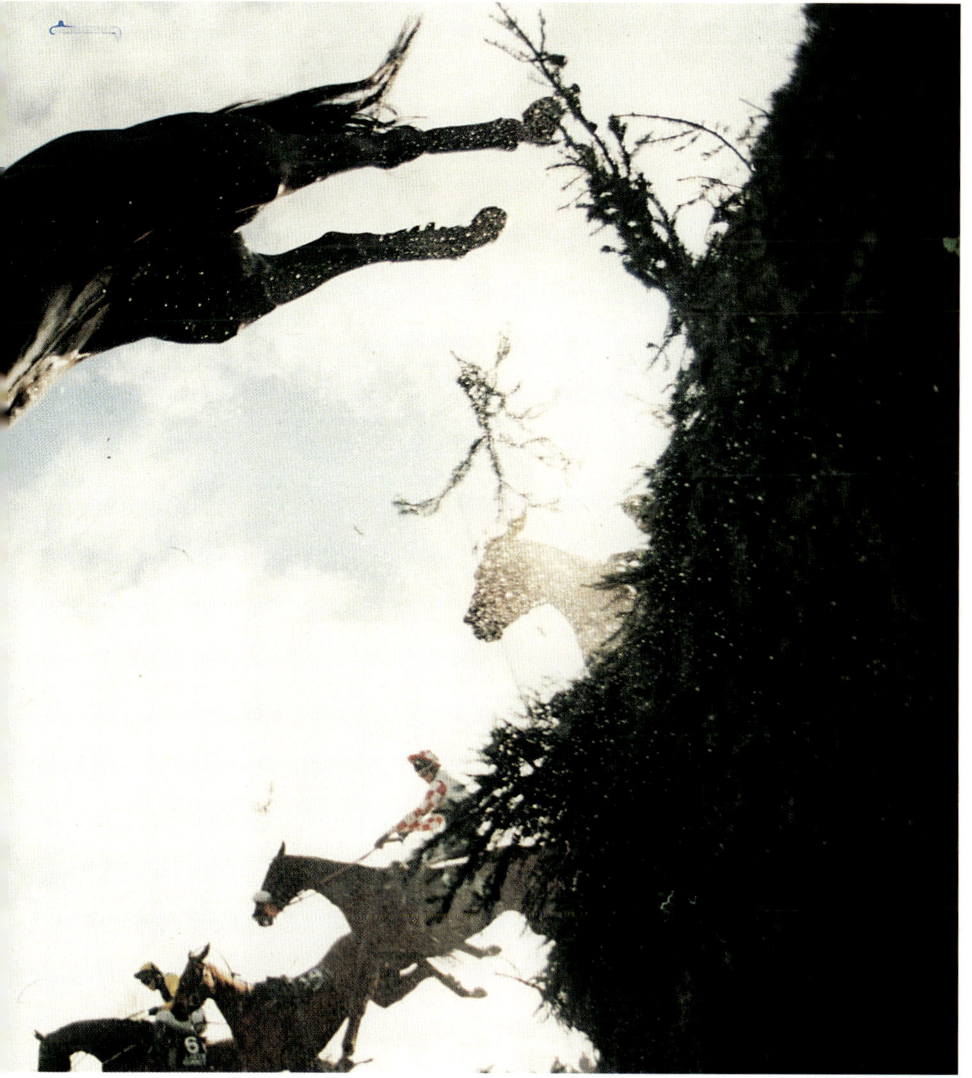

ROSS KINNAIRD/ALLSPORT

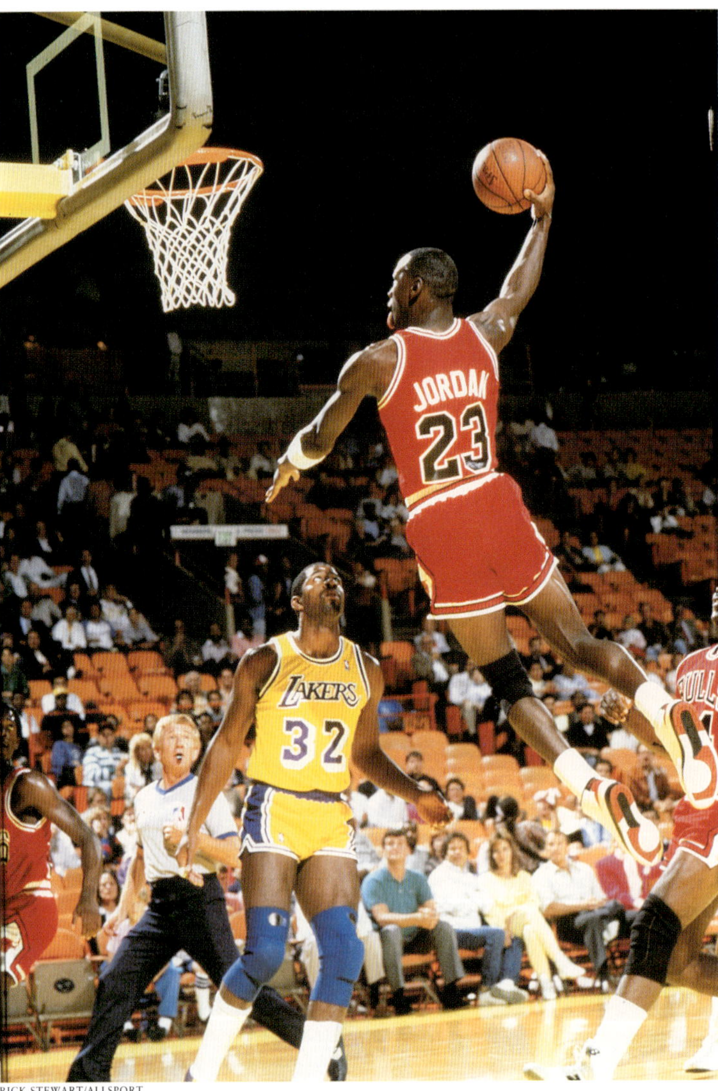

RICK STEWART/ALLSPORT

Battle of the giants. Magic Johnson of the LA Lakers (left) watches as Michael Jordan (Chicago Bulls) puts more points on the board.

Una batalla de gigantes. Magic Johnson de los LA Lakers (izquierda) contempla cómo Michael Jordan, de los Chicago Bulls, suma puntos al marcador.

Battaglia fra giganti. Magic Johnson dei LA Lakers (a sinistra) osserva Michael Jordan (dei Chicago Bulls) che fa canestro.

New kid on the block. Vince Carter of the Raptors leaps for glory at the NBA All-Star Slam Dunk contest, Oakland, California.

La nueva promesa de la cancha. Vince Carter, de los Raptors, realiza un salto glorioso en el concurso de mates de la NBA celebrado en Oakland, California.

Nuovi arrivati. Vince Carter dei Raptors salta verso la gloria durante l'All-Star Slam Dunk della NBA, Oakland, California.

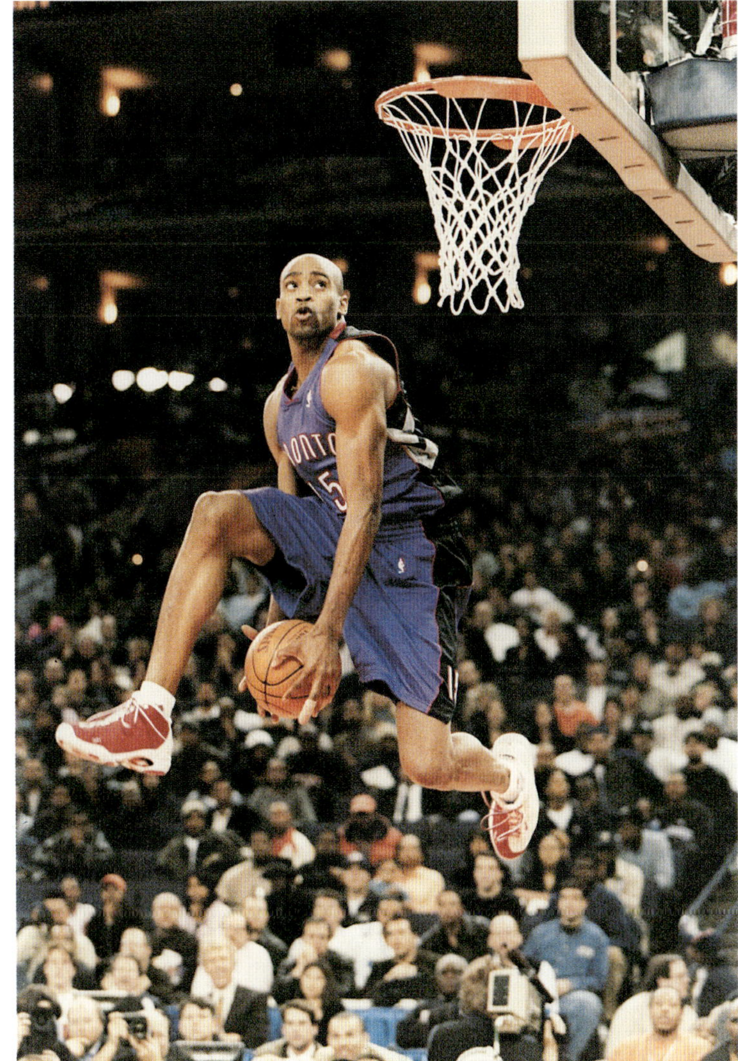

JED JACOBSOHN/ALLSPORT

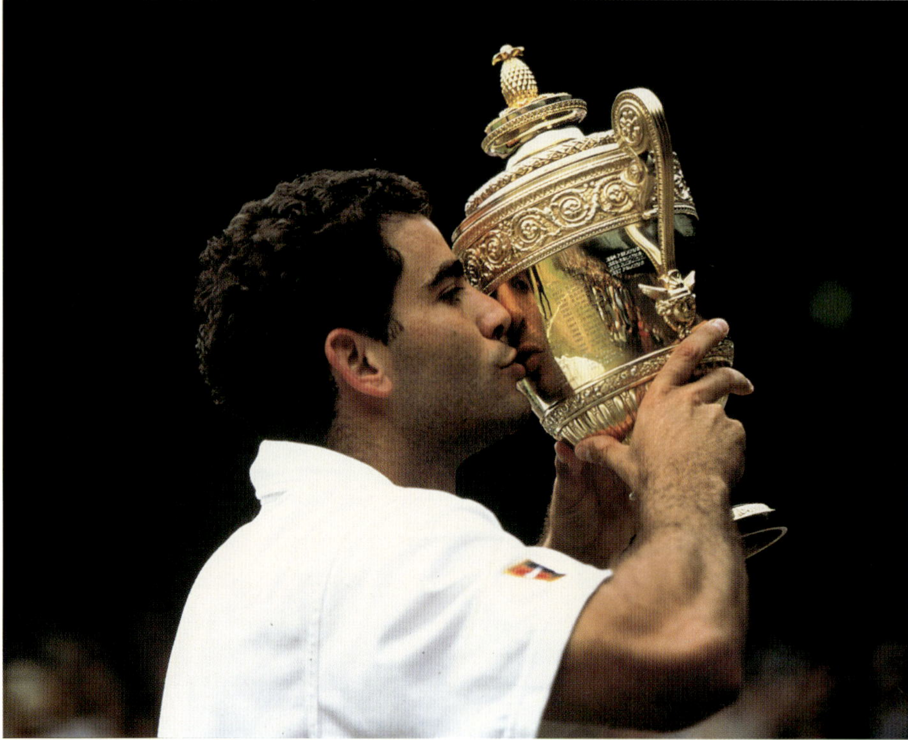

GARY M PRIOR/ALLSPORT

Pete Sampras plants a winner's kiss on the men's singles trophy after his victory over Goran Ivanisevic, 6-7, 7-6, 6-4, 3-6, 6-2, in the final at Wimbledon, July 1998. It was his fifth Wimbledon title.

Pete Sampras besa el trofeo de Wimbledon tras imponerse a Goran Ivanisevic por 6-7, 7-6, 6-4, 3-6 y 6-2 en la final individual masculina del torneo, disputada en julio de 1998. Era el quinto título que conseguía el tenista en esta competición.

Pete Sampras da un bacio da campione alla coppa del singolare maschile, dopo aver sconfitto Goran Ivanisevic per 6-7, 7-6, 6-4, 3-6, 6-2 durante la finale di Wimbledon, luglio 1998. Era la quinta volta che vinceva a Wimbledon.

The Sampras trademark slam dunk, this time at the Stella Artois tournament, the Queen's Club, London, 11 June 1999.

Remate con el sello Sampras. Esta vez, en el marco del torneo Stella Artois, en el Queen's Club londinense, 11 de junio de 1999.

Il classico tiro di Sampras, stavolta durante il torneo Stella Artois, al Queen's Club, Londra, 11 giugno 1999.

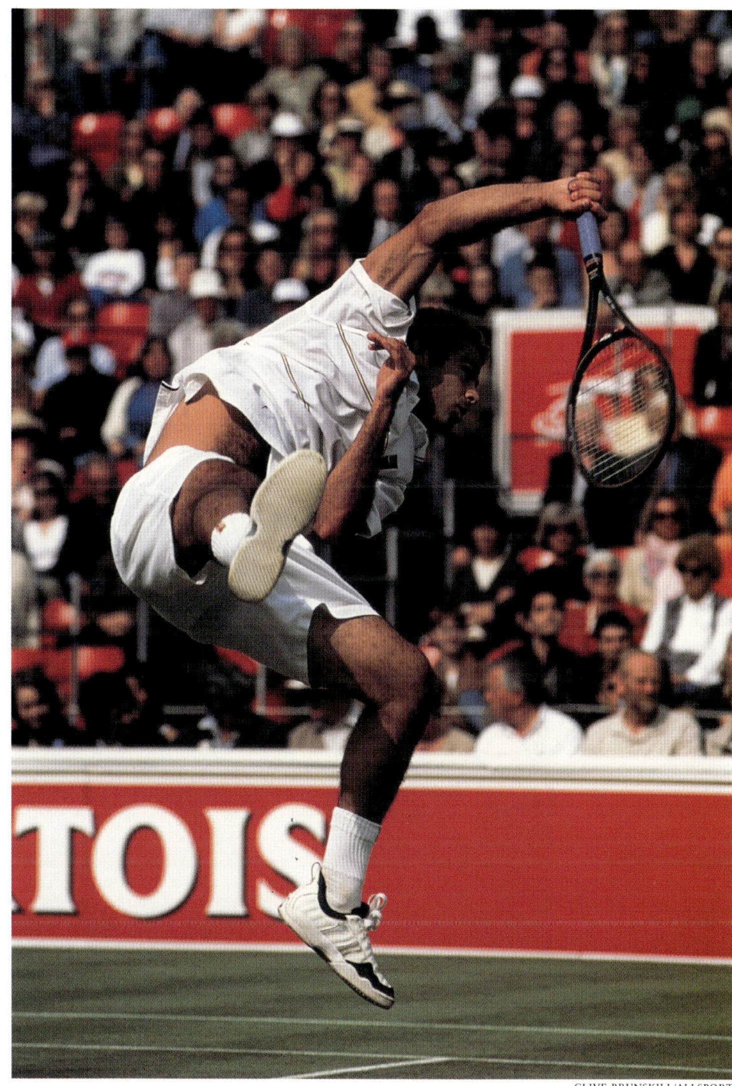

CLIVE BRUNSKILL/ALLSPORT

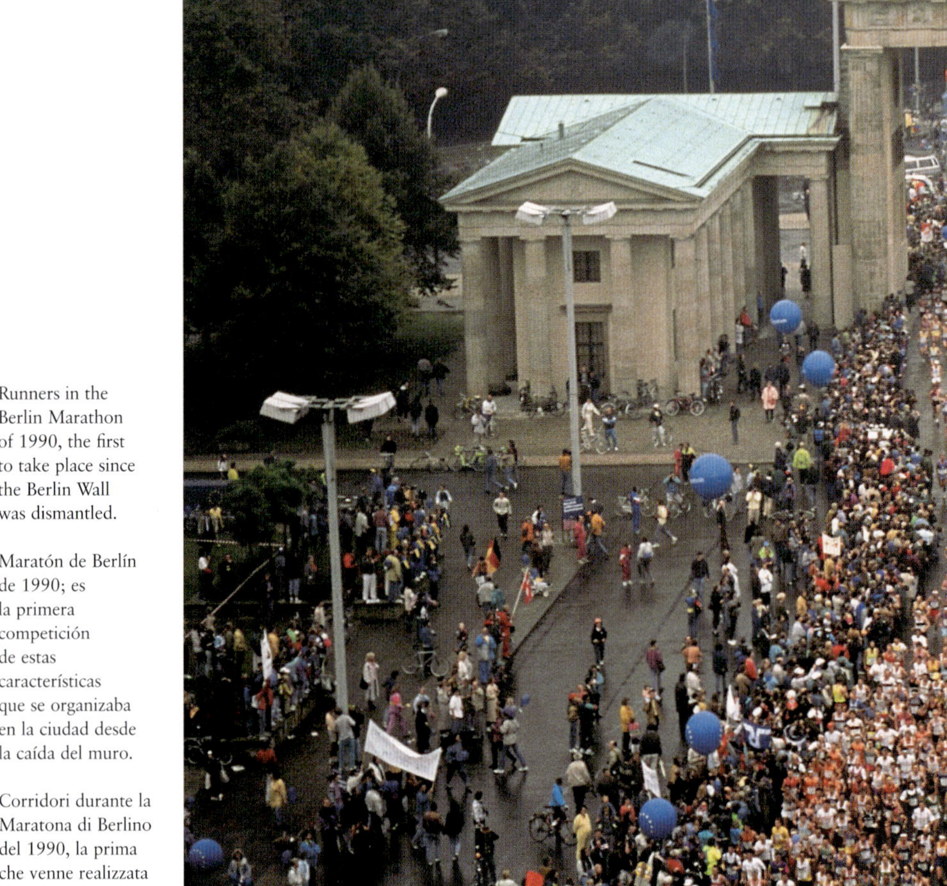

Runners in the Berlin Marathon of 1990, the first to take place since the Berlin Wall was dismantled.

Maratón de Berlín de 1990; es la primera competición de estas características que se organizaba en la ciudad desde la caída del muro.

Corridori durante la Maratona di Berlino del 1990, la prima che venne realizzata dopo la caduta del muro.

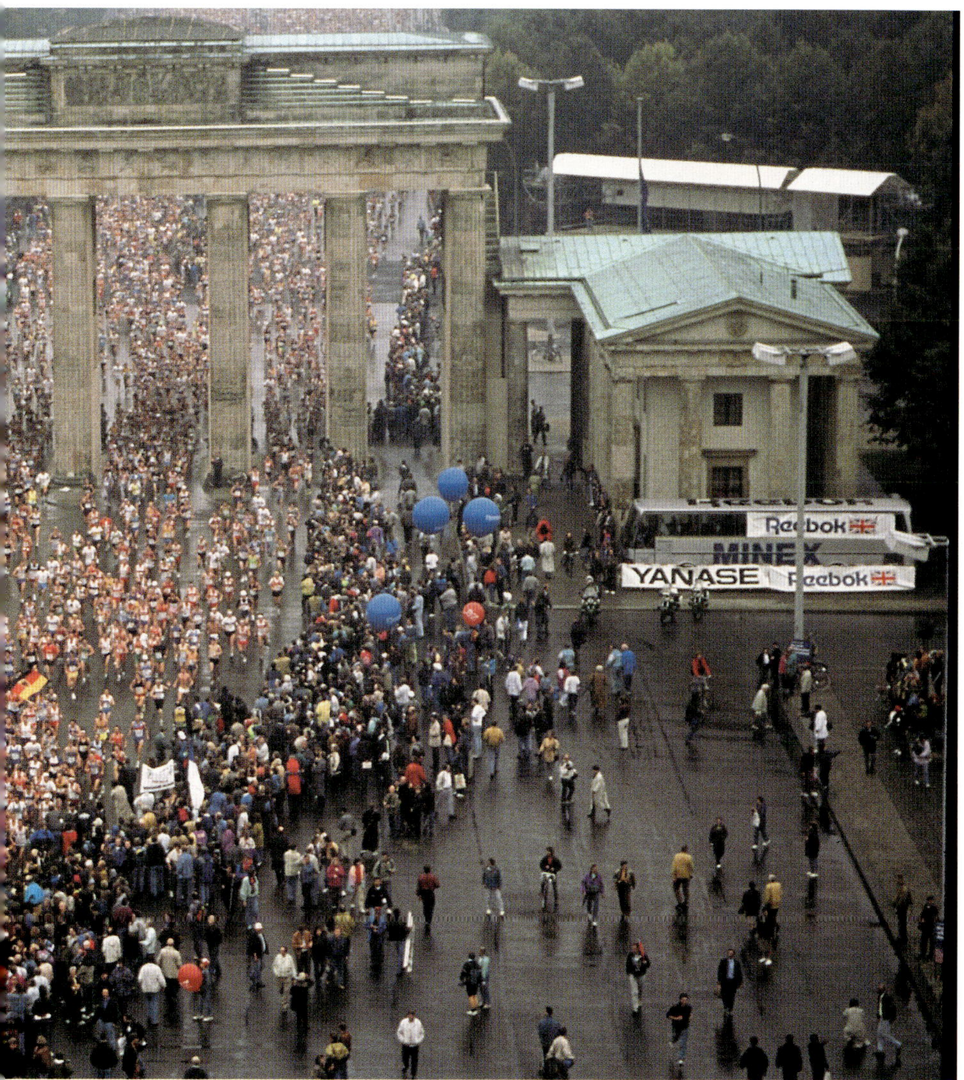

BOB MARTIN/ALLSPORT

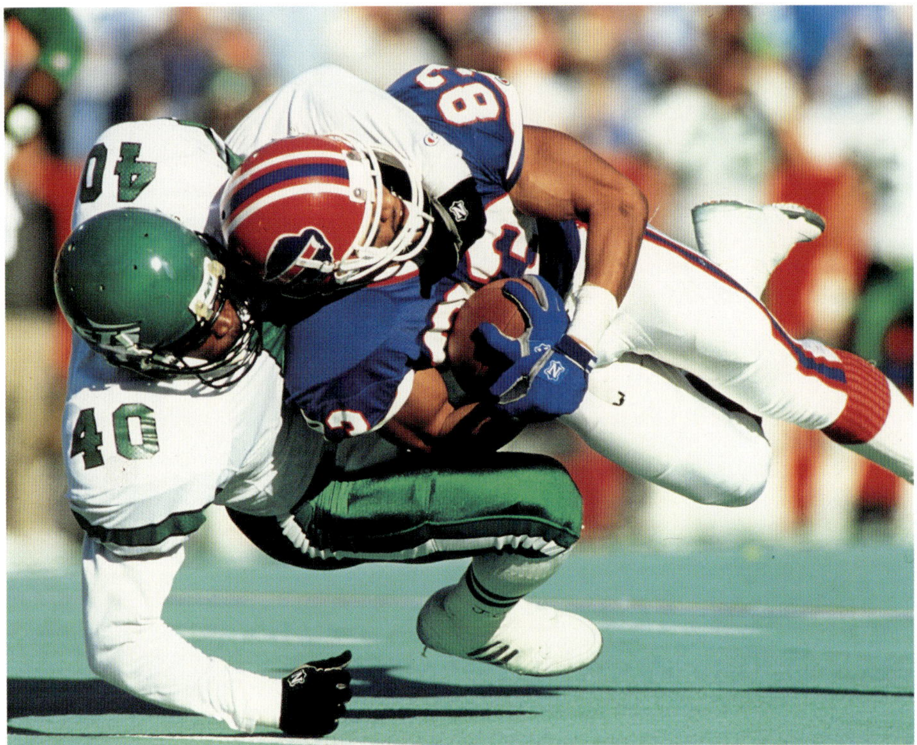

RICK STEWART/ALLSPORT

James Hastie takes out Andre Reed as the Buffalo Bills lose their Superbowl game against the New York Jets at Rich Stadium, the Bills' home ground, 1990.

James Hastie derriba a Andre Reed durante el partido de *rugby* de la Superbowl de 1990, encuentro que los Buffalo Bills perdieron en su propio campo (el Rich Stadium) ante los New York Jets.

James Hastie neutralizza Andre Reed, durante il Superbowl del 1990, nel Rich Stadium, quando i Buffalo Bills persero in casa contro i New York Jets.

Sammy Sosa hits his 63rd home run of the season as the Chicago Cubs beat the San Diego Padres 4-3, Qualcomm Stadium, San Diego, 17 September 1998.

El bateador Sammy Sosa consigue su 63° *home run* de la temporada en el partido en que los Chicago Cubs vencen a los San Diego Padres por 4 a 3 en el estadio Qualcomm de San Diego, 17 de septiembre de 1998.

Sammy Sosa tira il suo 63° home run della stagione e i Chicago Cubs sconfiggono i San Diego Padres per 4 a 3, Qualcomm Stadium, San Diego, 17 settembre 1998.

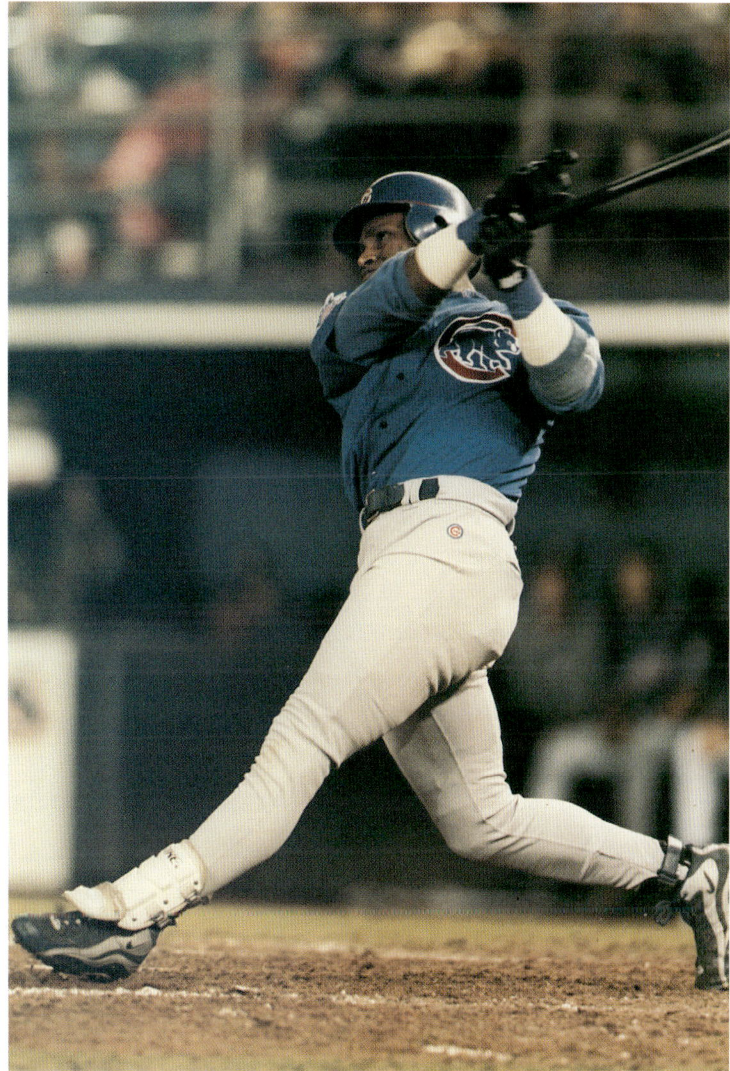

TODD WARSHAW/ALLSPORT

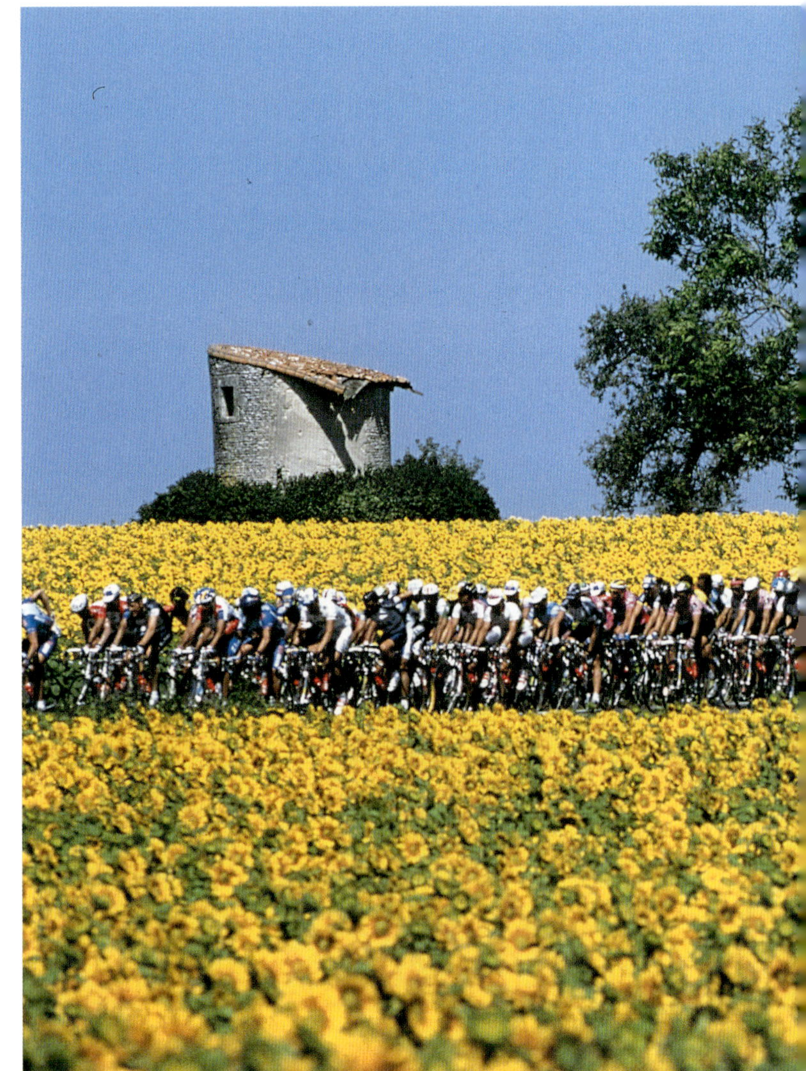

Participants on the eighth stage of the 1994 *Tour de France* speed between fields of sunflowers near Poitiers.

Corredores de la octava etapa del Tour de Francia de 1994 atraviesan un campo de girasoles cercano a Poitiers.

Partecipanti all'ottava tappa del Tour de France del 1994, mentre attraversano campi di girasole, nelle vicinanze di Poitiers.

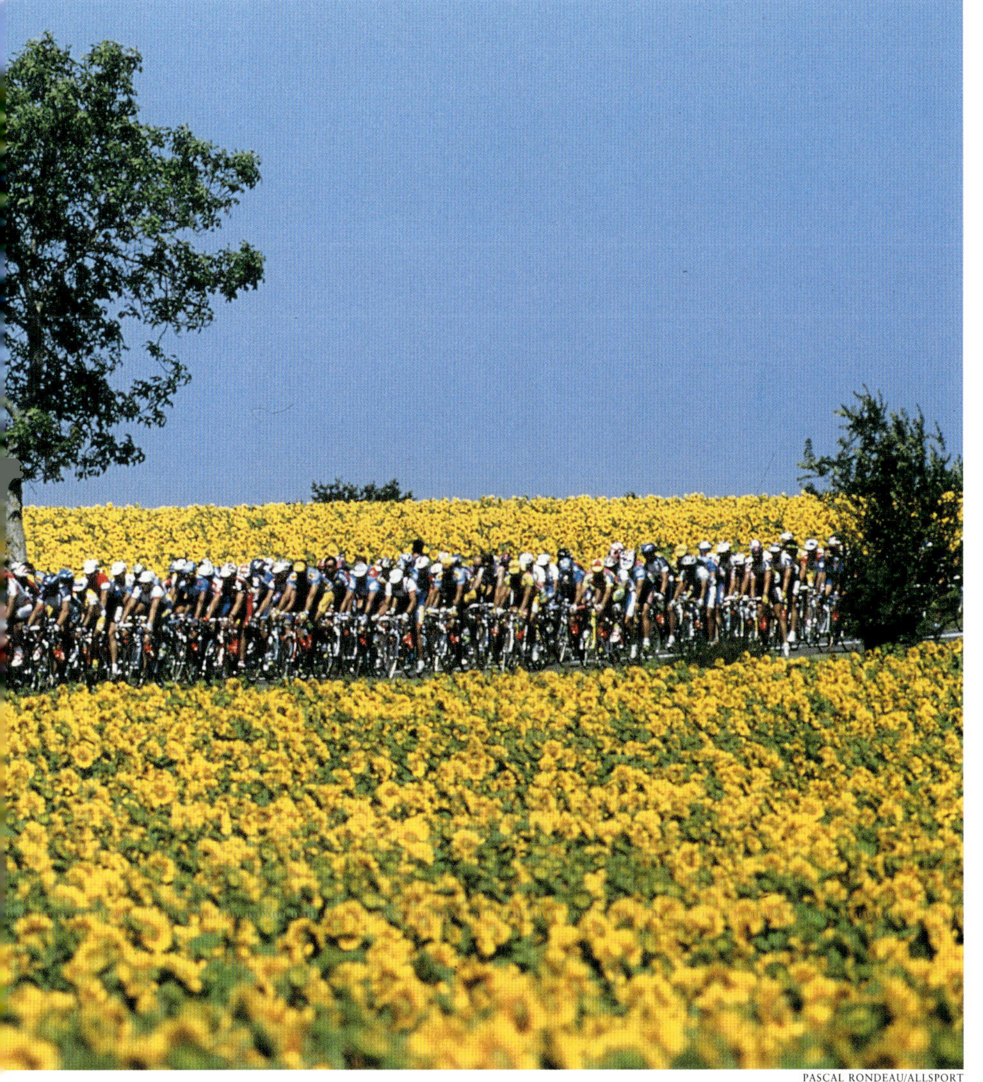

PASCAL RONDEAU/ALLSPORT

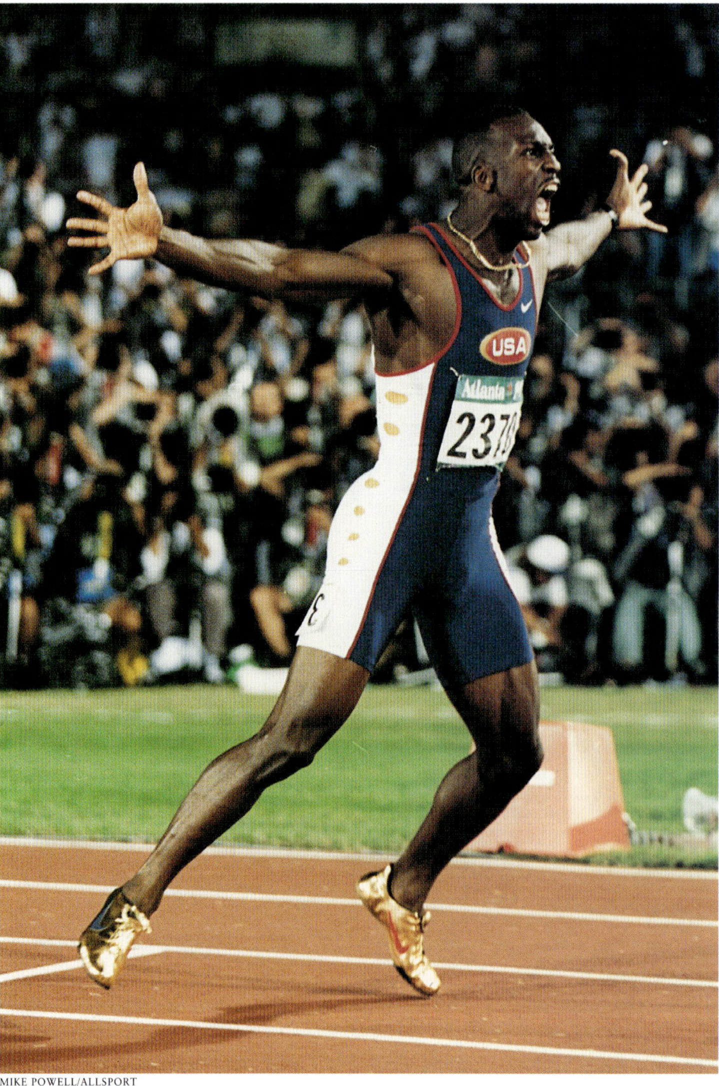

MIKE POWELL/ALLSPORT

A jubilant Michael Johnson celebrates his 200 metres world record in the Olympic Games, Atlanta, Georgia, 1 August 1996.

El atleta Michael Johnson libera su euforia al batir el récord mundial de los 200 metros en los Juegos Olímpicos de Atlanta, Georgia, 1 de agosto de 1996.

Un Michael Johnson esultante dopo aver battuto il record mondiale dei 200 metri, durante le Olimpiadi di Atlanta, Georgia, 1° agosto 1996.

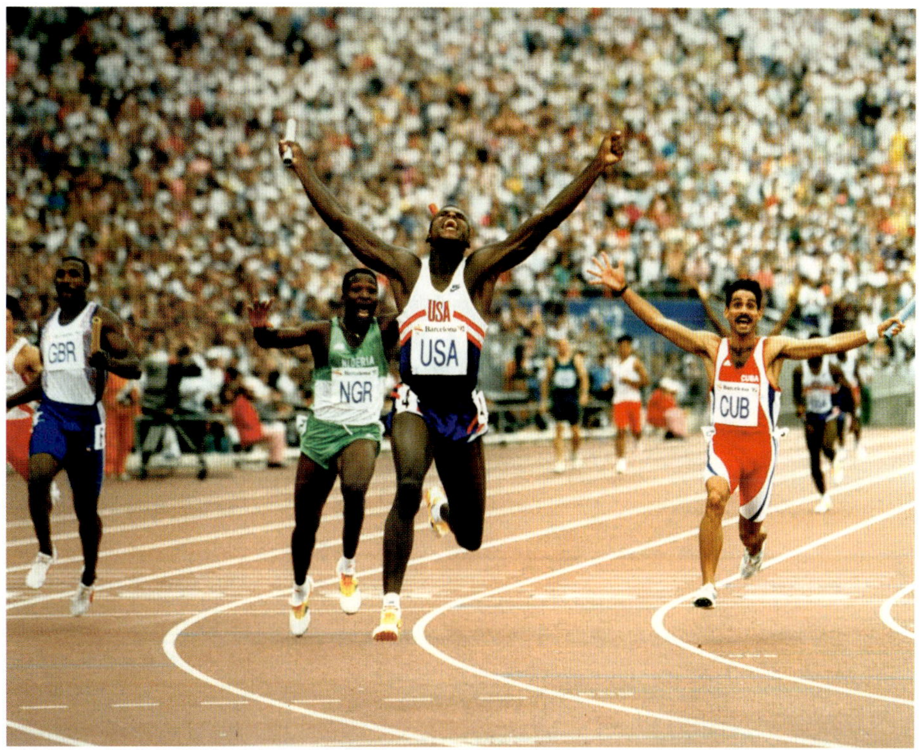

GARY HERSHORN/REUTERS/ARCHIVE PHOTOS

Carl Lewis completes the United States' victory in the men's 4 x 100 metres relay at the Barcelona Olympics, August 1992. The US team set a new world record with a time of 37.40 seconds.

Carl Lewis logra alzarse con la victoria para Estados Unidos en los 4 x 100 metros relevos masculinos en los Juegos Olímpicos de Barcelona, en agosto de 1992. El equipo estadounidense estableció un nuevo récord mundial con un tiempo de 37,40 segundos.

Carl Lewis completa la staffetta dei 4 x 100 maschile e regala la vittoria agli Stati Uniti, durante le Olimpiadi di Barcellona, agosto 1992. La squadra statunitense stabilì un nuovo record mondiale, con un tempo di 37,40 secondi.

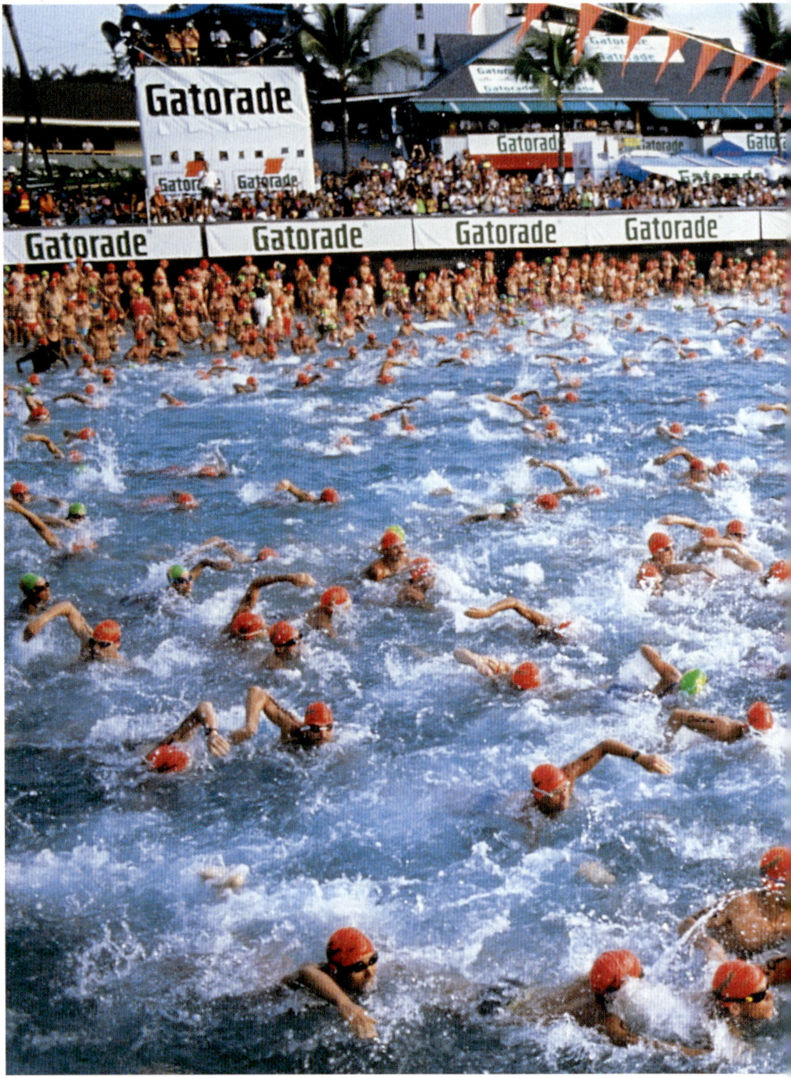

Competitors in the Ironman Triathlon whip themselves into a lather as they take to the water, Hawaii, 1991.

Participantes del campeonato de triatlón Ironman, celebrado en Hawai en 1991, se abren paso a brazadas entre la espuma al inicio de la competición.

Concorrenti del triathlon Ironman si fanno strada a bracciate nella schiuma mentre entrano in acqua, Hawaii, 1991.

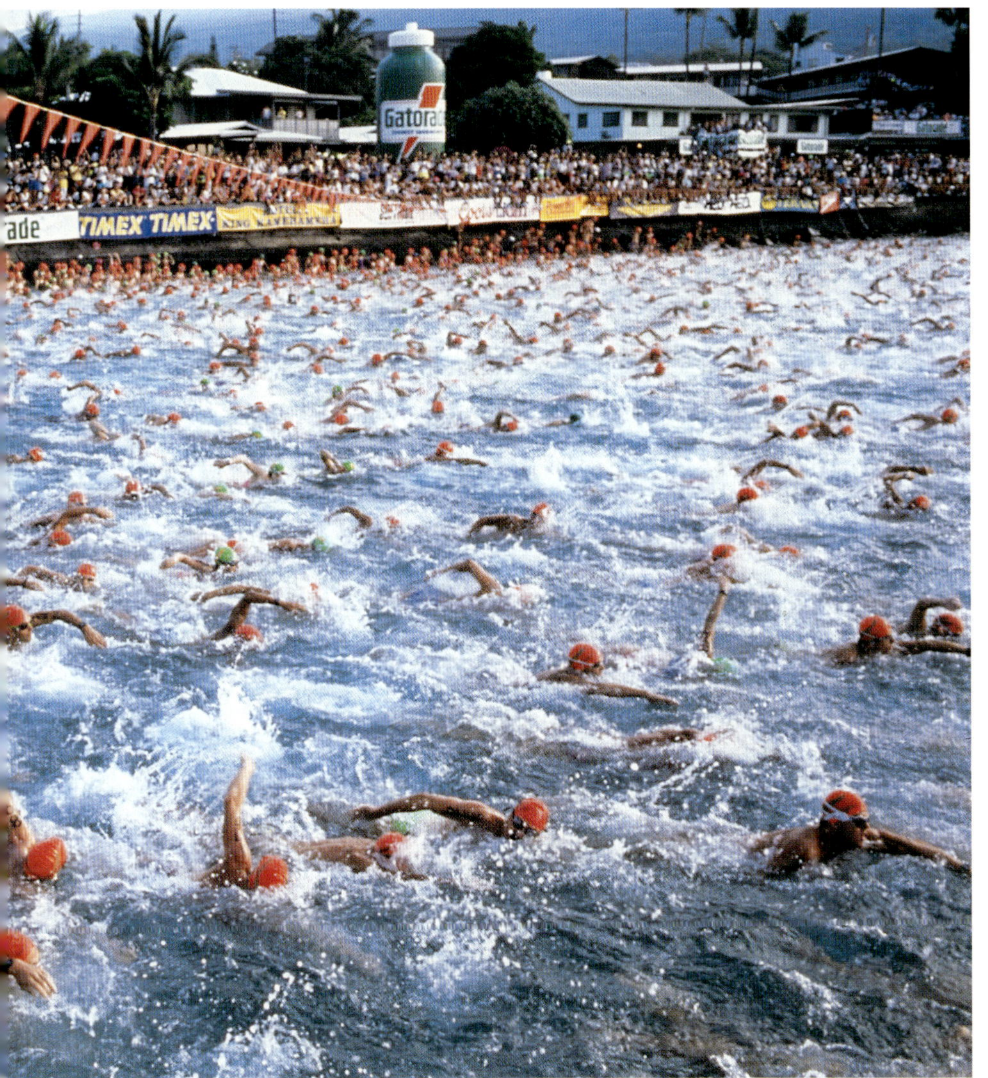

GARY NEWKIRK/ALLSPORT

11. Children
Los más pequeños
Bambini

At the height of the Kosovo crisis, a young ethnic Albanian refugee holds a Russian-made shell-case in his arms near the village of Kisna Reka, 12 October 1998.

En plena crisis de Kosovo, un niño refugiado de origen albanés sostiene en sus brazos un proyectil de fabricación rusa lanzado cerca de la población de Kisna Reka, 12 de octubre de 1998.

Durante il peggior momento di crisi nel Kosovo, un giovane profugo albanese tiene in mano un missile di fabbricazione russa nelle vicinanze del villaggio di Kisna Reka, 12 ottobre 1998.

ATTILA KISBENEDEK/EPA/PA

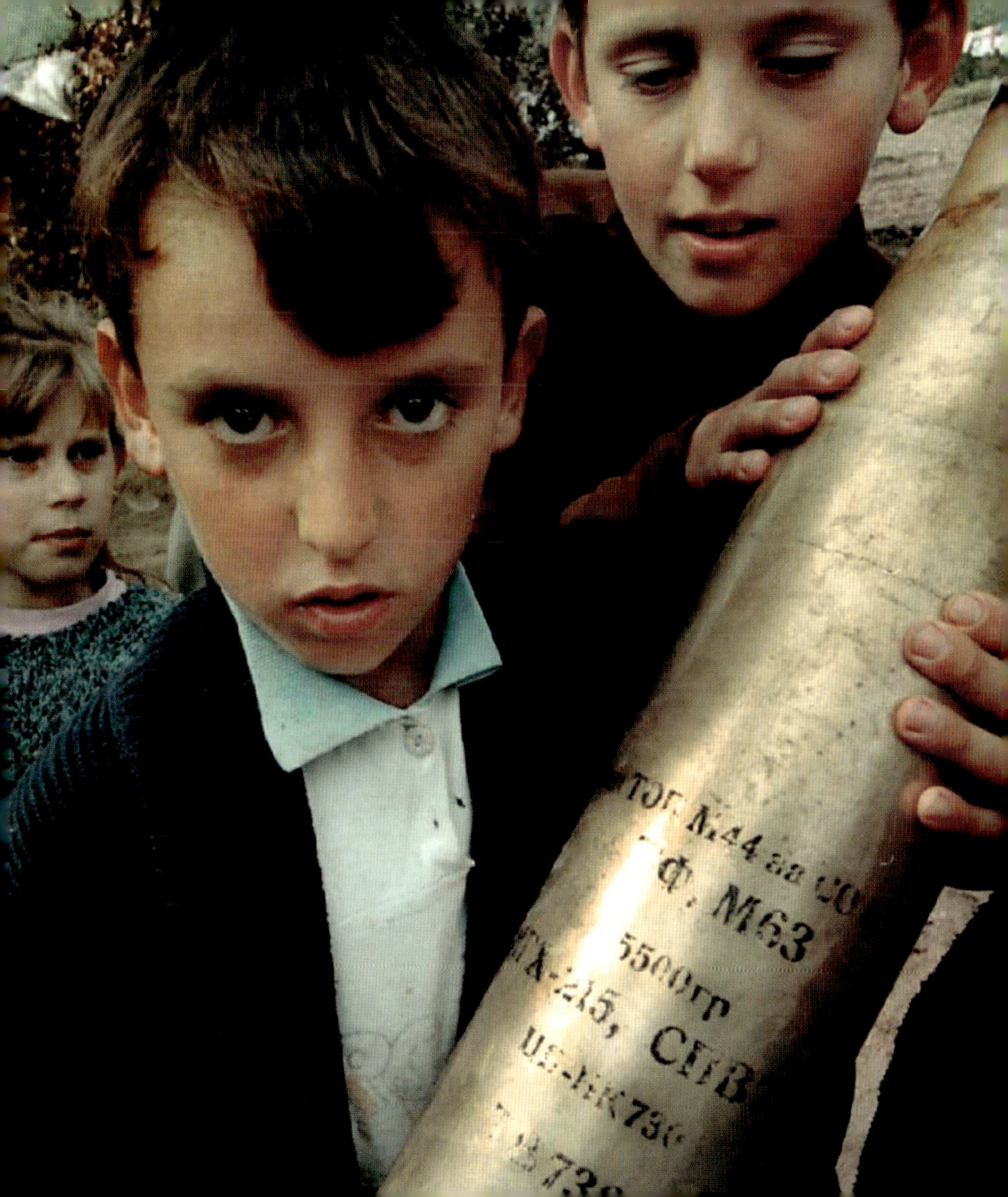
Ф. М63
5500гр

11. Children
Los más pequeños
Bambini

Childhood became a frenetic race to grow up. There was less time to play with toys before children were expected to play their part in fostering a nation's economy – as consumers of designer clothes, discs, snacks, drinks, PlayStations. Child prodigies sat more examinations at earlier ages than ever before, exceptionally were accepted by universities before reaching their teens, delivered bravura performances at musical recitals. The old evils of the past reappeared. Young children were overworked and underpaid in Third World sweatshops. Epidemics of killer diseases returned to slaughter the innocents. Child abuse was uncovered in the very institutions that had been set up to help children. And there was a new phenomenon – the establishment of armies of child warriors. Governments and rebels alike kidnapped boys and girls as young as 10 years old, trained them to kill, and sent them out to do battle for the 'cause'.

On a gentler note, children ate junk food, played Pokémon, pestered their parents for skateboards, worshipped the great, resisted their teachers, moaned, laughed, fought and dreamed that one day they would all be healthy, wealthy and wise.

En los noventa, la infancia se convierte en una carrera frenética hacia la edad adulta. La época para jugar con los juguetes se acorta puesto que los niños están llamados a impulsar la economía convirtiéndose lo antes posible en consumidores de ropa de marca, discos, *snacks*, bebidas y PlayStations. Los niños prodigio se presentan a los exámenes cada vez más jóvenes, en ocasiones acceden a la universidad antes de llegar a la adolescencia y hasta ofrecen recitales de música ejecutados con brillante maestría. También reaparecen viejos fantasmas del pasado: en las fábricas del Tercer Mundo se explota al menor y se utiliza como mano de obra barata; mortales brotes epidémicos causan estragos entre la población infantil;

se destapan abusos a niños llevados a cabo en el seno de instituciones creadas especialmente para proteger a la infancia y surge un nuevo fenómeno: la formación de ejércitos de niños soldados. Tanto gobiernos como grupos rebeldes gustan de secuestrar a niños y niñas de apenas diez años con el propósito de entrenarlos para matar y luego enviarlos a luchar por la "causa".

Una cara quizá más amable de la infancia es la de los niños que devoran comida basura, juegan a Pokémon, atosigan a sus padres hasta conseguir el ansiado monopatín, idolatran a las estrellas del momento y plantan cara a sus profesores; pequeños que se quejan, ríen y pelean, mientras sueñan que algún día serán todos ricos y sabios, y gozarán de una salud envidiable.

L'infanzia si trasformò in una corsa sfrenata per diventare quanto prima adulti. Ci si aspettava dai bambini che smettessero al più presto di giocare, per aiutare a migliorare l'economia del paese, divenendo piuttosto consumatori di vestiti di marca, dischi, snack, bevande e PlayStation. Alcuni dei bambini prodigio si presentavano agli esami con età mai viste prima, altri, in via eccezionale, entravano all'università ancora prima di entrare nell'età adolescenziale, e altri ancora tenevano magnifici recital di musica. I demoni del passato tornavano a fare atto di presenza. Alcuni fra i più giovani venivano sovraccaricati di lavoro e pagati miseramente nelle fabbriche del Terzo Mondo. E intanto apparivano di nuovo epidemie di malattie mortali che facevano strage di innocenti. Si scoprivano scene di abuso all'infanzia nel seno degli stessi enti che erano stati creati per aiutare i bambini e appariva un nuovo fenomeno – la creazione di eserciti di soldati bambini. Sia i governi che i gruppi ribelli sequestravano bambini e bambine di una decina d'anni, li preparavano per uccidere e li mandavano fuori a combattere per la "causa"

A un altro livello, i bambini iniziavano a mangiare cibo spazzatura, giocavano con Pokémon, tormentavano i genitori fino ad avere uno skateboard, veneravano le star, si ribellavano ai professori, piangevano, ridevano, litigavano e sognavano che un bel giorno sarebbero stati tutti ricchi, saggi e in buona salute.

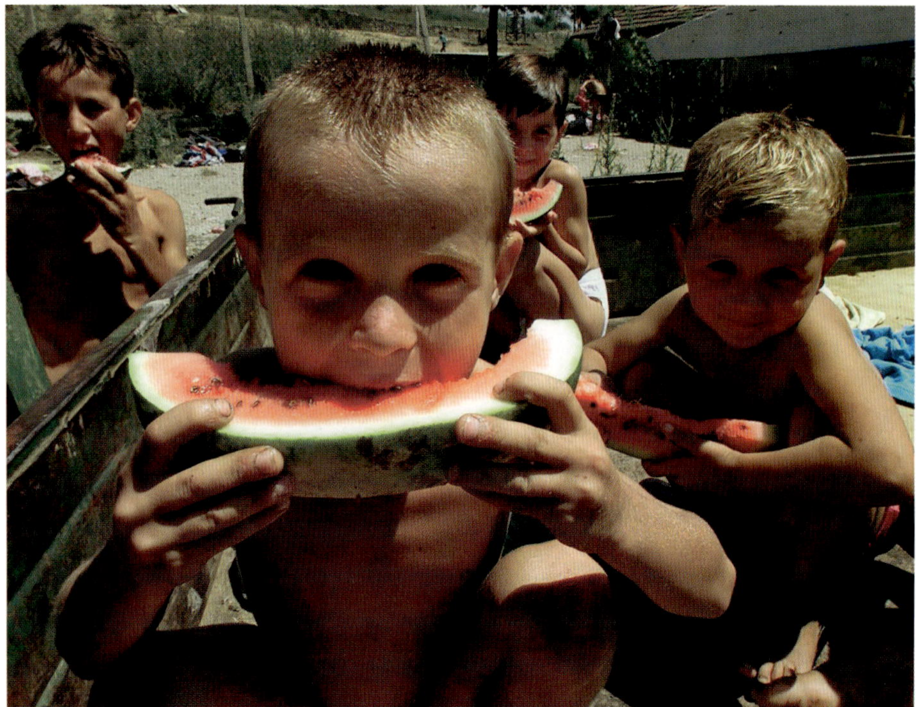

EPA/PA

Enough to go round. Seven-year-old Besart Javori (centre) shares the delights of a juicy watermelon with his friends in a tractor trailer on a farm near the spa town of Banje, central Kosovo, 22 July 1999.

Hay para todos. Besart Javori (centro), de siete años, comparte con sus amigos una deliciosa sandía en lo alto de un tractor de una granja cercana a la ciudad balnearia de Banje, en el centro de Kosovo, 22 de julio de 1999.

Ce n'è abbastanza per tutti. Besart Javori, di sette anni, (al centro) condivide con i suoi amici il piacere di una buona anguria fresca, nel rimorchio di un trattore in una fattoria, nelle vicinanze della città termale di Banje, Kosovo centrale, 22 luglio 1999.

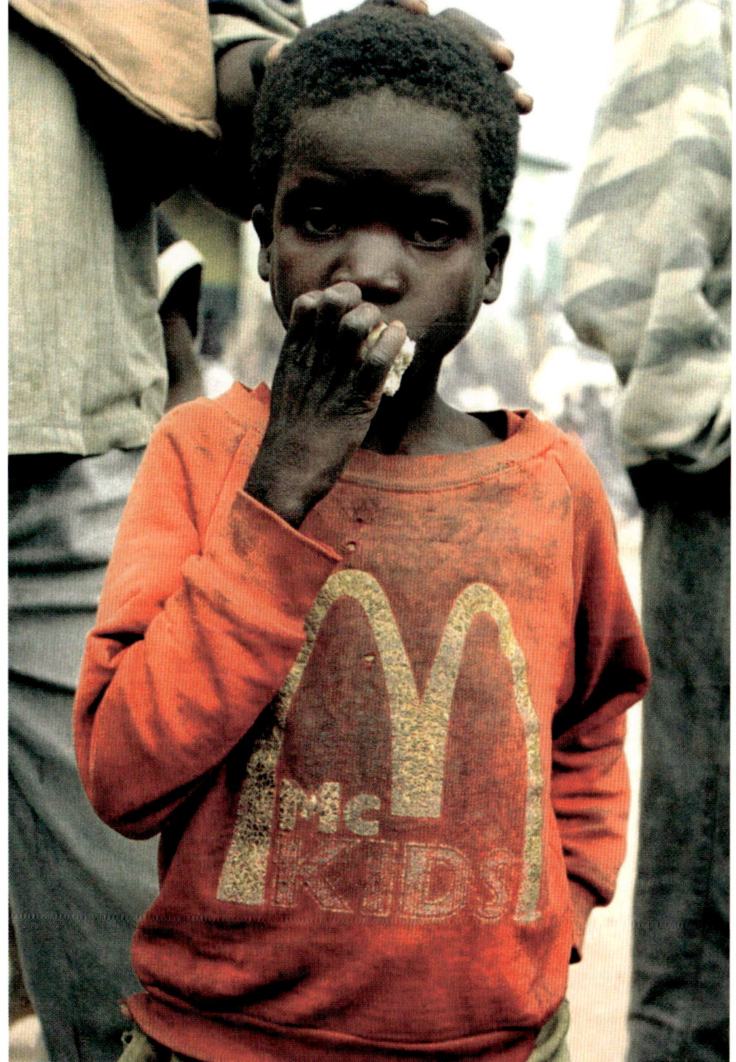

Not enough to go round. A malnourished child nibbles rations supplied by the World Food Programme, Luanda, Angola, 10 February 1999.

No hay para todos. Un niño desnutrido de Luanda, Angola, mordisquea un trozo de comida distribuida por el Programa Mundial de Alimentos de Naciones Unidas, 10 de febrero de 1999.

Non ce n'è abbastanza nemmeno per uno. Un bambino malnutrito rosicchia le razioni fornite dal Programma alimentare mondiale, Luanda, Angola, 10 febbraio 1999.

MANUEL DE ALMEIDA/EPA/PA

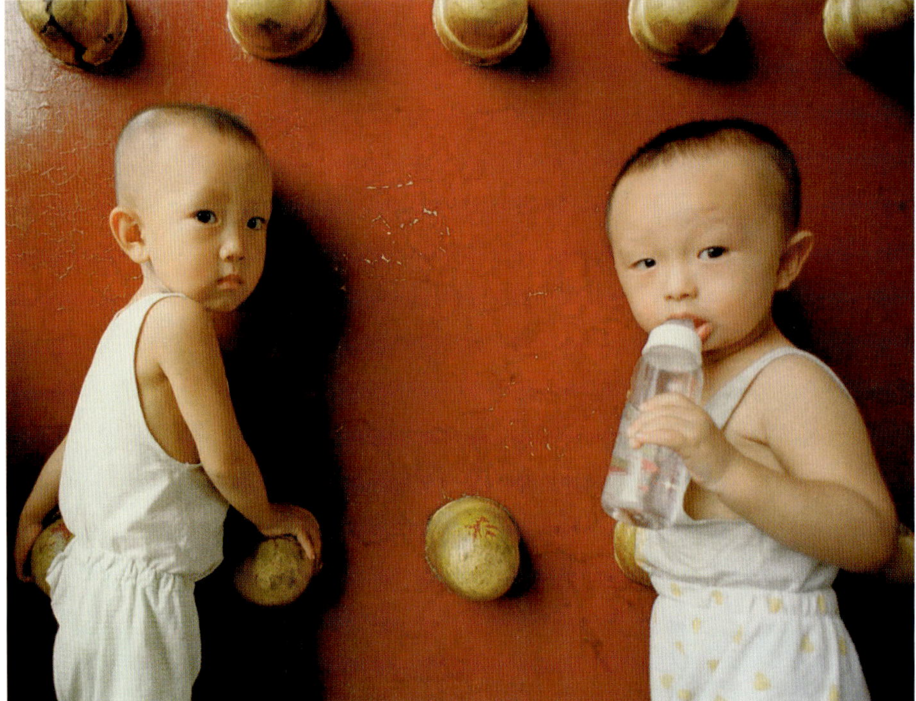

CHIEN-MIN CHUNG/LIAISON AGENCY

Formative years 1. Chinese children rub the doorknobs on the gate leading to the Temple of Heaven, Beijing, 5 August 1997, an action supposed to bring good luck.

Primeros años de formación 1. Niños chinos tocan los pomos de la puerta del Templo del Cielo, en Pequín, lo cual se cree que trae suerte, 5 de agosto de 1997.

Anni di formazione 1. Bambini cinesi toccano le maniglie del Tempio del Cielo, Pechino, 5 agosto 1997; secondo alcuni, un gesto di buon augurio.

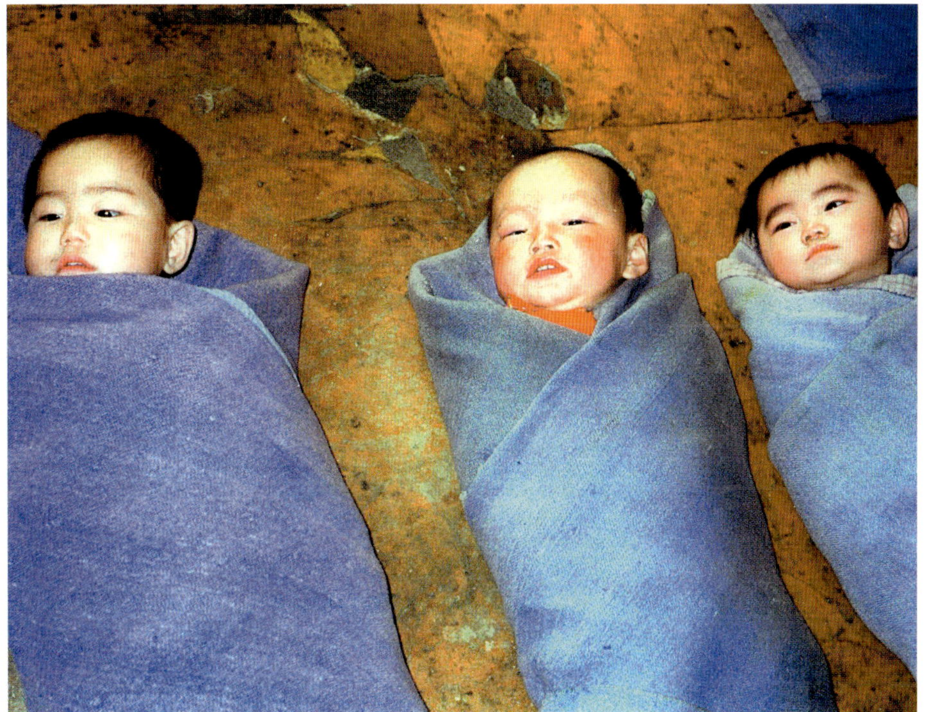

PETER SMERDON/EPA/PA

Formative years 2. A photograph for the UN World Food Programme showing children with stunted growth in a North Korean nursery at Kumchon, Hwanghae province, 25 March 1999. Famine had hit this isolated region.

Primeros años de formación 2. Esta fotografía del Programa Mundial de Alimentos de Naciones Unidas muestra a niños norcoreanos en una guardería de Kumchon, en la provincia de Hwanghae. Los pequeños padecen de raquitismo a consecuencia de la hambruna que asola esta aislada región.

Anni di formazione 2. Una fotografia per il Programma alimentare mondiale che mostra bambini rachitici in un asilo nido di Kumchon, una zona colpita dalla carestia nella provincia di Hwanghae, Corea del Nord, 25 marzo 1999.

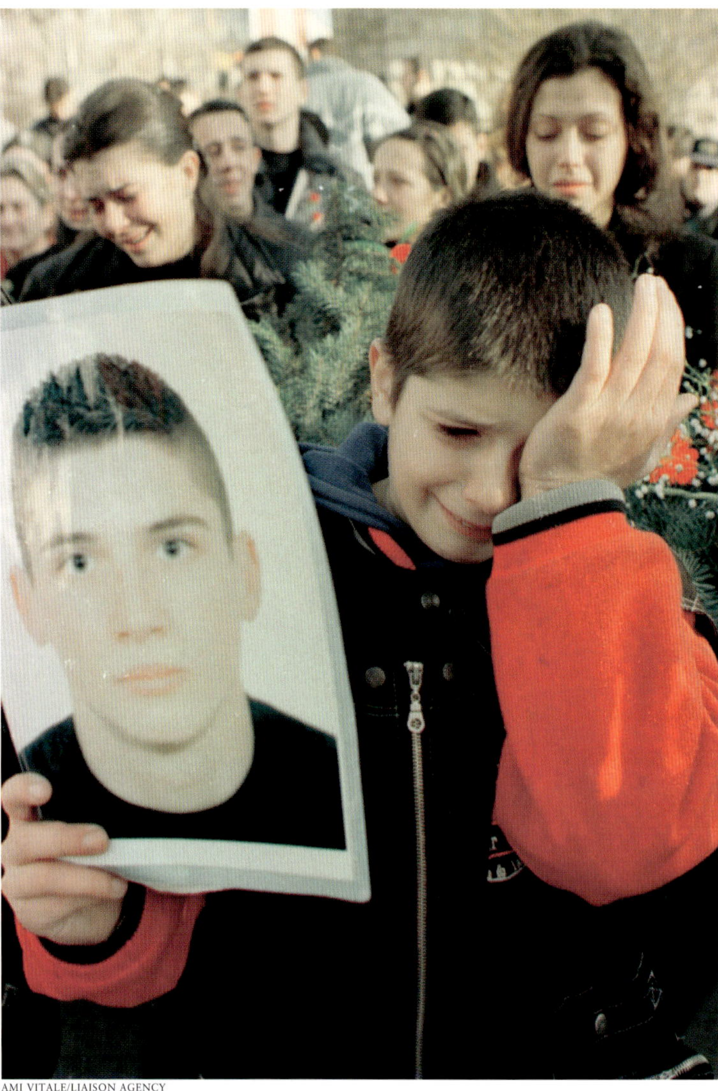

AMI VITALE/LIAISON AGENCY

Sudden death. Serb teenagers at the funerals of six friends killed in battles between Serbs and the Kosovo Liberation Army, 16 December 1998.

Muerte súbita. Jóvenes serbios asisten al entierro de seis de sus amigos muertos durante los enfrentamientos entre los serbios y el Ejército de Liberación de Kosovo, 16 de diciembre de 1998.

Morte improvvisa. Adolescenti serbi durante il funerale di sei amici uccisi in combattimenti fra i serbi e l'Esercito di liberazione del Kosovo, 16 dicembre 1998.

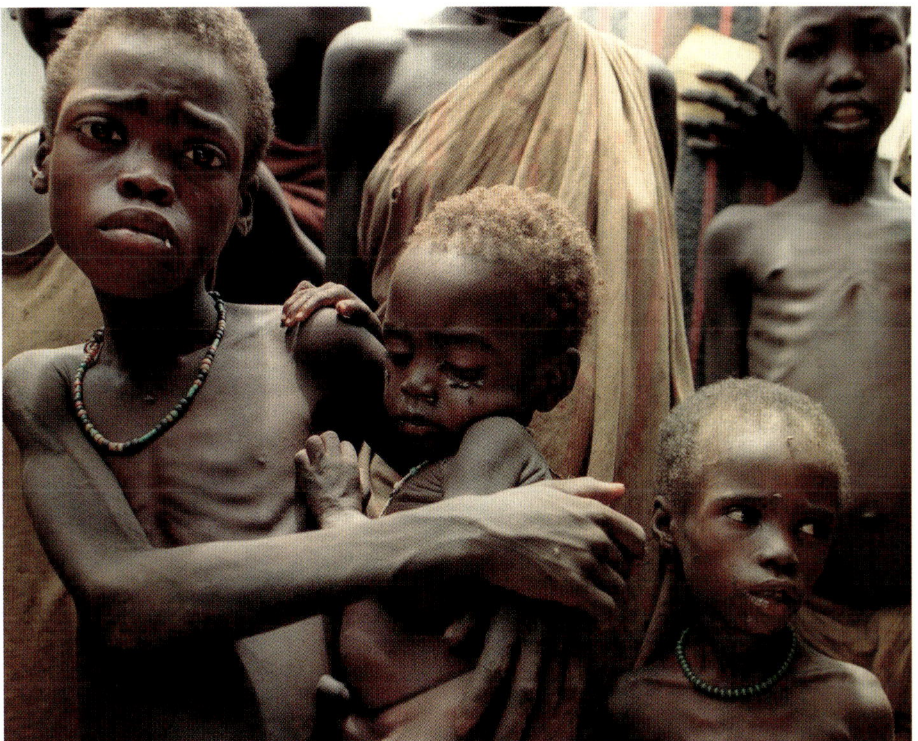

ERIC FEFFERBERG/EPA/PA

A lifetime of war. Sudanese children wait at a healthcare centre in Wau, southern Sudan, 20 July 1998. By then the war between the Sudanese Government and the Sudan People's Liberation Army had been going on for fifteen years.

Una vida entera en guerra. Niños sudaneses esperan ser atendidos en un centro de salud de Wau, al sur de Sudán, 20 de julio de 1998. El conflicto entre el Gobierno sudanés y el Ejército Popular de Liberación de Sudán duraba ya quince años.

Una guerra lunga tutta una vita. Bambini del Sudan aspettano in un centro sanitario di Wau, al sud del paese, 20 luglio 1998. In quel momento erano passati già quindici anni da quando era cominciata la guerra fra il governo del Sudan e l'Esercito di liberazione del popolo.

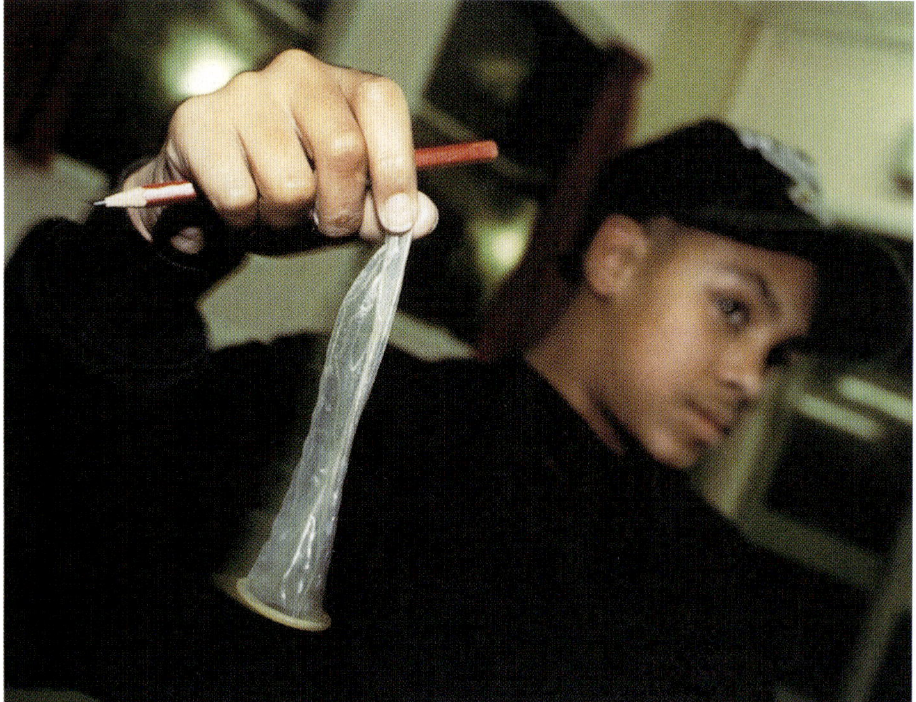

SIMON NORFOLK/PYMCA

The facts of life. A school pupil displays a condom to his classmates as part of a sex education and anti-AIDS programme. If you doubt the propriety of such happenings, study the page opposite.

La realidad de la vida. Un alumno de una escuela enseña a sus compañeros un condón, en el marco de un programa de educación sexual y prevención del sida. Si alguien duda de la conveniencia de estas iniciativas, que eche un vistazo a la siguiente página.

Cose della vita. Un alunno mostra un preservativo ai suoi compagni di classe in occasione di un programma di educazione sessuale e di prevenzione dell'AIDS. Se considerate sconvenienti situazioni di questo tipo, guardate la pagina accanto.

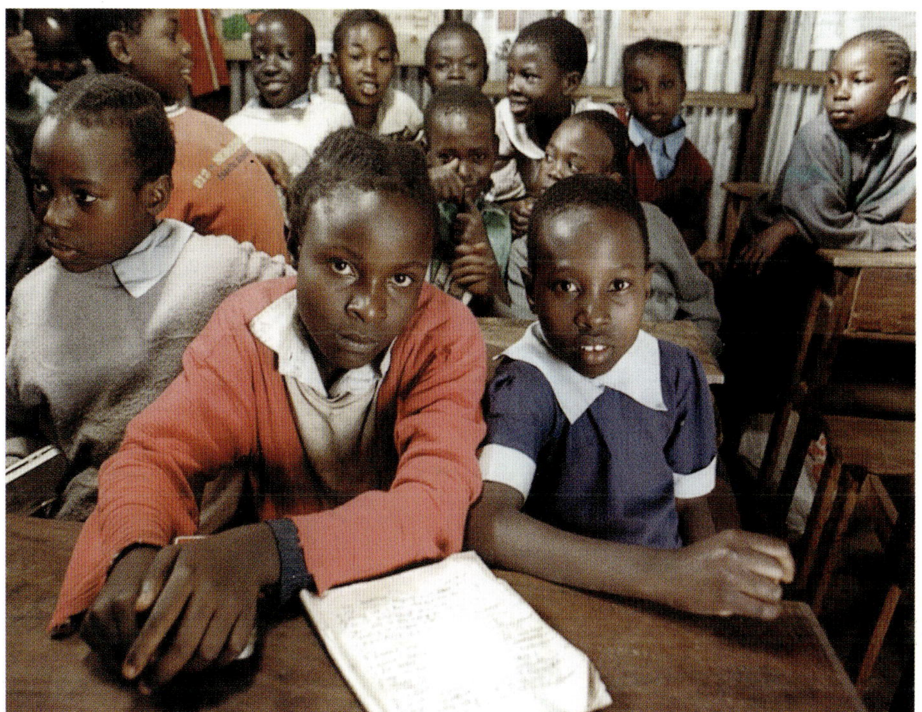

EPA/PA

Kenyan children at the Kikoshep school in the slum area of Kibera, Nairobi, 29 November 1998. All have lost at least one parent to AIDS; all are carrying the HIV virus.

Niños keniatas de la escuela Kikoshep, en el barrio pobre de Kibera, Nairobi, 29 de noviembre de 1998. Todos han perdido por lo menos a uno de sus padres a causa del sida y todos son portadores del virus VIH.

Bambini kenioti della scuola Kikoshep, in un quartiere povero di Kibera, Nairobi, 29 novembre 1998. Tutti hanno perso almeno uno dei genitori per colpa dell'AIDS, e sono tutti portatori del virus HIV.

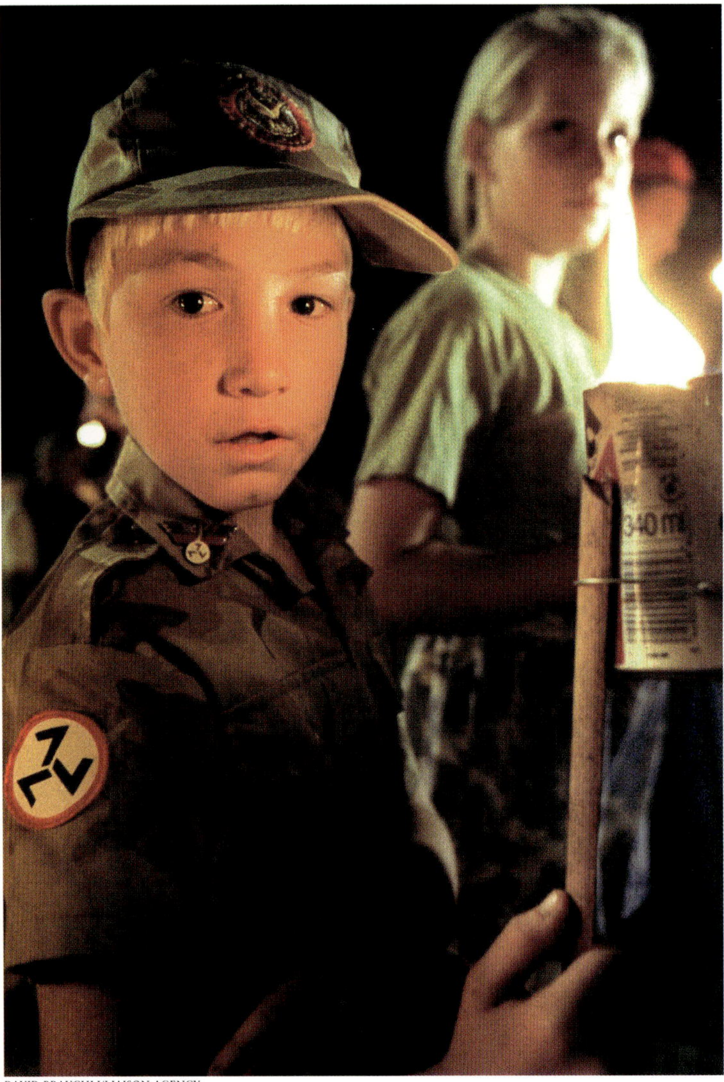

DAVID BRAUCHLI/LIAISON AGENCY

An AWB gathering on the 'Day of the Vow', Pretoria, South Africa, 5 December 1993. Afrikaaners celebrate a victory over the Zulus in 1838.

Congregación del neonazi Movimiento de Resistencia Afrikáner (AWB) en el Día del Juramento en Pretoria, Sudáfrica, 5 de diciembre de 1993. Los afrikáners celebran la victoria sobre los zulús en 1838.

Una riunione dell'AWB in occasione della "Festa del Giuramento", Pretoria, Sud Africa, 5 dicembre 1993. Gli afrikaner festeggiano una vittoria sugli zulù del 1838.

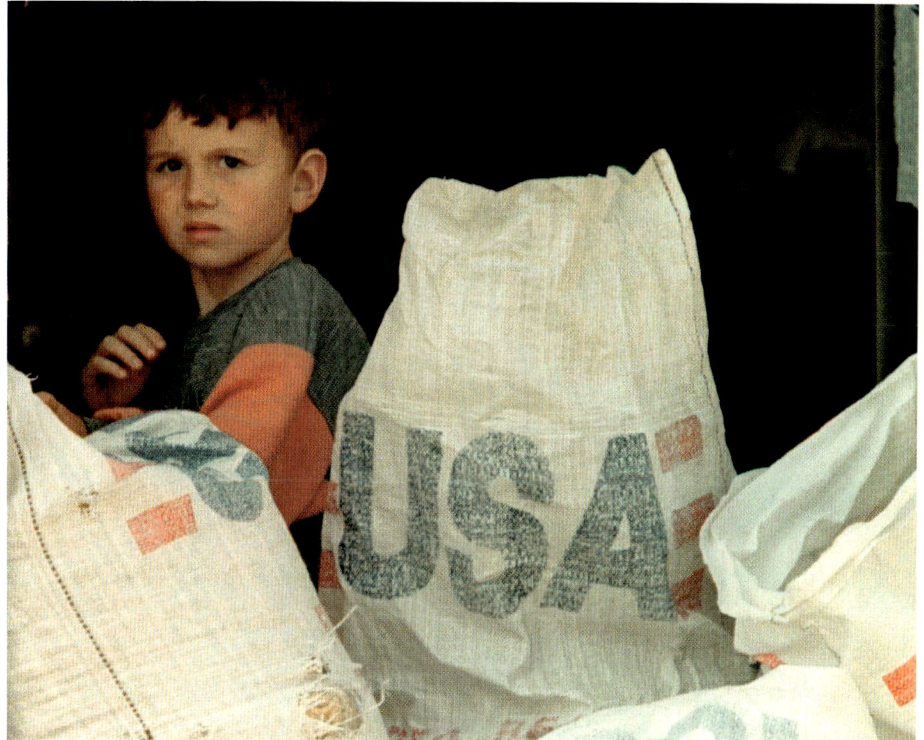

DAVID BRAUCHLI/LIAISON AGENCY

A young boy in a Sarajevo food store, 14 June 1995. At the time Sarajevans were stocking up on basic supplies in the belief that Bosnian and Serb troops would soon be fighting north of their city.

Un muchacho en unos almacenes de comida de Sarajevo, 14 de junio de 1995. Los habitantes de Sarajevo se abastecían de productos de primera necesidad ante la amenaza de un enfrentamiento inminente entre las tropas serbias y bosnias al norte de la ciudad.

Un bambino in un magazzino di viveri di Sarajevo, 14 giugno 1995. Era il momento in cui gli abitanti di Sarajevo facevano scorta di alimenti di base, pensando che le truppe bosniache e serbe avrebbero ben presto iniziato i combattimenti al nord della città.

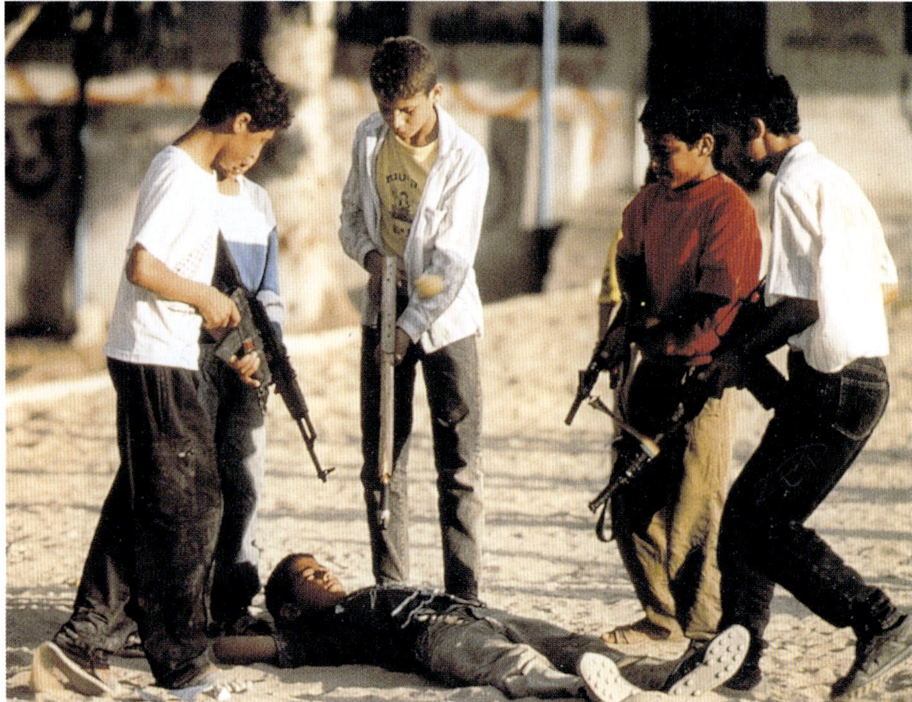

ROBERT SEMENIUK/BLACK STAR/COLORIFIC!

Children have always played with toy guns: these are home-made replicas of M-16s. Palestinian children traumatised by years of fighting and killing re-enact Intifada with a game called 'Arabs and Jews'.

A los niños siempre les han gustado las armas de juguete, como demuestran estos chavales palestinos provistos de réplicas de fusiles M16. Traumatizados por largos años de lucha y sangre derramada, reviven la Intifada mediante un juego llamado "Árabes y judíos".

I bambini si sono sempre divertiti con armi giocattolo: ecco qui alcune repliche artigianali dell'M-16. Giovani palestinesi traumatizzati da anni e anni di combattimenti e di morti, rivivono l'Intifada con un gioco chiamato "Arabi ed Ebrei".

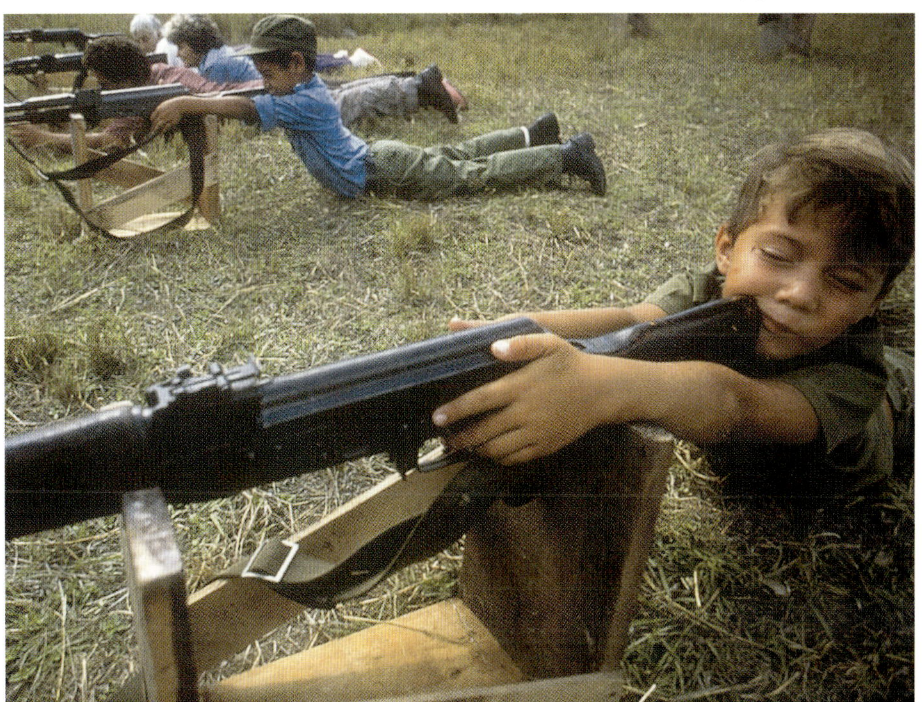

STAN GROSSFELD/BLACK STAR/COLORIFIC!

A Sunday morning militia training exercise in Cuba, 1990. The most powerful nations in the world rightly disapproved of the practice of arming children, but none of them was prepared to do anything to stop it.

Entrenamiento dominical de las milicias cubanas, 1990. Si bien las naciones más poderosas del mundo desaprobaban enérgicamente la práctica de dotar de armas a los niños, ninguna de ellas movía un dedo para intentar evitarlo.

Allenamento della milizia una domenica mattina a Cuba, 1990. Le nazioni più potenti del pianeta avevano giustamente condannato la pratica di armare i bambini, ma nessuna di esse aveva intenzione di fare qualcosa per evitarlo.

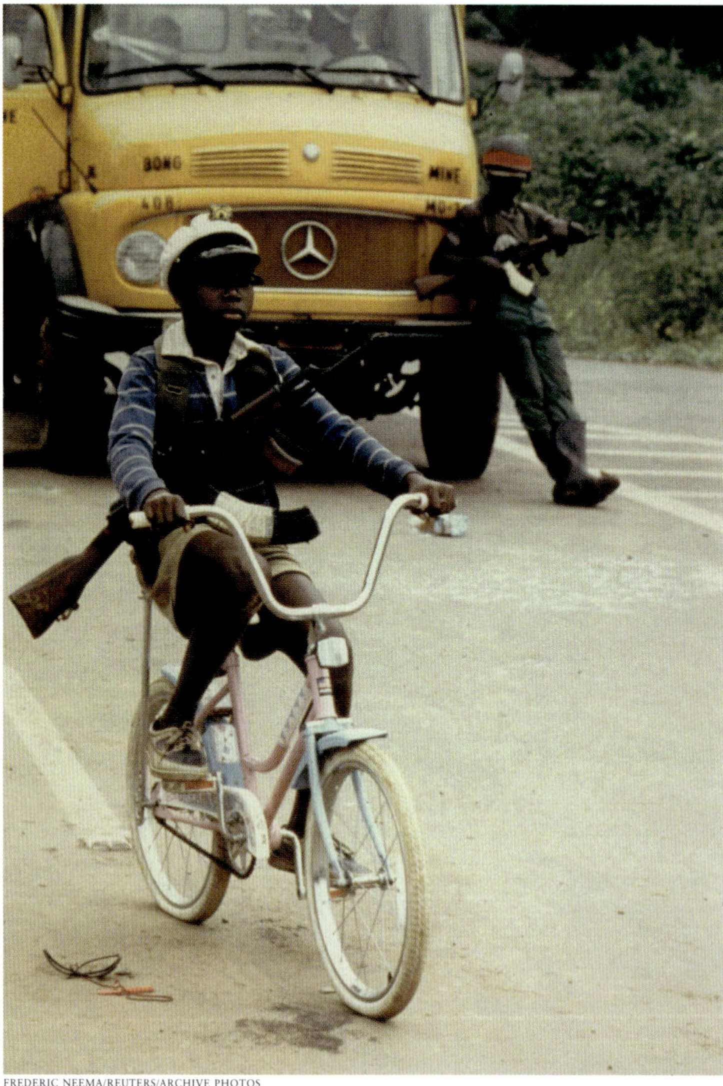

FREDERIC NEEMA/REUTERS/ARCHIVE PHOTOS

Junior Zoegee sets off to war. The 13-year-old was on his way through Monrovia, to fight Liberian Government troops, July 1990.

El pequeño Zoegee, de trece años de edad, parte hacia la guerra. Se dirige a Monrovia para luchar contra las tropas del Gobierno liberiano, julio de 1990.

Junior Zoegee parte per la guerra. Il bambino di 13 anni stava andando in Monrovia per combattere contro le truppe del governo liberiano, luglio 1990.

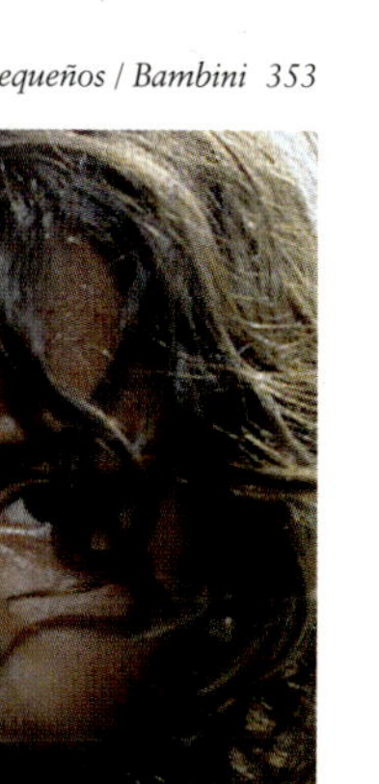

BEAWIHARTA/REUTERS/ARCHIVE PHOTOS

Australian troops of the International Forces for East Timor file past children near Dili, 21 September 1999. It was hoped that the new generation would be spared the horrors of a war that had already lasted twenty-four years.

Soldados australianos de las Fuerzas Internacionales enviadas a Timor Oriental pasan junto a unos niños cerca de la población de Dili, 21 de septiembre de 1999. Aún existía la esperanza de que las nuevas generaciones no tuvieran que sufrir los horrores de una guerra que duraba ya 24 años.

Truppe australiane della Forza Internazionale nel Timor Orientale sfilano vicino a un gruppo di bambini, nelle vicinanze di Dili, 21 settembre 1999. Ci si augurava di risparmiare alla nuova generazione gli orrori di una guerra durata già ventiquattro anni.

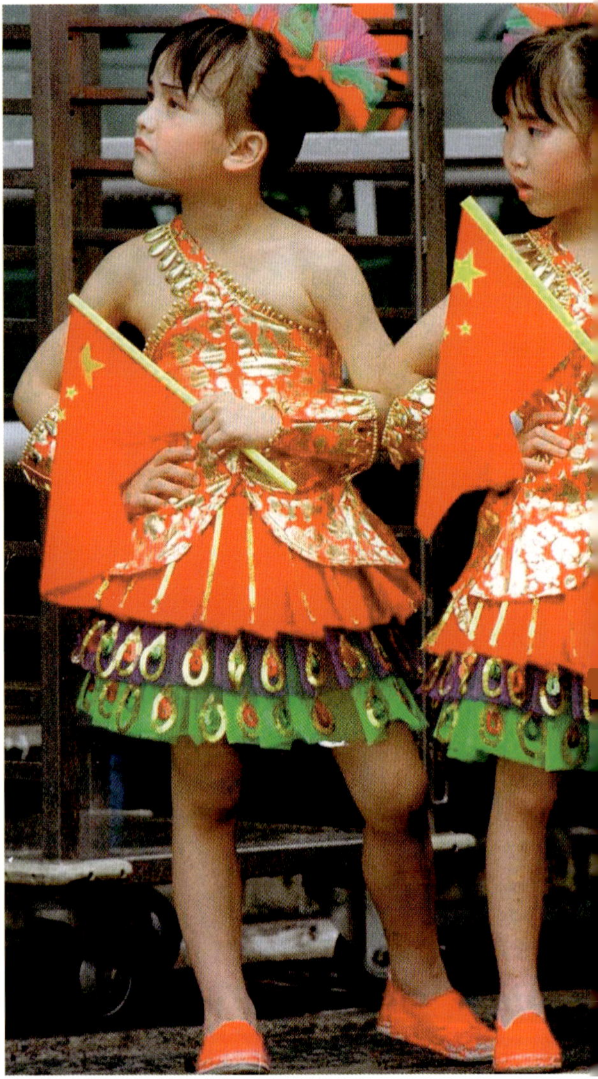

Young girls prepare to dance at a Buddhist festival in Hong Kong to celebrate re-unification with China, 1 July 1997.

Estas niñas se preparan para bailar en un festival budista en Hong Kong para celebrar la reunificación con China, 1 de julio de 1997.

Un gruppo di bambine si prepara per ballare in un festival buddista a Hong Kong, per festeggiare la riunificazione con la Cina, 1° luglio 1997.

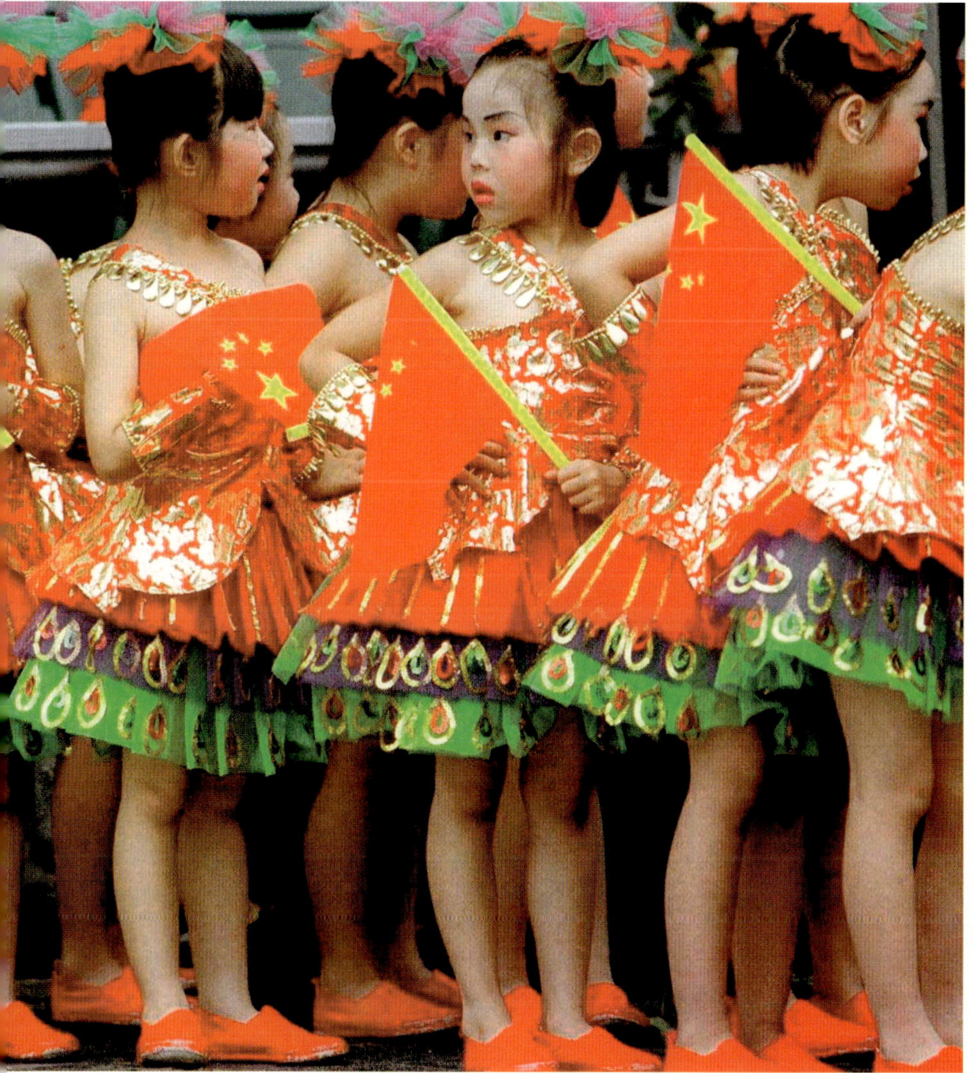

STEVE GRAY/REUTERS/ARCHIVE PHOTOS

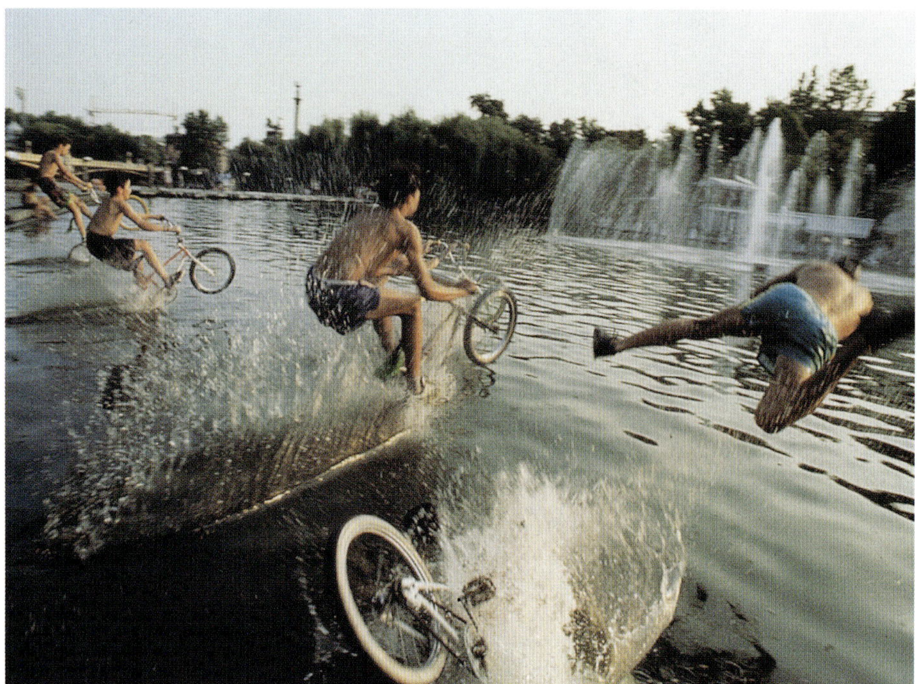

MANFRED HORVATH/ANZENBERGER/COLORIFIC!

The best playgrounds are always those that are discovered, adopted, adapted, taken over. Young bicycle acrobats take delightedly to the waters of the Stadwäldchen, Budapest, Hungary.

Los mejores lugares para jugar son siempre aquellos que se descubren, se adoptan, se adaptan y se ocupan sin más. Estos jóvenes acróbatas de la bicicleta se divierten en las aguas del Stadwäldchen de Budapest, en Hungría.

I migliori campi da gioco sono sempre quelli scoperti, adottati, adattati e invasi. Giovani acrobati in bicicletta si lanciano spensieratamente nelle acque dello Stadwäldchen, Budapest, Ungheria.

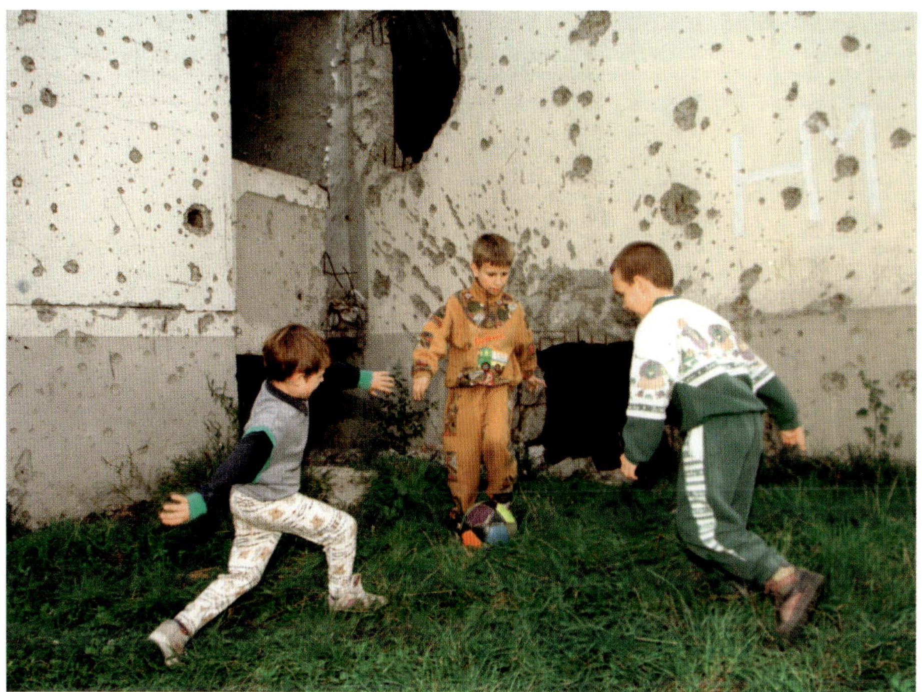

RUSSEL TADICH/LIAISON AGENCY

Undismayed by the bullet-scarred walls around them, Serb children play football in the ruins of Vukovar, November 1996. The town was destroyed during fighting between Yugoslav and Croatian forces.

Poco impresionados por las paredes acribilladas a balazos que los rodean, niños serbios juegan a fútbol entre las ruinas de Vukovar, noviembre de 1996. La ciudad fue destruida durante los combates entre las fuerzas croatas y yugoslavas.

Totalmente indifferenti ai muri scalfiti dalle pallottole, alcuni bambini serbi giocano a calcio fra i ruderi di Vukovar, novembre 1996. La città era stata distrutta durante i combattimenti fra le truppe jugoslave e croate.

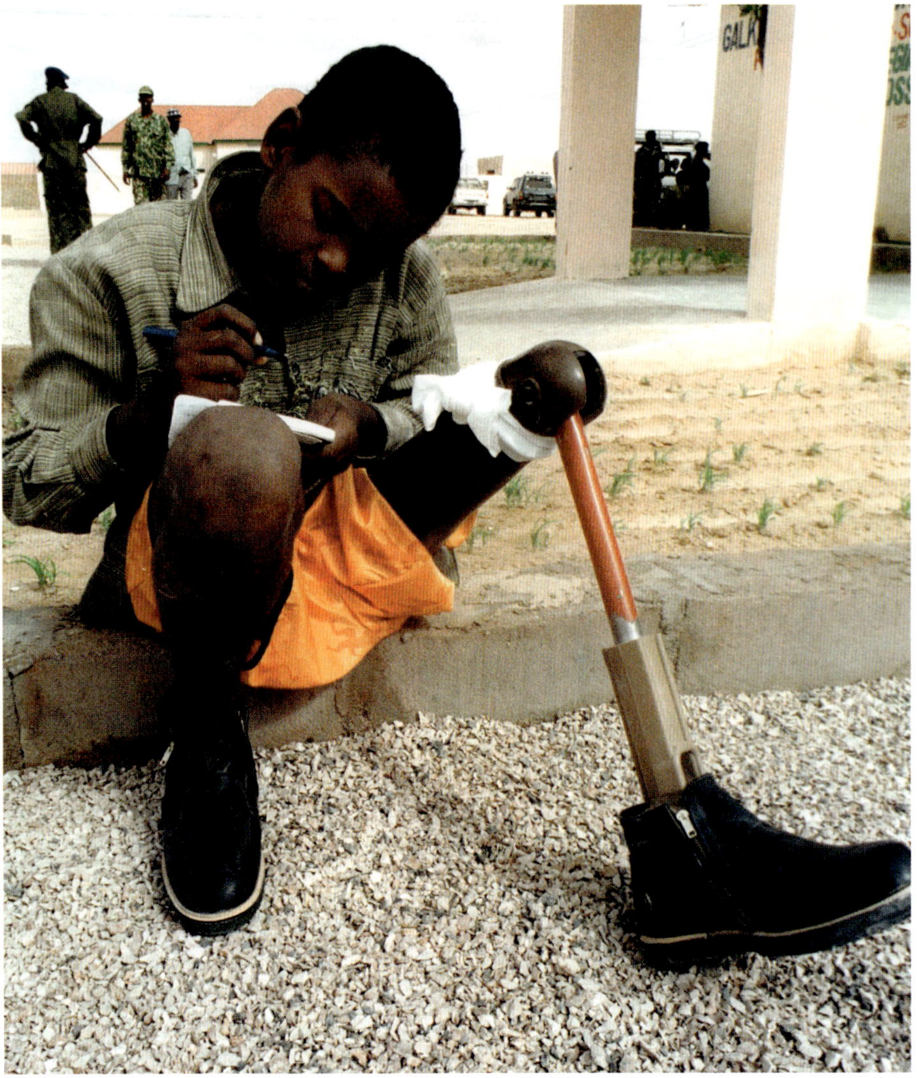

EPA/PA

(Opposite) Aweys Mohamed, 12, landmine victim, Somalia, 1999. (Right) A 12-year-old handicapped Bedouin – 'the family's shame', 1990.

(Página anterior) Aweys Mohamed, doce años, víctima de una mina antipersona en Somalia, 1999. (Derecha) Niño beduino discapacitado de doce años, la "deshonra de la familia", 1990.

(Pagina a fianco) Aweys Mohamed, di dodici anni, vittima di una mina, Somalia, 1999. (A destra) "La vergogna della famiglia" – un beduino handicappato di dodici anni, 1990.

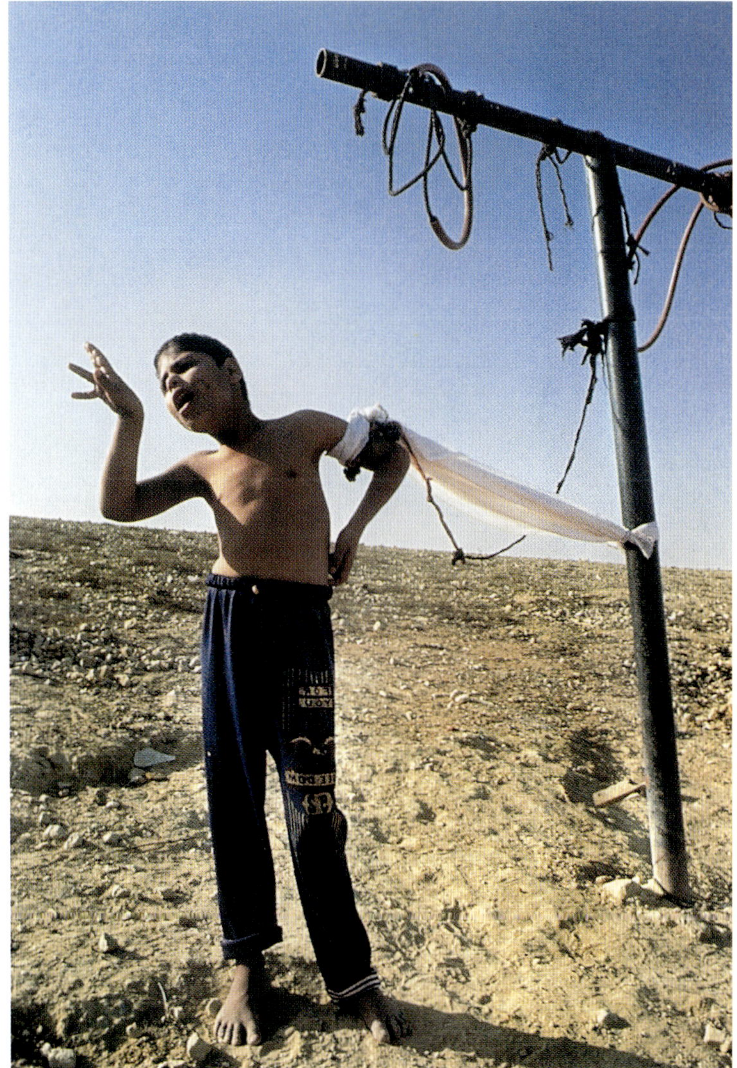

NITSAN SHORER/BLACK STAR/COLORIFIC!

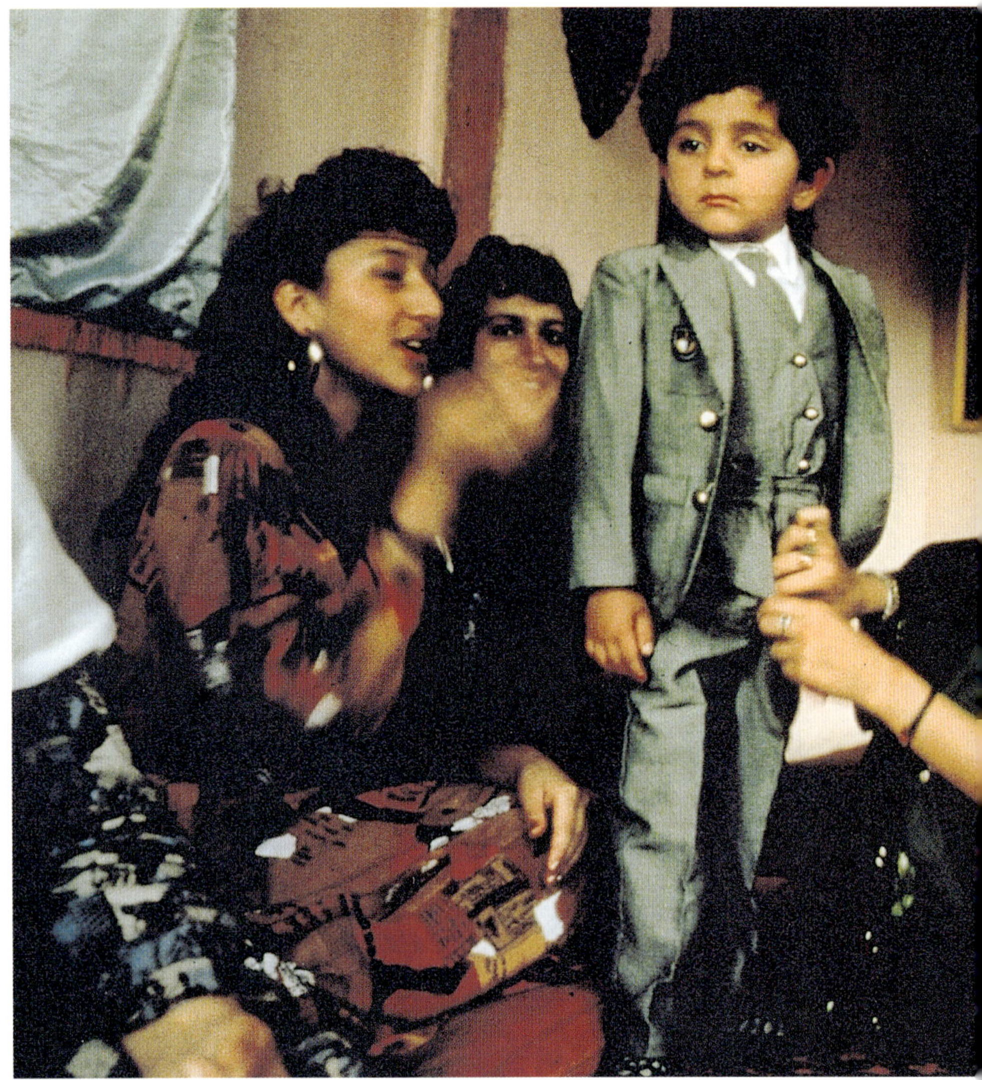

KLAUS REISINGER/BLACK STAR/COLORIFIC!

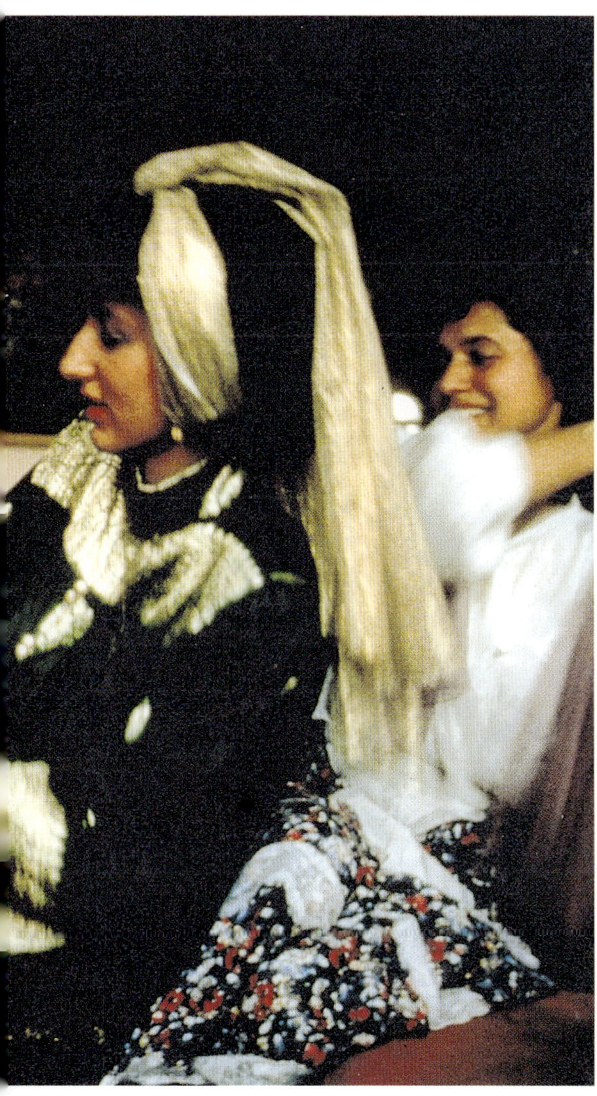

A young Muslim boy is prepared for a visit to the family patriarch, Afghanistan, 1992. He appears adjusted to the importance and solemnity of the occasion.

En Afganistán, un niño musulmán se prepara para visitar al patriarca de la familia, 1992. El muchacho parece plenamente consciente de la importancia y solemnidad que reviste el evento.

Un bambino musulmano viene vestito per una visita al patriarca della famiglia, Afghanistan, 1992. Il suo atteggiamento sembra accordarsi all'importanza e alla solennità dell'occasione.

12. All human life
Cosas de la vida
Fatti della vita

Seven-month-old Dolly, the world's first cloned animal, stands proudly in her pen at Edinburgh's Roslin Institute, 23 February 1997.

La oveja Dolly –de siete meses y el primer animal clonado del mundo–, orgullosa en su establo del Edinburgh's Roslin Institute, 23 de febrero de 1997.

Il primo animale clonato della storia, la pecora Dolly, posa orgogliosa a sette mesi di vita di fronte all'obiettivo nel recinto presso il Roslin Institute di Edimburgo, 23 febbraio 1997.

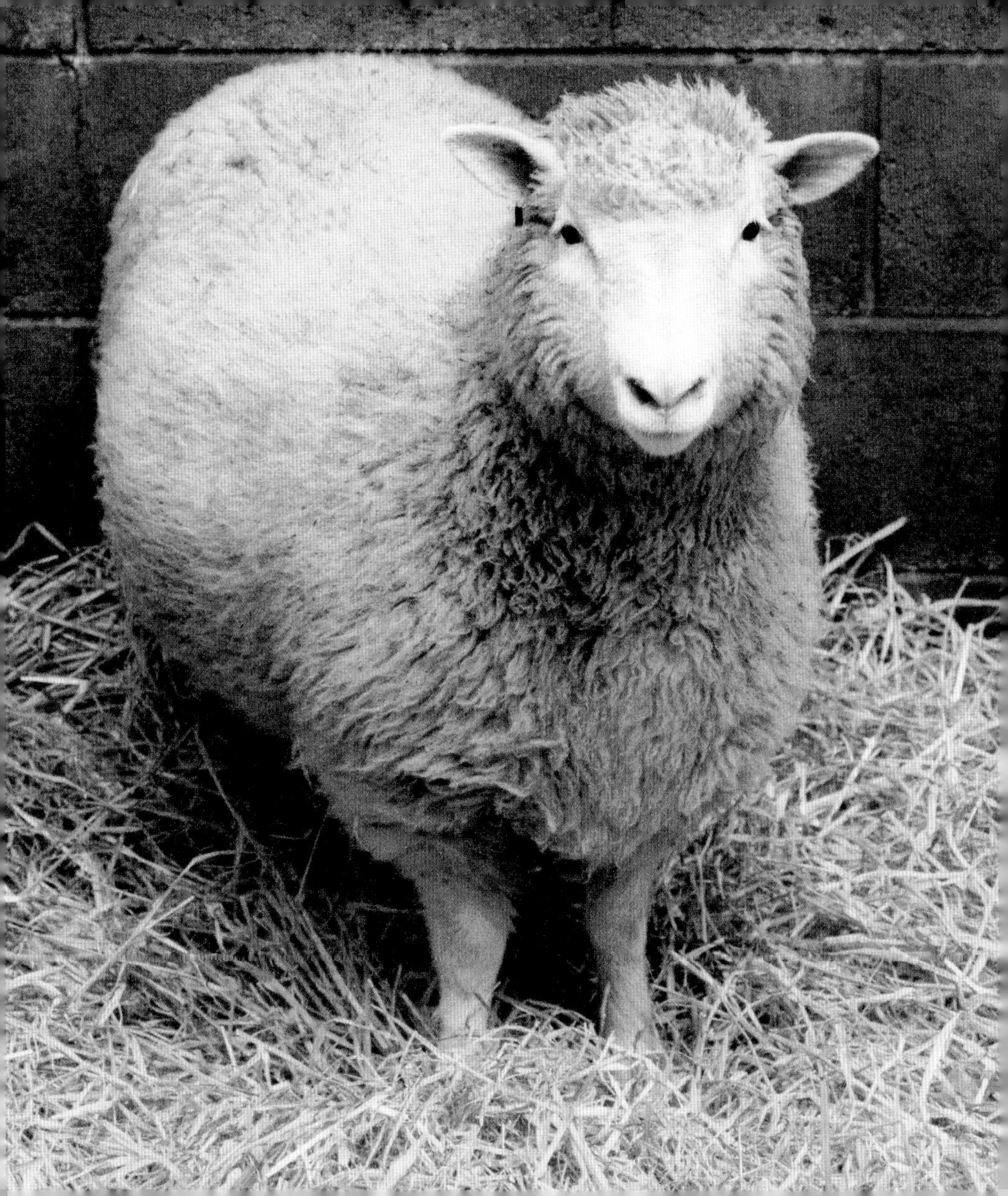

12. All human life
Cosas de la vida
Fatti della vita

As the century drew to a close, what was there left for human beings to invent, discover, demand, treasure or ill-use? It was a time of nostalgia. People recreated old journeys – walking across the Antarctic in the steps of Amundsen, Shackleton and Scott; sailing round the world in the wake of Drake and Magellan; climbing Everest in the ghoulish hope of finding the frozen remains of those who had perished in earlier attempts. It was time once again to plunder the carcass of the *Titanic*, search for the skeletons of planes shot down in the Second World War, restore old locomotives and revive the classic excursions by steam trains of the 1930s.

There were new vogues, new fads – the Trabant and the Jeep, smoked vegetables and ostrich meat, wild gardens and exotic pets, collecting telephone cards and Cold War memorabilia. And there were new problems. Mountains were being eroded by the very climbers they attracted. Venice was still sinking beneath the weight of its own tourists. Dozens of other glories had to be placed out of bounds to souvenir hunters.

And, at the Kyoto Conference in 1998, world leaders began the arduous process of rationing the world's energy resources…

A punto de clausurar el siglo XX, ¿qué le queda al ser humano por inventar, descubrir, reivindicar, apreciar o maltratar? Los noventa se abandonan a la nostalgia. Se recrean los viajes de antaño: recorrer el Polo Sur siguiendo los pasos de Amundsen, Shackleton y Scott; dar la vuelta al mundo en barco como lo hicieran Drake y Magallanes; escalar el Everest con la macabra esperanza de hallar los restos de quienes en tiempos pasados dejaron la vida en el intento. Otros se sumergen para explorar de nuevo los restos del naufragio del *Titanic*, buscan fuselajes de aviones abatidos durante la Segunda Guerra Mundial, recuperan viejas locomotoras y reemprenden las clásicas excursiones en trenes de vapor típicos de los años 30.

Aparecen nuevas modas y tendencias: el viejo Trabant y el Jeep, la verdura ahumada y la carne de avestruz, los jardines salvajes y las mascotas exóticas, las colecciones de tarjetas telefónicas y de reliquias de la guerra fría. Asimismo surgen nuevos problemas: las montañas sufren la erosión provocada por los alpinistas que las escalan; Venecia parece hundirse un poco más bajo el peso de los miles de turistas que la visitan y decenas de otros tesoros han de ser colocados fuera del alcance de los cazadores de *souvenirs*.

Y, en la Conferencia de Kioto de 1998, los dirigentes del mundo comienzan el arduo proceso de intentar racionalizar los recursos energéticos del planeta...

Man mano che si avvicinava la fine del secolo, quanto restava ancora che l'uomo non avesse già inventato, scoperto, chiesto, imparato o utilizzato in maniera sbagliata? Era il momento della nostalgia. La gente riviveva le emozioni di viaggi del passato – andare in missione nell'Antartico, seguendo i passi di Amundsen, Schackleton e Scott; circumnavigare il pianeta, imitando Drake e Magellano, scalare l'Everest nella terribile speranza di scoprire i resti congelati di chi era morto in tentativi precedenti. Era di nuovo il momento di recuperare i tesori del Titanic, cercare i relitti di aerei abbattuti durante la Seconda guerra mondiale, restaurare antiche locomotive e rivivere i classici viaggi dei treni a vapore degli anni Trenta.

Nascevano nuove mode, nuovi capricci – la Trabant e la Jeep, verdure affumicate e carne di struzzo, giardini selvaggi e animali da compagnia esotici, collezionare schede telefoniche e oggetti della Guerra Fredda. E nascevano anche nuovi problemi. Il processo di erosione delle montagne veniva accelerato da quegli stessi scalatori che erano attratti dalle loro altitudini, Venezia continuava ad affondare sotto il peso dei turisti; fu necessario vietare ai cacciatori di souvenir l'accesso a decine di altre glorie.

E durante la Conferenza di Kyoto, nel 1998, i leader mondiali si impegnavano nell'ardua impresa di amministrare meglio le risorse energetiche della terra...

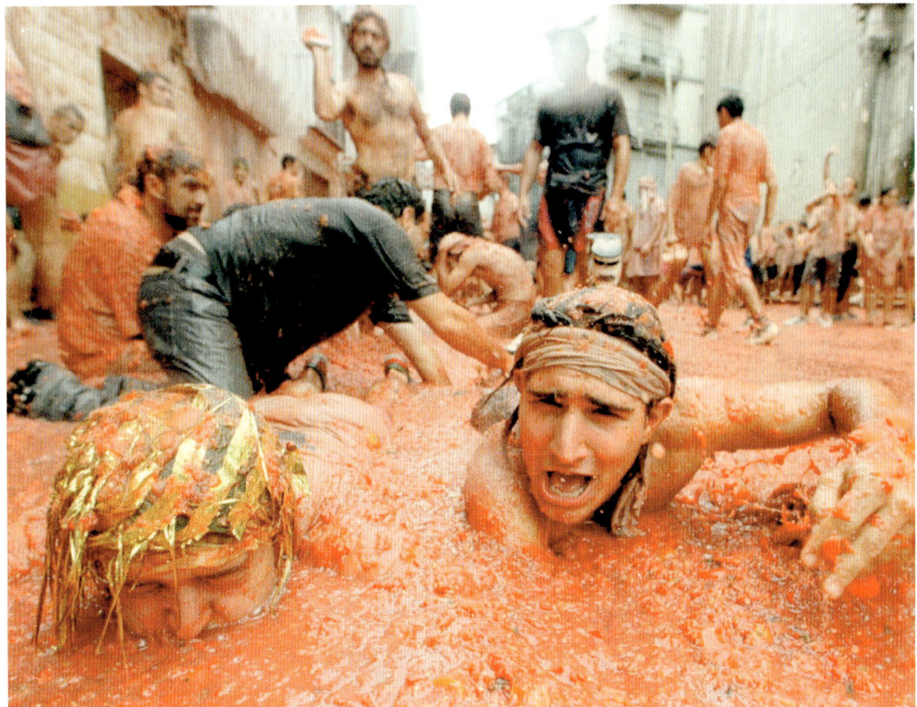

DESMOND BOYLAN/REUTERS/ARCHIVE PHOTOS

Every bad comedian's nightmare. Inhabitants of Buñol, near Valencia, Spain, flounder in the pulp of the 100 tonnes of tomatoes they have hurled at each other during their local festival, 28 August 1996.

La pesadilla de cualquier mal actor. Habitantes de Buñol, población cercana a la ciudad de Valencia, inmersos en la pulpa de las cien toneladas de tomates que se lanzan los unos a los otros durante la Tomatina, la fiesta más popular del pueblo, 28 de agosto de 1996.

L'incubo di qualsiasi pessimo attore. Gli abitanti di Buñol, vicino a Valencia, in Spagna, immersi nella polpa di 100 tonnellate di pomodori che si lanciano in occasione della festa del posto, 28 agosto 1996.

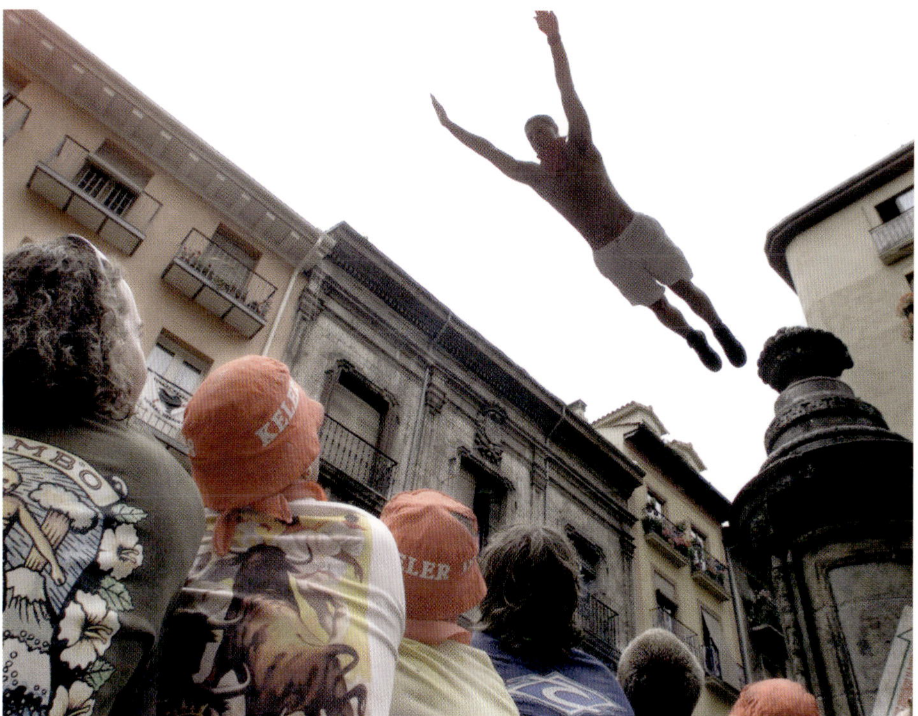

JIM HOLLANDER/REUTERS/ARCHIVE PHOTOS

In drunken memory of Ernest Hemingway. A visitor to the Fiesta de San Fermín, when the bulls run through the streets of Pamplona, dives confidently into the arms of waiting friends, 6 July 1999.

En memoria de Ernest Hemingway. Un visitante –a todas luces ebrio– de la popular fiesta de San Fermín de Pamplona, se lanza confiado en los brazos de sus expectantes amigos, 6 de julio de 1999.

Dopo l'ennesimo brindisi alla memoria di Ernest Hemingway, un partecipante alle feste di San Fermín, in occasione delle quali i tori corrono per le strade di Pamplona, si tuffa fiduciosamente fra le braccia ansiose dei suoi amici, 6 luglio 1999.

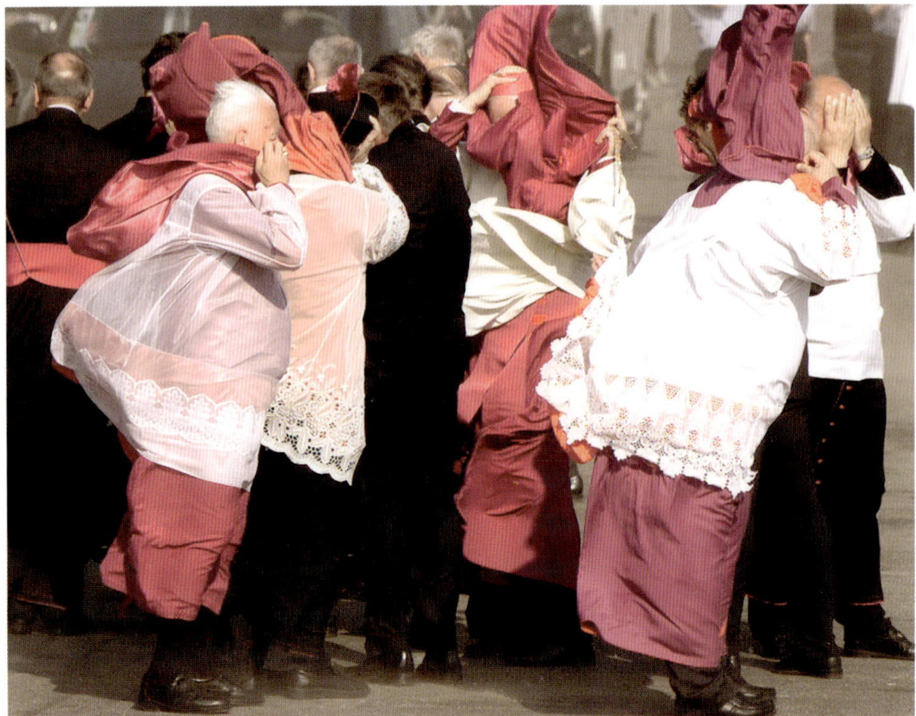

JERRY LAMPEN/REUTERS/ARCHIVE PHOTOS

(Above) A hurricane visit. Polish bishops battered by the rotor wash from the Pope's helicopter as they await his arrival in Elblag, Poland, 6 June 1999. (Opposite) Casting their fates to the winds. Graduates of the Air Force Academy commencement maintain the old tradition as they hurl their caps into the air, 2 June 1999.

(Arriba) Una visita airosa. Obispos polacos azotados por el aire del rotor del helicóptero del Papa, a su llegada a Elblag, Polonia, el 6 de junio de 1999. (Página siguiente) Lanzando sus destinos al vuelo. En la ceremonia de graduación de la Academia de las Fuerzas Aéreas se sigue la tradición de lanzar los gorros al aire, 2 de junio de 1999.

(In alto) Una visita al volo. Vescovi polacchi in attesa del Papa, fanno resistenza al vento del rotore dell'elicottero che lo trasporta a Elblag, Polonia, 6 giugno 1999. (Pagina a fianco). Gettare al vento il proprio destino. Ufficiali della Air Force Academy durante la cerimonia per il conferimento delle lauree, mantengono l'antica tradizione di gettare il cappello in aria.

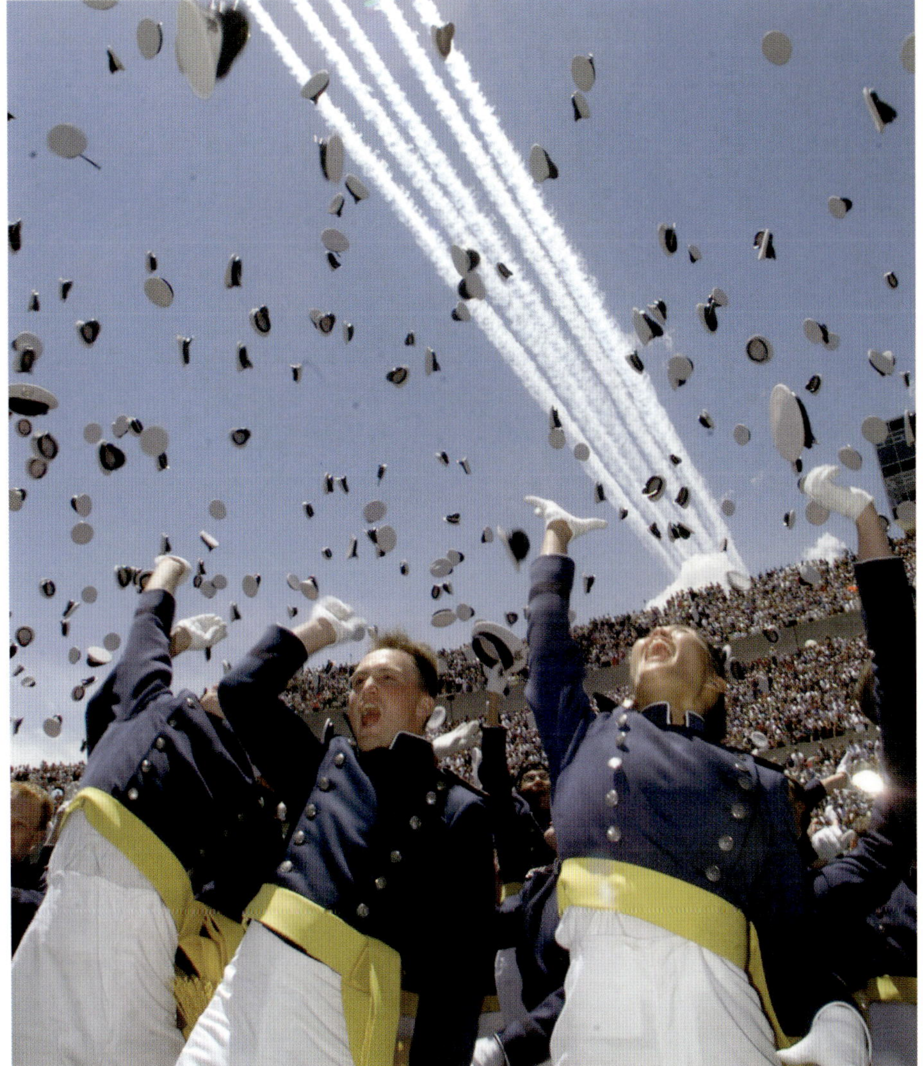

RICK WILKING/REUTERS/ARCHIVE PHOTOS

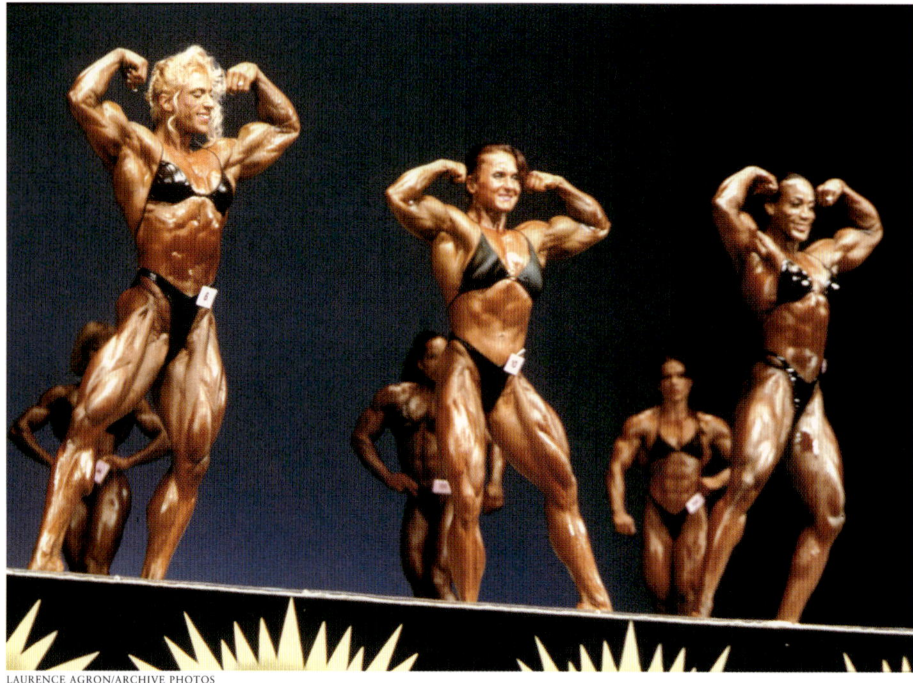

LAURENCE AGRON/ARCHIVE PHOTOS

Body-building. Kim Chivesky (USA – 1st) (left), Natalia Murnikoviene (Lithuania – 2nd) (centre) and Lenda Murray (USA – 3rd) (right) show what they're made of at the Ms Olympia Bodybuilding Contest, Chicago, 20 September 1996.

Todo músculo. Kim Chivesky (Estados Unidos, 1ª, izquierda), Natalia Murnikoviene (Lituania, 1ª, centro) y Lenda Murray (Estados Unidos, 3ª, derecha) exhiben sus cuerpos en el certamen de *bodybuilding* Ms Olympia en Chicago, 20 de septiembre de 1996.

Alla scoperta del corpo. Kim Chivesky (USA – 1ª) (a sinistra), Natalia Murnikoviene (Lituania – 2ª) (al centro) e Lenda Murray (USA – 3ª) (a destra) mettono in mostra il loro corpo durante il concorso di body building Miss Olympia, Chicago, 20 settembre 1996.

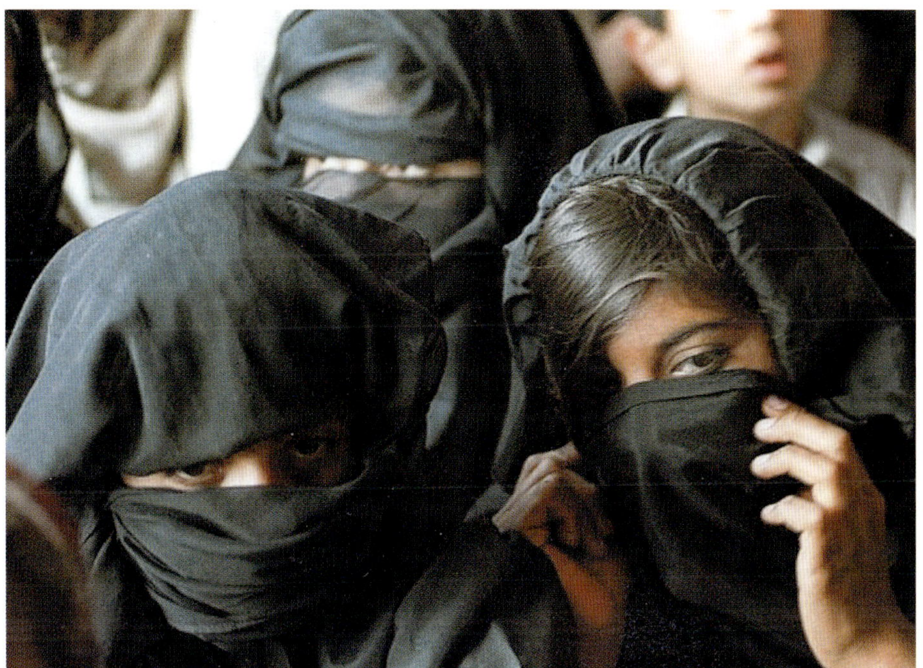

SAEED KHAN/EPA/PA

Body-hiding. Three members of the audience at an address by Benazir Bhutto, the deposed premier of Pakistan, Rattudero, 28 January 1997. The public meeting attracted a large number of women.

Todo velo. Tres asistentes al discurso de Benazir Bhutto –la primera ministra depuesta de Pakistán– en Rattudero, el 28 de enero de 1997. Gran parte del público presente estaba formado por mujeres.

Con il corpo coperto. Tre donne del pubblico durante una conferenza di Benazir Bhutto, Primo Ministro destituito del Pakistan, Rattudero, 28 gennaio 1997. L'evento pubblico attrasse molte donne.

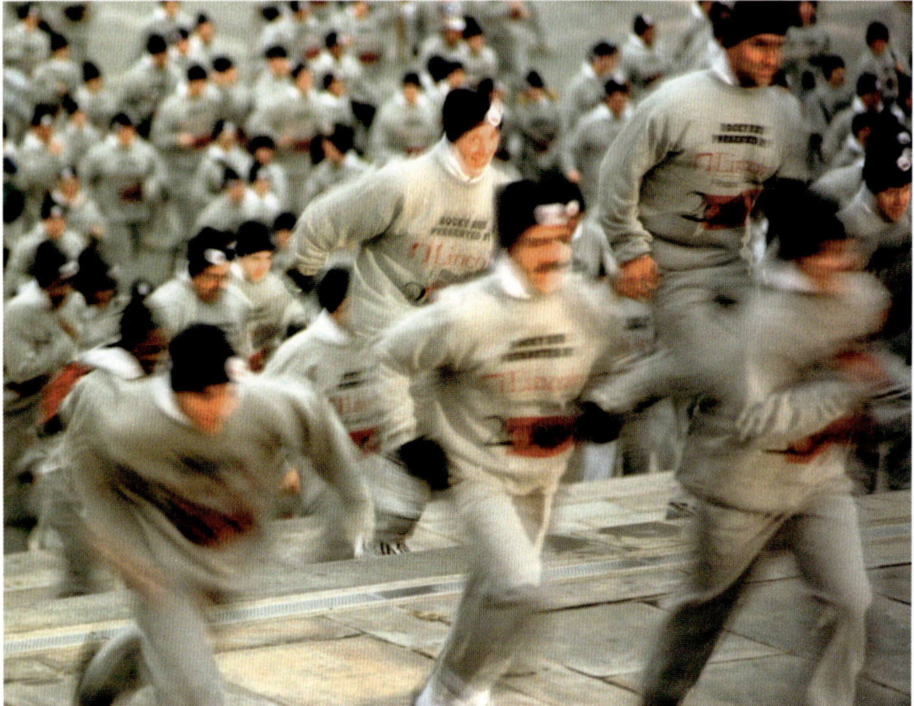

WILLIAM BRETZGER/LIAISON AGENCY

The sincerest form of flattery. Some 2,000 Rocky Balboa impersonators mount the steps of Philadelphia's Museum of Art as part of the Millennium celebrations, 31 December 1999. They were recreating a scene from the movie *Rocky*.

El halago más sincero. Cerca de 2.000 imitadores de Rocky Balboa suben la escalinata del museo de arte de Filadelfia recreando una escena de la película *Rocky*, como parte de los festejos del fin de milenio, 31 de diciembre de 1999.

L'adulazione più sincera. Più o meno 2.000 imitatori di Rocky Balboa salgono gli scalini del Museum of Art di Philadelphia durante i festeggiamenti del Millennio, 31 dicembre 1999. Rievocavano una scena del film *Rocky*.

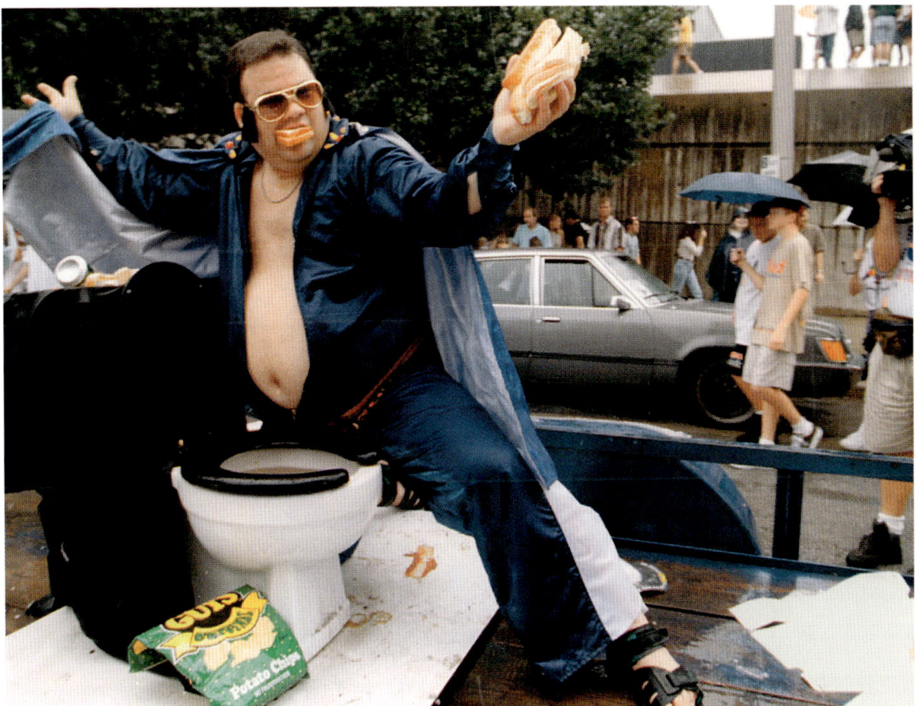

TIMOTHY J JONES/LIAISON AGENCY

'Down at the end of Lonely Street…at heart-attack hotel' Paul Rudy, the 'Jelly Doughnut Elvis', shakes it all about in the annual Elvis Parade on the anniversary of Presley's death, Kansas City, 16 August 1996.

Down at the end of Lonely Street… at heart-attack hotel. Paul Rudy –más conocido como el "Elvis de la gelatina y los donuts"– en el desfile anual organizado con motivo del aniversario de la muerte de Elvis Presley en Kansas City, 16 de agosto de 1996.

"Down at the end of Lonely Street… a heart-attack hotel". Paul Rudy, soprannominato "Jelly Doughnut Elvis" fa un movimento di fianchi durante l'annuale Elvis Parade per commemorare l'anniversario della morte di Elvis Presley, Kansas City, 16 agosto 1996.

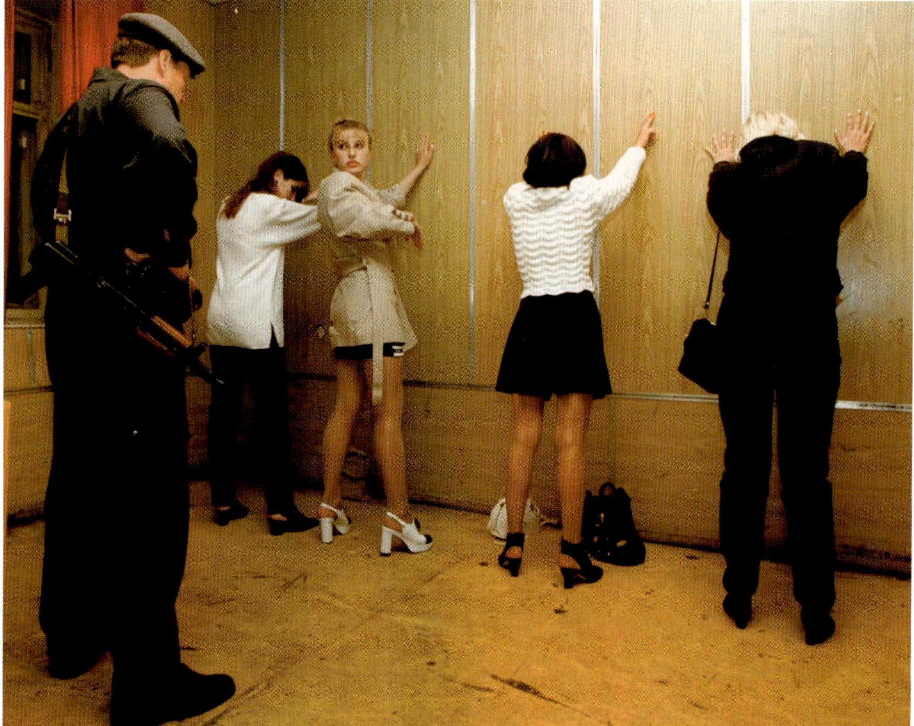

GEORGES DE KEERLE/LIAISON AGENCY

Fighting for a place in the market economy. Four young women arrested for prostitution parade before Moscow police, May 1997. Low wages drove many Russian women onto the streets.

Luchando por abrirse paso en la economía de mercado. La policía moscovita detiene a cuatro mujeres por ejercer la prostitución, mayo de 1997. Los bajos salarios arrastraban a muchas mujeres rusas a optar por prostituirse.

Lottare per farsi un posto nell'economia di mercato. Quattro giovani donne arrestate per prostituzione di fronte a un poliziotto moscovita, maggio 1997. I salari bassi costrinsero molte donne russe a scendere in strada.

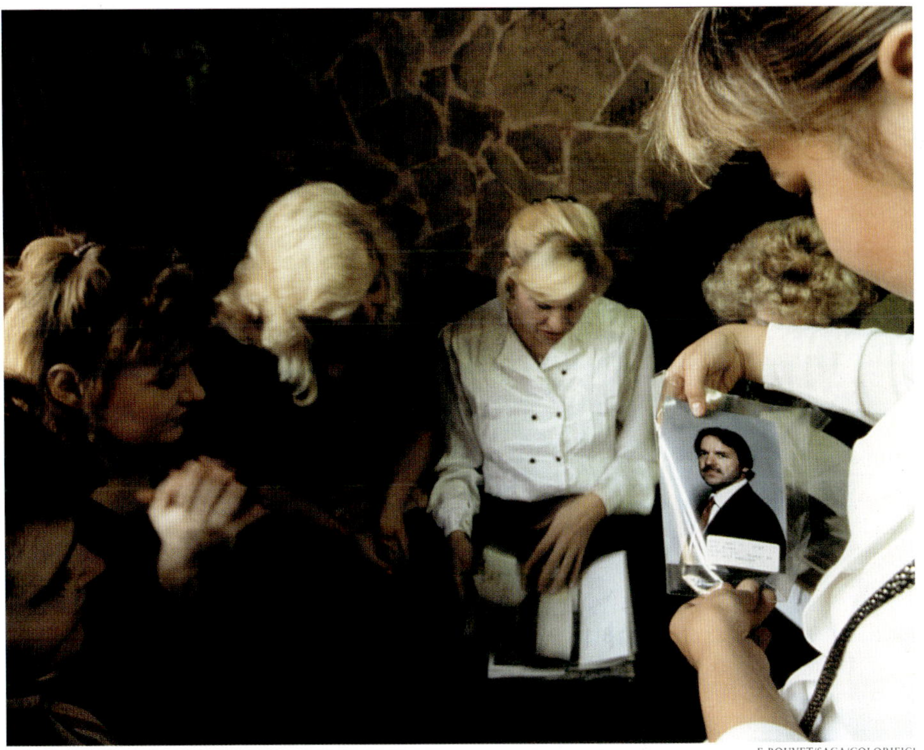

E BOUVET/SAGA/COLORIFIC!

'For better, for worse...' Russian women examine the files of available talent at a Moscow marriage bureau, October 1992, each of them searching for an American husband.

"En lo bueno y en lo malo..." Mujeres rusas examinan los archivos de una agencia matrimonial de Moscú, en busca de un marido norteamericano, octubre de 1992.

"Nel bene e nel male..." Un gruppo di donne russe esamina l'archivio di un'agenzia matrimoniale di Mosca, alla ricerca di un marito americano, ottobre 1992.

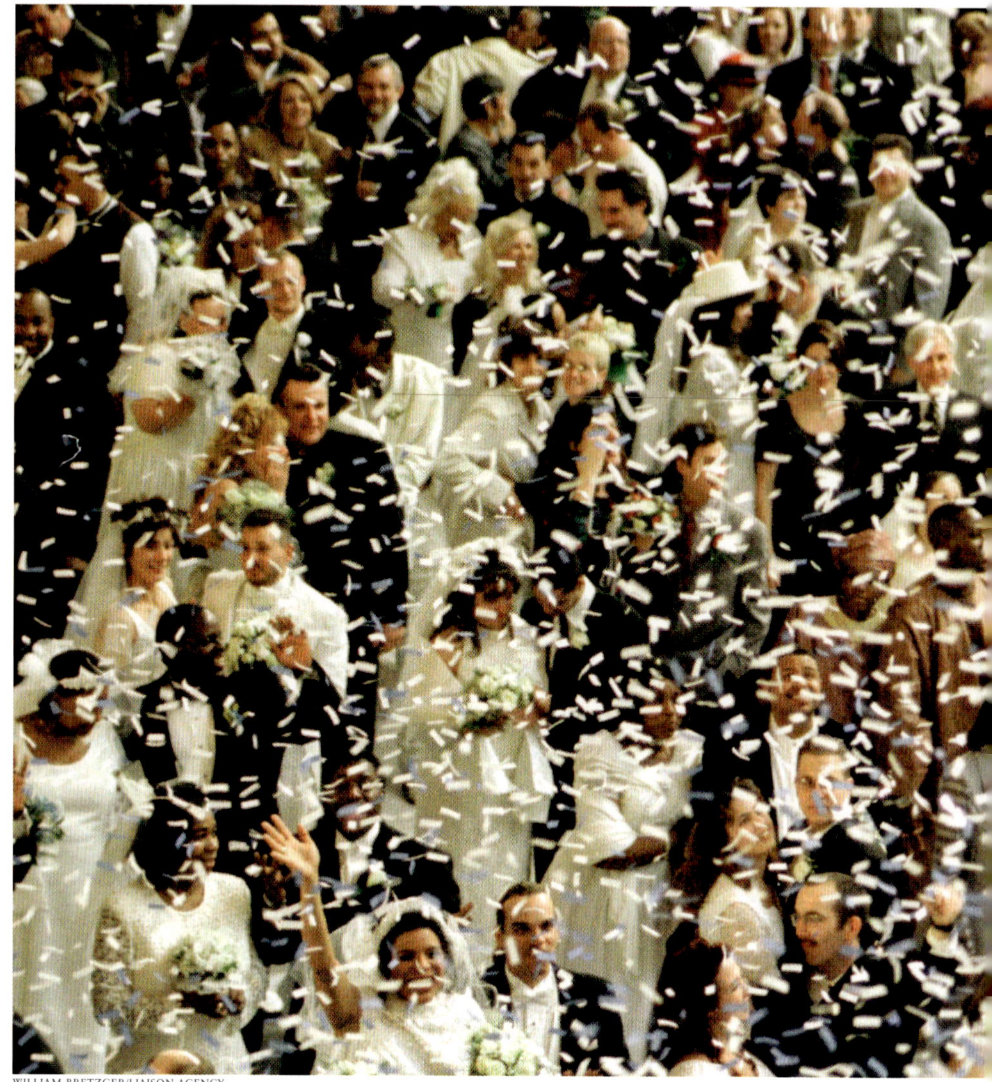

WILLIAM BRETZGER/LIAISON AGENCY

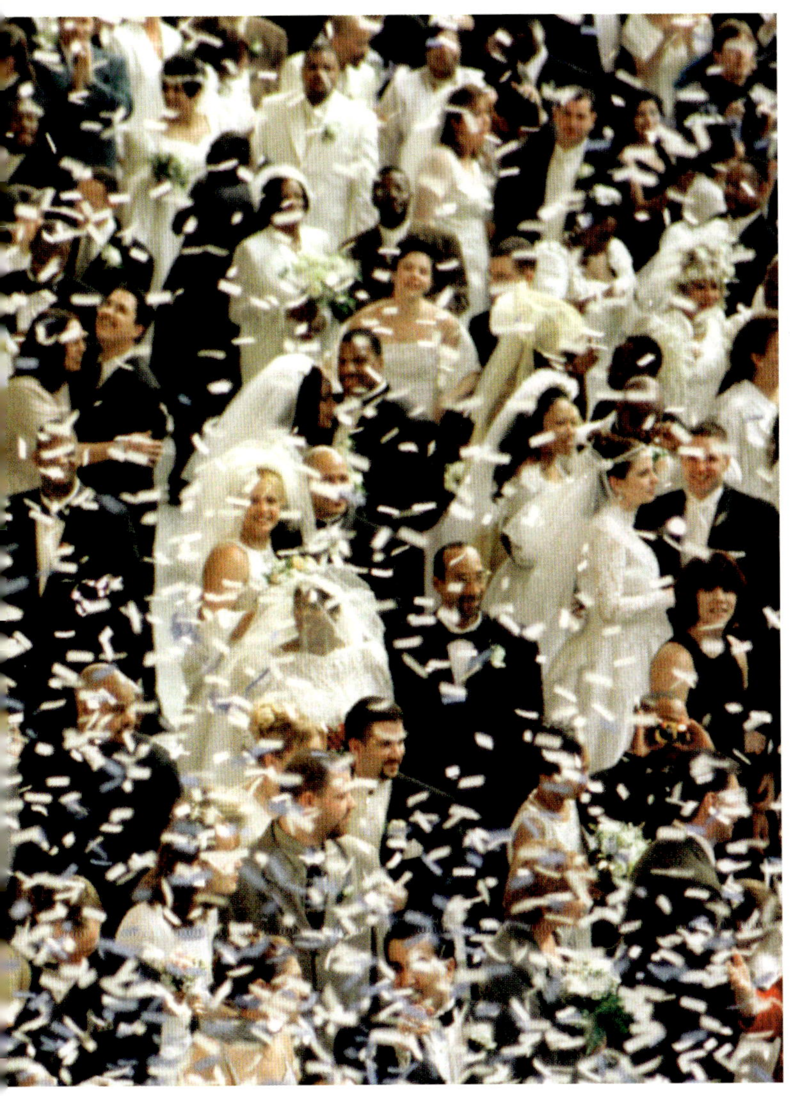

More than 1,300 participants at a mass wedding ceremony in the Pennsylvania Convention Center, 31 December 1999. Presumably all ended up with their intended partner.

Más de 1.300 contrayentes participan en una boda masiva celebrada en el Pennsylvania Convention Center el 31 de diciembre de 1999. Es de suponer que todos acabaron casados con sus correspondientes parejas.

Più di 1.300 persone presero parte alla cerimonia nuziale collettiva, celebrata nel Convention Center, Pennsylvania, 31 dicembre 1999. Si suppone che tutti passarono la notte con il rispettivo partner.

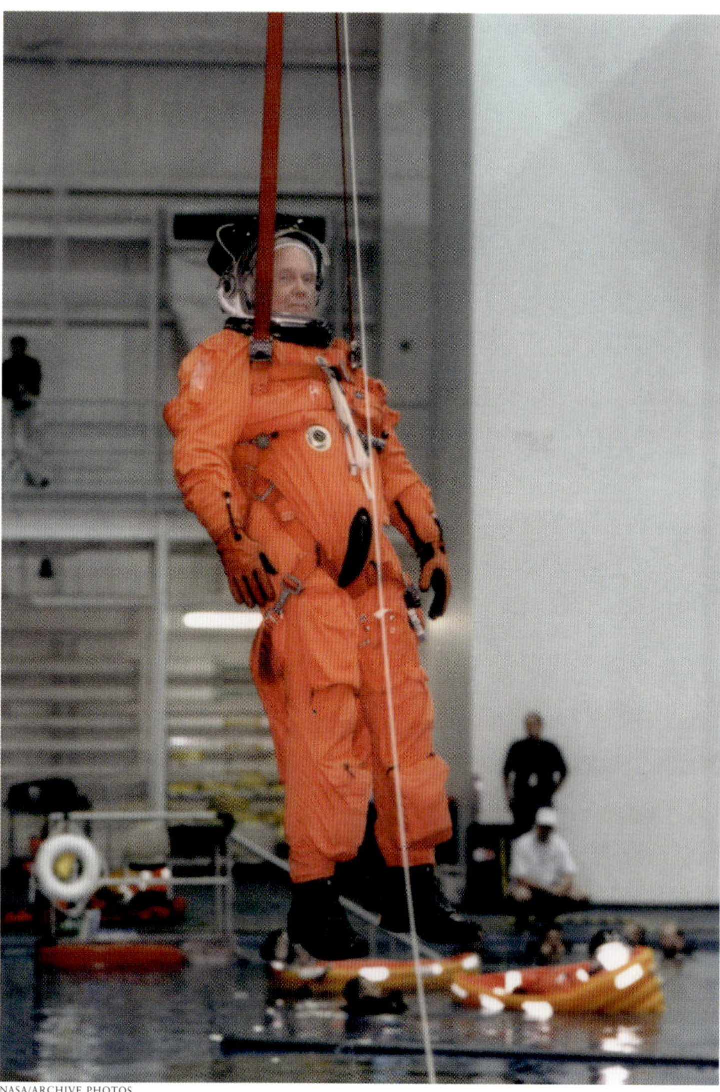

NASA/ARCHIVE PHOTOS

The turtle has landed. John H. Glenn Jnr simulates a parachute drop during training at the Sonny Carter Training Center.

La tortuga ha aterrizado. John H. Glenn hijo simula un descenso en paracaídas durante un entrenamiento en el Sonny Carter Training Center.

La tartaruga è atterrata. John H. Glenn Jr. in una simulazione di una caduta in paracadute durante l'allenamento presso il Training Center Sonny Carter.

Overturned turtles. Employees of a South Korean industrial instrument company participate in a morale-boosting workout on Daebu Island, 17 April 1998.

Las tortugas han volcado. Empleados de una compañía surcoreana de instrumental industrial participan en un ejercicio de motivación en la isla de Daebu, 17 de abril de 1998.

Tartarughe a pancia in su. Un gruppo di impiegati di una ditta di strumentazione industriale sud-coreana partecipa a una sessione per risollevare il morale sull'isola di Daebu, 17 aprile 1998.

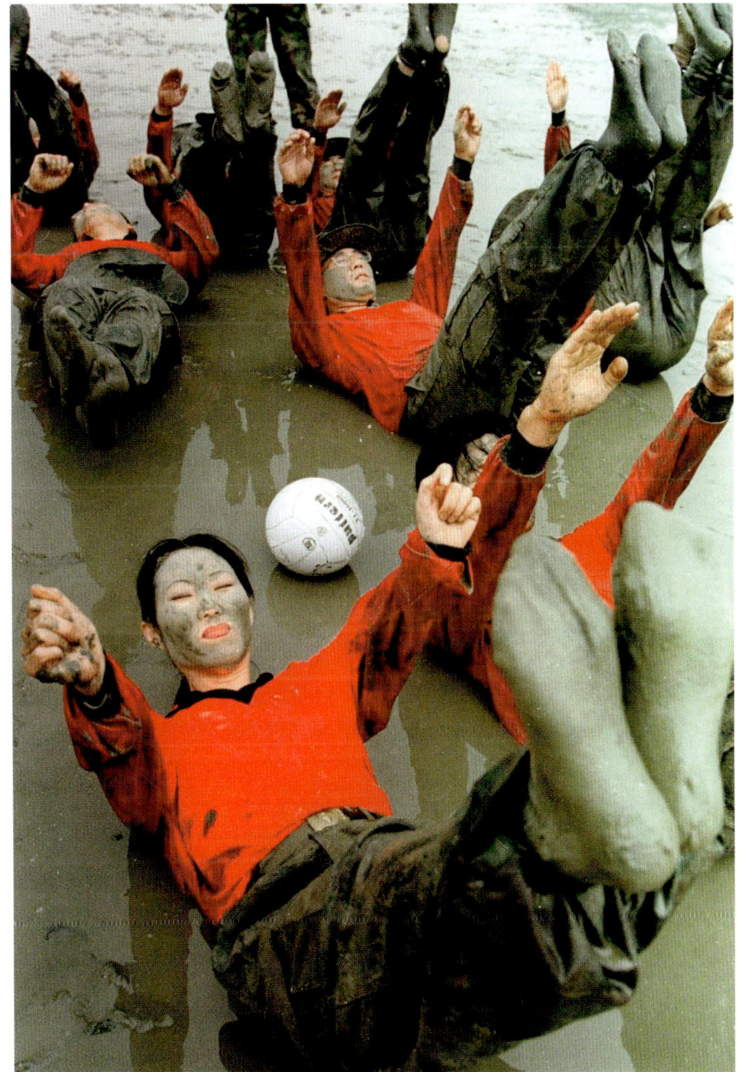

YUN SUK-BONG/REUTERS/ARCHIVE PHOTOS

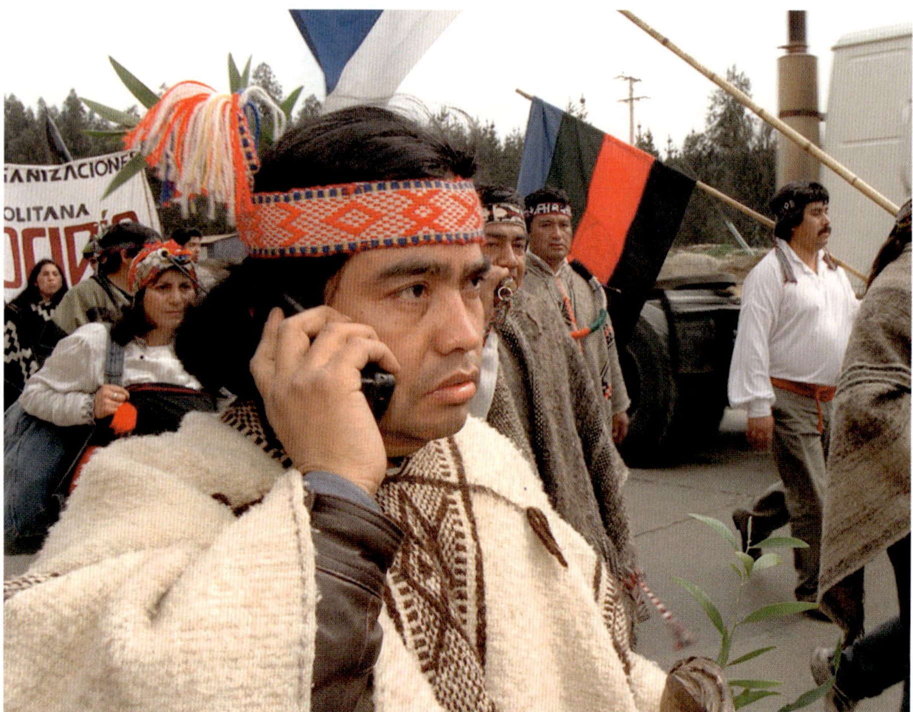

CHRIS BOURONCLE/EPA/PA

Native Chilean Indians take part in a march from Santiago to the National Congress in Valparaiso, 12 August 1998. They walked the 71 miles to protest against the building of a dam for hydroelectricity.

El 12 de agosto de 1998, nativos indígenas de Chile llevaron a cabo una marcha de 114 kilómetros, desde Santiago hasta el Congreso Nacional de Valparaíso, para protestar contra la construcción de una presa hidroeléctrica.

Indios cileni partecipano a una marcia da Santiago al Congresso Nazionale di Valparaíso, 12 agosto 1998. Percorsero 114 chilometri per protestare contro la costruzione di una diga idroelettrica.

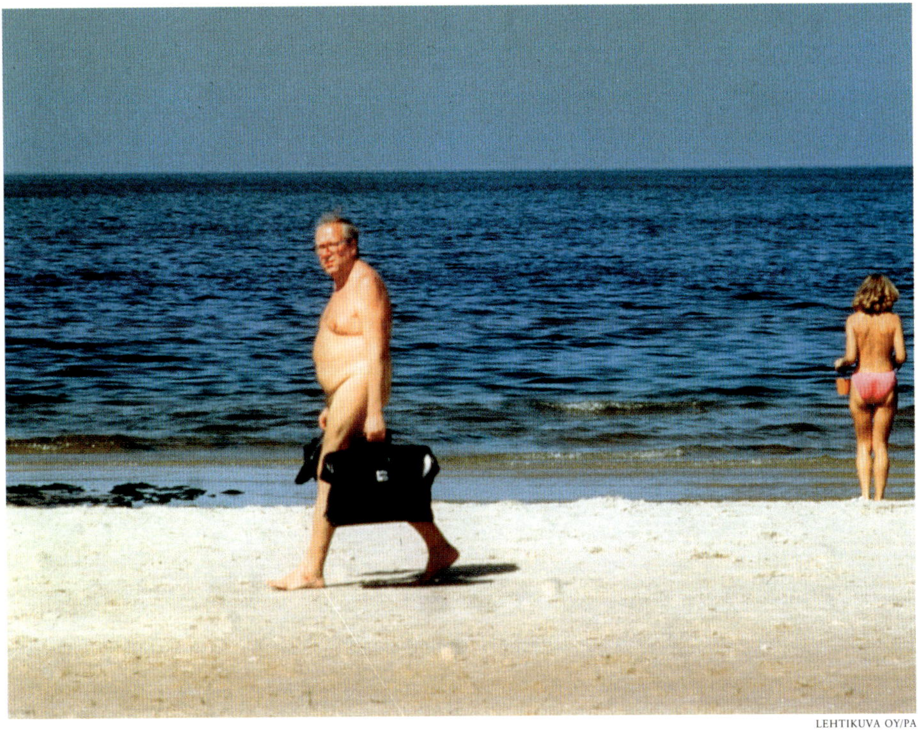

LEHTIKUVA OY/PA

Taking work home for the weekend. A Latvian executive strides along a stretch of beach at the Latvian Nudist Colony, Saule, 10 June 1992. After seventy years of Communism the whole exercise must have come as an enormous relief.

Trabajo para el fin de semana. En Letonia, un ejecutivo camina por la playa que baña la colonia nudista de Saule, 10 de junio de 1992. Tras setenta años de comunismo, la práctica de este ejercicio suponía toda una liberación.

Portarsi il lavoro a casa per il week-end. Un dirigente d'azienda lettone passeggia lungo la spiaggia della colonia nudista di Saule, Lettonia, 10 giugno 1992. Dopo settant'anni di comunismo, un esercizio di questo tipo doveva sembrare un incredibile sollievo.

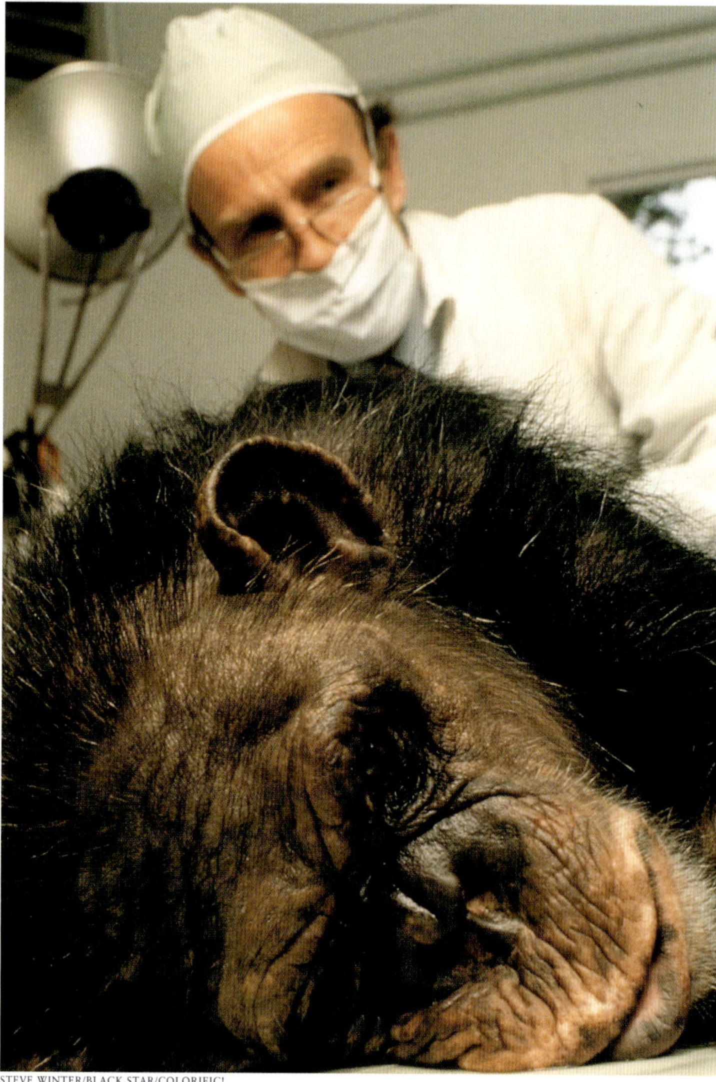

STEVE WINTER/BLACK STAR/COLORIFIC!

Doctor Jim Mahoney reluctantly submits an adult chimpanzee to AIDS research at the New York University Medical Center.

Con el corazón encogido, el doctor Jim Mahoney –del University Medical Center de Nueva York– somete a un chimpacé adulto a una investigación sobre el virus del sida.

Il Dottor Jim Mahoney utilizza, suo malgrado, uno scimpanzé adulto per realizzare ricerche sull'AIDS, nell'University Medical Center di New York.

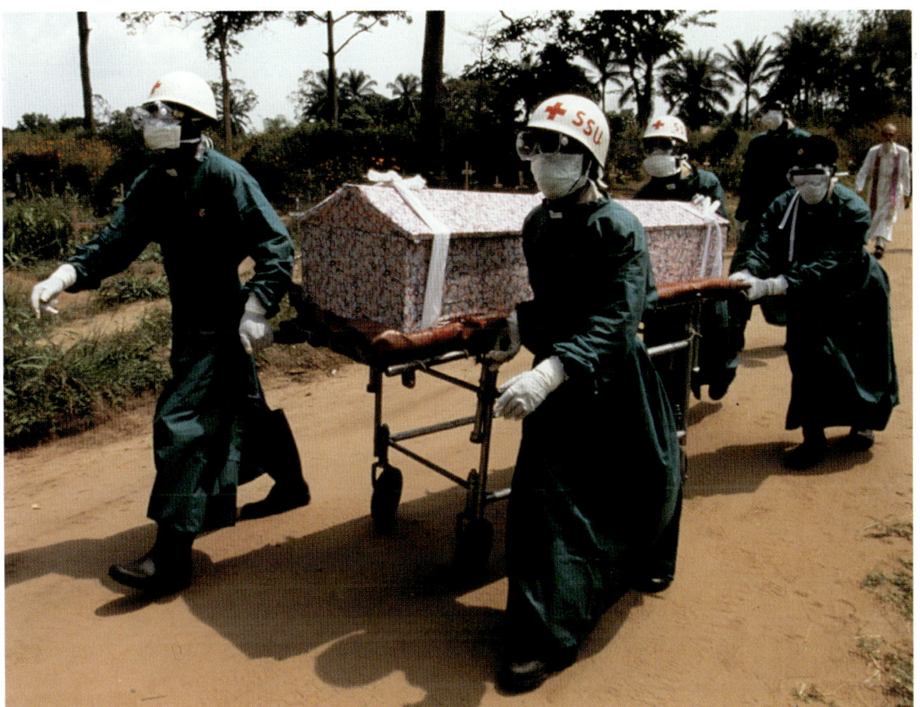

MALCOLM LINTON/BLACK STAR/COLORIFIC!

The funeral of Sister Dinarosa Bellerini, an Italian nursing nun, Kikwit Hospital, Zaire, 15 May 1995. She was one of the first victims of an Ebola virus epidemic which struck central Africa for the first time in seventeen years.

Sepelio de la hermana Dinarosa Bellerini, una enfermera italiana del hospital Kikwit, en el Zaire, 15 de mayo de 1995. Fue una de las primeras víctimas de la epidemia del virus Ébola que castigaba África Central por primera vez en diecisiete años.

I funerali di suor Dinarosa Bellerini, una suora infermiera italiana, Kikwit Hospital, Zaire, 15 maggio 1995. Fu una delle prime vittime dell'epidemia del virus Ebola che colpì l'Africa centrale per la prima volta in diciassette anni.

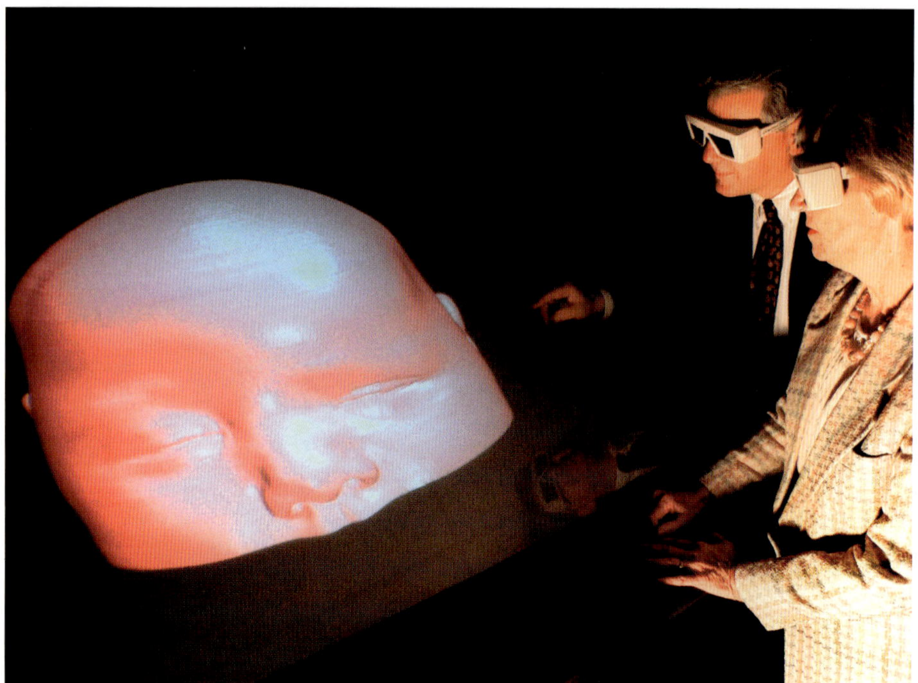

DARRYL BUSH/LIAISON AGENCY

Bulging baby image. Doctor Muriel Ross of NASA (right) and Dr Stephen S Schendel examine a 3D scan of a baby's head at NASA's Ames Research Center, 26 March 1997.

Un bebé en 3D. La doctora Muriel Ross de la NASA y el doctor Stephen S. Schendel examinan una imagen de escáner en tres dimensiones de la cabeza de un bebé en el Ames Research Center de la NASA, 26 de marzo de 1997.

Nasce il volto di un neonato. Il Dottor Muriel Ross della NASA (a destra) e il Dottor Stephen S. Schendel, esaminano un'immagine in 3D della testa di un neonato presso l'Ames Research Center della NASA, 26 marzo 1997.

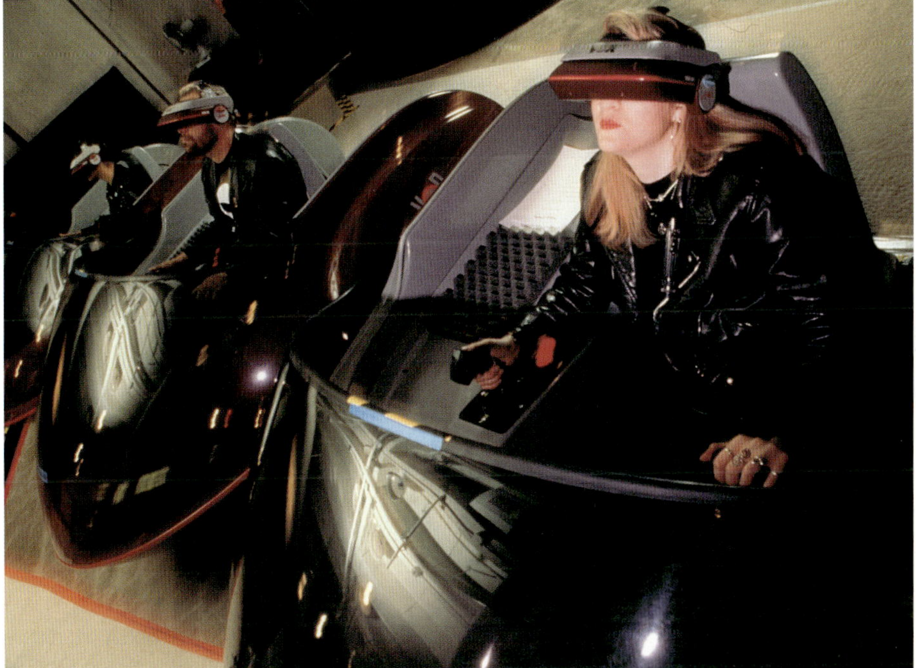

MAX RAMIREZ/BLACK STAR/COLORIFIC!

By the 1990s the computer was beginning to expand its impact on the world. Virtual reality was the name given by the ignorant to 'Cyberworld'. (Above) Visitors from Cyberworld take a trip back home.

En los noventa, la influencia del ordenador empieza a extenderse por todo el planeta y los más ignorantes denominan al cibermundo "realidad virtual". (Arriba) Visitantes del cibermundo se dan un paseo virtual.

Negli anni Novanta il computer iniziava già ad espandere il suo potere su tutto il pianeta. La realtà virtuale fu il nome che utilizzarono i profani per definire il "Cyberworld". (In alto) Alcuni visitatori del Cyberworld durante il viaggio di ritorno.

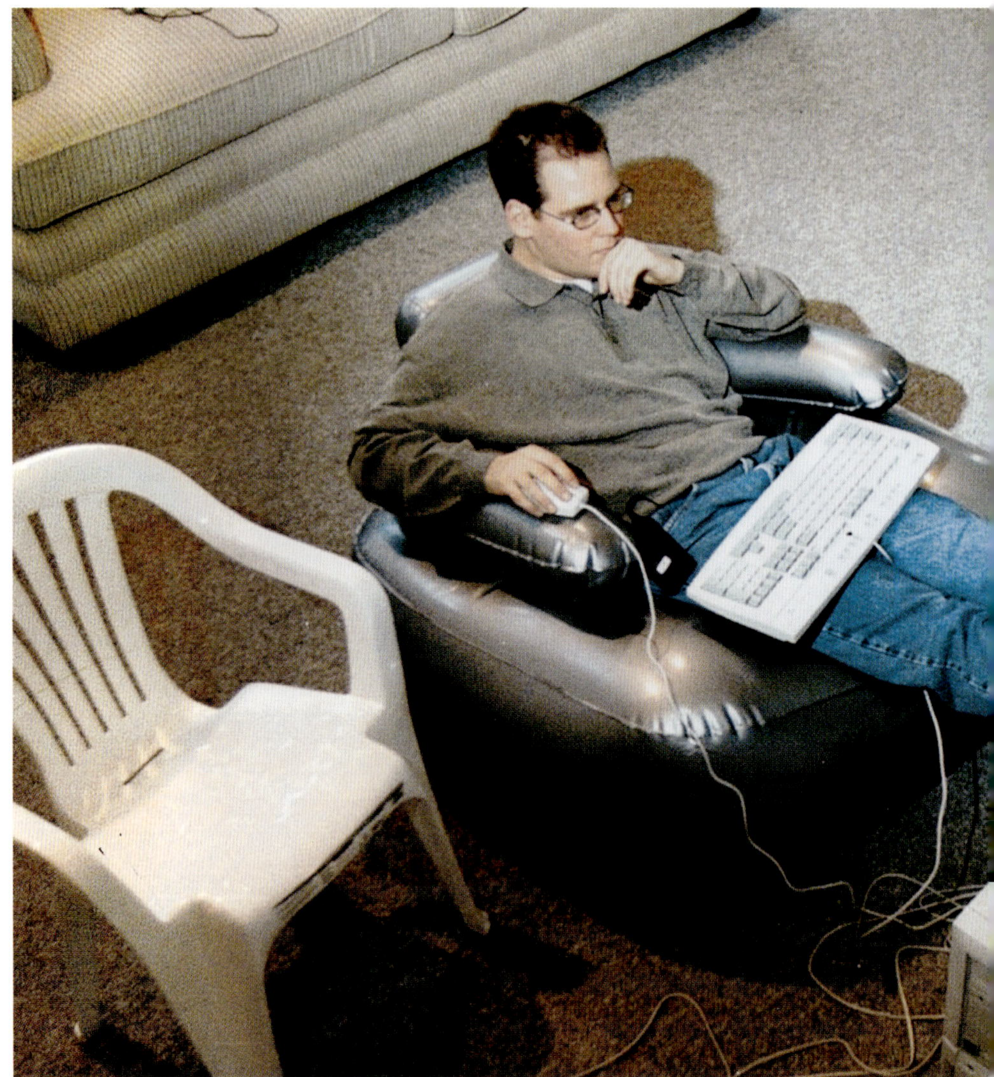

JON FREILICH/LIAISON AGENCY

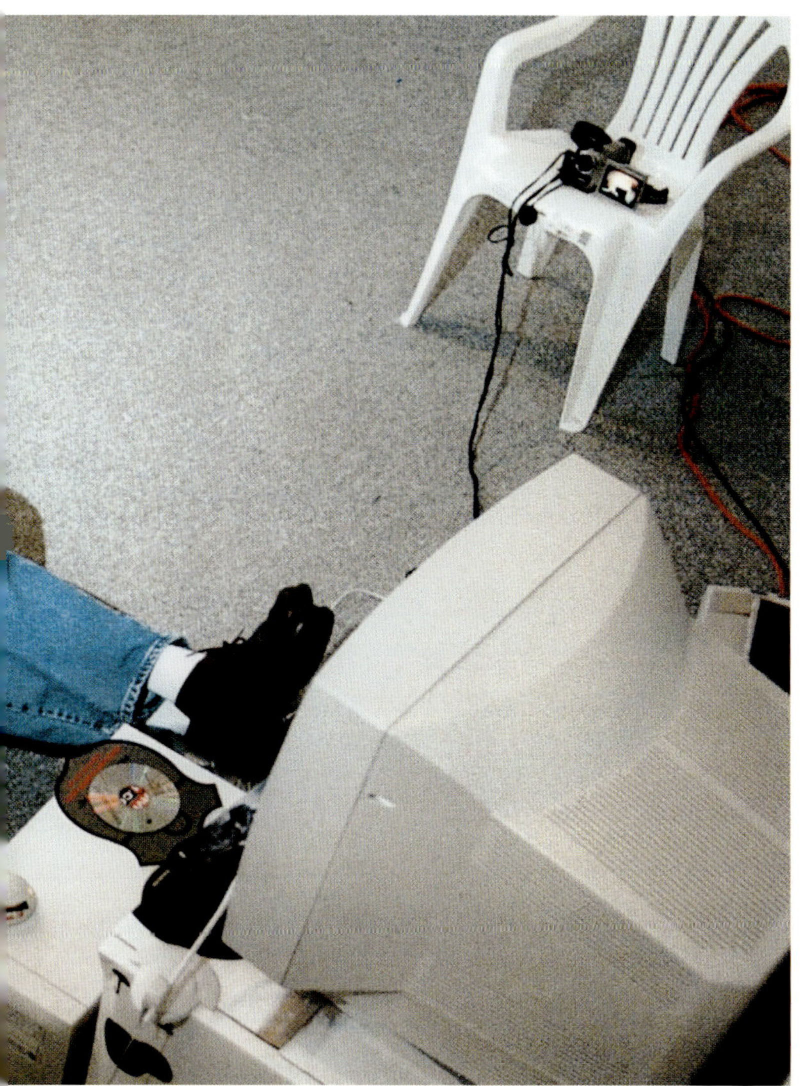

DotComGuy, the Texan who decided to live his whole life through the net, 16 December 1999. At least e-mail Christmas cards don't fall off the mantelpiece.

DotComGuy (o 'ChicoPuntoCom') es un joven de Texas que decide encerrarse todo un año en una casa con solo un ordenador y una conexión a Internet, 16 de diciembre de 1999. Por lo menos, las postales de Navidad electrónicas no se caen de la chimenea…

DotComGuy, il texano che ha deciso di vivere tutta la vita sul net, 16 dicembre 1999. Almeno, gli auguri di Natale ricevuti per e-mail non cadono dal caminetto.

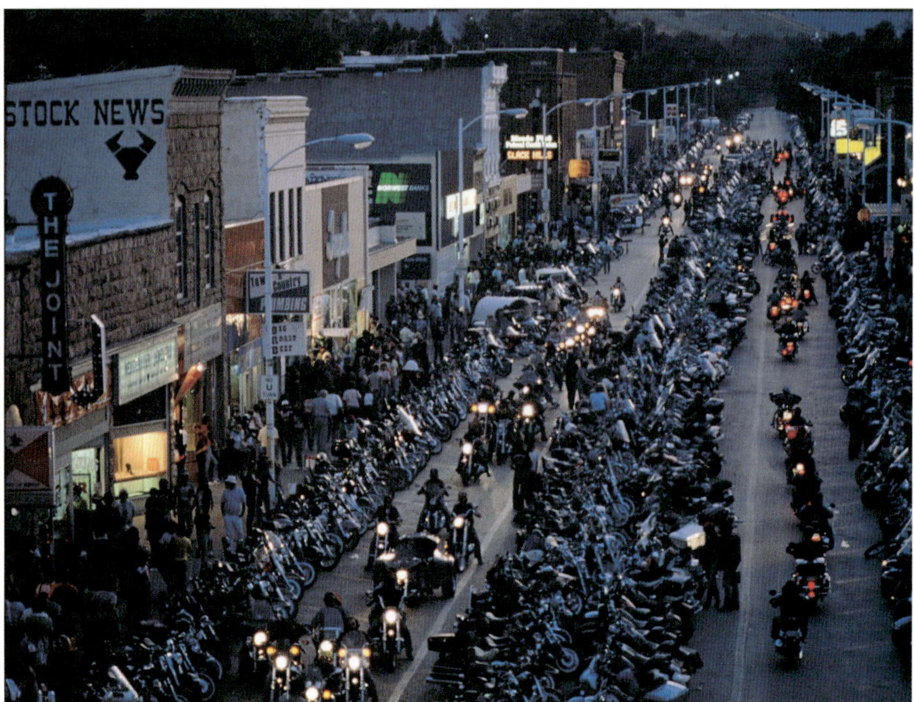

PAUL MILLER/BLACK STAR/COLORIFIC!

Three hundred thousand bikers invade the town of Sturgis, N. Dakota (pop. 7,000), for the 50th anniversary of the Black Hills Motor Classic. Every summer for a week Sturgis opens its minds, hearts and doors to bikers.

Trescientos mil motoristas invaden el pueblo de Sturgis –de 7.000 habitantes– en Dakota del Norte, para festejar el 50° aniversario del Black Hills Motor Classic. Cada verano Sturgis abre su mente, su corazón y sus puertas a las motos durante una semana.

Trecento mila ciclisti invadono la città di Sturgis (7.000 abitanti), nel Nord Dakota, in occasione del 50° anniversario del Black Hills Motor Classic. Tutte le estati, per una settimana, Sturgis apre anima, cuore e porte ai ciclisti.

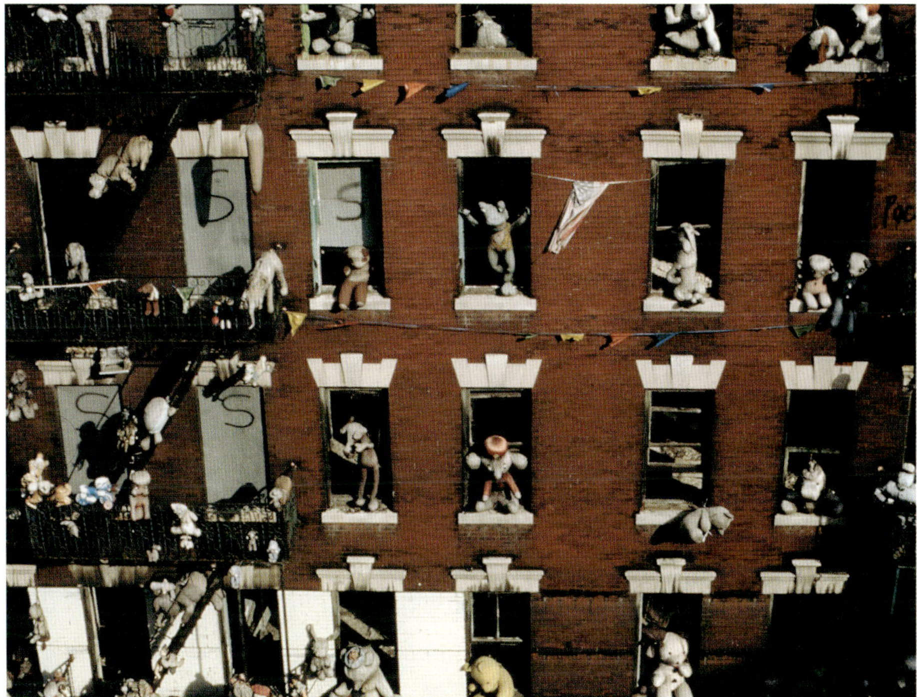

JOSEPH RODRIGUEZ/BLACK STAR/COLORIFIC!

A tenement block in the photographer's own El Barrio district of East Harlem, New York City. The windows have been decorated with soft toys by parents as a sign of defiance against local crack dealers.

Bloque de pisos en el distrito de El Barrio –en el cual vive el fotógrafo– al este de Harlem, Nueva York. Los vecinos habían decorado las ventanas con muñecos de peluche en señal de repulsa hacia los traficantes de droga que operaban en el barrio.

Appartamenti del Barrio, il quartiere di East Harlem di New York, dove viveva il fotografo che scattò l'istantanea. Le finestre furono decorate con peluche dai genitori in segno di sfida contro gli spacciatori di crack della zona.

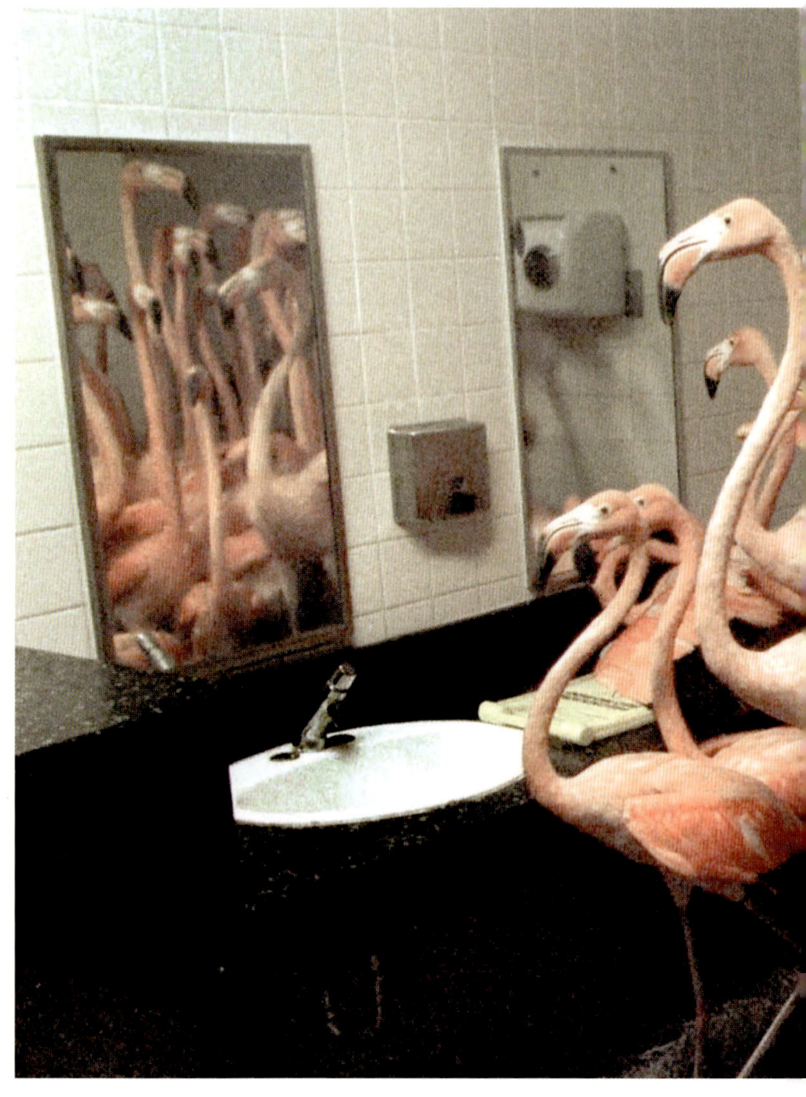

The usual queue in the Ladies. Flamingos shelter from Hurricane George in the restroom of Miami's Metro Zoo, 25 September 1998.

La típica cola en el lavabo de las chicas. Una bandada de flamencos busca cobijo en los servicios del zoo de Miami ante la llegada del huracán George, 25 de septiembre de 1998.

Come al solito, la fila per il bagno delle signore. Fenicotteri che si proteggono dall'uragano George nella toilette del Metro Zoo di Miami, 25 settembre 1998.

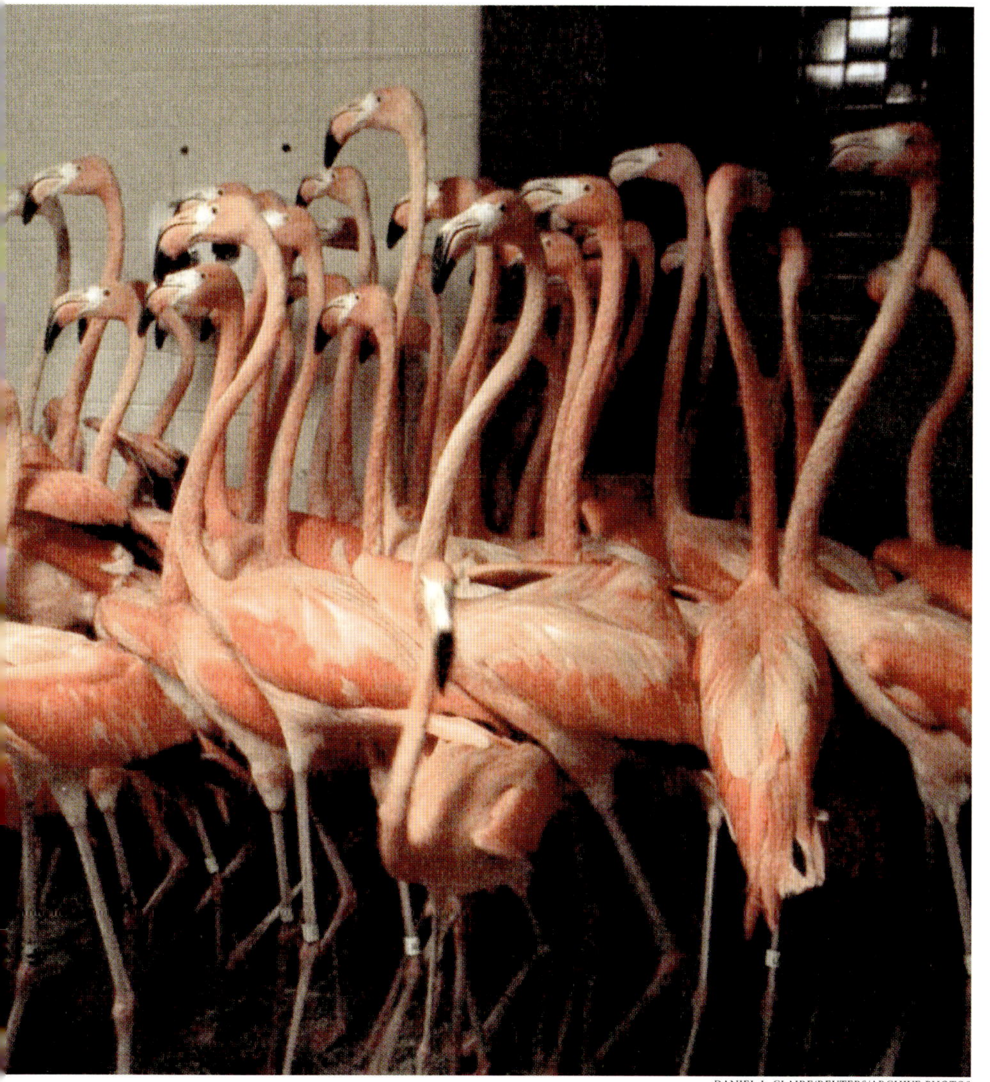

DANIEL LeCLAIRE/REUTERS/ARCHIVE PHOTOS

Index

gettyimages

Over 70 million images and 30,000 hours of film footage are held by the various collections owned by Getty Images. These cover a vast number of subjects from the earliest photojournalism to current press photography, sports, social history and geography. Getty Images' conceptual imagery is renowned amongst creative end users.
www.gettyimages.com

Más de 70 millones de imágenes y 30.000 horas de secuencias filmadas forman parte de las muchas colecciones que pertenecen a Getty Images. Éstas cubren un vasto número de temas desde los principios del periodismo fotográfico hasta la actual fotografía de prensa, deportes, historia social y geografía. Las imágenes conceptuales de Getty Images tienen renombre entre sus creativos consumidores.
www.gettyimages.com

Le varie collezioni di propietà della Getty Images comprendono oltre 70 milioni di immagini e 30.000 ore di filmati che abbracciano un ampio numero di soggetti: il giornalismo fotografico dalle origini ai giorni nostri, lo sport, la storia sociale e la geografia. Le immagini concettuali della Getty images sono rinomate fra gli utenti finali del settore creativo.
www.gettyimages.com

Acknowledgements

The picture editor is grateful to the following individuals and agencies or collections with which they are associated for their assistance with this book:

Christopher Angeloglou, Julius Domoney, David Leverton and Sally Ryall (Colorific!); Anh Stack and Michelle Hernandez (Black Star); Rosa Di Salvo, Richard Ellis, Bob Hechler, Hilary Johnston, Robert Pepper, Eric Smalkin (Liaison Agency); Rob Harborne, Lee Martin and Matthew Stevens (Allsport); Mitch Blank, Kathy Lavelle, Eric Rachlis, Peter Rohowsky and Arlete Santos (Hulton|Archive, New York); Antonia Hille, Sarah Kemp and Alex Linghorn (Hulton|Archive, London); Jake Cunningham (PYMCA); Martin Stephens and Milica Timotic (PA News); Gul Duzyol and Jocelyne Manfredi (Sipa Press); Judith Caul and Tony Mancini (*The Guardian*); Jim Docherty and Marianne Lassen (S.I.N.); Simon Kenton (Idols); and to Sara Green and Stephanie Hudson for their kind assistance in New York and London respectively.